Of Lizards and Angels

Other books by Frederick Manfred

The Golden Bowl (1944) (Mr. Manfred wrote under the name Feike Feikema from 1944
    through 1951)
Boy Almighty (1945)
This Is the Year (1947)
The Chokecherry Tree (1948)
Lord Grizzly (1954)
Morning Red (1956)
Riders of Judgment (1957)
Conquering Horse (1959)
Arrow of Love (stories) (1961)
Wanderlust (a revised version of three novels, *The Primitive* [1949], *The Brother* [1950],
    and *The Giant* [1951], published in one volume, 1962)
Scarlet Plume (1964)
The Man Who Looked Like the Prince of Wales (1965) (reprinted in paperback as *The Secret
    Place*)
Winter Count (poems) (1966)
King of Spades (1966)
Apples of Paradise (stories) (1968)
Eden Prairie (1968)
Conversations (1974) (moderated by John R. Milton)
Milk of Wolves (1976)
The Manly-Hearted Woman (1976)
Green Earth (1977)
The Wind Blows Free (reminiscences) (1979)
Sons of Adam (1980)
Winter Count II (poems) (1987)
Prime Fathers (essays) (1987)
The Selected Letters of Frederick Manfred, 1932–1954 (1989)
Flowers of Desire (1989)
No Fun on Sunday (1990)

Of Lizards and Angels

A Saga of Siouxland

By Frederick Manfred

University of Oklahoma Press : Norman and London

To
Wayne S. Knutson

Also to
Dwayne O. Andreas,
who once again helped when I was in need

The author's sincere thanks go
to the National Endowment for the Arts
for a grant given in 1983
to help write this novel.

Library of Congress Cataloging-in-Publication Data

Manfred, Frederick Feikema, 1912–
    Of lizards and angels : a saga of Siouxland / by Frederick
Manfred.
        p.   cm.
    I. Title.
PS3525.A5223303   1992
813'.54—dc20   '91-50865
    ISBN: 0–8061–2417–2 (cloth)   CIP
    ISBN: 0–8061–2514–4 (paper)

Text design by Bill Cason.

The paper in this book meets the guidelines for permanence and durability of the
Committee on Production Guidelines for Book Longevity of the Council on Library
Resources, Inc. ∞

2   3   4   5   6   7   8   9   10   11

Foreword

A word about resemblances.

It is impossible for any writer to make a faithful and complete portrait of any person he may have known, whether the writer be a novelist or a poet or a historian. A husband and wife can live together for fifty years, and be in love and live in happy "bondage" all that time, and yet not know each other completely. There is always a part of the husband the wife can never know, and there is always a part of the wife the husband can never know.

If one conceives of Jack and Jill as flesh prisms, each with many facets, and each with his or her own fire burning within, then Jack's fire will light up only those facets of Jill that face him, and Jill's fire will light up only those facets of Jack that face her. Their fires can never light up the dark side of each other's moons.

The novelist may take certain features of a person, the dimple in Jack's chin, the mole over Jill's eye, the cowlick in Jack's hair, the widow's peak on Jill's forehead, and still find he has not "got" either Jack or Jill. He has to fill in the dark side of the person's moon, light up the facets on the other side, with his general knowledge of human nature to present a fully rounded character.

That is why an author can say, truly, that any resemblance of any character in a book to real people in real life is purely coincidental.

FREDERICK MANFRED

Roundwind

BOOK ONE

1. Tunis

Tunis had a secret.

When Tunis was twenty he was quite sure he might have killed a grain hand while cutting wheat in eastern Siouxland. It happened in the deep bottoms along the Little Sioux River near Wanata.

The grain hand, a skinny bent man, had drifted into Siouxland during the 1881 harvest season. He hadn't given his last name, just said, "Call me Bud." Nor had he wanted to talk about where he came from or where he was going. He had shifty silverish eyes and lazy ways. He'd complained bitterly for several days about how hard he was working at the scything for the little pay he got, a dollar a day. He hated everybody, the guv'ment most of all.

Tunis finally got sick of the drifter's whining and told him to either shut up or get. But the tramp continued to complain, and when he'd at last accidentally nicked Tunis in the calf, Tunis dropped his scythe, grabbed the man by the throat with both hands, and gave him a good shaking. "Goddam you! I can't stand shirkers. Especially when they complain out loud." Only when the man turned completely limp did Tunis let him drop.

When Tunis's eyes cleared, and his furious breathing leveled off, he knew he might have done something terribly wrong. He looked around, up and down the bottoms as well as up to the great height-of-land to either side, to see if anyone had seen him choking the tramp. Not a soul in sight. He noticed the tramp's half-closed eyes gleaming silverish up at him from the ground. Kneeling, Tunis closed the tramp's eyes with a fingertip. Then Tunis ran, up the west bluff through a thick forest of ash and oak, until he came to the windmill in the Freyling highland pasture. There he pumped himself some water and splashed it over his face to cool off. He drank several handfuls of water, then vomited them back up. He sat down on the wellhead, shivering, shaking.

From his foster father, Old Dirk Freyling, with whom he was living, Tunis learned that his real father'd had bad blood in him. In a fit of rage, Tunis's father had killed his wife, choking her, and then, full of remorse, had killed himself. This had happened in 1862 when Tunis was but a year old.

Old Dirk might not have told Tunis about the wild temper of his father if Tunis hadn't got out of hand one day on the yard, almost clubbing a balky horse to death with a neck yoke. Old Dirk had remarked, quietly, "You better watch that temper of yours, boy, or someday you'll do something awful. Like your father, who had a touchy trigger in his head too."

At twenty Tunis Freyling had developed into a handsome fair-cheeked fellow with rusty hair, pearl gray eyes, broad heavy-muscled shoulders, thick thighs, and powerful hands with wide stubby fingers. He was five foot ten and weighed two hundred pounds. There was always an air about him that he was very much alive, with an active mind, with a quick way of seeing what a problem might be and of doing something about it immediately. His pearl eyes often flickered when he was excited. He walked lightly with a springy gliding motion. It all went with having a passionate nature.

At last, breath caught, heartbeat steadied, Tunis decided he'd better go back down the bluff and hide the body, and then pick up the scythes and bring them back to the yard. Down in the wet bottoms the scythes would soon begin to rust.

To his utter astonishment, when he returned to the scene he couldn't find the body. No sign of it anywhere. He couldn't imagine what might have happened to it. Scratching his rusty hair, shaking his head, he wondered if a cougar might have dragged off the body into the deep brush along the river. Several farmers had reported seeing a big prairie cougar working the bottoms. Or if possibly the grain hand might have revived, and in terror of his wrath had run for his life.

That evening when Tunis washed up for supper in the lean-to porch, he told Old Dirk that the tramp they'd hired had skedaddled for parts unknown. Old Dirk nodded. He'd half-expected it. Nothing more was said.

Tunis never did figure out what had happened to the tramp. As the weeks went by it began to bother Tunis more and more. If he ever lost his temper again he'd probably kill somebody for sure the next time. Tunis went out of his way to be kind and tender. When things started going against him, he'd quick caution himself to take it easy, go slow, smile, make light of it. At night, though, he was haunted by those silverish half-closed eyes. He could still feel the dampness of the man's wrinkled eyelids on his fingertip.

It took an extra effort of will for Tunis to get himself to work in the bottoms again. There were times when he wished his foster parents might have been religious. He wouldn't have confessed the wrong he'd done, but at least he would have learned how to pray. He needed to atone for what he had done. The harvest stiff had been worthless, yes, but he still was a human being.

Dirk Freyling and wife, Tressa, had been the first in the area to homestead two quarter sections along the Little Sioux River, well east of the Mill Creek Mounds and just west of the town of Wanata. Their land lay half in the bottoms and half on the tableland above the west bluff of the river valley. The valley was deep and the bluffs to either side were covered with ash, elm, hackberry, oak, and walnut trees. Here and there massive cottonwoods towered out of the bottoms.

There were no churches when Dirk and Tressa arrived, and they never acquired the habit of going to church. They rarely read the Bible.

Dirk and Tressa were well into their fifties when their next-door neighbor Tunis Alfredson had killed his wife and then taken his own life. Left behind was the baby, Tunis Jr. When no relatives came forward to claim the little tyke, Dirk and Tressa in their slow warm neighborly way decided to take him on as their own. They'd long wanted children and here now was a chance to raise one. The sheriff was relieved. He had been unable to discover where the Alfredsons came from. Dirk had once heard Tunis Sr. remark that they were related to some Alfredsons, pioneers, living by the Big Sioux River farther west in Siouxland, but just where he wasn't sure. Tunis's parents hadn't been religious either, and that had been one of the reasons why they'd made sure not to settle near Tunis Sr.'s religious relatives.

Old Dirk had also heard that Tunis Sr. had married a woman his relatives didn't like. She was always in a fret, always mad at somebody. She came from a violent family. Old Dirk had gathered, adding one thing with another, that the woman's father had killed someone in the Old Country and had had to flee, first going to Canada, and then secretly at night had walked across the border of North Dakota into the United States. So it wasn't just idle talk that young Tunis had hot blood in him.

Old Dirk was seventy-seven when one evening, just as they finished supper, his right eye slowly closed and he toppled sideways out of his armchair at the head of the table and fell heavily to the floor.

Old Tressa cried out, "Dirk!" She jumped up from her end of the table and knelt beside Old Dirk. It was one of the quickest things Tunis had even seen her do.

Tunis was quick to kneel beside the old man too. He leaned over him, rusty hair brushing into Old Tressa's sparse white hair. "Pa?"

Old Dirk's watery blue left eye looked up at them. "I think . . . I've had . . . a stroke."

"Oh, Dirk, not after all these years!" Old Tressa cried.

"I'm afraid so, Tress . . . I remember . . . when my pa . . . had his."

Tunis didn't want to believe it either. "You'll be all right in a couple of days. Here. I'll carry you to your bed." Easily, because Old Dirk was almost as light as a couple of dried cornstalks, Tunis carried him into the back bedroom. As Tunis straightened him out on the bed, he noticed several things. Old Dirk had no control over his right arm and right leg. There was also a wet spot on the front of his faded blue overalls. Tunis stood back and watched Old Tressa comb Old Dirk's thick brush of stiff white hair. Tunis clenched his teeth, so hard they cracked. Then, pinching his eyes shut, he whirled and left the room. Old Tressa would want to be alone with her man while she removed his clothes.

Old Dirk never recovered. But he didn't die right away. He lingered, and lingered, for two years.

Tunis wanted to help Old Tressa take turns bathing and dressing him, but she wouldn't hear of it. She fed the old man, emptied his pot. The only thing she let Tunis do was carry Old Dirk out to the rocker on the front porch when the weather was nice.

Tunis sometimes wondered what kind of life Old Dirk and Old Tressa had in bed at night. Of course they wouldn't be trying to make babies anymore. The closest he came to imagining them showing affection was Old Dirk kissing Old Tressa's withered paps with weathered lips.

There was one month though, in August, when Old Dirk recovered enough to be able to shuffle around the house without crutches. Even his cheeks turned pink. When Tunis cheered him on, Old Dirk smiled vaguely out over his land and shook his head. "I dunno, son. It still sits there close by. My dreams are turning muzzy." When Tunis later tried to cheer up Old Tressa about how good Old Dirk looked, she too smiled vaguely out over the flat prairie and said, "I'm not going to get my hopes up. It's like he's having a sunny hour now just before it gets real dark. The way he hangs there on those crutches . . . any day now he may fall over."

Watching the old man hitch himself around with his atrophied arm and leg was agony for Tunis. Tunis swore to himself that he was never going to let himself get that old. It was awful to be old and helpless, like a dog with all four legs crimped up. It was awful to have one's underclothes stink like a baby's week-old diaper. Tunis was sure he'd have the guts to end it all before he became that kind of bother to others.

The second stroke finished Old Dirk. And it finished Old Tressa too. After the undertaker had laid Old Dirk out in a pine coffin in the parlor, Old Tressa went to her bed and lay down. The next morning she was cold.

Tunis felt terrible. Both had died before he'd had a chance to square his conscience. He still felt guilty about having almost choked that grain hand and had often thought he should at least confess it to them. But now they were gone and he had no one to tell it to.

Tunis finished out the year on the farm, doing the plowing and harvesting the corn, baching it alone in the kitchen. Then on Christmas Day 1884, still haunted by what he'd done to that tramp, Tunis decided to sell out and skip the country. According to the clerk of courts at Storm Lake, he was the only heir. He hired an auctioneer in February and, except for Gypsy, the roan gelding riding horse, sold everything at a farm auction sale: land, buildings, implements, household goods, carriage, buggy, and animals. There had been no debts, and he cleared seventy-two hundred dollars. Tunis kept out two hundred dollars for pocket money and banked the rest at the Wanata Farmers Savings at four percent interest.

On the first of March 1885, he saddled Gypsy, packed his few belongings in a saddlebag, and headed southwest down an old Indian trail toward Cherokee. He'd heard at the courthouse in Storm Lake there was still some good open range left in the Floyd River valley north of Sioux City. That should be far enough away from where he'd choked the grain hand.

The weather remained clear though cold. Sitting on a warm horse, with his sheepskin coat buttoned up so that the furry collar protruded above his blue felt cap, and with his feet encased in long woolen socks inside a pair of high leather boots, Tunis rode along as cozy as a squirrel in a hollow tree.

There was a lot of open land around in 1885. Sometimes he traveled a dozen miles before he ran into a homestead where he could eat and sleep and put up his horse in a barn. He always helped with the chores where he stayed. He was so handy at it that invariably the farmer asked him if he wouldn't like to be his hired hand for the coming summer. The housewife too liked him. Tunis was neat and had good manners. He would smile, slowly shake his head, and say, no, he was heading for Sioux City way. They never asked him twice. An odd glow in his pearl eyes forbade further talk on the subject.

He followed the Little Sioux River, where he could, by taking the high table-land. The table continued to fall off into a deep valley, the side hills covered with an almost impenetrable forest of elm and ash and oak. Stands of huge cottonwoods persisted in soaring out of the bottoms, their tips reaching almost as high as the tops of the bluffs to either side. There were also many open fields in the bottoms, and where they'd been plowed the previous fall they were as black as soot. The plowed fields up on the table were brownish, tending toward gray. In some places pioneers had delved dugouts in the lower dropoffs along the river.

The trees provided shelter and fuel when he needed it. There was plenty of water for himself and his horse Gypsy. Where the river ran swift he and the horse had no trouble drinking, but where it ran slow he often had to chop holes in the ice.

He stayed one night in Washta in a rickety bug-infested hotel, and cursed it for miles afterward as he scratched all the bites.

In late March, when he hit Anthon, still feeling both guilty and sad, he learned he'd drifted well southeast of Sioux City. The Floyd River valley was some forty miles to the northwest. He turned his horse's head into the wind and in one day crossed a wide hogback into the valley of the West Fork of the Little Sioux.

He soon found himself in Quorn, an English settlement. The Queen's Inn was full of British talk and lost syllables.

Much of the conversation at the long dinner table had to do with British disappointment in the Chicago and Northwestern Railroad Company. The American railroad company hadn't liked the John Bull methods of the English Close brothers. Instead of going through Quorn, the railroad company platted out a town a mile east of Quorn and named it Kingsley.

"Well! That spelled the doom for Quorn," one red-cheeked Englishman intoned from the head of the table.

"Fred Close felt bad about that. He'd named Quorn after a place in Leicestershire, England, where he'd enjoyed many a holiday fox hunting, y'know."

"Wasn't the hunt at Quorn one of the best known in England?"

"The same."

Tunis learned from more talk at the table that there were English settlers everywhere. Despite their problem with the railroad, the Close brothers spent thousands of English pounds buying up choice land. The Close brothers then invited hearty English lads as pupils whom they'd train to run the farms, offering them a home and equipment and farm stock in exchange for half the profits. Sometimes the Close brothers sold the quarter sections outright to the pupils. Meantime, other British entrepreneurs bought land and established sheep ranches with elaborate mansions for the second and third sons of the upper classes, dukes and lords. The local people, making a pun on the word *pupil*, called all these places pup farms. One of the better known was Barlow Hall. The pups didn't have to work or worry about making a profit on the sheep. They lived on remittances sent to them by elder brothers, heirs to rich estates in England. The firstborn were only too glad to get rid of their sibling rivals. The pups lived a riotous life, fox hunting over the open range, carousing in the saloons, debauching women.

Tunis listened; said nothing.

Tunis left Quorn the next morning and headed straight west. He was told that if he followed the sun he'd hit Hinton on the Floyd River and that northwest of there he'd still find some open range. But he'd better hurry. Flocks of Frisians and Hollanders were coming in from Europe. They came by train to Le Mars and from there scattered everywhere, mostly in the direction of Sioux Center and Jerusalem.

By midday a late March blizzard came up. Tunis looked around for shelter. Just when he thought he was lost and might freeze to death, his good horse Gypsy smelled horses and snorted. Leaning forward, narrowing his eyes against the driving rice-hard snow, Tunis spotted a big mansion, a huge barn, lesser houses for hired hands and a cattleyard.

Someone was carrying a lantern from a shed to the large red barn. Tunis rode straight for the barn.

7

The face above the lantern turned and looked up. "You look lost."

"I was until I saw your lantern. What's this place?"

"Sutherland Hall." The fellow's nose lifted his upper lip into a smile of irony. "The new Eden in Iowa."

"Can you put up a horse and a man?"

"Climb down."

Tunis broke out of his stiff mold of a snow-plakked sheepskin coat and swung his leg over. The arches of his feet stung in his leather boots as he hit the ground.

"You're lucky you didn't start riding in circles in this blow," the fellow offered. He too was wearing a sheepskin coat with a high collar and a blue felt cap.

"Not with Gyp here. She can smell out horse sweat a mile away." Tunis shook his shoulders to get rid of the snow.

"I'm Galen Hurle," the fellow said. He opened a wide barn door leading into an alley and stepped aside for Tunis and Gyp to enter.

At the smell of fresh bluestem hay, Gyp whinnied in horse pleasure. A bay stallion at the far end of a row of stalls challenged Gyp. Gyp the gelding ignored it. Wavering cobwebs hung from eight-by-ten beams overhead. As the two men and the horse advanced down the alley hay dust rose underfoot.

Galen ushered them into a stall halfway down on the left. It had been neatly manured out and was well bedded with fresh straw.

Tunis saw that the stall was clean enough for a human being to sleep in, let alone a horse. "Thanks."

"Here, let me help you with the saddle. What'd you say your name was?"

8

"Tunis Freyling."

The moment Gyp's bridle was removed he nuzzled his nose deep into the sweet wild prairie hay to sniff the bouquet of it and then, with a shake of his head and mane, lipped up a fat mouthful.

Galen pointed to a sawhorse for Tunis to throw his saddle on. "Nice roan you got there."

"He'll do." The warmth of animal heat in the barn softened Tunis's cheeks. He opened his coat and shook off more snow.

There were some two dozen horses in the barn, and all leaned around in their stalls as far as their halter ropes would allow. They whinnied at the new-comer horse. But Gyp ignored them. He was too busy with the delicious hay.

"Have you eaten?"

"Not since morning."

"Dinner won't be ready yet for another hour. We here at Sutherland Hall have dinner in the evening, you know, not supper. But I'm sure Clara can set out a little tea and crumpets for you."

"British pups here then."

"That they are." The fellow tipped back his cap. Several locks of curly red-dish blond hair tumbled out over his high forehead. "I'm not British myself. I'm from Sioux City and was hired to show these pups how to run this stock opera-tion. But none of these British floaters want to work. Or can work. The duke of Sutherland, who hired me to straighten out this mess, told me that his pupils were the very pick and flower of British immigration. He warned me to go easy with them because they'd been gently nurtured. They were inexperienced. Had soft hands. Pah. Worthless, the lot of them. Drinking. And all the time trying to catch the maids up the back stairwell." Galen pulled his blue cap down over his forehead again. "All except Clara. Her they leave alone, for some reason."

"This Sutherland, is he rich?"

"A little. Though he lost his shirt in tea imports. He's trying to make up his loss here in America."

"You say there's hot tea in the house?"

"Come along." Galen continued to grumble. "His lordship warned me these no-good pups had a great amount of cheek. They sure as hell have. And I'm supposed to try and help them become successful at stock farming."

"This ain't a sheep ranch then?"

"No. Cattle. And polo ponies. Ha."

"Umm." Tunis had to hold his head away from the driving pricking snow. Except for two big cottonwoods there were no trees around to shelter the yard.

Looking up past the edge of his sheepskin fur collar, Tunis saw that the mansion was handsome. It faced south. It was three stories high, had a steep roof of red tile with wide overhanging eaves. A screened-in veranda circled the second floor and a glass-enclosed porch the first floor. The entire house was built of concrete walls and iron supports. Tunis had never seen the like. "Holy bells, what a house."

"Yeh. The Duke told me he had a house like that in England. Out in the country."

"A fellow would have a hard time screwing himself out of house and home with that one." Tunis got that thought from the tramp he'd choked. The tramp had muttered several times that he'd fathered too many children.

Galen let go with a short laugh. "Better watch your tongue around Clara in the house there."

"This fellow Sutherland must have been a top bull in England. With papers."

"That he was. And he tried to build up a little corner of Old England here. Right where you're standing is a clay tennis court. Out over there are his polo grounds."

"They really play polo here?"

"You bet, in the summers. Teams from England and Australia have played here. As well as from Fort Snelling, up at Saint Paul."

"Does his team ever win?"

"Just about always."

"Polo and tennis out here in the middle of nowhere, my God."

Tunis noted that the tops of two very old fat cottonwoods standing nearby were only a few feet taller than the two brick chimneys sticking up out of the red tile roof.

Galen led the way around to the back steps on the west side and then up into an enclosed porch. "Better take your boots off or Clara'll give you a look that'll sear your eyeballs."

Tunis, like Galen, took off his sheepskin coat and his felt cap and hung them up on a peg, then leaned down to unlace and remove his boots. "This Clara sounds like she might have a bad temper."

Galen lowered his voice to a whisper. "She's been disappointed."

"Men?"

"No. Fortune. She comes from Welton. That's halfway between Dubuque and Davenport. There was once another English settlement there."

"She's British then too."

"Yep. Comes from good stock. But her folks died when she was a kid. Diphtheria. And left her nothing."

"Where's the tea?"

Galen pushed open a ten-foot-tall door into a huge kitchen. The ceiling was twelve feet high and painted a light green. Oak cabinets and glassed-in shelves lined all the walls above work counters. There were two long worktables in the center of the room. Two young women wearing pretty red aprons flashed knives on the tables getting dinner ready. A short woman around twenty was filling the high black cookstove with chunks of wood. Galen announced, "Clara, found this stray out by the barn. So I brought him in. Looks like he could use a little tea to warm up."

The short woman at the stove closed the lid and brushed back dark auburn hair. "I just brought the tea tray into the great hall for their lordships." She spoke sarcastically.

"Then Tunis . . . it's Tunis, isn't it?" When Tunis nodded, Galen went on. "Then Tunis'll have to wait until dinner."

Clara spoke shortly. "The afternoon is bearing on." She fixed Tunis with a pair of grave gray eyes. After a moment she said, "Why don't you sit down at that little corner table there. By the window. It's where us girls eat. When we have the time. I've got a little pot here somewhere I can make tea in."

Tunis and Galen sat down. Tunis combed back his rusty hair with his fingers. The smell of the place was fragrant with baking apple pies, fresh bread, roasting wild fowl of some sort, oatmeal cookies. Tunis watched Clara as she set out white almost translucent cups and saucers, dropped several spoons of black tea leaves into a rose-dappled teapot, and then poured in hot water from a huge black kettle.

10

Tunis hadn't seen many women in his life—Old Tressa, and on occasion neighbor wives during harvest time—but he could see right away that Clara was different. She had a mind of her own about the way the kitchen should be run. The two young women hustled about as if in fear Clara might give them their walking papers at any moment. For all her short stature, Clara was well set up. Tunis couldn't see her legs because of the long white cook's dress, but from the way she walked she had to have good stout calves. Her waist was very thin. Old Tressa had had little or no breasts that he could remember, and he was surprised, and pleased, to see how full Clara's were. They looked like they might pop out of the top of her button dress on her least move, like romping puppies. But best was her face. She was beautiful. Good chin, full lips, straight nose, well-sloped cheeks, dark brows over searching gray eyes, round high forehead, and then that dark auburn hair, strands of which kept sliding out of the double knot above and falling in front of her eyes. A very handsome woman. And she was a crab? Hard to believe. She was probably only overworked.

Tunis glanced at the help. Both young women were taller than Clara, and stouter, with strong pink hands, about eighteen years old. They tended to flutter at their work rather than set to it. They kept throwing sidelong looks at Tunis, and then quick tended to the business at hand. They were both brunettes, blue-eyed, not really attractive.

Clara saw Tunis look them over. After a moment, she scolded the girls. "Greta, Lurilla, no looking out the window now. If dinner isn't ready on time, you know those pups will be in here fussing you again. And then only God'll know when we'll eat proper."

Looking out the frosted window, Tunis could see it had become dark outside, with an odd gray cast to it, as though the falling snow were carrying some kind of light down with it from the heavens. It was cozy inside the huge kitchen, and its warmth made him suddenly lonesome for the good old days with Old Dirk and Old Tressa. He missed having a home. Well, in a couple of weeks, after he found some acreage he liked, he'd build himself a sod shanty and start a new life.

Clara came over and lifted the lid to the teapot and looked in. She sniffed the aroma rising from it. "It's steeped. Would you like some?"

Tunis pushed his cup and saucer toward her. "If you please." He watched her pour the amber brew, both for him and for Galen.

"Cream? Sugar?"

"Just sugar, please."

"Maybe you'd prefer honey? The girls and I found some wild honey down by the crik last fall. In an old hollow willow tree."

"That would be just perfect."

Clara dipped a spoonful from a gray crock, whirled the spoon to spin the dark honey up into a ball, then released it over his steaming tea. The honey fell in two pulses, neatly, without splashing. Clara fixed Tunis with a look. "Where you headed?"

"Sioux City way, I guess."

"I hear Sioux City is infested with tramps. Let alone all those lazy lords from England."

"Actually, I'm looking for land north of there. More towards Sioux Center."

Galen took some honey too. "What you got cooking for tonight, Clara? It smells fit for a king."

"That's the one thing those big wigs in the other room will do. Hunt. When I told them that over in Welton we often had prairie chickens for dinner, they got their guns and actually walked down to the crik and shot me some."

The sound of revelry, of laughter and clinking glasses, could be heard through the tall oak doors leading into the great hall.

Clara went on. "Prairie chickens do have a strange wild taste, but they answer well."

Galen said, "So that's what all that hullabaloo was about this morning before the snow started."

"They bagged twenty of them and have been bragging ever since." The girls had stopped to listen and Clara caught them at it. "Greta, Lurilla, come, let's all clap to now and help out. Before our milords out there get too drunk."

Tunis sipped his tea. He looked out the window; then turned to watch Clara bustle about the huge black stove; and then looked out the window again.

Clara sensed him looking at her. "Do you have a place to stay tonight in this storm?"

"I can sleep in the barn."

Clara set out some fresh-baked bread. With a fork she caught up a large chunk of butter and dabbed the tops of the brown crusts with it. The better melted and in a moment the brown crusts shone in the lamplight. There was an instant smell of perfect baking. "There's a good sofa in the library."

"Thanks. But the barn will be all right. When you're on the move you can't be too particular."

Galen said, "I thought maybe I could put him up in my bunkhouse."

Clara came over. "A spot more tea?"

"Don't mind if I do." Tunis pushed his cup toward her.

Clara poured. The tea had turned darker. "Suit yourself. But I can make up a nice bed for you in the library."

It came over Tunis that Clara had taken a liking to him. Truth to tell he'd decided he liked her too. He wondered if maybe he shouldn't ask Galen for a job helping him teach the Britishers how to run a stock and horse farm. Tunis managed to smile up at her. "I think at that I'll take the sofa in the library."

"Good. When I get caught up here. I'll show it to you. In the meantime, if you want to clean up, there's the sink in the corner." Clara looked at Galen. "More tea?"

"You bet."

"Could you and Mr. Freyling here get me some more water from the well? I don't want to be caught short if this storm decides to last a couple of days."

"Will do."

Tunis wondered why Clara hadn't been grabbed up by some man. One of the rich lords should by now have spotted her as a good woman. Tunis wondered what Clara would think if she knew about what had happened up at Wanata.

Tunis and Galen thanked Clara for the tea, then went out on the porch and put on their boots again and stepped outside to get the water. They each carried two five-gallon cans.

Galen said, "Hey, you sure hit it off with Clara."

"Think so?"

"Usually she has no time for men. Atall. Even old Lord Sutherland, she bosses him around like he might be in his second childhood."

12

Galen set one of the cans under the nose of the rusted iron pump and Tunis began working the handle up and down. Water soon began to slosh into the can.

Galen said, "You know farming?"

"Some."

"You wouldn't want to help me?" Snow falling across Galen's red weathered face made him look especially appealing. "It's going to take at least two good men to pound some sense into those nuts. You won't believe what they'll do. Last summer, we're out with our walking cultivators, when one of 'em got to bragging about how fast his horses could run. Next thing I know, four of those fellows unhitched their heavy draft horses and proceeded to race them across the cornfield. They tromped under I don't know how many little corn shoots. And all for a side bet. Then when one of them offered to stand for drinks at the Prairie Club in Le Mars, they threw off the harnesses and galloped pell-mell all the way over there and got roaring drunk."

Tunis found himself smiling.

"They've even taken to shooting at our prize bulls Lord Sutherland paid hundreds of dollars for. All because the wild fox are now scarce, and the deer and the antelope have all run off." The first can was full and Galen shifted the second can under the spout. "They're endlessly complaining that they were told in England they'd be living the life of a country gentleman here in America, not this low mean life of a farm laborer. They do little dribs of work for an hour or so, and then they quit and dress up for town and ride into Le Mars to paint the place a rip-roaring red. Then they come home staring drunk and I've got to put 'em to bed. It's a miracle those gals in the kitchen haven't been raped yet."

Tunis quietly made up his mind he wouldn't ask Galen for a job after all.

"Clara knew what she was doing when she put a double lock and bolt on the door to her room."

Water in the second can welled up to the neck, and Tunis quit pumping while Galen shifted the third can under the spout.

When all four cans were full, Tunis helped Galen punch the lids into the can openings. Together, grunting, because the full cans were heavy, they started back to the house.

Galen muttered, "They can't tell a plow from a pumpkin."

"I heard over at Quorn, though, that some of them came over with a lot of money. And some still get remittances from their family estates in England."

"That's true. And Le Mars is having quite a boom because of it."

They shuffled heavily through the snow, up the steps into the back porch, and once again stomped off the snow and took off their boots. Galen led the way into the kitchen. "Well, Clara, here's your reserve water. Where do you want it?"

"Under the far sink there, please," Clara said crisply. "Thanks."

Tunis was careful to line up his two cans of water with Galen's to make it all look neat under the sink.

Clara saw it. "We'll be ready to serve dinner in a half hour. I'm just wondering, Mr. Freyling—you wouldn't want a bath first, instead of just washing up?"

Tunis thought maybe he smelled rank to her. "I think I will. That'll be just the ticket. I'll go get my saddlebags where I got some fresh underwear."

"Clara!" Galen exclaimed, "you ain't gonna let him take a bath in milord's tub?"

"I can tell Mr. Freyling is used to home conveniences."

So Tunis once more put on his boots and got his saddlebags.

Clara picked up a big black kettle steaming hot and a pail of cold water and then led Tunis up the back stairs to the bath. Someone had lit a fire in the fireplace and the leaping flames enhanced the bathroom with bouncing crimson.

The high-backed tin bathtub in the far corner stunned Tunis. It shone. A smell of perfumed soap rose from it.

Clara had to smile. "I never fancied it much myself. I prefer a washbasin in my room. But his lordship sure fancies it. Claims the high back keeps the draft off his old neck."

"Well salt my hide."

Clara edged toward the door. "When you've finished, bring your dirty duds down to the kitchen. I'll have one of the girls wash them after the dishes are done."

"Thanks."

Tunis undressed near the fire. The white terrazzo floor was cold to his feet. He first poured in the hot water and then added the cold until it had just the right temperature. He stepped in, shivered, then quickly settled into the steaming water. The four legs under the tub creaked. The long tub fit him perfectly. With the fire blazing in the far corner he knew why the old lord liked his high-backed tin tub. There was a cold draft coming down the wall behind Tunis and heading for the fire. The room had treated birch walls. Some of the foot-wide boards had warped a little in the alternating wet and dry room. A water closet bulked up square in the far corner.

Tunis soaped himself liberally with a bar of the lord's perfumed soap. He didn't particularly like the smell. Too sweetish. Something an old maid might like to let her think she was young again. He scrubbed his armpits and in between his toes and around his ankles. Vaguely, below in the great hall, he could hear occasional laughter.

Finished, Tunis stood up and toweled himself off. His skin had roughened over with goosebumps. He stepped out of the tin tub, quickly got out fresh woolen long johns from his saddlebags, and dressed. In a mirror over the washstand he observed that his brown woolen trousers were pretty baggy at the knees, even spotted with Gyp's saliva over the thighs. Well, the trousers would have to do until he got a chance to have them handwashed and ironed. His brown pullover sweater also sagged at the elbows and around the neck, though at least that was spotless. He rolled up his dirty duds and, carrying it all, water, bags, and clothes, took the back stairway down to the kitchen.

Clara and the two girls were lifting roasted prairie chickens out of the huge black oven. The smell set his mouth to watering. Clara said, "Why don't you just push through the swing door there. I've already told Mr. Sutherland that he has a guest. And Galen's gone in there."

"I bet you win all the prizes at a cooking fair."

"It don't take brains to be a good cook. It just takes a tongue."

She sure could be tart. It fit his own mood. Tunis cast a furtive look at her puppy breasts and then pushed into the great hall.

The first thing to catch his eye was the huge fieldstone fireplace with jumping flames. Where in God's name did they get all that wood? He hadn't seen many trees coming west from Quorn. He approached the fire slowly, holding up his hands to it to gather in the warmth. Here too the ceiling was a dozen feet high, with heavy oak crossbeams. The ten-foot doors leading off to different rooms were of solid birch with carved inlays. All the door handles were cast bronze, polished by use. There was a long built-in window seat with thick tan pillows. The entire great hall, as well as the wide curved stairway, had been finished with wood paneling. The stair rail ended in a large solid oak newel post. It was a big wig place all right, fit for a king.

A half dozen young men, mostly blond and pink-faced, stood on the red flagstones before the fire, smoking thin cigars, all talking at once. They were dressed for winter, stout tan corduroy suits with knee breeches and leather leggings and high leather shoes. A couple of the young men nodded at Tunis, but kept on talking.

An elegant old man in a brown twill suit sat in a red high-backed chair to one side of the fireplace, his slippered feet up on a brass fender. He had a luxurious mop of wavy brown hair in which there didn't seem to be a trace of gray. He smoked a long fat cigar, holding it to one side away from his face, elbow resting on the round arm of the huge chair. In his other hand he coddled a snifter of brandy.

A smile moved up over the old gentleman's swarthy face, lifting his long nose a little, making his dark eyes merry. "Care for a brandy?"

"No, thanks." A drink might unleash his wild nature, especially since he wasn't used to alcohol. The Freylings had never indulged in spirits. It was bad enough that he'd once got mad enough while sober to choke a grain hand to death.

Galen emerged from a water closet. "Tunis, you met everybody?" He proceeded to introduce Tunis around the circle of young men. The young gentlemen fell silent for a second, then went on with their rousing talk. They were plotting a raid on a shipment of young immigrant girls who were about to arrive in Le Mars from Germany. All were dressed in dinner jackets.

"And Lord Sutherland, this is Tunis Freyling, seeking his fortune north of Le Mars somewhere. Homestead some land."

"Really."

Tunis felt out of place in his baggy brown woolens, though at the same time he knew he was as good as any of those young dandies plotting to debauch young green girls. If not better. Their high-nosed airs particularly galled him. He could feel his gorge rising and he warned himself to be careful and not lose his temper.

Lord Sutherland flicked off an inch of gray ash from his cigar into the coal scuttle. "They offend you, do they?" He'd caught Tunis's look of contempt.

"Oh, it ain't the first time I ran into hot air."

"Hear, hear." Lord Sutherland took a smiling sip of brandy. He swilled the sip around in his mouth several times, then swallowed it. "Very good. But they mean no harm. Just high jinks. When you're blooded you can hardly help it."

Galen glanced at the tall walnut grandfather clock at the foot of the grand staircase. "Milord, time to sit down to dinner. You know how Clara is about wanting us to eat the food hot, not cold." He nodded toward the long oaken dinner table at the south end of the great hall.

Lord Sutherland threw his still mostly unfinished cigar into the fire and struggled to get to his feet, holding the glistening brandy snifter safely level. "I've been smelling those prairie chickens for an hour. Come." He gestured for the young gentlemen to follow him as he moved toward the high-backed armchair at the head of the table. He carried his brandy with such aplomb the brown liquid hardly swilled around. There was about him a fine ancient dignity. He settled with a comfortable sigh into the armchair.

The young pups, barely breaking off their talk, found their places at the table.

Galen showed Tunis to a chair directly across the length of the table from Lord Sutherland. It was where a lady of the house would ordinarily sit.

Tunis said, "Where you gonna sit?"

"Below the salt. Ha."

Tunis grunted. "I thought you told me these fellows boozed a lot. There ain't one drinking."

"Clara had something to say about that. Said she wouldn't serve dinners if they drank before meals. The old lord excepted."

In a moment the swing door to the left of Tunis opened and Clara advanced with a huge platter of roasted prairie chickens. There was a glad shout around the table. Behind Clara came the two kitchen maids, each carrying more food in trays, stacks of sliced bread, mounds of butter, wild turnips, apple pie, oatmeal cookies. Clara and the girls set the food at the head of the table near milord.

"Looks capital, Clara," Lord Sutherland said.

"Well, it's hardly an ice cream social," Clara said shortly.

"Delicious looking. Quite."

"Well, I tried my best, the girls helping."

Lord Sutherland drew a gold repeater watch from his fashionably cut vest pocket. "And as usual, right on time. You are to be commended."

"I go by the grandfather clock. Maybe you didn't hear it strike a bit ago. Tea later?"

"Please."

Clara clapped her hands. "All right, girls, back to scrubbing pots." Clara led the two maids back into the kitchen.

All the plates had been stacked at Lord Sutherland's right hand, and he proceeded to fill each one with a whole wild prairie chicken and portions of turnip before sending it down the table on his left. Finished, milord next sent the bread plate down the table.

The best-looking dandy at the table, whom Tunis remembered as being introduced as Harry Hillyard, relished the food. With a glance at Galen, he said, "As you Americans put it, this sure beats bacon and beans."

Tunis noticed the English had a different way of handling their fork and knife. They held the knife in their right hand for cutting and the fork in their left hand to hold the meat down, then lifted the meat to their mouth with the fork still in their left hand after they'd also packed on the back of the fork a bit of turnip. They mixed the food beforehand. The American took individual bits of first this, then that, and let the stomach do the mixing. The American also, after he'd cut his meat, shifted the fork to his right hand. Watching them all Tunis wondered if maybe the English way wasn't the niftiest.

The young bloods continued to josh each other about that fresh load of German virgins coming to Le Mars.

Harry Hillyard, ruddy with the glow of good eating, had a question for milord. "George, how come you never got married? If you don't soon have issue, that blood of yours will die out."

Lord Sutherland took a slow sip of his brandy and moiled it about in his mouth as he considered the question. "Oh, there's still plenty of time."

"But, George, you're almost sixty, aren't you?"

"Sixty-one."

"Isn't that getting to be a bit late?"

"No. No." Milord took another slow sip and savor of brandy. "There's still time. In fact, I've been thinking of going along with you fellows to have a look at those German virgins."

"Why you dog you, George. I say."

Lord Sutherland picked off a morsel of flesh from his half-devoured prairie chicken. "And then there's Clara, you know. Actually, she comes from good family, which only lately has fallen on hard times. Good blood there."

"Good for you, George. Have you talked to Clara?"

"Not yet. But I've been considering it."

"Don't wait too long."

"My father didn't get married until he was almost seventy. And then he had me. As you can see he didn't do all that badly."

Tunis stiffened. That old British dog marry Clara?

Harry Hillyard set aside his fork and knife. "That reminds me of an old story about a duke and a duchess." Harry deftly touched the grease from his lips with his napkin. "As the years drifted by and as they slowly dried up, the duke and the duchess saw less and less of each other. Bored. Finally they took to sleeping in opposite ends of their castle. Only at dinner did they meet, and even then they didn't speak to each other, but spoke through their help, the duke through the butler, James, and the duchess through the maid, Elsie."

Lord Sutherland's heavy gray-tinged brows peaked up, making his long red nose seem even longer. He held a juicy morsel of meat on the tip of his fork an inch from his mouth, awaiting the end of the joke.

"Now James the butler had been instructed by the duke that he was to awaken him at quarter till eight sharp every morning no matter what, as the duke liked to look at the lusty wenches walking past his window on their way to work in the village."

Galen's mouth fell open. For all his grumbling about the pups, he was intrigued with all their noisy goings-on.

"One morning the butler entered the duke's bedroom and called out, 'Marster, time to get up now.' When there was no response from the duke's four-poster, James moved to the windows and drew back the drapes, letting in the sunlight. Still no sound from the huge bed. James kept calling out, 'Marster? Marster?' When finally the duke still didn't move, James took hold of the bed-clothes and flung them to one side. There was a pause—and then James exclaimed, 'Marster, Marster. Look! Look!'"

Harry touched his lips once more with his napkin.

"The duke groaned. 'Yes, what is it?' James said, 'Look! Look!' The duke finally managed to lift his head from the pillow. There before him was a magnificent pillar. Indeed, a tower. The duke blinked; dropped his head back into the pillow. He whispered to himself, 'For heaven's sake.' James said, 'Shall I quick go call her ladyship? Hah? Hah?' The duke lay very still for a moment. Then he said, 'Uhh, no. No, bring me my baggy tweeds and we'll smuggle it into the village.'"

There was a wonderful uproar of laughter around the table.

Tunis had to laugh too. It so exactly fit that old buzzard Lord Sutherland.

Milord popped the juicy morsel of prairie chicken into his mouth, chewed several times, finally had to laugh himself, part of the chicken showing in his gold-tipped teeth. "Awfully clever. Very good. And just how old was the duke now?"

Harry waggled his head. "I don't know. That didn't come with the story."

Milord smiled. "Well, from such evidence as I have on hand he probably was in his nineties." And with that, milord nodded once, firmly.

Presently it was time to pass the pie. As the stomachs filled the animated jolly talk fell off a little.

Milord allowed himself one more comment when, pie finished, he quaffed the rest of his brandy. "Nevertheless, when all is said and done, I am determined, like the Close brothers, to make northwestern Iowa blossom like the rose."

Harry nodded. "And recoup the fortune you lost in tea."

Tunis found the made-up bed on the sofa in the library without trouble. Coals shimmered red in the fireplace. He'd never seen so many grand books in his life. He lit a small kerosene lamp to have a better look at the ornate volumes. Most were sets, bound in red leather with gold lettering. He read the names of the authors stamped on the spines: Dickens, Thackeray, Shakespeare, Chaucer, Spenser. The books made him feel uneasy, out of place. From Old Dirk he'd learned not to trust fancy pages. They belonged to people who had a way of making common people do most of the work for them. Various milords and their damned pups were bringing the caste system into America.

17

He'd just set the lamp down on a sideboard when there was a knock on the door.

"Come in."

It was Clara, wearing a long warm scarlet dressing gown. She was carrying his duds, neatly folded. The girls had finished cleaning and ironing them for him.

"Thanks."

"Don't mention it. Are you all right?"

"Just about to turn in."

"You're staying for breakfast?"

"If the cook don't throw me out."

"Good." Then Clara frowned. Her troubled eyes slowly swung toward the fireplace. "You still going north toward Sioux Center tomorrow?"

"Yes. Why?"

"You'll be going through Le Mars then."

"I suppose so."

She snuggled up her full breasts inside her arms. "I have half a notion to go with you and take the train east. Maybe I could find a better life in old Welton. I can't take much more of this life, cooking for this bunch of worthless fops."

Tunis couldn't resist a sardonic shot. "That old buzzard Sutherland admitted at dinner tonight that he's thinking of asking you to marry him."

"Oh, him."

Tunis began to tremble. Here, if he ever was to marry, was the woman for him. He wasn't in love with her, just nervous about her, yet he knew she'd be perfect. There was a style about her that he liked.

Clara went on. "If I stay here much longer, I'm on my way to becoming an old maid. Maybe back in old Welton there might still be a nice man left over for me."

"How old are you?"

"I was nineteen the third of this month."

"You're still a young chicken."

"In this country, when you hit nineteen and you're still single, you're an old maid." She fixed her grave gray eyes on him. "And how old are you?"

There was no evading her intent look. "I was twenty-four the tenth of last month."

"February and March. Just a month apart." Clara thought that all right. A smile turned up the corners of her lips. "Well, good night now. See you in the morning." Clara quietly withdrew.

Tunis stood by the sideboard a few moments, studying to himself; then finally, sighing, blew out the little lamp and crawled into the blankets on the sofa. Nineteen and twenty-four. That was just about perfect. But what could he do about it? He had a little money in the Wanata Bank, but otherwise no real prospects. First he had to find himself some good land. Then if he still felt warm about Clara, well, then he could come back to Sutherland Hall and look her up. If she hadn't been taken by then.

It was good to nest down for the night after a long hard day. He nuzzled his cheek and nose into the fresh white pillow. He stretched, groaning in pleasure, until he could feel his toes parting.

Clara surely had a cozy bosom. She'd make a wonderful nursing mother. She was a little short, he guessed about five foot four, but still well set up.

Trouble was, he didn't deserve her. He'd killed a man once. He had a terrible temper, and until he learned how to control it, got a little older, and maybe a little wiser, he could then think about finding himself a wife.

No.

2. *Clara*

Clara had just got the coffee started and was mixing batter for the pancakes when the door to the backstairs opened and Tunis stepped in. He'd shaved and his face shone under his neatly combed rusty hair.

"You're up with the roosters."

Tunis smiled sleepily. "Thought I'd get an early start for Le Mars, the sun having come up so clear and bright."

Clara glanced out of the tall windows. A dazzling golden white snowscape stretched west to the horizon. She couldn't blame him for wanting to get going. "Then you're not going to wait up for me to go along to Le Mars."

He set his saddlebags on the floor by the back door. "You really want to go?"

She turned to put more wood into the range. "I don't know what to do. Pretty soon the bees will fly around and make honey, and then the next thing you know summer will be over, and I'll still have got nowhere."

Tunis stood uncertainly by the door.

"Wouldn't you like some coffee and cakes first? I'll set out a plate where you had tea yesterday."

He let down his broad shoulders. His eyes blazed a light pearl gray at her for a moment. "If it's not too much bother."

"Milord's pups won't be mewling for food for another hour. So pull up a chair, I've got the time." She watched him settle at the little table by the window. She noted his powerful arms. He was the best man she'd seen so far, and that included all those sons of British lords upstairs.

"How far is it to Le Mars?"

"About a day's ride on a horse. You should get there by sundown easy." She set out a brown mug of fresh coffee. "Cream? Sugar?"

"Please." He tried to cross one leg over the other; couldn't quite make it. His thighs were too hefty.

She hid a smile. She wondered how often he'd tried before to cross his legs and failed. She poured four dabs of pancake mix on the sizzling griddle. In a moment all four dabs bubbled up and turned brown along the edges. She waited until the bubbles burst open and then turned the cakes over. Soon she had four well-browned cakes. She slapped them on top of each other and set them in a white plate and brought them to his table. "Butter and syrup?"

"Please." He smiled down at the inch-thick cakes. "The way to a man's heart is by way of his stomach all right."

She pounced on that. "Does that work with you?"

He couldn't look at her.

She went back to the stove, careful not to let her long white work dress brush against its polished black edges. "Wonder were those girls are? I called them when I got up." She shook her head. "Everybody is lazy but me and Galen, and sometimes I'm not so sure about him. What's he always doing out there alone in the barn so long?"

Tunis ate his cakes with relish, neatly, cutting them the American way into little squares.

She looked up at the ceiling. "If those two girls aren't down here in five minutes, I'm going to roust them out with a red-hot poker." She saw that Tunis's plate was almost empty. "More?"

He nodded, swallowing.

She poured out four more lily pads of mix. "Would you like some bacon to go with your cakes?"

"If you please, yes."

She reached for a frying pan from the top of the range and set it over the stove lid that was the pinkest with heat. She quickly sliced a half dozen strips from a plank-hard chunk of bacon. With a fork she placed the slices neatly in the bottom of the black pan. In a moment they were sizzling and curling over and changing color from striped white to delicious amber. She went back to the griddle and flipped the cakes.

She threw some more wood into the hungry ash-edged maw of the range. The flames took hold almost immediately and began to roar up the black stovepipes.

She spoke as though to herself, but meaning it for him. "I miss Welton, I surely do. Even though my father wasn't much of a farmer, we still had great times there. I remember Christmas. The silver knives Mother had, the copper and bronze pans hanging polished by the fireplace, the morning pudding pretty with burning brandy."

21

"What happened?"

"My father and mother died of diphtheria."

"Galen mentioned that."

"I know I must get out of here." She brought him the second batch of perfectly browned cakes, as well as the lucent curls of bacon. "I hope these are all right."

"Perfect. Couldn't be better."

"But even if my folks hadn't died we would probably have ended up on the poor farm. Dad just didn't have the knack for farming. He kept saying it was so different here in America." She glanced outside where the sun danced in lemon dazzles on the curving snowbanks. "Yes, I used to go to bed to read my sheets."

Tunis looked up puzzled, mouth full of food. "Come again?"

"We ran out of money for bed linens. So Mother made sheets out of flour sacks. And for quite a while a person could see where the lettering still showed."

"That's funny."

"Yes, it is, when you remember where my father came from." She shook her head. "And when you remember Mother brought bolts and bolts of cloth from the Old Country."

"What did you do with all your family's things?"

"Mother had to sell them bit by bit to the neighbors to pay our bills. After that, my father tried to raise flax. And what little flax we got, we women spun it for towels, which we sold. Not for our bedding."

Tunis sat very still.

What she couldn't tell this man was the other stuff. Her father, Cecil Short-ridge, had been kicked off the Shortridge estate near Yarmouth, England, not so much because as a second son he might be a threat to the firstborn, but because of all his escapades. He'd gotten more than one girl in trouble, and would never have married Clara's mother if there hadn't been a scandal about what he'd done to his own sister. He wasn't the only Shortridge to have done that. There were rumors that there'd been incest in his father's generation, on both sides. It seemed his family had a proclivity for it. Just as it also had a tendency to have weak lungs. Clara remembered that because of his asthma her father coughed a lot. It was hardly a wonder he became a victim of deadly diphtheria. And because her father hardly did a lick of work on their Welton home, her mother had to do practically everything, plow, sow, cultivate, harvest, in addition to the housework. Finally, worn out, she too succumbed to diphtheria.

Tunis crossed his fork and knife over his plate to signify he was finished. He pushed back his chair and stood up. "That was the best yet. Thanks." He stretched, extending his arms. "And now, to hit the trail."

"You're going then?" She knew it was a foolish question. It was obvious he was going. But she hated seeing him leave. What a handsome man. Pure in mind. Much better blood in him than there was in her veins. Perhaps having children with him would purify what tainted blood she had.

"So long." He knicked his head and then stepped out onto the porch, closing the tall oak door behind him.

She heard him stomp into his leather boots. Some rustling followed during which she guessed he was slipping into his long sheepskin coat and putting on his woolen mittens. In a moment the outer porch door opened, then closed.

She stepped to the window to watch him walk to the barn. He was following Galen's tracks in the new deep snow. He had to lengthen his natural stride to follow where Galen's longer legs had gone. She would never see Tunis Freyling again. The sun burned a glossy yellow off the angled slants of snow.

She brushed a tear from her eyes. She shrugged herself erect. "I mustn't think about him."

Then she remembered something. She went into the great hall and looked at the grandfather clock. "Seven-thirty? And those girls still aren't up?"

She set aside her pancake turner, pushed the griddle to the back of the range over the reservoir, and headed for the back stairs.

Halfway up the stairs she decided to go softly, on her toes. If they heard her coming the girls might pretend they'd been awake all along. She stole along the red-carpeted hallway to their door. As she reached for the door handle, she felt like a big cat out to catch some naughty mice.

She paused. She heard men giggling behind the door. Men? What? Pups in there?

She snapped open the door and let it flang against the wall. "What are you . . . oh, my Lord!"

Lurilla and Greta lay each with a young man between her upraised knees. Despite the chill in the room all four were naked. Morning light gleamed pink on the backs of the men.

Clara recognized the curly blond hair of Harry Hillyard. "So! scum will rise to the surface, ha?"

All four bodies stiffened.

"So that's why you two girls have always been such slugsabed in the morning. You slutsabed!"

Harry let go with a muffled chuckle into Lurilla's brown tousled hair and started up an undulating motion again.

"And as for you, Harry Hillyard, you aren't a gentleman, debauching a young girl while I'm talking to you. Och!" Clara whirled around, stepped out into the hall, and slammed the door shut after her.

She stood a moment, puffing, catching her breath, vision cross-eyed. "The only thing worse would have been if I'd caught the old lord in there."

It was obvious the girls were enjoying themselves. She saw again their lust-thickened eyes, their silly fat smiles, their bodies thrown open in abandonment. It instantly brought to mind what her father had done to her mother; that they'd then had to get married and leave England. She wondered if she'd been conceived in a moment such as she'd just seen.

Thinking of the old lord, she knew straightaway what to do. She stepped smartly down the stairs and then to milord's bedroom on the other side of the library.

She rapped sharply on his door. "Sir, may I have a word with you?"

Milord's old voice came faintly, ruckling. "Pardon?"

"Are you decent? I want to see you a moment."

"Of course. Come in, Clara."

Clara stepped inside. The odor of perspiring old skin was strong in the room. "I came to tell you that I am quitting. As of now."

Milord rose in his pillows. He was wearing a fluffy white nightcap over his thick brown hair. He was deathly afraid of night drafts. "Why, my dear, what's wrong?"

"If you could have seen what I just now saw. Upstairs there in the maid's room. Two of your pups . . . It was beastly . . . Och."

Milord's brown eyes opened bright and piercing. "Well, can you blame them? It's the way of warm blood, my dear."

"Then you've known this has been going on?"

"Naturally. It's quite charming."

"You old goat you."

"Thank you. I'll take that as a compliment. I still think young, my dear. As you might find out if you were to join me here in bed."

The black jet ring next to the gold wedding band on milord's left ring finger caught Clara's eye. The old devil was still, formally at least, grieving over the loss of his wife. "I mean that. I've been thinking of asking you to marry me."

"Me marry you! When you're still mourning the loss of your wife?"

"Oh, pshaw. That's easily removed." Milord quite handily slipped the black ring off his finger. "And why not marry you? I'll wager you have more gray hairs than I have."

Clara had oftened wondered if the old gentleman dyed his hair, it always looked so fresh and dark. Again she said it. "Me marry you?"

"Why not? I can't marry a commoner, which I'd be doing if I struck up something with one of the maids. But you're not a commoner. You've got the blood in you."

Clara backed toward the door. "Mister Sutherland," she said, using "mister" deliberately instead of "lord," and glaring at him, "I came in here to tell you I'm quitting. And I mean as of now. You, and your trollops, and your silly English lads gone wild from lack of parental care, can make your own breakfast."

"I take it then you won't marry me?"

"No!"

"Oh, pshaw."

"And I want one of your men to take me to Le Mars. Immediately. Today yet."

3. Tunis

As he approached the next rise in the land, Tunis saw less snow on the ground, and in some places, where the bluestem grass was as high as Gyp's gold mane, there didn't seem to be any white at all. Gyp moved easily, free at last of having to break through the hard crusts of snowdrifts. Arriving at the crest, Tunis saw that the wide valley of the Floyd River ahead was completely free of snow. A soft northwest wind moved over the tall rusty grass in rippling waves.

He was startled to see, down in the middle of the wide sloping valley, a considerable city. Le Mars. It was the biggest town he'd ever seen. At least three hundred houses. In the very center of the town stood several two-story buildings with imposing false fronts.

Looking to either side, he was pleased to see there still weren't many farmsteads around. There were two directly ahead, several off to the south toward Sioux City, three west of town, and off to the north, the direction he was interested in, he saw only one, nestled at the base of some high hills.

Gyp heard it first. A rumbling rushing sound. In a moment there was a moaning whistle. Looking off to the left, Tunis spotted smoke bubbling up over the edge of an intervening loaf of a hill. A train. The jumping smoke rose higher, blasting into spreading clouds of gray and black and white, and then under it a smokestack emerged, and finally the whole black engine, drive shaft pistoning, tall wheels flashing, green passenger cars and red boxcars following after as if, though inanimate, they were playing follow the leader. The train rushed toward Le Mars. Looking sharply, Tunis still couldn't make out the tracks. The wild prairie grass hid them.

Gyp watched the train with raised head, ears working back and forth, eyes started, nostrils flared open.

"What's the matter, Gypsy? Think it'll take after you?"

Gyp stayed nervous until he was sure the train wasn't coming their way. Then, content danger was past, he began to crop at the short grass mingled in at the roots of the taller bluestem.

Tunis was next startled to see a stagecoach coming over the far bluffs on the other side of the river valley. One of the two men sitting up on the driver's seat lifted something that glittered in the sun, and in a moment a horn sounded. The other man was holding the reins and lashing the four horses to a full gallop.

"I'll be strapped for skin," Tunis murmured. "A four-in-hand with someone winding the horn." The folk in the coach obviously wanted to be on time to meet the train in Le Mars. "Probably want to be sure they get first picks of those German virgins coming in."

As the coach started down the far bluff it kicked up several coveys of quail. The quail skimmed to either side like flat stones skipped across water. Moments later the coach chased up two wolves who'd apparently been stalking the quail.

Tunis pulled up Gyp's head and kicked him lightly under the belly with his heels. "C'mon, old skate, it's time we got into town ourselves. With everybody coming into town we may have trouble finding room for ourselves."

With a groan and a rippling shudder of roan hide, Gyp started up into a light gallop. Some hundred yards down the slope Gyp choused up two silver foxes. And a second later, a covey of some dozen prairie chickens cackled up out of the tall grass and slid in a long easy glide off to the right, vanishing into an island of cattails down in a wet draw.

In town Tunis headed for the livery stable near the House of Lords saloon. Gyp was chary about stepping into the big wide door. But when a horse whinnied from the back of the barn, Gyp whinnied back and stepped inside. Light brown powdery dung lined the floor of the long alley. The man in charge assigned Gyp to a far stall. Tunis took off the saddlebags and saddle and horse blanket and bridle, and after tying Gyp to the manger he fed him a panful of barley and some wild slough hay.

Curious to see the train come in, as well as wondering what all those imported girls might look like, Tunis wandered over to the green depot. He took up a spot at the end of the platform. Just as the huge engine nosed up, jetting steam, drive shafts clanking, iron crying, the four-in-hand chased in from the other side and pulled up with all four horses rearing. The driver cried a mighty "Whoa!" just as the steam engine whistled shrilly. The platform was already half-filled with joking young men eagerly scanning the windows of the coaches for a glimpse of the virgins. They too let go with a wild yell. Their rhuing was like the bugling of stallions.

The train crunched to a full stop. A conductor stepped down from the end of each coach. And in a moment a passel of young girls wearing gray bonnets and long gray frocks, obviously foreign, stepped down onto the cinder platform. They crowded together, eyes scrinched up in wonder and apprehension, looking at the men staring at them, at the depot, then at the town around, and then at the far hills.

Looking them over, one by one, Tunis didn't spot one that appealed to him, certainly not one that came up to Clara. Most had plain pink faces; several were downright scarecrows.

Just as Tunis started thinking about getting a room somewhere, he spotted Lord Sutherland coming up in a carriage driven by Galen. Four young pups were with him. And coming up in a brisk gallop behind milord were a half dozen more of his pups on horseback led by Harry Hillyard. The old lord's sharp brown eyes went picking over the huddled virgins.

Lifting a shoulder, Tunis turned and headed back to the House of Lords saloon, thinking that might be as good a place as any to get something to eat. He took a shortcut by way of an alley and after a dozen steps found himself holding his nose. Piles of filth nearly blocked the alley: empty whiskey bottles, empty bean tins, dog turds, human turds, torn clothes, strips of bloody rags, worn-through mittens, decayed potatoes, stinking wild turnips, half-eaten barbecued ribs. The worst were the decayed potatoes—their rotten sweet stink burned in the nose.

Tunis took the front steps up into the House of Lords saloon. The year before, the state of Iowa had passed a prohibition law, but it was obvious from the smell of alcohol that the proprietors were ignoring the law. Pushing through the second set of swing doors, Tunis wasn't surprised to see a dozen young men at a long dark mahogany bar drinking whiskey and beer. The tables off to the left were full too. The place was noisy with high-nosed English accents.

Tunis stepped up to the nearest barkeep. "Can an American get some grub in here?"

The barkeep, a heavy-shouldered fellow, wiped and wiped an already clean shining bar. "If you mean dinner, no. For that you'll have to go down the street to one of the cafes."

"Would such a cafe have a room for rent?"

"Might."

Abruptly there was a lot of banging against the outer swing doors, some cursing and shouting, and the crumpling clatter of shod horse hooves; then the inner swing doors parted and in thundered a man on horseback. It was wild Harry Hillyard, shouting, laughing, as with one hand he held back an almost crazed bay horse and with his other arm supported one of the newly arrived German virgins across the pommel of his saddle. "Tallyho, lads! I've found me a saint of a woman at last. Wait'll you see the pups out of this match."

The barkeep's fleshy eyes first opened, then closed. His heavy cheeks flushed a dark red. "For chrissake, Harry, you ain't proposin' to breed her right here on top of the bar, are you?"

"You bet your boots."

The barkeep hurried around from behind the bar. "Get that damned horse out of here! Before the marshall comes. It's stunts like this that'll be sure to close this bar down. Get out!"

27

Harry laughed down at the barkeep. "Oh, Tom, we're just out to paint the town red a little. Ain't we, Gerd?" He cupped up the German virgin around her bosom and shook her in a loving way. Gerd was utterly astounded, utterly embarrassed by what was suddenly happening to her in wild America. Harry's bay horse, meanwhile, was stamping and rearing, frothing at the bit, crinkling up the oak floor with its calked shoes.

"Get out! You're wrecking our new floor."

"What? You don't want to toast the bride?"

Tom the barkeep grabbed up a broom and began beating the horse and Harry and the German virgin with it.

The whole place echoed with shouts of laughter.

"Get out! G'wan, you damned drunken fool," Tom cried.

"Oh, well," Harry laughed, hugging his virgin, "if that's your mind, all right, we'll leave. But I'm not letting you kiss her at the wedding."

"Kiss her, my arse. Once those virgins find out what hellions you damned British are, they'll scatter out over the prairie like hens roushed out of a coop by a fox."

Harry backed up his bay horse, cutting and crimpling up the oak floor some more, finally got his horse to whirl around, then left the same way he came, swing doors flopping to and fro.

Breathing plumes of anger, Tom the barkeep threw the broom upright in a corner and went stomping around behind his bar again. He leaned heavily on the bar, puffing. Finally, getting control of himself, he noticed Tunis.

"And what'll you have?"

Tunis smiled. "Like I said, I was looking for a place to eat and sleep. But maybe I should wet my whistle first."

"What'll it be?" Tom the barkeep waved a hand at the stacked bottles of whiskey.

"Sarsaparilla."

Tom the barkeep paused; then raised his voice. "Hey, fellas, I want you to take note. In case the marshall comes in here to close this saloon, I'm serving sarsaparilla to this gent." He reached for a slim brown bottle, uncorked it, and set it before Tunis. "That'll be one nickel."

Tunis paid up.

When Tunis stepped outside again, dusk had fallen. He took a peek into the House of Commons saloon, saw that while it wasn't quite as stylish as the House of Lords establishment it still served only liquor.

Next came the exclusive Prairie Club.

A liveried red-haired flunkey blocked the ornate door. "Yes? What do you want here?"

Looking past the doorman, Tunis saw elegance such as he'd never before imagined. The first room, huge and with many tall windows, featured a fine glistening oblong pool table with a deep green billiard cloth. Fancy red-leather upholstered chairs ranged the walls. Four men stood around the pool table. One of the men chalked the point of his cue and then leaned over the table to make a difficult shot. All four men were dressed in white shirts, red vests, and black suits.

"Sir?"

Tunis resented the pompous doorman. "You mind if I stretch my neck a little?"

"Sir, this is a gentleman's club."

Tunis had to laugh. "How much will it set me back to join?"

"Twenty-five dollars. But of course the membership would have to vote on you application."

Beyond the gaming room, through some folding doors, another elegant room could be seen, a library of sorts, with tables, easy chairs and lamps, shelves of leather-bound books. Tunis sneered at all the folderol. "All this would be okay if you British weren't so dirty."

"Whott! Dirty? Piffle."

"Sometime take a gander at all that filth in the alley behind your club."

"But our alley is clean."

"It wasn't behind the House of Lords saloon."

"Awfully sporting of you to mention that. You Americans!"

"We Americans believe a true aristocrat cleans up after himself." With that Tunis turned and left.

Tunis found a boardinghouse not far from the livery stable. For dinner the cook served up salted pork, brown beans, green tea, and dark rye bread. It was poor fare compared to the country meals Old Tressa used to serve. And the bed was lumpy with old straw, though the sheets were clean and there were no bedbugs.

That night Tunis dreamt a strange dream. A tramp grain hand with silverish eyes came riding on a horse up the stairs and crashed into the room where

Tunis slept. The tramp saw where Tunis lay stretched out and from behind his back flourished a scythe and began taking swipes at Tunis. Tunis tried to duck away from the swipes, first one way, then the other. When the swipes came to within an inch of his nose, whistling, glittering, Tunis made an agonized dive for the floor. When a loud bang in his head woke Tunis up out of his dream, he found himself on the floor. He'd pulled the quilts with him off the bed.

"Goddam," he muttered, "that dummed tramp has sure got into me."

The next morning at breakfast Tunis had more pork and beans and green tea. He learned from two men who were traveling north by way of the stagecoach that the better farmland was rapidly being taken up along the West Branch toward Sioux Center and beyond. The two men were land speculators, and they went on to say that there was still some good farming country left near the town of Bonnie on the forks of the Rock River.

Tunis asked, "How do you get to Bonnie from here?"

"Follow the stagecoach trail. It runs from Le Mars to Sioux Center to Bonnie. From Bonnie on north into Minnesota they now have a train."

"A train? Already?"

"You got it."

When Tunis stepped outside he saw that it was going to be another sunny day out. But the stench coming from the alleys was still awful. Compared to the air on Old Dirk's farm, city air was an abomination.

Gyp was snorty when Tunis walked into his stall. Tunis curried the horse, brushed him down, and saddled him. Most of the horses nickered as Tunis led Gyp down the center alley and outside. It was as though during the night all the horses had become fast friends and now hated to part company.

Within minutes, trotting, Tunis found the stagecoach trail leading north out of Le Mars. He crossed the Floyd River and then climbed a height-of-land. He kept the West Branch of the Floyd in sight on his left. The wind had switched around to the south, at his back, and it wasn't long before he had to open his sheepskin coat. And Gyp worked up a sweat.

Tunis galloped Gyp two miles, then walked him a half-mile, then galloped him two miles. They put the country behind them at a rapid rate. The trail actually was several trails in the deep grass. When the tracks became deep ruts, stage drivers merely picked out a new route to either side on the virgin prairie.

There were no fences on the high ground, though there were farmsteads everywhere along the bottoms. Apparently every farmer used the high ground for a pasture in common. All the houses and barns were made of sod. Where a farmer was lucky enough to have a cutbank along the West Branch, he excavated a warm dugout for himself. It was all very primitive.

Checking the weathered mounds of the badgers and the pocket gophers, Tunis saw that the land was first-rate, all black soil, at least two feet deep even over the highest ground. There was no doubt that if it was farmed right, the whole country along the West Branch of the Floyd River would someday be a Garden of Eden.

It was noon when Tunis spotted a cluster of wooden houses in a valley ahead. The houses straddled a railroad track running east and west. The railroad upset Tunis. Maybe it was already too late to find good homestead land.

They descended the high ground and trotted across a flat slough. All trails converged on a sandy ford and from there headed into the cluster of houses. Tunis spotted a long sod house on the near side of the ford. It had a crudely lettered sign tacked over the doorway:

MAURICE POST OFFICE

AND ALL YOU CAN EAT FOR 25¢

Tunis decided to pull up. There were a dozen hitching posts out front made of ash limbs stuck into the ground. Gyp never liked being tied to a hitching post, and with a little smile at the willful nature of his horse Tunis decided to drop the reins to the ground and just let Gyp graze where his nose took him. Gyp liked human company too well to run off.

Tunis had to duck to enter the low dingy sod inn. The air was thick with smoke. The fireplace wasn't drawing too well, but what made it worse was the knotted grass being burned for fuel. The proprietor and his wife didn't have a stove or a range but did all their cooking over the open fire. Both of them were shorties, thin, and as quick as squirrels.

The proprietor showed Tunis to a table near the only window. "Special today is pork and beans."

Tunis saw that the only thing cooking over the fire was a huge blackened iron pot. "Well, I think instead I'll have some beans and pork."

The proprietor spoke over his shoulder. "Ellie, he prefers the beans and pork."

"Coming up, Maurice."

Tunis asked, "Do you have some tea?"

"Tea? Out here?"

The huge plate of pork and beans turned out to be tasty. Ellie had juiced up the mess with plenty of meat. The meat tasted wild. Tunis kept savoring it, trying to identify it. Finally with a fork he held up a strand of the meat. "Rabbit?"

"No. Skunk."

For a second Tunis almost threw up. Somehow he managed to keep his meat trap shut. "So that's what gives it the flavor."

"Yep. If you kill 'em careful and take out the stink sack careful, it makes for a nice tasty dish."

"Well, there's always a first time for skunk."

Both Maurice and Ellie coughed a lot. The smoke was getting to them. Every time they barked Tunis could almost see a tail snapping erect behind them.

Tunis managed to finish the strange meal. "How much?"

"Two bits. And we don't accept tips."

"Why not tips?"

"Because neither one of us is help. We own the place together."

"Will you accept a late March smile as a tip?"

"Only if you mean it."

"With me smiles are hard to come by."

"Got a guilty conscience?"

"More than you might know."

When Tunis stepped outside, he found Gyp had grazed off a couple dozen steps from where the reins had been dropped. Tunis mounted with his stomach feeling funny. And Gyp groaned that he had to run some more.

Gyp took the frozen ford in the West Branch on ginger hooves, the steel calks biting into the ice with crackling breaking sounds, then climbed the far bank. Gyp wasn't sure he wanted to cross the railroad tracks. He snorted down at the iron rails and cinder-sprinkled ties. Tunis urged him on, and at last with a long leap Gyp cleared the tracks. The two trotted through the cluster of houses with its one false-front store. Several women were hanging out clothes, fingers and noses red from the cold. The tracks narrowed to a point to the far east and to the far west. The tracks and the little green depot with its sign marked MAURICE seemed completely out of place, like children's toys tumbled out onto a clean tablecloth.

They mounted a slow rise. There were no trees in sight anywhere, only the everlasting waving tall rusty grasses. Some of the grass was higher than Gyp's tossing golden mane.

The wild prairie rolled a little in slow easy slopes. Again Tunis ran his horse easy, two miles on a trot, a half mile at a walk.

The sun was setting when they breasted over the last rise. Below lay a hamlet of several dozen houses, one church with a steeple, and four false-front stores. Two buggies and a carriage were lined up along a row of hitching posts. The horses were covered with blankets, heads down as they waited.

Tunis tied Gyp up to a hitching post. He noted the strange names on the storefronts: DeVries, Wayenberg, Vermeer, Oddink. The lettering on the false front immediately before him read: FABER'S FURNITURE & UNDERTAKING.

Across the street was Meademan's Cafe. Tunis headed for it, stepping across frozen dirty ruts.

A blond balding man, fat, looked Tunis up and down as he entered. The man had an enormous brown moustache, the tips of it curling up under his ears on either side. That man looked as if he wasn't exactly happy to see a stranger.

Tunis said, "Is there a hotel in this town?"

"Nope."

"No place I can put up for the night?"

"Noo."

"This Sioux Center?"

"Ya."

"How come you got no sign on the edge of town?"

"Everybody here knows this is Sioux Center."

A sign hung tucked into the edge of the big window. It read: WE ONLY STRIKE THE HIGH POINTS ON THE ROAD. LE MARS–BONNIE STAGE LINE.

Tunis asked, "Does the stagecoach stop here?"

"Ya."

"If the stagecoach should get stalled here in a blizzard, where would you put up the passengers?"

The bald man played it straight. "Vell, then we throw down some extra straw in a stall in the barn and pud 'em up there."

"That I believe."

There were no other customers in the place. Several more signs in a strange language hung over the sink and the cookstove. There were six wooden tables, each with four chairs. "Your name Meademan?"

"You hit it."

"No use asking then if I can put up my horse if I have to ride on yet tonight."

Meademan's upper lip made a little twisting motion, stirring up the elaborate moustache. Then Meademan stuck out a pale cook's hand. "You know, you look all right to me. Pud her there. I've got a room for you upstairs."

Tunis shook hands.

After he put up Gyp, Tunis came back for his supper. He wasn't too hungry. The skunk meat had gone down all right, but the thought of it hadn't. He asked for a menu.

"So you want a choice?"

"If there is one. I'm getting pretty sick of pork and beans."

"Vell, that's all you're gonna get here. Unless you'd like some *fet met stroop.*"

"Come again?"

"Dutchman's special. Pour a little melted hog fat, hot, into a prewarmed plate, next pour in a puddle of syrup, then take bread and break it and dip it in the mixture, taking up a little of both the fat and the syrup, and you got yourself a tasty thing there."

"Let's try it. There's always a first time for everything."

"Now you're talking."

Talk got around to what land was still available for homesteading.

Meademan said almost all the land around Sioux Center and Jerusalem was taken up. "Oh, there's maybe a little corner left here and there, a wet slough or a sandy hill, but you can be sure it ain't gonna be worth much."

Tunis dipped some more bread in the sweet mix in his plate. He liked it. He could feel himself being restored. "There still some left up north though?"

Meademan handed him a weekly paper, the Rock Falls *Journal.* He pointed to the lead article. "Read that."

Tunis read as he ate:

32

We are often asked, "How are we to reach Leonhard County?" We reply, "If you are coming with a team, why, Drive on of course." Never mind the rivers or sloughs, you can cross them almost anywhere at this season. Keep your eye on your compass to be sure of your course. Camp where night overtakes you, and in the morning, *Drive on.*

Bring all the stock along you have or can get. It will cost you nothing to feed them this side of the state at least, and when once here cut all the grass you please to winter on free. We have on our quarter section probably 100 tons of grass that will not be cut this year, except enough to cover our sod house, and you are welcome to cut all you please. *Drive on.*

To those who come by railroad we say, Buy a ticket to Le Mars (never mind Sioux City unless you want to see . . . but then what is there to see in Sioux City?) and from there take the Le Mars-Whitebone stage, and the gentleman driver will set you down safely at our sanctum (when we get it built) in Leonhard County. We have no first-class hotels yet at Rock Falls, but you can sleep with us unless there are too many of you, and then we can divide you among our warm-hearted log houses, and take care of you. So, *Drive on.*

Tunis looked at the date of the paper. "Why, but this is a couple of years old!"

"It's still the true dope though."

"But I heard there's a train now running down from Whitebone way. To Bonnie."

"Sure. And how far that track has been laid and ironed beyond that point I'm not sure."

Tunis helped himself to two dishes of hot fat with syrup and seven thick slices of homemade bread. He smacked his lips. He'd never before tasted anything like it. So long as the fat was warm, it tasted good.

"Anything else?"

"Coffee?"

"Just got in a fresh package of Arbuckle. Put hair on your chest."

Presently the coffee was ready. Tunis liked his with cream and sugar. He stirred the brew, had himself a sip. "Mmm. Hits the spot."

Meademan sipped some coffee with him. "It always does, don't it?" He shook his bald head, wiped his lips under his wide brown moustache. "We're lucky the wife don't know this came in today. She usually grabs the Arbuckle for the company at the house."

"Any Indians around?"

"Sometimes."

"Dangerous?"

"No. Mostly they're Yankton Dakota. They signed a treaty with the guv'ment to get out of here in 1851. When you see them they're usually hanging around in the river bottoms. Need water for their animals and theirselves just like we do. Fellow west of here had a band of Indians camp on his farm one evening. He watched them through the window of his sod house, making sure his kids were safe under the bed. All the Indians did was rope a calf that'd wandered too close, and butcher and eat it. Farmer said afterwards he felt he was lucky, if a person took into consideration that the land once belonged to the Indians. Said he'd be glad to trade one hundred sixty acres for a wandering calf any day."

Tunis held out his cup for more coffee. "How much is land going for around here?"

Meademan poured. "About five bucks an acre. Improved, it goes for maybe ten. It depends on what kind of year you've had around here. If there's been a grasshopper plague, it goes dirt cheap. A lot of people then want to move back to Wisconsin. Even to the Old Country. What hurts is those blixen land speculators."

"Cost much to get started farming?"

"Not really. If you've got horses and plow and some seed, you're ready to go. The sod house costs you only maybe a dollar fifty. And that's mostly for the window and the boards for the door. The sod for the walls you get free. Same for the branches and twigs and long slough grass and sod for the roof."

"Sounds easy enough."

"Say, are you in an awful rush?"

"No. Why?"

"Vell, you look like a puddy good feller. And the Lord wants us to try and save everybody we can. Vhy don't you stay over for Sunday and hear the gospel preached by a great preacher. Reverend Hollaar. Man, how he can reveal what's in that Bible at the same time that he's pounding some sense into you."

"I ain't been much for going to church."

"All the more reason vhy you should stay over Sunday then. You're saveable."

Tunis could still taste the fet met stroop. "He preach in English?"

"No, he preaches in Dutch."

Tunis shook his head. "For me to go to your Dutch service would be like trying to produce colts with a gelding. No shot delivered."

Meademan's head reared back. He was torn between wanting to laugh and being offended. He threw a quick look around, worried there might have been another patron in his cafe after all. Finally laughter won out and his wide moustache curled even farther under his ears. "Ha! Vell, maybe you're right. I shouldna been so pushy." He chuckled. "Reminds me of a story. There was this husband, see. He'd just learned that his wife was going to die and would soon face her judgment—when here all her life she's been a secret drinker. He paces up and down in their bedroom beside her deathbed, keeps asking her, 'Are you saved, Ma? Are you saved?' to which she keeps saying, patiently, breathing her last, 'Ya, Pa, I am saved.' Vell, you know, she soon gets tired of his carrying on, his sickening question 'Are you saved?,' so finally she rears up in bed and says, 'I've told you a thousand times, yes, I am saved! Now, shut your trap.'"

Tunis couldn't help but let go with a hearty laugh.

Meademan laughed with him. "Ya, ve Hollanders, ve can laugh at ourselves too, you know."

Tunis finished his coffee. "Where's the bed?"

"Come along." Meademan took the back way upstairs, Tunis following, and entered a room overlooking the main street. Meademan lighted a small kerosene lamp. The room was simple, whitewashed, with just a thick bed and a chair.

Tunis stared at the fat mattress. "A feather bed."

"Yep. You're going to sleep in the lap of luxury tonight. Ve aim to make Sioux Center famous for its sleeping accommodations. When ve Hollanders sleep ve wanna sleep on the best bedding there is. That's vhy so many of us marry fat wives."

"And indulge in *fet met stroop*."

"Ya. 'Night."

"'Night."

Early the next morning Tunis hit the stage trail going north. Again it was a nice day, clear blue skies, sun slowly warming the sleeping brown land, the tall rusty grasses on the high slopes waving in the easy southeast wind, frost slowly leaving the land.

He ran into two herds of cattle guarded by young boys on horseback.

Everywhere there were sod houses and sod barns near some plow-broken land. The diggings resembled dome-shaped muskrat nests. In the warming day, children came out and played being pioneers. A thawed-out pocket gopher mound was a place for a new play settlement. Match boxes served as houses and barns. The children caught field mice and pretended they were horses, tying a piece of twine string around their necks and staking them out in miniature pastures. Tunis remembered when he as a boy caught big yellow grasshoppers for make-believe horses and had hobbled them with store string.

For several hours Tunis galloped and walked Gyp across an utterly flat land. There were no hills, no trees, no streams anywhere. The grass was incredibly deep, and if it hadn't been for the stagecoach trail Tunis would have strayed from the direct route to Bonnie. The sun directly overhead at noon wasn't of much help to find directions.

It became warm out. He opened his sheepskin coat. The smell of a winter-confined body rose from his clothes.

Shadows had begun to appear on the right side of stalks of grass when Tunis came upon another railroad track. Ties and iron rails had been placed on the prairie with no grading. Looking east along the tracks Tunis could just barely make out the chimneys and spires of a little town several miles away. Another pocket of people already! To the west the shining tracks narrowed into blue infinity.

Gyp snorted at the tracks and once again was reluctant to cross them.

"I don't like seeing it any more than you do, Gypsy old boy. It could mean we're on a wild goose chase."

Gyp finally, with Tunis digging his heels into the horse's flanks, leaped over the tracks.

They continued going north. Soon the land began to slope down and away again, and little draws appeared, and then valleys and hills. The stagecoach trail followed the high ground, slowly veering northwest. Soon too little trickling streams appeared in the valleys. The water ran over and under ice.

They stopped at one of the bigger streams and refreshed themselves with ice-cold water, the man kneeling upstream from the horse and cupping up water in his bare hand and the horse curving its long neck down and sipping with its wide rubbery lips.

The wriggling trail swung down a long slope and headed for a river fringed by leafless trees. The trail crossed a sandy ford, climbed a short steep hill, and headed for a little town. The town lay on a table of land with the east side of it going up a long slow rise of land. There were some fifty houses and a half dozen false-front stores. Looking off the the left Tunis saw the trees of yet another river coming down from the northwest. It joined the first river a mile to the south. That had to be the forks of the Rock. A considerable grove of slender cottonwoods grew at the confluence.

Tunis headed for what looked like a small hotel on the near edge of the town. A dozen hitching posts stood in line along the sunny side.

Tunis climbed down and went inside.

A bearded man looked up from tending a wood stove. "Howdy."

"This burg got a livery stable?"

"Farther up town it does. Near the Bonnie Hotel."

"Two hotels here?"

"Yeh, worse luck. Ever since the damned Bonnie Omaha Railroad people decided to build a depot and a roundhouse north of here, the business center of Bonnie sprung up there. Instead of here. Old Man Rice built this little hotel, thinking this would be the center. But now even he has gone and built a second hotel near the depot."

"Well, I need a place for my horse. So I guess I better head for the main part of Bonnie. Sorry."

Tunis got aboard Gyp again. "Just a little ways more, old friend, and you'll have some sweet hay. Hup. Let's go."

Gyp followed a wagon trail in the soggy grass. After a couple of rods Gyp seemed to smell the sweet hay ahead and on his own broke into a gallop, heading straight for the taller buildings.

The few houses they passed were all one story and made from what looked like freshly cut cottonwood. Some of the siding was already warped, giving the modest cottages an old sagging look. Some children were out playing cowboy-and-indian in the tall bluestem along the edge of the dropoff to the west. There wasn't a single tree in town. The pioneers still hadn't gotten around to planting shoots and saplings.

Gyp nosed out the Bonnie Livery Barn before Tunis did, and whinnied ahead to a pair of spanking bays hitched to a flashy black buggy. The livery barn doors faced south under a staggered false-front peak. Within fifty feet of the barn Tunis could smell dried powdery horse manure. It was the kind of smell that always made him cough a little.

Tunis swung down just as the proprietor stepped outside with a customer. The two shook hands, and then the customer mounted into the buggy and with a flipping snap of the reins over the backs of the horses drove off.

The proprietor turned and eyed Tunis's roan horse. "What'll it be for you?"

"Need bed and board for the horse."

"Your horse got the heaves?"

"No."

"Then I got oats for him. And slough hay."

"I'll take it. Come, Gyp."

After Tunis had unsaddled Gyp and curried him down while the horse fed hungrily on the oats and hay, Tunis shouldered his saddlebags and headed around to the north side of the block to the Bonnie Hotel.

Tunis was surprised by the size of the hotel. It was larger than any building in Le Mars. Three stories high, with a lovely veranda on the north side, it boasted, according to a placard tacked beside the front door, that it had fifty-four rooms and was the favorite stopover of land agents, salesmen, and financiers. "Finest and largest in Northwest Iowa."

The lobby was filled with a variety of men: some dressed in fancy black suits and smoking long cigars, some in gray rough woolens and smoking pipes, some sportive and young, some sedate and middle-aged. The tobacco smoke mingling with wood smoke from an old potbellied iron stove was so thick Tunis had trouble getting his breath at first. Talk too was thick: about horses, "a fine stepper, and plenty of style and life"; about women, "we ought to import some wimmen in here like they do down in Le Mars"; about land, "the prairie along Mud Creek is so rich a feller ought to be able to get fifty bushels to the acre"; about the railroad, "those jealous fatheads north of here in Rock Falls can call our railroad 'a streak of rust' if they want to, but I tell you Bonnie now ranks as one of our finest western towns."

The talk excited Tunis. He got himself a room on the third floor, 312, overlooking the forks of the Rock to the south, emptied his saddlebags out on the bed to give the contents some air, shaved, had himself a quick bath, and then dressed for dinner, fresh shirt and string tie and new black button shoes. His brown woolen trousers were by now quite baggy over the knees, but if he quick sat down at a table no one would notice. He unfolded his black dress jacket and saw that the folds were more pronounced than the original press Old Tressa had put in them.

There was a knock at the door.

"Come in."

A pretty chambermaid entered. She was wearing a long white dress trimmed in red. She was blond, and chubby and cuddly like Cupid was sometimes pictured, and had pink dimpled cheeks and fat lips. "Would there be anything else?"

"Besides what?" The moment he spoke Tunis knew what she meant. He blushed. He'd never lain with a woman and here now was an offer for him to do so.

"The management wishes to make sure you're happy with your accommodations." She spoke as though she'd memorized it from a book of instructions.

What? When there was Clara to think about? "No, thanks."

She looked at the darkening window. "Did you find the candles? Here, I'll show you." She crossed the room and from a commode drawer found a candle holder and a long white candle. From a matchbox in a holder on the wall she extracted a wooden match.

"Don't light that. I'm going down to eat right now."

She hesitated, finally dropped the match back into its box. "If you say so." She tripped past him, swinging her hips. "Bye. If you should happen to change your mind, I'll be in the maid's room. Three-oh-one." She left, smiling over her shoulder.

As he slipped on his black jacket, he whispered, "For godsakes."

Once downstairs, he decided before eating to take a little stroll up and down the main street to see what the town was like. Bonnie might in time just become his town in which to trade and visit.

All the stores had falst fronts. Smell of beer and stale cigar smoke emanated from the billiard hall. The aroma of well-oiled leather coming out of the harness store was sweet. Even sweeter, almost sugary, was the smell of freshly cut timber from the lumberyard at the west end of town.

A boil of people crowded in and out of Rexroth's General Store. Horses under blankets, tied to hitching posts all up and down both sides of the street, whinnied to each other. The moist fermented stench of fresh horse manure was in odd contrast to the stuffy smell of old dried horse manure. Splotches of brown tobacco juice, some of it freshly spat, spotted the boardwalks everywhere.

Finally, having seen enough, Tunis went back to the Bonnie Hotel. In the dining hall he found himself sitting at a long table with several land agents and the ticket agent for the Bonnie Omaha railroad. The men tried to include Tunis in their talk, but he had little to say. He was a little disappointed that Bonnie was already so big. The town had just suddenly popped up out of the tall grass like a prairie dog village. It was almost a sure thing that most of the good land was already taken up.

37

The evening meal was surprisingly good. A hunter had dropped an elk by the river, and the steaks from it were tender and juicy. There was plenty of homemade bread and imported plum jam. But the meal was somewhat spoiled by the stink of the kerosene lamps burning in their sockets along the four walls. The aroma of the hard-coal burner in the center of the dining hall didn't help any either. There was also in the air a curious mingling of odors from strong shaving lotions and acrid sweated-in woolens.

One of the men was a biter of lips. He wasn't too sure he liked the new railroad coming to town. "Not until horses get used to that puffing monster."

"Well, yeh, that. But give it time."

"And drunks. You remember how Jack Mahoney, drunk, fell into a cattle guard and couldn't get out—"

"Mel! Why must you always bring up stuff most people want to forget? That kind of talk don't help progress."

"—and the train came along and ran over him? His remains had to be collected and carried to his residence in a tub. I know. I helped his wife go around picking up the pieces. We only found two of his teeth. One of them gold."

Tunis grimaced to himself.

A heavy man across the table cleared his throat. He was dressed in a brown suit and white shirt and blue tie. The tie and vest were spotted with cigar ashes. His head like his belly was fatter and heavier at the bottom than at the top. He resembled two huge turnips, the lesser one perched above the other, especially since his jowls were flushed almost the color of a turnip. His voice was rough, as though he had a growth in his throat. "Mel, because of the railroad we have the boom, and it's going to stay. You can hear hammers going at it from early morning until late at night. There are at least six bunches of carpenters at work here. The fact is, this is a great little town to start life in."

"Poor Jack, he never knew what hit him."

"This spot here on the Forks is not so far north it gets too cold in the winter and not so far south it gets too hot in the summer. And best of all it lies between two mighty rivers, which we can use for transportation."

"Christ, Boughers," Mel growled, "now you're letting your big belly get the best of your brains. Just like all you land agents, you're full of bullshit. Blowing up things so you can sell land at a big profit."

Boughers carefully cut himself another piece of juicy elk and lifted it into his cavernous mouth. He chewed a couple of times. "Mel, what the devil are you doing in a young town like this with your old-town talk?"

"Somebody's got to bury the dead."

"Well, even there, as undertaker you're gonna have it rich in time."

Tunis grimaced some more.

The man next to Tunis had a dark walrus moustache. He nudged Tunis lightly. "Where you headed?"

Tunis didn't like being touched. "None of you business."

"Oh. Just asking is all."

Mel leveled sour fish eyes at Tunis. "Ha, got something to hide like the rest of us, eh?"

Tunis cautioned himself not to snap at the man. He still had land to buy and he'd better not get those land agents mad at him. "And what are *you* hiding?"

"I was once a doctor in Fort Dodge. Until I discovered that doctors were more morticians than physicians. So then I took up undertaking." Mel sighed elaborately, with the sigh at the end breaking into a loud belch. "I'm still thinking of heading to New York, where I can be a doctor again."

"Go then," Boughers pronounced. "We have no time for cynics and backbiters."

Tunis threw a wondering look at Mel. Fort Dodge wasn't too far east of the Wanata area, where Old Dirk and Old Tressa had lived. Maybe Mel might know that a tramp had been killed, that the tramp's bones had been found after the cougar had got through with them.

Later, Tunis followed Boughers out to the lobby. He touched him on the shoulder. "Do you think there's still some land left to homestead around here?"

Boughers turned heavily. He had legs like logs. "Plenty. Why don't you come to my office in the morning? It's a block and a half up the street. Say after breakfast around eight and I'll show you a map where such land might lie."

"I'll be there."

Tunis spent a restless night. He rooted around in his straw ticking like a hot-blooded boar, thinking about Clara and her firm bouncy way of running Lord Sutherland's kitchen, about the chambermaid who wanted to light his candle for him. Also he was afraid he might have come along too late to get a good piece of land near Bonnie.

Tunis got up at six, shaved, had himself a good breakfast of cakes and coffee, then set off up the street with his coat open, he was so warm.

He found Boughers in. "'Morning, sir. I talked to you last night. Tunis Freyling."

Boughers looked up heavily. "You're up bright and early, Mr. Freyling." Boughers's voice was even more coarse in the morning.

"What is it they say, got to strike while the iron is hot?"

"Pull up that chair and I'll show you the map, Mr. Freyling." The fly of Boughers's brown pants was speckled with odd rings of white as if he'd spilled some mucilage on it.

Tunis twitched in his chair. The huge heavy man had a smell about him that made Tunis's nostrils work like a rabbit's.

Boughers pulled a tube of paper from one of the pigeonholes in his oak rolltop desk and spread it out on a pullout board. It was a professionally drawn map of Leonhard County. "Most of the land along these railroads is taken up." He pointed to the Bonnie Omaha line running from Bonnie up to Rock Falls, and to another line running from the southeast corner of the county into Rock Falls. Still another railroad ran across the top of the county from Yellow Smoke through Rock Falls to Sioux Falls. "The U.S. government, and the state of Iowa, to encourage growth, and to get the railroad bigshots in the East to run their lines through here, gave them free every other square mile of land on both sides of the track, like a checkerboard, which they could sell to help pay for the cost of laying down the iron." Boughers pointed with a blunt forefinger. The nail on the forefinger was thick and scoured with rough growth lines. "They've already sold quite a lot of that land. The tracks usually follow the banks of a river, and people need water." 39

"Look, sir, all I want to know is, can a fellow still get a homestead in Leonhard County?"

Boughers didn't like being interrupted. His semen-colored eyes glinted. "How much money you got to spend?"

"Hey, that's none of your business."

"Have you got it on you? There's no bank here yet, you know. There may have been one where you came from, but not here."

"Again, that's none of your damned business!"

Boughers studied Tunis's eyes, and after a moment a look of respect came over his face. He saw Tunis was not one to trifle with. "There are three ways of obtaining land. Homestead, tree claim, and preemption."

"Homestead, I asked."

"There isn't much of that left. Only on the high ground, away from the rivers. Where you'd have to dig to China to get water. Most of that right now is being grazed by the herd. You know, where everybody puts in their yearlings and fatteners, everthing except the cow they milk, and they hire cowboys—"

"Yeh, yeh. I saw some of that near Sioux Center." Tunis hitched his chair up closer and pointed at the Big Sioux River valley. "No good land left there, I suppose."

"Hardly."

"Then maybe I ought to go on out to the Dakotas."

"That's pretty well taken up just cross the Big Sioux. Farther out the land isn't as black. And it's dry there."

"Do you have a piece you've picked up on speculation I might buy?"

Again Boughers fixed sheening eyes on him. "It all depends on how much money you got."

"Or want to spend."

"How much?"

"Why don't you tell me about your best bargain and then I'll see if I can handle it."

Again admiration appeared on Bougher's heavy countenance. "Tell you. Ahh . . ." He reached for a cigar box, offered a cigar to Tunis, and when it was refused helped himself. He lighted up elaborately, first biting off the closed end of the cigar and spitting it accurately into a spittoon, then stroking a big matchstick on the sole of his leather boot, then holding the flame to the blunt end of his cigar and puffing mightily to get the cigar started. Clouds of smoke wisped up around his face. "Ahh . . ." Boughers extracted from yet another pigeonhole a long tan business envelope. He drew out the letter. It was fat, seven pages of legal size, written in an elegant hand, with many a flourish of the letters L and F and T done in both hairline and broad strokes. "Mmm, let's see . . . 'and delivery of these presents by the said parties of the second part, the receipt whereof is hereby acknowledged, and the said parties of the second part, their successors and assigns forever released and discharged from the same by these presents, have granted, sold, aliened, released, conveyed, and confirmed' . . . umm"—Boughers looked up to see if he'd impressed Tunis, and when he saw he hadn't, went on—"in sum and substance, Mr. Freyling, a lady in New York, a certain widow named Betsy Worthing, wants to unload a whole section of land just three miles northeast of Bonnie here."

"That's four quarters."

"Right, Mr. Freyling."

"But I'm only interested in a quarter."

"Hmm." Boughers let his spit-colored eyes run down the page, then went back to a note pinned to the first page. "Yes. She wants to get rid of it all in one package. It seems her husband, James, and his two brothers, Joseph and Robert, and she herself bought the four quarters from the Bonnie Omaha Railroad in 1873. They bought it on speculation, you see, and came out here one summer by stagecoach from Le Mars, and it seems"—he read to himself a moment—"they fell in love with it and resolved among themselves that it should never be separated, that the whole section should be sold to one person. So, Mr. Freyling, it's all or nothing."

"How much?"

"Well, at ten dollars to the acre, sixty-four hundred dollars."

Tunis stood up. "Too much." He could afford it, what with his seven thousand dollars in the bank at Wanata, but he wanted some money left over to build a good house and a warm barn.

Boughers smiled cavernously up at Tunis. "You do have a temper, don't you? Sit down, my man."

Tunis bit back a smart crack. Slowly he sat down.

"How about seven dollars an acre?"

Tunis saw it was going to be a game of dare. He hated bargaining. Old Dirk usually had but one price, and then stuck to it once he'd decided what it was. It hit Tunis that Boughers had been instructed by the widow Worthing to keep the difference between her price and whatever he could sell it for. Plus his usual sale percentage.

"Well, my man?"

"I've got only one price." Tunis remembered what Meademan in Sioux Center had said. About five bucks an acre. "I'll give you four dollars an acre." Tunis did some rapid calculation in his head. "I'll give you twenty-five hundred and sixty dollars. And that's it."

Boughers took a pencil from his vest and did some figuring on a scrap of tan butcher paper. "How about five dollars an acre? Then I can make myself a little profit and look myself in the mirror tomorrow morning."

Again Tunis stood up. "Four dollars an acre and that's it."

Boughers sighed a rough ragged breath. "You're a hard man, Mr. Freyling." He sighed again. "All right. You look like you'll do justice to it. That was another one of the widow's requests, that the place go to someone who would make a Garden of Eden out of it."

Tunis stared down at the map. He spotted something.

"Say, I see that the Bonnie Omaha Railroad cuts across it. How many acres would that right-of-way be there?"

Boughers's eyes opened in more surprise. "Oh, that's right. I forgot about that." He checked the deed. "The right-of-way is a hundred feet wide and about a mile long." He consulted a measure and weights scale. "It comes to twelve-plus acres."

41

"That cuts the whole thing down to six hundred and twenty-eight acres, give or take a few square feet."

"Something like that."

Tunis grimaced, working his tongue between his upper lip and his teeth. He began to feel hot with excitement. "Can you give me directions out there? I think I'll go have a look at it yet today. The weather is still nice."

Boughers reached for a key caught on a nail. "The summer the Worthings stayed there, they built a log cabin on it. Ten by twelve feet. It's on the left side of the railroad tracks and just about in the center of the section. Here's the key to the cabin."

Tunis took the key. "You know, I'm not sure I like the idea of a railroad running right through my property."

"Ah, but think of the convenience. You want to go to town, Bonnie or Rock Falls, you can flag down the train for a ride."

"But what about railroad bums coming through? I don't feel too kindly about tramps."

"Buy yourself a shotgun."

"If I take some grub along, can I stay overnight? I'd like to get the feel of the place by sleeping on it."

"Sure. Fine by me. There's two one-legged beds in the cabin. And some bedding. If the mice haven't got to the bedding."

"How will I find the section corner stakes?"

"Well, where the stagecoach trail, what they now call the King's Trail, crosses the tracks, that's the south boundary of your section. Follow that boundary either to the left or the right and you'll find them."

Within the hour Tunis set off aboard Gyp. Whinnying with other horses during the night had refreshed Gyp. Packed in the saddlebags was a paper bag of sandwiches and several aromatic strips of jerky.

The old stagecoach trail followed the railroad on the right. The ruts were deep in places. There were varying hills on the right, some of them resembling the bulges of long yellow squash. On the left across the tracks twinkled the watery ice of the Big Rock River. The river wound through intermittent groves of trees. A south wind at Tunis's back moved through the grass, into the short rusty buffalo stems on the hills and the tall dark brown bluestem in the bottomlands.

The hills on the right began to slope more gently, and presently Tunis spotted where the stagecoach trail took a sharp left across the railroad tracks. Some ways down the left side of the tracks stood the Worthing log cabin.

Tunis pulled up. Looking down carefully, he spotted a steel stake some fifty feet east of the tracks. He then urged up Gyp across the tracks and found the first west stake. By lining up the two stakes, he sighted out the south side of is section line, using a certain ash tree along the river bank as a mark to go by. He pushed Gyp through the tall grass going west, watching carefully underfoot. After a while, with luck, Tunis found the southwest corner stake of the section. Looking north, he picked out another tree, a tall cottonwood, where the northwest corner stake should be. And looking east, he made out where the southeast stake should be.

The sun fell warm on his cheeks as he looked around. Gyp grazed underfoot. More than half of the section lay west of the tracks, and that half was as flat as the top of a black range stove. The other half on the east side of the tracks was hilly, and that land would probably not be as good.

He decided to trace out the west side of the section first. He urged Gyp into a walk. Within a dozen rods they hit the river bank. The cutbank showed that the top layer of black soil was at least two feet deep. It would take centuries to exhaust the fertility of that rich humus. He was pleased to see that there was no gravel under the black dirt.

The ice on the river was becoming mushy on the surface but was still frozen below. Gyp crossed the ice without question. They climbed the far bank and proceeded north. He kept Gyp walking toward the single tall cottonwood he'd marked out as his target. They passed through a patch of gooseberries. A thrust of chokecherry brush reared up out of an Indian mound. The river kept wriggling back and forth on his right. The trees were mostly ash and box elder and cottonwood sapling. Soon they crossed the river again where it swung west.

Everywhere they kicked out rabbits. The cottontails spurted a dozen feet, then stopped to nose the air with quivering nostrils. Jackrabbits exploded up in a first long leaping bound, then zigzagged, first right, then left, long mule ears popped straight up, eventually vanishing in the tall grass.

"Just think," he whispered, "this land has never been touched except by wild animals and Indians. They left it as pure as rainwater."

It took him a while to find the northwest corner stake. He found it hidden in some wolfberry bushes. It was when Gyp tried several of the dried white berries and snorted at the taste of them that Tunis saw it. So. Tunis looked around to see what the sights were from that corner. Off to his left, west, the land slowly rose to a considerable hogback some miles off. He loved the sweep of the slow sloping valley of the Big Rock River. Already it felt like here was land he should have known all his life.

Off on his right, east, beginning within a dozen rods, loomed a thick grove of trees. Even without leaves it seemed an unpassable mass of timber. A wasteland. Well, every farm should have a wasteland. A jungle. If only to remind a fellow that open land was a privilege.

He dismounted to have a closer look at the wasteland, letting the reins drop so Gyp wouldn't wander too far off. He pushed through the wolfberries and entered the edge of the jungle. The first dozen feet it was almost tight, like a stake-and-rider rail fence. Vines of wild grape, some of them as thick as the thews of a horse, braided up through the random growth like the work of a mad weaver. Some thirty feet in he found deer trail and various paths large animals had worked out through the otherwise impenetrable brush and saplings. Here and there a single tree had managed to get most of the overhead sun and had considerable girth.

The sensation of fear came over him. He stopped in his tracks. Danger lay near. He could sense it. An animal was nearby and was looking at him. Cougar?

Carfully he worked himself backward through the thick underbrush, watching to either side, also looking back over his shoulder, until he got to where he no longer sensed danger. Funny that Gyp hadn't snorted, even spooked. But then, the wind was from the west.

He found Gyp where he'd left him. He climbed aboard and turned Gyp's head east. They skirted around the south curving edge of the wasteland until they hit the river again. Where the river entered the wasteland it disappeared under an umbrella of branches and twigs and brush so thick and tight, leaning down, that it seemed not even a canoe, were the river thawed, would have been able to make passage. As Tunis worked his way east to the railroad tracks again he could see that the jungle was actually quite large, a good eighty acres of it. It probably had the best soil around. It would take a lot of work to clear it.

43

When they hit the railroad tracks, Tunis pulled up and let Gyp graze some more. Tunis turned in his saddle to look back and study the jungle from a distance. He could see that it extended some eighty more acres to the north into the next man's land.

"Well," Tunis murmured, "maybe I ought to leave it there for the wild animals. They had the land first, even before the Indians. If we plow up all the land, the wild animals won't have any place left to live. The only thing I don't like about the idea is that the jungle is where cougars can hide out. Thank God, cougars don't care much for human flesh and only chase venison."

They crossed the tracks and moved up the hills to the east. It took Tunis at least an hour to find the northeast corner of his section. It was at the very top of a steep dropoff. Here the grass was short, almost all of it true buffalo grass.

He looked down at his land, spreading away to the river. Not counting the wasteland, and the land along either side of the river, which he'd have to make into pasture, and the hills along the east side of the tracks, he'd still have some three hundred acres of rich bottomland to cultivate. He was going to be a rich man with all that land.

The sun glanced pink off the rowan grass, made luminant the pink ends of his fingertips, glistened in Gyp's golden mane. He sat pricked erect for several moments, caught up in a dazzling bubble of happiness. His eyes glowed, his heart beat faster.

He let his eyes rove over the hills to the south, where they shouldered down, hairy with grass, from the tableland above. The hills were like a herd of buffalo emerging from underneath a brown blanket and slowly grazing westward. In a way the hills were remindful of the Little Sioux River bluffs around Wanata. He smiled. He had to have hills nearby.

Movement caught his eye. On the second hill over. Gophers? Out already? There were also mounds. But pocket gophers were almost eyeless and never played out in the open. He gave Gyp the knee and they cantered over, dropping through a grassy draw and then up toward the critters.

The little creatures saw him, chittered at him in protest, and then flip! disappeared into the holes at the base of the little mounds.

"Prairie dogs!" He surveyed the hill. "A regular city of them. Well, I'm going to get rid of them pronto. Galloping across here an animal can break a leg."

Gyp knew what they were too. When Tunis gave him the knee to go on, Gyp carefully skirted the entire colony, snorting at their smell.

Tunis found the southeast corner stake easily. It stuck up out of the grass like the point of a sword, gleaming a little in the falling sunlight. Again from that point Tunis surveyed his property. As he watched the light slowly change into a falling yellow, he saw what appeared to be a cloud rising farther south down the river. Presently there were two clouds. The first cloud was black, the second varicolored. As the clouds approached, rising and falling, they began to break up into separate bits, thickening together and thinning out. They were birds. The first cloud turned out to be blackbirds and second one pigeons. They were coming up from the Missouri River. They were bringing spring.

Watching the birds come toward him, he spotted two sod houses about a mile away, one to the east of the railroad tracks and one to the west. Somehow in coming out he'd missed seeing them, probably because of the horse-high grasses. In each case a pioneer had broken out a small plot of prairie grass near the sod houses with a breaker plow. The freshly tumbled-up earth shone a glistening black.

Out of the corner of his eye something red next caught his attention. Some kind of rock. He turned Gyp toward it and rode over. It turned out to be a huge red boulder about the size of a horse lying on its side.

"What a rock! Wonder how that got here? Even if the river got high enough, ice in it could never have shoved it up here." It was a strange rock with faint lines of orange flowing around in the basic red. Looking closer he made out scratches on the slick surface on the west side of it. Narrowing his eyes . . . "By God, if that don't look like somebody's pecked out the stick figure of a man on it. With a kind of a prickly halo above the head."

He studied it a while. "No white man would have bothered to do that. If a white man is gonna peck out something on rock, he usually carves his initials."

Gyp reaching for grass underfoot reminded Tunis he hadn't eaten since morning. Time to put on the feedbag. And check out the log shanty the Worthings had built. Again Tunis gave Gyp the knee and they descended.

When he approached the shanty, he was surprised to discover that the

Worthings had also built, a couple of rods north of it, a shelter for animals open to the south. It was a log lean-to covered with a thick layer of matted bluestem grass.

"Well, Gyp, old hoss, it looks like you too got quarters for the night. When here I was afraid I'd have to put you up on one of those one-legged beds in the shanty."

He climbed down and led Gyp into the shelter. Gyp snorted at the unfamiliar smells, stepped around gingerly on the dirt floor. Tunis stripped Gyp of the saddle and blanket, then curried and brushed him down. There was a little pile of slough hay in a corner and Gyp was soon munching away at it. The hay had a good smell, of dried wild clover balls and rosehips. Gyp shuddered his hide in pleasure, rippling first over his shoulders, then under his veined belly.

Tunis picked up his saddlebags and headed for the door on the east side of the log shanty. He found the key in his pocket, opened up, and stepped inside.

The smell of wintered wood and dried mouse dung hit him. Light from the door and from the little square glass window in the south wall was just enough to see things by. The log walls were chinked with a mixture of stringy grass and clay. The one-legged beds were in place all right. Each bed had three of its corners nailed to the two walls, with the fourth corner resting on a wooden leg. Each was big enough to sleep two people. Tunis wondered a little about the sleeping arrangements the Worthings might have had, three men and one woman in the same room. Surely the two brothers and the husband wouldn't have taken turns sleeping with Betsy. He did remember hearing stories from Old Dirk about strange doings on the frontier where women were scarce, sometimes a ratio of one woman to every three men.

The mice hadn't worked too many holes into the bedding. If he used all of it on one bed he'd sleep warm that night. Some kindling and a dozen small logs were piled up against the wall near the fireplace. A double-bitted axe topped off the pile. Digging out a match, he soon had a snapping fire going. It lit up the place with a rosy light, matching the light coming in from the red sunset.

The Worthings had also carved several chairs out of fat log ends. He drew one up to the fire, and getting out the sandwiches and jerky, he sat down to eat. The log chair wasn't too comfortable, but it was better than sitting on one's heels. The jerky was tough, and after a while he got out his jackknife and cut himself some very thin strips for easier chewing. He ate slowly but lustily. Too bad he didn't have something to drink to wash it down.

Sleep overcame him about the time it turned dark outside. He crawled into the one-legged bed in the southwest corner. The mice soon let him know he was an intruder and rustled around under the bed; once one chasing the other ran over his belly. He slept heavily despite their scurrying about.

Gyp awakened him at dawn, pawing at the ground by the door, sometimes striking the side of the log cabin.

"Comin', old hoss."

Tunis laced on his leather boots and got up and opened the door. No wonder Gyp had got nervous. It was snowing out. "Hey, we better hit the trail. Unless we wanna stay here for a couple of days. Be right with you."

Tunis gobbled down the one sandwich he had left, stuck the last strip of jerky into a pocket of his sheepskin coat, and was set to go. He locked the door and,

45

carrying his saddlebags, hurried Gyp to the horse shelter. He quickly threw on the saddle blanket and the saddle, bridled Gyp, and led him outside and hopped aboard.

The snow fell thick with a shoving wind from the southeast. Within fifty feet Tunis lost sight of the shanty. They had trouble locating the railroad tracks. Gyp didn't like facing into the wind, but Tunis held him to it. Finally Gyp stumbled over the tracks.

"Ah, now I feel better." Tunis pulled on Gyp's right rein. "All we gotta do now is follow these into town."

They'd bucked sideways into the driving snow for a while when Tunis remembered he hadn't gone to the privy.

"That reminds me. Wonder where the Worthings did their jobs. There was no privy there."

Gyp snorted, bucked a little, worked sideways into the quartering wind.

"They must've sat in the deep grass behind the shelter." Tunis shrugged one shoulder. "Or maybe they didn't go at all. Them high monkey-monks in New York sometimes think they're above such mortal concerns." Tunis pulled the sheepskin collar up around his face on the left side. "If one can believe the papers coming from there."

Gyp hated walking down the wooden ties between the tracks. Three inches of snow already fallen made the footing uncertain. Once Gyp's right front hoof caught between two ties and almost got stuck.

The snow thickened even more, came down as though someone was deliberately dumping sacks and sacks of white flour on them. Sometimes the wind came up and flicked snow in Tunis's face.

46

"Keep going there, Gyp. When we get to town you'll have your oats."

About a half hour later there was a clinking sound. Gyp began to limp.

"Hey, what's up."

Gyp began to limp badly on his right front hoof.

"Whoa." Tunis slid off the horse, lifted up the front hoof and had a look. Gyp had thrown a shoe. Getting it caught between the two ties had done it.

Tunis swore. "Holy balls. What a time to have this happen." He hated delays, being put out of joint; had no patience with fate. When he made up his mind to do something, he wanted to do it right then and there.

He studied to himself to cool down. Losing his temper in the middle of a raging snowstorm wasn't exactly smart.

"Gyp, you stand right here now, you hear?"

Tunis dropped the reins. Then he went back up between the two steel rails, kicking through the snow, trying to find the lost shoe. But kick and shuffle along as he might he couldn't find it.

He went back to Gyp. "Well, old friend, I'm not going to ride you with a shoe off. I'll have to hoof it with you." Tunis threw the reins up over the pommel of the saddle and tied a knot in them. "Think you can follow me? I'm not going to lead you."

Tunis turned and led the way. He needn't have worried about Gyp. The horse followed him so close his nose sometimes almost rested on Tunis's shoulder. Having to walk himself, Tunis understood better why Gyp had snorted at the going between the two tracks.

"Hel—lo-o-o!"

Tunis stopped. Peering west, wind behind him, he made out movement in the flying snow. A man. The man was standing beside a sodhouse, one of those Tunis had spotted from the red boulder hill. Tunis saw right away he had the look of a deadbeat, a sponger.

The man started to waddle toward Tunis in the deep snow. He was dressed in a shabby sheepskin coat and leather boots. When he came up close and looked up, brown eyes peering out of a hairy face, nose working, he looked more like a muskrat than a human being. The man puffed. "I see you're headin' for town. Could you tell Doc Wallance my wife is having a baby?"

"Well, why don't you go get him?"

"She's having an awful time and I don't dare leave her."

"All right. Consider it done."

"Thanks a lot. Oh. I'm Hack Tippett, in case you're wonderin'.'."

Tunis looked at the man. Since they might someday be neighbors he better tell him who he was. "Tunis Freyling."

"Thanks again, Tunis."

Tunis nodded and started walking toward Bonnie again. Gyp limped along behind him, sometimes almost stepping on his heels.

Soon the snow fell even thicker. It plakked both man and horse white on the left side. Walking warmed Tunis, and he kept debating with himself if he should open his coat and cool off and also get wet with snow, or keep it buttoned and have his underwear get sopping wet with sweat.

In another half hour Tunis began to notice the blurry outlines of houses to either side of the tracks. Then the railroad roundhouse loomed up huge and dark. They'd made it. It wasn't long before they came upon the Bonnie depot. From the depot Tunis led Gyp to the livery stable behind the Bonnie Hotel. He hung up the saddle and blanket to dry and groomed Gyp. The horse's coat of roan hair was clotted with lumps of snow. Then he fed Gyp oats and hay.

"Gyp, I'll be back later to have your foot fixed."

On his way to Boughers's office, he spotted Dr. G. C. Wallance's door. It was on the same side of the street. He left word about Hack Tippett's wife's having a baby.

In Boughers's office he stomped off the snow, removed his sheepskin coat, and shook it free of frozen pellets of moisture.

Boughers turned lumpily in his swivel chair. "See you made it."

"Yep."

"Get a chance to look at the Worthing place before the storm?"

Tunis drew up a chair. He wished Boughers could have been a nicer fellow. "Yeh, I had a peek." Tunis worked his upper lip. "I got a question to ask you."

"Fire away."

"When people travel from here to Rock Falls and don't take the train, how do they go?"

"Follow the old stagecoach trail."

"Don't that run mostly where the tracks are now?"

"It does."

"That means if they build a highway someday it'll parallel those tracks then?"

"Might."

"Can I see that county map again?"

Boughers reluctantly dug out the rolled-up map once more.

Tunis studied it. Sure enough the stagecoach trail had been traced in lightly as following alongside the Bonnie-Whitebone railroad except where it crossed it. He pushed back his blue felt cap and scratched his forelock. "If the county builds a regular highway along there, that'll mean another twelve acres gone, won't it?"

"Might."

"Well, I'm only gonna pay for six hundred sixteen acres then."

"No, you'll have to pay for six hundred twenty-eight. The county still hasn't bought it."

Tunis bounced to his feet. He began to pace back and forth. He cautioned himself not to let his temper show too much.

Boughers selected a long cigar for himself and lighted up. He mouthed several smoke rings. "Look at it this way, Freyling. By the time the county buys it you can make a profit on those extra twelve acres. Sell them for a hundred an acre."

"But it'll break up my property even more into two parts. The railroad is bad enough."

"And another thing," Boughers continued, "the way the law now reads, the county will have to build a fence along that right-of-way. With gates. And eventually the railroad will have to, too. With cattleguards."

Tunis paced up and down a couple more steps, then slowly sat down. Maybe by the time the county put in the road he might just be pinched for money. Inside he began to smile, though outwardly he kept up a gruff appearance.

Boughers puffed himself a mighty smoke ring. "What I must know, because of what has been entrusted me, is this: do you like the place?"

Tunis knew he had to give just the right kind of answer. He couldn't show he was hot to buy it, because the price might go up; but he still had to show he would be the good husbandman or Boughers might rule that the Worthing request for the right buyer hadn't been fulfilled. "At first I wasn't sure I liked that big wasteland on the north end there. But then I decided it was okay. We all have a piece of wasteland in us and it would stand there as a kind of reminder."

"Good thinking, good thinking."

"About that shanty, did all four of those Worthings live there at the same time?"

"So far as I know, yes."

"Hmm. Makes a man wonder a little what their sleeping arrangements were." Boughers's heavy face closed over.

Tunis continued to ruminate out loud. "Husband James and Betsy wouldn't have had much privacy with brothers Joseph and Robert around all the time."

Boughers studied the red end of his cigar with nearly closed eyes.

"Know anything about that?"

"Not a thing, not a thing."

"Aha. Then there was something funny going on there, wasn't there?" Tunis had another thought. "How did the three brothers die?"

"That's a matter of confidentiality."

"Damn, just so the place ain't haunted." Tunis bounced up out of his chair again and began pacing back and forth. "Now maybe I'm not so sure about it."

"How much money can you put up for an option?"

"Right this smack-dab minute?"

"Yes."

"One hundred dollars. I've got more with me, but I'll need that for running money until I bring the rest from Wanata."

"You've got cash? Don't need to take a loan?"

"I've got the cash for all of it."

"Good." Boughers's face cleared up. "While you were out there looking at it, I drew up an option." He pulled a thin roll of papers from a nearby pigeonhole. He unrolled them out on his desk. He motioned his big pocked nose at a goose quill and a black inkstand. "At your service."

Tunis paced some more. Once that hundred dollars disappeared into Boughers's cavernous pocket, it was done. Everything was really fine about the Worthing place, even the railroad. And maybe someday the highway. Except that the place might be haunted. The place he'd left was haunted with the memory of the tramp he'd killed and whose body had disappeared mysteriously. But then, maybe that was life. There probably wasn't a place on earth but what it didn't have a spook or two. His real father had known one too. And if the truth be told, Boughers also probably had a spook or two in his life. Tunis couldn't for the life of him imagine any woman, even a whore, letting Boughers get between her shafts. Maybe Boughers had some other way of getting rid of his ashes. He noted with an inward smile that Boughers's vest was clean of ashes that morning.

"Well, my man?"

Tunis made up his mind. "Hell's bells, why not?" He picked up the option and read it carefully. Boughers beside him sucked wetly on his foul-smelling stogie. Tunis saw the figures, six hundred twenty-eight acres for $2,512.00. "But you haven't written in the option fee."

"That's right." Boughers picked up the quill and in a flourishing hand wrote in, ". . . for the consideration of an option fee of one hundred dollars . . ."

Tunis dug into his pocket and from his roll of money peeled off five twenty-dollar bills. Then he signed. "And now to find myself a good blacksmith. My horse threw a shoe."

"Oh. We got a good blacksmith in town. Pete Smucker across the street from the depot. He can brad and rivet with the best of them. Hard and fast. And as for shoeing a horse, when he's through rasping 'em down, it looks like the horse was born with his horseshoes on."

"Good. I'll be back from Wanata as soon as I can."

"Don't let the trail robbers make a raise of your money."

Tunis led the limping Gyp across to the smoky blacksmith shop.

Pete Smucker wasn't too busy at the moment, said he'd be happy to oblige with a new shoe. Smucker had sloping shoulders and a drooping brown moustache.

With a quick maneuver Smucker picked up and caught Gyp's hoof between his knees, exposing the inside of it. "Gonna have to do more than put on a shoe, mister."

Tunis held Gyp's nose in the crook of his arm to keep him calm. "How so?"

"Look at that horny pad there." Smucker pointed a crooked finger at a triangular growth in the sole of the hoof. "That looks sore. Might have been the reason your horse threw the shoe in the first place." Smucker touched it with the end of a long pincers, and right away Gyp stirred and tried to lean on Smucker. "See, it's sore. Gonna have to chisel some of that away."

"Do it then."

"Gonna be sore for a while unless you put a kind of covering on it."

"What've you got in mind?"

"I could slip of piece of sheet metal under the shoe to cover that pad until it heals. Be like if you was to put an extra layer of felt in your shoe where your heel is sore."

Tunis had been wondering where he could hide his money once he withdrew it from the Wanata bank. There weren't many places on the human body where a man might hide money from a highway robber. And it wouldn't take a thief long to explore every last nook and cranny of a man's saddlebags. Here now, under that pan of sheet metal, was the perfect place to hide money. Not even the Devil at his cleverest would think of that spot. "Put it in."

Smucker dropped Gyp's foot and began searching for a piece of sheet metal and the right-size shoe. "Hear you're gonna buy the Worthing place."

Tunis lifted an eyebrow. "Here I was hoping Boughers would have a hitch on his tongue."

"Ain't much you can hide in a small town." Smucker picked up Gyp's hoof again and began trimming it with a pincers and a hoof knife. "You didn't see the stagecoach coming in, did you? Jack the driver is supposed to bring in a shipment of shoe calks for me today."

"Not in the heavy snow. In fact, I doubt if a driver would want to be out in it."

"Oh, I'll get my shipment all right. Because Jack's got the ribbons today, and he'll come or die." Smucker fitted the plate of sheet steel under a horseshoe and began to nail the two in place, driving the flat nails into the hoof and then clinching them where their points showed through. "Too bad about our drivers Jack and Lon."

"Oh?"

50

"Jack Church drives for the Bonnie-Le Mars line and Lonnie Brandon drives for the Bonnie-Wodan line. Apart neither one is a bragger. But when them two get together, they've got to brag. The one has to outbest the other. No help for it either, I guess. Jack Church and Lonnie Brandon are like two bulls in a pasture with only one heifer between them. They've got to show off in front of her."

Tunis liked the smells in the blacksmith shop. There was something appetizing about the heated metal; the taste of baked apples was in it. The drifting smoke from the pink burning coals in the bellows made him think of a fabled city in dream.

There was a rattling sound in the falling snow outside, then the muffled clopping hooves, then a great shout, "Whoa!" in front of the Bonnie Hotel.

"There he is now. Good. Now I can make me some more horseshoes."

Gyp seemed to understand something good was being done for him and quit leaning on Smucker. He nickered in pleasure at the stagecoach horses outside.

Smucker rasped the edges of Gyp's hoof even with the shoe. "There," he said, dropping Gyp's hoof to the dirt floor. "That's better than it was before. That'll be one dollar."

Tunis paid up, then led Gyp back to the livery barn.

That afternoon, when the snow let up and the sky cleared, creating a blue made dazzling by the pure white fallen snow, Tunis heard loud voices in Wilter's Saloon. They were boasting voices, roaring what they could do. Tunis guessed it was Jack Church and Lonnie Brandon at it again. Tunis stepped down off the boardwalk and shuffled through the snow-streaked rutted street and then up the steps into the saloon. Sure enough, the two drivers were bragging about who had the fastest horses.

"Jack, you're a goddam liar. Your watch must've stopped."

"Lonnie, nobody calls me a liar."

"But Jack, you couldn't have done it that fast."

"Ask Ockie over at the livery stable. And then ask Quimby down at Le Mars. They'll tell you."

Just when it looked like the two drivers were about to come to blows, Wilter the saloon keeper interposed. He warned the boys he'd throw 'em both out himself if they didn't shut up. "So make up, or else."

With hanging lower lips, knowing all eyes were on them, the two shook hands. Then they went back to drinking.

Tunis saw the truce wasn't going to last. Their handshake'd been too limp.

Just before supper, Tunis went out to the livery stable and fed Gyp. Gyp whickered in pleasure, standing solid on his new horseshoe.

Tunis had just started up the alley to leave when Lonnie came chasing Jack into the barn entrance. Lonnie was brandishing a heavy singletree, cursing like a madman, foam at the corners of his mouth. "No sonofabitchin' skinny shitepoke is gonna tell me I don't know how to shake hands like a man."

Jack nimbly avoided Lonnie's wild swings, his blue eyes turning light. Jack spotted a pitchfork standing near a wooden upright and jumped for it. Then he whirled on Lonnie. He made several stabbing motions with the tines of the fork; finally managed to get in a thrust that nicked Lonnie in the side.

"Ow!" Lonnie roared. And then seeing his singletree was no match against a pitchfork, he dropped the wooden bar and ran out of the livery stable.

"That son of a bitch," Jack murmured.

Ockie the proprietor came out of his office with a white face, shaking. He'd witnessed it all through a dusty window. "Jack, you better stay out of sight for a while."

"Why?"

"Lonnie will be back. And the next time he won't come with just a club. I know. He carries grudges."

"He also carries a big mouth."

"Just get out of here. Because he'll be back."

Jack's neck and head came up. "Well, first I'm gonna feed my horses."

"Suit yourself. But don't say I didn't warn you."

Jack shook his head, as if to say, wasn't that the limit? He started in feeding his four horses.

Tunis stopped to tell Ockie he'd be leaving early in the morning and that he'd probably better pay up that night for the keep of his horse. Tunis had just handed over the money when there was another bellow behind him in the doorway of the livery stable.

It was Lonnie Brandon carrying a shotgun. "Where's that braggin' son of a muskrat bitch . . . oh, there you are. So you thought you could stab me in the guts with a pitchfork, huh?"

Jack was standing between two of his chestnut bays. "Now, Lonnie, let's not use guns. You shouldna come after me with that singletree. Then I wouldn't have grabbed that fork."

"But you were still gonna spill my guts with that pitchfork, warn't you? Well, I'll never forgive you for that." Lonnie was so engorged with rage his gray eyes were almost shut. He raised the shotgun; aimed; pulled the trigger.

There was a bright flash of light, a roar that shook the rafters of the livery stable and made every horse in the place rear up at the end of its halter ropes. A big hole showed up where Jack's nose and mouth had once been even as Jack was blown back. Jack slid out of sight. A blue cloud of gunpowder smoke slowly drifted up toward the rafters.

Lonnie lowered his shotgun. "You don't tamper with my guts, goddam you."

Tunis jumped for Lonnie, jolting him from the side. Tunis's weight carried the two of them down, the shotgun flying off to one side. Tunis straddled Lonnie as Lonnie lay sprawled on his belly. Tunis grabbed Lonnie's wrists and jerked them up behind his back.

Tunis said, "Ockie, call the marshall."

Ockie came walking over. He looked down at Tunis and Lonnie, then over at where Jack had fallen between the two chestnut horses. The chestnut horses had begun to jump around. Ockie went over and pulled Jack out from under the trompling hooves. "Yeh. And we better call Mel the undertaker too."

Faces began to appear in the doorway, wondering eyes as big as goose eggs.

A man stormed past the faces. He was carrying a tablet, pencil caught under his blue cap. "My God, Jack's shot!"

Ockie grimaced sourly. "You newspaper men can't help but smell blood, can you? Like hyenas."

The newspaper man began to scribble furiously in his tablet. "Cold-blooded murder," he muttered as he wrote. "Jack Church is shot down like a dog in the local livery stable."

Presently Marshall Brandt appeared. He collared Lonnie Brandon and led him off to the cooler.

Tunis went to his room. He wanted to hit something.

4. Clara

Clara Shortridge sat between Lord Sutherland and Galen the driver in the front seat of the carriage. All three had their legs and feet wrapped in a huge brown buffalo robe. Lord Sutherland was wearing a black top hat and a black cutaway coat. Crowded into the back seat were four of the lads. Milord kept smiling at all the rough talk coming from the back. Milord had announced that he too was going to Le Mars to look over that shipment of German virgins. Perhaps there might be one among them who would not mind being known as milady.

That dirty old perfumed goat, Clara thought. It was bad enough that his worthless pups had such foul mouths. What was especially galling was that the pup she'd caught lying on Greta was one of the four in back. Harry Hillyard, who'd lain on Lurilla, was riding on horseback alongside the carriage with five other scamps.

The carriage wheels dropped into a badger hole, jostling everybody. Clara resettled into her own spot, careful not to sit too close to milord.

She still hadn't made up her mind what she was going to do when she got to Le Mars. Tunis's piercing pearl gray eyes were still much in her mind. What a handsome stand-up man he was. If only she could live somewhere near him so they could see each other casually from time to time and thus get acquainted in a natural way. But that was probably wishing for the moon.

As they finally rode up over the last hill, Le Mars lying below them in a shallow valley, Lord Sutherland slowly turned and said, "You're sure now, my dear, you do not want to accept my offer?"

"No." Clara set her chin away from him, hiding her face inside the drawn-down brim of her woolen bonnet.

"And you're sure you do not want to continue as our housekeeper?"

"My mind's made up."

"What will you do? I'm concerned about you."

"Maybe take the train to Welton and see if I can pick up my life there again."

"And if you don't find any old friends there?"

"In that case, come back here to Le Mars and look for some kind of respectable work. Just drop me off at a hotel somewhere until I decide what I must do."

"So be it then." Lord Sutherland turned to Galen. "Best drop her off at the Regent Hotel."

Galen nodded and gave the reins to the matched gray horses a light flip. He didn't like seeing Clara leaving, and he showed it by the way his underlip pushed out. It was apparent that he too, in his quiet way, had had ideas about Clara.

When they pulled up at the Regent, it took but a minute for the rowdy lads to untie Clara's trunk from the back of the carriage and set it down on the board-walk. Clara herself carried the small suitcase and her purse.

Lord Sutherland had one last word. He leaned out of the carriage. "Our accounts are all squared up, are they?" Milord had paid her just as they left Sutherland Hall.

"They are."

"All right, Galen, let's have a go at those German virgins."

Galen dipped the reins, "Giddap," and the carriage careened off for the depot.

"Good riddance to bad rubbish," Clara said to herself.

A red-faced porter emerged from the front door of the gray clapboard Regent. "Some help, miss?"

"Yes. Could you store this trunk of mine in the hotel here until I make up my mind what to do?" Clara saw the cocked wise look in his eyes. "Don't worry. I've got the money to pay for my stay."

"Not worrying, miss. Just that a lot of people are passing through who've gone belly up out east."

"Women too?"

"Well . . ."

"Carry it in while I get myself a room." She held the door open for him while he, grunting as he lifted, shagged the trunk inside.

She rented a room for a week at a dollar a day. A week would give her time enough time to make plans. The trunk was stored in a room off the lobby. She gave the bellboy a quarter for carrying her suitcase up to her room.

After she'd refreshed herself, she went downstairs to ask if there was an Episcopalian church in town.

The desk clerk said there was. "But Father Alton is out of town just now."

"Pshaw. And I wanted to talk to him. It's been so long since I've been to church." She flipped her gray knitted mittens against her black fur cape. "You wouldn't know if there was an Episcopal church in Bonnie, north of here?"

"No. Nearest one that way is in Whitebone."

Clara nodded. She went back upstairs to her dingy room. It was when she sat down she noticed something. She went to the water closet and there discovered it was that time of the month for her.

Except to go to meals Clara hardly left her room the next several days. She read in her book of Common Prayer, reciting aloud certain of the morning and evening devotions.

". . . the Scripture moveth us to acknowledge and confess our manifold sins and wickedness; and that we should not dissemble nor cloak them before the face of Almighty God our heavenly Father; but confess them with an humble, lowly, penitent, and obedient heart; to the end that we obtain forgiveness of the same, by his infinite goodness and mercy."

She watched the yellow stroke of sunlight from the tall narrow window move across the dark-stained oak floor.

"Is it nothing to you, all ye that pass by? behold, and see if there be any sorrow like until my sorrow which is done unto me, where in the Lord hath afflicted me."

Outside her window, down on the street, men were cursing one or another of their horses for not pulling its share of the load.

"We have erred, and strayed from thy ways like lost sheep. We have followed too much the devices and desires of our own hearts."

Down the hallway she could hear the shrill laughter of loose women. Soiled doves.

She next read some of the Litany, reading the part of the minister silently, and speaking the responses aloud.

> Remember not, Lord, our offenses, nor the offences of our forefathers; neither take thou vengeance of our sins: Spare us, good Lord, spare thy people, whom thou hast redeemed with thy most precious blood, and be not angry with us for ever.
> *Spare us, good Lord.*
> From lightning and tempest; from earthquake, fire, and flood; from plague, pestilence, and famine; from battle and murder, and from sudden death.
> *Good Lord, deliver us.*

When the worst flow was over, she began to take short walks up and down Main Street. Below her black cape, her long gray silk skirt billowed about her high black button shoes. She looked in on the General Goods Store, the Westminster Mercantile, and the Ladies Millinery Store. She stopped in a Drugs & Sundries and had herself a pink ice, sitting on a wire-steel chair at a glass-top wire-legged table.

She decided that perhaps Lord Sutherland was right. There was really no reason for her to go back to Welton. At the same time she couldn't get Tunis Freyling out of her mind. She hated being the one to do the chasing, but if she didn't do something about finding him she'd never have him.

The desk clerk at the Regent said no such person as she described, a man with rusty hair and burning gray eyes, had registered with them. She checked the House of Lords Saloon. Yes, there had been such a man there. The barkeep remembered specifically because the man had ordered some sarsaparilla, a rarity. The barkeep suggested she try the livery stable. They might know where he stayed overnight. The barkeep also remembered that he'd told the man there was a good cafe down the street.

At the livery stable Clara learned that Tunis had left for Bonnie four days before. That meant she and Tunis had been overnight in town at the same time. Too bad she'd had to keep to her room or she might have run into him somewhere.

She also learned the stagecoach was leaving for Bonnie the next day. She promptly bought a ticket. She gave little thought that Tunis might not like it she'd chased after him. She was glad to be shaking the dust of Le Mars from her feet.

On the way back to the Regent she ran into a drunken Englishman who took a liking to her. He followed her doggedly, calling after her, loud enough for everybody along the street to her. "Won't you at least go walking with me on the boardwalk, lady?"

Clara gave him a chilly back, drew the brim of her gray woolen bonnet close around her face.

A half block farther down, the town marshall, a silver star on his chest, spotted the pest dogging Clare. Quickly he interposed his huge bulk between Clara and the young tousled drunk. "All right there, young feller, that's enough of that. We can't have you molestin' women. It's off to the calaboose with you."

After the marshall had grabbed the drunk by his collar, he said over his blue shoulder, "Sorry, lady. But you know how it is when King Alky takes over. They just ain't responsible anymore. Sober, this slunker might be a prince of a fellow."

"I wouldn't know. I never fancied alcohol much."

Clara hated the smells wafting out of the alleys. The stink was worse than the stink of a clogged sink. It was strange that the town marshall didn't get after the stores and saloons for being so careless with their debris and garbage. Twice she saw rats chasing through sacks of decayed fruit and moldy bread.

She took a bath that night to feel clean again. She washed her clothes in a large slab sink in the water closet.

She went to bed early. She dreamt of Tunis several times, and always he was walking away from her, face averted, and when she called after him he hurried away even faster. Each time, disheartened, she gave up and sat down on a stump and cried. Wetness on her checks awakened her.

The more she thought about Tunis the more she had to have him. His strong sturdy legs and wide short hands were a perfect match with her own short strong body. They would have wonderful healthy children. His strong blood would help breed out the weaknesses her line had, of a bent toward incest and asthma. She herself had never had a brother or a sister and so couldn't say if she had the first tendency. She surely didn't have any unnatural affection for her poor father. And she certainly didn't have the wheezing cough of the asthmatic. As for her poor overworked mother, Clara felt nothing but sorrow for her sad life. She regretted she'd never put her arms around her mother and comforted her.

56

But Tunis Freyling must never know about these dark thoughts. She'd take them with her to the grave. She'd watch their healthy children grow up knowing that the asthmatic strain in her blood had been overcome by the powerful seed of her husband-to-be.

The owner of the stagecoach line had hired a new driver. Something had appeared to have happened up the line to Jack, the usual driver. The new driver, Bollicky Bill Undersides, grumbled a little when he had to tie Clara's trunk onto the rack behind the stagecoach. Bollicky Bill had a roving eye for women, and when he gave Clara the eye she was quick to be crisp with him.

There were only two other passengers, both of them heavyset land agents, and they never once glanced at her. Both were wearing dark broadcloth frock coats and black silk hats. They smoked cigars like they might be the vents for a pair of volcanoes, and talked about how, after they'd made a killing in selling land, they'd retire to New York and live the life of Reilly. Clara ignored them. The rest of the stagecoach was filled with gray canvas mailbags.

It was a good day out. The sky was a little misty and there were milky fogs in the valleys, but the sun was shining and trying to clear the air. The snow had all melted and good-size streams, glancing brilliant and nickel-like, ran in the draws. The ice had also gone out of the Floyd River and in some places the river was out of its banks. Great wavering arrows of geese, honking and dipping and reforming, came up out of the south and went by overhead, following the river flyway below.

The stagecoach stopped at Maurice, where Bolicky Bill left some mail and picked up some more.

Clara got out too. She asked the woman Ellie in the smoky eating place and post office if she'd seen a horsebacker come by who had rusty hair and sharp gray eyes.

"Yes. Came by here about a week ago."

"Did he say anything about where he was going?"

"No. We just noticed he headed north towards Sioux Center."

Back in the red-trimmed stagecoach again, Clara suffered the stogie smokers. The coach rolled, and rose and sagged on its springs, and jolted through axle-deep ruts, and rattled across old hard pocket gopher mounds.

At Sioux Center it began to rain and Bolicky Bill elected to stay overnight.

In Meademan's Cafe the bald-headed proprietor remembered Tunis. "Ya. Square-set fellow. Had his first Dutch dish of *fat met stroop* here."

Clara looked puzzled, and after Meademan explained what the Dutch dish was she had to laugh. It sounded like Tunis. Willing to try something new at least once. She didn't want a husband who'd be too particular about what he ate.

Meademan looked at her with a knowing smile. "Your sweetie?"

"Not yet."

"You're quite a perky gal, ain't you? You'll do." He leaned an inquiring smile at her. "Would you want to try the dish?"

"Yes, I think I will." It would be fun to know what Tunis had tasted. It would give them something to talk about when she saw him. "Did he mention where he might be going?"

"Just north. Following the stagecoach trail. Looking for land."

After a while she had her first taste of the strange Dutch dish. She pronounced it good. But she worried a little it might be fattening.

57

Meademan rolled his head and laughed. "Not if you burn it off with hard work."

Clara was given the same room Tunis slept in upstairs.

The next morning the sun was out again and Bollicky Bill pronounced the trail dry enough to proceed north. It was from Bolicky Bill that she learned about the dreadful business where Tunis had overpowered the man who'd shot down Jack, the previous driver. She wasn't too surprised. She'd already spotted that Tunis had a lot of daring in him, that he would be just the one to jump in when trouble came. Some muscular men were cowards. But apparently not her Tunis. She wanted a brave husband. It would take a lot of bravery to start up a new family life in a wilderness.

The stagecoach pulled up in front of the Bonnie Hotel late in the afternoon. Clara had Bolicky Bill bring her trunk inside, where the desk clerk stored it in a side room. She rented a room on the first floor fronting on the long veranda facing Main Street. The wallpaper had a pretty pattern, luscious pink roses climbing over fragile white trellises. The wooden floor was covered with a colorful Persian carpet. The bed's brass ends glistened. The white pitcher standing in its wide white bowl gleamed, it was so clean, and in the soft light from the window it seemed almost transparent.

After she'd cleaned up a little, Clara went back to the main desk in the lobby. She asked the desk clerk if a Tunis Freyling were registered there.

The clerk looked her up and down as though he were wondering if she were a scarlet sister.

Clara fired up at his look. "Don't worry. I read the Bible."

"Well, one can't be too cautious these days. All sorts of spare ribs coming through."

"Is he here?"

"No. Checked out yesterday."

"Do you know where he went?"

"Tell me, are you his sister?"

"Why do you ask?"

"You look like you might be related."

"No, we're just friends." She decided to add a little innocent lie. "We agreed to meet again after he'd found some land."

The clerk's bland face opened with interest. "Oh, then you still don't know he bought some land."

"He did?"

"Yeh. Three miles northeast of here. Bought a whole section of land. Went back to where he came from to get the money and bring some supplies."

Clara's heart began to beat strong in her neck. "Mercy me, then he moved faster than I expected." Clara suddenly felt very happy. She hadn't gone on a wild goose chase after all.

"Yeh, it's hard to keep a secret around here." The clerk's face turned bland again. "Was he supposed to leave a message here for you?"

"No. I came earlier than we'd planned." Another little lie. She favored the clerk with a confidential smile. "I wanted to surprise him." She thought a moment to herself. "If a person was to go and look for this section of land, how would he go about it?"

58

"Just follow the railroad tracks north out of town. And then about three miles out you'll see a shanty on the left-hand side. That's it. Too bad the Bonnie Omaha didn't come back from Whitebone the other day because of the storm, or you could've caught a ride out to the shanty. You see, it leaves here in the morning for Whitebone and comes back in the evening."

"Thank you very much."

Before it got dark, Clara took a walk, east up Main Street to the last house halfway up the slow hill, then west down Main Street to the lumberyards beyond the Bonnie Omaha Railroad tracks. She saw no church spires and that she regretted. If Bonnie was going to be their town it was going to be a bleak life without some kind of religious ritual-and-song and pastoral instruction.

She had supper alone. A couple of the men in town had gone ice fishing in the still-frozen Big Rock River and had come back with two long strings of fat pickerel. They'd sold half of their catch to the hotel. Clara loved fish and ordered the pickerel. Since there was also fresh bread with apple butter she relished the meal.

Back in her dainty flowered room, she sat a while in a chair by the window, watching the figures of men walk past in the dim gas-lit street.

She wondered what Tunis would say when they met. She'd learned, watching the pups at Sutherland Hall, and remembering her father's ways around women, that men turned skittish when women did the chasing. It wasn't fair, but that was the way God made men. Everything had to fit their notion of how things should be. Maybe she was being a bit forward at that.

She went to bed. The feather tick was soft and giving. She lay on her right side, carefully drawing up her knees and feet inside her long blue flannel nightgown. Outside men continued to saunter past her window beyond the veranda. Sometimes there were loud shouts, and boasting taunts, and occasionally even rough raw talk.

That was another thing she'd liked about Tunis. He hadn't sworn once during his visit at Sutherland Hall. He seemed to have such control of himself. The power was there but it was in control. She wanted a man of control.

She nuzzled her head in the pillow.

Times and ways were different on the frontier. So maybe the usual rules of behavior weren't called for. Women were called upon to do all sorts of hard labor on the virgin prairie, and so maybe it was all right if a woman spoke her mind about the kind of man she wanted. Priscilla did it when she told John Alden, "Why don't you speak for yourself, John?"

She dreamt some more about Tunis. Yankton Indians spotted him traveling alone and that made him fair game. Desperately she tried to wake up to warn him that he was being watched from behind some tall grass on a low ridge. She thought she could make out four braves, each with a single pink feather, each with a bow and arrow. After a moment, peering closer even as she was trying to shriek to get Tunis's attention, she saw that all four were naked, not even a breechcloth. Her shriek broke into a choked sob and she awoke, slippery with sweat.

She lay awake and troubled for a long time. Her heart beat funny. She heard the last drunk come stumbling down the veranda outside. She felt lonesome and lost as she lay alone in a strange room in a strange town. Finally exhaustion took over and she again fell into a deep sleep just before dawn.

In the morning the first thing she heard was a voice in her head, a loud one, saying: "You're a silly goose to be chasing after a man you hardly know. What will people say? Your father, were he alive, would give you that odd look of his, thinking to himself that you weren't any better than he was, having a roving eye."

The feather bed was comfortable. It was like sleeping on a mother's ample breasts.

She thought about the dream again and once more felt the horror of not being able to call out a warning to Tunis that four naked Sioux, each with a single pink feather, were about to ambush him. The terrible lost stuck feeling almost took over again.

Why should she have dreamt about Indians when she'd never seen any? And why four of them? And why naked and each with a pink feather? She had the strong feeling that she'd dreamt something unwholesome.

Shaking her head, she bounded out of bed. "Dare to be a Ruth." She washed herself harshly in the cold water from the white pitcher.

They were serving pancakes for breakfast in the dining hall. Pancakes she loved. It would be fun to have pancakes served to her for once instead of having to make them for a horde of young English rapscallions. She remembered the pancakes she'd served to Tunis. She was lavish with the syrup and ate until she felt thickish over her cheeks and under her eyes.

She went back to her room.

It was strange that she should think about Ruth of the Bible. She got out her small leather Bible and read some of the passages from *the Book of Ruth*.

"Entreat me not to leave thee, or to return from following after thee: for whither thou goest, I will go; and where thou lodgest, I will lodge: thy people shall be my people, and thy God my God."

59

And wasn't that a wonderful passage where it was described how Ruth happened to glean wheat in one of the fields belonging to Boaz? And then her words to Boaz when he had been kind to her: "Why have I found grace in thine eyes, that thou shouldest take knowledge of me, seeing I am a stranger?"

Later on Naomi the mother-in-law told Ruth what to do. "Wash thyself therefore, and anoint thee, and put thy raiment upon thee, and get thee down to the floor; but make thyself not known to the man, until he shall have done eating and drinking. And it shall be when he lieth down, that thou shalt mark the place where he shall lie, and thou shalt go in, and uncover his feet, and lay thee down; and he will tell thee what to do."

And it had all happened as Naomi had foreseen. "And it came to pass at midnight, that the man was afraid, and turned himself: and behold a woman lay at his feet."

Ruth had revealed herself to Boaz then. "I am Ruth thine handmaid: spread therefore thy skirt over thine handmaid; for thou art a near kinsman." And after some thought Boaz had said, "My daughter, fear not: I will do to thee all that thou requirest: for all the city of my people doth know that thou art a virtuous woman." Later on Boaz told his elders, "Ruth the Moabitess have I purchased to be my wife."

The only trouble with that story was that she, Clara Shortridge, had neither a mother nor a Naomi to lean on for counsel. She had to do it alone.

Yet with a good breakfast in her stomach, and the happy thought of Ruth, she began to feel more optimistic about having followed Tunis to Bonnie. If Ruth could do a brave thing, find her man in the manner she did, then Clara Shortridge could do likewise.

She put on her high black shoes and buttoned them up with a buttonhook and then slipped on her one-buckle arctics. Looking outside she saw that the sun was shining and that it wouldn't be too cold out, so she put on a light green jacket over her gray full-length dress, drew her gray woolen bonnet warm around her face, pulled on some flannel-lined gloves, and set out.

Finding the railroad tracks by the depot she headed north. The dry crisp cinders between the ties crackled under her rubber arctics. The ties lay placed just right for her short stride; she didn't have to break step to keep from catching her feet between them. Several housewives were already out hanging up clothes to dry. They stared at her as she went past.

The snow that had fallen a couple of days before had mostly melted and left on the wet earth the strange smell of washed linens. The odor of water from melted snow wasn't the same as water just fallen from the sky. Rainwater often had the vague blue smell of electricity in it.

About a mile north of town, where the Big Rock River curved in toward the railroad, she ran into various flutters of birds in the deep faded grass, grackles and robins and song sparrows. Slim swallows with their gunmetal wings were already pecking new holes for nests into the black walls of the river banks.

The ice had suddenly gone out during the night, and great gray chunks the size of house roofs were banging into each other with crushing sounds, shelving up on each other with pinching screaks, parting and colliding, and slowly floating away. In the open patches of water ducks were dipping in, trailing webbed toetips, then, hearing a small iceberg crack apart, were flutting up and forming whirling circles above the budded trees.

Clara rejoiced at the sights and sounds of spring. The sun on her cheeks was like the warm kiss of a big-lipped man.

"Reminds me of when I was back home in Welton," she murmured, "how the ducks used to fly around like everything."

She passed several sod houses. She didn't see anybody, though, and wondered where the people might be. Perhaps they were having a morning cup of tea before pitching into the next set of chores. On each place the several cows and horses hung bunched together like they might be family.

Soon she saw the shanty ahead, on the left side of the railroad tracks. It was just beyond where the stagecoach ruts crossed the tracks.

She approached the shanty warily. So this was where she might soon be living if all went well between Tunis and herself. Compared to the sod houses, the log shanty was a palace. It had a real roof with thick curling cottonwood shingles instead of layers of sod.

She walked around the log shanty and spotted the lean-to for animals. She noted the fresh droppings of a horse. Tunis's roan gelding. It pleased her to see this evidence of her man's horse.

She approached the door. More evidence that someone had just been there—fresh horse tracks and the heel prints of a man's boot in the dirt just off to one side of a wide red door stone. She tried the door. Locked.

A thought came to her. With a little wise smile she withdrew a hairpin from her hair and, bending the hairpin open and fixing a hook out of one end of it, made herself a sort of key. She tried it, wiggled it around several times in the keyhole, trying to find the trip to the inner mechanism. She tried angling the bent hairpin into the side of the keyhole, and though the hairpin bent there finally was a click and she was in.

61

The mouse smell almost gagged her. She hated the mice and their smell with a sudden hot anger. Give a mouse the least hole and it would poke its nose in. If she came to live in the log cabin the first thing she was going to do was get after those mice. Poison. Traps. Small club.

She liked the two beds in the south corners. Until they got married Tunis could have one and she could have the other. At that thought she sat down in one of the carved log chairs near the fireplace and began to wonder how she should handle their being alone together. Maybe she shouldn't live here right away. People might talk. Also it might make him think he could have her without a marriage license.

It was chilly in the cabin. She looked around. There was still a little kindling left on the flagstones to one side of the fireplace, plus several small logs.

"Now for a match." She nosed around the place, noting the various shelves and ledges. Finally, on the right side of the fireplace, she noted what looked like a little door that had been expertly fitted into the log wall, made to look like it was part of the log. She took off her glove and caught at the edge of the little door with a fingernail. The tiny edge gave reluctantly; finally, spilling dust, it opened.

"For heaven's sake."

Whoever had made the little door and the cavity behind it had to have been a master woodworker. She leaned down to look inside. A box of matches. Several candles. A pad and pencil. A pearl necklace. A pearl-handled .38 pistol, loaded. And, of all things, a brown leather-bound diary with gold trim.

She forgot about a fire for the moment. The writing in the diary with its fine feminine hand caught her eye. There were daily entries. One sentence caught her eye: "Who do I love most?" Clara blinked. Apparently the writer loved more than one man. Clara read on for several pages. There seemed to be three men: James, Joseph, and Robert. Lord in heaven? the woman writer loved all three. And loved them more than just as brothers.

Clara clapped the diary shut. More she didn't want to know. Fornication. Probably adultery. Even incest. Again? She regretted having peeked in the thing. She didn't want a cloud hanging over a place where she might be living for the rest of her life. She wrinkled her nose at the diary and put it back into the hiding place. She wiped the dust of the diary from her fingers, even blew on her fingers. Then she picked up the matchbox to start the fire.

When she got the fire going briskly, the flames and gray smoke shooting swiftly up the chimney, she put the matches back. She was tempted to reach in again for the diary and throw it into the fire. But she still was not absolutely sure that Tunis owned the place. Suppose the owner of that diary came back for it someday and it couldn't be found. The woman writer would go wild with worry that someone had come upon that messy secret.

Curious to see who really did own the diary, Clara got it out once more and looked at the flyleaf. In the same handwriting was the name: *Betsy Worthing.* Clara started at the name, trying to see in her mind what the writer might have looked like. From the handwriting the writer had to be some kind of lady of fashion.

Clara couldn't resist a further look. She read, fascinated. It seemed Betsy was the wife of one named James Worthing, that the two of them had come west with his two brothers, Joseph and Robert, who'd helped build the log cabin, and that they'd lived together in the cabin all of one summer.

Again Clara clapped the brown leather-bound diary shut. What she'd read made her shiver. One thing she was right away sure of. The moment she knew Tunis owned the place, and if she were going to stay with him, she was going to burn that Worthing woman's terrible secret. She didn't want the ideas in it branded into Tunis's brain. She pushed the diary deep into the secret hiding place behind the pearl-handled pistol and closed the little door. The diary in its secret compartment was like a bad conscience for the log cabin.

She drew up one of the log chairs and sat by the fireplace for a while. She watched the flames pulse up the black fire hole.

"When will I ever get my life straightened out? Have a husband to help keep a good home? A home like my grandparents once had in Merrie Old England? It is taking so long. So long."

She gave a good hard long thought to Tunis. She saw him again in her mind's eye. A handsome rusty-headed powerful man. Piercing pearl gray eyes. Wonderful wide hands with short thick fingers. Wide short nails, neatly trimmed and clean. She could already feel those safe chubby hands touching her.

She got up and looked out of the two-foot-by-two-foot window to the south. The sun was still shining but it was past noon. She opened her coat and with a pinch flicked open her gold lapel watch. Already one o'clock.

She wished she'd taken along some sandwiches. She poked around in the place to see if perhaps the Worthings might have left some food behind. Dried fruit the mice would long ago have nibbled away. Her eyes were pulled toward the beds. She knelt and looked under the bed in the southeast corner. Nothing.

Swinging around on her knees, she looked under the other bed. Aha. A deep cache in the dirt floor. So frost wouldn't get at food. She peered down in the deep hole. There were packed-in layers of bluestem grass for insulation. Under that tins in a flat wooden traylike box. She lifted the tray up. Pork and beans in most of the tins. Several tins of pears. The ends weren't bulged out, so they were still good. A nickel can opener stuck up tucked in between the beans.

A gaming idea came to her. Why not stay overnight? It'd be an adventure. If she locked the door no tramp coming down the railroad could get at her. Why not? She now had food. And there was a bed.

Using the can opener she pried open one can of pork and beans and smelled it. Yes, no poison there. She set the can on a stone near the fire to heat up the beans. She also opened a can of pears. Good too.

When the beans were warm, she used the can opener as a spoon. The beans tasted good. Even the strings of bacon still had good savor. She finished off the meal with the pears. Each pear felt like an extra tongue in her mouth. She drank the juice thinking of it as her after-dinner beverage.

Sleepy, needing a nap, she threw a small log on the fire, held her hands briefly to the crackling flames, and then went to the beds. All the bedclothes were on the bed in the southwest corner. Apparently that was where Tunis had slept. She took the other one. It was instinctive in her to take the bed on the right-hand side of the man. She picked up the bedding and threw it on her bed and slipped under. The mouse smell still disgusted her. It was worst in the woolen blanket, while the quilt seemed to be almost odorless. She made a few sliding motions with her shoulders, and within moments fell sound asleep.

A whistle awoke her. A train. That had to be the Bonnie Omaha coming back from Whitebone. She looked at her watch. Almost six o'clock. She slipped out of bed and went to the door and looked out. There it was, a black engine with a high smokestack, black coal car, two red boxcars, a baggage car, and a yellow passenger car. The cars rolled and swung after each other with low grinding sounds. They rambled along like sleek sows with an old black boar leading the way.

She saw people looking out at her from the passenger car. It thrilled her to see them. From what far places on earth might they not have come: New York, Boston, Philadelphia, Chicago, Minneapolis? She was glad that the railroad cut across part of Tunis's land. She and the children wouldn't feel so isolated. One of the things she didn't like about Sutherland Hall was that it was so far from anywhere.

Another thought came to her. The desk clerk at the Regent Hotel in Le Mars had said there was an Episcopal minister in Whitebone. Perhaps on a Sunday she and her family could flag down the train in the morning, go to church in Whitebone toward noon, then come back home in the evening.

She brightened at still another thought. She and Tunis could also go to Whitebone someday to get married. She hoped Tunis wouldn't fight her about the Episcopal church. She had to keep her church. It tied her back to her family and to her ancestors in old England. Because of that secret malady in her family she needed the church all the more.

The big black engine whistled again, shooting off a quick rising plume of white steam. Looking, Clara saw why. Some boys were driving a small herd of cows across the tracks heading for a dugout along the river. That pleased her too. She and Tunis would have cows some day. Milk. Butter. Cheese. She watched the train vanish around the long curve of the low southeastern hills. Its black plume of smoke dispersed into the clear falling sunlight and wisped away.

Standing there in the door, she realized that the hotel clerk had said the Bonnie Omaha had been stalled in Whitebone because of a snowstorm. That was why she hadn't seen any train tracks in what was left of the snow on the railroad. Well, if she had to, she could always flag the train down tomorrow afternoon for Bonnie.

She built up the fire from the hot embers. Hungry again she had herself some more pork and beans and pears.

The cold pears made her wonder where Betsy Worthing might have gone to the toilet. Clara went outside to have a look around. No privy that she could see. Unless Betsey had used the horse shelter. With a quick look around, even though she knew there probably wasn't a soul around for at least a mile, Clara settled in the tall faded grass behind the shelter and relieved herself.

The sun was just setting on the brown waving bluestem as she turned to go back to the shanty. The sun's rays made the brown grass gleam like auburn hair. Against a red-purple sunset budded river trees traced sharp bizarre squiggles. It was all glorious. Already she loved the valley.

She still worried a little that she'd been too bold in following Tunis; further, had even dared to have a look at the land he had purchased. What would he say?

She measured again in memory the look he'd given her that last morning at Sutherland Hall when she'd fed him breakfast. He hadn't been very talkative, as though he regretted something, or had wanted to mention something but hadn't quite dared.

She hoped it was because he'd been smitten with her just as she'd been with him.

She had to have him.

With that thought, and an extra log on the fire, she went to bed for the night.

5. Tunis

Early in the afternoon, as Tunis came around the low line of east hills, he was startled to see smoke rising from the chimney of his log cabin.

"Goddam! A claim jumper."

Tunis was driving a team of bays. He rode easy on an undulating spring seat high atop a spanking new green two-box wagon with yellow wheels. He was proud of the rig. Behind him Gyp followed, tied with a lead rope to the back of the wagon.

He looked down at the floor of the wagon to where his new shotgun and a box of .10-gauge shells lay. Load the gun? He cautioned himself not to get out of hand. One man in the grave was already more than enough. Maybe it was just a tramp off the railroad. If it was a tramp he'd soon learn he'd made a very bad mistake. Tunis's jaw set out as he jounced along on his high spring seat.

Up until that very moment everything had gone perfect. Not a hitch anywhere. Everything had gone as loose as goose grease. Like the earth turning without a squeak.

After Tunis took his money out of the Wanata bank, he'd gone to the nearest implement shop and bought the wagon. Then he'd gone to a farm sale, where he bought the team of bays, Fred and Bill; a breaking plow; several shovels and spades; a garden rake and hoe; and other assorted tools piled in a storebox. The night before he left for Bonnie he went to the livery stable and secreted most of his money inside the piece of sheet metal under Gyp's right horseshoe. The rest of the money he hid in his saddlebags.

The trip from Wanata to Bonnie had also gone well. The bays proved to be stayers. Tunis had been a little worried at first that Fred might turn out to be a winded horse. But once Fred got to sweating he'd pulled his share with ease. As the crow flies, which was the route Tunis took, it was some sixty miles, first past some Indians mounds, then through Gaza and Primghar. He'd slept out in open near Archer, not wanting to call too much attention to his new rig. From there it was some more driving into the northwest, past Sheldon and Matlock and finally a colony of Quakers in the southeast corner of Leonhard County.

Even Boughers had been most accommodating once Tunis had handed over $2,412.00. Boughers quickly wrote out the bill of sale as well as the notice of sale to the county recorder, Boughers's eyes had ovaled open a sheening gray when he saw Tunis's horses and rig. But he'd said nothing, only nodded his head on a good deal made for both sides.

But now that smoke rising from his chimney.

Tunis pulled up some twenty yards from the log cabin, careful not to say whoa, only pulling up on the lines. He reached down for the new blue gun, quietly inserted a shell, then stepped down from the wagon. He whispered, "There, there, Fred," and touched Fred on the rump to let him know everything was all right. Then, gun cocked, Tunis headed for the door.

Two steps from the red door stone, the door suddenly opened. He snapped up the gun, ready.

"Clara!"

"Tunis!"

"For godsakes, woman, I was afraid you might be a claim jumper."

"For heaven sakes yourself, sir, I thought you might be some kind of dangerous stranger."

Then they both burst out laughing. She pushed back a strand of dark auburn hair that'd slid out of the double knot above. He set down his gun.

She said, "You aren't a stranger, but with that gun you still look dangerous."

"Well, I didn't know what I'd find here."

"Suppose I had been a claim jumper, what would you've done?"

"It would have gone mighty rough for him."

"Is that gun loaded?"

"It sure is."

She frowned. "Well, I suppose you probably had to do that." She looked past him. "I see you now have a team of horses and a wagon. And there's still your Gyp."

He wanted to brag about his new possession, but his puzzlement over how come the only woman to so far catch his fancy should be standing in the doorway of his new home was the stronger. He made a little questioning motion with his hand, looking first at her and then at his cabin.

Her face sobered over. "Well, I was first going back to Welton. You know, where my folks lived? But then I got to thinking about us . . . about how maybe it would be years before we'd meet again if I didn't try to find you . . . the way things work out in this world . . . anyway, I decided to grab the bull by the tail and make sure we'd meet again." A smile brightened her grave gray eyes. "I meant to walk out here only for the day. But I liked it so much that I decided to stay the night. And it looks like you caught me before I could walk back. Or catch the train this afternoon."

"Train?"

"Yes. It leaves Bonnie in the morning for Whitebone, comes back in the evening. But it got caught in that storm up north and it didn't show up again until last night."

"Oh." He smiled at her. What a perky plucky woman. He liked that in her. "Grab the bull by the tail and look him straight in the eye, eh?"

She didn't like the vulgarity he'd made out of her remark, and showed it. "Out here I've learned a person has to be his own matchmaker."

"Suppose I'd decided I didn't like you?"

"I knew you would though." Again she smiled.

"What happened there at Sutherland Hall that you quit so quick?"

She grimaced. "His royal highness himself proposed the day you left. The old goat. And then I ran into something disgusting upstairs."

He looked back at his horses and then back at her. "What do you have in mind? I mean . . ."

"I've thought about that. If I stay here, we can hang a curtain . . ."

"Until what?"

"Until we get better acquainted."

He managed to keep a poker face. "And then?"

"Get married of course."

He bit his upper lip. "Meanwhile, what about the gossip? They're fiends for it in little towns."

"And not in big towns? They even gossip in heaven, you know." She looked past his wagon at the tall rusty grass and then at the east hills and then north to where the river curved off through a wide flat plain. "Out here there can't be much gossip. And what little there'll is, I can stand it if you can."

He held up a mittened hand. "Look, lady, don't get me wrong. I think it's pretty swell I found you here in my cabin. Instead of a tramp. I'm only thinking of your good. Especially since like me you've had a roughty time so far in life." He cocked his head at her. "You sure you don't want to live in town for a while and have me come courtin' you all regular and proper?"

"Where would I stay?"

"In the hotel. Maybe you could cook there some. Until I get things squared away here." He quirked a smile at her. "Why, I haven't even had time to dig a hole for the privy. Let alone build an outdoor palace proper for a lady."

"Tunis, I'm not cooking for anybody ever again. Unless it's for my husband-to-be."

He looked at her steadily. "How did you open the door?"

"A hairpin is to the woman what a jackknife is to the man."

"Ah. Then we're going to have to get a better lock."

She looked askance at his gun. "Must you still carry that like you're going to shoot somebody?"

"Oh." He uncocked the gun.

"Tunis, I will not be trifled with. Do you want me or don't you want me? I want to know right now."

He swallowed. His nerves raced with light. "Today yet?"

"Yes."

"Well, all right, you can stay. It'll at least save you a trip walking back to town."

"Good." A sweet womanly smile opened her face. "What have you got in that wagon?"

"Come." He led the way. "I'm afraid I ain't got much for the lady of the house." With a laugh, he added, "I wasn't expecting you so quick."

"That's all right. Later on when we get my trunk from the hotel we can get the needed supplies."

She helped him unhitch Fred and Bill and unharness them in the horse shelter. While he fed the two horses along with Gyp, she gently petted them on the rump. The three horses seemed not to mind her, which Tunis thought a good sign.

Next she helped him unload the wagon. She was astonished at the great weight of the breaking plow. But she was most interested in the box of odds and ends. In it she found a meat grinder, a washboard, a lard press, a butcher knife, a flensing knife, and a knife sharpener. All these she promptly brought into the log cabin.

She also helped him store the shovels and spades, the hammers and level, and all the other tools that might rust, into the cabin. When they finished, the place had a cluttered look. Both frowned at all the handles sticking up.

He spotted a nail in a log above the fireplace. "Ha, it looks like the Worthings had a gun here too." He was about to hang up his shotgun, when a thought occurred to him. "Maybe I should go out and shoot us some game. I'm hungry."

Clara said, "Maybe I should show you the cache I found under your bed." She knelt and pulled out the box of canned goods. "That's how I could stay overnight."

"I'll be cow-kicked. Now I never noticed that. And here I thought I looked the place over pretty good. Think there's enough there for us for a meal?"

"I think so. Though if you want to shoot a rabbit, go ahead."

He let his shoulders down. "No, after all that jolting on the wagon, I'm tired. I'll hunt tomorrow."

"Good. I'll quick warm us up some beans." She placed her hands on her hips. "But there's one thing I wasn't able to find."

"What's that?"

"A sheet to hang between us tonight."

He glanced at her bosom. "Maybe we can use one of those blankets."

"But there already aren't enough blankets. Besides, they're so holey you can see through them like they might be a slice of cheese."

"Then we'll have to do without that wall."

She glanced at the diminished pile of wood beside the fireplace. "You'll have to get us more wood."

"I already thought of that. I'm sure I can find some down limbs along the river."

She sighed. "I don't want you to get the wrong idea either. I want everything between us to be right and proper. That way we'll always have respect for each other." She let fly a little laugh. "Though at the same time, I'm not as shy and back-numberish as you might think."

He liked everything she said. It surprised him that he should right away take to her. When, except for Old Tressa, he'd always felt ill at ease around women. He wished now he'd paid more attention to girls back then, so that he might better understand this Clara, if what she was doing was the usual way frontier girls behaved. She was both proper and bold. She certainly was no tramp. It was probably because she was a lady from Welton.

She said, more to herself than to him, "I was just thinking. What would my mother think if she could see me now? Staying overnight in a cabin with a man and not married to him. She'd say it was dreadful. That we were both going to perdition."

He wanted to put his arms around her. "Maybe it would be worth perdition."

She saw the motion in him. "No. You go get us some wood. And I'll get our supper ready."

He found a fallen ash limb along the river and carried it in on his shoulder. With the double-bitted axe he chopped it up into proper lengths. When he threw the largest chunk on the fire, it instantly gave off an almost savory aroma, reminding him of thoroughly dried jerky.

Clara served the pork and beans on the flagstones. He sat on one side of the fireplace and she on the other. With no forks and knives, they had to tip the cans up and let the food slide into their mouths.

Tunis said, "You know what would go good with this? Rusk with butter and sugar on it. Old Tressa used to serve that on Sundays."

"And some tea."

"Yeh. Dark tea or green tea, either one."

"I'm glad you like tea. That's my main drink."

Soon it was time to go to sleep.

He said, "I'll go have a look at the stars while you climb in bed."

"I'd like a look at them too. I'm no different from you."

He repressed a smile. "All right. I'll go check the horses first then."

When he returned she was already in bed. He saw that she'd taken the bed in the southeast corner and would lie on his right. How had she known that that was what he wanted? He could just make out her face in the pink light from the fire. Her gray eyes looked like soft little holes of light. He put a couple of logs on the fire for the night. When he started to undress, he saw that she had turned over, facing the wall.

He slid in under the thin lumpy bedcovers. He lay a while in thought. "I suppose we ought to make plans for a trip into town tomorrow."

She was almost asleep. She murmured, "Why don't we talk about it in the morning? Then our heads will be clear."

"Good thinking."

The fire crackled and fluted and rustled. For the first time he found himself wonderfully excited about a woman. How would they go about it if the day ever came? He'd seen stallions mount mares and bulls their cows and cocks their hens and boars their sows. But how did a man go about it with a woman? He wondered if she'd ever given thought about how it might be. Did she ever wonder what he might be like naked? He found himself ready, aroused. Just think, he'd found himself the right woman and she was already sleeping in his house.

He let go with a great sigh. It took him a while to go to sleep.

6. Tunis

"A new day and new weather," Tunis murmured, as his eyes opened to the light pouring in through the little window above his head.

"I was wondering when you'd wake up," Clara said from her bed in the other corner.

"You been awake long?"

"An hour or so." She smiled with sleep-softened lips. "Why don't you get up and light us a fire and I'll make us breakfast?" She rolled over so as not to be facing him.

"All right." He stretched mightily, until his toes curled up, and sighed deeply, and then, yawning, swung his legs over the edge of the bed. "Man, did I sleep." He dressed quickly in the cold.

Presently he had a good fire going. He kept his back turned while Clara dressed.

Clara soon had breakfast ready. With a little laugh, she said, "I thought I'd try something a little different this morning. I hope you like bacon and beans."

"I do if you'll serve them with some canned pears."

"About our plans for today. We are going to town, aren't we?"

"Then you're still of a mind to ignore the gossips?"

"Oh, pshaw, Tunis, at worst all they'll be able to say is, 'If you can believe all you hear about her, then she's no better than she should be.' I know. I used to hear that at home about women who had a mind of their own."

The Bonnie Omaha went by on its way north to Whitebone just as they finished breakfast. The engineer must have noticed the smoke rising from their chimney because he whistled two quick toots.

They rode into town perched together up on the spring seat. The bays Fred and Bill trotted along briskly, chain tugs clinking, celluloid rings on their hames flashing red and white and blue. The sun came over the east hills in a wide throw of yellow warmth.

Things were bustling on Main Street when they arrived in town. There were buggies and wagons of all makes and descriptions on both sides of the street, with the horses tied to the long row of hitching posts. The smell of morning wood fires lingered in the air. Children had gone off to school and all one saw were grown-ups. Everybody was wearing winter clothes unbuttoned at the throat.

Tunis drove straight to the Bonnie Hotel. With Clara helping, her trunk was soon loaded into the wagon. Next they went to Rexroth's General Store. They had a little argument about who was to buy what. Clara wanted to spend some of her money too. He insisted they spend only his money. He had plenty.

Clara said, "There are some things a woman likes to buy without the man knowing."

"Here," he said, digging out his purse, handing her a hundred-dollar bill, "take this."

She pushed the bill aside. "No, for those private things I want to spend my own money. Until we get married."

"Can I know how much you've got?"

"Well! the nerve of you." Then she laughed. "Well, I guess it will be all right for you to know. I managed to save several hundred dollars." She bit her upper lip in thought. "I suppose now I should ask you how much you got. But remember, I'm asking only after I've already told you that I liked you."

There wasn't the least hesitation on his part. It was something he noted with pleasure. "I inherited some money from my foster parents. After paying for the farm, and for the horses and wagon and so on, I've still got almost four thousand dollars left."

A wonderful look of both surprise and satisfaction spread over her face. She not only had a fine man, she had a rich man for a husband. Or at least one that was well set up for life. "Still and all, I want to spend my own money for my personal things until we get married. All right?"

"Well, if that's the way you want it."

She stepped up close to him. "I have a question to ask though."

"Fire away."

"There's no bank here in town. Where did you put that extra money?"

"I've got it hidden on our place. But I hear they got a good safe bank in Rock Falls, the county seat. Someday when we go for supplies there, ones we can't get here, I'll put it in that bank."

"Are you sure it's in a safe place?"

He told her where he'd hidden it, under the shoe of his horse Gyp.

She laughed. "I declare. If that wasn't a right smart thing to do."

"That's what I thought."

While they were talking, the storekeeper Rexroth came up. "Aren't you Tunis Freyling? The man who bought the Worthing place?" Rexroth was a stocky man some thirty years old.

"Yes."

"Well. Happy to see you." Rexorth had a smile that truly meant nothing but good. "And this is Mrs. Freyling then." He waved a hand to indicate the whole store. "Madam, it's all yours if you want it."

Tunis said, "Yeh, if she can afford it."

Rexroth went on. "And if I don't have it, let me know and I'll order it. Now that we have regular train service on the Bonnie Omaha, we can usually get our orders filled in seventy-two hours."

Clara said primly, "Thank you."

Rexroth bowed, and then went off to the back of the store where a cash register gleamed a bronze gold in the light coming through a side door.

The general store was a paradise of things to buy. There were baskets of fresh gleaming eggs, big jars of fresh butter just in from the farm, large chunks of nectar-smelling maple sugar, strings of curly dried apples. Filling an aisle were barrels of flour and middlings, coarse fluffy cornmeal, buckwheat shorts. In another aisle were sacks of dusky potatoes, purple turnips, powerful-smelling onions. The air was so heavy with the wonderful aromas of good things to eat it made the nose thicken.

In another section were barrels of dried and salted fish, salt pork in a huge crock with a large stone on top to keep the pork below the level of the brine, thin strings of jerky almost a transparent brown, smoked ham, packages of dried beef, smoked bacon, kegs of gray lard, a whole smoked hog's head smiling down benignly from a meathook, jars of headcheese. Almost all the customers in the meat area licked their lips.

And then there was the section where one could buy overalls and dresses and mittens and coats and hats and caps. Right in the middle of it were stacks of bolts of cloth for the woman of the house who had to make her own dresses as well as clothes for her children. There the smell had an inky scent of dye in it.

When they finished their shopping spree, Tunis brought the wagon around to the door on the east side, and he and Clara loaded up: potatoes, dried meat and fish, eggs, salt, sugar, tea, coffee, butter, cheese, flour, yeast, syrup, baking powder. They also bought utensils: a white enamel pail with a dipper, coffeepot, pots and pans, teakettle, frying pans, coffee grinder, meat grinder, shakers, rolling pin, a set of forks and knives and spoons, and a soup ladle. Clara made sure they had a box of mousetraps, a shiny nickel alarm clock, a packet of various-size needles, a sharp regular scissors as well as an eyehole scissors, several thimbles, and bedding for two. Tunis made sure they had a square, carpenter's folding rule, saw, nails, staples, pincers, pliers, crowbar, sledge, wedges, two tin pails, two pitchforks. He also bought a sack of seed corn and a sack of wheat.

Rexroth helped them load up after Tunis had paid for everything. "I guess I don't need to tell you that your business is most welcome, Mrs. Freyling."

Clara nodded.

"And that you pay in cash, Mr. Freyling." Rexroth clapped his white hands together. "Come again."

Tunis nodded.

When they had both climbed aboard the spring seat Tunis remarked, looking back at their full load, "One thing we didn't figure on. To leave enough room for some lumber. For the outhouse."

Clara said, "The train goes by our place. Can't we have them drop it off across from our house?"

"Great idea. Let's swing around to the lumberyard and order up what we need."

The lumberyard boss agreed it was possible to drop off the lumber near their house. "So you're the couple that's taken over the Worthing place. Engineer said he'd seen smoke coming out of the chimney there."

"That's us." Tunis was careful not to look at Clara.

"Tell the engineer to give us a couple of toots like he did this morning and we'll pile out and help unload the order."

"Will do."

On the way home, a little after twelve noon, Clara reached into one of the grocery sacks and dug out some dried apples and crackers for them to nibble on to still their hunger.

Tunis was the first to remark on it. "It looks like we don't need to worry about the gossip about us. Everybody's got us married."

Clara gave him a quirked look. "I hope that don't give you ideas."

"I didn't mean it that way."

"Because when the right day comes, you and I will catch the train outside our house and go to Whitebone and get married."

Tunis raised an eyebrow. "Whitebone?"

"That's where the nearest Episcopal church is. And I mean to get married as an Episcopalian. By a father."

Tunis rode in silence for a while. A couple of times he lightly flipped the lines, not really to urge Fred and Bill and on but to be doing something with his hands. "You're that religious, eh?"

"Yes, I am. And if you object, then it's all off. I'll just be your housekeeper for a while. Until we've got you settled." Her chin set out. "And then I'll try again somewhere else."

"You keep surprising me."

"There are many things I have not spoken of."

"Maybe I'll be surprising you too sometime. For one thing I suffer from the anger of a too proud heart."

"I've got used to adversity. And now I need adversity to keep me nerved up."

When they arrived on the yard, Gyp whinnied from the horse shelter. It felt good to get a greeting of some kind from someone left on the yard.

As soon as they were unloaded, Clara got out the box of mousetraps. She baited the traps with bits of cheese and set all twelve of them in strategic places. "If I don't do this right away they'll sample all the food. How I hate mice. That's the one mistake I know for sure God made when he created the world. They're of no earthly use that I can see."

Tunis unharnessed the horses and set them and Gyp free to graze where they would, sure they wouldn't run off too far. Then he promptly got a spade and began looking for a spot to dig the privy hole. After some looking around, he decided to dig the vault on the edge of the slight dropoff behind the house. First though he got Clara outside to have a look at the spot and agree on it.

"This should be about right, not? Not too close for the stink and not too far for the cold."

She wrinkled her nose. "Why must you men always be so explicit?"

He huffed at that. "I'm not a schoolmarm."

"But I guess it's all right. Though I sure wish we could have some lilac bushes on both sides of the path. To cut down on the wind in the winter and to smell nice in the summer."

"In time, lady, in time."

"Where do we get the water? Out of the river?"

"Until I get a well dug. That's next on the docket."

She went back into the house to get the pails and he started digging.

He was down about a foot when his spade struck a bone, Curious, he dug carefully around it, even getting down on his knees and using his jackknife to unearth whatever it was. It turned out to be the skeleton of a man. It had to be that of an Indian, not a white man. The sight of it gave him a queasy stomach. He stared down at it. There but for the grace of God and chance might have lain the tramp he'd killed along the Little Sioux River.

He called Clara outside again.

Clara stared down at the rusty skeleton as though she in turn were thinking of something sad. "Maybe we shouldn't disturb those bones. Certainly not where we want to put an outhouse."

"I agree. I'll fill it in again."

Clara had tears in her eyes. She held a hand over her eyes and looked around. "This spot is a little too close to the horse shelter anyway. Why don't you dig it more to the south, so that when the women have to go, we go around the side of the house away from the barn."

"The women?"

"Me. And my daughters to come."

"All right."

She watched him fill in again. She whispered, "Rest in peace, whoever you were. We didn't mean to disturb your bones." Then, gravely, she turned and returned to the house.

He began a new hole where she wanted it.

He had it completely dug, four feet on each side and six feet deep, by the time she called him in for supper. He noted again how deep the black topsoil was, a good two feet before it slowly changed to light brown, then to yellow clay. He'd lucked onto some wonderful land. The frost was out and the long winter deep freeze had worked up the ground soft and marly.

That night Clara cooked up a succulent meal: boiled potatoes in the skin, boiled fish, thick brown flour gravy, cut string beans. She'd set it all out, using a storebox for a table, at which they had to sit sideways on the stump chairs. Tunis looked at it all with tongue ready and tight against the inside of his teeth. Just as he picked up a fork and knife to set to, Clara raised a hand.

"Tunis, would you mind if we prayed at each meal? I've missed that so much since I left my father's house in Welton."

Man, was she religious. It probably meant she was still pure in heart. "If that's what you want."

"I don't want this to be a fishbone in the throat between us now."

"No, go ahead."

74

"Will you ask the blessing then? As the head of the house?"

"No. That's something I shouldn't do. I won't mean it like you will."

"Do it awhile and then you'll get used to meaning it."

"No. You pray." Tunis threw a look upward. "He's more apt to listen to you than to me."

She studied him with her grave gray eyes, then closed her eyes and folded her hands. "O almighty God, look down upon thy humble servants and see the work that they do. Bless our labor so that it may redound to thy honor and glory. This food that has been prepared for us bless it also. May it give us health and strength, and the desire to live the good life inspired by thy holy spirit. Forgive us our trespasses. We ask it in Jesus' name. Amen."

Tunis was touched.

She opened her eyes after a moment. "Tunis, after we've finished eating, can we read a little from the Bible and have a little talk about it?"

"If you want."

They relished the meal together. It became dark out and Tunis threw several logs on the fire. They talked about the day in town and how much they were pleased with the big general store.

Clara said, "Rexroth seems to have everything a body would want."

Between bites Tunis mused on the fire. "One thing we forgot. Some kerosene. And a lamp for the house and a lantern for the yard."

"We can get that the next time we go to town."

A trap snapped. Pop.

"Aha!" Clara cried. "Got one." She jumped up and leaned down near the groceries stacked in the far corner. She picked up the trap by a corner and with her face drawn up in distaste carried the mouse outdoors. When she came back she reset the trap with cheese bait.

Tunis had to smile.

For dessert Clara served a dish of boiled dried apples garnished with brown sugar. Then she poured them each a cup of hot steam-wisping tea.

Finished, Clara decided to read from The Book of Common Prayer instead of the Bible. She chose a passage from the Gospel According to Saint John, chapter 15: "I am the true vine, and my Father is the husbandman. Every branch in me that beareth not fruit he taketh away: and every branch that beareth fruit, he purgeth it, that it may bring forth more fruit. . . . If a man abide not in me, he is cast forth as a branch, and is withered; and men gather them, and cast them into the fire, and they are burned . . . These things have I spoken unto you, that my joy might remain in you, and that your joy might be full."

The reading didn't mean much to Tunis, but the warm clear tone of Clara's voice did. For once her voice wasn't sharp, abrupt, but tender and honeyed.

Another trap snapped. The trap flapped around a few times as the second mouse struggled. Then it fell silent. Again with a mixture of distaste and glee Clara got rid of the crumpled mouse and reset the trap.

Tunis helped himself to more tea.

Clara sat down again. "Well, what did you think about what Saint John said there?"

"I never worked in a vineyard, so I don't know."

"But the idea of it. That if you prune back a vine you get more grapes than if you don't. And if you prune it back real hard, you get a lot of grapes. And better grapes."

Tunis pushed out his lip in thought. "Well, I know it happens with apple trees. I used to watch Old Dirk cut back his apple trees in the spring. In the fall we'd have so many apples, we had to let the cows in to eat the windfalls."

"Then you do see the lesson in what we just read."

He found himself stubborning up. He hated being led.

"That when you have children you've got to prune 'em back a little."

He had a thought. "Maybe that passage also means you shouldn't take on too many things at once. But settle for just one thing at a time."

Her grave eyes opened in pleasure. "Good." She closed the book. "Now, wasn't that nice? Oh, how I miss those after-dinner meditations I used to have with my father and mother."

By the time they went to bed, both very tired, six more traps snapped and six more doubled-over mice were dropped in the grass outside.

Clara had completely remade the beds. She'd burnt the old holey bedding and replaced it with fresh sheets and blankets. She'd also scented the sheets with some kind of soft subtle perfume.

Tunis had just barely turned on his right side, his favorite way to fall asleep, when he was gone.

The next morning he awoke to the smell of boiling coffee. He sat up. "Clara."

"Time to get up. A new sun and a new sky."

"Wow. Did I sleep."

He washed his face and sat down to breakfast. While he'd slept Clara had ground some wheat in the meat grinder and boiled it for porridge. He dropped a dab of butter on the steaming brown cereal and then sprinkled on some sugar. "Isn't this a little coarse for you?"

"A body needs roughage or the spirit will falter. Now. Shall we pray?"

When they'd finished eating, Clara announced that she'd trapped ten more mice. "I was up half the night with those mice. But I think things have quieted down now."

As Tunis sipped his coffee, mind full of drifting prisms of thought, he heard the train whistle outside. Two toots. "By gosh, is it that time already? Well, I better get going. I promised I'd help them unload."

Clara said, "I'm coming with."

Both slipped on their boots and sailed out to the tracks. The train had stopped directly across from the house. The great black engine breathed steamily, occasionally letting go with a long vast sigh of escaping power.

The engineer smiled down at them from his iron perch. "C'mon, you boomers, time's a-wastin'. I believe in running a train on time."

Tunis smiled back, nodding.

The brakie and the conductor had already slid back the side door of a freight car just ahead of the red caboose. Both men were surprised to see that Clara had come out to help. They began to hand out lumber of various sizes: one-by-sixes, two-by-twos, and four-by-fours.

When they finished Tunis had a question. "I forgot to ask in town where I could get some well casing."

"Wood or cement?"

"Cement. Wood don't last long."

"They make cement casing up in Whitebone."

"Could you bring some down?"

"Yeh." The conductor pushed back his black cap as he let his eye rove over the flat land. "You're probably gonna run into water pretty quick here. When they put in this roadbed, they ran into some gravel a dozen feet below this black soil and yellow clay." He mused on the land some more, pursing up his thick lips. "I'll just bet if you was to dig along the edge of where your land drops off a little there, you'd hit water within ten feet. In fact, you might start off a spring."

"How wide do those casings run?"

"You probably should start with a casing three foot in diameter and then as you go down put in narrower ones. They're two feet deep. Let's see. Six of them would be sure to do you."

Up ahead the engineer pulled on the cord to the whistle, a long impatient blast.

"Coming, coming," the conductor growled. Then to Tunis he said, "Shall we drop you off some tonight on the way back?"

"Yep. And just to be sure, make it nine casings. And have the bill with you."

"Will do." Then the conductor waved a go-ahead signal to the engineer and headed for the caboose, the brakie following.

Tunis and Clara carried the lumber to the vault he'd dug, and then Tunis set to work with hammer and saw and nails.

Tunis had a good eye for design. Sometimes his eye was so good he didn't need the square. With Clara sometimes helping him hold a board in place, he had the whole privy built by four in the afternoon. It was a two-holer, with the big hole for grown-ups and the little hole for children. Tunis cut a cute quarter moon in the door and put on a turnknuckle for easy opening.

Clara looked at the door. "Why not a full moon?"

"Then you wouldn't know it was a moon."

"With that quarter moon I think you men are making sport of our curse."

"Why don't you go in and be the first to try it? While I bring the tools into the house."

"That's just what I'm going to do."

They had finished supper and read the word when they heard the Bonnie Omaha whistling again in the distance to the north. Quickly they scrambled into their outdoor clothes and hurried out to the tracks. They got there just as the train pulled up, great engine pulsing with steamy restless power. The conductor and the brakie let down a ramp out of a red boxcar. Soon the two men were rolling down the two-foot-deep well casings, with Tunis and Clara catching them on the roll and stopping them in the deep grass. When they were finished the conductor presented the waybill.

Bills already stuffed in his pocket, Tunis paid for the casings. "Thanks a lot. If you ever hanker for a cup of coffee, you know where to pull up."

"Will do." The conductor glanced toward Tunis's log cabin. "I see you got your altar built already."

"Yep. And one of us has already worshiped there."

"How did you like the shingles I brought you?"

"Just fine."

"Cedar shingles cost more but I didn't dare bring you the homemade kind for fear you'd take a shot at me coming by some morning. Fellow in town has a shingle mill. But he makes his shingles out of boiled cottonwood. If you boil cottonwood it can be sliced as easy as cutting cheese. Trouble is—"

Tunis broke in. "—cottonwood shingles when they get wet warp off the roof and crawl all over the county."

"Oh, so you know about that. Yeh, they're guaranteed to keep the house dry provided it don't rain."

"Thanks for thinking of the cedar ones for us."

"Don't mention it."

With charges of power, huh! huh! huh!, steam whooshing straight up in the air, black smoke crowning it, the engine slowly drew away, the charges coming faster and faster, until the train was back to its usual speed, h-h-h-h-h-h.

Tunis studied the gleaming almost-white concrete casings. He gave one of them a push. "They're pretty heavy. I think what we'll do is roll them over one at a time, as we need them."

During the night, rolling on his side and waking slightly, Tunis realized where he should dig his well. He didn't believe in witching for water. Witching was a pile of hookum.

The next morning right after breakfast he started in. It was fun to be working with a brand-new spade. It was sharp and it flashed in the sun.

Clara came outside. "Why are you digging the well there?"

He leaned on his spade. "It's my idea to add onto the house someday. What I thought—"

Clara interrupted. "Good! I was hoping that would be your thinking. It's so crowded and junky in there."

77

"Hey, hey. You're lucky I'm thinking of the house first. Most farmers build a palace for the cows long before they build a hut for their wife."

Clara shut up.

"So. Anyway. What I thought I'd do is make a sort of shanty or lean-to out of our cabin there. And then hook the house, the new part, onto the southeast corner of it and build it in this direction. That way your north door has got a little protection. What you'll do is step in through the present door, take a left, and then step through a door into the kitchen of the main part. We'll put that kitchen door where you got your bed now."

"I hope you're thinking of putting a floor in that cabin someday."

"I'm going to make that a cement floor. Then we can use it as a milk house too." He smiled teeth at her. "The house will come right along beside the well here, with the main front door here and the cement stoop there. Later on, I'll dig us a cistern north of the cabin there, catching the water off the roof of the whole shebang. That'll give the lady of the house soft water for washing clothes and dishes, and well water for drinking and so on."

"You're not going to water the animals right in front of the house here, are you?"

"No, no. I'll dig another well farther down the yard. Where I build the barn and the hog house. No, this well is for drinking. You can sit on the stoop in the evening after a hot day's work and have a cool drink of water."

Clara admired his foresight.

He dug a hole three and a half feet wide and some three feet deep, and then rolled and lifted in the first casing. Once he had that done, he merely had to dig out the center of the hole and then under the casing along the sides. The casing kept working down as he cleaned out the sides. Presently it was time to drop another casing on top of the first one. Again some more digging and the two casings, weightier, worked down easier, almost by themselves.

Clara helped him roll the casings over one by one from where the train had dropped them in the grass. The deeper he dug, the harder and hotter the work became. By noon hour he was some five casings deep into the earth. It became difficult to heave out the dirt and he hit upon the idea of using a pail with a rope. After he'd filled a pail, Clara hauled it up and emptied it.

About two in the afternoon, when he was seven casings deep, he hit water-bearing gravel. At first it seeped in, but then as it pushed the gravel ahead of itself, it started coming in faster. The next thing Tunis knew, he had water up to his knees and still rising. He scrambled up the casings as fast as he could, catching his toes where the edges didn't quite overlap exactly, and had just managed to get out when the water came to within four feet of the surface.

"Holy buckets!" Tunis cried. "Do we have water."

Clara came running out of the cabin where she had gone for a moment to get Tunis some crackers and cheese. "Tunis! you're soaking wet."

"Yeh. Take a look in there. So high you can almost dip it out."

She stared at the slowly diffusing water. It was clear as air. "Isn't that wonderful? I'll quick get us a clean bucket."

Within moments, using the rope, Tunis hauled up their first good drinking water. They savored it as though it were holy sacrament.

Clara said, "Has a good taste. Not too hard either."

Tunis swirled the water around in his mouth with his tongue. "Yeh. Like it's been run over green stones."

"Like water flowing over steaning stones." She mused to herself. "I always wanted a stream with steaning stones."

"What in the world is a steaning stone?"

"Like in a stone jug. Gives it a special taste."

Tunis collected the wood left over from making the outhouse and soon hammered together a cover for the well. He put a lid in the cover through which they could dip up water. "We don't want any animals falling in and fouling up the water."

"What a horrid thought."

Tunis looked down at his wet pants and shoes. "I better change clothes."

"Yes. And while you're doing that, I'll start supper."

7. Clara

The next morning, right after breakfast, Clara got out the new rake and new hoe and leveled the blacker dirt Tunis had thrown up out of the well. The soil was wonderfully crumbly and worked well. She made two neat square plots, five feet by five feet, and raked and reraked it all until the dirt was as fine as flour. Then she got a couple of packets from her trunk she'd been saving. One was lettuce seed and the other radish. She sowed the seed evenly and then got down on hands and knees and patted the soil firmly down over the seed. From her mother she'd learned that if one packed it down firmly one got quick results.

From her mother she also learned about using fresh-turned soil. When her father and mother first arrived on their virgin prairie home in Welton one hot August, it was too late in the year to break virgin prairie and to plant crops. But an old Fox Indian had come by and showed them that if they were to throw radish seeds into the mounds freshly heaved up by pocket gophers they still could have fresh vegetables before frost time.

The weather couldn't have been better for Tunis's spring work. Usually April brought showers. But a quirk in the weather brought them nothing but a series of sunny days. There was to be no wasting of those God-given planting days. Tunis decided that the first virgin sod he'd break would be just west of the cabin. There was just enough room, he said, for a plot of twenty acres between the cabin and the river.

But first he had to get rid of the tall grass to make for easier plowing. The dry weather was perfect for burning off the prairie. With no wind out it was easy to keep the fire under control. He first backfired around the cabin. Once he had that done, he let the fire burn as it would toward the river. It took a whole day for the twenty acres to turn an ashen black. Burning slowly, it also gave the animals, mice and rabbits and gophers, time to escape to either side.

As Tunis plowed the next day, Clara sometimes heard him talking to his horses Fred and Bill and Gyp. From the tone of his voice, she could make out that he was barely able to keep his temper. And it wasn't because of what the horses were doing either.

She decided to bring him some food for his lunch break. She fixed some tea and a dried-beef sandwich and carried it out to him. "I hope you're not mad at me."

"You? No. It's just this turf. It's as tough as a leather belt six inches thick. Man! One minute I'm too deep in, and the next minute I'm skimming over the surface." He pointed to a single strip a dozen rods long of very uneven plowing. "I'm strong enough but I'm not heavy enough."

Clara looked down at the long gleaming share of the breaking plow. "Maybe it's not sharp enough."

"Hoo, it's sharp enough all right. I could shave with it if I had to."

Clara knelt down to look at the thick turf. There were so many intertwined roots the turf looked like a thickly woven house carpet. Some of the roots were as thick as rat tails. Dozens of pink angle worms were already at work sucking out tunnels toward the surface.

Tunis coughed. "How busy are you there in the house?"

"Why?"

"Maybe you won't like this, but how about you riding me piggyback? That way there'll be enough weight to hold the walking plow down."

Clara didn't know whether she liked that or not. Her valuables would be right up against his neck.

"Look, I'll show you." He rehooked the knotted lines over one shoulder behind his back. "Fred! Bill! Gyp! Giddap."

The three horses groaned and leaned into their collars. Tunis quick aimed the point of the huge heavy plow down to catch into the woven turf. The point caught and dug in, and then, as the horses really began to pull, it suddenly went straight down, hurling Tunis for all his two hundred pounds of broad stubby weight up in the air and dropping him between Fred and Bill. The startled horses stopped dead.

"Oh! Tunis! Are you hurt?" she cried.

"No!" Tunis cursed, then got to his feet. Rubbing his shoulder he walked back around behind the plow.

"I see what you mean," she said.

"Well?"

"Oh, but you can't hold me up and drive at the same time."

"Try me."

She felt a giggle coming on and quick made it into a laugh. She hated gigglers. He was a powerful man, that she knew. She'd several times had a glimpse of his body as he undressed for bed. She hadn't meant to peek; it had happened accidentally as she tried to find the right soft valley in her pillow.

"Well?" Tunis wasn't laughing.

"All right. How do I climb aboard?"

"Like this." He settled on his heels. "Okay, swing your legs around my neck."

She drew up her long gray dress to her hips and one leg at a time climbed onto his broad shoulders.

"Sit up closer. That's it. Now catch your toes under my arms and back around behind me. Good. Here's the lines and you drive. I'll be too busy holding down this wild bronco of a plow to drive."

"Like a stagecoach driver."

"You bet. Now. Slap those lines and yell at the horses. Let's go."

Laughing, trying to be serious, Clara slapped the reins up and down. "Giddap. Fred. Bill. Gyp."

The three horses didn't move.

"Put the growl of a bear into it, woman."

She tried again. Still the horses didn't move.

Tunis under her let go with a strong command. "Get!"

The horses got and the plow dipped in, then dug in, and when it wanted to head for China, Tunis powerfully clutched the long handles and, aided with Clara's weight, held them firmly fixed at a certain angle and kept the great plow exactly level. There were tearing anguished sounds in the turf. A strip of sod some eight inches thick and sixteen inches wide rose up and, getting caught on the long moldboard, slowly curled over and fell, grass down. The long strip of sod jostled around like some long live black python. And it kept writhing after Tunis and plow passed by.

Clara could feel Tunis's power with every step. And with every step her valuables snuggled closer in toward the back of his neck. She wondered if he was aware of how intimate it all was. Probably not. Too busy holding down the plow. She thought it all rather homey.

At the end of the round he'd marked out, he tipped the plow on its side and it popped out of the ground. "All right there, lady above, turn the horses left, tight, and we'll start the back round. That's it. Now. Once more." He lifted the plow a little and then jabbed it down. Again the plow wanted to dig itself down out of sight, but Tunis powerfully held it at the right angle, muscles thickening over his back and neck and shoulders, giving Clara a vigorous rolling ride.

Clara could feel herself first softening toward Tunis, then swelling in love for him. She feared she would dampen his neck. She worked herself back an inch.

When the round was completed, he shouted, "Whoa."

The three horses stopped dead. They had begun to breathe heavily. Each horse stood on three legs, resting the fourth leg.

"How you doing up there?" he said, muffled under her.

"Fine."

"Enjoying the ride?"

She tried not to laugh. "Sure am."

"Well, down here I'm slowly turning into a nigger. All that burnt grass."

"I can smell it up here."

"By the time we get done we'll both look like we came out of darkest Egypt. Even the horses' legs are black."

She smiled. "We'll just have to get out the tub and scrubbing brush."

"Will you scrub my back?"

"Maybe."

He wriggled his neck around. "Lady, you got scratchy underwear, you know that?"

"Maybe I should go put on my flannel ones."

"Well. No. I got you up there now and we can wait until noon." He looked ahead at the horses. "I sure wisht I had another horse. With a four-horse hitch instead of three, we'd move through this stuff as easy as pushing a paring knife around a potato." He inhaled a deep breath, tossing Clara about a little. "Well, let's go. Get!"

They plowed until noon, making twenty full rounds, all of it some fifty feet wide. When Tunis settled to his heels to let Clara to the ground, he estimated they'd turned over about two acres of sod.

"Not at all bad. At this rate within a week we'll have turned over enough for a start this year." He hardly puffed after all the work of holding down the plow and carrying Clara. "I figure I'll put ten acres to wheat and ten to corn. After I get the crops in, I'll turn over another twenty. And that second twenty I'll let set through the next winter. There's nothing like letting frost act on fresh-plowed prairie soil. It cures it of alkaline at the same time that it softens and sweetens it. Besides getting that turf to rot into soft mulch."

It took them seven days to turn over the first twenty acres. The three horses became gant from all the hard pulling. Tunis too seemed leaner and Clara was hard put to keep him satisfied at the table.

A two-day rain set in. It turned the burnt black to earth black. Tunis welcomed the rain. But with Tunis underfoot all day in the tight cabin, Clara became nervous. After all the intimacy of her riding on his shoulders and of their scrubbing each other's backs each night to get rid of the black ash, she was sure he had ideas.

But Tunis didn't make a move toward her. He was content just to fatten up a little again.

The moment the rain ended and the birds were singing once more, meadowlarks and redwings and robins, Tunis got the hoe and went out to the plowed ground.

"Too bad I don't have a harrow. So the hoe will have to do. I've got to loosen up the dirt on the black side of the turned sod so the wheat kernels can catch in." He chopped away furiously. "It's only ten acres. When we do the ten acres for the corn we'll use the spade every few feet."

Clara saw that Tunis was going to wear himself to a frazzle if he hoed the whole ten acres alone, so she dug through an old storebox, where she found an ancient hoe. She joined him. Between the two of them they managed to scratch the black soil loose in a couple of days.

She watched him sowing the grain. It was a sight she would never forget. He'd made a sling for the sack of wheat and carried it on his left side. The sun shone on his rusty hair and his pink hands and his glowing tanned cheeks. First one hand dipped into the sack and came up with wheat and made a sideways spraying motion, and then the other hand dipped in and sprayed. It was like he was stepping to music and was waving his arms to either side like a child lost in a dreamy waltz.

83

Finished with the sowing, he got out the garden rake and swiftly began covering the wheat. He had to hurry because the blackbirds had begun to help themselves. Clara quickly made a scarecrow out of an old pair of pants and a shirt of his, and then she too dug out an extra rake and helped him.

In April the days became longer and green shoots began to show at the base of old dead stalks of last year's grass. Fuzzy purple mayflowers popped out over the hills to the east. The rounded slopes appeared to have been decked out with a series of silken coverlets. In some low spots the rain had rotted fallen bluestem along with trailing wild roses and the smell of fermenting gave the air a heady bouquet.

One morning early at dawn Clara was awakened by a strange booming sound. It couldn't be the train crossing the trestle a mile to the south. It still wasn't time for the train.

She sat up. There it was again. Brum-boo-boom. Brum-boo-boom. It wasn't the sound of someone blowing on a flute or of someone beating on a leather drum. It had a distinct sound of its own. In between those two.

She looked over at Tunis. Sound asleep.

Quietly she slipped out of her long flannel nightgown and got into her day clothes, long gray dress and sweater and stockings and high leather shoes and bonnet. She helped herself to a couple of sips of sweet cold water from the pail and then stepped outside, careful not to let the door squeak.

The sun wasn't quite up. But the rim of the horizon on the east hills was already a burnished pink-bronze, as though a vast fire were burning on the other side of the world. There was no wind out. It was so still she could hear the songbirds along the river in the trees trilling the morning wake-up serenade.

There it was again. Brum-boo-boom. It was like someone was playing an ocarina beyond the horse shelter.

Curious, Clara headed for a sandy knoll to the north. Tunis had remarked that he thought the knoll might be an old Indian mound. Dawn light bloomed all around her as she walked.

When she came within a dozen rods of the almost bald knoll she saw them. Prairie chickens. Barred yellow-brown birds. With light feathers below the beak. The males had begun their spring mating rituals.

Clara stood stock-still.

Two of the cocks made a rush at each other; stopped just short of actual combat. Feather tufts on either side of their heads stuck out like horns, tails were raised and spread, wings drooped. On both cocks orangelike sacs about the size of a big plum became inflated just behind the head. Then with sharp almost violent jerks of the body both cocks emitted the booming she'd heard earlier. Close up it was almost as if they were loudly calling a man's name, "Bum Muldoon! Bum Mul-doon!" Off to one side a half dozen other cocks were warming up for their displays.

Several hens appeared out of the deeper grass below and wandered up into the bald spot. They were like young girls pretending there weren't any boys around.

Immediately the cocks began to act like wild dandies at a dance. They bowed toward the hens as if at a high court nuptial, prostrating themselves with wings spread out, bills almost touching the ground, stamping the ground with their feet.

The hens ignored the vanity. They pecked at some grass seeds on the left, some seeds on the right.

One of the cocks who'd been standing off to one side, head down, in what seemed to be a subdued state, suddenly leaped straight up with a noisy excited cackle, then, alighting, made a long drawn-out pathetic squawking sound as though it had been caught in a trap. Then it made another sudden move, completely startling the other displaying cocks, also surprising one of the hens, because before she could move he jumped her. She tipped up her tail and the act was done. That was the signal for the other cocks. At least four of them mounted her one after the other before she could collect her feathers and escape.

"Them sneaky devils!"

But then, after a moment, Clara realized how beautiful it all was, the booming sounds, the prancing, the mating.

"Too bad Tunis couldn't see this."

Walking back to the house, she made up her mind.

Tunis, head down in the washbasin, was swilling his face with cold water, blowing moisture from his nostrils, grunting at the effort of leaning over. He reached blindly for a towel and, when he couldn't find it, said, "Is that you, Clara?"

She handed him the towel.

When he finished drying his face, he picked up a comb and began to groom his rusty hair. "Where were you?"

"Out watching prairie chickens."

"Yeh. They woke me up."

"Tunis, I got to talk to you."

Tunis settled sideways at their storebox table.

"It's time we decided something." She set the coffeepot in the fireplace and then poured some cornmeal and water into a small kettle and hung the kettle on an arm over the hot flames. "You know, about our living together."

He became shy.

"You've never really had a girl, have you?"

"Is that bad?"

"No. I think it's wonderful. But we can't go on this way, Tunis. One of these days . . ."

He turned red. She couldn't tell if it was because he was embarrassed or because he was angry.

"Tunis, I've been thinking a lot about us lately."

"I guess I have too."

The water began to boil in the kettle. Clara got a spoon to stir the cornmeal to keep it from clotting. "Tunis, tell me, do you like me?"

"You know I do. Yes."

She became nervous herself. "I wonder, do we like each other enough to get married?"

He tried to cross his short thick muscular legs; couldn't quite make it.

"Well, we better make up our minds pretty soon, Tunis, or I'll have to leave. It's just getting too dangerous."

"I know."

"You too?"

"Yes."

"Well, the way I know why I want to marry you is that I want your children. You're the first man I felt about that way."

"I want your babies too."

The corn porridge was done. She poured some into two bowls, one for Tunis and one for herself, and brought the bowls to the storebox table. But she didn't sit down. She stood beside him waiting.

Tunis struggled and struggled with himself. Finally he looked up, cheeks red, pearl gray eyes troubled. "What do you want me to do?"

"You could kiss me. And then you could propose to me."

He stood up as though he had rheumatism in his knees. He stood facing her. Finally he leaned his flushed face forward and touched his lips on hers. His full lips were dry, just as hers were. But though dry, a tiny spark jumped between them.

"Oh, Tunis." She melted. She threw her arms around him and pushed her full breasts against his chest, and reached up and kissed him again, allowing her lips to open a little, wet, yielding. Then he hugged her, hard, responding with a moist kiss too. The bump she'd seen several times in his gray work trousers began to push at her.

Tunis broke away for a moment. "Clara, will you be my wife?"

"Yes, Tunis. And the sooner the better."

"I suppose we better look up a justice of peace."

"No, I still want to be married in Whitebone. At the Episcopalian church there."

"If that's what you want." He pursed his lips. "Though I better warn you. I'm not much of a churchgoer. And I may never join it."

"I won't like that, but I will accept it."

His ruddy face softened above her. A holy dark yearning look suffused his face. He began to hug her demandingly.

"No, not now, Tunis." She shook her head vigorously. "But after we're married, anything."

He didn't like being blocked, and showed it. He certainly had a temper. But he also was in control, and so would make her a powerful husband. A stalwart man in time of need. Their children would be wonderful.

"My," she said, "we're forgetting about the corn mush. It'll be cold the next thing we know."

When they'd finished breakfast, Tunis said, "I suppose we better go to town today and get you a wedding dress."

She smiled with a wink. "You remember in town when I said I wanted to spend some of my own money on something private? Well, in one of those packages I got me some purple silk cloth. I've just about got one finished."

"Not white?"

"Oh, I have the right to wear white. It's just that I have a hankering for purple. I guess I got that from my grandparents who were somebody in England." She smiled mischievously. "Sometimes, when you were busy outside, I'd quick sneak out the purple cloth and work on my dress. And if I work hard on it one more day, I can have it done by tonight."

"Hmm. Too bad I don't have a new suit."

"The train has a layover of about four hours in Whitebone. That should give you enough time to buy a suit."

"Hey. That's just what we'll do."

The next day was the first of May.

Shortly after eight in the morning, Clara and Tunis flagged down the Bonnie Omaha. Clara carried a big dress box and Tunis had the pocketbook. They mounted the steps into the passenger car.

The conductor said, "Gonna do a little shopping in Rock Falls, I see."

Clara said, "Tunis needs a new suit and we've decided to go all the way to Whitebone for one."

"Yeh, they got 'em there too."

A toot up ahead from the big black engine and they were off.

The passenger car was filled with travelers, most of them drummers for clothes, machinery, tools. The drummers had faces as smooth as worn thimbles. The several young women on board had heavily made-up faces. Clara wondered if they were soiled doves.

The train rolled up along a winding valley. The Big Rock River sometimes flowed near the tracks, sometimes off in a distance, and always with a thin fringe of trees bordering it. Off in the distance on either side the land sloped up into smooth heights-of-land or long hills. It was soothing land to look at.

Presently Rock Falls appeared. As the seat of Leonhard County it was twice the size of Bonnie. The train stopped long enough to drop off passengers and pick up new ones. Just before the train took off, the engine backed down a side-track to pick up a boxcar loaded with produce, and then, puffing mightily, spreading up a thick cloud of smoke that threw irregular shadows over the passenger car, it set off north, still following the Big Rock River valley.

The monotony of the crackling wheels below made Clara languorous. She wondered if she dared rest her head on Tunis's shoulder. That intimate they hadn't become yet, and after some thought decided it could wait until after they were married. She brushed off the sooty windowsill and leaned against the window instead.

Watching out the window she saw how birds of all kinds, prairie chickens, meadowlarks, killdeer, sprayed out to all sides as the train with its pointed cowcatcher advanced through the tall prairie grass. After a short flight the birds disappeared into last fall's still standing russet bluestem. Bright sunlight glanced off their shiny wingtips.

Farther out she spotted various sod houses, log cabins, two-room frame houses, and out along the first dropoff under the hills dozens of dugouts. Women were hanging out clothes and men were breaking prairie sod.

The train crossed the river to the west bank. Sitting beside the window on the right, Clara could make out far to the north in the distance what looked like a low mountain range. She wondered what it could be and asked Tunis to have a look.

A businessman, overhearing them in the seat ahead, turned and smiled. "Them's the Blue Mounds. Lot of red rock sticking out of the earth. When you stand on top of that you can see miles in all directions. It's what gave that river here its name. Big Rock River."

Tunis asked, "Is Whitebone still on the other side of that?"

"No. We're just about there. The Blue Mounds are two miles on the other side of Whitebone."

The train pulled into Whitebone, engine puffing easily around a curve to the right. It whistled twice, then coasted in. Brakes slowly set and iron cried on iron and, with a final metal shriek, the train stopped in front of the high brick depot.

Clara and Tunis stepped down onto a brick platform. All the other passengers seemed to have friends waiting for them. From the depot agent Tunis got directions on how to find the largest general store as well as the Episcopalian church, and then they set off.

Nelson's Department Store, like Rexroth's store in Bonnie, seemed to have everything. The place had a high gray stamped-tin ceiling with huge support pillars. There was a wholesome smell in the store, of freshly woven cloth and peppermint candy and oiled wooden floors and Old World cologne.

A slim dandy of a man with thin brown hair ran the men's department. Even as they approached him, he was already measuring Tunis for a suit. When Tunis, blushing, explained what they had in mind and didn't have much time, the dandy had a ready answer.

"We have suits to fit anybody. Even a humpback dwarf." The dandy got out his tape measure. "Step this way, sir."

After he'd measured Tunis, with many a cluck over the size of Tunis's arms and legs and thick shoulders, he began to poke into the rows of suits hanging on a long iron rod, looking at the figures marked on tags. Finally he came up with three suits, brown, blue, and black.

Clara liked the blue one right away. It was a herringbone and its blue was deep like the blue over a crow's back. It also caught Tunis's eye.

The dandy clerk was quick to catch what they liked. "Yes, this should fit. Come, I'll show you our dressing room." He led Tunis away.

Some ten minutes later Tunis stepped out into the aisle where Clara waited. She could hardly believe her eyes. He was always handsome to her, but dressed in a snug-fitting blue-black suit, gleaming white shirt, black shoes and black socks, and a red tie that was more a scarf than a tie, he was positively a prince. It struck her at that moment, for the first time, that Tunis had to have real blood lines in him. His real parents, far back, had to have been people of some importance. Good. That made it all the more likely that their children would be good ones. His blood lines would wipe out the defects in her own line. Of one thing she was sure. She had lived with him for more than a month and not once had there been a hint that he had asthma. He was as healthy as a wild horse.

Tunis strained not to show off in the new clothes. "Like it?"

Clara winked back tears.

The dandy stood on one leg, the other leg set off at an angle, stylish. "Your husband should run for president."

Then Tunis paid up and they set off for the jewelry department. For wedding rings Tunis bought them each a plain wide-band ring, a heavy gold with a sharp yellow hue. Next they hurried out to find the Episcopalian church, Clara carrying her package and Tunis his old clothes rolled up in a bundle.

It was two blocks to the church. Neither said much. Clara kept pinching Tunis's arm as they walked along.

There weren't many trees in town, ash and maple, and all were just barely started. But every one of the little trees had its bird singing out its prairie claim, the oriole its silver song, the cardinal its piercing challenge, the thrush its modest fluted lyric, the meadowlark its cheerful glee.

They found the pastor, Father Garlington, at home in the parsonage next to the church. The parsonage was small and white, and very neat. The pastor answered the doorbell himself. He invited them in. He was a slender man, about thirty, brown hair, healthy pink cheeks, and brown eyes that were instantly alert and sympathetic. When he learned what they wanted, and that Clara was still a member of the Welton church, he warmed up even more. He asked Tunis, "And you? What church do you belong to?"

Tunis shook his head. "I never went to church, mostly because my foster parents never went."

Clara worried. "Tunis doesn't have to be a member, does he? You can still marry us, can't you?"

Father Garlington smiled. "Rest assured, Miss Shortridge, I have no objection. Though I would suggest that Mr. Freyling take instruction."

Tunis became nervous. "But we live so far away."

Father Garlington nodded. "Just come when you can."

Clara said, "I have our church Book of Common Prayer and I always read out of that to him."

"Good." Father Garlington smiled on them both. "We'll need witnesses, won't we? And a marriage license. I'll call my wife, and when we go to the church we'll also ask the sexton to stand in." Father Garlington left to find his wife.

Within minutes his wife appeared. She was as blond as a burst milkweed pod and full of wide smiles and excited for Clara and Tunis. She led Clara into their bedroom so Clara could put on her wedding dress.

Father Garlington led Tunis off to the church, where they would await Clara and Mrs. Garlington.

Mrs. Garlington exclaimed over the quality of the material of Clara's wedding dress. "I like your choice of purple. So many brides always choose white when pastor and I know perfectly well they are no longer virginal."

"Well, I am," Clara said. "Tunis agreed we shouldn't."

"How very charming! He must be a rare one."

Soon Mrs. Garlington led the way outside and across to the church next door.

One look and Clara fell in love with the purple stone church. Her dress went well with it. The high-pointed colored windows reminded her of pictures she'd seen of Anglican churches in England. It was a small church but perfect in its design: the tall tower, the steeply pitched roof, the huge oaken outer door, the lovely stone lancet arch over the entrance.

Inside there was an instant smell of fading incense, and drying cracked oak, and oiled oak floors. Clara almost cried. It had been so long since she'd been to church in Welton. She was actually getting married in her church.

Through the second set of doors she saw, at the end of the aisle, Tunis waiting for her, face flushed, a smile so wide it dimpled his cheeks. Beside him stood a strange man wearing an old black threadbare coat over a pair of overalls. The stranger had to be the sexton, who'd quick put on his church coat. Behind Tunis up on a dais stood the smiling Father Garlington.

As Clara and Mrs. Garlington slowly walked down the aisle, Father Garlington stepped over to a small organ and played "Here Comes the Bride."

89

Clara's eyes brimmed over. Through the film in her eyes she saw how the colored arched windows, all primary colors, blue and red and yellow, blurred together into little rainbows. She walked in dream. She tried to arrest the moment, make each step last a long time. She tried to make it all mean something deep and lasting and wonderful. She kept moving in dream: it wasn't happening, it was happening.

Father Garlington finished playing the organ.

Together Tunis and Clara faced Father Garlington.

It went too fast. Clara kept trying to slow it down.

Father Garlington was speaking. "I require and charge you both, as ye will answer at the dreadful day of judgment when the secrets of all hearts shall be disclosed, that if either of you know any impediment, why ye may not be lawfully joined together in matrimony, ye do now confess it. For be ye well assured, that if any persons are joined together otherwise than as God's word doth allow, their marriage is not lawful."

Impediment? Well, there wasn't on Tunis's side.

"Tunis Freyling, wilt thou have this woman to thy wedded wife, to live together after God's ordinance in holy estate of matrimony?" Father Garlington smiled gravely down on Tunis. "Wilt thou love her, comfort her, honor, and keep her in sickness and in health; and, forsaking all others, keep thee only unto her, so long as ye both shall live?"

Tunis almost squeaked. "I will." It surprised Clara: ordinarily he had a winning baritone voice.

"Clara Shortridge, wilt thou have this man to thy wedded husband, to live together after God's ordinance in the holy estate of matrimony?" Father Garlington's warm brown eyes pulled at Clara. "Wilt thou love him, comfort him, honor, and keep him in sickness and in health; and, forsaking all others, keep thee only unto him, so long as ye both shall live?"

Forsaking all others? There were no others to forsake. "I will."

Father Garlington helped Tunis's right hand take hold of Clara's right hand.

"I, Tunis Freyling, take thee, Clara Shortridge, to my wedded wife, to have and to hold from this day forward, for better for worse, for richer for poorer, in sickness and health, to love and cherish, till death do us part, according to God's holy ordinance; and thereto I plight thee my troth."

"I, Clara Shortridge, take thee, Tunis Freyling, to my wedded husband, to have and to hold from this day forward, for better for worse, for richer for poorer, in sickness and in health, to love and to cherish, till death do us part, according to God's holy ordinance, and thereto I give thee my troth."

In dream Clara saw them exchange rings.

"O almighty God, Creator of mankind, who only art the wellspring of life; Bestow upon these thy servants, if it be thy will, the gift and heritage of children . . ."

Tunis's knees shook. Out of the corner of her eye Clara saw sweat break out on his forehead.

" . . . I pronounce that they are man and wife, in the name of the Father, and of the Son, and of the Holy Ghost. Amen."

Clara gave a glad cry. She leaned up on tiptoe and kissed Tunis. She kissed him with parted wet lips. Then she threw her arms around him. If she hadn't been wearing the long floor-length purple dress she would have leaped upon him, catching her legs around his hips.

It was time to go. Looking at his watch, Tunis said they'd just have time to catch the train if they walked fast. Clara picked up her skirt and they hurried out.

When they arrived home shortly before six, with the sun shining sideways across the valley in throws of amber lucency, both were still in nervous dream. All the way home they hadn't said much. But they'd sat close together, hip to hip, aware that other passengers were smiling at them.

Tunis dug out the key and opened the door. "Wait," he said, and he took her package as well as his own and set them inside. Then he swooped her up in his arms and carried her over the threshold, ruffles and flounces and high-button shoes. He set her down beside her bed.

It was an awkward moment. She wasn't quite ready. "Mustn't you do some work outside yet tonight?"

"Well, yeh, call up the horses to make sure they haven't wandered off too far."

"Why don't you quick light us a fire and then go check your horses while I set out the dinner."

"Good idea."

"You won't have to change into yard clothes, will you?"

"No."

"Good. Because I want us both to be fancy for our wedding dinner. And when we cut the cake."

"Cake? I didn't know you baked a cake."

"What's a wedding without a cake?"

"You're full of surprises, woman."

All too soon dinner was ready. Clara wanted to delay and to delay the wonderful moment that was coming.

When they'd finished their meat and bread, Clara unveiled the cake. It was a two-decker, some six inches high, covered with white frosting. Clara smiled. She picked up the cake knife she'd inherited from her mother.

"Come," Clara said, "help me cut the cake. It's the custom."

He stood beside her. He took the knife.

She placed her hand on his and helped him push the edge of the knife down into the cake. She remembered what her father had once said at a wedding, under his breath. "The bride's hand on the groom's hand to cut the cake really means she guides his member into herself." She smiled. "That's good. I'll take over from here. You sit down and I'll dish it out."

Finally the sun sank and only the fireplace gave off light in the log cabin. It was time for bed.

Tunis asked, "Well, which bed do we sleep in?"

"The bride's, of course."

They undressed facing away from each other, hardly knowing where they placed their clothes. She slipped into her nightgown, he into his nightshirt.

She kneed herself into bed first, quickly. He got in next, stiff-limbed.

They lay side by side for a while. Then very slowly she reached around and drew his face toward her and kissed him. He kissed back. He hugged her close. They lay breathing, she faster than Tunis.

After a while, when she sensed that he didn't know what to do next, she whispered, "Don't you want to try it?"

He lifted himself over her, hesitating. "There doesn't seem . . ."

"Here," she said. "Just push it in."

Again he tried, and then held back a little as if afraid of hurting her.

"Just push it in and hope for the best. I can bear it. Someday I'll have to bear children through that small place. And that'll surely be much worse."

He tried again.

Something gave way, broke, a punch pushing through kid leather.

"Ah," she cried.

A little later he cried, "Ah."

She bled a little all night. He had to keep bringing her basin after basin of warm water from the water pot beside the fireplace.

Clara was very happy. "Don't look so sad, my husband. My mother would be very happy at the sight of this blood. And so should you be. I truly was a virgin. Just as you were."

8. Tunis

1885

For the next months he worked from can't see to can't see. When the wheat began to show soft green in his first plowed twenty acres, he broke another piece of land, again twenty acres. It could lie fallow for the year, the grass manure sweetening it below and the rain and the frost of the coming winter sweetening it on the surface.

Next he hired a carpenter, Lars Frisholm, a lost Norwegian in the Anglo-Saxon town of Bonnie, to help him build onto the house. Lars was a taciturn fellow, lanky legs and arms, sunken cheeks, and eyes with just enough bluing in them to keep them from looking like two little pools of milk. He had great long blunt fingers. He started off all conversations with the words, "Naw, I don't think so," and then proceeded to do it anyway. He had a keen eye for design and on the back of a piece of brown wrapping paper drew what he thought Tunis had in mind. Curiously enough, he spoke with a flawless English accent. He'd once sailed for the British mast.

"Like you say, we hook the northwest corner of your kitchen onto the southeast corner of this cabin we're in now. Then we put a door leading out of the kitchen into the living room here. Have the parlor come off the south side of the living room here. Like so. And then we tuck the bedroom onto the southwest corner of everything. How's that?"

Tunis crooked his head to one side. "Clara?"

Clara nodded. "Yes. That way, if there's a lot of noise in the kitchen, say, where the kids're playing, we won't hear it in the bedroom."

Lars allowed himself a sardonic smirk. "Yeh, and the other way too. Any noise you make in the bedroom, like say, snoring and such, they won't hear it in the kitchen." Lars said the word "snoring" as though he meant "snorting."

Tunis avoided looking at Clara. "What about the upstairs? What are we going to do up there? Where's the stairway?"

Lars said, "My idea would be to keep the house a low one. There's lots of wind out here on the prairie. You don't want a house that sticks out big and square like a banker's. Maybe in town it's all right, where there's plenty of trees, where you can protect it a little. But out here, you ain't gonna have trees. Too much gravel here for trees."

Clara was concerned. "Tunis, is that true about trees?"

"Could be."

"Oh, dear. And I so fancied a grove around our house. Maybe we should plant lilacs around it then."

"Naw, I don't think so," Lars said. "What do you want to stink up the place with them for?"

"Oh, Mr. Frisholm, how can you be a good carpenter and not like flowers?"

Lars said up erect. "Are those two supposed to go together?"

Tunis said, "Clara, we'll try both the trees and the lilacs."

Lars then drew the floor plan for the upstairs. It showed two bedrooms and a storage room, all with dormer windows. A side-view sketch of the house showed a low-pitched outline that would slip the wind.

Early in July the Bonnie Omaha began dropping off lumber across from their log cabin, all of it tough well-cured ash, with some soft maple. The white ash had a beautiful grain and Clara decided she'd keep it unstained and varnish it plain. With the lumber came Lars and an apprentice, or gofer, as Lars called the stripling lad.

Tunis helped dig out the basement, really only a root cellar, and pour the footings. He also helped set up the studdings and then the timbers for the gable roof. After that Lars didn't want his help. Lars wanted it to be his house, his making. "When I get done with that thing," Lars said, "not even a cyclone can take it down. It'll either have to take it all, the whole house like a railroad station in the sky, or leave it alone."

By the middle of July the wheat began to turn. What had been for a few weeks a silvered green gradually changed to a light yellow-green. The tender spikelets fattened with milk-heavy kernels. As the milk hardened the wheat turned into a tessellated gold.

Both Tunis and Clara watched the skies for grasshoppers. There'd been rumors in town that certain areas in the Dakotas across the Big Sioux River had been hit by great clouds of them. Thus the moment Tunis felt the wheat was ripe enough to cut, he was into it with his cradle scythe. The stand of wheat was so beautiful he hated to touch it. But it had to be done. He moved rhythmically around the ten acres, left foot forward, a swaying motion to the right with the scythe, then a sweeping cutting motion to the left with the slender stalks falling in swaths like ranks of soldiers shot down, the right foot following. Once a man got the rocking rhythm down pat, like the momentum of a weighted flywheel, the work really wasn't hard.

Clara followed after him, making a binding out of a handful of wheat stalks and tying up bundles. At the end of an hour, Tunis would stop his cutting and join her in setting up shocks, six bundles upright with a seventh bundle as a topper.

The birds soon caught on that the wheat was ripe for the taking too, and they came in from all corners of the sky, crows, redwing blackbirds, pigeons, turtledoves, quail, prairie chickens.

After that Tunis was in a rush to get the wheat threshed. He and Clara rigged up a small threshing floor near the horse shelter and, using weighted leather flails, beat out the wheat as fast as they could. Sweating, tired, they managed to store some two hundred bushels in the near corner of the shelter. They poured it on the dry ground and covered it with canvas. Once the wheat was in, Tunis took his time hauling most of it to town in his three-box wagon, scooping up a load in the morning, driving to the grain elevator in town, picking up some groceries and other supplies, and then rattling home with an empty wagon in the afternoon. He sold 150 bushels at sixty-four cents for a total of ninety-six dollars, a tidy sum, and enough to pay for the grocery staples for a long time. They had enough wheat left over for making bread and porridge, as well as an occasional treat for the three horses.

Later in July, during the hottest of the dog days, when Sirius was sharpest in the northern skies, Tunis cut enough hay to top out four large stacks near the horse shelter for the winter.

Meanwhile Lars worked slowly. Both Tunis and Clara became impatient with him at times. They were afraid he wouldn't get the house done before the snow would fly, though both did note that he was thorough, and that his work was expert, if not beautiful. It was going to be a modest-size house, not too big, one that, like an Indian mound, fit into the prairie.

When Jarl the gofer didn't quite have things ready for Lars exactly as Lars needed it, Lars would shake his head. "One boy is only half a man. I'd hire me another, but shiit, two boys is no man atall." Or if Lars would call down for a rattail file to make a hole in a two-by-four and Jarl would be slow to find the file, Lars would mutter, "That slowpoke has got the gumption of a tired louse."

Jarl was as freckled as a tiger lily. He loved to climb. When he wasn't running errands for Lars, he was climbing all over the gable timbers or the ridgepole, making faces at the sky. Lars would cuss him to come down before he broke his neck. "The more a monkey climbs the more he shows his tail."

Poor Jarl meant well. He had to drop out of school because he couldn't read and often was in tears over the way Lars treated him. His eyes were as soft and brown as a weepy pup's and his lips were always drawn back.

Tunis several times thought of taking Lars to one side to ask if he shouldn't quit tagging the boy. But something would happen to throw Tunis off his purpose. Once it happened that Lars couldn't quite reach a spot where he particularly needed to place a spike in a crosspiece. He growled, "Kid, get me a piece of paper to stand on. I'm either too short on one end or not long enough on the other."

Every now and then Jarl would address Lars by his first name, not his last. This brought ice into Lars's already pale eyes. "Kid, would it put a blister on your tongue to say mister?"

But always the work progressed. And early one day in September, before the first frost, Lars knocked on the door of the old cabin, where Tunis and Clara were sitting wondering what groceries they should get from town, and called in, "Well, you two love doves, come and look at it. She's ready for the paint brush."

They hurried outdoors. Without paint, the new addition glistened a tan-gold in the sun. The windows gleamed.

Clara said, "If I knew it wouldn't weather so, I wouldn't paint it on the outside."

Lars said, "Naw, I don't think so. In this part of the country the rain and the sun will raise perfect hell with wood. Make it curl up so the water will get inside."

Lars took them on a tour inside. "Here I got the chimney for your cookstove. There you can put a table. And in the living room here, you can put in a longer table for company. And in the parlor there's room for an organ and a loveseat for the kids. And here in the bedroom, there's room for the commode and the breeding pole."

Tunis choked back a laugh.

The way Clara's eyes darted around it was plain she had other ideas about how she would feather her nest.

They next went upstairs. "See how I made them steps? Wide enough for a man's foot, not just for milady's little toes. Here's a storage room. For your sugar and flour."

Clara hadn't been watching the finishing of that room and was surprised by what she saw. "Why, you used tin for a kind of wallpaper."

"Sure. To keep the mice out. See, I even backed the inside of the door with tin."

"I can paint it though, can't I?"

"Like you paint a flour bin, sure."

Lars showed them the two bedrooms next with their sloping ceilings and dormer windows. "Push the beds under the sloping part there and the kids can walk around in the tall part of the room."

Clara and Tunis had little to say. But both were immensely pleased. Lars Frisholm was a good carpenter.

Lars scratched himself. "Everything all right?"

Both Tunis and Clara nodded.

"Here's my bill. My gofer and me worked here for nine weeks, six days a week. That's fifty-four days at two-fifty a day. Two dollars a day for me and fifty cents for the kid. Comes to one hundred and thirty-five dollars. That seem right to you?"

"I'll take your word for it." With the wood from the lumberyard plus the concrete, the entire addition had cost them around four hundred dollars.

"Good. And now while I go outside and tap, you write out the check, hah?"

Again Tunis nodded.

After Lars had gone outside, Clara asked, "What's he mean, go outside and tap?"

Tunis smiled. "He means, pass his water."

"That man. Sometimes . . . I dunno."

Tunis decided to pay in cash and not by check. He asked Clara to go get the money from where she'd hidden it. Earlier she'd decided that keeping his extra cash under Gyp's shoe wasn't a good place—too smelly and also, suppose Gyp threw that shoe someday? She kept it in the cache hole under Tunis's bed.

When Lars came back into the house, he accepted the folded money without counting it. "When you gonna build yourself a barn for the animals?"

"That's next."

"Can I give you a piece of advice?"

"Shoot."

"And I can build it for you?"

"You got it."

"I was looking at those trees you got in your pasture. A lot of fine ash there. Why don't you cut down a couple dozen, them that's about a foot thick and thirty foot long. Haul 'em home and let 'em dry out over the winter. Then next spring we use them for supports for your haymow. Again we'll build a sloping thing to slip the wind. And one that'll hold hay upstairs like you wouldn't believe."

Tunis nodded. "I can do that I guess."

"Ash logs will be better than any four-by-fours or six-by-sixes from the lumberyard. I made one with ash logs for a British rancher west of Le Mars. I fixed it so you could drive a manure wagon through the center. To save on all the work of carrying out the manure on a fork. And you throw the hay down in front of the cow stanchions and the horse mangers."

Tunis caught the picture instantly. "I'll have the logs ready for you come spring."

"Jarl, let's get a move on. Time to catch the old Bonnie Omaha back to town."

Within the week, Tunis began selecting and then cutting down the ash trees Lars wanted. With his team of horses Tunis shagged home each tree and trimmed it on the yard. He kept the trimmings and the branches for firewood. It took him a month. He piled the huge logs crisscross over one another.

While Tunis was hauling home the logs, Clara used a flat varnish on the grainy ash inside the house. She finished painting the outside of the house with white about the time Tunis hauled in his last log. Together, in the cool weather of late October, they papered all the rooms. They finished the house by mid-November. Quickly, before the weather got bad, they traveled to town and hauled home various loads of furniture; hard-coal burner, kitchen range, double bed, four chairs and a table for the kitchen, bedclothes and dishes.

They'd been sleeping in separate beds all the while, but now suddenly finding themselves in a big double bed, they had trouble finding sleep. Just when one was about to drift off, the other would move a leg or an arm into a more comfortable position, and that would erase near-sleep. For several nights they tossed about the first hours, until finally, discovering both were wide awake, they quite naturally began fondling each other, and soon were making love. It was all right, since both desired children; except that it was hard on sleep.

As each month went by Clara became more and more disappointed. Her periods came as regular as the coming of the full moon. Several times, just as they were about to fall asleep, she talked about it.

"Maybe it's in my blood for our line to die out."

Tunis grunted. "Our line?"

"I mean my father's line."

"Well, it could be my fault too, you know." Remembering the story about that wild temper of his father, he added, "Perhaps it's meant to be."

"There was a weakness in our family, so it's probably my fault."

"Weakness."

She stirred uneasily beside him. "Like I said, there was some asthma in our family."

"Lots of families have that. Tain't really a weakness. More a question of nerves." He reached for her, his hand landing on her belly. "But you don't have it and that's what counts. The way you bustle around here, always busy, always working, I'd say you're as healthy as a horse."

"A horse?"

"A handsome filly."

"Handsome?"

"Pretty then."

She placed her hand on his, slowly moved his hand to her breasts. "My breasts are ready for life."

"Everything will be all right. We just haven't made the right connection. It's hard to figure out what's the right time with the human bein'. Now with the animals—horses, say—you can tell when the mare is in heat."

"Have you been watching me to see when . . . I might be . . . in heat?"

"A little."

She lay silent in the dark for a while. Finally she sighed. "I so want children. I so want at least one boy and one girl."

9. Clara

It was early March 1886 and Clara was home alone. Tunis had gone to town to get some new wheat seed he'd seen advertised in the Bonnie *Review.* The new seed had been guaranteed to be free of grain rust. Once rust got into a field, the crop was lost.

Finished taking some fresh bread out of the oven, Clara happened to look out of the north window. And looking, gasped. Indians!

She brushed back her hair for a closer look. A dozen Indians. Four males walking, each leading a horse. With the women and children riding horseback. The men wore buckskin clothes and a red plume in their black hair, the women bright red woolen blankets over their shoulders. Behind the Indians trailed a half dozen horses carrying stakes and folded leather tents. One of the trailing horses was dragging a travois made of two poles and a wicker basket on which lay a very old feeble woman. All the horses were small, ponies, and all were gaunt. Looking still closer, Clara saw that the Indians were gaunt too. They'd had a hard winter.

They were headed straight for her back door. When they came to within a hundred feet of the house, one of the four male Indians gestured and the whole band stopped. Then the male Indian placed his gun on the ground and approached the house alone, his spotted pony trailing him head down.

Clara had been scared to death, until she saw how the headman lay his gun down. Ah. That meant they came in peace. And in hunger. They were probably coming to beg for food. She fought off the trembles. No use wishing Tunis was back from town. This was something she was going to have to handle alone.

She decided to talk to them. She stepped outside.

The headman stopped. He had light skin and blue eyes. He held up his right hand. "Could we camp on your land for the night?" He spoke good English.

"I expect my husband home any minute. But I don't know what he'd say."

"We used to set up camp under that cottonwood tree next to the river"—he pointed—"when the Worthings lived here." For all his light skin the headman had the high sharp cheekbones of the true Indian. His violet-blue eyes were tired. He waved a hand toward the railroad tracks. "That iron road was our old trail. From Talking Water to Santee. We had it before the white man. My mother is very old. She needs the rest. She speaks of a thing called porridge and we do not know what that is."

Clara glanced in the direction of the travois. For the first time she noted the old woman had faded gold hair with a lot of silver in it. A white woman. Clara gave the man a closer look. He was so emaciated he stood bent like an old man. "May I see her?"

"She cannot talk. She has lost her mind."

"But you said she spoke of porridge."

"It is one of the few words she knows."

"I would still like to see her."

"Come. I will show you."

Clara followed the tall half-breed. She glanced at the faces of the other Indians as she passed them. Their eyes were like dried puffballs filled with brown powder. She followed the headman around the last horse and looked down at the old woman lying in the long reed basket. The old woman was white, all right. "What happened?"

"She has grieved all these years for my father, Scarlet Plume. He was among those hanged at a place called Mankato. She said he had nothing to do with the uprising. He was only bringing her back from having been captured by bad Yankton Sioux."

"Why!" Clara exclaimed. "You are speaking of the Great Indian Uprising of 1862."

"It is the same. After he was hanged, my mother, Judith Raveling, returned to Scarlet Plume's band to live with them. She hated the whites for what they'd done to him. Also, she loved the Yankton way of life better than the white man's way. It was cleaner, she said, and the tepee let the sky in."

"What did your mother call you?"

"Sometimes she speaks of me as Her New Man. When she remembers."

"We have names like that among the English. Newman."

Her New Man shook his head. "It is not the same."

She looked him up and down. "You must be twenty-three then."

He nodded. "Before my mother's mind broke, she had counted twenty-three winters for me and my twin sister." He looked ashamed at the ground. "All of us need the food badly. Can we put up our tepees under the cottonwood tree?"

"Yes. Yes. And while you're doing all that, I'll see what food I can spare." She worried to herself what Tunis might say. "When my husband returns, I shall speak well of you."

Old Judith stirred in her long basket. A vague smile moved out from her lips and her face broke into wrinkles. She had heard something familiar. "Porridge?" Her once-lovely lips were swollen and cracked from too much sun. Four white hairs in a bunch draggled down from her upper lip. Her white skin was blotched with what looked like rust spots.

Her New Man said, "What is porridge?"

"I shall bring her some and then you shall see."

"It is good. We await it."

"Is your sister with you?" Clara wanted to see what the other twin looked like.

"No. She has gone to live in Paha Sapa." Her New Man went over and picked up his gun. "Come," he said to his people, and then led them toward the cottonwood.

Clara went back to the house. She had sometimes thought about the Indian question. She had heard ministers preach on the subject. The Lord had meant for free land to be used, not wasted, therefore it had been a good thing when the white man took possession of the land, just as the Israelites had done when they pushed out the aborigines in Canaan. Had not that turned out to be a fortunate thing? So too here in this New Canaan, this America.

She wondered what Tunis would say about having an Indian encampment under one of their cottonwood trees along the river. He'd never mentioned Indians. Maybe he thought them a nuisance, like coyotes or gophers. Or those pestiferous crows come to eat up one's crop of wheat.

She decided to give the Indians the fresh four loaves of bread she'd just baked. She placed them in a basket. Tunis had killed a deer the week before and it hung freshly smoked in the back porch. That too she got down from the rafter where it hung. Next she got down on her knees and looked through her tin-lined flour bin in the cabinet. Her New Man could have her flour too if his women knew how to use it.

"If only Tunis was here. I hate to do something he might get mad about." She rested a moment on the protruding breadboard. "But those poor people need help and I'm going to do it." Next she made a batch of porridge with cracked wheat and set it ready in an old bowl she had planned to discard.

She heard Tunis drive onto the yard with his team of horses and the wagon. She heard his grunted "whoa" and then his firm step in the back door.

His first words reassured her. "I see you've invited some neighbors over for a picnic in our pasture."

She looked up with a cautious smile. "Yes. Will you help me carry it over? They're starved."

"Did they come begging?"

"No. They just asked if they could tent under their old tree. Seems they used to stop there when the Worthings lived there. They're on their way to Santee."

"That's in Nebraska. How come you're offering 'em all this food?"

"I took one look at that old woman they're shagging along and then I knew I had to do it. She's a white woman, out of her head, who keeps asking for porridge." She told him about her talk with Her New Man. "You should see her hair. It's almost white. A snowball."

"I suppose they figure besides the tree that this land I bought is theirs too?"

"Her New Man didn't mention that. Come, we'll set all this food on the ironing board and then you hold one end while I hold the other."

Together they carried out the food. The tepees had been set up, three of them, and three little mink-eyed children were playing out front. The children fell silent when they saw all the food. The oldest one, a boy, finally cried out a single sound in a strange tongue.

Her New Man stepped out of the nearest tepee. A wonderful glad smile spread over his hollow high-cheeked face when he saw the food. Then he saw Tunis. His face became guarded. He threw a questioning look at Clara.

"It's all right," Clara said. "Tunis, let's set it all out on the grass here." Clara quickly, with Tunis helping, moved the food from the ironing board onto the plakked-down grass. Last she took up the old bowl of still-warm cracked-wheat gruel and handed it to Her New Man. "I brought the porridge. Do you have a spoon?"

He nodded. "My mother thanks you." He turned and disappeared into the nearest tepee.

Tunis watched two red-blanketed women approach the food. A wry smile worked his lips. "You were pretty liberal with our smoked ham. I'll have to go hunting again tomorrow."

"They needed the food. Poor creatures." She gave Tunis a side smile. "I was afraid you might get mad."

"I never get mad when something's done right. And good."

"But when it isn't?"

His upper lip worked over his eyeteeth. "Sometimes I guess I do have a quick flashpoint. Like an old musket. But I've been thinkin' on it."

"Only children have a quick temper."

"There's more to it than that." He shook his head. "I could tell you some things."

The two dark mothers began cutting up the dried meat with old knives. Their knives were worn back so far they resembled thin flat awls. They handed slices to the little children, who ate greedily, black eyes shining as they watched their mothers' knives work into the smoke-empurpled flesh. Presently, happy to be eating again, the children began to skirl in play around their mothers, yelling and cooing in glee.

The brown mothers next fed the men, giving them liberal slivers of the smoked meat. The dark men chewed deliberately, slowly, as if to extract every last savor of the meat.

Meanwhile the gaunt spotted ponies, released from their burdens, cropped hungrily at the winter-flattened grass. They tore at it with sidewise grazing motions. Sometimes one or the other of them would lift its head and look off into the distance as if waiting for the distant whinny of an old friend.

When the Indian mothers next began to slice the bread, Clara could take no more. "Come, Tunis. It's hardly polite to watch one's neighbors eat."

Tunis said, "I was hoping to get a peek at the white woman."

"Maybe tomorrow when she's feeling better. And they've all slept on a good meal."

They walked back to the house together.

Tunis unloaded his sacks of seed wheat into the back porch and then unhitched the horses, while Clara got supper ready.

That night, probably because both felt good they'd done a fine thing with the Indians, Clara and Tunis were tender with each other, and coupled twice in love, both hoping that at last she'd catch.

The next morning after breakfast, Clara and Tunis walked over to the Yankton encampment. They were surprised to find the two Indian mothers wailing and scarifying themselves, the children standing silently to one side, and the old men staring at the hills to the east where the sun shone warm and yellow.

"What seems to be the matter?" Clara asked.

An old wrinkled man, face as stiff as cured horsehide, wept copiously. Yellow tears ran down the zigzag cracks in his cheeks.

Her New Man stepped out of his mother's tepee. He'd loosened his braids and his yellow hair hung straggled down to his shoulders. He resembled Christ. The only decoration on his mother's tepee depicted an Indian chief hanging from a gallows.

"What has gone wrong?" Clara cried.

"Hi hi he he," Her New Man intoned, "my mother has gone to join my father, Scarlet Plume, and I am trying to be happy for her. Thank you for the gift of porridge. She will need it for the long journey ahead."

Tunis stood stiff beside Clara.

Her New Man began a strange slow dance, hardly lifting his moccasins from the earth, eyes fixed on the sun, singing to himself. "I-ye, I-ye. The spirits came to my mother in the night, while she slept, and carried her off to That Other

Place. I am happy. She has found the peace with my father of the good heart. I am content."

Clara thought the Indian words of grief hauntingly Episcopalian.

Presently Her New Man stopped his slow death dance. He looked at Clara and Tunis. "My mother came to love this great cottonwood." He waved his hand up at the long gnarled ochre-colored branches of the tree overhead. "May we ask the white man if we can bury my mother here?"

Clara and Tunis looked at each other.

Tunis nodded.

Clara asked, "Did she die in her sleep?"

A strange smile lifted the corners of Her New Man's lips. "She awoke suddenly in the night and sat up. It was when the wind changed from the south to the north. I threw some old leaves on the fire to see better. Her face was young again. She said she regretted one thing—that she never got to shoot General Sibley for what he did to my father. This was strange to me. My mother hated the guns. Even the arrow."

Clara could feel the bottom of her belly opening up in sympathy. Some old unresolved memory had awakened in the dying Judith.

"It seemed she meant to get to her feet and still do the shooting. Then the youngness left her face and she fell again and she cried out, 'Where is love?' and at last her spirit departed."

Muscles in Tunis's cheeks worked.

Her New Man looked up at the cottonwood. He pointed at a long low branch that hung out over them. "Her bones will be safe there."

Clara was startled. "Tunis? Aren't they going to dig a grave for her?"

102

"They don't do it that way, Clara," Tunis said. "They first wrap the bodies up and expose them to the elements on what they call scaffolds. Or else tie the bundles up in the trees. So the animals can't get at them. Later on they come back when there's nothing but bones left and they bury the bones."

"Are we going to let them bury this white woman the heathen way? On our property?"

"I guess we are. If that's what they want."

"But for a white woman it isn't Christian."

Her New Man caught on. "It was her wish. She despised the white man's way. She said only the red man knew the true road to the Great Spirit."

Clara and Tunis stood back and watched.

Her New Man took down his mother's old leather tepee. Carefully he cut away the design of the Indian chief hanging from a gallows and folded it up and put it to one side. Then gently, with the entire band watching, tears running, he rolled her body up in the tattered leather. He tied both ends very tight with leather thongs. Next he tied two braided leather ropes to the bundle. Then he climbed up into the cottonwood tree and slid out on the long hanging thick branch. One of the old braves flipped the ends of the braided ropes up to him. With two braves lifting up Judith's body, he drew the body up into the tree and tied it securely to the branch. Done, he leaped lightly to the ground.

Tunis blew his nose in a red handkerchief.

Her New Man pled to the skies, hands lifted, head thrown back, long yellow hair flowing down to his shoulders. "Old Mother, we give you to the seven winds of the skies, to where the sun rises, to where it sets, to where the cold builds, to where the warmth melts, to the stars above, to the earth below, and to where your bones now rest. Rest happy. Soon we shall join you. Be happy with my father. Do not look back but hurry on to see him. I wish it myself. Hurry. Let your flesh become speaking dust so that your dust may once again laugh with his dust. It is all one. Soon too your bones will become the speaking dust. It is all one. The dust knows. Yelo. I have said."

Clara shivered. She'd never heard a funeral sermon as eloquent.

Her New Man approached Clara and Tunis with hands spread out, palms up. He pointed to the highest hill to the east. "There is a great stone on that hill. It is *wakan*. It has the image of a god on it for those who grieve. While my people rest a little, my heart tells me I should climb to that high place and talk with the great stone and tell the image on the stone that my mother has gone to join my father. The great stone already knows, but I must still tell it to pay my respects. My father and mother have gone to join all the little spirits that cannot be seen by the human eye. The little spirits are too small to be seen. Yet they are everywhere."

Tunis waved a hand for Her New Man to look and go where he would.

While the troop of Indians cried and wept, and while the women continued to scarify themselves, Her New Man walked quietly away toward the Freyling yard, crossed it, then crossed the old stagecoach trail and the railroad tracks, and finally ascended the high hill. He stopped at the top beside the red boulder. In a moment Her New Man kneeled before the red boulder and began to pray to it.

Clara remembered the red boulder was something that Tunis thought he should remove someday. It would be in the way of the plow should he decide to turn that land over too. Clara made up her mind to persuade Tunis not to touch that sacred boulder, to leave it resting in the wild grass and keep that area for hayland.

103

Presently Her New Man returned to his band. He spoke sharply in Yankton Dakota. Very quickly every one began to scramble about, taking down the two remaining tepees, rounding up the spotted bay-and-white ponies, packing parfleches.

Clara approached Her New Man. "Where are you going?"

"It is not seemly to abide near the body while it is turning to speaking dust. We will remove a short distance around the bend of the river. May we?"

Tunis said, "You are welcome to rest where you wish on the Worthing land. Someday perhaps you will come to live with us."

"That someday will never come for me. My doom has been foretold. Me and these old ones do not have many days left. That is why we are bringing the little children to the Santee."

Clara and Tunis watched them move down the river, around the bend, and then set up camp near some clumps of chokecherry trees.

"It is all so strange to me," Clara said.

Tunis cuffed at the grass with the side of his leather boot.

"I think he wants to die," Clara said.

"All of them do. They know they're done."

Clara said, "You know, I surely expected you to be hard on them."

"Indians used to stop on my foster father's farm when I was a kid. Many a time. Old Dirk and Old Tressa were soft touches and the Indians knew that."

"Did they look as defeated as these Indians?"

"No. They still had the old air of the watchful wolf about them. Black eyes looking back and forth, nose shot open, ears perked out."

"Poor souls."

"Yeh, the white man hasn't been very Christian to them."

"You still really don't think much of religion, do you?"

"No, for a fact, I sometimes don't. Except when I see how you're living your life."

Clara took his arm. "I think it's time you and I caught the Sunday train to Whitebone again and visited Father Garlington."

That night as they were about to fall asleep, they heard Her New Man lamenting in the dark beneath the bundle of his mother. Quite clearly they could make out his profound anguish.

They lay listening quietly. Neither said a word. Her New Man cried aloud for an hour.

Her New Man's voice fell off in slow quavers, as if he too were about to expire.

Then all was silent.

10. Tunis

Spring, then summer, came with a rush right after Her New Man and his band left for Santee.

Tunis had barely got his wheat sown and dragged when Lars Frisholm and his gofer Jarl showed up to build the barn. Tunis helped them pour the concrete footings and set up the powerful log frame and the gable roof line. But from then on Lars and his helper once again took over. Lars would let Tunis clean up around the site at the end of the day but nothing else.

Clara meanwhile fed the men. With their house built they had room to put up Lars and Jarl. It kept her busy. She'd been somewhat surprised by Tunis's hearty appetite when he was working, but when she saw how Lars and Jarl could stow away the grub she had trouble believing it. Especially that Jarl. When she mentioned the boy's appetite to Tunis, Tunis laughed. "He's probably got hollow legs. All young growing boys have. You should have seen me when I was his age. It was nothing for me to have two steaks for breakfast along with fried potatoes and a bowl of oatmeal. And for dinner at noon, three steaks and boiled potatoes and gravy and six slices of homemade bread and home-canned beans and whatnot. And for supper, two more steaks with fried potatoes with more bread. Not to forget dessert, home-canned fruit of some kind. I never had eyes bigger than my stomach."

"Uggh," Clara murmured. "That's almost being a pig."

Lars still like to rip away at his helper. "Trying to make a carpenter out of you is worse than trying to teach a ball of twine how to think."

Tunis bought a wagon load of barbwire. Barbwire was a brand-new invention to help keep one's horses and cows to home. It would also keep the neighbor's stock out of the grainfields. There was no way of course to keep the fence-leaping deer from nibbling at the first tender shoots of wheat. For fence posts Tunis dropped some young ash trees and cut them into seven-foot lengths.

He anchored the corner posts with a deadman, a huge stone buried in the ground and tied to the top of the post with a twist of heavy wire. To make sure that winter's frost heaves wouldn't loosen his taut fences, he invented a new way of bracing the corner posts with braided wire and a crossbar.

He first fenced in what he thought would always be his pasture, the acreage through which the Big Rock River flowed, up to the wild wasteland in back. Then he fenced in what he figured would be his first arable land, a piece of sixty acres south of the house and a piece of forty acres to the west near the river.

Taking the train on a shopping trip to Whitebone with Clara one day, he shipped home four black-and-white Frisian-Holstein cows and a bull, along with a crate of white Wyandotte hens and a rooster, four red Hampshire sows and a boar, and two more draft horses, mottled grays, Sue and Sal.

He put the cattle in the pasture and let them run. The hogs he gave free rein until he could build a shed in the fall. Meanwhile Clara built a small chicken coop out of the odds and ends she found around the rising barn. The chickens had a glut of a time eating all the bugs around, and a week after arriving they began laying eggs in the old horse shelter. Clara began serving eggs for breakfast with the usual cracked-wheat porridge.

Tunis learned from a passing traveler, out walking for his health, that they could get their wheat ground at a mill that had just been built at Klondike, on the Big Sioux River some fifteen miles west. Together in late August he and Clara took some twenty bushels of freshly harvested wheat, sacked, in their spring wagon and rode through islands of yellow prairie flowers to Klondike. On the way they came upon occasional settlers living in sod houses. They had to cross two swelling hogbacks before they arrived at the brink of the Big Sioux River valley. Plunging slopes led down to the wriggling river. The mill, painted red, straddled one end of a manmade dam. The masonry of the dam and the millrace, though crude, was carefully constructed, strong enough to resist even the heaving ice of the most severe winters.

Christian Kruger the proprietor turned out to be a witty man, his warmth going well with his girth. Kruger noted the hint of fall in the air. "I don't care much for winters around here. But, yeh, I like the fall. Fall is spring made into good wine."

Kruger had four sons, Fred, Otto, August, and Lou, all of whom worked for him in the mill. They were covered with flour dust, face, backs of the hands, clothes, and when one of them removed his cap a moment to scratch his hair, the contrast between the white flour and black hair was so sharp, so incongruous, that it made Clara laugh out loud.

Kruger laughed too. "Yeh, well, it's still better that they are all white with black hair than the other way around."

The big waterwheel in the millrace turned slowly and inexorably, making soft crunching sounds like a cat munching mice.

When their wheat was ground into flour, and sacked, Clara couldn't help but marvel at the fine flour, its clean white quality. "It's better than the flour coming out of Minneapolis."

Kruger nodded. "If you find any mouse dirt in it, you get it for free."

"Which," Tunis wanted to know, "the turds or the flour?"

"Both." With a broad flour-whitened hand Kruger wiped a smile from his mouth, fixing his lips into sobriety. "Our dusters and purifiers are mouse-proofed by a little trick I took with me from Germany. Besides lining them in tin, I've set a bunch of hidden mouse traps around. Never fails. Them mice ain't figured it out yet."

Tunis said, "What about a cat?"

"Cats don't like all the flour dust. They're always wiping it off their noses and finally they just fade away."

Tunis paid for the milling.

"Don't forget to come again."

On the way home, in the dark under myriads of stars, Clara wondered out loud, "I hope Lars found enough food for himself and Jarl."

"Don't worry about Lars. He'd eat sacramental bread if it came to that."

"Well, I hope he doesn't take it into his head to kill one of the chickens."

"If he does I'll chop off his head, tit for tat."

It was eleven on the clock in the kitchen when Tunis hauled in the sacks of flour. Clara made them a quick supper of dried beef and biscuits.

Two days later Lars Frisholm, standing in the open haymow door under the south peak, hallooed out to where Tunis was fixing fence. "Got a team of horses handy?"

"Yeh. Why?"

"Come. I'll give you a ride up into mouse heaven."

Tunis hung his pinchers on a strand of barbwire and walked over. Sure enough, Lars and his boy had finally finished building the barn, including installing the slings, carrier, rail, and long rope.

"Get the horses," Lars said, "and we'll try it out once. Give you a ride up there on a sling."

"Better yet, let's try it with some hay first. Will that rope reach out to that first pile of slough hay there?"

"Let's try it."

They spread a sling out near the pile of hay and mounded it full. Tunis got out his new team of grays, Sue and Sal, and hooked them onto the evener at the other end of the rope on the far side of the barn.

It worked like a charm. The huge mound of hay first dragged across the ground until directly below the peak, then it rose in slow majesty, twisting around slightly, and when the sling hit the catch in the carrier on the rail, it swung into the huge mouth of the haymow and disappeared. When Lars pulled the trip rope, the sling opened and the hay dropped to the floor with a fluffing thud.

Lars nodded. "Couldn't be better." Lars turned to his helper. "Okay, kid, pack up the tools. We catch the train yet tonight."

By the time Tunis unhitched the horses, Lars had the bill ready for him. Tunis stared at the figure. "A hundred and sixty-three dollars."

Clara had happened by to watch the hay enter the barn. "Why, Tunis, that's more than you paid for the house."

Lars laughed. "That's because the pantry for the animals is twice as big."

Clara allowed herself a mite of a smile. "My father said it already, that in America the cow is more thought of than the wife."

"Do you give as much milk?"

"You don't have much time for the human being, do you, Lars Frisholm?"

"Live in town like I do, lady, and you'd think like me. You're lucky you live out here where there can't be much corruption."

Tunis didn't like Lars being so free with Clara. He frowned. But, holding his tongue, he went into the house and dug out the money in cash.

Lars stared at the cash a moment. "You know of course, Tunis, that you're a damn fool to keep so much cash around in your house, don't you?"

"You mean robbers? Let 'em come. I got a gun and Clara is a hex. Between the two of us we'll fix 'em."

There was a whistle up the valley. It was the Bonnie Omaha on the way back from Whitebone. Lars and Jarl hurriedly grabbed their carpenter toolboxes and hustled toward the tracks.

Tunis and Clara almost had their first wrangle about what color to paint the barn. They were riding on the spring wagon to town to get the paint. Clara said she'd been sick of seeing red barns everywhere back in eastern Iowa. Why couldn't they, in this new country, this virgin land, paint all their buildings white?

Tunis fought off an impulse to snap at her. Wasn't it after all mostly his money they were using? But to say that out loud would hurt her feelings. With an effort, biting back his temper, he managed to say in a low voice, "But I didn't tell you what to paint the house."

"One always paints a house white."

"Suppose I told you I really wanted the barn painted red?"

She fell silent.

Tunis set a little flip of motion into the reins out to the grays, Sue and Sal. He tried to envision what a white farmstead would look like. In the winter, with snow on the ground, it would all blend together. In the summer, with crops green all around, the white buildings would stand out in sharp contrast. It would be different all right.

Tunis first drove to the hardware store hitching posts. Then he led the way into the store, Clara tagging along with her lips set thin.

"What'll it be today?" the proprietor asked.

"Need some paint for the barn."

"Yeh, heard you had a new one. Lars was in yesterday. He ordered what he thought you might need."

"He did?"

"He gave me the figures. And there's your paint. Two coats' worth. Fifteen gallons."

"What color?"

"Well, the usual, red."

Tunis shook his head. That darned Lars. If Lars hadn't built him such a good barn he had half a notion to look him up and sock him. "Naw, not red. Me and the Missus have decided we'd like to paint it white."

"Oh. Hmm. I think I got that much white around. Been an awful run on house paint, you know, the way this town is booming."

"Well, white it is. And I'll need some brushes. And putty with a putty knife. And some turpentine." Tunis felt a touch on his elbow. He allowed himself a sliding look at Clara. She was smiling. Thank God it wasn't a victory smile. Just a warmly pleased smile. She liked it that he'd surprised her with a change of mind. So. It did seem they'd always get along.

Working together, they finished putting on both the first and second coats of white by middle October, just before the first deep freeze. Tunis next built a small granary, which they also painted white. They moved the grain piled on the floor of the old lean-to horse shelter into the new granary. The old place had begun to attract rats. They also moved all of Tunis's haycocks and haystacks up into the haymow.

When the first snow began to slant in from the north, they rounded up all the livestock and put them under one roof of the barn: horses, cattle, hogs, chickens. With hay above in the mow for insulation, animal heat kept the barn as warm as toast.

Clara noted that both the cows and the sows seemed extra plump. "Looks like they've had a good fall."

"Yeh. And the bull and boar have had a good fall breeding."

"You mean?"

"Yep. They'll all be coming in sometime during the winter."

Clara winced.

Tunis noticed that lately she'd become touchy about whether or not she'd caught.

11. Clara

Early in December their nearest neighbor to the south, Hack Tippett, came blundering into their kitchen with his hairy rusty face. "We gonna have another baby, but Doc Wallance has gone to Sioux City for the week. What should we do?" He looked at Clara with pleading brown eyes.

Clara looked at Tunis. "Maybe I should go."

Tunis frowned, blackly. Somehow he managed not to say what he thought. He had never liked Tippett.

Clara said, "I'll get my coat and purse."

Tunis said, "Tippett, you've been around cows when they needed help. It's the same thing."

"No, it hain't the same thing. My wife is 'uman."

"It would be to me."

Clara said, "He's right though, Tunis. We aren't cows."

Tunis continued to look black.

Clara said, "I'm going. Sometimes it can be complicated."

Tunis said, "What do you know about calving?"

"I was born knowing it."

"All right, go then."

Clara found the Tippett sod house a mess. Children everywhere in the kitchen. Clara counted seven. The oldest could hardly have been more than eight. The two littlest ones had wet pants and runny noses. The next five on up had their clothes on misbuttoned. They too whimpered with colds.

Hack didn't come any farther into the sod house than to stand by the kitchen door with his muddy boots. "The Missus is through there. Well, I got the stock to feed and my barn to clean." Then he turned and bungled outdoors. It was obvious Hack Tippett was truly afraid of birthing.

Picking her way around playing blocks and snotty children, Clara pushed into the second room. Again everything lay in a mess: chair tipped on its back, chamber pot half under the bed filled to the brim with brown disintegrated feces, clothes on the floor, sheets slipping off the mattress, pillowcases only half-covering the pillows, top quilt partly hanging down to the floor, a disarray of powder boxes and perfume vials and medicine bottles on the dresser. And it didn't help to have only a vague light coming in through the two small square windows high off the packed-dirt floor.

The woman on the bed had pale brown hair pushed up on the back of her head from lying on the pillow. Her eyes were so pale a blue they resembled huge drops of water. The eyes had a flat look about them, which probably meant she was far-sighted. Her face was mottled and scabbed over the nose and along one side of her forehead. She was small but her belly was huge. She looked like a great butterball, out of which stuck a head on one side and a pair of skinny legs on the other.

110

"Well!" Clara said, trying not to shake her head. "First, though, I better get your name. I can hardly go around calling my neighbor Mrs. Tippett."

"I'm Malena."

"Well, Malena, let's see how things are coming along with you." With her thumb and forefinger Clara discretely lifted the blanket and sheet and had a look. "It's coming all right. How long have you had birth pains?"

"Since about one this morning."

"Coming close together?"

"No. They seem to be slowing down."

"Well, at least let's straighten out the bed here a little. And have you got a rubber sheet?"

"The rubber sheet we got is on the children's bed."

Clara got the rubber sheet and washed it in the lead sink in the kitchen. When she had it clean, she went back into the bedroom, the children following her. The children had a look about them as though they never talked; just dumbly followed people around.

Malena said, "Yes, I guess my man is awfully busy in bed all right. I've just barely got one born when bang there's another one on the way."

Clara wanted to say: "Busy in bed, my eye. This is plain brutality." Then, with a little ironic humph of a sound to herself, she next thought: "My man is a bull in bed. Yet for all the good it's done us we could've used a little of Hack's brutality."

The two littlest children began to suck their thumbs.

Clara wondered about the thumb sucking. There was a smell of milk in the air, wet and intimate. It struck her what the matter was. "Are you still nursing, Malena?"

"The two youngest ones."

"For heaven's sake."

Malena picked at the bedcover. "They cry so."

"Good gracious, woman, what are you going to feed the new one?"

"Sometimes I wish it born dead."

"Now, now. I didn't mean for you to be thinking that. Does Hack have a cow in the barn?"

"She's about dried up."

"You're next, if you're not careful."

Malena said, "Children, you play out in the kitchen, you hear."

The children didn't move; only stared. One of them, the oldest, a girl, wiped her nose with the back of her hand and then wiped the gray string of snot down the back of her faded yellow dress.

Clara said, "All right, children. We can't be having you in here. Shh, get along now, scoot."

The children gave her an odd look and slowly went into the kitchen.

Clara lifted, then had to shag, Malena onto the rubber sheet, though even as she did so she saw that the sheet underneath had already been partially befouled.

Malena had her next contraction.

Clara watched a minute. She remembered helping her mother as a midwife at a neighbor's house. It seemed to her Malena's contraction was weak. "Do you have coffee in the house?"

"No. Hack says it costs too much."

Clara nodded. She proceeded to clean up the room. It took a while to restore some order. The worst was bringing the contents of the brimming chamber pot out to the privy in back. The smell made her promise herself she was not going to eat in the Tippett house.

Malena's next contraction came earlier and stronger. Apparently the cleaning up around her relaxed her.

Clara then went after the first room. She changed the diapers of the two youngest children, straightened out the buttoning of the others, washed their faces, combed their sticky blond wispy hair, and wiped their noses. As she worked, Clara resolved to herself that never, never, would she let her household get that slipshod and filthy. Just imagine, she thought to herself, what these little kids are going to remember about their childhood in this dump of a home.

Besides the smell of human milk, and of wet diapers piled into a diaper pail, there was yet another disagreeable odor. It wasn't so much a rotting smell as it was one of slow disintegration. She decided after a while that it was the white-washed sod walls. They would never hold up like stone, nor even, for that matter, like wood.

After a while, as she tidied up the place, Clara saw insects: occasional silver-fish, dull brown beetles, feathery-legged centipedes. The crickets she heard. The sod house needed some insecticide; and if that wasn't available in Bonnie, a toad.

Malena's next contractions continued to come stronger but not faster.

Clara said, "When you feel them coming on, try to cough. Real hard."

"It hurts under my ribs so."

"Try it anyway."

Clara made them a meal of sorts at noon: watery rice with nutmeg sprinkled on, some bread Hack had tried to bake but which turned out unleavened and stringy, and some canned venison reheated. Hack bolted his food and vanished. The children ate slowly, picking at what was in their plates. Clara herself couldn't eat any more than a small portion of the soppy rice.

After dishes were done, Clara told the children to go take a nap, whether they wanted to or not. They lay down but didn't close their eyes.

Clara kept watch beside Malena's bed.

Malena puffed between contractions.

The windows were too high in the sod wall for Clara to look out at the countryside. All she could see were occasional fleecy clouds sailing across a blue sky. She became lonesome for her own sweet-smelling house. She missed Tunis. She smiled thinking about him. He was so strong. She often had the sense of some kind of power humming in him, as though there might be a hulking top spinning in his chest.

Malena spoke weakly. "I hope I ain't getting on your nerves."

"Well, a social hop this ain't."

"I didn't know my life was going to turn out like this. A thin old sow pooping out one kid after another."

"What did you expect when you married Hack?"

"Flowers and a good laugh now and then. Good times. You know. Like all the girls dream about."

Clara nodded. Malena had a point. For all she was proud of Tunis and their wonderful farmstead, she did miss the old days in Welton when she was a girl. "Yes, like you, I used to dream about good times coming."

"I used to love to dance, flying from one man's arms into another man's across the shining floor. Someone playing the fiddle under the lanterns."

"I know. I could dance too. I was so light on my feet. I specially liked the highland fling."

"The what?"

"Let's have another look at you."

Around four, Clara heard the children murmuring in the kitchen, complaining about something. She went to look. The two oldest children had their noses up because the two youngest were sopping wet. Clara cleaned the young ones and then filled the stove with wood again.

A few minutes later Clara heard an odd squeak in the back room; then a sound as though an egg had broken open.

Clara dashed into the back room.

Malena lay with her legs as wide apart as she could get them. Tumbled in between them, head down, back up, lay a freshly born baby, still in its translucent bag of waters.

Clara pounced on the infant. With a fingernail she punctured the bag. Silky fluid spilled everywhere. Clara pulled the bag away from the baby as though stripping off loose underwear and tipped the baby's head back. She tenderly pushed a finger into the baby's mouth. Instantly it began to bawl. "There, there. That's better."

Malena raised her head. "Is it born?"

"You didn't feel it coming?"

"I napped a sec. And then I coughed. Then I woke up and I guess it had already happened."

"My goodness, you surely must've loosened up in a hurry. I never."

Clara tied the umbilical cord in two places with store string and then with a scissors cut the cord between the two knots. "There, there. Everything's going to be all right, my little coney."

Hack took Clara back in his democrat late that night, he driving the horses and she holding up the lantern.

Clara felt she had to say something in Malena's behalf. "Mr. Tippett, you're going to lose a wife if you are not more considerate of her."

"How come?"

"She's all worn out bearing you so many children."

"Hum." His face stuck out at her like an outraged squirrel's. "The Bible says, 'Be fruitful and multiply, and replenish the earth, and subdue it: and have dominion over the fish of the sea, and over the fowl of the air, and over every living thing that moveth upon the earth.'"

"Is your name Adam?"

"You know it hain't."

"Is your wife's name Eve?"

"You know durn well it hain't."

Clara persisted. "God telling Adam to be fruitful and replenish the earth back then was one thing, because Adam and Eve were the only human beings on earth and they had to do it alone. But God ain't asking you and Malena to do it alone today."

"Goldurn, woman, I don't like the way you talk."

"Think about it though, Mr. Tippett."

113

"Hum."

"Suppose you lose your wife, then what?"

"Well, then me and the kids will just have to hold the fort the best way we can. We'll stick it out." Hack pulled up in front of her door. "And thankee for helpin' out."

"I'll drop around tomorrow and have another look at her." Clara handed him the lantern and stepped down.

"No need. I can take care of the rest now. It's only the birthing I can't stand."

"All right, Mr. Tippett. Good night."

"Hum. 'Night." With a slap of the lines, Hack drove off into the pitch-black night, holding up the lantern high with his left hand.

Tunis had left the kerosene lamp lit. After all the raw Tippett smells, the soft odor of kerosene burning in her kitchen was like sweet incense. The ashes in the kitchen range were still alive, and she held out her hands over the warm stove lids.

Tunis called from the bedroom in back. "Clara?"

"It's me."

"Throw some wood in the stove. I'll be out in a minute."

When Tunis appeared out of the gloom of the living room, he was dressed to go outside.

"Something going on in the barn?"

"One of our cows is having twins. I need you to help me."

"Well, now that it seems I'm in the birthing business, I might as well help another life into this world."

"Good gal."

114

"It isn't Lily, is it? The one with the red brockled face?"

"That's the one."

"Funny she should have red blotches on her white face when she's a full-blooded Frisian-Holstein."

"I heard say once that originally the Frisian cow was red and white. Far back."

"Lily's cute. It's like she knows she special."

"Well, she'll be special all right if she always throws twins."

Tunis carried the lantern and a pail of warm water taken from the stove reservoir. Clara followed him, carrying a basin and some soap.

All the animals perked up when the lantern light bloomed in the barn. The horses whinnied, the chickens chucked irritated, the sows honked, and the cows lowed. The black-and-white bull, in his separate pen, got heavily to his feet.

Tunis led the way to the end of the stanchions where he'd prepared a little corner for Lily. Tunis expressed surprise to see Lily standing, reaching down her red nose, licking at something. "Look at that, would you!"

Clara nodded. She'd already spotted the two mounds of still numb flesh. The black-and-white calves looked like they'd been freshly shellacked.

"She had twins alone!"

Lily left off from her licking to look at them. Her mostly broad white face looked exactly like it might have huge red freckles.

Tunis set the water down and hung the lantern on a nail. "Well, I better get a fork and carry away the afterbirth."

Clara said, "I think she's already eaten it."

Tunis kicked around through the straw. "You're right. It's gone. How come you guessed that?"

"I just got through helping the Tippetts, you know."

Tunis stared at her. "You don't mean to tell me Mrs. Tippett swallowed her afterbirth?"

Clara's throat made a funny clicking sound. "Well, I wouldn't blame her if she had, there's so little food in the house."

"Yikes."

"I read somewhere in my father's library that the reason some animals eat the afterbirth is because it's loaded specially with rich nourishment."

Tunis said, "Before we throw this warm water away we should probably have a look at the other critters in a family way." He looked under the tails of the other three cows. "Still a couple of weeks away here." He next examined the sows across the alley. "They're piggy all right. But still a week off. So I guess we can throw the water away." He picked up the pail of warm water and spilled it in the cow gutter.

Clara smiled to herself. "It's going to be fun to have all that young stuff around. Newborn. They're so innocent. Born pure. Without sin."

"Animals can't sin in the first place."

Clara gave that some thought. "That doesn't seem fair, somehow."

"Though I suppose you'd have to say a wolf with rabies is evil. But you still can't say he's sinning when he bites you. Because he don't know no better."

Clara mused. "I wonder, are there any sins that are all right?"

"I don't get you."

"Well, the way we are in bed lately, knowing that no children are coming of it, knowing it's been mostly for fun . . . could that be counted a sin?"

"Well, love, we're still hoping, ain't we?"

"That's true." Clara took several deep breaths, reveling in the fleshy animal smells, in the dry sweet aroma of fresh straw. It was ever so much more clean and bracing than the Tippett smell. Though she had to admit that the aroma of Malena's broken bag of waters had been all right. The waters' smell was something dark and true and tender in the very Garden of Eden. Thinking about it Clara could feel her breasts stir.

They walked back to the house. It was surprisingly warm out for that time of the year. Something about the warm pitch-black night made Clara walk close to her husband.

After washing their hands they went directly to bed. Clara blew out the night lamp on her side. Again the deep black made Clara seek the comfort of being near her husband. She moved over in her nightgown until her hip touched his.

She could feel him warm up in his nightshirt. "Husband?"

"Yes, wife."

"With all that luck in the barn, might we not try it again to see if we can't have the same kind of luck in the house?"

He turned and kissed her, and she let herself be possessed, abandoning herself to it.

115

12. Tunis

By late March 1886 they knew. Clara was going to have a baby by early fall. Both hoped it would be a boy. At the moment, Tunis needed a boy more for his work than she needed a girl for hers.

Clara began getting the baby clothes ready. She ordered a cradle at Rexroth's store, made ready several maternity dresses, bought a new washboard and several washing tubs.

Tunis meanwhile was in a fret. He'd discovered rats on the place. They'd burrowed under the small granary and from there had chewed their way up through the wooden floor and were helping themselves to the stored wheat.

"Where the devil did they come from?" he raged at dinner one noon. "There are no rats out in nature. The Indian never knew the rat. They must've come with the white settlers. But how? Hid away in their covered wagons? Hid in their bread bins? How?"

Clara spoke out of the marvel of her condition. "Can't you buy some traps?"

"Well, I'm gonna have to do something. Or all our work will be for nothing."

The next time he went to town he bought traps and a .20-gauge shotgun. "If I don't get them with the one, I'll get them with the other."

He set three traps around the hole the rats had chewed in the floor. He was careful to use gloves to keep his smell off the traps.

The next morning when he went out to check the traps, he discovered the rats had chewed out a new hole in the floor not more than a foot from the old hole and right under the chain of one of the traps.

"Those dratted devils. They got brains!" He shook his head. "Well, they had to have brains in the first place if they was able to figure out how to get to our farm by just following the railroad tracks."

He decided to bait the traps by dipping some kernels of wheat in butter and then putting the treated kernels on the trip plate of the trap. He set three more traps around the new hole.

The next morning he found that the rats had chewed a new hole in the floor and had helped themselves to more wheat, but had ignored the treated wheat.

A fiendish grimace curled back his lips. So. The rats were still smelling him on the traps. Well, he'd fix that. He took all the traps and the gloves he'd handled them with and buried both in the earth. Then while the shining steel traps and the gloves were picking up natural smells, he took to shooting the rats. Right after supper, just as it was getting dark, he went to the granary with his shotgun, a handful of shells, and a milking stool, and sat himself in a corner and waited. He left the door open for light.

He sat very still for maybe a half hour. Light faded slowly. Several times an itch set up on his back but he fought off the impulse to scratch it.

Finally he saw a pointed white-whiskered nose poke up through one of the holes.

He waited. He already had the gun pointed.

There was some squealing below the wooden floor. It sounded more like playful squealing than hurt squealing. The body belonging to the poking nose was bumped from the rear and the whole head showed.

Bam!

The head and part of the shoulder of the rat disappeared. The rest of the body dropped out of sight.

Tunis's grimace deepened. Quietly he reloaded his .20-gauge.

There was silence for a while below the floor.

Tunis waited.

Gradually the rats got over their consternation and it wasn't long before the playful squealing started up again.

Tunis pointed his gun once more. He could hardly see. He wanted to get at least one more. If he could knock off two for the night and two more the next night, the rats might decide it was getting too hot for them and leave.

A whiskered pointed nose, sharp gleaming teeth beneath showing in a slanted mouth, slowly pushed up through the second hole. There appeared to be some wrestling going on behind the nose as though other rats were anxious to have a look too. Slowly the whole head showed.

Bam!

Again the head of a rat vanished. Extra BBs pelleted across the floor into the sloping mound of wheat.

Silence.

Tunis reloaded his gun.

117

"Tunis?" It was Clara calling from the house.

He continued to sit.

"Tunis? I heard you shoot twice. You all right?"

He nodded to himself in the dark. It was time to go. There'd be no more rats to spot that night.

"You didn't hurt yourself?"

Tunis stood up. Carefully he ejected the full shell from his gun and dropped the shell into his pocket. He'd learned from Old Dirk Freyling never to walk around with a loaded gun in the dark. He stepped outside and locked the granary, then walked slowly across the yard toward where Clara stood in the lighted doorway of the back porch. She had one hand over her brow to see the better into the dark and the other hand over her belly.

"You're all right?"

"Yes."

"Any luck?"

"I shot two of the sonsabitches."

"Will that chase them away?"

"We'll have to see."

While his traps and gloves were soaking up earth smells, he was back shooting the following night and the night after that. Each time he blasted two rats to bloody smithereens. He also enlarged the two rat holes with the gun blasts.

It seemed to him that for every rat he killed the mother rats produced two more young to replace them. Every night there appeared to be more squealings and flouncing around of bodies and hard bony tails.

When he judged the traps and gloves had lain in the earth long enough, he carefully baited the traps and set them around the two holes. He also set two traps at the edge of the sloping pile of wheat and covered them with a gentle sifting of kernels.

Still nothing. The rats arrogantly chewed out a third hole in the floor and helped themselves to more of the precious wheat.

"I'm going to get some strychnine. And soak a couple of cups of wheat with it and then pour the lot through the holes to the dirt below. That should get 'em."

He got the strychnine, soaked the wheat, and poured the treated kernels down the three holes.

Nothing happened. There were more squealings than ever.

"That damned squealing is driving me crazy. Because I know what they're doing, squealing like that. Breeding more young. And having fun while they're doing it."

Clara had a suggestion. "Why don't we get a couple of cats and lock them in the granary at night?"

"Hah! They'd better be big cats. You realize how big a rat is? Some of them are bigger than cats."

"Seems to me though that the minute the rats learn there's cats around the rats will go."

"Hmm."

The next time he and Clara went to town for groceries, he inquired around for cats. He found two yellow male brothers at a Mrs. Suddaby's, who had a houseful of cats.

118

For a couple of days he kept the yellow cats on the front porch and fed them in the kitchen to get them used to the Freyling smell as well as get it in their heads that the Freyling place was home.

The yellow cats loved the warm porridge and the fresh milk and all the attention. They were constantly underfoot in the kitchen.

The fourth night Tunis decided it was time to put the two cats to work. He took them out to the granary with a pan of fresh milk and closed the door behind them. He went to bed hoping that when he looked in on them in the morning, they'd be fat with rat meat.

To his great astonishment, when he opened the door the next morning the cats had vanished. Tunis went back to the house baffled.

Clara saw his disgusted expression. "What happened?"

"The rats must've et the cats."

"Not really!"

"There ain't any sign of them anywhere. Neither hide nor hair. Just pfft! gone. They didn't even bother to finish the milk I brought out with them."

"How could they have gotten out?"

"I don't know."

"Could they have escaped through one of the holes in the floor?"

"And run the gauntlet through enemy lines?"

"That's true." Clara poured him some coffee. "Well, maybe later in the day they'll show up at our door meowing for warm porridge and fresh milk."

The two yellow cats never returned.

One night, ruminating in the dark together, a warm May night, Clara wondered if maybe they shouldn't try another idea with cats.

"I don't want to hear about it," Tunis said.

"Wait me out. My father told me that before I was born my mother so wanted to go back to England. He said he almost listened to her. But then, he said, I came along, and Mother suddenly changed her tune. And Father thought it was because she had me in a certain place. If a mother has a baby in a certain place she tends to want to stay in that place. It's like she's suddenly tied to a place where she'd had pain and where the afterbirth is buried. Where the only world the children know is that place. To the kids home will always be where they were born and the mother goes along with that."

Tunis sat up in bed. Now there was a good idea. That Clara of his, she sure had a sharp head screwed onto her shoulders. "So you think when we have our babies here, they'll always call this home."

"They're bound to."

"So if we're good parents, we won't have to worry they'll run away on us."

"I think so."

"Hmm." Gently he placed a warm hand on her belly. The swelling in it had grown some the last couple of weeks. He'd noticed that when she walked she walked with an extra swing, as though she might be carrying a basket of clothes. "How is the little one getting along in there?"

"Fine. Giving me no trouble. I've been waiting for morning sickness, but it never came." She took his hand in both of hers. "The best part is, I'm feeling so full of pep lately."

"Good sign. But any more pep and you're going to be hard to handle."

"Hoo. That'll be the day. I can't think of anybody you couldn't handle."

"Am I really like that for you?"

"Yes. There are times when I'm afraid of you. The way you can sit there and smolder. I'd sure hate to be around when you got mad." Her belly laughed under his hand. "I was afraid there for a while you were going to declare real war on those rats."

He withdrew his hand. "But I have declared real war on them. And if it's the last thing I ever do, I'm gonna get those sonsabitches. Tomorrow I'm gonna ransack Bonnie for a couple of female cats in a family way."

It took two trips to find the pregnant cats. When Tunis couldn't find any in Bonnie, he caught the next train to Rock Falls. It was late in the afternoon when he came home with a small wicker basket heavy with two fat cats. He was careful to first close the kitchen door before removing the cover of the basket.

"Dark gray ones," Clara remarked. "Never saw cats that color before."

"Fellow was telling me that that was the original color of the cat. He said the gray cat was the tougher cat. There's more jungle in her." Tunis remembered the first time he'd explored his acreage, especially in the wasteland in back, when he'd felt the presence of a big cat.

"Heavens, they won't attack us?"

"Might. If you show your tail."

"You!"

The dark gray cats proved to be very tractable so long as they were heavy with young. They had very white whiskers and a vivid white tail tip. They liked to rub their shoulders and then their tails against Clara's ankles, all the while purring like a couple of kettles about to boil over. Tunis found some sand in a gravel spit behind the barn, where the land fell away to the river bottom, and made a sandbox for them in the back porch. He also whacked up a small box bed for them and Clara placed a blanket in it for them to sleep on.

The grays, as both Tunis and Clara called them, decided after the second week they liked their new home. When anything new was brought to them, food, bedding, they always nosed around it a few times, and touched it with a deft paw, which was instantly snapped back, and mewed a little, and it was only after they'd wrestled with it or on it that they accepted it.

Tunis was also pleased to discover that despite their lumpy bellies the gray cats were great mousers. Mice liked to make the back porch or the old cabin their home, and Clara had been fighting them for months. But the grays took care of the mice. They slunk around; they waited, patient mounds of gray resembling old mops; they pounced. And gobbled. They were good predators, all right.

In June one morning both grays greeted Tunis with weak mewings. Looking closer, he saw that both had given birth to young and that the young were already stuck fast to their dugs. Eyes shut, pink corners of their little mouths wet, the tiny kittens were sucking away for dear life.

"Clara, come out here at once."

Clara came sleepily, housecoat pulled up snug around her. "Yes?"

"Look, love."

"Ohh." Her grave gray eyes took on a warm color. She held her large belly with one arm and her filling breasts with the other arm. "They look so helpless." She knelt and reached a finger toward the little pulsing bundles, not quite touching them. "And they're all gray too. With a white tail tip."

"Yeh, they bred true. I hope that all of them turn out to be cougars like the man said."

120

"A person would never believe such little helpless creatures could ever grow up to be ferocious mousers."

"And let's hope ferocious ratters."

"They're so sweet." Clara stood up and brushed back a strand of auburn hair. "I suppose now we can let the door open and they can go outside and get some sun." Her nose wrinkled up. "I'm getting a little tired of cleaning out their sandbox. The smell here isn't of the best."

Tunis knelt down and counted them. "By the Lord, they had six each. That means we now got fourteen cats."

A month later the little kittens began to gambol around in the house, out in the back porch as well as on the linoleum floor in the kitchen. Tunis sometimes for the fun of it played cat-and-mouse with them, sliding his hand under a throw rug and making suspicious movements under it. The moment the kittens spotted the movement, they assumed the pounce attitude, crouched down, tail flicking from side to side, head suddenly bent ahead; and then, humped up, they jumped, pouncing on the bump in the rug. And when one jumped, they all jumped. Sometimes Tunis found his arm buried in tumbling playing kittens.

Tunis and Clara need not have worried about the grays running away once they were given the run of the place. Taking the kittens with them, the two gray mothers went mousing in the grass around the yard, each day taking them farther and farther afield.

It was in August, when Tunis was ready to cut the ripened wheat, that he spotted it. He'd bought some planking and sheets of tin to put a new floor in the granary, and was wondering if he shouldn't first lock all fourteen cats in the granary overnight to chase the rats away, when it hit him that he hadn't heard any squealings under the granary the last couple of days. Investigating, tearing out some of the flooring, he discovered the rats had left. Their nests and droppings were old.

Carrying a hammer, he called into the house. "Clara? Guess what."

Clara came to the door. She looked like she had a hound curled up asleep under her apron. "Yes?"

"The rascals are gone."

"You sure?"

"Yep. Gone."

"The rats didn't go hiding under some other building?"

"Nope. They hang around only where there's food."

Clara had to laugh. "And now we have all those cats."

"Yeh, if each of those female young has six kittens, we'll be hip deep in them."

"What will you do about that?"

"For a while I'm going to keep the cat population up to around a dozen. Just to make sure the rats don't come back. But anything over that I drown. Put 'em in a sack and throw 'em in the river."

"Oh."

A couple of days later Tunis discovered how the rats had come to the place earlier. He was near the railroad tracks, putting in a new fence, when the Bonnie Omaha came by pulling several cars loaded with golden wheat. Hanging onto the back car, just ahead of the caboose, he spotted the familiar scabby tails and the pointed whiskered noses of rats.

"Those pesky devils," he told Clara afterward. "There they were, hitching a ride on that train like a couple of wise old hoboes. The guts of 'em."

Clara bent over heavily and picked up one of the gray kittens rubbing its tail against her ankles. "Well, we're both blessed. We got rid of the rats and the mice."

121

13. Clara

On the sixth of September, as Clara was looking for eggs in the haymow, the first pains came.

Her first thought was: "How in the world am I going to get down that ladder. I'll never make it. I shouldn't have come up here at all. Drat those hens, always trying to hide their eggs."

She knew Tunis was out turning over another piece of virgin prairie with the breaking plow down in the bottoms north of the barn. He'd never hear her yell for help.

She set the pail of eggs down on the slick floor of the haymow and slowly settled down on a fresh mound of wild hay. She puffed. She held her belly firmly as the strong gripping convulsed in her. She'd never before felt anything like it. It was a final kind of pain. With judgment in it. The usual kind of belly-ache one sometimes got during dog days was nothing like it. In the middle of the gripping her sense of smell suddenly became keen. There was the aroma of faded wild roses in the hay, the gutter smells coming up from downstairs, and the smell of sweat in leather horse collars.

The smells of the barn, the pain, brought a passage of the Bible vividly to mind. Mary'd had Jesus in a manger.

The pain passed and she could breathe easier. With the edge of her apron she wiped sweat from her brow. She stared at the open mouth of the trap door where the ladder began. Were one of those pains to hit her halfway down she'd lose her grip and fall and hurt the baby. If only Tunis were on the yard. "Because we've got to get Dr. Wallance. Malena Tippett had her eighth easy, after a cough, but I know the first one is always tough."

Another contraction swept up out of the bottom of her and seized her innards. "Ohhh. Tunis?"

The next thing she knew there was Tunis standing over her. "Woman!"

She had to wait to say something until the seizing had left. "I thought you were out plowing."

"The evener broke and I had to come home to make a new one. We hit a big boulder and those four horses broke the evener into flying toothpicks. Then just as I was leading the horses into the barn, I heard you."

"I'm so glad you came. I don't want to have this baby up in the haymow. I'd never live it down."

Tunis helped her to her feet and led her to the trap door. He started down first to catch her in case she slipped on the ladder. She followed jerkily, with trembling hands. When she hit the straw-covered floor she heaved a sigh of relief.

"You better quick get Dr. Wallance."

Just then they heard the Bonnie Omaha whistling north up the valley, where it crossed the old stage trail near Lakewood.

Tunis said, "Hey, I'll stop the train and tell the conductor to quick send Doc out here. That'll be faster than riding Gyp in." Tunis left on the run, darting out of the alley of the barn, heading for the tracks.

"Come back right away," she called after him.

She had another contraction as she headed toward the house. She stopped and leaned over till it passed. She almost fainted.

Tunis came running back. "They're gonna tell Doc Wallance to come out pronto. Here, let me help you." He put his strong arms around her and led her into the house.

Once she reached the bedroom Clara felt better. As she slipped off her long maternity dress, she told Tunis what to do. "There's a rubberized sheet in the commode there. After you pull the quilts back, put it on the sheet."

"Yes, milady."

"And you better make sure there's plenty of hot water."

"Done, milady."

"And now if you'll help me into my nightgown. For some reason I'm having trouble lifting my arms."

Patiently he slipped a white flannel nightgown over her head and shoulders. He was very tender. His pearl gray eyes shone.

She lay down carefully, on her back, letting her legs lie apart. She smiled at his considerate hands. "Do you remember the other time you ran all night with a pan of water to staunch the flow of blood?"

123

"I thought sure I'd ruined you."

She found it hard to laugh. The baby in her kicked and kicked. Also the weight of it pushing up into her lungs held laughter down. "That's the way we women are made. But we're tough."

"Well, I guess I better get things ready."

"And oh, yes, don't forget to get those eggs. I left them standing on the floor of the haymow."

Another pain came along.

Suddenly she could feel that the baby had moved down from the high part of her into the bony cradle below. It was in a rush to come.

She called him back. "Tunis!"

"Yes, love."

"I don't think we're gonna need a doctor. Quick come with the water."

He was in the room in an instant. His eyes had become very light with intensity.

"Do you think you can help instead?"

"I can sure try."

"You'll be looking at my shame. I may dirty the bed."

"Try me."

"Just so I don't lose your respect."

"Try me."

The other being in her was now the boss. It decided to shove against the bone cradle with force. "It's going to come naturally all right. By itself. Oee. I'm beginning to feel like the Red Sea. Splitting apart to let the Israelites through."

Something gave and something popped through. "There. Do you see something?"

"Quick. Another push."

She pushed. She groaned. She pushed. "Akkh!" she yelled, "Truly, we are born in anguish."

There was a wet burbled cry.

"It looks like a big bubble," he said amazed. "Oh. There it broke. There's water all over."

The cry cleared. Then the baby let out a bellow. "Bwaa!"

Tunis laughed. "Another country heard from."

The baby drew itself up as though it were going to give a great final kick at the end of a long swim. Then it surged forward and there was a slushing sound and then there was a vast relief of burden. It was born.

"It's a boy," Tunis said softly.

"Wonderful."

"And he's got one tooth showing already. In the bottom gum."

Clara spotted it too. A little speck of white showing through what seemed a skinless ridge of pink flesh. "I'm going to have to teach him not to bite." Clara could feel herself sinking off into a sweet easy dream. "Do you know how to cut the cord?"

"Coming up. Just relax, milady." He placed the baby on her belly head down. "I'll be back in a jiff with some silk thread and a scissors."

The baby lay wailing on her belly. It sobbed in a series of compressed jerks.

Gently, with sure steady fingers, Tunis separated mother and child. "What a racket you're making there, young feller. Man, has he got the lungs."

124

Clara lay a soft hand on the baby's bottom. "Now wash him with just a touch of soap. And careful not to get it in his eyes."

Tunis cleaned up the baby. "He has your auburn hair, love." The baby quieted down after Tunis diapered it and wrapped it in soft flannel. It sighed involuntarily from all the hard crying. "Yow!" Tunis couldn't help but exult. "We did it without a doctor. What a mother you turned out to be, wife. I knew you were first-class the very first time I saw you."

"I thought you were pretty good too, the first time I saw you."

Tunis handed her the baby, placing it in her arms. "There you are."

Clara listened to the baby breathing. No rasping sound that she could tell. No hint of asthma. Tunis's sturdy blood had won out. "But it is a sweet anguish."

Tunis next cleaned up Clara. "Are you hungry? I can make you something."

"Some broth. It's in the bottom of the cabinet." She smiled up at Tunis, very happy. "But if you're hungry, please go make yourself something too, my husband."

"I'm too excited to eat." He looked at the baby some more with swelling pride. "Our son has come."

"Our prince and heir."

"Have you thought what we might name him?"

"Yes. Have you?"

"Not really." He combed back the baby's rusty hair. "Oh, a couple names maybe."

"Like what?"

"Oh, Dirk. And if it was going to be a girl, Tressa. My foster parents, you know."

She savored the names in her mind. Dirk Freyling. "Somehow this boy doesn't look like a Dirk to me. How about Tunis Junior, seeing he has reddish hair and your build."

"Absolutely not. That I'm absolutely against."

"But why?"

"Then the kid has always got to be measuring himself up against his old man."

"But we're starting up a whole new family tree. Tunis the first. Tunis the second. Tunis the third."

"Nope!"

The baby began to stir in her arms and to make sucking motions with its lips. "Well, I do declare, someone's hungry." With an indulgent smile, she lifted out her left breast, fat with milk, the teat running a little pinkish, and pushed the baby's mouth up against it. The little mouth took hold instantly.

Tunis had to laugh. "Look at that, would you? He's even better at it than a fresh calf. And I always thought nothing could match a calf for pure hard sucking. Look at that."

She had to adjust the baby to get it to lie snug. "Ow. Oee." She winced. "Does my bottom still hurt!"

"Have you thought of any other names for him?"

She smiled down at the eager suckling. "Well, I once saw a name in an old English paper I thought was catchy. Tane. Would you like that? Tane Freyling?"

"Never heard of it."

"It means 'immortal.' It also could mean 'tooth.' At least according to my mother, who fancied names."

"Tane." He savored it in his mind. "That's pretty good. Tane Freyling." He looked down at her. "You women sure have a knack for naming children. When a mother names a baby, it's almost as though it was born with that tag on it out of her belly."

"Well, with one tooth showing like that, I couldn't help but think of Tane."

"All right. Tane it is."

"Good. That's settled then. Will it be all right to have him baptized by Father Garlington?"

"Of course. We'll catch the Bonnie Omaha in."

She felt something letting go inside of her and then sliding out. "Oh, dear. There!"

"Yes. The afterbirth. That's a good sign. That's one of the things you have to watch out for with cattle. If she don't clean right, she's gonna show ribs all summer long."

She quirked an odd smile at him. "You sure like to compare women to cows, don't you?"

"Except that one of you has a chance at heaven."

Little Tane slowly fell asleep. His soft sucking mouth opened a little and several drops of pinkish milk ran down his chin.

"Would you give me that washrag on the commode there?"

Tunis obliged.

"That broth. I think now I'm ready for it. I'm starting to feel hungry."

"That's right. Come to think of it, I could eat a bite myself." He ran off to the kitchen.

Clara lay smiling to herself. She thanked God she had full breasts for her child. One thing she was not going to do—have another baby started before Little Tane was weaned. Malena Tippett was lesson enough for that.

When Dr. Wallance finally arrived, he found mother and child doing well. He grumbled that he'd come for nothing. "The usual story. I'm always called too late, for the dying and for the just born."

14. Tunis

It was the middle of November, that time of year for cozy sleeping, when husband and wife think of each other as a little stove in bed. But to Tunis's surprise, Clara stayed on her side. When he reached across to touch her, she quietly but firmly pushed his hand away.

He held himself in, somehow managed to speak with a lover's soft voice. "Does it still hurt?"

"I'm not breastfeeding little Tane while swelling up with another baby."

"Oh, we won't get a baby right away. Look how long it took before Tane came along."

"That's what you think. I've often heard from women that once you start bearing children, there's no stopping them."

He hated being blocked. He could feel where her hand had pushed back his hand. So far he'd managed to live with Clara without feeling he wasn't getting his way. They'd been a good team together mostly because they each had their own work, she inside and he outside.

Clara slowly turned on her side away from him.

"Wife, how long is it this going to go on?"

"Tane is going to be at least a year before I consider it."

He sat up in bed like a suddenly released jack-in-the-box. "Me to go without my bed rights that long?"

"You did it before we got married."

"Before I got used to the joys of love with a sweet wife, it was possible. But not now."

"I'm sorry. But that's the way it's going to be."

He fell back into his pillow. "So that's my reward."

"You've been well repaid with the son you now have."

The baby stirred in the cradle at the foot of the bed. After a moment the baby whimpered.

She sighed. "I suppose I better rock him a little."

"No," he said, "don't. He mustn't get used to being pampered the minute something doesn't go right."

"Is that how you got to be such a man?"

He sat up suddenly again, wishing he could hit her. "Woman, you sure have a tart tongue. Worse than the bite of horseradish."

The baby gradually quieted down.

She said with an edge of iron in her voice, "But if you need to indulge yourself in concupiscence so bad, go find yourself a soiled dove somewhere and do with her whatever it is you need to do. But . . . . don't tell me about it."

He lay down again. Of course he'd never do that. He'd never had another woman. He loved Clara.

All through that winter she denied him.

She was sweet to him during the day: at the table, when they drove to town to go shopping, while sitting around the stove in the evening.

She was especially loving and tender the Sunday they caught the Bonnie Omaha to Whitebone and had Tane baptized in the Episcopalian church. She pinched Tunis's arm in love several times during the ceremony, and smiled up at him as though he were king, and spoke lovingly of him to Father Garlington. Even during supper that night after they got home she was all smiles as she served him venison and potatoes, several times resting her hand tenderly on his shoulder.

But then, when they went to bed, she gave him the cold treatment again.

"Good God," he said into the dark, as they lay awhile in silence, "I might as well gnaw off my balls for all the good they're doing me."

She said nothing.

"Clara, really now, can't we do it in such a way you won't get caught?"

"I don't trust that. I've heard of too many stories where that doesn't work."

"Lord, I don't know what I'm going to do."

"Forbear."

"For who?"

"For Jesus."

He fell silent. He never quite knew how to handle her religious remarks.

He became grim around the house. His lips slowly set in a slow scowl.

The one time they did have lively talk together, and behaved as if they had no bedroom problems, came when they received a much-fingered letter in the mail from Her New Man. Someone at the Episcopalian mission had written it for Her New Man, and he had then signed it by affixing his mark to it, a small pictograph, the stick figure of a man with an arrow through his heart from which blood spurted copiously:

Kodah,

   It is time to take the bones of my mother from her tree and bury them in our Great Mother. I am going to visit my sister in Paha Sapa and cannot bury the bones myself. By now my mother has given back to the sun and the winds the sweetness of her flesh and now the bones must go to their rightful home. I thank you.

Her New Man

Clara said, "Are the bones still there?"

"I saw 'em there a week ago."

"But the ground is so frozen now."

It was the middle of January and the thermometer outside their kitchen window read thirty-six degrees below. "I can use the axe and chop out a hole."

"You'll do this in the dead of the winter?"

"Of course. We owe them at least that much."

Clara stood musing out of the kitchen window. A magnificent frost blossom resembling a flowered fern curved around the bare spot through which she was looking. "You're a good man, Tunis."

He growled uneasily, not wanting a compliment from a wife who would not be cozy with him at night.

She turned and went to where he sat in his swivel armchair and ran her hand through his hair. She ruffled his hair with cool affection, in a manner he could not misinterpret.

But he felt good about the gesture, and later on, when he went out in the cold with an axe and a spade and buried Judith Raveling's bones, he smiled wryly to himself.

Except for that January, the winter of 1886–87 was a mild one. Tunis managed to get a lot of winter work done: repairing the harnesses, cleaning out the various stalls in his great barn, winnowing the wheat and selecting the best of it for the coming spring's planting, resetting the door frames in the barn now that the building had finally settled.

In May one morning just at dawn they were awakened by a tapping on the picture window in the parlor next to their bedroom. Coming out of a deep sleep, Tunis first thought it was the wind tugging at the screen door out front, that they'd forgotten to hook it. But when he awakened a little more, he realized there was no wind out.

He sat up in bed. Could it be someone knocking on the front door? A visitor that early?

Clara said beside him, "I think it's out there where I got that shelf outside the bay window for my flowerpots."

He looked at their clock. "Anyway, it's time to get up. I'll go see what's going on."

"So will I."

In their white night clothes they stole into the still-dusky parlor and carefully, on bare toes, approached the bay window.

It was a male meadowlark. He was walking up and down the shelf between and around Clara's flowerpots and staring at something in or on the window, first with one bright bead eye, then with the other. The meadowlark whicked around on his long spread toes, then opened his long pointed beak and sang.

"Listen to that," Clara whispered. "He's saying, 'There it is! Spring!'"

The meadowlark turned and peered at the bottom of the window, exactly opposite where he was standing on the shelf. He waited a second, then angrily pecked at the window. Several times. Then he sang again.

Tunis said, "Sounds more like he's saying, 'This is all mine! Y'hear!'"

They watched some more as he sang and pecked at the window and sang.

"Oh, I get it," Tunis said at last. "It's dark in here and that makes the window a perfect mirror. He's pecking at his reflection. He thinks it's another male meadowlark invading his place. But he can't figure out why that other rival ain't fighting back. His enemy just mocks him. And doesn't even sing back at him."

"Can it really be that?"

"He and his mate have a nest near here, in the grass somewhere. And while she's setting, he's standing guard."

"That's hard to believe. Birds don't think."

"But they know."

"Well, you know so much more about animals I guess I better shut up."

The meadowlark continued to sing and then to peck at its reflection. Its breast was a vivid yellow intersected by a black V. Its gray beak was as long as its longest gray toe. Judging by the size of its foot it should have been a bigger bird.

Tunis said finally, "We can't be letting him rob us of our sleep. I'm going to put a little board outside at the base of the window so he can't see himself."

"Good," she said. "I was afraid you'd shoot him."

"You sure don't know me yet, do you?"

"You walk around mad all day."

"I wonder what other men do when their wives pull a 'don't touch me' stunt on them."

"I wouldn't know. And I don't care to know. All I know is that I'm not nursing a baby while I'm carrying another one. That is final."

They went back to bed. It was getting more and more light out. Neither could sleep. They each lay in their own tangle of thoughts.

Tunis looked at where his clothes hung over a chair, then over at where Clara's clothes lay over the arm of a love seat. He smiled to himself. "Reminds me of a story."

"I don't know if I want to hear it."

He went on anyway. "There was this couple, see. They went together for a long while before they got married. All the while they stayed pure. And all that time he never had much to say. She did all the talking. But finally they did get hitched and they took the train to Sioux City on their honeymoon. They had their first night together in a hotel. She did an awful lot of wiggling, and some squealing, and some bossing around about who was going to do what, but finally the marriage was consummated. And then they fell asleep. The next morning, waking up together, the sun coming through the window, he pointed to their clothes. 'Well,' he said, 'there's the pants on the chair there, and there's the petticoat on the love seat there. Which one are you going to put on this morning?'"

Clara said nothing.

Tunis smiled some more and got out of bed. He pulled his nightshirt off over his head and then went over to their love seat and slipped on Clara's white petticoat. He managed to get the petticoat down over his hips and adjusted it to fit.

"A perfect fit," she said from her pillow. Then she got up and went over to the chair, pulled her nightgown off over her head, and stepped into his underpants. It was the first time she'd ever let him see her stark naked.

"Hmm," he said, "I guess it's up to me to make the breakfast then."

"Yes, and I'll have to milk the cows."

"And I'll have to clean the house too."

"Yes, but if I have to manure out the barn, I quit." Then she burst out laughing. "Oh, Tunis, can't we have peace in our wonderful home?"

"Until when?"

"For the sake of our baby Tane?"

"Until when?"

"You mean when you get your bed rights back?"

"Yes."

"Until our Tane is at least a year and a half old. Like I said."

"I'll be goddamned. Woman, you are tough. You drive a hard bargain."

"Well, you drive a hard one yourself."

"Well, I should be able to. If a man doesn't get hard once in a while, you got nothing. Not even children."

She sighed. "You men, you're bound and determined to turn any conversation into dirt."

"Thank God for dirt farmers. Without them you'd have nothing."

She stepped out of his underpants, again showing her short voluptuous body. It was a lovely white. "I was thinking of hymns and psalms."

"And I wasn't?" He stepped out of her petticoat.

She asked, "What do you want for breakfast?"

"Whatever the pot serves up."

The little board Tunis put up along the bottom of the bay window didn't work. The next dawn the twitchy meadowlark hopped up on the board and once again above the board saw its imaginary rival. Incensed, it attacked the glass some more.

"You'd think he'd get a headache, banging his beak like that," Tunis said from his pillow.

"Or knock his beak loose," Clara said.

"He's robbing us of about an hour's sleep every morning." Tunis was thinking they shouldn't waste the hour. "By the Lord, I know what I'm going to do. Put my pants to work. They ain't doing any good in here." He got up, picked up his work trousers, and in his nightshirt stepped outside through the front door. He carefully draped his trousers above the board he'd placed under the window.

The tapping stopped.

Clara had to laugh. "Smelling your pants out there, he now knows for sure he's got a rival. And a big one." She laughed some more. "I suppose the next thing you'll do is move out there with Mrs. Meadowlark and help her sit on the eggs."

"And I suppose you'll invite him in here and ask him to help you change Tane's diapers."

"Tunis, why don't we put a scarecrow out there?"

"Sure, might as well. Nail me to a post out there. Because that's all I am to you in here."

They gave each other the silent treatment most of the summer.

Tunis worked like a fiend in the field and on the yard, taking it out on the machinery and the earth, though he was kind with the animals.

He built fences around all his property, the whole section, and around each field, both plowed and still virgin, and around the barnyard and the houseyard. He broke another forty acres of prairie sod. He dropped trees and cut them into logs, getting them ready for winter splitting and chopping.

He was short with his neighbor Hack Tippett, though he wasn't short with Malena Tippett. Malena was still very skinny and walked with that weak begging aspect that attracted men. Tunis could see why Hack couldn't let her alone.

Meanwhile little Tane thrived. Soon he was sitting up in the highchair Tunis made for him, and sat with Tunis and Clara when they had their meals. Both Tunis and Clara occasionally spooned him some of their wheat porridge and fed him bits of their mashed potatoes. Clara had plenty of milk for him, which he loved dearly, but he was also hungry enough to try adult food.

"Look at those fat legs," Clara said with smiling indulgence. "He's going to be a monster."

"He sure has the shoulders all right. Good. I can use that on the yard, you know."

"Suppose he's gifted, then what?"

Tunis remembered his own restless days. "Let him follow his own nose."

At first little Tane had dark reddish hair. It soon gave way to blond hair, a soft gold. As it thickened Tane's brows came in, a darker gold, almost brown. His blue eyes were wide-set. His nose started out as a little bump but gradually it took shape and became well-shaped and firm.

Little Tane rarely cried, and when he did it was because he'd been wet for some time. He gurgled to himself a lot, and waggled his arms and legs in phantom baby races, and smiled at anything that moved.

Tunis said, "Someday, if he's lucky in love, he's gonna have a happy life."

Tane began to stand up on his own at eight months. He'd skedaddle sideways crawling until he came to a chair, then with his strong chubby fists haul himself erect and then hang on, smiling in baby triumph. He'd hang on with one hand and wave with the other. When his hand happened to let go of the chair, he had the happy ability to just sag down with a plop to the floor.

He started walking in September, a few days after his first birthday. By October he was streaking everywhere through the house. Clara had to set things out of his reach in all the rooms.

He said, "Mama" by Thanksgiving Day and "Papa" on Christmas Eve.

He loved his Christmas present, a boy doll, and called it "Dumno." Dumno went with him everywhere, to bed, at the table, on the floor, where Tane tried to teach it to play with blocks. Dumno went along a few times the Freylings went to church.

Tunis loved the boy.

Then, New Year's Eve 1887, Tunis sensed a change in Clara. Her eyes kept straying to Tunis's hands. With a laugh she spoke of how Tunis's big toe had become a thorn in her life because that was the part of his sock that always wore out first. If she could have a New Year's wish, she would wish that somehow the sock makers could invent socks with a double-thick toe. "And while they're at it, the heel too, since that is always next to go."

She even hinted that she would like to have gone to the social hop the new bank in town was putting on, but of course, with the baby around now, they could hardly go.

"Oh, I dunno," Tunis said. "I read that in the paper too. Holding it there in the Bonnie Hotel, they'll probably put all the babies in one room and have the maids take care of them. You wanna go?"

"How cold is it out?"

"That shouldn't bother us. We can bundle up in the bobsled with a lot of fresh straw. And we got three buffalo robes now."

Clara looked at Tane in his highchair. "Maybe we better not. He's had the sniffles lately."

"Suit yourself."

"We still have some brandy left, don't we?"

"About four fingers. Though I was kind of saving that for medicinal purposes."

"Maybe at midnight we can treat ourselves with a little medicine."

He nodded. He began to understand something.

For the first time in a long while they stayed up long after Tane was put in his trundle bed, talking, reminiscing about the old days when they were kids. Clara laughed at the least hint of a joke.

At eleven o'clock, Tunis began to yawn. "I don't know if I can make it to midnight."

Clara yawned too. "Let's pretend our clock's an hour late."

"Good idea. Shall I get us that shot of brandy?"

"Why must you men always call it a shot? Why can't it be a sip?"

"Sip coming up." Tunis dug out the bottle of brandy from the side cupboard in the living room, found two small slender glasses, and poured them each a little drink.

They clinked glasses, standing beside the glowing blue-titted hard-coal burner.

"Happy New Year, Tunis, my husband."

"Happy New Year, Clara, wife."

"Many happy returns."

"Same."

While Clara checked to see if Tane was still covered, Tunis put some more coal in the burner and dropped a last chunk of wood into the kitchen range. Tunis also held a lamp up to the kitchen window to see what the thermometer outside read. It was twenty below.

"Good thing we didn't go after all."

When Tunis turned down the night lamp and climbed into bed in his nightshirt, he was surprised to find Clara on his side of the bed. He could just barely manage to tuck the blankets in under the mattress on his side. She didn't move either when he with a little wriggle indicated it was tight quarters for him. She was facing him and that made it even harder to ask her to move over.

"What's this?" he said.

She smiled.

"Have you begun to wean Tane?"

"I start tomorrow."

"I think I forgot how. It's been so long."

"No mean remarks now."

"Maybe you can show me. Then I'll know for sure you think it's all right."

"Husband. Now, now."

He hadn't forgotten. Nor had she. All the cold winter days they were man and wife. Tunis bloomed as a man.

15. Tunis

On the morning of January 12, 1888, Tunis couldn't believe his thermometer. It read seventy-two degrees above zero. Snow was melting everywhere. The top four inches of the earth became a layer of sloppy grass-lined mud.

Around ten in the morning it was decided Tunis should go to town to get some supplies. Clara was running out of salt and sugar and vegetables. Tunis didn't like the seventy-two degrees. Heat in the winter days always meant danger. Also there was an odd smell in the air, reminding him of a horse that had overheated after a hard run.

Just as he left the yard, sitting on the high spring seat of the wagon, he had a long look around at the entire horizon. Not a cloud. Not even a stray wisp of a mare's tail. He shrugged; then clucked up his mottled grays Sue and Sal into a trot.

As he approached Tippett's lane, he noticed across the road Clate Bartles standing outside his sod house. Clate and his sister Hettie had bought the quarter section east of the Tippetts. They had managed to build a sod house and a horse shelter just before the deep frost set in the past fall. Tunis didn't think much of the quarter section they'd bought. One look and a fellow could see it was mostly sandy hills. Both Clate and his sister Hettie had a secretive look about them.

Clate waved him down.

Tunis pulled up on the lines. "Whoa."

"Can you help me catch one of my horses? It's Beaut. She's in that draw behind the shelter there. Every time I get close, she runs off." Clate had a pale blond moustache. His light blue eyes shied away just when it seemed he was about to look directly at you.

"Sure."

They found the horse nibbling at the bark of some young cottonwoods. It was an old bay mare, with wise leering lips and almost popped moon eyes. Twice as they were about to grab her around the neck, she jumped away.

Tunis asked, "Have you tried using a little sand on her?"

"You mean, like salt on her tail?"

"No, no. Just watch now." Tunis swallowed to clear his throat. He took a deep breath, settled his chin down to his chest, and let go with a growling roar of sound. "*Beaut!! Get!!*"

Beaut's old gray head came up, she almost backed a step, then she whirled around and headed straight for Clate's horse shelter. She sidled up beside the other bay horse and stood obedient.

Both Tunis and Clate hurried after her. While Tunis blocked the entrance to the horse shelter, Clate went in and grabbed Beaut around the neck and secured her with a halter.

"Thanks," Clate said. "I don't know what I'd a done if you hadn't come along."

"Think nothing of it."

Clate began to harness both horses. "How'd you do that? You almost scared the bejaises out of me."

"Get a handful of sand from the river, pour it in the back of your throat, then let go with your best roar."

"Quite a ways to go for sand when you're in a hurry."

"You got plenty of sand up in your hills here."

Clate's face saddened over. "Yeah, maybe we made a mistake buying this."

Tunis scuffed the muddy crumbly earth. "If you've got the money, you might be wise to buy several more quarter sections in these hills. And then make a ranch out of it. Graze fatteners. Except along this draw here, I wouldn't plow one acre of it."

"I might just do that."

"Need me any more?"

"Nope."

As Tunis climbed onto his spring seat again, he saw Clate's sister Hettie standing in the door to their sod house. She surprised Tunis with how tall she was. She completely filled the doorway. She wasn't heavy; just tall and long-armed. Her complexion was even lighter than her brother's: hair long and stringy to her hips like the white tail of a horse, blanched-white cheeks, eyes more holes than blue, a freckled brown nose. Tunis waved to her with two fingers. She didn't respond.

Tunis was almost in town when, looking back, he saw Clate coming rapidly up behind in his democrat. Mud was flying high from all four wheels and all eight hooves like little clouds of black grasshoppers.

Tunis still didn't like the January heat. It was so warm he had to open his sheepskin coat and unbutton his gray woolen shirt almost down to his belt. That odd sweated-horse smell was even sharper. He checked the horizons to all sides. Still clear everywhere.

Tunis tied his grays to a hitching post on the east side of the new brick First National Bank. He'd barely emerged from between his horses onto the wooden sidewalk when Clate pulled up beside him and tied up as well. Tunis was afraid Clate was going to want to chum around with him as he shopped, but Clate read his mood and with only a nod went his own way.

People in town talked about the crazy January weather. There were a lot of jokes about it. "Why move south for the winter?" "The earth must've slipped a couple of cogs to the south." "The good Lord must've piled on the coal in good old Sol." All thought it wonderful luck not to have to chop wood for the stove.

Tunis finished shopping early. It was just high noon. For old times' sake, he decided to have himself a dinner at the Bonnie Hotel, just to see who might be around and what the talk of the day was.

Boughers the land agent with his spotted vest and Mel the undertaker with his sour fish eyes were eating together in a corner. They nodded noncommittally at Tunis. The pretty cuddly blond chambermaid had graduated into becoming the head waitress. She pretended she didn't remember Tunis. She was all business about seating people, impersonal, as chilly as a dried-up old maid.

Most of the talk had to do with the way homes were springing up all around town like white mushrooms. Because of it, two new business establishments, a harness store and a grocery, were being built on the upper part of Main Street.

It was just one o'clock when Tunis untied his grays and prepared to head for home. Not much to his surprise, Clate appeared from nowhere and untied his horses too. Clate followed Tunis out of town.

Tunis had just taken the curve onto the angled trail going northeast when, looking up, he was surprised to see, low on the northwest horizon, some sinister gray-edged clouds rushing toward him. It looked a little like a thousand moles were coming at him just underground, recklessly throwing up grayish dirt as they advanced.

"Hey," Clate called loud from behind Tunis. "Look at that coming!"

Tunis stared at the oncoming woolly turmoil.

"End of the world?" Clate cried.

"Blizzard," Tunis pronounced. "Sonofabitch." Tunis snapped the lines over the backs of his grays. "Get!"

The grays got. Clate also whacked up his bays.

It came on thickening. The earth across the river, the melted fields and lingering snowbanks off knolls, appeared to be unraveling as the rolling edge of the storm came toward them. It came on so hard, so fast, it sucked up wet dirt and mixed it with the oncoming swirling snow.

Tunis slapped his horses into a gallop. Clate did the same behind him.

But it was too late. Within seconds the world was a whirl, and horse and man were lost in it. Tunis couldn't even see his hands. His eyelashes became so heavy with snow and dirt they stuck together.

Wiping his eyes, he looked around to see if he could spot Clate. He couldn't. Clate had vanished.

136

The grays stopped.

Tunis geed and hawed at them. He jerked on the lines.

The grays wouldn't move. They doubled up their heads against the blasting snow and dirt.

Quickly he buttoned up his gray woolen shirt, snugged up his sheepskin collar around his head and face. He pulled down the earflaps of his woolen blue cap.

He hoped Clara had been looking out the kitchen windows and had seen the storm coming. The livestock would be all right. When he left he'd locked up everything in the barn. With little Tane to think of surely she'd have the sense to stay inside and wait out the storm. He thought about it awhile; finally nodded his head. Clara was one of those women who could take care of herself no matter what was up.

It was his business to survive. Since the horses wouldn't move, he decided to get down and lead them. He tied the lines loosely onto the center post on the wagon and stepped down. He found his way around to the front of the horses by following first the left trace and then the lines to the bridle. He took Sue by the bit and spoke firmly into her flopping ear. She was the most tractable of the two grays. "Steady, old girl. I'll try to find the ruts home for you. Everything's going to be all right."

Leaning over, he managed to make out the edges of the ruts in the mud he and Clate had made earlier in the day. Stumbling, continually shaking his head to free his eyelashes of snow and dirt, he worked his way north a dozen rods, the grays following him trustingly. He hoped to God that Clate had the sense to latch onto the endgate of his wagon.

The storm thickened even more. It roared. The wind became so powerful it pushed him up against Sue again and again.

Then the upper half of a massive vise of ice came down out of the heavens, right down through the whirling snow, and met the lower half, clamping together tight. Within moments the snow and dirt, frozen, became piercing BBs. Tunis could feel his cheeks stiffening. His lips turned into hard little cucumbers; he couldn't even manage them to cluck at the horses.

The worse came when he lost the rutted trail. Well, the Bonnie railroad tracks had to be off to the left a couple of rods. He'd find them and follow them home. Though how Clate would know when to turn off to the right for his lane was something Tunis didn't care to think about.

Finally he stumbled over the near track. He was stunned to discover they were almost covered with low drifts of new blackish snow. My God. This was the worst he'd ever seen. Why, another hour of it and there'd be three feet of snow. And with that wind there'd be snowdrifts a dozen or more feet deep.

Finally he had to drop down to his knees to make out the near track going home. The grays trusted him, floundering behind him, snorting only when they sensed they'd nearly stepped on his heels.

Another dozen yards and the tracks vanished under hard rusty snow. Soon the pellets let up and the blasting snow turned a ghostly bluish white. Hurriedly he scratched around, back and forth, trying to find the tracks. It was no go. He stopped and turned his back to the storm. He put his arms around the head of good old Sue. Sal felt neglected and pushed her nose into their embrace, ruckling a low mumbling sound.

They were dead ducks. It if lasted a couple more hours there was no getting out of this one.

He wondered what Clate might be thinking back there.

A little snort of laughter broke from him. Well, well. He hadn't lost his temper at the storm. That head of cabbage between his ears had gone soft. He smiled some more. His wild temper was being leeched away drop by drop because Clara kept pulling him on top of her every night.

There'd be no more nights of Clara's thighs if he, Tunis, didn't get home alive. Nor of little Tane's hugs and kisses.

The grays sensed something. They whinnied. Some animal was nearby. Puma?

As if to scare away whatever it was, Tunis threw out an arm against the busting storm. To his stunned surprise, his fingertips hit something solid. What! He took a step forward and felt again. Godalmighty. A solid wall. Sod house. Why, that had to be Hack Tippett's diggings. Somehow they'd lucked it out to run right smack dab into Hack's place.

Tunis pulled up his cap part way and placed an ear against the prickly sod edges. Vaguely he could hear children crying inside, with sometimes Hack's high-pitched voice cutting through to tell them to shut up.

Tunis turned and yelled back. "Clate!"

No answer.

"Clate? You still there?"

Clate suddenly showed up beside him. "We're done, ain't we?" Clate had to shout to make himself heard.

"What?" Tunis had to shout too. It was like trying to talk with one's tongue shoved back. "Hell, no. Here. Look, feel."

"I'll be damned. That's Tippett's soddie."

"You bet."

Clate heaved a sigh of relief. "Well, from here I know my way."

"How? When you can hardly see the end of your nose?"

"Het and I live right across from here."

"You'll never make it. Best thing is for us to work ourselves around to Hack's front door and get inside where it's warm."

"What about our horses?"

"I'm gonna cut mine loose and let them run with the wind."

Clate considered this. "I think I'm gonna chance it across to Het."

"You're a goddam fool if you do."

"If I keep the wind on my left cheek, I can't help but bump into my buildings. Or the fence around them."

"Well, it's your neck."

Clate turned and vanished into the roaring wind.

Tunis unhitched his grays and then unharnessed them. He threw the harnesses into the wagon. Then he gave the horses each a whack on the butt. When they didn't move, still stood stunned by the storm, he made a jump at them, waving his arms around, yelling at them. "Get! Get! If you don't keep moving with the wind, you'll freeze. I'll find you when this blows over."

It took a moment for the grays to catch on. Then with a wet whoofing whinny they ran off, disappearing utterly, their snow-plakked gray hides fading off like a pair of dreams into the great bluster of white.

For a moment he considered making sure Clate had got off all right. Yet to take one step away from the solid wall of the sod house was to invite disaster. Clate had made his choice.

138

Tunis felt his way around to the right, around the first corner, at last found the rough wood door. He pounded on it with his fist to let those inside know someone had come, kicked piled-up snow away from the bottom of the door, then edged the door inward, and as quickly shut the door behind him. For a moment he felt blinded in the dim inside. A candle burned on the wood stove in the kitchen part. Gradually his eyes adjusted.

Hack Tippett and his wife Malena sitting near the candle had jumped to their feet. Hack quick grabbed his shotgun; Malena grabbed up their youngest baby to her breast.

"Hack?"

"Oh. It's you. My God, man, I could have shot you."

"It was either that or freeze outside."

"Malena said she thought she heard something bump against our soddie. But I said naa, it's only the wind."

"You don't mind? You can put me up for a bit?"

Hack still held the gun half-presented. "Pull up a stump and sit down by the stove here."

Tunis clasped his arms around his chest to warm his fingertips; finally removed his sheepskin-lined mittens. "Crimininty, but it's good to be safe inside. You wouldn't believe how wild it is out there." Tunis saw that Malena was heavy with child again. The baby she was holding fit snugly on top of her swollen belly.

Hack said, "I know. I saw it coming and just got the stock inside in time. Then I skedaddled back to the house here."

Malena said, "Daily a thousand dangers surround us which may strike at any time."

Tunis nodded. He had trouble hiding his disgust at the smell in the place. It was as though dirty diapers had been rinsed out in a pail of sour milk. He hoped the storm wouldn't last too long or he'd be vomiting all over the floor. Compared to Malena, his Clara was a queen for cleanliness. Again he noted how Malena drew on a man. There was an appealing pathetic air about her that invited a man to mount her.

Hack asked, "Did Clate make it back in time? I saw him leave for town right after you went by."

"Damn fool. He followed me home until we run into your house here. But instead of coming inside, he decided to work his way home across."

Hack's muskrat nose quivered up into a sneer. "Well, it don't surprise me none. He ain't quite all there. He's bound to be froze stiff by morning. And so will his horses."

"Unless he turns 'em loose."

"Where's your horses?"

"I turned 'em loose. God knows where they are by now."

"Well, take off your coat and make yourself to home."

Somehow Tunis managed to stomach the sourness in the house the rest of the afternoon. Hack for all his haphazard work habits had managed to keep a sizeable supply of wood on hand behind the stove. They were warm all through supper. The pale limp children stared at Tunis all the while. They said nothing; ate slowly with little appetite. Tunis almost wished he'd picked up the habit of smoking so he could have surrounded himself with his own atmosphere.

The storm raged outside. Roared. Every now and then they could hear bits of the north and west edges of the grass-and-mud roof disintegrate. Dropping cold pressed down outside. They could hear the walls cracking. The cracking sounds inched inward. Hack loaded in the wood, keeping the little stove red-hot around the stove lids. But the cold gained on the little trembling stove.

The children finally decided Tunis was all right. All eight crowded up around his knees, the oldest hanging over his elbow, smiling palely up at him, expecting him to be good to them. Maybe the children knew, sensed somehow, he had a little boy at home and that he liked his little boy, so would like all children.

Presently Hack showed his muskrat teeth. He was jealous. He started to give orders to the two oldest children, a boy and a girl, to button on their clothes straight, to change the diaper of the littlest one clinging to Tunis's boots, to red up the corners of the place.

Tunis tried to look hard at the tykes to discourage their attention.

At ten they ran out of wood.

Hack said, "Well, I guess now there's nothing for it but we have to go to bed to keep from freezing."

That's what they did. All the Tippetts crawled into one bed and got under several layers of blankets.

Tunis stared at the menagerie. It resembled a huge bedbug with ten heads for legs. He nearly laughed out loud. Wait until he got home and told Clara about it.

He sweat thinking about Tane and Clara.

With the stove out and the air cooling off, Tunis had to put on his heavy

139

sheepskin coat again, finally even his sheepskin mittens. He huddled near the black box stove intent upon absorbing every last bit of its expiring warmth.

When the walls began to crack even on the inside, he blew out the candle and lay down on the floor and pulled up his legs inside the sheepskin, much as a rooster on a perch might draw its legs up into its feathers.

He slept fitfully. He kept dreaming that Clara was in some dark trouble. Curiously the threats to Clara had nothing to do with snowfall, only black winds. Somehow above it all, like a wraith, little Tane floated, stark pink naked, carrying a little bow and arrow, singing a child's song. Once Tunis managed to make out the words:

> Meadowlarks,
> Meadowlarks,
> What do we do
> When the white wolf barks?

All night the blizzard roared and soozed and blasted and moaned and blustered.

When the alarm went off at seven the next morning, Hack sat up out of his end of the layer of blankets, shut the clock off, and with a defeated groan slipped back under the covers.

Tunis shivered. He straightened out his legs for a moment to get the kinks out of his thighs, then quickly pulled them back inside his sheepskin coat.

Tunis slept for a couple more hours. His nose felt parched from breathing the cold air. The children also had the sense to know it was death to get out from under the blankets. They slept soundly.

140

Around ten in the morning, Tunis awoke from one of his drifting naps to see that it had lightened up outside. He pushed back a flap from his ear and listened. Ah, the wind had died down. The storm was letting up.

He stirred. Knees cracking, back aching, the side he was lying on numb, he worked himself up to his knees, then stood up. Stiffly he stepped over to the high window. The upper right-hand pane was the only one still clear of drifted snow.

The sky was clearing off rapidly from the west. Already a bluebird color was showing all along the horizon. Rising on his toes, he saw a strange new white drifted world. He hardly recognized the hills to the southeast.

Hack reared up from his corner of the bedcovers. "You see anything of Clate or his horses out there?"

"Not a sign of 'em."

"Take a peek out of the other window and see if you can make out my woodpile. Hraa, it's cold in here."

Tunis stepped across the room. The bad smells of the day before seemed to have been frozen down. "Yeh, there's a big corner of it sticking out. I suppose you'd like for me to get you an armful."

"Well, you're up."

"Thanks."

Tunis pulled the front door inward, to find a bank of snow as high as his chin blocking the way. He found a shovel and began to push out a path.

"Close the door," Malena called out weakly.

"I will when I've got the room to turn around."

He finally found a shallow winding path to the woodpile. Loading up a big armful, he trudged back, pushed in the door, closed it behind him, and dumped the wood at the foot of the stove. He found some wrapping paper, dug a match out of the Tippett matchbox, and started the fire. Within moments he had a fire roaring in the black box stove. He held his hands over the rising warmth.

"Set the coffeepot on," Hack called muffled from under the bedclothes.

Tunis resented taking orders from Hack. Who did that mattress pounder think he was? But Tunis wanted coffee himself so he stepped over to the water pail and broke through the ice and poured some water in the speckled blue coffeepot.

"There's some coffee beans in that tin above the cabinet there. And the grinder is next to the flour bin," Malena called from her side of the bed.

Tunis growled, "For godsakes, what would you folks have done if I hadn't come along?"

Silence from the bed.

After a while the coffee was boiling and filling the room with its sweet aroma and the whole place began to crack with warmth. Gradually too the various Tippetts crawled out from under the thick bedcovers and began to move around. They reminded Tunis of chilled flies thawing out on the sunny side of the house.

After some hot coffee and hard bread, Tunis and Hack bundled up and went outside to check up on things. A huge snowdrift starting at the left edge of the sod barn had swelled up over the house, almost up to the chimney opening. The only part of Tunis's wagon showing was the spring seat; all the rest, including the groceries and harnesses, were buried under seven feet of snow.

Smoke from the chimney wafted gently upward until some fifty feet high it dispersed. It was so calm out they could hear a crow caw a mile across the river.

Hack went to look at his thermometer tacked onto a nearby post. "Holy buckets! Forty below."

"That's a drop of a hundred and twelve degrees since yesterday!" The thought made Tunis breathe faster. "We better watch each other's noses for frostbite. It can sneak up on you when it's as cold and still as this."

There seemed to be new hills where the railroad tracks ran. Looking beyond the tracks, they saw that Clate Bartle's house too was almost buried under a vast long snowdrift.

"See any sign of him?" Hack asked.

"Nope."

They started walking toward Clate's place, climbing over the hard frozen snowbanks, sliding down through the hollows. The only place they could see any railroad tracks was off to the left where a bridge spanned a dry creek.

They knocked on Bartle's front door. It was half-buried behind a snowdrift.

The door opened inward and a startled Hettie looked out at them. She looked first at Tunis, then at Hack. "Ain't Clate with you?"

Tunis shook his head.

She clutched at her throat, eyes as gray as mouse holes. "Then he's still out there somewhere."

Tunis became sick to his stomach. He should have forced Clate to come with him into Hack's house. "We better start looking."

They looked beyond Clate's horse shelter, to either side; found no trace of him. Next they looked in the little grove of cottonwoods in the draw farther on. Still no sign of him or his horses.

They were plunging through a particularly deep drift on the way back to Clate's house when Tunis noticed something. On the other side of some gooseberry bushes, in what looked like another snow-filled draw, Tunis saw movement. "Look."

They crawled on their knees over a loose snowbank and brushed through the gooseberry bushes. There was Beaut, the old bay mare, with her wise lips and popped eyes, still alive and trying to free herself from being tied to her partner hidden in the snow. Tunis also spotted a man's arm sticking up out of the snow and holding on to the cross line to Beaut.

Hack's nose quivered. "There he is."

"Yeh."

Quickly they dug down. They found Clate alive, in an air cell under the crust of the drift, pale moustache filled with snow.

"You must have Indian blood in you," Tunis said.

Clate looked up at Tunis. For once his light blue eyes didn't shy off. "How so?"

"Crawl into a snowbank when it storms. And if possible with an animal."

"Yeh. And if Beaut would have only stood still, I would have made it."

"Well, you're here, ain't you?"

"Help me out of this once."

Tunis and Hack reached down and grabbed Clate by the shoulders and heaved him up out of his snow prison. It was instantly apparent that Clate was frozen from the knees down. His legs were doubled under him and he couldn't bend them.

"God, Clate."

142

"Yeh. That goddam Beaut. But she knew it was either her or me, and she kept wiggling to stay alive."

"Is the other horse dead?"

"She quit breathin' during the night sometime."

Tunis unsnapped the cross lines and then the tugs to free Beaut. Clate's democrat was completely buried. Tunis reached down into the snow and felt the other bay's chest. It was stone stiff. Tunis tied up Beaut's tugs and threw the lines over her hames and then gave her a whack on the butt. Beaut whinnied, reared a little, then stiffly galloped toward her animal shelter.

Clate asked, "Did your grays make it?"

Tunis said, "I hope so. They're probably miles southeast of here somewhere." Tunis looked at Hack. "We better carry him to the house."

Clate was as heavy as an ash log. The three of them kept breaking through the crust of the snow. Each time Clate's stiff legs went in bent and came out bent. Each time he looked down at his legs and groaned.

Hettie saw them coming. Quickly she shoveled out a path. She helped them into the house, holding the door open and then pulling up a chair to the red-hot range. Once she had Clate sitting down, Hettie scrabbled at his pants, trying to take them off. She got them and his underwear down over his knees but couldn't remove his leather boots. She couldn't bend his ankle. Six inches above his knees and on down his legs were frosty white. They resembled cured bacon. Hettie became frantic. "Get me a pan of snow. We've got to rub the frost out of them."

Clate said, "First get that jug I put under our bed."

Hettie hurried to get it.

Tunis raised an eyebrow. Our bed? And they were brother and sister?

Clate removed the wooden stopper from the brown jug, sniffed the contents, took a mouthful. He coughed. The contents of the jug were so strong tears filled his eyes. Then he swallowed, making a throat-clearing sound as though he'd been burned inside. He took another slug and then set the jug down. "Ah, that's better."

"Whiskey?" Tunis wondered. Then he picked up the jug and had himself a sniff too. "Criminy, man, this is straight alcohol." Clate looked down at his crotch. "Well, at least I didn't freeze my tassel."

Hettie rolled her eyeholes away from glancing at where Clate was looking. "We've got to get the doctor, not?"

"You bet." Tunis gave Hack a firm look. "You're elected. You get him."

"Why me?" Hack squealed.

"I don't know your horses. Get out your best horse and ride into town and find Doc."

"I can't leave my wife and kids alone that long."

"I'm doing it. What do you think my wife's thinkin' all this time? And my grays gone too?"

Hack still hesitated.

"Besides, Hack, you owe me a favor. Remember that time when we first met? In another snowstorm?"

"That's right." Hack lowered his head and left.

Tunis got a pan of snow from outside and began rubbing Clate's legs with it, up and down. He rubbed and rubbed. "I hope our Hack don't weasel out on us," he muttered to Hettie. He rubbed gently with the full palm of his hand. Where the flesh wasn't frozen it turned a deep pink, then slowly reddened. Where it was frozen it stayed as pale as the white-painted leg of the kitchen table.

143

"I'll have another shot," Clate said after a while.

"But you'll get drunk," Hettie said.

"What's the difference now? I'm probably a dead duck anyway."

Hettie swung her eyeholes up to the ceiling; then pitched in and helped rub snow, she on one leg and Tunis on the other.

"I said, I'd like another shot," Clate remarked after a minute had gone by.

"Yes, Clate, dear." Hettie handed him the brown jug.

Clate helped himself to four long swallows. He didn't cough or flinch this time. His breath began to stink like a rotted cucumber.

An hour later they heard horses breaking through the crusts of the snowbanks outside. In a moment the slim figure of Dr. Wallance with his little black satchel slipped in through the doorway, Hack following him.

Dr. Wallance removed his sealskin cap, buckle boots, gray gloves, and black overcoat. Tunis had seen Doc uptown several times and had always liked his looks. There was a fine fastidious air about him, of neatness and precision, no nonsense. His eyes were the color of deep blue snow; they were open and warm in greeting, and narrowed and unblinking in examination. He had long slender but strong fingers. He wore the black suit of a lord, with black bow tie and white shirt.

One glance at Clate and Dr. Wallance knew what was up. He studied to himself. It appeared he was trying to find the right words to break some bad news gently.

Hettie saw the look. "We've been rubbing him good with snow, doctor."

"Hmm." Dr. Wallance leaned down and touched the frozen portion of Clate's legs, finally pressed firmly down on the iron-hard skin and muscle. The frozen portion didn't give. "The rubbing is probably all right. But not the snow. The snow only makes sure you're keeping it frozen. Warm water is much, much better."

Hettie pointed at the steaming kettle of water on the stove. "I'll quick get a pan of that."

"Wait. Let me think." Dr. Wallance pursed his elegant lips. "Couple of years ago I lost Jack Little because I didn't have the courage to do what I knew should have been done."

"What was that, doctor?"

"I let him thaw out first, thinking that I could amputate him then if it became necessary. Ten days later he had gangrene so bad I couldn't save him."

Hettie reeled. "You've got to save him, doctor. He's all I got in this world. We have no other relation."

Hack shivered. What he'd just heard was too much for him. "I've got to get back to wife and kids. Tunis, you know they need more wood right away."

Dr. Wallance placed his slim hand on Hack's shoulder. "No. You stay. We need you."

"What for?" Hack squealed.

Clate said, "What have you got in mind, Doc?"

"Well, no doctor has ever been successful in amputating a limb. At least not in this country. But I think I know why. They wait too long. A thawed-out frozen limb has no circulation. So gangrene is bound to set in. Now, if we were to amputate it right away, we'd have a chance. Also, having it frozen like this, it'd serve as an anaesthetic."

"Oh," Clate said.

"You won't feel a thing."

Hack backed a step. "You mean . . . you're going to saw it off where it's frozen?"

Dr. Wallance pursed his lips again. "No, an inch from where it's frozen. There won't be any feeling there either. And the blood will be just chilled enough not to flow much."

Hack backed another step. "I'm going home. I can't stand blood." He snarped around at Tunis. "You know I can't. Your Clara had to midwife my Malena once when Doc here had gone to Sioux City." He whirled and bungled out through the door, slamming it after him. They heard him hop aboard his horse and go thrashing off through the crusted snow.

Silence.

Dr. Wallance looked at Hettie. "Well, it looks like you're going to have to help Mr. Freyling here hold your husband down."

"He's my brother. I'll do it."

Dr. Wallance turned his iceberg eyes on Clate. "I think I can save your life if I amputate now. It's up to you."

"You're sure, Doc? These are my legs, you know."

"It isn't even a gambling matter, Clate."

Clate sucked a long slow breath. He threw Hettie a private look. "Doc, I've got a lot to live for. Let's cut 'em off."

Dr. Wallance smiled down at him.

Clate said, "Begin, Doc."

Tunis was suddenly full of admiration for his strange neighbor.

Dr. Wallance's eyes narrowed to thin icicles. "All right. Hettie, do you have any aprons or smocks? We're going to need them. Because blood is going to fly."

"Clate has a canvas smock for when he makes sausages. And I've got a couple of gingham aprons."

"Get 'em."

Soon Dr. Wallance, having removed his jacket and vest, was dressed in the heavy tan canvas smock. Tunis and Hettie each put on an apron.

They hoisted Clate onto the kitchen table. Dr. Wallance opened his black bag and laid out various items on a nearby chair: lancet, clamps, hacksaw, cauter. Dr. Wallance lifted a stove lid and slipped the point of the cauter into the hot coals.

Clate blinked at the sight of the cauter. "Doc, can I have another shot out of that brown jug?"

"As much as you want."

"What little I had before don't seem to have taken hold." Clate drank deeply from the jug. He wiped his lips with his sleeve. "All right, Doc, commence."

"Sorry I don't have any chloroform for you, Clate. I used my last bottle to set a bone."

It did turn out bloody. Dr. Wallance cut and cauterized as he went down into the legs. But the big blood vessels weren't so easily stemmed. Sometimes the cauter wasn't hot enough and it had to be put back into the hot coals, while the blood continued to spurt. When Dr. Wallance used the clamps to pinch off a thick vessel, the clamps gradually slipped off. It was slow work. Clate lay groaning, jaws gritted together in awful mortal stress.

Once Clate broke out singing a hymn:

> "God moves in a mysterious way
> His wonders to perform:
> He plants his footsteps in the sea,
> And rides upon the storm.
>
> "Behind a frowning providence
> God hides a smiling face.
> The bud may have a bitter taste,
> But sweet will be the grace."

To make sure flesh and skin would cover the severed bone, Dr. Wallance had to strip back the flesh. It was like pulling back a massive foreskin to expose the glans. The sawing went slowly.

"Damnation, Clate, but you've got hard bones. Harder than the bones of a workhorse."

Clate managed a smile at Hettie. "Told you the Lord meant for me to be a beast of burden and not a high monkey-monk."

Dr. Wallance finally finished sewing Clate up with silk thread. Dr. Wallance's smock ran with both dark blood and fresh blood. The aprons of Tunis and Hettie ran with blood too. And the kitchen table was awash with crimson.

Clate lay breathing fast on the kitchen table. It was as though he'd just had a long hard run. "What are we gonna do with them legs, Doc?"

"Bury them."

"With the ground frozen like it is?"

"Then you can put 'em in a snowbank until spring."

"Naw. The wolves'll smell them there."

Hettie too had been breathing hard. "I can axe a hole in the ground."

"Do that then."

Hettie said, "What about your leather boots, Clate?"

Clate turned on his side a little to look at his severed legs. "I won't have any use for them any more. So bury them with the legs."

Hettie fell on her brother's neck and kissed him. "My darling brother. What will we do now?"

Clate's lips writhed back into his cheeks. "There's nothing for it now, I guess, but for me to do the house work and for you to do the yard and field work."

"Oh, Clate."

Dr. Wallance and Tunis stood back, wordless for the moment.

Finally Hettie looked at Dr. Wallance. "But he'll live now?"

"Well, we can at least thank heaven for small favors."

Afterward, Tunis and Dr. Wallance stood for a moment together outside. They looked up at the sky, then at the blue horizons around, then at Dr. Wallance's bay riding horse.

Dr. Wallance smiled a pinched smile. "That's got to be the first time any physician ever amputated legs in quite that manner. While they were still frozen. If Clate survives, other doctors will follow suit."

Tunis frowned. Until then he hadn't expected to see vanity in Dr. Wallance.

Dr. Wallance said, "You all right, Freyling?"

"Yes."

146

"Where's your horses?"

"To hell and gone. I unhitched them yesterday and let them run with the wind."

"Then you're gonna walk it home."

Tunis nodded.

"Watch your nose. You're walking into the wind."

"I know."

Tunis started out over the snow, taking his bearings from the row of high hills on the right and a tall gaunt river cottonwood on the left.

When he arrived on the yard, Clara was looking at him through the bay window. She hurried to open the door and threw her arms around him. The noon sun held them in its golden-snow ambience.

"Sorry to be a little late," he said. "Tain't good for the cows to skip their milking."

"I milked them this morning."

"How'd you manage that with the baby tyke in the house?"

"I took him with me. He loves to watch the chickens chatter up on their roosts."

"Then everything's all right here?"

"Yes. But how are you? Where's the horses?"

"Gone galley-west somewhere." He lifted her up and swung her around. "No, that's not right. They drifted east with the wind. They'll be all right."

"Won't they be lost?"

"Tomorrow morning early I'm going looking for them." Tunis heard something fall to the floor in the house, a tin of some kind with fluid in it. "Tane?"

"Goodness," Clara exclaimed. "I hope that little dickens ain't pulled the tea-kettle off the stove."

Both ran into the kitchen.

It wasn't the teakettle. Blond little Tane had tried to help himself to a dipper of water from the pail under the spout of the cistern pump. He looked with baby astonishment at the splash of water he'd made on the floor.

Tunis rushed forward and picked the boy up and hugged him. "Boy, am I glad to see you alive."

"What happened, husband?"

Tunis told how he and Clate got caught out in the storm on their way home; told about his smelly night in the Tippett household; finally, reluctantly, with halting words, told of the awful fate of Clate and his legs.

"What a strange thing to happen to that family."

Tunis went outside to check the yard. Clara with a grain shovel had neatly chopped out a path to their privy. She had also worked out a route to the barn around the various shoulder-high snowdrifts on their yard. All the animals seemed content to be inside.

An hour latter, as the sun sank in an utterly clear windless sky, Clara had a dinner ready for him: venison, potatoes, corn bread, coffee. They ate with happy smacking sounds.

While Clara washed the dishes and swept the kitchen, Tunis trudged in the dark along Clara's path to the barn and milked the cows. He also fed the cows and horses hay and the chickens and hogs some grain. Barn secure, he carried two buckets of milk back to the house. Clara helped him pour the milk into settling pans so cream could rise to the top.

147

After they'd been in bed awhile, after making love, Clara mused aloud in the dark. "Wonder what kind of life those two have together. They never go out, I hear."

"Who?" Tunis murmured almost asleep.

"That Clate and Hettie. Something unholy there." Clara sighed. "Whatever it is, we don't ever want it here."

Tunis opened an eye in the dark. What mysterious thoughts was his sweet chunk of a wife having now? He decided not to mention Clate's slip of the tongue about "our bed."

The next morning very early, Tunis saddled Gypsy and set out over the hills to the east. Draped over the horn of his saddle were two halters along with two long lead ropes.

He climbed the first hogback just as the sun came glancing across the snow world in streaks of gold. He had to shield his eyes against the glittering dawn. Looking under a mittened hand, he made out what looked like a thick clump of cottonwood saplings in a turn of the Little Rock River some five miles away. If the grays had survived it would be in that clump.

Touching Gypsy under the flanks with his boots, he started down the long sliding sweep of land, working his way around occasional snowdrifts. So far no one had settled on the sloping land. Nearer the river he could make out several sod shanties from the way the huge drifts had piled up behind them.

When he reached the river, he was surprised to see how high the bank was.

Some ways farther upriver and on the other side of it, a considerable yellow cliff rose off the turning stream. Another clump of growth stuck out of the snow beneath the cliff. Willows. If he didn't find the grays in the sapling cottonwoods, he'd check that next.

There wasn't a sound out except the unching of Gyp's hooves in the hard snow. No wind. Not a bird. Usually even in the most intense cold a crow could be heard cawing somewhere. But not that morning.

He called down toward the thicket of sapling cottonwoods on the other side of the river. "Sue? Sal? Huh, girls! Hi! Hup!"

Nothing. No movement or whinny.

He spotted some fresh tracks going into the cottonwoods. From where he sat he could see they were the tracks of a puma. In fact, two sets of tracks, one larger than the other. It meant a papa and a mama puma were working the brush. If the grays were in the brush they'd be standing as still as graven stones. Damn. He hadn't thought to take his gun with him.

He checked the puma tracks again. They came in from the northwest, almost the same route he'd taken. Could they have come from the wasteland in the northwest corner of his own land? Most likely. There wasn't much other cover around.

Gypsy raised his head. His roan ears shot forward, flopped back, shot forward again.

"So you know they're in there too, huh?"

Gypsy whinnied; then fluttered his nostrils.

There was an answering whinny for a moment; then it was shut off.

"Get!" Tunis dug his heels into Gypsy's underbelly. "Maybe we can roust 'em out of there before the big cats get 'em."

They galloped around off the high bank; plunged through the deep snow across the frozen river; then entered the edge of the thick cottonwood saplings. Branches whipped against horse and man.

"Get outa there!" Tunis roared.

There was an answering whinny, then another, and the next second Sue and Sal burst out of the brush and deep snow, casting up shawls of white. They came straight for Tunis and Gypsy, breasting through the drifts, heads raised high, whickering low grunts of happiness to see them.

"So you two birds did make it after all."

Tunis soon had them haltered. He tied their lead ropes to the horn of his saddle. Seeking out the shallow snow and barren spots, he took a roundabout route out of the brush and across the river and then back up toward the height of land. He'd been right that they could take care of themselves in a storm provided they were free of harness and wagon.

They were halfway back up on the rise when behind them an unearthly wawl rose. It was piercing; it hurt the ear. In a moment a second wawl rose with it, an octave higher. Cats all right. And they were sad that he'd robbed them of a meal. Another half hour and he would have been too late.

Tunis shook his head. Suppose those two cats had found Clate half-frozen in the snow. They would have chewed him off down to the frozen part.

Tunis decided not to tell Clara about the two cats. Someday he'd have to go into his wasteland and shoot them before they had kittens.

Two days later he walked the grays over to Hack Tippett's place and dug out his wagon from the snowbank. He rode home under a melting sun.

Four days later the Bonnie Omaha with a huge gleaming snowplow up front came bucking up from Bonnie to blast through the snowbanks lying across the tracks. Sometimes the drifts were so deep the engineer and his boys had to back up a quarter of a mile and then start forward again to take a fresh whack at them. Occasionally the snowplow jumped the track or got stuck; then men would clamber up front and scoop the plow and engine free. It was hard work in bitter cold weather. Men were moving white mountains.

In April one night just after they'd climbed into bed, Clara with a little laugh had an announcement. "Husband, maybe by the time the snow flies in November, we'll have a daughter to celebrate."

"Oh. Are you sure?"

"I've missed two months now."

He lay silent for a while. Tane had fallen asleep in his cradle at the foot of their bed. A soft wind outside touched the corners of the house lovingly. "How can you tell it's going to be a girl?"

"Just watch."

She first said no to him in August. It was hot. When he persisted, she told him she had to think of the coming baby.

In November, on the fourth, when Tunis came into the house for a cup of tea at five, before milking, he smelled it—a birthing smell, the broken bag of waters. Whether in the barn or the house, it was unmistakable: like the extract of freshly cut rhubarb.

He rushed into the bedroom in back. "Clara?"

Clara, a bit gaunt, smiled up from her pillow. "Yes, husband?" Then she smiled down at what at first resembled a rubber doll's face, a bit red and raw, little pink lips working in a soft sucking motion as if just finished suckling the mother. A filmy trickle of milk ran out of the corner of its pure mouth. Clara quickly wiped it up with a corner of the pink blanket.

149

"You're all right, wife?"

"Couldn't be fitter, husband."

"That fast!"

"Yes. I was pounding the bread dough in the kitchen. You know how I like to lift the lump of dough up to the ceiling and then let it drop in the breadpan? Well, on one of those drops, I had the feeling that the bottom had dropped out of the bread pan. But come to look, I found out my own bottom had about dropped out. So I quick ran in here and had her."

Tunis knelt by the bed. He smiled down at the little thing. "A pink blanket?"

"It's a girl all right. Like we wanted."

"Everything all right?"

"You can empty it out of the pot, husband."

Later, after milking, and after making supper for himself and Clara and feeding the boy Tane, he asked, "Have you thought what you might name the baby?"

"Thea."

"Thea Freyling. Hmm. Why Thea?"

"We can use a healer in our family."

"Is that what it means?"

Little Tane had been watching them with wide blue wondering eyes. He lifted a chubby finger and pointed at the baby. "Tea? Tea?"

Clara laughed. "Yes, little son. A medicinal Thea."

Tunis looked at his children, first his son, then his daughter. Far back, almost as if he were looking at them from the back of a cave, he got to wondering if either of them had inherited his one great fault: a hot, even murderous, temper.

And once again, for more than a year, Clara denied Tunis his bed rights.

BOOK TWO

16. Betweentimes

So it went the next dozen years. By the end of the year 1900 they had six more children. Dirk was born on August 7, 1890; Tressa on December 5, 1892; Rolf on October 21, 1894; Ana on November 11, 1896; Mallie on July 6, 1898; and Geoffrey on Christmas Day, December 25, 1900. All of them were born in the same bedroom and all of them without the aid of Dr. Wallance. By the time Tunis and Clara thought of calling the good doctor, it was already too late. Clara had her babies easy.

Tunis named Dirk and Tressa after his foster parents and Mallie after a girl he'd dreamed about one night. Clara named Rolf after a distant hero relative on her mother's side, Ana after the first named woman before Eden times, and Geoffrey after Chaucer and because it went well with their family name of Freyling.

With one exception all bore a strong family resemblance, brow and chin, a touch of rust in the hair.

The exception was Rolf. The moment he was born, Clara knew she had an odd one in him. He had black hair, like the hair of a wild horse, which bristled straight up. No amount of combing could make it lie down. His hair looked much like the bristle brush it was groomed with. He had a low receding forehead, thick jutting brows, a bull neck, and a receding chin. But his body was perfect and it had the delicate skin of a girl.

Tunis was as puzzled as Clara about the boy. "He looks like a throwback of some kind. One of our great-great-grandparents must of mated with a Neanderthal."

"Tunis!"

"It happens in the animal world, you know. Every now and then a mare will throw a gray colt with stripes like a zebra."

"For goodness sakes, husband, don't say that out loud in front of the other children or they'll start calling him Zebe."

"I won't mention it again. We're just going to have to live with it. And hope that he learns to live with it too."

"He will. I'll see to that."

"How are you going to do that?"

"By teaching the other children never to pick on him. They're going to learn to accept him as though there's nothing different about him."

"Good luck. If we notice it they sure as God will."

"I'll be right there to thwack 'em. But you've got to help."

Dirk soon showed winning ways with the smile of a confident lover. He almost always got his way with a witty remark and a boy's wet kiss. Tressa was born with a soft heart and was perfectly willing to share her cake with Dirk and to let the other kids play with her favorite doll. Ana had a way of storming around when she couldn't get her way, whacking her brothers and sisters over the head with her rag doll and screaming until they gave in. Mallie was born with thickish lips, a pudendum like an apricot, and a forgiving nature. And Geoffrey, within a year after he was born, began to look like a little gentleman.

All the children were baptized by Father Garlington in the Episcopal church. Clara was determined that their children got the right start. Later on when they became older, Clara thought, she could talk them into becoming confirmed. The baptisms took place in the summer. They caught the special Sunday train that carried the Bonnie baseball team to Whitebone. The train always left early in the morning so the players could get in a full game. This gave the Freylings time to see Father Garlington. Riding with baseball players up and back queered the Freylings forever on sports. The baseball players were mostly ruffians; they swore like corporals, told utterly filthy stories, and bragged like General George Armstrong Custer.

Tane meanwhile grew up broad-shouldered, heavily muscled, with a gleaming blond complexion and pink-tinted gold hair. At six he was milking his first cow and at eight was driving his first pair of horses. It was Tane who helped his father break the last of the wild prairie, so that out of 640 acres the Freylings ultimately had 450 under cultivation.

Thea grew up slender. She was often lost in herself. There was an air of a goddess about her. She knew very soon what was the proper behavior for a lady.

Both Tane and Thea started school a mile to the northeast. They walked along the Bonnie Omaha tracks more often than they traipsed down the mud road paralleling the tracks.

154

A man named Adam Erdman and wife Eveling homesteaded the section to the northeast of the Freylings with the set purpose of making it an orphanage for lost boys from the big cities. Both Adam and Eveling had been born and raised in Saint Paul in a Christian family that had long been interested in doing social work in the slums. Adam had finally got around to the idea that outdoor life far from the fleshpots of the city was the only solution for young malcontents and potential criminals. Adam and Eveling called their place the Siouxland Home. They built small cabins for their boys. They built barns for the cattle and horses and hogs and chickens, and only at the last built themselves a brick house. They became especially dedicated to saving orphans when it became apparent after awhile that Eveling would never have children.

Some of their orphans, five of them, were young enough to attend the same country school with Tane and Thea. The orphans ranged in age from seven to fourteen. The instinct to form gangs was deep in them.

The teacher, Velda Fikes, a woman of twenty-five, single, tall, was a gracious disciplinarian. All the kids liked her right away. They knew they'd get a fair shake from her at the same time that they knew she would tolerate no nonsense. There were to be no teacher's pets or hates. She had long blond hair, wide gray ox eyes, and a large mouth. What made her teaching effective was that she was an actress of sorts. She was forever dramatizing the lessons. She acted out the parts of Hugh Glass and the grizzly bear, Ichabod Crane and the headless horseman, Carrie Nation and her axe, Paul Revere and his midnight ride. She was particularly vivid in her presentation of how the biblical Jael hammered a nail into Sisera's head, fixing the head to the ground. But best of all was her powerful rendition of the crucifixion of Christ.

During recess hours the oldest boy from the orphanage, Jud Artus, began to wonder how it might have felt to have nails driven through one's hands and feet, how it felt to hang from those nails on a cross. And what did one do if one had to pee. And if the one nailed to the cross would truly see God at last. And was it true that after one died on the cross, one would rise on the third day and fly straight to heaven to sit on the right hand of God, ready to judge the quick and the dead?

One morning Jud Artus came to school with a hammer and a handful of ten-penny nails and a spade. The four boys with him carried two long two-by-fours. They were careful to stow it all behind the woodshed out of sight of teacher Fikes. The five orphanage boys were especially quiet all forenoon long.

Miss Fikes caught their mood soon enough. The five boys were up to something. She wondered what it might be. The two blond Freyling children, Tane and Thea, she read like they might be primer books. But not dark Jud Artus with his black sometimes obsessed eyes.

During the noon hour she usually ate alone at her desk from her lunch bucket as she corrected papers, while the children scattered over the acre of school ground to eat their sandwiches. As long as she heard talk and laughter coming through the open windows she knew everything was all right.

That noon it wasn't long before she became aware of a strange silence outside. Worried that it might have something to do with Thea, the only girl in school, Miss Fikes decided to have a look. What she found stunned her.

At the stroke of twelve the five orphans had quickly gobbled down their sandwiches, urging Tane to do the same. They had something for him to do later on, they said, something that would make him famous not only in America but in heaven as well. Jud could be very persuasive, especially when he took up a pinch of flesh just above one's elbow and twisted it.

155

While Jud held Tane close, the other four boys hammered the two two-by-fours into a crude cross. Taking a spade they dug a hole in the tough prairie sod some two feet deep. They were careful to do the hammering and digging behind the woodshed.

When Jud laid Tane on the cross and asked each of the four boys to hold down one of Tane's limbs, Tane finally got the idea. "Well, you're not going to nail me to the cross."

"Wal, they did Jesus."

"But he was God and he probably didn't feel the nails going in."

"But then this won't be a real crucifixion."

"Can't you tie me on with ropes?"

"We ain't got ropes. It won't hurt all that much."

"But I'll bleed. And my ma won't like that. Getting blood all over my overalls."

"But it won't make all that much difference. Because by that time you'll be up in heaven."

Tane looked up at the blue sky with his blue eyes. "I will?"

"Sure. That's where Jesus went. He's up there now waiting for you."

Tane didn't like it. He tried to wrench himself free of Jud's pinching grip.

Thea spoke up. She'd been sitting in the deep grass watching those crazy boys from the orphanage. "You leave my brother alone or I'll go tell Teacher."

Jud stood very still for a moment. His eyes narrowed to glittering slits. "If you don't shut up, we'll crucify you next." When Thea made a move as though to get to her feet, he added, "You stay sittin'. And if you don't like to look and watch your brother ascend to heaven, then turn around and look at the girl's outhouse."

Thea refused to turn around. She sat thickening with child hate.

Jud looked down at Tane. "Jesus wasn't a sissy, so you better not be one either. Or God won't want you in heaven. Buley, hold his right hand open for me." Jud took up the hammer and a tenpenny nail and knelt beside Tane. He held the point of the square-headed nail in the exact center of the palm of Tane's right hand. He flicked a look at Tane, then made a quick chopping swing of the hammer and drove the nail through Tane's palm and down an inch into the wooden cross. While Tane looked astounded at his transfixed hand, Jud swung again, driving the nail deeper into the wood.

Despite the four heavier boys holding him down, Tane rolled over on his right side and stared at his hand. His mouth opened, set to scream.

"God don't like sissies, bo!"

Tane began to struggle, careful not to move his right hand, kicking with his feet and striving with his left hand. "You're not putting any more nails into me, you Judas Iscariot!"

Jud next tried to drive a nail through Tane's left palm, but Tane fought so hard, and wiggled so much, Jud couldn't get in a good swing at the nail. "God's watching you and he ain't likin' it atall."

Thea got up from the grass and began to pound Jud on his back. Silently. Furiously.

Jud reconsidered. "Wal, Tane, maybe we can crucify the rest of you just using our belts. But I hardly think God'll set you at his right hand. He'll probably just barely let you in through the pearly gates."

"I don't care. My pa needs me to get the cows and my ma needs me to get the eggs."

Thea said, "But, Tane, I get the eggs at home."

Tane said, "Well, I help you find the hard ones. In the weeds along the yard fence."

Jud snapped, "Buley, you and Flop and Rance, take off your belts. We gotta crucify him yet today. The Lord has spoken."

The fourth boy, Bruni, protested. "How come you don't want my belt?"

"Because you ain't wearin' one. You lost it in the haymow last Sattidy when we was playin' Revolutionary War."

"Oh. That's right."

"Tie him down, boys."

Tane was soon tied securely to the cross.

Thea looked down at Tane's nailed-down right hand. "Don't it hurt awful?"

Jud pushed her to one side. "Get out of here. Can't you see we're awful busy crucifying? All right, Buley, Bruni, help me lift him up. That's it. Now set the bottom end of the cross down in the hole. Good. Flop, quick grab the shobel there and fill in the hole while we hold him straight up. Rance, you stomp down the dirt. Hard. So the cross won't tip."

It was at that point that Velda Fikes stepped around the corner of the woodshed. "For heaven's sake! What are you children doing?"

Jud fixed his eyes steadily on Miss Fikes. "We're playin' crucifixion."

Miss Fikes clutched her breasts. "Gracious!"

"Stand back, teacher. In a minute he's gonna ascend and if you stand too close you won't be able to watch him go all the way up."

Miss Fikes slowly shook her head. "Ascend? What you kids won't think of next!" She looked down at Thea. "Why didn't you come and tell me?"

"I didn't want to be a snitch and a tattletale."

Miss Fikes spotted some blood running out of the palm of Tane's right hand. "What? You actually . . . oh, Tane boy, what did they do to you!"

Jud stood back. "Well, Teach, this ain't a perfect crucifixion, you know. Because he wouldn't let us, the sissy. So he didn't bleed as much as Jesus."

"As much as . . . ! Oh, dear!" With one hand Miss Fikes held her ample breasts and with her other hand she held her forehead. Her gray eyes seemed to circle in their sockets like onions rolling in boiling water. Not a single course in teacher's college had prepared her for what she was looking at. "Jud, you lower that cross! Right now!"

Reluctantly, Jud threw his hammer in the grass and with his buddies helping lifted the cross out of the hole and lowered it to the ground.

"Now untie him!"

Jud loosened the belts holding down Tane's left arm and his two ankles.

A gushing sigh escaped Miss Fikes. "Now, how are we going to get that nail out?" She picked up the hammer and looked to see how she might extract the nail with it. Gingerly she hooked the claw of the hammer under the square head of the nail. She saw right away she had no leverage with which she might pry up the nail. "Oh, dear, look what you've done, Jud." Finally, in a frenzy, she took hold of the wooden handle of the hammer with both hands and, pinning down the right arm of the cross with straddled feet, wrenched the hammer straight up. There was so much anger in her that her back and arm muscles swelled with power. With a screaking noise the nail came out of the wood, and the hand came up with the nail.

"Ouch," Tane said.

"So sorry, Tane, darling boy." Miss Fikes stared down at the nail. "But now, how do we get the nail out of your hand?"

Tane's face screwed up. "Let's unhook the hammer first." Gently he freed the nail from the claw of the hammer. Then he got to his feet.

Everybody looked at the dull blue nail protruding through Tane's right hand.

Thea said, "We better call Dr. Wallance."

Tane said, "I'm going home. My pa will know how to get it out." Tane turned and picked up his dinner bucket and started for the gate by the road.

"Wait!" Miss Fikes cried after him. "Do you think you can walk all the way home without fainting?"

"Sure," Tane said sturdily. "If I don't look at it. Thea, get your bucket and let's go home."

Miss Fikes watched them go, a hand to her throat.

Jud and his orphan cronies sagged back on one leg, disgusted that their game had been spoiled.

Miss Fikes collected her wits. She whirled on Jud. "Mister Jud Artus, for you and your friends, school is out for the day. And I want you to go directly home and tell Mr. Erdman that I want to see him immediately. Now, no ducking into the cornfield somewhere until four o'clock with you pretending then you've just come home from school, you hear? Because I'm going to stay here in the schoolhouse, seated at my desk, until Mr. Erdman shows up. All night, if I have to. And if he does not show up by morning, then I'm catching the Bonnie Omaha"—she pointed at the nearby tracks just east of the school yard—"to Rock Falls to see the sheriff."

Jud stared at Miss Fikes with city impudence. "Shucks, Teacher, we were just playing. 'Cause the next game we was gonna play was to cast Satan into hell."

"Never mind. Just hustle home. Right now."

When Tane and Thea arrived on the yard a half hour later, Tunis was pitching off a load of alfalfa into the barn, with Clara pushing back the hay inside the haymow. The other children were playing in a sandpile in the shade of a scrawny ash tree south of the house.

Little Dirk was the first to see the nail protruding from Tane's hand. "Hey, you look like they tried to crucify you."

"You might say that," Tane said.

"That ain't funny," Thea said.

Tane walked straight for Tunis. "Pa, can you pull this nail out for me?"

Tunis stared down from the half-empty hayrack. "What the hell . . . ?"

Clara saw it too. She leaped out the side door of the haymow onto the load of hay, then slid off to the ground and ran to Tane. Gently she picked up the boy's impaled hand.

"It don't hurt much, Ma," Tane said. "It's just that I won't be able to milk my cow."

Tunis dropped from the load of hay and stomped over. "How in Christ's name did that happen?"

"Be careful we don't blaspheme now," Clara warned.

158 Tane stared down at his hand a little cross-eyed. Some blood had dried to black along the bottom of his wrist. "It don't hurt much, Pa."

Thea said it. "Those orphanage boys tried to crucify him. Then teacher came and caught them."

"Crucify him! For Christ's sake. What the devil kind of kids have they got there over at the orphanage?"

Clara said, "Let's not get excited now. And please, watch the language." She held Tane's hand tenderly. The tiny little wrinkles that had begun to show with age under her eyes deepened. "Tell us about it."

Tane and Thea took turns reporting what had happened.

Tane said, "Really, Pa, it don't hurt much. It's so funny. Can you please pull it out for me?"

Tunis quivered with outrage. "Sure, son. Come with me to the house."

Tunis picked up a pincers from the toolshed on the way to the kitchen. "Clara, do we still have some brandy in the house?"

"You're not going to give the boy a drink?"

"You bet. And I'm also going to use it to purify the wound."

Clara with some reluctance dug out a dark bottle of apricot brandy.

Tunis poured an inch of the tan brandy in a glass and handed it to Tane. "It's gonna bite. So drink it all in one swallow."

Tane looked in the glass, then with his left hand lifted it to his lips and drank it down. He didn't cough. It was done in a manly way.

"Good boy." Tunis next set the boy in a chair across the corner from his own swivel chair, where the light was the brightest coming in through the west kitchen window. He asked Clara to hold the boy's hand. She placed her one hand firmly around the fingers and the other hand tight across the wrist, just high enough off the table so the point of the nail wasn't touching the yellow tablecloth. Gently with the pincers Tunis took hold of the nail. Then, with a tight grim smile, he flicked a look at the window and said, "Hey! there goes a deer." When both Tane and Clara, startled, looked out of the window, Tunis suddenly jerked the pincers upward—and out came the square nail.

"Ow!"

All three stared at the puckered hole. Then Tunis took up Tane's hand and poured a spurt of brandy into the wound. Some of the brandy oozed through the hole.

Clara said, "We should get it to bleed. One's own blood purifies it best."

Tunis said, "How are we going to get the blood to run? When that kid punched that nail through there, he pinched off all the little veins and arteries."

Clara squeezed around the edges of the wound trying to get the blood to flow.

"Ow! That hurts, Ma."

Tunis said, "But we got to get the blood to run, boy."

Tane hid his hand behind his back.

Tunis said, "Well, maybe the brandy will have done the trick, Clara."

Clara got some bandages from her ragbag, pieces of a white sheet torn in streamers, and bound up the boy's hand carefully.

"Now I won't be able to milk Switcher, Pa."

"We won't worry about that, boy. Let's just hope that wound heals over good." Tunis's jaw set out. "Now to find out what the devil went on at that school." Tunis stood up and headed for the door.

159

"Wait," Clara said. "Nothing wild now, please."

"I was thinking of riding Gypsy over, but he's getting too old. So instead I'll walk there. By the time I arrive I should be pretty well cooled off."

But he wasn't. If anything, when he stalked into the white country schoolhouse, he was even more outraged. "Miss Fikes?"

Miss Fikes looked up with her wide gray eyes. "Oh, Mr. Freyling. I was expecting Mr. Erdman."

Tunis walked up to her desk and glared down at her. "That my boy should be crucified! My boy!"

"I know, Mr. Freyling. I'm sorry it happened. Maybe I should have been out there on the school grounds watching them during noon hour. But they've all been so well behaved until just now that I didn't think—"

"That my boy should be crucified by some shitty city kids!"

"I can well understand your being upset—"

The door opened behind Tunis and a short slender man stepped in. His blond hair was caught under an old straw hat. He had gentle eyes with a firm mouth and easy way of walking. "I was told you wanted to see me, Miss Fikes."

Miss Fikes stood up, pushing back her chair. "Yes, Mr. Erdman. I'm glad you came. And you too, Mr. Freyling. We can get this thing settled right now." Miss Fikes looked from one to the other. "Have you two met? Mr. Freyling, this is Adam Erdman, head man at the orphanage." She went on to explain what she thought had happened.

Erdman offered his hand but Tunis refused it. Erdman shrugged. He looked at Tunis with a bemused air.

Tunis didn't like Erdman's lackadaisical air. Tunis glared at him with blue-rage eyes. It was all he could do to keep himself from hitting the fellow. Just in time he remembered the tramp he'd killed. "I want those kids thrown into the boys' reformatory!"

Miss Fikes said, "Mr. Freyling, I can well understand—"

"The hell you can. That my oldest boy should be crucified!"

Erdman turned serious. "Neighbor, I apologize for my boys. When they're sent to me, I don't know what fanatics may have already bent their minds. It takes time to know them."

Miss Fikes said, "Actually, though, they were just acting out things they learned from the adult world. Like playing Indians-and-cowboys."

"Bull! That boy of mine has a hole in his hand."

Erdman said, "What can I do to make up for it?"

Tunis stomped around on the board floor. "Nothing. I just wish my kids didn't have to go to school here."

Erdman said, "I'm trying to raise good Americans too, Freyling."

"Well, good luck. A man can see you've made a good start," Tunis leaned into Erdman. "Are you going to pound that kid?"

"No. But I will talk to him. And so will my wife, Eveling." He measured Freyling with a cool smile. "By the way, my wife and I would like you to come visit us some evening. I've got some dandy new horses in. Belgians. With rump muscles like oak limbs."

Tunis glared at him. Then, out of the corner of his eye, he saw that the expression on Miss Fikes's face had changed. She'd turned pale. Ah. She'd spotted that he could go over the edge in rage. She thought him scary.

160   Tunis muted his blazing eyes. He looked down at his hands. "One thing you want to remember, Miss Fikes. It's going to take a long time before kids Tane's age are going to quit picking on him that he was once crucified. If his hand heals up, he's always going to have that scar in the middle of his hand to remind him. Until he dies. That's why I got so mad."

"I think I understand, Mr. Freyling." The look of fear did not leave her wide gray eyes.

Tunis ground his teeth. It was too bad she'd seen his inside fires. Clara had sensed his quick melting point but she hadn't seen him get so mad he could kill somebody. "One thing I'm going to ask you to do."

"Yes, Mr. Freyling."

"Don't give any orders that the kids are not to talk about it. That'll make all the more sure they will. Tane's just got to learn to live with his own bunch."

"You're right."

"Kids think straighter than we do. I know I did when I was a kid."

Miss Fikes nodded. Slowly the white-edged look began to leave her eyes. She cleared her throat. "I have a confession to make. It's as much my fault as Jud's. Perhaps more. You see, I have a reading hour every Friday afternoon. If they've studied good, and if they've been well behaved all week, then I read them a story from some book. Sometimes I tell a story and act it out. Well, I've been dramatizing some stories from the Bible. About how Jael drove a nail through the head of Sisera. How Christ was crucified. And so on—"

Erdman jumped a little. "It was you then who put that in Jud's head."

"I'm afraid I did."

Erdman said, "And it wasn't the religion he was raised in."

Tunis exclaimed, "Why are you always reading stories with a nail in it? You must have nails on the brain."

"No," she said. Then she blushed.

Tunis looked right through her. Here was a good-looking woman who was badly in need of a man; while at home he had a wife who every now and then had shut him out. What a twisted world it was.

Erdman turned and gave Tunis a smile. "Maybe there isn't much difference between us after all. You know, here we've been neighbors for a couple of years, and yet we've never visited back and forth. We shouldn't let that river come between us."

Tunis asked, "Miss Fikes, what kind of people do you come from?"

Miss Fikes said, "Normal people. My parents live in Le Mars."

"Oh." Tunis turned and stomped out of the schoolhouse. "Le Mars!"

Tunis walked off more of his rage on the way home.

Lately he'd noticed that his rages had come over him more often. He knew why too. That darn Clara kept giving him the cold treatment in bed. In the past it'd been her, not him, who'd decided it was time to start another baby.

All he had left to live for was the memory. Those times had been as sweet and as tender and as delicate as a flower hungry for its bee, a slinky Delilah seeking a Samson's seed. During those breeding times he'd been happy, and all man, and there wasn't a chance he'd fly off the handle no matter what the provocation might be. So long as the juices of life could flow out of him his fires were dampered. It would have been easier to start a fire in a tub of water than for him to break out in a terrible rumpus. But all too soon there would come again that time when she would shut the door on him. Month after month after month he'd suffered her denial of his bed rights.

Luckily he somehow had managed to have the good sense to quick take a long hard stomping walk. When a singletree broke, or a tug on a harness broke, he'd jump up and down a couple of times, roar out: "All right, stop. Everybody go in the house. I knew it, I knew it. Today everything's going to go to pieces. No use, no use." Then before he struck somebody, or hurt his fist striking a post, he'd run out into the open field, cursing, waving an arm at the sky. If he could have waved a leg and run at the same time he would have done it. Once he ran a quarter of a mile, hard, until his breath burned in his throat; then, cooled down, he walked quietly back and with sure fingers fixed whatever had gone wrong.

He knew that the children were quite aware of the differing moods in the house. In the past when he'd had his bed rights, then the evening sun had struck brightly through the west window over the steaming supper table, and there were smiles and lively stories as the family ate, and Pa was a benign patriarch and Ma was the kindly earth mother, both of whom had time for all kinds of trifling talk.

It was not good for the kids to have that up-and-down kind of life. Too bad he couldn't naturally be an even-tempered man. Too bad she couldn't naturally be the ever-submissive wife.

At the same time, and it was something that was both sweet and bitter to him, she'd become a remarkable woman. She ran the house well. The girls were taught to be neat and to be helpful in the house. The boys were taught that once they stepped through the back entry (the cabin Tunis and Clara had first lived in) there would be no roughhousing. They were to remove their dirty boots or muddy shoes at the door and behave like gentlemen. They could tease the girls. But no rough words. No dirty stories. Clever stories, my, yes, that was all right. They could read the newspapers and the magazines that came in the mail, but they had to make sure their chores were done first, in the house, out on the yard.

Clara also saw to it that the family went to church when the weather was good. They'd flag down the Bonnie Omaha and ride up to Whitebone. Once in a while, after Tunis bought a new carriage, they'd ride into Bonnie and attend one of the churches there, usually the Congregational.

Sitting of an evening at the supper table, with the sun glowing a soft saffron in the west, with the children all talking and laughing about something they'd seen on the yard that evening (a white rooster had chased Bill, their mutt of a dog, into the house), with even little Geoffrey gurgling wet smiles in his high chair, Tunis surveyed his eight little duckies.

Geoffrey sat at his left across the corner of the table and next to Clara. That way both he as father and she as mother could take turns spooning Geoffrey food. Mallie sat beyond Clara at her left. At the far end of the table were Ana and then Rolf. On the right side of the table sat Tressa and Dirk and Thea and Tane, with Tane sitting at Tunis's immediate right. Tunis with his big swivel chair had the whole north end of the table to himself.

Well, Tane had shown that he didn't have a wild temper when Jud Artus drove that nail through his hand. He hadn't gone into a boy's rage.

Thea didn't have a hot temper either. She had merely stood by and watched with a sad hurt face.

The boy Dirk with his soft sly smile and his jokey manner was too witty to have it. He made wisecracks when he got hurt instead of striking out. Tressa had thrown a bucket of cold water over him one day and all he'd done was to shake the water out of his eyes and hair, and said, "Well, now I don't have to wash my hair Saturday night."

Tressa liked to tease in a loving way and liked to be teased in turn. She didn't have that wild fire in her either.

Rolf the throwback lived in a world of his own. With his wild black hair and his wild wide flashing mouthful of teeth he was untouchable. His dreams were different and his siblings knew it and they left him alone. Besides, they were never sure just what he would do if provoked. The few times they'd tried sticking it into him a little he'd acted as though he hadn't even heard them; went trudging to the toolshed to invent something for Pa.

In Ana there was a hint that she might have a temper in time because she allowed no one to touch her, not even her mother. The joke in the family was that only Jesus could comfort her, but then he'd have to wear gloves.

Mallie was the loving kisser. She was always hugging everybody and trying to sit close to one, snuggling and wiggling. Once she'd asked Dirk, after she'd seen him touching Tressa, if after supper they couldn't play pinching. So she didn't have that killer instinct in her either.

And the baby, gurgling Geoffrey, well, he was too little for one to tell what he had in him.

What a menagerie. Really, Clara had done very well with their eight children. She never took time off. Their kids had kept her as busy as the schoolchildren kept Velda Fikes busy. Mothers and teachers didn't have it easy. Just imagine.

That Velda Fikes had seven children to teach and each one in a different grade. And each grade had six classes: reading, writing, arithmetic, spelling, history, geography. Raising kids was tough titty.

Tunis's left cheek began to twitch. Something on that side . . . it wasn't a mosquito, so . . . He flicked a look at Clara. Ah. She had her grave gray eyes fixed on him, fixed so hard he'd at last felt it. She'd been alerted that he'd been looking for something in his duckies and she wanted to know what it was. Was she watching him because she too on occasion looked for something in the natures of their children?

He flicked a second look at Clara.

Her eyes had closed down and she was busy dipping up some food for Geoffrey from his baby plate and lipping it a moment to make sure it wasn't too hot and then spooning it into his pink smiling mouth.

Tunis felt a sneeze coming on. Quickly he pressed a finger into the narrow grooved depression under his nose, until he felt a tingling up between his eyes. That always stopped it if he pressed there hard enough. When the little seizure passed without becoming a loud snortch, he almost regretted it. Lately he had taken pleasure in sneezing.

Thought of his loss of bed rights welled up in him again like a burning belch. Gallish. Too bad Clara was so religious that she could argue that husband and wife should not couple unless they had procreation in mind. Too bad she didn't have a little of the whore in her so that she could enjoy with him the pleasures of sweet lust. What was wrong with lust? Only preachers and priests condemned it. And dried-up unfructified old maids. If it weren't for good old lust there'd be no population. In the human kingdom as well as in the animal kingdom.

He wondered if Velda Fikes were coupling with a man somewhere. She was boarding at the Pullmans' a half mile east of the school. Old Charlie wouldn't bother her of course; he had a beautiful wife with a wonderful yielding smile. And that long-legged boy they'd just taken on as a hired hand, Alfred Alfredson, was still too green to know what a woman was for.

Tunis next wondered if maybe he shouldn't try to become friends with Velda Fikes. That is, if he could convince her that she hadn't really seen a wild man in his eyes. Maybe he should drop in on her after school some nice warm day. A lonesome schoolma'am her age might welcome some attention from a man. She might also know how to use a halved lemon to keep from having children.

Smiling to himself, he slowly sipped his tea.

"What are you laughing about?" Clara asked sharply.

The kids shut up. Gone was their loving innocent chatter. They looked from Ma to Pa and then back again to Ma.

Tunis deliberately let his smile deepen. "Oh, when I was town the other day, I heard a funny story about H. B. Pierce. He was down from Rock Falls in his new Milwaukee Steamer. I guess we missed seeing him come by here down the old King's Trail."

Clara crooked her head at him. "You mean that new kind of buggy with a steam engine in it?"

"The same. It seems he gave fat old Boughers—you know, the land agent who sold me this farm?—he gave him a ride in his new jitney. They were speeding along for fair, when the air pressure in the gasoline tank got too high and the burner automatically turned on under the boiler. Soon there was so much pressure the flames came out of the rear of the contraption instead of

163

going up through the boiler. Old Boughers heard the roar and looked back. Then he yelled, 'My God, Pierce, she's on fire!'"

Clara slowly let laughter overtake her, and finally sagged back in her chair. The children caught the change in mood and joined in the laughter.

Tunis flicked another look at Clara. Yes, she'd taken his magician's pass. His secret was still safe. "Yeh, I don't know what this world's coming to when our bigshots think cars will replace horses."

Rolf's grave eyes woke up under his straight-up black hair. "Don't you like inventions, Pa?"

"Sure. But this one won't work. I heard tell that Pierce never goes riding in it but what they don't have to pull it back to town with horses."

"What's it look like, Pa? How does it work?"

"It's a one-seated thing. Has two steam cylinders that drive a chain attached to the rear axle. You get the steam by lighting a gasoline burner under the steam boiler. There's a barrel of water in back."

"How do you get the water into the boiler?"

"You pump it by hand as needed."

Rolf rolled up his head. He understood.

Again that valley under Tunis's nose itched. He scratched it with a finger. It reminded him that if he had a moustache it probably wouldn't itch there anymore. Maybe he ought to grow one. Clara might not object. She'd banned kissing too. Kissing led to coupling. It made him wonder if all the moustached and bearded men he met uptown had bedroom trouble with their wives.

He wished they might have ended their married life together like his foster parents Dirk and Tressa had come to a peaceful end in theirs. In their last days the late Dirk and Tressa had been like two old doves together.

164

Tunis looked over his children yet again with damp eyes. As far as he could tell, none of them had the wild one in them. Good. Maybe it would die with him. It was always a good thing to breed out bad blood. By marrying Clara he'd thinned that out of his line.

17. Clara

Clara had given Tunis that sharp look because she too had been ruminating about their children, had been looking them over for hereditary defect, from Tane around to Geoffrey. Had Tunis read her eyes? God only knew what he would do if he found out. He had such a temper. Thank heaven he never struck women.

Two of her children were suspect in her eyes. She'd noticed it at night when they were sleeping. Dirk and Tressa. There was an odd ruckling sound in their breathing during sleep. Daytimes there didn't seem to be anything wrong with their breathing. What had made her wonder about them, and had caused her to check their beds after they'd gone to sleep, was that when little, and as time went on, they liked to give each other little hugs, innocent enough, and often walked across the yard, or got the eggs together, with their arms around each other. Very gently she'd suggested, hinted, that it didn't look proper outdoors where someone might be passing along the King's Trail. In the house, maybe. Dirk and Tressa did quit being close on the yard, so far as she knew, but they kept it up in the house, at the table, while cleaning up the tins in the milk porch.

She would have to watch them.

But they were so loving about it. They made sure each got his share at the table. One day she'd be sure it was pure Christian love she was seeing between those two children; then, the next day, she was afraid she was seeing something that could turn to lust, especially on the part of Dirk. Dirk was after all a son of his father, a wild man in bed, and Dirk was sure to have inherited some of that concupiscence.

But at least for the moment, Dirk and Tressa were like two loving puppies together.

What those two little tykes were to each other made Clara all the more determined not to have any more relations with her husband. She didn't want a ninth child around who might succumb. And anyway, eight was enough.

It was a hot fall Saturday. When the Bonnie Omaha came by in the morning heading north for Whitebone, Clara had barely noted its whistle for the crossing. She had remarked to Thea, who was helping her with the wash, that it was very dry out and that they needed rain for the pastures. She had just hung up the family underwear, noting how the south wind filled out the arms and legs, making them seem they were still full of flesh, when she smelled smoke. They had a fire going in the entryway for the wash, but that was north of her. She turned to look to see what might be burning to the south. Could the Tippetts or the Bartleses be having a serious fire?

Clara was stunned to see a grass fire racing toward her about a mile away on the west side of the railroad tracks. A spark from the Bonnie Omaha must have started it. A great cloud of heavy black smoke was already lifting skyward and leaning toward her as the wind got behind it. Tunis and Tane hadn't got around to plowing the stubble in the south field. But worse was the tall grass growing in the virgin prairie between their farm and Hack Tippett's spread, as well as along the tracks.

Clara had several clothespins in her mouth. These she spat back into their pail and dropped the wet underwear she was holding into the reed clothes basket. She ran toward the house. "Thea! Thea? Where are you? Oh. There you are. I want you to run like the dickens and get your father and Tane there from behind the barn. I think they're hauling manure. Tell them a prairie fire is headed straight for us and they better come quick if they want to save the house and barn."

Thea took one look at the black cloud of smoke about to cover the sun, then turned and ran like a scudding jackrabbit.

Clara next spotted Dirk and Tressa checking the grapevines along the north end of the garden. "You two! Quick get pails and start pumping water."

Dirk and Tressa let go of each other's hand and hurried to obey.

Clara got a five-gallon can. She had barely got it half full by dipping it in the rain barrel when Tunis and Tane came running up, puffing, eyes looking wild at the oncoming horror.

Tunis swore. "I knew I should have plowed us a fire guard around the yard, it was so dry. Tane, get us those grain sacks from the granary. We'll soak 'em in the rain barrel and fight the fire with them."

The great plume of black smoke soon hid the sun and passed high overhead. The smell of burning bluestem grass came toward them acrid and sharp. Soon they heard the crackling of the fire.

166

"Lord, if that jumps the tracks," Tunis said, "there goes Pullman's buildings."

"And our school," Thea said.

"And the orphanage," Clara said.

Tunis shook his head. "I don't think it'll jump the river. Not enough wind behind it."

Tane came with an armful of empty sacks. Quickly Tunis dunked them in the rain barrel. "What I'm gonna do now is backfire here south of the house and out across the yard. What I want you guys to do, Clara, is swat out the fire I make when it creeps up to the house."

"But my clothes hanging there . . ."

"They're too wet to burn."

"But they'll get all black."

"Well, it's either that or the house."

Clara nodded. He was right. As usual. He always had good sense in a pinch.

Tunis grabbed the five-tine potato fork standing behind the house and also snapped up an old newspaper from the back porch. He caught the newspaper onto the tines of the fork, lighted the paper with a match, and, once he had a good blaze going, ran in a semicircle south of the house, dipping the burning paper down into the tall grass, gradually starting a chain of little fires. The little fires quickly spread toward one another. They crept slowly against the wind but ran faster with the wind.

When the backfire came close to the house, Clara and the children began beating it out along the edges with their soaked sacks. It was surprising to see how fast the fire seared along the ground even though the grass in the lawn was short. The fire burned off everything, even the stumps of old weeds.

Tunis ran the line of little fires well out toward the railroad before be began curving it north to the east of the barn. Clara and the children followed the backfire behind him. When he thought he had gone far enough in that direction, he ran to catch up more paper on his fork tines and set it on fire and then started another backfire west of the house. Finally, when he'd set enough fire going against the oncoming rushing main prairie fire, he dropped his fork and picked up a wet sack to help with whacking out the little creeping fires near the buildings.

The great fire came on with a whooshing roar. The wind seemed to have picked up and tongues of flame licked ahead into the tall wild grass. Birds and rabbits and two deer squirted out of the tall rushes in a swamp. The deer squeaked and bleated in fear.

Soon the front edge of the racing prairie fire ran into the rim of the creeping backfires, and with a soft hiss the tall flames collapsed and gently whipped out, leaving only a few wisps of very white smoke where the thick root of a weed or a sunflower continued to smolder.

The whole family watched the great prairie fire rush past the farmyard on either side, the arm of it on the east flaming along the railroad and the arm on the west running toward the river pasture.

"My washing," Clara wailed. The clothes hung gray and black on the clothesline.

"Yeh. And my cornfields," Tunis said.

Tane said, "I don't think the corn will burn, Pa. It's too green."

"Let's hope you're right, boy."

They watched. The rushing edge of the fire jumped through the fence; it licked up all the grass at the end of the field. But within moments it fizzled out in the first rows of corn, setting up an awful stink of burnt green leaves.

The east arm of the fire continued to race northward, following the King of Trails road and the Bonnie Omaha railroad embankment.

"It's gonna burn our school!" Thea cried. "Poor Miss Fikes."

Tunis nodded.

Tane pointed. "Hey. Lookit. Somebody's backfiring around the schoolhouse and between the river."

Tunis said, "That must be Erdman and his bunch of bobtail orphans."

Looking carefully, Clara could make out what looked like tiny stick figures flitting to and fro, bobbing and jumping and waving something."

"Good for Jud," Thea said. "He's not such a bad boy after all."

Even as they watched, the big rushing wall of flames ran into Erdman's backfired area and drooped, then dropped away, with little veils of yellowish smoke wisping up and vanishing into bluish air. But the higher-flying black smoke kept rising into the skies, slowly forming a wide strange cloud that kept revolving like a ghostly kaleidoscope, the ends worming into the middle and the middle exfoliating outward.

Clara stood close to her husband. She heaved a sigh of relief. "Thank God you were home."

Tunis's lips worked as he bit on the insides of them. "Yeh. Reminds me of when I was a kid. When Old Dirk just before he went to bed at night would step outside and sweep the entire horizon for signs of flame."

Clara heard coughing behind her. Dirk and Tressa. Both had a distressed look in their eyes. She had better watch them. She didn't favor giving any one child more attention than she gave any of the others, but perhaps with those two she might have to.

That night when she went to bed, after Tunis had fallen asleep, she went with a night lamp upstairs on bare feet to see if her two coughers were all right. The four boys slept in the west bedroom, two to a bed, and the four girls slept in the east bedroom, also two to a bed.

She looked in the boys' room first, lifting the night lamp to let the soft light bloom over the sleeping bodies. Tane and Dirk always slept in the bed on the right and Rolf and baby Geoffrey in the bed on the left. To her surprise, Tane was sleeping alone. Where was Dirk? What!

Quickly she barefooted it into the girls' room across the narrow hall. She lifted the light high. Sure enough. Tressa wasn't sleeping with Thea either, though Ana was sound asleep beside little Mallie. Where in the world?

She heard a cough behind her. It came from the linen closet in the hallway. Quickly, softly—she didn't want to make too much of a fuss over it—she could be wrong—she looked in the linen closet. There they were. Sound asleep in each other's arms, Tressa in her long white nightgown and Dirk in his long-pipe underwear, their lips pale pink and smiling in angelic innocence. They looked like a pair of cupids in smiling sleep together.

She set the night lamp on a stand in the hallway. First she reached down for Dirk, extricating him from Tressa's clasping arms, easily and slowly, so as not to awaken her, and then lifting she carried him to his own bed. My, the boy was heavy.

168

Then she carried Tressa to her bed.

Tressa woke up a little. She seemed to sense that maybe she shouldn't have been where her mother found her. "We was both coughing so much, Ma, we kept the others awake. And so when I went to lay down in the linen closet, Dirk came too. We coughed so."

Clara whispered. "Shh. It's all right. That was thoughtful of you." She hugged Tressa dear, smelling her daughter's sweet little-girl flesh. "But pretty soon you and Dirk had better not always be so close."

"But we love each other, Ma. He's my brother."

"I know, child. Shh. Now go to sleep." She brushed back Tressa's red-brown curly hair. "Sleep." She covered Tressa and gave her a gentle touch on the shoulder.

Clara picked up the little lamp and slowly went downstairs. She had to be careful not to waken Tunis. She wondered again if maybe they shouldn't sleep in separate beds; or even separate rooms, if she wasn't going to let him in.

There was really only one regret about denying him. During those ten years when she'd had eight children, she'd had her period but a half dozen times. That at least had been a good thing. She hated having her periods.

She had just barely begun to drift off to sleep, had already caught a glimpse of a tall tree strangely covered with rose blossoms, when suddenly Tunis rolled over to face her. His hand swept up under her nightgown and dropped down on her privates three fingers wide. Before she could react his middle finger found her. She grabbed his hand with both her hands. "You cut that out! Tunis!"

But he was strong and found her even more. His hardness burned against her hip.

"Tunis! I'll call the kids."

He said nothing. He tried to part her knees with his big powerful knee. His hand pushed in on her. There was a sound in him as if far back in his head he were both laughing at her as well as snarling at her. It was dark but she didn't have to see his face to know it was wrinkled in lust.

She fought him. "Tunis! No more children."

"Sure. But I must have relief."

She reached for his privates and gave it all an awful jerk. "No!"

"Do you want me to visit a whorehouse then?"

"That's up to you. If you can abide the sin of it."

He growled. He rose over her and managed to set his knees inside her knees. He pushed down at her, trying to find her. He moaned like a stallion. She held onto him with both hands and steered him first to one side then the other. She tried to dig her nails into him. Too bad she kept them short for housework. He kept getting closer. He was so powerful. Even as she was proud of his marvelous power she hated what he was trying to do to her.

She cried out, muffled under his humped head, "Husband! You're raping your own wife."

He kept surging down at her.

She squeezed him with all her might, digging her nails deeper into his member, especially over the egg-sized head.

Of a sudden he moaned, seeming to collapse over her, his brow touching her neck and shoulder. She felt him throbbing in her hand. In a few moments he slackened in her grip, became limp. And when she let go, finally realizing what had happened, she felt a little puddle of semen drop on her belly just below her navel. 169

"Uggh! You dirty man. Och!" She pushed him off her. She bounced out of bed, holding her nightgown up and away from her body, and in the dark found her way through the parlor, then through the dining room, then into the kitchen. Selecting a match out of the matchbox over the stove with a thumb and forefinger, she scratched it alive into a flame, and lighted the hanging lamp over the table. She went to the reservoir in the back of the stove and poured some warm water into a basin and again with one hand worked up some suds with the family bar of tar soap. She could smell the semen. It reminded her of the smell of a canful of angleworms. With a washcloth she went after the spurts of semen.

She rinsed out the washrag. There went a possible child down the drain. But she didn't care. She was not going to have another baby even if it meant Tunis might divorce her.

The next morning, Sunday, Clara hustled all eight children into their Sunday clothes and caught the morning train to Whitebone to attend church.

After the service, Father Garlington in his kind way asked where Mr. Freyling was. "Is he ill?"

"No. My husband just didn't care to come to church today. Men aren't all that religious, you know."

18. Tunis

After the family had caught the train north, Tunis decided to have a look at his corn in the field north of the barn. There'd been a hint of frost during the night and he wondered if maybe his corn might not have been nipped a little in the bottoms near the river. The corn should really have another ten days of warm weather to mature. Corn nipped too early turned out soft and shrunken, and sometimes, if shelled and stored in a bin too early, moldered into gray rotted clusters, unfit for the stock to eat, and worth nothing as seed for next year.

He also thought he might have a look for signs of cougar in the tangled jungle of the wasteland along the river. He was sure he'd heard their unearthly scream one night a week ago. He took his shotgun with him.

He walked down a row of corn a dozen rods away from the road, watching as he went along for noxious weeds as well as for frost-crimped leaves. There were occasional cockleburs. He was going to have to get after them soon or they'd be a pest. Get out his army of children and go up and down the fields pulling them out. He found some islands of pigeon grass. Well, there was no fighting that. He found no morning glories or creeping jennies. Thank God. When those two got started, they could choke corn and grain to death.

There was a light wind out from the south and it tossed the coarsegold tassels about above his head. Corn ears with hairy ends hung heavy toward the ground. A great crop was coming, provided the frost could just hold off for at least one more week.

Emerging from the cornfield, he carefully laid his shotgun under the fence, then slipped between two of the barbwires. Picking up his gun again, he entered the jungle. He found a deer path. Grapevines almost shut off the sunlight. Deer fur hung caught on some of the branches of prickly ash.

He spotted fresh deer droppings. That meant the deer were moving about freely. Perhaps he hadn't heard a big cat screaming after all.

He followed the winding deer trail all the way to the river. He heard the running water before he saw it. The lapping noise came from a gravel ripple. Sight of the gleaming translucent water made him thirsty. He slid down the steep black bank, carefully holding his gun out from his body, and stopped at the edge of the gravel. He looked up and down the stream. It was an Eden, he thought, with all the tree branches hanging heavy with green leaves almost touching the water in places. There weren't even any flies or mosquitoes tippling the surface of the mirror water. He knelt and with cupped hand caught up several swallows of water. The water had the taste of tree roots in it and the smell of it was that of a woman with child.

It came over him that eyes were watching him. He didn't jerk up. He pretended he hadn't noticed. When he let his hand down, he slowly stood up and let his eyes pick up objects to either side peripherally.

Nothing that he could see. Probably just his imagination.

As he dried his hand against his brown work pants, he happened to look at where the deer trail took up again on the opposite bank.

There. A cougar. It too had come for a drink. It stared at him. A male. The sun caught its eyes just right to make them glow opalescent, as if a tiny candle had been lighted inside them.

They stared at each other.

Then, as Tunis started to lift his shotgun to his shoulder, the cougar vanished. It was as if it had just simply erased itself.

"Shucks. I should have fired from the hip." Tunis grimaced to himself. "Well, I was right. I did hear him then. I suppose I ought to count the newborn calves. Though generally the big cat only likes wild meat."

Another deer trail led off to the right along the river bank. He followed it. Huge grapevines hung down from elms and cottonwoods. Some of the vines had the girth of a horse's thigh. They were loaded with blue-ripe grapes. He grabbed up an occasional cluster and, holding tight to the stem, raked the grapes off into his mouth with his teeth. The wild grapes were tart and strong, with only a little sweetness in them. Yet they were good. It made him smack his lips and suck his tongue, both to hurry the taste along as well as to get rid of it.

The trail debouched onto the King of Trails where a wooden bridge spanned the river. He climbed carefully through the four-strand barbwire fence and pushed through deep bluestem grass onto the road and turned south to go home.

Happening to look over to the east, he spotted smoke rising from the schoolhouse chimney. What? Someone had lit the stove in the schoolhouse on Sunday? Tramps, perhaps. That was no good. He decided to roust them out. They'd no doubt followed the railroad tracks out from Bonnie.

He opened the door suddenly to surprise them, letting it bang against the wall, only to be surprised himself. There sat Miss Fikes behind her desk.

She jerked up. "Who . . . ? Mr. Freyling!"

"Sorry," he said. "I didn't know it would be you. I was sure some railroad bums had made a nest here for the night. They sometimes come walking down the tracks, you know."

Seeing his bewildered look, she smiled. "I had some papers to correct. The Pullmans have company up the hill and I couldn't concentrate."

His eyes fastened on her large lips. Here maybe was a woman who would not deny her man bed rights were she married. "You're really out to be a good teacher then, aren't you?"

"What else should I do with my life?"

"May I ask how old you are?"

"Twenty-five."

"How come a good-looking woman like you ain't married?"

"That's what they all say."

He liked her quickness. "You want to remember you can't kiss anybody on the other side of the grave."

She pinkened. "Maybe I don't want to kiss anybody."

His eyes fastened on her lips again. "A woman with your looks . . ." He shook his head. "That would be hard to believe. Everybody needs a sidekick. Even the Bible admits that, where it says—"

"It is not good for the man to live alone," she broke in.

"Well?"

"I just didn't run into the right one, I guess."

"Or maybe you were too picky."

"Maybe."

He found himself leaning down at her. "Don't tell me you don't like men."

She reddened; said nothing. She bit on her lower lip.

He straightened up. "Excuse me for pushing in. It's just that . . . Well, you're such a nice-looking woman and it would be a shame for that to go to waste."

"Ha."

"Ah. Then you've had a beau."

Her eyes blued over with anger. Her blond hair done up on her head in the top-heavy mode of the day seemed to swell. "Why, Mr. Freyling, you almost sound like the chairman of a school board. I don't have to answer that."

He liked the way she was dressed: old-fashioned white-barred dimity and leg-of-mutton sleeves and long flaring skirt trimmed with a furbelow. Off to one side on her desk lay her wide-brim straw hat decked with imitation violets. "Excuse me again. But, you see, I think you're a nice woman." To himself he thought: "Lord, how I'd like to get at her furbelow."

Again an odd look came over her face. She was still afraid he might go over the edge.

The wood stove in the northwest corner crackled softly. There was a smell of oak wood burning, as well as of cast iron being heated.

Her eyes continued to show deep blue. But her lips said, "Well, Mr. Freyling, I like you too." Quickly she added, "You have such lovely well-behaved children. You should be proud of them."

172   He looked down at the oiled floor. "Well, at that it ain't all cream and roses being married. Especially when the good wife shuts the door on you."

"You mean, you two sleep in separate rooms?"

"I mean, she won't let me in." He could feel his neck thickening. "You know, coupling."

Her red lips parted. "Oh."

He knew that something could happen between them that both would be sorry for later on. It would be so easy to walk around her desk and pick her up and lay her on the floor. He sighed, so deep he shuddered involuntarily. "Can I ask you something? With that name, Fikes, where did you come from?"

"I was born in Le Mars."

"Ah, Clara came from there. She's British, you know."

"So am I. My father was a British pup. And my mother was one of those lower-class maids shipped over for hired help."

"Then you still have relatives around here."

"No, most of them have gone back to England. They just weren't cut out for the kind of work you have to do in America to be a success at farming."

"Hmm. I'll have to tell Clara about this."

Her lips closed.

The moment for possible coupling passed.

If he was going to step out on Clara because of great need it had better not be with the teacher of his children. He nodded. Better a prostitute in Sioux City.

After a while he excused himself and walked home.

19. Clara

As Rolf grew older his heavy brows bulged out more; his hair got thicker and stiffer and rose straight up off his skull like the black brushy mane of a horse. His gray eyes appeared to look right through one and to focus on something behind one's head, far and deep into one's soul. His lips also thickened and widened so that his horse teeth flashed very white. At the same time, below his neck, his body developed into a remarkable specimen of manliness: wide shoulders, powerful forearms, heavy thighs and calves, small hands and small feet. His skin remained delicate and burned easily in the summer.

Rolf was by no means dumb. Miss Fikes confided in Clara that he was the best student in arithmetic she ever had. He was wonderful at doing sums. One glance at a column of figures and he'd have it all added up. Always accurate. He was also very good at reading, provided it came at him in story form. He didn't care to read essays or poems.

Rolf graduated from the eighth grade at the age of thirteen. From that moment on he became, along with Tane, another right hand for his father. He liked pigs and became the pig man on the farm. He thought little pigs wonderfully clever and pretty. He read articles about how to raise pigs in *Farm and Fireside*, and when he found something that made sense he applied it to hog raising. He invented new feeds, combining ground corn with ground wheat or ground barley. He knew how to make great slop, mostly from skim milk, potato peelings, apple cores, and other edible garbage from the kitchen, mixed in with linseed meal. His hogs became fat very rapidly and always brought the best price at the stockyards in Sioux City, where they were shipped via the railroad.

He learned how to imitate pig sounds so accurately that Clara couldn't tell the difference between Rolf's imitation of a boar's rutting grunt and the real thing. In fact he was good at imitating many animal calls.

Once Rolf spotted a cougar sitting on its haunches at the end of the pig pasture. Somehow the young pigs had not spotted it. Very calmly Rolf sent out a mother hog's warning grunt, piercing and true, so that every one of the hundred little pigs perked up their pointed ears, then turned and ran straight for the hog house door, yipping, "Hgohnee! hgohnee!" Then to chase off the big cat, Rolf imitated the yowls and barking of a half dozen hounds hot in pursuit of something, "Arf, arf! ipf, ipf!" The big cat instantly whirled and shot under the fence at the end of the pasture and dropped out of sight behind the riverbank.

Later that night Clara and Tunis talked in the dark about the boy. "He is a strange one," Clara said. "I just don't understand where he came from."

Tunis grunted. "Probably a morphodite."

"What's that?"

"Both boy and girl."

"I diapered him many times and saw no sign of that."

"Wal, then maybe like I said before, he's a throwback."

Clara shivered. "You mean, a savage brute came out of my flesh?"

"And out of my loins."

Clara shook her head in her pillow. "Anyway, I worry about him a little."

"How so?"

"What woman will marry him?"

Tunis grunted again. "You might be surprised."

"Meaning what?"

"You women sometimes hook up with the damnedest-looking men. Goofs. And the better-looking you women are, the worse your pick is."

There was some truth in what her husband said. One could only hope that it would prove to be true in Rolf's case. Except that the woman would have a surprise in Rolf. Aside from his strange brute face, he was everything a woman could want. Especially that delicate skin of his.

Tunis said, "I have noticed one thing. He's really well hung." Tunis sometimes in the summer took the boys swimming in the river on Saturday evening. "There has to be some woman somewhere who'd appreciate that."

"You would mention that."

"A man naturally checks things like that. Like in stud poker you always check where the ace is."

"Oee. Now you're trying to be funny." Yet Clara had to smile to herself. Good thing Tunis couldn't see the smile. She didn't want him to know that she often did appreciate his sarcastic punning. In bed she had to keep his dog at bay somehow.

"If I can't have any more children myself, then I want grandchildren."

174

"Well me, I first want to see how our children turn out."

There was a considerable silence from his side of the bed. "You aren't worried about something in them, are you?"

"Not more than any other mother might be."

Through the bedspring she could feel him tense up. Then to her shock he let go with a long fart, starting out first in an oblative basso, climbing next into a worried tenor, rising into a tremulous alto, and finishing off into a squeaky soprano.

Clara bounced up on her side in disgust. "Good gracious! I didn't know you were a crowd."

Tunis didn't respond.

Clara said, "I hope that that slip isn't going to be the start of a bad habit. Because I won't stand for it! You understand? I won't, Tunis. Not in my house."

"Don't worry."

"But I mean that, Tunis. I just will not have it."

"I'm worse off than a turtle in love."

She was afraid to ask why.

"You know, those turtles we sometimes find on their backs in our pasture by the river?"

She held her tongue.

"I used to think maybe the cougars did it looking for a different kind of meat. But now I know better."

She gritted her teeth for what was coming.

"I looked carefully at one of them one day. Got down on my hands to do it. Turns out every one was a man turtle. Not one woman turtle. All men turtles."

It slipped out before she could stop it. "That's funny."

"Well, I would never have found out either, except that this summer I happened to catch one of the men turtles mounted on a woman turtle. You should have seen it. He was tipped straight up to get at her. Then when he gave her his final shot, he fell over backwards."

"Ohh! That I believe."

"S'fact. S'truth. As I lay here beside you for all intents and purposes a neutered male."

Clara decided to change the subject. She gave herself a shake in bed. "Take Ana now. She's going to be so pretty the boys are going to be chasing after her like bees after a plum tree in blossom."

It took him a moment to follow her lead. "Ha! Hardly. She already acts like an old maid around her brothers. Completely different from the way Tressa acts around Dirk."

So Tunis had noticed something there too then.

"By the way, we may have to watch Dirk and Tressa when they get a little older."

Clara ran her tongue around the outside of her teeth but still inside her lips. The alarm clock ticked quietly on his side of the bed. Yes, he had seen something then. And, yes, she would have to keep them separated. "Well, maybe you're right about Ana. She's such a fussbudget. She might even have it in her to become a nun."

"Stepfather Dirk used to call such pure-born Baptists."

"She hardly eats more than a sparrow. And if it isn't cooked just right, she pushes it to one side. And when she sets the table, she always makes sure she gets the shiniest plate. If she gets a little spot on her dress, she's right away got to run to the sink and dab it out."

Tunis stretched and yawned beside her. "I've noticed too that when she comes out of the privy, she always acts like she's just undergone a terrible tragedy of some kind."

"Yes, she hates being human. I really believe that deep down in her soul she feels she should have been born an angel." Clara sighed. "The funny thing is, when I was carrying her I had dreams almost every night about a nun wearing a tight black hood. You could hardly see her face, it was so tiny. And she walked with pretty little steps two inches apart."

"I didn't know you dreamt like that."

"I didn't tell you because I didn't think it important." Clara played with the silk edge of the quilt. "Do you think a mother's dreams might have something to do with what they become later on?"

"Maybe it's the other way around. What they are already in your belly might color your dreams."

"Oh. Then maybe that's why I dreamt the way I did when I was carrying Rolf."

"What did you dream with him?"

Clara hesitated. "Well, it really was about you. When I conceived him, I dreamt you were chasing me around in our pasture. First you'd be a stallion. Then you'd change into a man, except that your head looked more like an ape's. And the heavier I became with him, the more you took on a side I didn't like at all."

"Like what?"

175

"That you were going to bite me into line. You showed such awful teeth, husband, white and sharp."

"Why didn't you tell me about those dreams?"

"I didn't want to burden you with them."

"I could've loved you up a little to let you know your dreams were just dreams."

"But they didn't turn out to be just dreams."

"I could have still given you some nice warm hugs."

"I didn't want to encourage that either. You know how you are."

"You damn right I know how I am. I need bed rights."

She nuzzled her head in her pillow. What a persistent man he was. "Anyway, it's fun talking to you like this. We should do it more often. Remember how we used to talk in the dark?"

"I remember all right. Especially when we still lived in the cabin part. You were even ahead of me then in wanting to couple."

"I was?"

"You know damn well you were. You used to grab hold of me first."

"Don't swear so, husband. That and those indecent noises I will not abide. And now, let's go to sleep."

He lay in silence for a while. Then he bounced up, high, and came down with a thump, and in so doing knocked loose several slats beneath them. The mattress sank in the middle and they were thrown together, willy-nilly. "Darn!" Then he laughed and began hugging her.

Clara deliberately held back her laughter. Laughter always made her weak, and weak she couldn't afford to be with him in the same collapsed bed. Quickly she knapped her knees together, tight, to keep him from getting between them. Already she could feel his aroused member. "We better get up and stick those slats back into place."

Thea called from the living room. The blush of a night lamp appeared through the partly open bedroom door. "What's the matter, Ma?"

Clara caught her breath. Gracious. Maybe Thea had heard them other nights. Especially that time when Tunis tried to rape her. "Nothing." Quickly Clara laughed a little laugh. "Some of the slats let go. There always was one slat too short, you know."

"Oh."

"Good night, Thea. See you in the morning."

Thea withdrew, the weak light from the night lamp fading away.

Together Clara and Tunis got out of bed, and while she held up the mattress, Tunis crawled under the bed and slipped the slats back into place.

The cold floor must have cooled off Tunis's ardor, because he fell asleep almost immediately after getting into bed again.

Clara lay brooding to herself. She felt sorry for him. Perhaps the Bible was right to let a man have a concubine or two. Or those Mormons in Utah were right.

But for her, eight children was a God's plenty.

20. Tunis

It was raining out, too wet to pick corn. Everybody was in the house that Saturday and Clara was crabby with the whole family underfoot.

"Can't you find something for the boys to do in the barn? Get them out of the way? I can't get the girls to do any housework."

Tunis shook his head. He swung back and forth several times in his swivel chair. "The barn is as clean as a Dutchman's bedroom."

Dirk and Rolf and Ana were playing city under the table in the dining room. They had arranged their playing blocks into streets and alleys, with houses and stores along either side. They used smaller blocks for buggies, pushing them about, racing, going to parties.

Tunis thought it strange that those three should be playing city when they'd been brought up on the farm. Maybe it meant something about who they'd become someday.

Mallie and Geoffrey sat off to one side watching.

Thea and Tressa were dusting the furniture. Tane was sitting by the bay window chewing his nails.

All of a sudden Mallie with a soft loving smile decided to join the city builders. She got up and toddled straight across the streets and alleys, wrecking one whole corner of the city. It looked as though a tornado had whizzed under-through the table.

Ana set up a howl.

"Now what's the matter?" Clara cried from the kitchen.

"Clets is always spoiling things for us."

"Take your blocks out to the granary then and build your city there."

"It's too wet in there too, Ma. Can't you keep her there with you in the kitchen?"

"No. Get out of the house."

"Oh, Ma."

"Makes no difference. Get out. I got too many things to worry about just now. All in the house at the same time during the middle of the day . . . ugh!"

Ana got to her feet and came into the kitchen where Tunis sat in his swivel chair. She held his eye unflinchingly with her enamel blue stare. "Papa, it ain't fair that because Clets is just a dumb baby she can do anything she wants. She's got to learn the rules too."

Tunis held his head to one side like a Solomon. He pushed out his lips as though in deep thought. He couldn't help but admire the fight in Ana's slim sinewed body. Ana was always sure of what her rights were. He remembered how, when he'd diapered her as a baby, she seemed to have such a very small pudendum to go with her small mouth. Even little Mallie already had twice the lips of Ana.

"Papa?"

Tunis looked up at Clara. "Wife, the kids can stay in the house, can't they?" Outside the rain was coming down in trailing sheets of gray water. "If it's too wet for me, it's certainly too wet for them."

Clara said, "I'm working in here and I don't want to hear any complaining from naughty kids."

Tunis got to his feet and went over and picked up Mallie. "Come here, you little bundle of love. Maybe Papa can give you some horseback rides, hah?"

Mallie lolled in his arms, smiling with her thick lips. Both her lips looked as if they'd been stung by a bee. As Tunis resettled in his chair, she threw her little arms around his neck and gave him a kiss under the ear.

Tunis laughed. "What a little kisser you are. Someday you're gonna make some man very happy."

Clara said, "Careful with that talk now."

Tunis laughed some more, then set Mallie on both his knees, giving her his forefingers for reins to an imaginary bridle.

Pleased, Ana retreated to the block city under the table and began helping Dirk and Rolf rebuild the houses.

Tunis gave Mallie a series of quick hops on his knees. "That's how a trotting horse goes." Next he gave her several undulating lifts in the air with his knees together. "And that's how a galloping horse goes." Finally he gave her a series of irregular quick hops. "And that's how a pacing horse goes."

Mallie's eyes blued over with wonder and her soft lips opened in child bliss. "More."

178

Tunis played with Mallie until the sockets in his hips hurt.

Geoffrey all the while sat stoically under the bay window. He had his own play blocks on which the original color was still sharp, blue and red and orange and yellow and green. The letters and numbers on the blocks were also still clearly defined. Geoffrey would pick up one block at a time with his slim fingers and stare at it, examining all six sides carefully, especially the lettered sides. It was almost as though he knew what he was looking at. Of the eight children he was the only one left who wasn't quite housebroke. He knew about number one, that it should be done in a pot or out of sight around the corner of the house, but number two was still done in his diapers.

Sometimes Tunis caught Geoffrey staring at him as though the boy saw him as someone else. The boy's stare was disconcerting.

"Now Clets," Tunis said to Mallie, "isn't that about enough for you? Jeffy wants a turn too, you know."

Without hesitation, unselfishly, Mallie slid down from his knees to the floor. With a child's warm chuckle she watched as Tunis swooped up Geoffrey.

Tunis set the boy precisely on his knees.

"Give him the galloping ride first," Mallie suggested with a happy laugh. "That's a good one."

"Wanna gallop some, boy?" Tunis set in motion what resembled a horse galloping madly over the hills.

"Oh, goodie," Mallie cried. "Ain't that a good ride, Jeffy?"

Geoffrey sat with a stiff back. He kept looking down at Tunis's bouncing knees. It was as if the boy had to inspect it all first before he was going to enjoy it.

Tunis got tired after a while. He looked at his youngest with a wry smile.

"You are a rare one, boy. I don't know what's gonna become of you."

Clara said, "He's going to be the one we send to college."

Dirk under the table heard that. "And why not me?"

"You too, if you want that," Clara said. "But we got to have at least one go on to higher education."

Tunis said, "Provided we can afford it."

"We will," Clara said.

It rained for another couple of days, just enough to keep the family in the house most of the time.

During the rains, Tunis let his beard grow. Looking in the mirror one morning, he thought he looked quite handsome with it. He knew he should shave soon, but wondered if it wouldn't be fun to at least let his moustache grow. Maybe Clara would smile at him again.

She didn't smile. When he tried to give her a kiss in the kitchen, she said, "Go away with that sandpaper."

He laughed. "It's a cookie duster, wife. You know, brush off the cookie before you eat it."

The next time he went to town he bought a plug of tobacco. Columbia Brand. He bit off a corner on the way home. At first the taste wasn't very good and he found himself spitting a lot with the wind. If Clara wouldn't let him touch her, he'd indulge in one of the other transgressions.

He was careful not to chew around the house, keeping the plug hidden in the horse medicine cabinet amidst the harnesses hanging on the inside wall of the barn. Tane and Rolf saw him break off a small bite several times but said nothing. What men did in the barn was none of the women's business.

Tunis soon began to like it enough to take a chew a couple times a day.

One morning he forgot he was chewing tobacco when he brought in the milk to be separated. He spat several times in a slop pail standing near the separator. Each time he managed to hit the slop pail dead center with a plinging sound.

"What in the world are you chewing there?" Clara suddenly said from the door. She was bringing him a clean shining pail in which to catch the cream.

"Oh. Yeh." Caught, Tunis decided to be bold about it. He hit the slop pail dead center again. "So you noticed."

"How could I help it when I saw you coming up the yard, spitting almost every other step. Like you had a bad cold or something."

Tunis ran his tongue around inside his lips. "Mmm, it's good. Cleans the teeth and keeps them from decaying. No bugs can stay alive in a mouth that's well-greased with tobacco juice."

"Rahhch!" She scathed out her throat several times. "That's one of the filthiest habits there is!"

"It is wonderful comfort though for a man who's had to give up one of his favorite vices."

She set the shining pail down. "I don't know which is worse, you making . . . Rahhch!"

"Make me happy at night and I'll quit. That's a promise."

Her eyes glittered. "I won't be bought."

"And I won't go without indulging myself in something. Otherwise why live?"

That night at supper table, Rolf asked Tunis what seemed to be an innocent question. "Pa, are you sure you know when it's the proper time to breed the sows?"

"Something you read in that *Farm and Fireside* again?"

"No, I was just thinking about how we always have our little pigs born in cold weather."

Tunis carefully cut himself a slice off his pork chop. "What do you have in mind?" He savored its juicy meat warmth.

"We should probably top off the sows a little later in the winter."

"Trouble is, son, the market ain't always right later on. Also, the little tit-suckers would be coming in just when we're busiest in the field."

"Yeh, but you got me now as your pig man."

Tunis helped himself to another corner from his pork chop, along with a dab of mashed potatoes and gravy. "By gum, son, you're right." He flashed a look at Clara. "Okay. From now on you choose the day when we let the boar mount his ladies."

Clara dropped her fork in her plate. "That's enough of that rough talk now."

Tunis wrinkled his nose at her. "We're only talking about natural things. You know, we can't have pork chops every year unless we—"

"Not in front of the girls! They're already getting too much information on the farm here."

"What they're learning here on the farm will make them wonderful understanding wives."

"I want my girls to grow up to be ladies."

Tunis glared at Clara and she glared back at him. Had she been a man he'd have asked her to stand up so he could knock her down.

The older children twisted nervously on their chairs. Finally they broke into hysterical laughter. They sometimes behaved the same way when a storm hung threatening in the skies outdoors. Theirs was a hilarity engendered by terror. Pa and Ma break up? That would be the end of the world.

The small children began to cry, Mallie a high shrill keening, little pink tongue showing like a thirsty bird's, and Geoffrey a tight piercing wail.

Tunis could feel wrath coiling up in his belly. His impulse was to strike at heads around him left and right. Just in time he remembered that time with that tramp back on Old Dirk's farm. He swallowed to keep down his gorge. Swallowed again.

"Pa?" Clara called from her end of the table. "Pa?" Her voice could just barely be heard over the rilling children.

Tunis lowered his shoulders. "All right! That's enough of that racket." He forced a smile under his moustache. "Ma, all four of your girls are certain to grow up ladies." He started to laugh. "And all four of my boys will grow up to be softhearted peedoodlers."

Everybody laughed then, Clara, even the little children, who hadn't the least notion of what Pa meant.

That summer the local school board announced that the country school by the river would be closed. Adam Erdman had decided that his wife could teach his orphan boys and had got permission from the county school superintendent to construct a small schoolhouse on the orphanage yard. Meanwhile the two Pullman children, Gordon and Grace, were being sent by their parents to special schools, Gordon to an academy near Des Moines and Grace to a girl's finishing school near Sioux City. That left only the Freyling children of school age. There weren't really enough pupils to justify hiring a teacher full-time. Miss Velda Fikes would have to look elsewhere for a job.

"Good," Tunis said when he heard the news. "Now we won't have to worry about any more crucifixions."

Clara was equally satisfied with the news. "I'd been thinking anyway," she said from her side of their bed, "that our children should go to that new school they got in Bonnie."

"You don't mean that Christian Grammar School of the new Little Church?"

"That's just what I mean. They'll get good religious instruction there."

"That's almost four miles from here. How are the kids gonna get there?"

"By horse and buggy, what else?"

"But it's mostly Hollanders going to that school."

"I know."

"But you're English. Don't that kind of grind you a little?"

Clara moved in little quick jerks. She'd taken to doing that lately, even in her sleep, often awakening him. In the old days when she moved at all she moved gently, even serenely, so that he hardly noticed. "No, it doesn't grind me. Not when I remember how Lord Sutherland and his foul-minded English pups behaved around their hired kitchen help. At least the Hollanders try to live a Christian life and that's what I want for our children. All the more so when it's so hard to go to our own church in Whitebone."

Tunis swore to himself. "Those damned Hollanders are spreading out in all directions in our part of the country. All the way from Sioux Center."

Clara took up the problem the next evening at their supper table. She told the kids the news about their school. There was an instant clamor all around the table. Only Mallie and Geoffrey remained silent. Finally all eyes swung to Tunis to see what he might have to say.

A sliding smile crept in under Tunis's moustache. He glanced around at the older kids, from Thea on down to Ana. "Unless you kids don't mind walking those three and a half miles."

Thea noticed that Tunis's look hadn't included Tane. "You mean Tane don't have to go to school any more?"

"Not if he don't want to. He'll be sixteen come September sixth." Tunis winked at Tane. "My oldest boy is now my right-hand man on the yard."

"That ain't fair."

Clara broke in. "You don't want him to go on through high school then?"

"Ask the boy."

Clara directed a searching look at Tane. "Don't you want to go to school?"

Tane rocked his wide shoulders back and forth. "What would be the use of it? School ain't gonna help me be a better farmer."

"Then you really want to be a farmer?"

"I sure do, Ma. It's the life for me."

"You're sure about that now? You're casting the die for your whole life."

"I don't care to read books, Ma. Except that big one outdoors. There's an awful lot of pages out there I have to turn over yet."

Clara slowly let down with a sigh. She threw a severe look at Tunis. "I hope you know what you've done, bending that boy's mind."

Tunis leaned forward in his chair, anger flaring up in him again. "And you're not bending anybody's mind in this family?"

Clara retreated in her fleshes. After a moment she said, "Will someone please start the beans around?"

The following Sunday morning at breakfast, Clara announced that she'd like to go to church. In Bonnie. Could Tunis hitch the driving team to the carriage? It was such a lovely day for worship.

"To what church, for godsakes?" Tunis asked.

"Since we're sending our children to the Christian School there, I think we should have a look at the form of worship in the Little Church."

"Sit down haunch to haunch with those baggy pantaloons?"

"Why not?"

"Even after what they did to your British friends? Push them out of Plymouth County? Let alone Sioux County?"

"My British friends, as you put it, weren't meant to be Siouxlanders. They just didn't have the Siouxland step."

"For godsake."

"Yes, for God's sake, I'd like for our whole family to attend worship in the Little Church this morning."

Tunis heaved his heavy shoulders twice. "Tane, will the yard be all right if we all leave it for a couple of hours?"

"I think so, Pa."

"All right, get up the trotters Bess and Belda."

"But Pa, we just got them this summer. We haven't tried them out yet on the road. What if they scare when the Bonnie Omaha section men come along in their speeder?"

"They're just gonna have to get used to living near a railroad track."

Somehow they all managed to pack themselves into the two-seated carriage. Pa with his plug hat and Ma in her black frock coat sat in front, with Mallie in between them and Geoffrey up on Ma's lap. The other six were piled in back, Dirk holding Tressa on his lap, Rolf sitting alone in the middle, Tane holding Thea on his lap. Ana disdained sitting down; she stood all the way to church just behind the front seat. There was much laughter all three and a half miles. Clara tried to quiet them down by reminding them that they were on their way to worship in a tabernacle of the Lord. But if it wasn't Belda the right-hand Morgan lifting her tail and letting go with a merry musical toot every time her right rear leg hit the road, then it was Dirk making a joke about what a sharp tailbone Tressa had—it was digging into his leg like a cold chisel.

The bunch quieted down as they entered Bonnie. They watched the houses go by. Tunis handled the ribbons expertly and kept the swift bays in hand despite all the strange sounds down the main street.

Once on the churchyard, Ma led the kids into the white church through the south door, while Tunis unhitched the horses and led them into the red church barn.

When Tunis peeked around inside the south door to see where Clara and the kids had gone to sit, he couldn't find them at first. It embarrassed him to stand there like an old cock trying to find where his hen had settled herself in tall grass. Strange blond faces stared at him, the eyes in them already sobered by what they expected the minister to say in his sermon. Then a figure stiffened by piety caught his eye. Ana. Quickly he spotted Clara sitting to Ana's right. There was an opening for one more at the end of Clara's bench. Tunis walked up the aisle and sat down. Their family of ten exactly filled the bench.

Tunis felt uncomfortable. He could feel eyes behind him staring at the back of his head. Little children ahead turned shyly about to look at him. Soon a mother had to place a hand on the head of the staring child and turn it around to face the front. It wasn't long though before the little blond head wyed around once more. The church seemed to be full of mothers with bared tits nursing babies and fathers gravely fingering spade beards.

Tunis had on a new blue serge suit. It felt tight. He wished he could loosen his red tie and white shirt collar. Clara would have a fit if he did. Little Geoffrey, also wearing blue serge, sat quietly obedient next to him. Clara kept a brood hen's eye on the others sitting to the left of her. The Freylings were going to have style or else.

The sun struck through a round window high in the south wall and down at the seats ahead. It lighted up the white hair of an old man with a silverish trans-lucent effect, as though Judgment Day was about to come for him and he needed only to listen to one more sermon and then he could be transfigured into immortality. The stroking round column of sunlight also, by reflection, made the golden pipes of the organ gleam softly as though each pipe were lighted from within by a tall candle.

Presently the janitor, a bent old man with long gray hair, came down the north aisle carrying a glass of water. He moved on such an even keel that the water remained perfectly level in the glass. His old filmy gray eyes, his whole being, was concentrated on making sure not a ripple showed in the glass. He carried it down the farther curve of the long aisle, then climbed the steps to the rostrum and set the glass on the right-hand ledge of the oaken pulpit.

Five minutes to go, the organist, a pretty woman with a wide gray hat, climbed into the console and began playing some music from medieval times, softly. The whole church quieted down, even the babies.

Presently at 9:30 the minister, Reverend Graves, came down the north aisle, followed by six elders and six deacons, all dressed in freshly pressed black suits, limbs stiff with Sunday decorum. Reaching the front of the church, the six elders and the six deacons sought out their two reserved benches, while the minister, a huge block of a man, stopped at the foot of the stairs to the rostrum. He prayed to himself, great gray head bowed. The rostrum was the holy of ho-lies of the Lord, and during worship no one ascended it without first squaring accounts with the Almighty. Finished, the minister ascended the steps. Lifting the tails of his black coat, he slowly sat down on a carved wooden chair with a black leather seat and back.

When the organist finished her prelude, Reverend rose to his feet and ap-proached the pulpit. He opened a large black hymnal and announced they would open the service by singing Psalm 68. He spoke in the Dutch language.

Tunis waited for Reverend Graves to translate what he'd just said into Amer-ican, but when he didn't Tunis glanced over at Clara with a questioning look.

Clara looked back with the same bewildered look.

Tunis leaned over and whispered, "Is this all gonna be in the Dutch language?"

"I hope not," she whispered back.

The organist played the opening note, once, then with the congregation joining in, deepened the notes. Wonderful voices singing in an Old World tongue swelled into the psalm.

Tunis was moved.

Singing finished, Reverend Graves made what appeared to be some announcements, again in Dutch.

Tunis frowned.

Clara sat as still as a prairie chicken caught out in the wilds by a change of weather. The children too sat very still, eyes and ears taking in the strange babble.

It went on and on. Finally, some ten minutes into the sermon proper, Tunis couldn't stand it any longer. With a look of apology at Clara, he slowly rose to his feet and headed for the south door and went outside.

When the service was over and they were all safely aboard the carriage again, Clara said, "You might have had the decency to at least wait until the benediction."

"What? Never." Tunis glared at her. "You might have known it would all be in Dutch. I met those Hollanders once in Sioux Center, and they're a stubborn lot. They're still thinking that America is one of the colonies of the Netherlands."

Clara bounced Geoffrey hard in her lap. "I still think it was good to go once, though. At least the ritual of the thing was welcome."

"About as bad as going to a Roman Catholic church where everything is done in Latin."

"Now, now."

184

"Really, for me to go to a Dutch service is like having to go to a whorehouse without balls."

Tane and Dirk almost smothered with laughter.

"Not in front of the children, please!"

Tunis said, "The children hear this kind of talk in the barn all the time."

"But on a churchyard?"

"There's a church barn not forty feet away."

Clara lifted her nose. "Anyway, while you were getting out the horses, I talked to Reverend Graves a moment. He assures me they do not teach in the Dutch language in their Christian School." She pointed toward a two-story concrete-block building on the corner of the church lot. "It's a state requirement that all instruction must be in the English language."

Tunis sent a little slap into the reins. "Get, Bess! Belda!"

The dark chestnut horses leaned into their collars, the great muscles of their rear quarters doubling and redoubling.

Clara said firmly, "I still want our children to have Christian instruction. They're getting enough of the other from the rough life around us."

Tunis waited until they were almost upon the Bonnie Hotel before he said, "If I hear once more about someone wanting to crucify any one of my children, the children are staying home and we'll hire Miss Velda Fikes to come live with us and instruct them."

Clara waited until they turned past the flagpole before she said, "That I'll agree to."

The children looked from Pa to Ma and back again. They wished Pa and Ma would get rid of their storm clouds.

Tunis looked up at the sky. "I did notice the Little Church has a pretty good barn to stall our horse in while the kids are in school. They even have a feedbox in the mangers."

"Good," Clara said.

That night, going to bed, with Clara already under the blankets and only her head showing, a white nightcap on, Tunis settled on the end of the bed before he blew out the lamp. "Wife," he said.

"Yes, Mr. Freyling?"

"You don't ever say husband anymore, do you?"

"No, I do not."

"Why don't you just call me brother then . . . sister."

Clara stared at him, daring him to proceed.

Tunis loved her. Yet here she was, in their very own bedroom, denying him touching and kissing. What was truly amiss? They didn't have to have children if he withdrew in time like Onan once did. "Wife," he said, "wife, really, we can't go on living in a state of near war all the time. It isn't good for us. It isn't good for our children. They know something is wrong between us."

"I am aware of that and I wish it wasn't there and the best way to get rid of it is for you to begin behaving like a Christian husband. The time for procreation is over. Finished."

A great sadness welled up from his belly. He looked at her with pleading eyes.

"There you go again with that look. Maybe you better go sleep on the couch in the parlor tonight."

185

21. Tane

Tane and Pa finished milking their last cow at about the same time, and one after the other emptied their pails into a big five-gallon milk can. The smell of raw milk and moist mastication was sweet on the air.

Tane said, "That new Frisian cow is giving more every time I pail her. We ought to get more of them, Pa, now that Dirk and Rolf are helping with the milking. And with Tressa stripping those we're drying up."

"I've thought of that, son. But I just wonder if we shouldn't add a couple of Guernseys instead. A Guernsey gives out richer milk. It's so rich with cream it's almost yellow. If we add their milk to what we get from our Frisians, our cream check will fatten up some."

"Where would we get some Guernseys?"

"The next time I ship hogs to Chicago, I'll go along and see if I can't find some there."

Dirk and then Rolf stood up from their last cows too and, throwing their one-legged stools to one side, poured their milk into the big five-gallon milk can.

Tane noticed that Dirk had a red welt near his left eye. "What happened to you?"

Dirk turned his head away to hide his eye. "Nothing."

"I hope the other fellow looks worse."

Dirk looked down at where Tressa still had her head buried in the side of a skinny cow. She was stripping each teat with thumb and forefinger.

Tressa felt Dirk's eyes on her and finally looked up with a twisted smile. "My wrist hurts so. I can't pinch hard enough. There's always a couple drops left."

Dirk quick gave her a quirked look to shush her.

Tane caught the exchange. "What happened to you two?"

"Nothing."

"C'mon."

Pa was alerted too. "What now?"

Tressa finally had to laugh. "Those public high school kids, they're such devils."

"What happened?" Tane had noticed earlier that when the kids came home from school in their gray cab they'd all looked a little flustered. Late that summer Pa had got hold of an old buggy and had timbered up an enclosed cab on its running gear. He'd put a door in back, with a little window or driving hole in front. He'd built a narrow bench along the inner wall on both sides, so that the kids, except for the driver, sat facing each other. Thea and Tressa had painted it all a flat gray. It was cozy inside and already the kids declared it a comfort against the November winds. Tane asked further, "You didn't have a runaway with Bess now?"

Tressa said, "Well, she didn't like what happened."

Tane rocked back and forth on his stout legs. He'd become a broad slab of a young man, with muscles in his forearms and over his shoulders like the muscles of a Belgian horse. He had wide hands with stubby thick fingers. His thumbnails were twice as wide as they were long. In the flesh of his thumbs his nails looked like the tip of a full moon just barely showing over the edge of a horizon. "You better tell us what happened. We're not going to have any more of that dummed persecution of us Freylings."

Tressa finally decided she'd got the last drops out of her cow. She stood up, tossed her one-legged stool to one side, and poured what little milk she'd got into the big galvanized can. She poured mostly with her left hand, the right hurt her so. "Well, them high school toughs swarmed around our cab just as we were driving past. One of them grabbed Bess by the bridle and then two others quick unhooked her tugs. Well, you know what happened next. When they let go of Bess's bridle she took off, with Dirk hanging on to the lines. He flew out of the driving hole and we girls flew out of the rear door. With our dresses over our heads like a bunch of chickens blown out of the coop by a whirlwind." Tressa had to laugh so much she sat down on her one-legged stool again. "And I landed wrong on my right wrist."

"So that's how," Tane said. "Where was you all this time, Rolf?"

Rolf was laughing too. His big horse teeth shown white in the dim illumination shedding down from a lantern hanging on a nail in an overhead beam. "You know what Pa's said to me, that I wasn't to stick my nose into things, so they wouldn't be so apt to call me names."

Tane shook his head. "You two guys, when you saw trouble coming, you shoulda popped out of your cab and stood up to those city shits."

Dirk said, "It wasn't city birds tormenting us so much, as it was those dirty Mud Crickers."

"You mean those miserable excuses for human bein's living along Mud Creek there?"

"Yeh. Those Schellers. They're a noisy lot. And the names they call people. You know what they call us?"

"What?"

"Frycakes. Can you imagine? All because we go to a Dutch school. And because the Dutch are supposed to eat a lot of frycakes."

Pa had been leaning against a support pole and listening with a scowl on his dark weathered face. "The name calling ain't all that bad. That's just plain human nature. But I don't like it they touched Bess. Maybe I better talk to the town marshall."

Dirk said, "Oh, don't do that, Pa. It'll only make it worse. We can take a different route through town."

"Never," Tane growled. "We Freylings don't have to skirk around like beaten dogs. There's got to be some way to fix those Mud Crickers." His wide body shook back and forth. "We'll think of something."

Pa said, "Nah. Standing here like this, the milk's gonna get cold before we run it through the separator. Tane, grab hold of the other handle and let's haul this big can to the milk shed."

Tane let his anger down slowly and helped his father carry the full can to the house.

But Tane wasn't done with those Mud Crickers. The next afternoon around two o'clock he told Pa that he was going to the pasture and check out the fence line before the snow blew in. Once out of sight of the yard, he followed the willows south along the Big Rock River for a mile, then cut across to the Bonnie Omaha tracks. Once in town he headed directly for the churchyard near the Christian School. He had just barely crawled into the Freyling gray cab when school let out. When Thea opened the back door to the cab, he greeted her with a smile and a finger to her lips, warning her not to say anything and to tell Tressa and Ana to shush too.

Dirk and Rolf soon had Bess hitched up to the cab, and when they crawled inside the cab Tane also shushed them not to say anything. Tane whispered, "The school kids here don't need to know I rode with you tonight. But by gummy, those rascals up at the high school are sure gonna know about it."

Dirk said, "I was thinking of taking a different route home, like I said last night."

Tane said, "And like I said last night, we Freylings don't have to skirk around like beaten dogs. Now, let's get going. Pa is probably wondering where I've gone already."

Dirk began to smile. "Ha! Boy, do I want to see the faces of those Schellers when you come flying out the back. Especially that big Bors. He spits when he talks. Like a leaky faucet with the wind blowing out of it."

Both Dirk and Rolf smelled of old dried horse manure from the church barn. Tan dust from the barn floor lay over the toes of their shoes. The girls, Thea, Tressa, and Ana, felt the chill in the air and began to slip on their mittens. Ma had tied a string to their mittens and had run the string through the sleeves around over the backs of their necks so they wouldn't lose them.

188

Dirk sent a ripple down the lines to Bess. "C'mon, you old skate, let's shake a couple of legs."

They rattled off the churchyard and headed up the first street going north. Soon the roof of the high school showed through the trees. The ash trees and the maples were turning, green shading off into lemon yellows and rusty ochers. Several oldsters, men and women, were raking up the first fallen leaves into neat piles on their yards. A single cumulus cloud, white with an underside of gray, hung over the white cypress water tower high on the hill east of town.

The corner of the high school grounds appeared.

Tane crawled to the end of the left bench near the door in the rear, crouched, ready to spring out.

Dirk began to laugh at what was coming next. "C'mon, Bess old girl, get going there."

But Bess was remembering what happened the day before. She tried to shy off and take the street to the left.

"Hyar!" Dirk cried. He pulled hard on the right line, jerking it, so that the bit in Bess's bridle almost came out of that side of her mouth. "Get back on the track, you old bitch."

"Please," Thea said, "no swearing now." She and Ana and Tressa sat very straight on the bench along the right side. They'd turned white over their cheeks remembering what had happened the day before. "And Tane," Thea added, "please, don't lose your temper either. We all know how strong you are."

"Never mind now," Tane said. "I know what I'm doing."

Bucking a little, shying from right to left, Bess slow-trotted toward the wide main sidewalk leading up to the big white front door of the white high school. She'd spotted the gang of bad boys lolling on the front steps.

Tane leaned forward to get a good look at the gang of young toughs. "You're sure that's the same bunch?"

"Positive," Dirk said. "See that big one up front? That's Bors Scheller, the meanest Mud Cricker of them all."

All Tane could see of Bors was a bristle of wild twine-colored hair and a high nose.

Sure enough, just as their cab was about to draw even with the wide main sidewalk, the gang of toughs poured down off the front steps and came running toward them. Bors headed for Bess's head while the others converged on the tugs tied to the shafts.

Tane waited until they'd stopped Bess and the cab, then hopped out and, leaning down, snaked up past Bess. He caught Bors by the throat and with a single powerful flip plopped him down on the hard gravel street. "You dummed bully, ragging my kid brothers and sisters! I'll teach you to torment them." Tane bopped the back of Bors' head up and down on the gravel. "Take that, you miserable excuse for a human bein'. And that! And that!"

Bors gulped. "Oww!" His huge nose turned purple and his thin slit lips turned sheet white. "Cut it out."

"You bet, I'll cut it out," Tane gritted between set teeth. "Calling us frycakes, you deserve to have your tongue cut out."

Ana stuck her head out of the driving hole. "Kick him in the knots!"

Tane was shocked. But then that was Ana's way. She didn't think much of men and boys. Her cry cooled him down some.

Dirk and Rolf piled out of the cab too and tackled the other fellows trying to unhook Bess's tugs. They went at them with such fury the gang retreated, and when they saw what was happening to their leader in the hands of the powerful Tane they took flight.

Drops of spittle shot out of Bors's mouth as Tane bopped him some more on the hard earth. Bors tried to squirm out from under Tane, but Tane's weight and power held him firmly fixed to the ground.

Suddenly there was a commanding cry directly above Tane. Already the boys Dirk and Rolf as well as the girls Thea and Tressa and Ana in the cab had fallen silent.

"Tane! Let him go. Do you hear me? Let him go! Right now."

Tane looked up. There was Pa sitting horseback on Belda.

"Let him go!" Pa roared again. Pa had the strangest look on his face. "Get up from there. Right now!"

Tane thought Bors should have a couple of more bops; he hadn't been punished enough. But Tane decided to listen to Pa. He let go of Bors and stood up. A little deflated, yet grinning a little, Tane said, "Why, Pa, you sound like you was afraid I was gonna kill him."

Pa's face was all worked up. His pearl gray eyes looked as if they'd turned to steam. "You didn't tell me you was gonna do this."

"No, I didn't. And I didn't because I knew you'd tell me not to. But I decided I had to."

"After this you tell me, you hear? I don't want you getting into bad trouble."

"Why Pa, you really do sound like you was afraid I was gonna kill him, for godsakes."

Pa's whitish eyes glowed down from Belda's back. Pa sucked both lips inward and bit on them.

The other kids, Thea, Tressa, Ana, Dirk, and Rolf, also stared at Pa. The high school toughs stood with open mouths along the sidewalk. Bors slowly picked himself up off the ground and crestfallen joined his bunch again.

Tane said, "I only meant to shake him up good, Pa. It was time to teach him something. Those Mud Crickers are so wild they're only one jump ahead of the Indians."

Pa said, "Don't compare them to Indians. Your Ma and I knew some good ones."

"Oh, that's right. We got a good one buried in our pasture." Tane rocked back and forth, feeling his power. He'd done something wonderful. "Yeh, maybe you're right, Pa. I shoudna been so rough on him. But you might as well tie a knot in a dog's tail as to expect a Mud Cricker to be a sensible citizen."

Pa chewed on his teeth some more, though it could be seen he was much relieved to see that Tane could joke about what he'd done. Funny that Pa should be so afraid that his oldest boy would get out of hand. Pa said, "Let's all head for home. Ma will be worried about us being late."

Ana had to make one last gesture. Leaning out through the driving hole, she stuck her tongue out at the roughs from Mud Crick.

Rolf laughed a wide white tooth laugh. "Why, Ana, I didn't know you had a tongue with such a sharp point to it."

Pa said from his saddle. "Ana, let's have no rubbing it in. We want to get along with people. You never know when we may need a Mud Cricker to help us out at threshing time."

22. Thea

Thea had been aware of trouble brewing in Pa and Ma's bedroom. It had something to do with what Pa and Ma did in private. Also that it had to do with the difference between a man and a woman.

Thea had only the past summer learned there was a big difference between her and Tane, just as there was a difference between all the other boys in the family and her sisters. Thea had begun to have her periods. In particular she'd learned the difference when she helped raise Geoffrey, changing his diapers and such. Little Geoffrey had that pretty little dingle.

Thea wanted Pa and Ma to be happy. She cast around in her mind how she could say something to help. The Bible said it was not good for men to live alone. But it also was not good for man and wife to be always quarreling. Pa really was a wonderful man, a rock of strength for the whole family. She knew that if she ever found a man like Pa and married him, she'd give him what he wanted. Whatever that might be.

She loved Pa. She was most grateful that when she became old enough to help with the milking, Pa had smiled and said that, no, she should help Ma in the house. "Turn and turn about," he'd said. "I got Tane to help me with my work; now it's Ma's turn to have help." Thea hadn't cared much for barn work and such. She hadn't even cared much for getting the eggs or washing the milk pails. She liked dusting and making the beds. She liked knitting and crocheting. She liked setting a good-looking table for dinner.

Thea had learned much about being a woman of the house by just watching Ma, and of course from playing with her dolls and the little dollhouse Pa had built for her one winter day.

She remembered the time she'd played she was a mother with a newborn child. Pa and Ma had given her a brand-new doll for Christmas. Of course having a baby meant the baby would go ackyfeese in its diaper and she would have to change it. To make it more real she'd stealthily gone to the kitchen with her doll and poured a little spurt of what was left in the coffeepot into the doll's diaper. Then she'd shaken her head, like any good caring mother might, and in a warm loving voice had scolded her doll. "Dolly, Dolly! Tchh, tchh! Look at what you've done. When are you going to be housebroke? Tchh, tchh. Now we're going to have to change your diaper again and give you a bath." She'd undressed her doll by the stove. As she carried it on the way to the sink past where Pa was sitting, she saw the affectionate smile on her father's lips. She'd said, "Papa, you mustn't look now," and she held the doll to one side so her father couldn't see the doll's bare poopet part. A moment later, Pa had burst out laughing; and then with a quick hand to his face had tried to hide that he was laughing.

It was Saturday. Looking out the kitchen window to the west, toward the Big Rock River, Thea saw it was snowing. So early in the fall? Goodness, it meant they were going to have a spell of squaw winter. Squaw winters, unlike Indian summers, didn't come around very often. The falling snow made her want to hug herself, to feel cozy. Better yet, maybe she and Tane and Dirk and Tressa could go sliding on the hills across the railroad tracks. Pa had timbered up a sled for them, which Tane and Dirk mostly used. The girls preferred to sit down with their coats wrapped tightly around them and then slide down. The only trouble was, it made Ma so mad that their coats wore out so fast over the seat.

She was half-done with the breakfast dishes. Pa and the older boys were out on the yard somewhere, and Ma and the other girls were upstairs making up the beds for the day. Little Geoffrey was toddling around under the long table playing with a boy doll.

As she watched through the window, the snow began to fall thicker, in flakes as long as chicken feathers. If it kept up much longer they could go coasting down the east hills. A surge of joy filled her. They'd have a high old time. The Freyling kids knew how to have fun together. And Pa and Ma didn't seem to mind so long as the chores were done and the fun wasn't a bad thing to do.

Tane came stomping into the back porch, then into the kitchen, wide pink face open with a big smile. "Do you see what I see outdoors?"

Thea smiled. She looked down at his shoes. "You forgot something."

Tane looked down at his feet. "Oh, yeh, take off my shoes. Or sweep them off with a broom." He quick stepped back into the porch and began whisking the snow off his shoes. Then he popped back inside, closing the door behind him. "Are you kids done in the house with your morning work?"

"I about am."

"Well, we are. Dirk is getting out the sled. And I found a long piece of tin up in the haymow that Old Frisholm the carpenter left behind. We can slide down on that too."

Thea suddenly had an idea. "Say," she said, "I know what us girls can do. And I'm going to ask Ma if we can have it."

"What's that?"

"You'll see. Why don't you guys just go ahead. We girls will come as soon as we can."

"Good. Where did you girls put our buckle boots last spring after the last snow?"

"Where else but where we always hang them? Behind that door you just went through. Up on the wall there."

"Good. Dirk and Rolf want theirs too. See you in a couple of minutes then." Tane whirled and was gone.

Thea hurried to finish the dishes. Oh, joy.

She remembered once asking Pa what it meant to have a squaw winter.

Pa'd said, "Well, honey, that early snow makes for easier hunting for the Indian brave. Early snow melts slowly into the ground and softens up the dry leaves and twigs. Everything is matted. That way he can stalk his game without being heard."

"But Pa, if it's the brave who does the hunting, why call it a squaw winter?"

"The brave brings down the game, and then the squaw goes out and cuts up the meat and brings it home."

"Doesn't the brave help carry it home?"

"Sometimes."

Ma couldn't resist making a comment. "The brave gets all the fun and glory, and the squaw does all the bloody work. Just like in the white world."

Pa had to laugh. "But the squaw owns the meat and she doles it out. All the brave has is his bow and arrow."

Tressa came running into the kitchen. "Thea! It's snowing."

"I know. Tane was in already to ask if we wanted to go sledding."

"Are you going?"

"Of course. Tell Ana to hurry up with making the beds."

Soon Ma came into the kitchen. With her hair caught up in a dust cap and a dustpan in her hand, she looked like a witch. "When did I say you could go sledding?"

"Ma, I know you don't like it when we slide down in our coats. Can we have that old bread pan hanging out in the porch?"

"What for?"

"We can slide down in that."

"What you kids won't think of next." Ma heaved a big sigh. "All right, go ahead. It's got a hole in it anyway. I was hoping Arie Makkum the tinsmith would come by one of these days and mend it for us."

"Oh, Ma, we won't hurt it more sliding on the snow."

An inward thought darkened Ma's eyes. "All right. But dress warmly now, you hear?"

"We will." What Ma meant was to be sure to put on extra underclothes so the boys wouldn't get ideas in case the dresses slid up.

Soon they were all up on the highest hill east across the tracks and standing near the big red boulder. The boys had already slid down the hill several times on the homemade sled and the long strip of tin.

Dirk had to laugh when he saw the big wide bread pan. "What are you gillies gonna do with that?"

"Just you watch." Thea clapped the pan to her seat, made a few running jumps forward to the lip of the hill, sat down where the snow was deepest with the pan under her, and began sliding. As she gained speed, the bread pan began to turn on her, and by the time she reached the bottom of the hill she was spinning around like a top. She let out a long pealing yell.

Tressa watched closely. After a moment she decided she'd rather ride on the strip of tin with Dirk than sit in a spinning bread pan. "I get dizzy so easy." And down she went with Dirk, also shrilling with joy.

Ana stood with her usual air of being self-sufficient. "Good. That'll give me and Thea more turns at the pan."

Thea climbed back up the hill. A lively north wind had raised roses to her cheeks.

Ana took the pan next, clapped it to her seat, made several quick running leaps, and then plopped down with the pan under her. She too began to trill with excitement as she sailed down the hill. She held her knees to her chest. As she went down, the wind of her going caught at the blue shawl around her neck and gradually unwound it. She looked like a descending spider slowly releasing a trailing thread. And she too began to spin like a top the faster she went down.

It was Tane's turn to take the crude homemade sled down the hill. Carrying it sideways, he made a short run, getting up good speed, and then with the sled against his chest threw himself forward. He hit the snow-packed earth with a thud and started sliding. Pa had reinforced the runners' edges with strips of iron and after a dozen feet the sled seemed to pick up extra speed because of it. Iron mashed through the snow better than did plain wood. Near the bottom of the hill Tane let go with a wonderful yell of triumph.

They all slid down and climbed back up, and slid down and climbed back up, for a couple of hours. The more they played the more tireless they felt. They laughed and laughed. Slowly too, as more snow fell, and as they rolled off into the damp snow at the end of each run, they became sopping wet over their seats and arms. Mittens shrank, and if one took a mitten off one couldn't get it back on. Fingers turned red and tingled.

Thea noted that Tressa kept sliding down with Dirk on the strip of tin. "Don't you want to try the pan once, Tressa?"

"No. The tin is fine. I can't tell which is the most fun, with Dirk on top and me on the bottom, or the other way around."

Thea was a little jealous. "Let's trade once."

A frown showed between Tressa's dark eyebrows. But she was a good-natured soul, and softened, and said, "All right. Just once then." Tressa took the pan and like Thea and Ana clapped it to her seat, made several running jumps, sat down, and down the hill she sailed.

Thea turned to Dirk. "C'mon, brother, I can go down with you once. That much you ain't stuck on Tressa, are you?"

Dirk's lips broke into a twisted smile. "Well, all my sisters are good looking. I guess I'm lucky at that." He gestured down at the long strip of shiny tin. "You wanna be on the bottom, or what?"

"I'll do like Tressa. On the bottom." She pulled the tin to the edge of where the hill began to tip down and then lay down on the tin.

With a yielding laugh, Dirk lay down on her. "Work your arms like they might be fins. To pull us forward. That's right. There. And away we go."

Thea was instantly aware of the firm bump in the front of Dirk's pants. So that's what Tressa was feeling every time the two of them went down the hill together. It was wrong of Tressa to like that. Certainly with her brother. Thea became so conscious of the warm bump that she was hardly aware of how fast they were flying into the spraying snow. Yes, it was wrong of Tressa. And of Dirk. But how was she going to warn them without getting them mad at her. Could be too they didn't know it was happening, were just having a lot of fun. But the bump was warm. And it was big.

Thea and Dirk slid to a stop. Dirk rolled off into the snow, feet and hands up in the air like a playful puppy. She rolled off the other side of the sled. She looked at Dirk sharply. But, no, he was only laughing up into the falling snow, at the fun of it all. Thea blinked snow out of her eyes. Maybe it was all in her head.

When Thea and Dirk had climbed back up the hill, Tressa had already given up the bread pan to Ana and had come over to await Dirk with the strip of tin.

Tressa said, "Now, ain't the tin more fun, Thea?"

Thea looked Tressa in the eye. But Tressa's face was innocent with a warm smile. Tressa didn't seem to catch on why Thea was looking at her that way. "It was all right," Thea said finally. "Though I think if I go down again I'm going to lay on top of Dirk. He lays so heavy on one."

194

Tressa laughed. "He sure does, don't he? That's why I sometimes get even with him by laying on top and bouncing on him when we get to the bottom so he knows what I'm going through."

"Oh."

Tressa asked, "You going down with him again?"

"No. You go ahead. You like it better than me. I like the good old bread pan."

It was Rolf's turn to go down with the homemade sled. He was a faster runner than Tane. He also backed up farther to get his running start. When Rolf finally slid forward with the sled, horse smile glittering as white as the snow, he was already going full tilt. He too let out a triumphant yell when, halfway down the hill, the iron runners sang on the snow and, where there were little bumps of pocket gopher mounds, the sled took off a few feet, sailing in the air each time.

Tressa and Dirk went down next. Their stocking caps were covered with frozen crusts of snow. Dirk was on the bottom, and after they'd got a good start Tressa began to bounce on Dirk as they went over some rough spots, to emphasize them, laughing, going ungh ungh. It struck Thea that if Dirk had done that with Tressa under him it would be wrong.

It also struck Thea what was probably wrong with Pa and Ma in their bedroom. It horrified her to think that Pa and Ma might still be coupling. Pa putting himself into Ma? Uggh. Of course they must have done that some time in the past to have had eight children. But that was back then. It was impossible to imagine them doing it now.

Poor Pa. Poor man. He should pray to God for help to get rid of lust. For lust it had to be if one could believe Father Garlington.

And poor Ma. Bedeviled by a man she loved. Ma was probably the worst off. Ma had to fend off a man and at the same time try to hold him to help her raise the children. Ma couldn't let him do it and she couldn't let him get angry.

Thea became aware someone was calling her name. "What? What?"

Ana was standing in front of her with wide blue questioning eyes. "Thea! It was like you was in another world. I called you and called you."

"What do you want?"

"It's your turn. 'Course, if you don't want your turn—"

"Gimme that pan." Thea snatched it away from Ana. "'Course I want my turn." She took several quick jumps forward, clapped the pan to her seat, added yet another jump to get up some real speed for once, and then plumped herself down seat first. She hit an icy spot and found herself losing the pan under her. She tried to right her body, but couldn't quite get herself centered in the pan. She leaned ahead, leaned ahead, trying to catch up with the pan. Because of all the sliding they'd done so far, the path down the hill had become very slick. The pan with her trying to stay on it began to gain real speed. By the time she hit the bottom of the hill wind began to burn her cheeks. About then she caught up with the pan. And just when she'd centered herself on it, she noticed she was still going with great speed past the spot where they usually came to rest. The pan had also begun to spin. And on one of the spins she saw, scaring her, that she was headed straight for the railroad tracks. On the next spin around she found herself going up the small grade of the railroad. She tried to tumble out of the pan; finally managed to do so. But it was too late. She went head first into a partially snow-covered iron rail. Bang! Stars! Gone . . .

When she came to, she found herself lying on the brown sofa in the parlor. There were faces hovering over her. Pa. Ma. And a strange face with light blue-snow eyes and a bow tie. Dr. Wallance.

"How did I get here?" Thea asked.

"Tane carried you in," Ma said.

Pa was smiling.

Whirlwinds were circling in Thea's head. Inside it was like she was full of smoke. Like a chimney was backing up. "Pa," she said, "why ain't you nice to Ma?"

Pa stiffened.

"Now, now," Ma said. "Just lie still now." Ma turned to Dr. Wallance. "She's still out of her head a little."

Dr. Wallance grunted.

Thea felt of her head. Dr. Wallance had wrapped a thick bandage around her forehead. "I sure gave myself a bump, didn't I?"

Dirk said from the foot of the sofa, "Good thing the Bonnie Omaha didn't come along just then. You'd have derailed it."

Ma said, "That's enough now. No more joking about it."

Thea wondered if while she was out of her head she'd said something about what Dirk and Tressa were doing.

Ma said, "She'll be all right now, Doctor?"

Dr. Wallance's old veined Adam's apple bobbed over his black bow tie. "She'll be fine."

Pa said, "What do we owe you?"

"Oh, five dollars." Dr. Wallance smiled as he rubbed his chin with slender veined fingers. "No rush about it though. I wasn't put into this world to make money." Dr. Wallance picked up Thea's hand and took her pulse. "How do you feel?"

Thea's tongue had a mind of its own. "I'm still worried about Pa and Ma."

23. Tunis

March 1903

"You've come at the wrong time. It's too late for breakfast and too early for dinner," Tunis said.

"I'm not trying to work you for a meal," the peddler said. "Though I never refuse one." The fellow was driving a stylish pair of black flyers in front of a blue hack. He had black hair slicked back, a high forehead with a long thin nose, and eyes like slippery buttons. He was dressed in gray striped tails and black leather boots.

"Maybe you better move on before I lose my temper."

"Come now," the fellow said, "you wouldn't want me to take to drink because I couldn't make a sale today, now would you?" The fellow's long nose had the discolored look of a drinker. "My name is Phineas Quimby."

"Can't leave it alone, huh?"

"Oh, I'm on the wagon now. But it ain't easy to stay aboard, let me tell you." For a moment Quimby's eyes softened with reflection. "The worst thing about being on the wagon is that when you get up in the morning that's the best you're going to feel all day."

Tunis had to smile. The fellow was a kind of curious skate after all.

Quimby looked at the Freyling yard, noting the big barn and the fine house and the full granaries. "You haven't done so bad, have you? And you still look young."

"Well, you know what they say, only the good die young, and so far I've beat Satan out of it."

"Lucky you."

"What kid of trash you peddling? And let me tell you, I hate all peddlers." Tunis had stepped outdoors without putting on his blue denim jacket, and the chilly air began to penetrate his clothes. The sun was out but it still hadn't risen high enough to warm things up.

"Mostly this set of Mark Twain's *Complete Works*. Surely you've heard of him."

"Yep." Mark Twain was a funny man with deep thoughts.

"One of the great humorists of all time."

"I could stand a little humor around here."

"You ain't happy with this layout? I'll trade you."

"How much?"

Phineas Quimby tied up the reins around the whip socket and with long fingers quickly opened a paper carton on the seat beside him. He pulled out the first volume, a gleaming red book with gold lettering. "There's twenty-four volumes to the complete set. That'll cost you fifty cabbage leaves."

"That's pretty steep." Tunis knew Clara was watching them through the kitchen window. She wouldn't approve of paying that much for a set of books by a humorist. "How about a couple of smoked hams?"

"How many pounds each?"

"Twenty pounds."

"Make it four and the set is yours."

Tunis rolled his shoulders against the cold. He thought of inviting the fellow in but decided against it when he remembered the stories about how salesmen were known to seduce the women of one's household. He took the book from the fellow. It was volume one of *Roughing It*. Tunis opened it at random, eyes falling on the sentence: "Here, right by my side, was the actual ogre who, in fights and brawls and various ways, *had taken the lives of twenty-six human beings*." Twain was telling about a famous desperado known as Slade. Tunis remembered hearing Old Dirk Freyling talk about Slade. Tunis cleared his throat. "Is that all you're peddling?"

"I'm also selling a set of Charles Dickens."

"Ain't he British?"

"That he is."

Tunis considered. If he bought a set of Twain for himself for winter reading, he'd better buy a set of Dickens for the Britisher Clara. "I better have him too. Only trouble is, I doubt if I can let you have more than four hams."

"What else you got to trade?"

"Let's take a walk over to the smokehouse. But first let me get a jacket."

The smokehouse had once been a small chicken house. It'd had to be fumigated for lice and it was then that Tunis had decided they might as well smoke their meat in it. Tunis and Phineas Quimby both had to stoop through the door and could just barely stand up under the low ridgepole. Various kinds of smoked meat hung to either side of them, ham, sausage, jerky, and several quarters of beef.

198

Phineas Quimby spotted the quarters of beef right away. "Whew! What nice chunks of meat. I'll take one of those for Dickens."

"What'll you do with both the ham and the beef?"

"Sell 'em to some store in Bonnie for cash."

"Hmff." Something caught in Tunis's mind. "Hey, your last name Quimby, there's a town by that name on the other side of Le Mars. British settlement. You British too?"

"You hit it."

"What a cohinkydinky. Okay, you get the quarter of beef for Dickens."

Together the two men carried the meat to Phineas Quimby's buggy. Then the fellow set the two boxes of books on the stoop. They shook hands. Tunis continued to feel Clara watching them through the kitchen window. He smiled to himself when he thought about what Clara would say when she saw the set of Dickens.

Phineas Quimby climbed aboard his blue hack. He loosened the lines, picked up the whip and flourished it lightly, making a whistling sound with it, and clucked up on the black trotters. The trotters responded instantly and they were off up the lane.

Tunis carried the box of Dickens into the house first. "Wife, here's something for you." He set it on the kitchen table.

Clara and Thea were busy at the sink. They turned to look. Clara had her hair done up in a knot on top of her head and Thea had done hers up in a long golden braid. Clara said, "What worthless thing did you trade for now?"

"Open it. It's for you."

Clara wiped her hands on her gray red-trimmed apron. She got a butcher knife out of the utensil drawer in the cabinet and with a guarded grimace cut the box open. She folded the paper leaves back and lifted out some packing. A long row of red leather-bound books came to view. Clara stared. "I don't believe it." She pulled out one of the volumes. It had gilt edges and the pages were uncut. "Dickens. My father's favorite."

"I thought you'd mentioned that once," Tunis said.

Clara read the title. "*Dombey and Son*. For some reason my father loved this one the best."

Thea beamed at her father and mother.

Clara said, "And what's in the other box?"

"Just a minute." Tunis stepped outside and brought in the Mark Twain. "Have a look."

Clara picked out a book, *Innocents Abroad*. "Isn't this the one where he pokes fun of the Old Countries?"

"I don't know. That's what I'm going to find out. There's nothing else to do winter evenings." He picked up volume one of *Roughing It* again. "I think I'll read this one first." He flipped through the front matter. Some printed handwriting caught his eye: *This is the authorized Uniform Edition of all my books, Mark Twain.*

Clara caught the shaft he'd shot at her. "What we can do at night, when we're about to go to sleep, is talk about what we find in our favorite author."

"Yuh," Tunis grunted.

Thea sensed an argument coming on. She asked brightly, "Can I read these books too? After you've finished them?"

Clara nodded. "Sure, child."

Thea reached to pick up one of the Dickens books.

Clara held her off. "Are your hands clean? Books by writers like these are precious gifts and you must treat them like they're babies dressed for church."

Thea quickly wiped her hands on her gray apron.

Tunis smiled. It had worked. Clara wasn't going to eat him out for a foolish purchase. "Do I get permission to sit in the house then to read? If I sit quietly in a corner somewhere? I know you don't like men underfoot during the day."

"I have no quarrel to pick with anyone who wants to read. You know that, husband." Then Clara drew up her brows. "But I do have one complaint to make."

"What's that?"

"It is the usual winter complaint. By March the food rots so in the cellar. No matter how we wrap the apples in newspapers, they rot into each other. And the potatoes are all sprouted out. Same with the onions and carrots. And it don't help to go to the stores in town. They don't get in fresh vegetables until summer."

Tunis chewed on his lip. "Wife, you're right. Through no fault of yours, the grub lately hasn't tasted very good. What we need is to build us a root cellar. One we can use as a cyclone cellar too."

The next time Tunis went to town he asked around if there might not be a mason who knew how to build root cellars. Boughers the land agent finally gave him the name of an immigrant named Alfred Alfredson V.

"Can he talk American?" Tunis wondered.

"Speaks better English than you or I. He's a Frisian and once sailed before the British mast," Boughers said.

A little bell began to ring in Tunis's head. Alfredson. Say. Dirk and Tressa Freyling had once told him that that was his real father's name. In fact, Tunis had been named after his true father and he really was Tunis Junior. Tunis Senior, it was said, was related to some Alfredsons living somewhere in West Siouxland. So. This mason was probably some kind of cousin of his.

Tunis sought out Alfredson in his home in southeast Bonnie. One look at the Alfredson house and Tunis recognized in the architecture a touch of the Old Country, especially in the steep roof and the set of the windows.

Alfredson was home, and invited Tunis in for a cup of Frisian tea. His second wife, a bulky woman with frizzy white hair, set out the tea cups. Tunis and Alfredson sat across from each other at the kitchen table.

Alfredson was related to him all right. He had his same build, except that he was shorter. Alfredson was perhaps a bit wider in the shoulder and his stout legs were a bit more short-coupled. His reddish brown hair had begun to turn gray. He seemed to have trouble with his gray eyes, as if his sight were going. He smoked a corncob pipe upside down, with the open bowl aimed down.

It was apparent that Alfredson had taken an instant liking to him. "So you want a root-and-cyclone cellar combined."

"There's not too many ahead of me, are there?"

"No. But I'm a part-time gandy dancer on the Bonnie Omaha section."

"Say. The Bonnie Omaha cuts right through my land."

"I know." Alfredson sucked on his corncob pipe. Holding his hand under his pipe he made sure no hot tobacco crumbs fell in his lap. "I have to make a run up the line with my speeder next week and I'll stop and have a look at where you should put your root cellar."

"What day?"

"Monday."

"Make it around dinnertime noon. We're going to start field work next week. Weather permitting."

"Done."

Tea had finally steeped enough and Mrs. Alfredson poured them each a cup of wine red tea. Thin wisps of steam trailed off the tea. The smell of it was like just-cut rhubarb. Tunis noted that while Mrs. Alfredson used cream and sugar in her tea, Alfredson just used sugar. Just sugar in tea was his custom too, something he learned from Old Dirk and Tressa.

Tunis asked, "How much will it cost me?"

"I work by the hour. And you furnish the materials. The cement blocks and bricks and mud."

"When you built one for someone else, how much did it amount to for them?"

"Couple hundred."

"That's reasonable enough."

"It'll outlast your children's children."

"You built your own house here, didn't you?"

"Yep. I made the blocks first and then set them up."

"Did you work from a plan you took with you from the Old Country?"

"All from my head." Alfredson spoke as if he didn't want to take much credit for being original. Alfredson kept focusing and refocusing his gray eyes on Tunis as if he were trying to get a fix on him of some kind.

Mrs. Alfredson finally said it. "Do you know, you two look like you might be related."

Tunis sat up. He ran a finger back and forth across his moustache.

Alfredson snorted. "Impossible. He comes from another part of this country and my people come from Friesland."

Tunis decided not to tell what he knew. There'd be time enough to tell Alfredson what his foster parents had told him. Also Tunis spotted that Alfredson might have a temper, a quick flash point, like himself. He'd have to be careful around him.

Alfredson placed his corncob pipe carefully upside down in a little brass ashtray. He sipped at the edge of his tea to see if it'd cooled enough to drink. When his tongue discovered it was still too hot, he blew lightly over the surface of the wisping sepia tea, eyes fixed past his nose on the little flowing ripples, then tried sipping again. "You got some good land there, Freyling."

"It's tolerable."

"Reminds me of the land in Friesland. So black it was purple. Rich with thousands of years of cow manure. Plus the fact that it once was under the ocean."

"The land around here was well manured too."

"How so?"

"The Indians say it was once black with buffalo. For thousands of years."

"That accounts for it." Alfredson drew his lips up under his brown moustache in an elegant sneer. "Well, all I can say is, it's too good for the Americans."

201

"How come you didn't homestead a place?"

"I did. I once owned a quarter section a mile north of Chokecherry Corner."

Mrs. Alfredson lowered her cup of tea and set it gently into its saucer. "He traded that quarter section for some worthless land in the Bad Lands."

Alfredson's gray eyes glowed at her. "That happened before I got hitched to you."

Tunis had to say it. "Don't you like it here in America?"

"Well, it's better than living under a monarchy. I have no time for kings and queens. In three or four generations they breed themselves down to dumbbells. Every other generation they'd be wise to let the milkman deliver the milk in the bedroom."

Mrs. Alfredson took another sip of her creamed tea. "Or maybe have the mason build a new fireplace in the queen's bedroom."

Tunis exploded with laughter, almost blowing the tea out of his cup.

Alfredson slowly fixed his opalescent eyes on his fat wife. "By God, my seed would improve the line at that. All you have to do is take a look at the kids I had with my first wife."

Mrs. Alfredson looked her husband in the eye, daring him to stop her. "Your first wife looked like a horse, judging by her picture."

"She . . . she . . ." Alfredson stammered, "she . . . was beautiful. That picture you saw of her doesn't do her justice."

"That oldest son of yours has got a nose like a horse."

"She came from a high-class family."

"How come you married me then?"

Tunis began to squirm in his chair. Their argument reminded him of his problem with Clara. Why couldn't what looked like good people get along? Goddam human nature and all its twisted brains. Tunis said, "My wife and I once went to the Little Church in town here. You go there?"

"Attend church with those pious bigots? Never."

Mrs. Alfredson had to stick it into her husband some more. "Since you understand the Holland language, it might do you good."

"Bullshit." Alfredson swung his swimming gray eyes on Tunis. "What did you think of their service?"

"Couldn't understand it. It was like trying to pick corn without a hook. Though I liked the singing of the psalms."

Alfredson picked up his corncob pipe and lightly clapped out the ashes into the brass ashtray. Then he packed in fresh tobacco with a punching forefinger. The stringy tobacco smelled like sweet whiskey. He lit his pipe, bowl held down, letting the flame leap up into the tobacco with each deep suck. "Be careful around the Hollander. They're all out for the dollar."

Tunis said, "Maybe that's what this country needs. They work hard. And I hear uptown they pay their bills."

Mrs. Alfredson glanced needles at her husband. She chirped out of her fats, "And I suppose a Frieshead ain't all for the dollar?"

Alfredson puffed up several smoke rings. "We Frisians believe in being free first. No slavery and no royalty. Rather dead than slave."

Tunis asked, "Where are your children?"

Before Alfredson could answer, his wife said, "He farmed most of them out." It was obvious that she was taking advantage of the fact that her husband stammered. She was the quickest to pick up the talk. "I've told him he could have them all here and I'd mother 'em."

"I didn't farm out Gerda and Abbott." Alfredson looked at Tunis for understanding. "They're out playing with the neighbor's kids right now."

Tunis recalled something. "Don't your oldest boy work at Pullman's, north of my place?"

"That he does."

"Good kid. Works like a horse." The moment Tunis said it he knew he'd said something wrong. He tried to smile over it.

Alfredson caught the look. Slowly he smiled. "It's funny how the human tongue likes to make slips when talk gets touchy."

Mrs. Alfredson said, "Well the one I really would like to have kept is your oldest, Karen. She could have helped me in the house. Instead of placing her with that rich Hamilton family. Where they'll teach her how to be high toned. Up there in the Silk Stocking district."

Alfredson placed his pipe carefully in the brass ashtray. His face turned red. "Look. I want you to shut up talking about my children."

"Well," she pouted, "I always dreamed of having a lot of little kids underfoot. And if you'd still been any good I could have had one of my own yet."

Alfredson stood up suddenly, almost upsetting the table. "I've said the last word on this now, you hear?"

"Hah. What can you do to stop me?"

"Leave for the Bad Lands again with Gerda and Abbott."

She shut up.

Tunis could feel the hair over the back of his neck prickle. He was glad Alfredson was married to the witch and not him. At least Clara was a lady. Tunis pushed back his chair.

Alfredson sat down. "Do you have to go?"

Mrs. Alfredson said, "Stay for another cup of tea."

Tunis hesitated.

Alfredson said, "Pour the man a cup of tea." Alfredson tried to cross his short-coupled legs; couldn't get either leg to hook over the knee. His thighs were just too wide.

Tunis had to laugh. "I can't do that either."

"See," Mrs. Alfredson said, "you two are related then. Especially when I look at your moustaches. They're exactly alike."

"Pour the tea," Alfred said.

Alfredson came out the first week of June to start on the cyclone cellar. He drove a pair of chestnut hackneys. The horses were small but powerfully built, with hindquarters like short oak logs. No matter at what angle Alfredson set his scraper, the two chestnuts pulled up the load of dirt.

Alfredson selected a spot for the storm cellar just west of the house and not too far from the door of the back porch. He piled up the dirt, first black loam, then clay, then sand, in four heaps, one to each side. Once he had the hole deep enough, head high, he leveled out the bottom.

He told Tunis, "You're lucky having that sand down there. Because now your storm cellar will always be dry. A clay bottom will eventually make the floor of your cellar sweat, but not this sand."

The next day Alfredson brought out his mixing trough and trowels. With Tane and Tunis helping, he poured the footings and then the whole floor. When the Bonnie Omaha stopped to deliver the bricks and concrete blocks, Alfredson also helped unload them. Alfredson began to enjoy himself. He became very fond of the Freylings, especially Tane.

"You've got a good one there," he told Tunis as Tane walked past with a double load on a hod. "I bet he can push over a tree."

Tunis had to laugh. "Yeh, I've decided that I'm never gonna pick a fight with him. Thank God he's slow to wrath."

Alfredson also liked Clara. She held him at some distance at first. But as the days went by she gradually relaxed, and finally invited him to take his meals with them.

Alfredson endeared himself to Tunis when he began walking to work, altogether four miles from his home, instead of driving out with the chestnuts. Alfredson didn't need the horses once all the materials were set ready to hand.

When the children weren't working they sat up on the mounds of dirt and sand to watch. Alfredson sometimes posed riddles for them. "What is it that has only one leg and is red all over?" Thea and Dirk offered up the most guesses; all of them, of course, wrong. When no one was able to guess, Alfredson laughed. He stroked his red-brown moustache several times. "Well, maybe the riddle wasn't fair. You had to know about how a page in a book is set up. You see, some books have the page number on the bottom of the page. That's called a leg by printers. And the page is read by you."

Dirk caught on right away. "I'm gonna try that one on our teacher."

Tunis overheard the riddle. "Then you once worked for a printer?"

203

"Yep. I guess I've tried a little of everything. Sailor, blacksmith, farmer, carpenter, mason. And printer's devil. The one thing I haven't done is be a preacher. I have no time for preachers. They can go to work like the rest of us, and then on Sunday, if they still have something to say, they can then get up and say it. Like the Quakers do it. When they're moved to do it."

For the walls of the step-down entrance Alfredson used fieldstones. With Tane helping, and using one of the Freyling teams of horses, he hauled in the stones from the fields on a stoneboat. He built the cellar door of thick wood, slanted to shed rain, with a wide overlap slat to cover the crack between the two halves.

Finally the storm-and-root cellar was about done. On that last day Alfredson came out with his steady powerful chestnuts again. He hooked them onto the scraper and began filling in around the structure set in the earth. He first filled in the sand, then the clay, and finally the black dirt all over the top.

He told Tunis, "You might sow a little grain over it. To keep the dirt from running when it rains. Or blowing off when the winds come up. But within a year, grass will grow over it."

"Without seeding in grass?"

"That black dirt is just chuck full of wild grass seeds. It hasn't been plowed for thousands of years and during all that time billions of seeds have settled down into it, in that thick sod."

Clara came out to inspect the cellar. She liked the easy way the two halves of the door lifted up, each with its little iron ring for a handle, the wide steps down into darkness, and clean cement smell inside.

Alfredson leaned on a shovel. "Have you ever had much to do with one of these?"

"No."

"Can I give you some advice?"

"Of course. I'm all ears." Clara crooked her head to one side.

"Keep both doors closed as much as possible, both these outside halves as well as that one down there. You want to keep it as dark as possible for the potatoes so they won't sprout. And dry. Stick your carrots pointed down in damp sand, in a drum, and cover tightly. If you store apples down there, don't put them next to the carrots; if you do they'll turn bitter. Paraffin your turnips; otherwise they'll stink up the place something terrible. Also your apples should each be wrapped in paper and kept in a slatted box. And every now and then sprinkle water on the box to keep them damp. And beets, leave about two inches of the tops on them or they'll bleed out."

"What about freezing?"

"Not down there. The floor down there is at least three feet below the lowest frost line. And the earth underneath will keep the place around forty degrees. Just right."

"Can we whitewash the place?"

"If you want." Alfredson's eyes brightened. It was obvious he liked it that Clara was one of those housewives who wanted a bright and shining place. "Be sure to paint that top outside cellar door. Or in time it'll warp on you and then you'll have water puddles all over the floor below."

"Thank you so much. It'll be wonderful to have almost-fresh vegetables in the middle of a blizzard."

"That it will."

The rattling of a carriage by on the road alongside the railroad tracks caught Alfredson's attention. It was a new carriage with fancy red trim on black. The gray horses had on new black leather harnesses with tinkling bells and glancing celluloid rings, red and yellow and blue. "Who's that?"

Tunis said, "That's Pullman. Where your boy works."

"Hmm. His horse and rig make as nobby a turnout as one can see in any of the large cities."

Clara said, "You'll stay for one last supper?"

"You won't need to invite me twice for that."

Just before they sat down at the table, Alfredson got a small fruit jar from his runabout. He sat down at Tunis's right. He opened the jar, everybody watching. "I thought maybe this called for a celebration. I have here what we Frisians call *boerejonges*. Translated, it means 'farmboys.' Raisins soaked in brandy." He winked at Tunis. "One soaked raisin will be enough for you to speak in tongues. That's why we sometimes call it 'naughty boys.'" He handed the fruit jar to Tunis.

Tunis looked at the contents. There were hundreds of white raisins floating around in an amber fluid. Tunis looked at Clara. "We don't drink in this house, do we?"

Clara said from her end of the table, "No, we don't."

"But this is a special occasion."

"Yes, it is."

"It won't hurt if we each have one raisin."

"I guess it won't."

"The children each one too?"

205

Clara hated to hurt Alfredson's feelings. She threw him a warm look. She truly liked him. "Go ahead."

Tunis said, "Wife, will it be all right if I also give each child a bit in a teaspoon besides the raisin?"

"Go ahead."

The children, from Tane down to Geoffrey, were already licking their lips at the sight of the fat floating raisins. Tunis gave them each a spoonful of the special drink, going around the table behind the chairs.

"Mmm," the older children said, "mmm."

Mallie ran her tongue up around the edges of her thick soft lips. "It bites." Little Geoffrey savored it slowly, said nothing. His wondering eyes looked down past his nose at his own pushed out lips.

Clara took a sip too, quickly, like a hen not sure if it was safe to take a peck at a cat.

With a smile, Tunis helped himself to a full teaspoon. Mmm. It was good. And it was sharp. As he bit into the raisin it exploded in his mouth with liquid heat waves. Tunis sat down with a gratified sigh.

Clara asked, "How's your wife these days, Mr. Alfredson?"

Alfredson said, "Why do you ask?"

Clara said, "Sometimes you look so terribly lonesome."

Alfredson said, "Maybe it's because I'm denied grief in my own house."

Later, when Alfredson left, the west began to cloud over. A storm was brewing in that corner. Soon great thunderheads like heavy sows came wallowing in.

The sinking sun lit up the dark wine bottoms of them, varnishing them with sudden red purples and yellow-shot pinks.

Tunis watched Alfred Alfredson V ride away toward the southwest. "Perhaps it's just as well," he whispered to himself, "that he doesn't know we're related. We're so much alike it scares me."

24. Dirk

1906

Dirk was sixteen and lay troubled at night with sweet dreams. He slept with Tane in one bed while Rolf and Geoffrey slept in the other bed. There was only one window and even when it was open it was stuffy in the room, full of the summer smells of sweaty underwear and yeasty youth. Of the four boys, Rolf the horse smelled the sweetest. Geoffrey the six-year-old also smelled sweet. Tane didn't smell too bad either. But Dirk knew he was the worst. That's because in the mornings there was often a stain in his underwear and in the sheets.

It was something he couldn't help. Tane teased him about it when their door was closed and the room was dark, about that little post augur Dirk always unlimbered in sleep. Tane claimed it was like having a fifth brother in bed with them. What set off Dirk's strange hunger was what he sometimes saw in the girls' room. When Pa called them to get up in the summer mornings, it would be just light enough from the red dawn opening outside the window of the girls' room for Dirk to make out the forms of his sisters in their two beds. After a hot night, when all eight children complained about how sticky it was upstairs, and they weren't allowed to sleep downstairs on the screened front porch because Ma had said no, Dirk would sometimes stop for a peek at the naked bodies of his sisters lying sound asleep on top of their sheets, their skin rosy luminant in dawn's light. Tane never did stop. Tane always stoutly stumbled on past the girls' door knowing it was wrong to look at his naked sisters.

But Dirk had to look at Tressa. Tressa was fourteen. Her breasts had just begun to fill out, and lying there asleep innocent in dreams her breasts moved with every breath she took as though they were pears alive with heartbeats. She had a waist as slim as a fawn's. Her hips had begun to set out, widening in perfect curves. Her legs too had begun to fill out, in the thighs, in the calves, and she had perfect little pink toes. Dirk would look at all these every morning, admiring them. But finally his eyes always settled on her pudendum, where curly tufts of short brown hair shimmered red in the light, with a shadow running down the center. Sight of her naturally thick vulva lips made him so aroused it hurt. Again and again he thought: "If only Tressa was alone in there. I'd go in there and just push it in. She likes me too and she would like me to."

Dirk also looked at the other girls. All four lay with their heads near the window and their feet toward the doorway he was standing in. Thea was well built too. But her pubes weren't as pronounced. They were thinner. While Ana had hardly anything at all; just a little mouse of blond fuzz. And little Mallie, she had what looked like a little girl's puckered lips.

"Dirk?" It was Pa calling softly up the stairwell. "You didn't fall asleep on us now, did you?"

Dirk had to tear himself away from the girls' door. Good thing Pa always checked to see if he was really going to get up, or some morning he would have gone in. What a ruckus that would have made.

Tane chided him about it. "You know it's a sin to look in there, don't you?"

"Yeh."

"Someday you're not going to be able to hold back."

"I know."

"A terrible sin. Something the Lord's gonna punish you for."

"Tane, it's well worth the sin of looking."

"Boy! you better not let Ma hear you say that. Or Pa."

Dirk allowed himself a slow smile. "Now about Pa, I dunno. He ain't so blind. He knows what goes on."

"C'mon."

"Why do you think he's got that breeding calendar tacked up in the alley for? He knows when the bull socks it home."

Tane fell silent.

The two boys were manuring out the calf pen. It was sticky hot work. The manure was matted and hard, and sometimes they had to use the hay knife to cut it in squares to pull it free from the dirt floor. They sweat like coal heavers on a train.

Tane said, "You'd be better off if you married your right hand."

"Is that what you do?"

Tane turned red.

One Sunday, Ma got it into her head that they should all go to the Episcopalian church in Whitebone again. They could go up again with the Bonnie Omaha special that was carrying the Bonnie baseball team with their fans to play Whitebone, going out early in the morning and coming back late at night.

Pa didn't say anything at first at his end of the breakfast table.

"Well, Pa?" Ma said.

"I guess it'll be all right. Though we got one thing to worry about."

"Oh? And what's that?"

"Adam Erdman over at the orphanage was telling me the other day that there's been some rustlers working this county. He got it from the sheriff. They come in across the Big Sioux River, at that ford near Starum, quick cut out what cattle they want, and then chouse 'em into South Dakota."

"Hmm. Then maybe Tane better stay home to watch the yard," Ma said. "Thea can get a big supper ready for us when we get home."

"Oh, Ma," Tane said, "let Dirk stay home. I'd kind'f like to get away once. I hardly ever go anywhere. I'm always working."

Thea said, "Me too, Ma. I never get away."

Ma considered.

Dirk said nothing. He didn't dare look at Tressa to see what she might be thinking. Maybe she felt like Thea that she too never got away. He thought: "Please, let Tressa want to stay home with me."

Ma sat thinking hard on her end of the breakfast table. "Well then, maybe Rolf and Ana can stay home. Rolf is a big strong boy now."

Dirk cast his mother a swift glance. Did she know he peeked at his sleeping sisters in the morning?

Rolf moosed up his thick lips. "And I suppose I ain't good looking enough to go to church, hah?"

Ma gave him her extra-patient look. "No, Rolf boy, I didn't mean that. I meant—"

Ana spoke up with her over-fine voice. "Oh, Ma, I've told you already that I want to be a missionary someday. I don't go to church nearly enough. I could go every day."

For once Ma didn't look to Pa for help in what to do. "Tane, Thea, can't you two wait until—"

"No," Thea said. "I want to get away from this dump at least for a couple of hours. We're like lost pioneers on an island here."

"Same here," Tane said.

"Children!"

"I don't care," Thea said. "You taught us to speak up when we felt strong about something. Well, I feel I must get away for at least part of one day. Then I can stand it again."

Ma turned sarcastic. "Is it really all that bad living on our own property? Where not even a banker has a right to tell us what to plant? Or when to breathe?"

Thea and Tane looked down at their cereal bowls.

At last Ma had to turn to the head of the house. "Pa?"

Pa helped himself to another spoon of oatmeal. Finally he looked up, eyes a high pearl gray under heavy red-brown brows. "It sounds to me like Dirk and Tressa are elected. They don't seem to be all that sorry about staying home."

Ma took a deep breath; held it a while; finally let it all out in an old sigh.

Pa said, "And another thing. The Bonnie Omaha special might be coming back late in case those baseball bums have to play an extra inning game. And that would mean somebody had better start the milking on time. You know how particular I am about that six-on-six routine. You gotta keep to that schedule or the cows will dry up on you." Pa threw Tressa a look. "So if you stay home, you can help Dirk milk, once you get supper for us under way."

Tressa smiled. It was a smile Dirk sometimes saw on her lips as she lay asleep in the pink dawn, "All right, Pa."

"Good," Pa said, "then that settles that then."

Ma turned silent for the rest of the morning. She had everybody out by the railroad track by the time the steam engine whistled coming out of Bonnie.

Dirk and Tressa stood on the front stoop and waved good-bye as Pa and Ma and kids climbed into the green passenger car. They watched the train start up, the engine coughing huge clouds of black smoke as the great driving wheels clanged with power. The baseball players and their supporters were all piled into a special yellow car hooked on at the end. There was a lot of yelling and cheering and pennant waving.

When the Bonnie Omaha with its wavering plume of gray smoke disappeared beyond the fringe of river trees, Dirk turned to Tressa with a glad smile. He wasn't sure what came next; he was only glad that he was with Tressa alone for a while and that they were going to have a lot of fun.

Tressa said, "I guess I better get busy. Ma gave me a lot of work to do."

"Like what?"

"Make all the beds. Do the tins in the milk separator. Scald the milk pails. Dust the parlor. Then start thinking about what to have for supper."

He gave her a shy push. When the folks were around he felt freer to hug her up now and then, and push against her shoulder with his shoulder, all in fun, but now that they were alone at last, things were not the same. Both were a little nervous. "C'mon Tress."

"Maybe we can visit when I make us something to eat at noon. Can't you find something to do on the yard? Like oil the windmill? Check the fence lines?"

"Rolf oiled the windmill last week. And you know Tane. If there's a staple missing from a post somewhere, he knows about it."

"Well, me, I'm going to get busy."

"Why don't I help you? I'm kinda handy in the house. Maybe I can do the dishes for you."

"Well, okay. But we're on our honor today to get the work all done before Ma gets home."

"I know. Show me where the soap is and I'll get at the sink stuff."

They worked hard. Dirk could hear Tressa bustling around upstairs as she moved the beds out from the wall to get at where she could not tuck in the sheets on both sides of the bed.

He waited for her to come downstairs. But she didn't come. She kept finding things to do. Then he knew she was thinking the same thing he was thinking.

A little sadly he decided he'd better check the yard as Pa had suggested. He fed the chickens some extra ground corn for Ma. He made sure there was plenty of drinking water for the hogs in the special fountain Rolf had invented. He turned on the windmill to make sure there was plenty of water for the horses and cows in the concrete water tank. Again he used one of Rolf's inventions—a wooden lever tied to a long heavy wire that ran all the way out to the windmill beyond the night yard. Poor Rolf. He might have the soul of Christ and the brain of an Edison, but that didn't change fact that he was as ugly as a gorilla.

Dirk put up his foot on the water tank. He looked out to where the cattle were grazing in the pasture. First one cow would move forward four steps and begin cropping, then another cow, then another, taking turns moving slowly across the flat meadow on the near side of the high river banks. Everything seemed to be all right there.

Dirk happened to look up just as Tressa was heading for the privy. He smiled to himself. Women too when they had to go had to go. To his surprise she didn't enter the privy. Instead she stepped into the grass on the north side of the privy, took a quick look over at the road to see if anyone were coming down it, and then, lifting up her green dress at the sides and pulling down her bloomers, squatted in the grass. From where he stood, with the forenoon sun catching her just right, it looked like she was sitting, for a brief moment, on a shimmering icicle. What a pretty thing to see. Sight of it made him shiver.

He dropped his foot to earth and slowly started toward the house. He noticed dried milk spots on his overalls. The spots had turned hard, like drops of paint sometimes did. He thought: "You know, I ought to dress up a little. Tressa would like that. She always wears nice dresses, day in day out."

He spotted a commotion in the tall weeds on the edge of the yard toward the railroad. Curious, he strode over. Coming close, he saw it was a rooster pecking and jumping at a bull snake in the weeds and then fluttering up, wings outspread. The white rooster was enraged; some of his pet hens were nearby and he was out to protect them.

The spotted brown-and-yellow snake tried to ignore the fluster of the rooster.

But when the angry white cock landed a couple of pecks near its eyes, it suddenly convulsed, whirled on its tail, and nosed its way into deeper denser weeds. Gone.

Mister Cock pranced around on his toes, snapped his wings up and down several times, let out an ear-cracking clarion call, "Errh!! cuk cuk cuk, karoo!" The hens, four of them, knowing that now all was safe, came running up close, heads down and beaks pointed out, wings opened and lifted a little. Before they knew what hit them, he mounted them each in turn, driving home his seed. Then, proud of himself on the defeat of an enemy and the successful propagation of his own kind, he strutted about as vain as a president.

Dirk had to laugh right out loud. Men! as his nun sister Ana would say.

Being a man though was wonderful. He couldn't wait for the day when he'd have a wife.

Something caught his eye off to one side. Looking quickly, he saw it was Tressa in the kitchen window looking at him. She waved her hand at him a little, held her head wonderingly. What was going on? That kitchen window gave the women in the family an unfair advantage. The men didn't have a window to look in on the women at their work. Unless a man went up close and pressed his nose against the glass. It was usually hard to look inside, especially when it was very light outside. The women always cussed a fellow out when he did press his nose against the glass to see if the tea was steeped—the nose always left an oily smudge on the window.

Dirk pointed at the rooster as the culprit who'd made him laugh.

Tressa shook her head to show that wasn't it. What else was out there in the deep grass?

Dirk made a sinuous motion with his hand. Then, seeing that was not working, he decided to go back in the house. There was nothing more to do on the yard.

Tressa had a merry smile for him as he entered the kitchen. She looked up from the sink, where she was getting some meat ready for the oven. "What was so funny out there anyway? You looked like a goof the way you were bent over."

He told her.

"Oh," she said. "Snakes I don't like. Uggh. That's even worse than having mice underfoot."

"It was a bull snake. And actually he's a friend. A bull snake in the garden eating grasshoppers and gophers is like having an extra gardener around."

"I still don't like 'em. You remember what that snake did in the Garden of Eden."

Dirk smiled. He went over and put his arm around her and shook her a little. "Well, anyway, Mister Cock chased him off into the tall weeds. So everything's going to be all right." He gave her a smooch in the neck through a parting in her curly auburn hair. My, she smelled good. Like ripe corn in the autumn did when its silk began to hang down brown and aromatic.

She laughed and wriggled her shoulders for him to get away. "Now, Dirk. You know."

"No, I don't know. I just know I like being close to you. I can't help it but I do."

"I like that too. But we mustn't." She became aware of the bump that had grown in his overalls. She leaned away from it one moment, then pressed against it the next.

He slipped his hands around her from behind and cupped her breasts. He'd

211

done that before in front of the family, always with a laugh, shaking her breasts as if they were live creatures, and calling her "Hufty." This time, calling her Hufty, he held her breasts tenderly, in love. They were like a couple of puffed-out cheeks filled with breath. "You're so nice to hold."

"It's terrible," she said.

"What is?" he asked muffled, thickening.

"That we can't get married."

He hadn't expected her to come to the point that quickly. "Would you marry me if you could?" he asked into her musty hair.

"Are you asking me to marry you?"

"Would you?"

"If I could, yes. You know I would. I love you so."

He kissed her in the nape of the neck, where the hair was parted and flowed to either side. It looked very much like the shadow running down the center of her pudendum. "And I love you, Tress."

"I could marry you and live with you pure in love."

"You mean, and never do it?"

"Yes. Couldn't you?"

He pushed his bump gently but firmly against her round bottom. "You'd be asking me to give up an awful lot."

"Dirk, you." She pushed back against him, more to push him back in his place than in need. "Besides, it's time we ate. Why don't you quick go out in the garden and get me some rhubarb. You like it so much."

"Must I?"

"Yes."

Reluctantly he let her go. He took the pan she held out for him, with a knife, and trudged out to the garden south of the house. The rhubarb was easy to find amid the flourishing vegetables. He broke out a dozen juicy red-purple stalks, cut off the leaves, and headed back for the house.

"Thanks," she said, when he handed her the rhubarb. To keep him busy, she added, "Why don't you set the table for two."

"You in Ma's place and me in Pa's place?"

She wrinkled a smile at him. "If you want."

The rhubarb cooked while they each had a pork chop and a potato and tender pole beans. The aroma rising from the steaming rhubarb reminded him of the faint sweat smell in Tressa's green dress.

Dirk had asked for a blessing when they started the meal. When they finished eating, Dirk wondered out loud if they couldn't skip reading the Bible, and instead just go straight into the prayer of thanks.

Tressa crooked her head at him. Her blue eyes were clear and open. "Well, since we are sitting in Pa and Ma's places, we probably should read the Bible like they do."

"Well, if you say so." Then Dirk had an idea. There was a certain passage in the Bible that would fit. He got Ma's old King James Bible from where it lay on the shelf next to the clock and looked up the passage, II Samuel, chapter 13. He read in a lover's winning voice:

"So Amnon lay down, and made himself sick: and when the king was come to see him, Amnon said unto the king, I pray thee, let Tamar my sister come, and make me a couple of cakes in my sight, that I may eat at her hand.

"Then David sent home to Tamar, saying, Go now to thy brother Amnon's house, and dress him meat.

"So Tamar went to her brother Amnon's house; and he was laid down. And she took flour, and kneaded it, and made cakes in his sight, and did bake the cakes.

"And she took a pan, and poured them out before him; but he refused to eat. And Amnon said, Have out all men from me. And they went out every man from him."

As Dirk read, Tressa's clear dark brown eyes slowly became troubled. Her lips thinned. Her back arched erect.

"And Amnon said unto Tamar, Bring the meat into the chamber, that I may eat of thine hand. And Tamar took the cakes which she had made, and brought them into the chamber to Amnon her brother.

"And when she had brought them unto him to eat, he took hold of her, and said unto her, Come lie with me, my sister."

Dirk closed the book, and with a goofy smile looked across the table at Tressa.

Tressa said, "Why didn't you finish the passage?"

"Isn't that enough from the Bible today?"

"No." Tressa got up and came around the table and picked up the Bible. "I'll show you why it isn't enough." She returned to Ma's chair and paged through the books of Samuel until she found the same chapter. Then she read:

"And she answered him, Nay, my brother, do not force me; for no such thing ought to be done in Israel; do not thou this folly.

"And I, whither shall I cause my shame to go? and as for thee, thou shalt be as one of the fools in Israel. Now therefore, I pray thee, speak unto the king; for he will not withhold me from thee.

"Howbeit, he would not hearken unto her voice: but being stronger than she, forced her, and lay with her.

"Then Amnon hated her exceedingly; so that the hatred wherewith he hated her was greater than the love wherewith he had loved her. And Amnon said unto her, Arise, be gone.

"And she said unto him, There is no cause; this evil in sending me away is greater than the other that thou didst unto me. But he would not hearken unto her.

"Then he called his servant that ministered unto him, and said, Put now this woman out from me, and bolt the door after her.

"And she had a garment of divers colours upon her: for with such robes were the king's daughters that were virgins apparelled. Then his servant brought her out, and bolted the door after her.

"And Tamar put ashes on her head, and rent her garment of divers colours that was on her, and laid her hand on her head, and went on crying."

Tressa looked up from Ma's Bible and leveled grave blue eyes at Dirk. "That's the whole story."

"Oh," Dirk said.

"If you're gonna read a story, read all of it."

Dirk remembered something. "Give me that Bible again." He reached across the table for it. He paged through the Bible until he found II Samuel again. "You know how Ma and Pa sometimes like to discuss what was just read in the

213

Bible? Let's talk about the last part of verse thirteen. Where Tamar says, 'I pray thee, speak unto the king; for he will not withhold me from thee.'"

"You know very well, Dirk, Pa would never agree to such a thing. And Ma certainly wouldn't."

"Anyway," Dirk said, "you sure knew where to quick find the last part of that whole passage."

"I've heard the Bible read so many times, I couldn't help but remember."

"But you specially remembered the passage."

"Maybe I did. But I'm not going to have you bolt the door to your chamber against me. I want to keep it the way it is with us, that we love each other very much."

"Only as a brother and sister?"

"Certainly not with that Amnon and Tamar thing in mind."

Dirk knew she was right and fell silent.

"Now," Tressa said, "you asked for the blessing. Now it's my turn to give the thanks." She slowly closed her eyes and offered up a grave prayer. She thanked the Lord for his many bounties, thanked him especially for the gift of love between brother and sister. Amen.

Dirk wilted inside. "I think I'll go take a nap."

"Are you all done on the yard?"

"So far as I know."

Dirk went into the parlor to lie down on the leather sofa.

Tressa called after him, "Not with those milk-stinking clothes you don't. You should've really put on fresh clothes for dinner. You know how Ma is about stinking duds in the house."

"You're getting to be kind of a boss, Tress. Now I'm not sure I want to marry you."

"Oh, g'wan with you. Change clothes."

With a little smile to himself, Dirk took off his spotted overalls and folding them, threw them in a corner of the parlor. Then he lay down on the hard sofa in his underwear.

Tressa appeared after a moment, head around the corner of the door. "I thought as much. You get a pants on of some kind. I'm not having you lay around here half-naked."

"Tress."

"I don't care."

He got up and started for the stairwell. He noted that she was quick to look the other way.

Up in the boys' room he muttered to himself, "I could just as well have gone to church with the rest. I would've at least pleased the Lord in that." Before reaching for a decent pair of pants, he leaned down over one of the two beds and looked out the window.

What caught his eye puzzled him for a moment. Their cows were all gathered in a bunch at the end of the lane leading into the pasture. Almost out of sight was a commotion of some sort. Then he heard it. Two bulls bellowing, clamoring in beast jealousy. The cows parted after a moment and Dirk got a good look at the thundering bulls. Why, it was their own tom bull, a huge black-and-white Frisian-Holstein, fighting with a red-and-white bull. The other bull had to be Clate Bartles's. Now that Clate was a cripple he probably hadn't been able to get his sister Hettie to keep up the fences, and was too poor to hire a man to do it for him. Luckily both bulls had been dehorned or they would have by now gutted each other.

Dirk wheeled and tumbled downstairs. He grabbed up his dirty overalls and shot into the kitchen.

Tressa looked up from where she was sweeping the dust out of the kitchen into the porch. "What in the world?"

"There's some bull in our pasture fighting our bull. Bartles's, I think. God, I better do something about it."

"Dirk! you be careful now."

Dirk fastened his suspenders and hurried outdoors. First he ran to the barn and got a pitchfork. When he took the turn into the lane to the pasture, Tressa showed up with a broom. Together they raced down the lane.

The cows saw them coming and opened into two bunches. The cows were silent, heads up, eyes shiny alert, intent on the fight.

Tressa said, "Don't get too close now!"

Dirk said, "I just want to prick that Bartles bull in the ass a little. Catch his attention so our bull can win."

"Just so they don't both take out after you for interrupting them. Like two bullies fighting on a schoolyard."

"Hey. That's right."

The two huge bulls banged into each other, broad triangular heads booming dully. Their bellowing took on a hysterical edge. Both sounded a little like Pa when he got mad when things were going wrong for him on the yard. Both were outraged.

Dirk finally dared it. He took a run at them and jabbed his fork into the behind of the red-and-white Shorthorn. Bartles's bull hardly noticed. It continued to push and bump and grunt into Freyling's black-and-white bull.

Dirk next took a run at their own bull and pricked him too in the rump just over the flailing tail. Their bull hardly noticed; continued to bump and bellow into Bartles's bull.

"Be careful," Tressa warned. She waved her broom at both bulls as if she hoped that would distract them.

Dirk said, "God, what must we do? They're gonna fight until one of them drops dead."

"I don't know," Tressa said.

The cows behind Dirk watched the fight standing in two neat semicircles, head beside head. The high afternoon sun shone brilliantly on the raging bulls. The bulls had begun to kick up a little dust out of the pasture grass and the sun caught the dust particles, giving them a shine like floating fireflies.

"I'm gonna stick 'em one more time," Dirk said. "And if that don't work, we better get help."

At that moment their dog Shep showed up. He was a beautiful collie with a long nose and long flowing gold hair streaked with touches of brown and a tall white tail. He slunk between Dirk and Tressa; then, nose down, teeth showing white, on quick white feet, he headed straight for the nose of the Bartles bull.

"Shep!" Dirk cried. "Look out."

Shep snaked in with a humped-up neck, then bit in, sinking his teeth into the rubbery nose of the big red-and-white Shorthorn. "R-r-r-rr!"

The Bartles bull bayed in pain. Angry, he waggled his great head back and forth, trying to shake off Shep.

Shep hung on.

The Freyling bull, astounded by the help he'd suddenly gotten from friend dog, backed a step, lifting up his head, sneering up a great black lip.

Again the Bartles bull tried to shake off Shep.

Shep had got in a good deep bite. Frothy blood showed in the shining black edges of Shep's mouth. "R-r-r-rr."

Dirk began to cheer. "Wow. Atta boy, Shep. Sic 'em. The son of a bitch."

The Freyling bull bellowed with a great guttural roar. He pawed the dirt with his front feet. He lowered his great broad triangular head and charged. He hit the Bartles bull in the side of his belly and completely knocked him over, freeing him of Shep. He continued to butt the Bartles bull as if he were rolling a barrel along the ground, legs around and over, around and over. For a good thirty feet the Freyling bull rolled the Bartles bull. At last the Bartles bull fell into a little ditch, and in it managed to get his hooves set under himself again. He gathered himself forward and escaped the butting skull of the Freyling bull. At that moment Shep joined in once more and nipped the heels of the Bartles bull. The Bartles bull then really set his hocks into it and took off for home, Shep barking and darting at his heels. The Bartles bull sailed over the first pasture barbwire fence like a deer in high flight. He also took the fence by the road in one leap. Then, crying in brewling defeat, he loped home.

The Freyling bull, sure that his enemy was on the run, snorted to himself a few times. Then he returned to his admiring cows. The cows nosed up to him, almost as if they meant to kiss him. The Freyling bull rolled his great head around and up and down. Slowly he went around smelling under the tails of his admirers, lifting his nose, musing to himself about what he was sensing. Finally he found two ripe cows with slightly lifted tails. Without further ado, he mounted the first one and drove home his pink rapier with a loud thunk, so hard the black-and-white cow almost collapsed under him. Then, turning, he mounted the second cow and drove home another thwat of seed.

Dirk couldn't help but laugh. "Man, did he stick it home to those two. They sure know they got bred right."

Tressa wasn't amused. "You men. You would think that funny."

"Well," Dirk said, "that's life. That's nature."

"Sometimes we women in the house get sick and tired of what we see all day long on the yard. Roosters jumping on poor hens. Boars climbing onto sows. Stallions mounting poor beautiful mares. All you men know is to double up your neck, cross your eyes in heat, and ram that stump home. Bppf! Really, we get so sick of seeing all those pink pickles disappearing into all us poor women!"

"Well, Tress, that's all we poor men got."

"That's why we sometimes like to go to church. Because at least that is for once different."

Dirk fell silent. He loved Tressa, and was inclined to let her have the best of the argument.

They walked back up the lane together, he carrying his pitchfork and she carrying her broom. Shep padded along behind them, now and then catching up with Tressa and licking her fingertips. When they were almost back on the yard, Tressa began to forgive men, and Dirk too, and she took Dirk's hand in her hand and gave it a warm squeeze.

She said, "Sometimes, Dirk, when you're real nice, then I love you very much."

"Well, Tress, I sorta like you too."

He managed to get in a nap at last and Tressa finished the housework.

When the train didn't come down from the north at five o'clock, Dirk knew the ballgame had gone into extra innings. "Hufty, I think we better start pailing them cows. So we finish up at least one about the time we usually do when all the men are home to milk."

"I'll throw some more wood in the stove and then I'll be right with you."

Dirk fed the cows some ground feed, a mix of corn and oats, to get them chewing and feeling content. There were twenty-two of them, neatly in a row, heads caught in wood stanchions, nose down in the long feeding trough.

Both Dirk and Tressa milked with their heads buried into the side of the cow, in the hollow between the hipbones and the end of the rib cage. Both sat on one-legged stools, milk pails caught between their knees.

Enough light came in through the west windows to cast a mellow rosy glow over the backs of the black-and-white cows. The smell of fresh straw underfoot and the sweet aroma of fresh milk spretting into pails hunt sweet on the air. Foam rose creamy on the rising milk in the pails.

Dirk finished his first cow before Tressa did. He set his stool to one side and emptied his pail into a five-gallon can. He'd been brewing on what Tressa had said earlier. "Well, maybe you're right, Hufty. All that breeding going on here on the farm, it's hardly a wonder that we men are always thinking about it. Fact is, I even dream about it." Dirk settled under his second cow.

Tressa got up and dropped her stool to one side. "Well, I dream about it too. All because I see you boys laying there naked on your beds."

"When?"

"When I have to get up and go to the privy."

"In the dark?"

She emptied her pail into the five-gallon can. "In the moonlight. All those pink stumps sticking up while you're all sound asleep. Sometimes four of them at the same time. Like toadstools nodding. I tell you, it's all a girl can do to stand it."

"For godsakes, then you peeked too."

"Too? Then you've been peeking at us."

"Yeh, in the morning. When I get up. When you're laying there all pink and rosy in the dawn. I tell you, from my side too it's all a man can do to keep from climbing in bed with you."

She stood very still for a moment. "Dirk, that's really wrong, isn't it?"

He squeezed the cow's long fat teats in easy rhythm. Ping pang. Sping spang. Splett splutt. Foam rose in his pail like rising miniature cumulus clouds. "But I tell you, it's like I've thought before, it's well worth the sin of looking at it."

She sat down under her second cow and began pinging milk. Presently she said, "After seeing how our bull did it, it makes one wonder a little how it would be with human beings."

"I've wondered about that too. How it really goes."

They finished their second cow at the same time. Dirk let her pour out her milk into the can first. As she did so, he set his pail down and embraced her from behind, slipping his hands cuppingly around her waist and then slowly up around her breasts. He held her tight against him as she finished emptying her pail. The yeasty smell of just-poured milk rose in their faces. He kissed her in the neck, under her auburn hair, then her pink cheek. "Hufty is the perfect name for you. It fits your tits. Just like they fit snug into my hands. Real handfuls."

Tressa let the pail drop to the cement floor.

"And you smell so nice, Tressa." He saw again their great bull, slowly musing through his herd of admirers. "So ripe." He could feel himself swelling against her firm curved buttocks.

All of a sudden she turned around in his arms. "Ochh!" she said. "Pinching those cow tits one after another, when they feel so much like those toadstools I see in your boys' bedroom, ochh!"

"Hufty."

"Oh, Dirk, let's do it once."

"What?" he said, voice muffled in her hair.

"Come, lie with me, my brother. But do not do with me as Amnon did with his sister Tamar."

"Amnon didn't really love her."

"But you do me?"

He began to feel hot and pointed. "Where?"

"Up in the haymow. That way they won't catch us should they come home suddenly."

"But if they see us both coming down the ladder?"

"We can tell them we were both looking for eggs. You know, that one hen who's always hiding her eggs up there."

"We're looking for eggs right in the middle of milking?"

"We heard her cackling up there." Quickly, with a nuzzling chubby hand she reached into the side pocket of his overalls and caught hold of him and squeezed him gently. "Wouldn't it be fun to see how it really goes at last?"

"Yes," he whispered. "And I suppose we can hear the train whistling at the crossing by our old schoolhouse."

"Easy," she said.

"Oh, Tress, what else can I do seeing you naked on your bed asleep in the warm summer mornings."

"I know. I know."

He reached down and lifted up her long green dress and, slipping his hands inside her cotton bloomers, filled his hand with the wonder of her. It was his first time. He was surprised about how it all was. He found a valley of wet delight.

"Quick," she whispered. "Let's go up in heaven. I mean, the haymow."

"All right."

Both were so thick with it their hands fumbled on the rungs of the ladder. She was first and almost slipped and fell back on him. The aroma of her was like the perfume from a just-opened milkweed blossom.

She found the right place. A sloping wedge of alfalfa in the farthest dark corner. She drew him down beside her. She slipped off her bloomers, then reached and unsnapped one of his suspenders. "Let's play a little first." She kissed him, little wet edges of her lips catching at where his lips were moist. "But if tomorrow you bolt your door against me, I'll tell Tane what you did to me. So that he, like what Absalom did to Amnon, can kill you."

"But I'm not forcing you, Tress."

She laughed thickly. "I guess that's right. Oh, Dirk, I guess it's because I truly love you."

"I love you too, Tressa."

They didn't play long. She opened for him and he found her curved offer and he reached deep into her.

"Maybe we better quit now," she whispered. "Before you . . ."

"For godsakes, not now! I've only just started."

"All right."

Slowly he climbed into heaven.

Afterwards, they lay sighing together. Slowly thickness ebbed away.

He smelled the alfalfa beneath them. They'd stirred it up enough for old hayfield aromas to rise, dried wild-rose blossoms, dried burdock, dried alfalfa leaves. Age was in the smell. The smell hinted of a far future time, when they'd both be old and gray and wrinkled.

They breathed in unison, softly, at ease.

"I love you, Dirk."

"And I love you, Tressa."

"What if there's a baby?"

"If there is, we'll just have to have it, that's all."

"Oh, Dirk, why can't we run off together?"

"I agree."

"To the Bad Lands. Or even high Montana."

"Or some desert somewhere. Prospect for gold."

"Then you won't bolt your door against me?"

"After this, Tressa, never. You don't know how wonderful it was. Between brother and sister it's got to be the best. Because of the special way we love each other."

They heard a train whistle in the distance to the north.

219

Both sat up, listening; then both scrambled to get their clothes in order again. They hurried, more slipping down past the rungs of the ladder than taking them. Dirk emptied his pail that he'd left standing and sought out his third cow. Tressa settled under a cow at the far end of the cow barn.

They were almost finished with their third cow when Pa and Tane showed up.

"Well," Pa said, "I see I left two good hired hands home today." Pa pulled out his pocket watch. "Right on the dot, too."

The cows were soon milked.

Ma in the house had been pleased too to find the Sunday evening meal practically ready when she came home. She officiated from her end of the table near the hot stove with warm beaming smiles on all her children. She'd had a holy day in church with her family.

Dirk had trouble eating. Once the rest of the family was home, he didn't once look at Tressa. He knew he should probably glance at her once in a while to avoid suspicion, since he and Tressa were always joshing each other at the table. But the aroma of the roast was just too meaty for him. His tongue kept wanting to cleave to the roof of his mouth. He kept swallowing. He loved Tressa more than ever. He now knew something special about her.

Pa asked, "Anything out of the way happen while we were gone?"

"No, not really," Dirk said, eyes shying down at his half-filled plate.

"Oh, Dirk, there was too something out of the way," Tressa said. She had an even wider smile than usual for him. "Out in the pasture?"

Pa was instantly alert. "What happened out in the pasture?"

Tressa said, "That awful red bull of the Bartles's got in with our cows. And naturally our bull wasn't gonna stand for that. So they had a butting contest. They sounded like two hills colliding."

Pa said, "Dirk?"

"Yeh, it's true."

"What happened?"

"Well, I went after the Bartles bull with a pitchfork. And Hufty"—Dirk allowed himself a warm snort of a laugh—"Hufty went after him with a broom."

Ma was aghast. "A broom? What did you think you could do with a broom against a bull?"

Dirk said, "That's what I thought. He already had a tail to brush off the flies."

Tressa shot back, "Well, you were just as silly going after him with that pitchfork."

Pa's high grayish eyes leaned into Dirk. "Well?"

Tressa laughed. "Shep saved the day. He bit the Bartles bull in the nose and so tore at him that he forgot about our bull. So then our bull butted him over and rolled him into a ditch. From there the Bartles bull took off and sailed over a couple of fences and disappeared down the railroad tracks."

"Wow!" Rolf broke in. "You guys had a lot of fun."

"Yeh," Tane said. "I wish I could have seen that."

"Yes, it was a wild day all right," Tressa said, with a sidelong look at Dirk.

Dirk was afraid Ma wouldn't read the sidelong look right. He quick looked down at his plate. But he still couldn't eat what was left. It was like his innards were all plugged up.

220

25. *Tressa*

Ma was first to notice it. "Tressa, didn't you just have your period?"

"What?"

The girls Thea and Tressa were doing the dishes. Pink sunset bloomed through the west windows of the kitchen. The pink light gave Thea's gold hair the look of angel hair.

Ma said, "Well, just look at yourself there, girl."

Tressa looked around over her shoulder at the seat of her green cotton dress. Sure enough. A small spot of blood. It surprised her. How could that have leaked there without her knowing it, when she always could feel when her period was starting? Quickly she made up a lie. "I sometimes have that in betweentimes."

"I never noticed it on you before."

"Well, I always quick clean it up. Like you taught us. Be ladies. Neat."

Ana looked up from where she was reading the Book of Ruth. Ana had lately taken to reading those passages in the Bible that dealt with heroines. "That's a lie, Tressa, and you know it."

Ma said, "Ana, you keep out of this."

"Well, it's still a lie. Because I help you wash the clothes, Ma. And I always watch for stains in the seats of underwear. Soak and rub them up special."

Tressa bit her lip. Ma was watching her close. "You would, Ana. When you never have to go to the privy because you're so pure."

Ma said, "I tore up some more old sheets for you girls and put them in that bag behind your door upstairs."

Tressa said, "Ana, you finish drying the dishes then. I'm going upstairs."

Ana glared at Tressa. "Nosiree. It's your turn and it stays your turn, no matter what."

Tressa lifted a shoulder. She looked at Ma. Tressa managed to look at her without shying off. She hated pretending but it had to be done.

Ma put down the sock she was darning and stared at Ana. She stared hard.

Ana snapped the Bible shut. "Oh, all right. But you always favor Tressa. All because she's so pretty. While me, with my plain looks, me you stick in a corner." Ana got up and snatched the dish towel from Tressa. "But just you wait. I'm the one girl of yours, Ma, that's gonna turn out to be Cinderella."

Thea lifted a dish out of the sudsed-up water. She snorted a soft lady laugh. "More like a Clinkerella, I think."

"Girls!" Ma said.

Tressa went upstairs and got out several strips of torn-up sheets. Little white threads trailed off the strips where the tear had jumped the weave. She removed her green dress, then her white cotton bloomers. There hadn't been much bleeding, thank goodness. She hadn't remembered that Dirk hurt her. It had all been sweet and melting. But there must have been some kind of maidenhead there after all. She explored herself; couldn't find a sore spot anywhere. Well, if now she got married someday she could never show her husband evidence she was a virgin. She would have to pretend again come that day.

That Ma. She sure kept track of everything about her girls. So far as Tressa knew, Ma didn't keep a written record of her girls. Ma must have a wonderful memory to remember every last little thing about them. She was a good mother who meant for her girls to grow up ladies and be pure when they got married.

Tressa next examined her smile in a mirror. She had no regrets. Except that there had better be no baby.

Bending over, she discovered that some silky fluid had run down the inside of her thigh. That had to be Dirk's seed. Precious issue. She couldn't resist a little smell of it, and dipped up some of it with a fingertip. Ah. What a deep inner flesh smell. Like smelling down into a wound. Carefully she wiped it up.

She fitted an elastic belt around her waist and safety-pinned a strip from the torn-up sheet to it. The strip of cloth fit her as snug as a loincloth. Then, with a smile to herself, happy in her love for Dirk, she went downstairs. And after making sure that the chores in the kitchen were done, she went outside to join Pa and the boys on the stoop on the east, or shadow, side of the house.

The next morning at breakfast Tressa was quick to see that Dirk only picked at his food. His lips shaped themselves into a thin grimace of distaste.

Ma saw it too. "Dirk, don't you feel well?"

Dirk jerked up his head. "Who? Me? Oh . . . yeh."

"Maybe you don't like the way I make breakfast."

Dirk pushed part of a fried egg and a strip of curled bacon around in his white plate. Already the bacon grease had stiffened into a gray paste. "No. Your cooking is fine, Ma."

Pa gave Dirk a searching look too. "I can't have any shirkers around today. When the hay is down, you gotta get it up."

Tane put in a word too. "Gotta make hay while the sun shines, you know."

Dirk lifted a small square of egg into his mouth. It was all he could do to chew on it. "Don't worry. I'll handle my end of it."

Again at noon Dirk picked at his food. He managed to down a glass of milk and a slice of bread with butter.

Tressa thought it strange that Dirk didn't put on some jelly. He had a sweet tooth. She guessed what the trouble was. If only he could feel the way she did about what they'd done. They'd done it out of deep love for each other. She hoped to God he wasn't going to pull an Amnon on her.

Once more at suppertime, Dirk poked his fork around in his plate at the fried potatoes. He had to close his eyes to swallow. His Adam's apple clicked.

Tressa could see Ma make up her mind. Ma was going to have a talk with her boy. Before the sun set, no doubt. Like a good Christian.

Well, Tressa made up her mind about that too. She'd have a talk with Dirk before Ma did. Dirk had to be warned to be careful. He just might let slip something if he wasn't told to watch his tongue.

When Tressa had finished the dishes with Thea, she hurried outside to the privy. She was quite sure she'd seen, out of the corner of her eye, out through the kitchen window, Dirk head in that direction. She hoped, fervently, that he had a stomachache and not a heartache.

Just as she approached the door of the privy, with a quarter moon cut into it, the door opened and Dirk stepped out. Dirk's lips were down at the corners.

Tressa blocked his path. She looked him in the eye. "What's the matter with you anyway?"

"Nothing that a good crap wouldn't take care of."

"You constipated?"

"Yeh."

"Since yesterday afternoon?"

"Yeh."

Tressa swallowed. "Look, let's you and me take a walk up the lane out toward the crossing. A good fast walk might loosen it up."

"If you wanna."

"'Course I wanna."

They started out, kicking up dust in the lane, trying to smile at each other.

Tane sitting on the stoop called after them. "Hey, where you guys going?" Pa and Rolf looked up too.

Dirk whispered, "Don't answer him."

Tressa said, "I think we better." She called back over her shoulder, "To see if the tracks are still there. If they ain't we're gonna warn the engineer in Bonnie."

Tane laughed.

The sun ovaled down toward the green fringe of trees along the river. It caused the grass to cast shadows as tall as bushes. Light skittered off the edges of fence posts in dazzling bits of yellow-gold.

They'd walked a good ways before Tressa finally asked, "Is what we did yesterday bothering you?"

"Not really."

"'Really' usually means it is."

Dirk's upper lip thinned out wide under his fine straight nose. "It's just that I feel all clogged up, mostly. And that ain't good. Next thing you know I'll have a broken 'pendix."

"Now, now. Don't be so gloomy."

"Well, I ain't crapped since yesterday morning."

Tressa took his arm and drew it against her. "You silly boy, why don't you take some of Pa's Epsom salts?"

"You mean that stuff he uses to tan leather with?"

"Sure. It's the same thing they sell in the Bonnie Drugs and Sundries." She scuffed her high-laced brown shoes in the dusty road. "I know. Because I saw an ad in the Bonnie paper telling about it."

Dirk glanced at her. "It won't make me sicker than I am?"

"Epsom salts is Epsom salts. Try a half a spoon first. If that don't make you sick, then increase the dose."

"Maybe I oughta. Because I sure feel all blocked up inside. I pushed and pushed, and didn't even let a . . . gas."

Tressa pinched his arm to show she was glad he didn't use the dirty word. "Do."

They walked a mile farther on. When they were out of sight of the house, behind a brush of willows, Dirk slipped his arm around her waist and gave her a warm hard hug. He tried to kiss her but she wouldn't let him. She did return the hug.

"It's gonna be all right, Dirk. I feel fine."

Again he tried to kiss her, as well as slip his hand under her long green dress.

She pushed him off with an indulgent laugh. "What a nut you are. One minute you look like you just tasted some bile, because of what we done, and the next minute you're all fingers at the rubber band of my pants."

He released her and began to walk a few feet away from her. "I know. I can't figure it out myself. I guess I'm just plain selfish when I start thinking about how you look bare naked in your bed mornings."

She nodded. "That's old news to me too, you know."

The sun sank behind the river trees and instantly cool air descended from the skies. The light turned a deep red-orange. It turned the iron railroad tracks into two long shimmering strips of pure gold.

Soon they'd walked far enough, and together turned and headed back for the house.

They strolled past some dusty sunflowers and both began to cough. The coughing was catching and in a moment both began to retch with deep heavy expulsions of air. Both brought up ragged strings of phlegm.

Between coughs, Dirk said, "Sometimes I think my asthma is getting worse."

"If it ain't pneumonia."

"Funny thing is, after I've coughed like this, my conscience always seems to feel better."

Tressa bent over to cough easier. "Don't . . . say . . . that."

"If you get a baby, I'm gonna wish I'd gnawed off my balls."

"Oh, Dirk, please."

Dirk reached up and ran his fingers through his dark brown hair. "Maybe I am some sort of animal. I've got a bump here that's exactly like the one Shep's got in the back of his head."

224

"Dirk."

"I've got the morals of a dog."

She took him by the arm and drew him close to comfort him. She felt terrible. She wished now she'd resisted him in the cow barn. In a way it was more her fault than his. It was true he'd pushed at her some, but it was she who said the fatal words, "Let's do it once." She'd even suggested where, up in the haymow. All because of pinching those six-inch-long tits every night. "Dirk, listen to me. No sane person desires to do bad on purpose. It just happened. And don't think it hasn't happened before."

He seized on that. "You mean, maybe Tane and Thea?"

"No, not them. Never them. But I heard in school that it has between Clate and Hettie Bartles."

"Naw. Them? He ain't got any legs."

"That doesn't prevent him from becoming a father."

"But they don't have any kids."

"I heard Ma whispering with Malena Tippett that people have noticed Hettie has showed a couple of times. Then later she mysteriously didn't show again."

"Then they've been murdering them."

"Shh. Not so loud. We're almost on the yard. And by the way, be careful around Ma."

"I know."

The sun slipped down behind the horizon in a great burst of scarlet throws of light. The fringe of trees along the river resembled a crowd of marching people carrying umbrellas.

Pa got to his feet just as Tressa and Dirk stepped up on the concrete stoop. "Glad you got back. It's time to go to bed. Tomorrow is another hard day of work. We've got to get that hay in before it rains."

A few days later, Tressa sought out Dirk again. "How about another walk before going to bed?"

"If we take too many of those walks, Ma is going to wonder about us. Let alone Pa."

"Oh, Dirk, they know we're close. Buddies."

Dirk wrinkled up his lips. It was almost a sneer. "Well, all right. I could use a walk. Like Pa sometimes says, when he offers to get the cows instead of me, 'time to jostle the bowels again.'"

Again sunlight was flowing in from the west, over the winding river trees, throwing long brown shadows, filling the air high overhead with coarsegold light.

They took a left at the end of the lane and headed north up the road toward their old country schoolhouse.

Finally Tressa asked, "Did the Epsom salts work?"

"A little."

"I notice you're eating a little better."

"Yeh. But all the salts does is bore a little hole through the middle of you. It don't scour you out."

"You men. Always so flat-out rough with your talk."

"Well, that's the way it is. It don't scour out the sides, Tress. I want to feel completely scoured out."

"Well, then take a little more."

They walked in silence until they came to the edge of the wasteland across from the schoolhouse. The sun had settled to within a hand's breath of the horizon. It lighted up the green trees from behind and lacquered them with a bluish sheen. Shafts of saffron light speared straight up into the skies, giving the heavens above the farm a Judgment Day illumination.

They stopped to watch the sky.

Tressa heard the river trickling nearby. "When you boys go swimming with Pa after supper on Saturday night, do you all go swimming naked?"

"Sure. How else would we soap ourselves up?"

"Pa too?"

"Yep."

"Does he kind of turn away from you boys, to hide his shame?"

"He has no shame different from us. He's got what we got. And he ain't ashamed of it."

"Just like you boys?"

"Just like us. Except that he's a little more weathered."

She listened some more to the trickling water. A mother thrush low-whistled a good-night lullaby. Tressa said, "Sometime I want to go swimming with you."

"You know what that would lead to."

"It would be so much fun. We could play tag and skip through the water. And dive into that deep hole you boys found in the wasteland here."

"The fish would faint."

Tressa laughed. "You nut you."

Dirk slipped a hand around her hip and pulled her up close. He began to bunch up her breasts. "I just love these little kittens of yours. No claws to 'em."

"You might be surprised."

He pushed against her.

She broke out of his arm. "Quit it."

"Tressa."

"I wish you could make up your mind. One minute you're sick about what happened and then the next minute—"

"I want you. Let's."

"No!"

The sun dropped behind the ball of the earth. Darkness misted up rapidly out of the citron wasteland. Bird song fell away. Crickets squeaked.

Tressa said, "We better turn back."

"Yeh." Dirk kicked at a clump of sunflowers. One of the blossoms broke off and fell at their feet. "Pa thinks there's a family of cougars in the wasteland. He says that sometimes you can hear them at night. The most unearthly yell you can imagine."

They turned and started for home. The cut grain to either side glowed a dull gold, with the road and the railroad track slicing through the fields like a series of long brown threads. The tops of the high hills on their left shouldered up cinnamon against a darkening east.

Pa and the boys were still sitting on the stoop telling stories. Ma was sitting inside the porch with darning in her lap.

"Well," Tane greeted them, "you guys get lost?"

"No," Tressa said brightly. "We just thought we'd like to see what's happening to our old abandoned schoolhouse."

Ma said, "Tressa, you forgot something."

Tressa started. "What, Ma?"

"You threw the dishwater just outside the back door again. We don't want that. We want the grass to grow there too. Throw it farther out by the fence after this. Where the grass is deep."

"All right, Ma."

Pa cleared his throat. "I was talking to Bert Faber of the township board the other day. He says the railroad bums are taking to sleeping in the old school-house and that we better take it down. Or sell it. So you kids better be a little careful out there. No telling what one of them might do to you."

"All right, Pa. We'll be careful."

A week later, in early September, on a soft mellow Friday morning, Dirk came home from getting the cows with a handful of wild grapes. He was eating them as he rode bareback on old gray Pearl.

Pa asked, "Was there a lot of them?"

Dirk said, "The place is hanging purple with them."

"I've always wanted to make some wild-grape wine." Pa brushed the ends of his moustache with his fingertips. "Hmm. Tane and me can easy do the work for a couple of days, plowing and hauling manure. Why don't you and Tressa go graping back in there? And I'll dig up some old crocks and buy us an extra sack of sugar."

But Ma shook her head. Ma and Tressa happened to be out on the yard just then. "There's so much fall work to do yet. Get the hard-coal burner ready. Clean out the stovepipes and then paint them with liquid stove blackening."

Pa cleared his throat. "Wife, wouldn't you like a little spiritus vinum of our own making for Christmas? Once?"

Ma said, "You and your fancy words." Ma drilled a high clear look into Tressa. "Well, all right. Go, you two. But don't dawdle around. Pick and nothing else." Ma threw a frosty look at Pa. "There's too much work on a section of land for anybody to loaf."

Tressa looked to see how Dirk was taking it.

Dirk was idly combing Pearl's black mane with trailing fingers. His eyes burned a light blue along the edges of his lashes.

They went the next morning with Pearl hitched to the runabout. Pa found a half dozen light gray gunnysacks for them to fill and Ma gave them two old pails to climb up into the trees with.

Tressa opened the gate by the house and closed it, and again opened the gate at the far end of the pasture and closed that. Pearl trotted along easily, the muscled halves of her rump rising and falling. She passed several long plumes of gas, which made both Tressa and Dirk pretend to faint. Dirk turned Pearl down a narrow trail into the dense jungle. Soon the trail closed over. Dirk got out and unhitched Pearl so she could graze in the wild grass while they picked grapes. He gave her a long lead strap so she would have plenty of room to crop.

Tressa carried the sacks and Dirk carried the pails.

Trees closed over them.

Tressa looked around. "Where are they?"

"Just a couple of steps more."

"You mean one of our cows got out and you followed her into this wilderness?"

He nodded. "I had to walk in and chouse her out."

A clearing ahead lightened the sky.

"See," Dirk cried, pointing.

All around the edges of the clearing grapevines as thick as a man's arm climbed up into the towering elms. Every vine was knopped over with hundreds and hundreds of bunches of ripe grapes. The blue smooth-skinned grapes were unusually fat for all their being wild. The air in the clearing took on a bluish hue, there were so many.

"Umm," Tressa murmured.

"I told you. And they're pretty sweet too."

Tressa reached up and sampled a bunch. Blue juice spurted from between her teeth. "For once a wild grape tastes good. Doesn't pucker up your mouth."

They set to work. There were enough grapes within reach so they didn't have to climb. Every tenth handful they'd thrust a bunch into their mouth and then, using their teeth, strip off the grapes as they pulled out the stem. Juice ran down their chins. Their lips turned so blue they looked like they might have a severe case of rheumatic fever.

Overhead hundreds of birds were feeding on the higher grapes. Robins, tanagers, bluejays, blackbirds scolded down at Tressa and Dirk.

Tressa marveled to herself. "If Ma saw this she'd have everybody out picking grapes."

"Thank God not."

"Verily, this is a land flowing with milk and honey."

They took turns carrying the grapes to the runabout. Within the hour they'd filled all six sacks packing full. They also filled the two pails.

Dirk said, "We broke a record picking so fast."

Tressa looked up at the sun. "Maybe we still have time for that swim."

"You wanna?"

"They probably won't expect us until noon."

"All right."

Smiling, they leaned toward each other, foreheads touching, straight noses side by side, grape-stained lips kissing. They swayed from side to side.

Tressa's period was almost a week late. She was a bit worried about it, though she'd been late several times before. "If we do, you gotta promise there'll be just swimming. No funny business."

"Sure."

"We can tease each other but no more."

Dirk said, "I think there's another ford near here."

"I was hoping there'd be one right in the middle of the wasteland. That way we wouldn't have to worry about anybody seeing us."

Dirk moved Pearl a dozen feet farther down the lane to some fresh grass to make sure she wouldn't break the hitching strap. "All right, follow me. I think I know a trail through here. Tane showed me one once."

"What about the cougars?"

"They don't like human flesh. Only wild game."

"You're kinda wild, Dirk."

They had to duck to get under the first wall of grapevines. The animal trail wriggled back and forth past the trunks of huge ash trees. Soon they could hear ahead the river talking. Once they had to get down on their hands and knees and crawl. At last, like an explosion, they emerged on a sunny river bank. Below them the river glittered and rippled over several pink sandbars.

Dirk laughed. "Ain't it wonderful? Not even the Garden of Eden had a stream like this."

"The Bible never mentions if there was a stream or a spring in the Garden of Eden."

Dirk hopped down the steep black bank, and then held out a hand to help Tressa down. They removed their shoes and set them neatly at the edge of the water. Taking each other's hand, with a little yip of joy, they skipped across the rippling ford. On the other bank they found a flat sandy spot.

Tressa waited for him to be the first to undress. If he decided not to, then that would be all right too.

Dirk jumped around on the sand. "Next time we boys go swimming I'm gonna tell them about this spot."

"Don't."

"Why not?"

"Let's just keep it for ourselves. Our hidden garden."

Dirk unhooked a suspender and dropped his overalls.

"Dirk! You ain't wearing underwear."

"No. Sometimes I don't. It just gets in the way."

"Does Ma know about this?"

"I don't care if she does." He took off his shirt and stood sideways to her. "C'mon, last one in is a shitepoke."

"You go ahead. I'll be with you in a sec."

Dirk raced into the water, splashing up silver sprays. "It's cold. Yow!"

Tressa laughed watching him. She admired his slim body with its knots of muscles. She loved his narrow deep hips, his slender wide shoulders. He was a most handsome lad. She loved him because he was all winning man.

"C'mon, Tress!"

"I'm coming."

She slipped out of her long green dress, then her white cotton slip, then her white fluffy bloomers. The tight elastic band in the bloomers had left a pink mark around her waist. The mark itched and she rubbed it. The sun caught her auburn pubic hair, giving it a shine like polished rosin. She saw that Dirk was about to look up from his skipping about in the running water and quickly ran for the ripples, kicking up glittering sprinkles. Dirk saw her coming and ran for where the water was deeper. He settled into a shallow hole, plashing up a curl of water. Tressa settled in with him. Both were careful not to get their hair wet. Wet hair would be a dead giveaway when they got home.

They played like sunfish chasing grains of light.

Finally Tressa, looking up at the sun, let out a gasp. "How long have we been in here?"

"Not long."

"C'mon, we better get home." She rose and skipped out of the water.

"Let's see, when it's high noon on our clock, the sun still ain't quite overhead in this part of the country." Dirk held up a hand and measured what was still left of the arc for the sun to climb. "I'd say it's exactly eleven o'clock. Still plenty of time for us to get home before we catch billyheck."

"I say we go home."

"All right."

They dressed slowly on the sand, back to back. Tressa kept waiting for Dirk to peek at her, even love her up. She hoped he wouldn't; hoped he would.

Dressed finally, they turned and looked at each other. Slowly smiles for each other grew. They'd had a great time being just a good brother and a good sister together. Everything would be easier for them from then on.

They crossed the river through the ripples, slipped on their shoes, climbed the high black loam bank, and retraced their steps through the jungle. An occasional mosquito wafted out of the green leaves and brushed their cheeks and then drifted away.

Again Tressa opened and closed the gate as they moved into the pasture. They crossed the river near where Pa and the boys went bathing on Saturday evening.

Tressa said, "Sometimes I'm gonna sneak to the end of the cornfield here and watch you men."

"There ain't all that much to see with us."

"It's just that I'd like to see how you guys behave when you're naked together."

"Why?"

"See if it's any different when we girls go bathing in our spot."

Dirk smiled to one side. "Let me tell you that in this family every pecker gets a fair shake."

"Dirk."

They were almost home, going up the lane past the night pasture, when Tressa had a question. "Dirk, you know, don't you think it's a little funny you never asked me if I'd had my period?"

Dirk flicked a look at her, then looked at the trotting Pearl. "Well, I meant to. But you girls are so mysterious about your secrets, it's hard to figure when you got the rag on."

"Dirk!" She bounced so hard on the spring seat she set it to rocking.

"You are. So I decided that everything was all right."

"You men!"

"Is it?"

"I don't know for sure."

Dirk turned pale. "What?"

"It's been a while."

Dirk pulled up Pearl to a stop. "Holy bells. Now we'll have to run away somewhere and get married."

"Ha. Where would we go? At our age? We could never make anybody believe we were of age to get married."

"In Kentucky the girls are married the minute they show titty."

"How would you know that?"

"From the boilerplate of our Bonnie astonisher."

"You can't always go by what it says in the newspaper."

Dirk fixed her with an anxious look. "You're sure about being late?"

"Yes."

"Oh, boy."

Tressa took him by the elbow. "You really would run off with me and get married?"

"If we had to, sure."

She gripped his arm, hard. "Oh, Dirk, then we really do love each other, don't we?"

"Was there ever any doubt about it? You're for me, gal. I'll never find anybody like you to marry."

Tressa pinched his elbow again. "I think somebody's looking out the kitchen window at us and wondering what we're talking about."

Dirk said, "I saw that too. Look, we're close enough to the gate for you to hop out from here."

"That's right." Tressa quickly leaped down from the runabout and ran to open the gate.

Tane saw them coming. "Well, you guys are back early." Tane was jealous of the way she and Dirk had become buddies. Thea wasn't that interested in Tane. "Pa thought you wouldn't be home until well after dinner."

Pa and Ma stepped out of the back porch and came over to have a look at the haul. Pa opened one of the gray gunnysacks. His eyes opened wide at the fat blue grapes.

Ma flicked a look at the grapes and then at Tressa. Ma was careful not to look at Tressa's lap. "You two must've worked." Then she saw their blue teeth and blue lips and had to laugh. "You two look just like when Pa and I first found some grapes. That first year." She sighed. "My, how time flies."

The rest of the family came pouring out of the house. Thea and Ana stared at all the grapes. Rolf right away helped himself, with his thick lips daintily nibbling off single grapes. Mallie had to climb up the runabout wheel to get at the blue fruit. Geoffrey stood waiting for someone to give him a bunch; when no one did, he finally cried out, "Don't stinge me."

Ma quickly put a stop to it. "No eating these grapes now. It'll spoil your appetite."

Dirk tried his winning smile on Ma. "Dessert first, Ma. Why wait for something you enjoy?"

Ma shook her head. "If you wait for the best last, the best will taste even better."

The grapes were carried into the back porch. Dirk unhitched Pearl. Tressa ran off to the privy.

When Tressa emerged from the privy she went straight to Ma. "Give me a minute, will you, before you sit down to dinner?"

"Why?"

Tressa whispered in her ear.

"Oh. Good."

Tressa knew that Ma was counting back to that time when some blood had shown up unexpectedly in her green cotton dress. Ma would know that sometimes big commotions threw a woman's period off.

A month later, right after Pa had finished making wine and just as the menfolk were about to start picking corn, Dirk wouldn't get out of bed. Tane and Rolf, even little Geoffrey, had got up at Pa's first morning call. All the girls had gotten up too, Thea and Tressa and Ana and Mallie.

Ma finally became edgy. "What in the world is wrong with that Dirk?"

Pa said, "Maybe he's got a bellyache again. One day he's got the runs, the next day he's all bound up." Pa finished his coffee and slipped into his blue denim jacket. "I remember I had that too when I was his age."

Ma turned to Tane. "Did he say anything to you?"

"No. Just groaned and turned over and buried his head under the pillow."

Ma was measuring out oatmeal for the double boiler. "I don't like it. He's starting to act spoiled."

Tressa didn't dare open her mouth. She slipped into her blue yard jacket.

Ma stopped Tressa. "He listens to you better than anybody else. So you go up there and find out what's the matter."

"Oh, Ma—"

"Uk, uk, just go."

"Oh, all right." Tressa had to make sure she was acting just right, not too reluctant and not too eager.

She went up the stairs slowly and entered the boys' room. The boy smell in it was like that of a boar's nest. Except that it was sweeter. She went to the foot of Dirk's bed. She could just make out in the opening morning light Dirk's lank form under the blankets.

She gave his toes a push through the blankets. "Wake up, you slug-a-bed. Time's a-wastin'."

Silence.

"Dirk, you're gonna get us in trouble acting like this."

Light breathing.

"C'mon, Dirk, get up."

"No."

"Ah, you can still talk."

"It's no use."

A knowing smile grew on her lips. "You're not fooling me. I know what's really the matter with you."

Suddenly the pillow over his head flopped to one side and he rose up like a Lazarus. "What do you know?"

"You're mad because we stayed decent swimming."

He glared at her. His blue eyes were squared in their sockets, his dark brown hair stood straight up because of the way the pillow had shaped it. "Well, in the meantime I'm not gonna marry Madam Palmer. Tain't natural."

"But what we did is?"

"You said you loved me."

"Sure I did. And I do. But I don't want to love you the way you want me to."

"Who was it who said, in the cow barn, 'Quick, let's go up in heaven'?"

She smiled. It had been wonderful.

"Hah? It wasn't me, you know."

"Dirk, I think we should try to be with each other the way it was when we went swimming. Innocent."

He flopped down and pulled the pillow back over his head.

"Dirk, please, get up. Freylings are never lazy."

He snorted under his pillow.

"Get up."

"It's no use. What's there to live for if I can't have you once in a while. I was really hoping you'd get caught, you know."

"Now you're being selfish. And foolish."

He lay so still she feared he'd deliberately quit breathing.

She flipped the covers off his feet and reached up and tickled him on the inside of his thigh. "This'll get you up."

Just then Ma called up the steps. "Is he getting up? The others have left to milk, you know."

"No, he isn't." Tressa quickly pulled the covers down over his legs.

Ma came up the steps. She entered the bedroom. She stared at the form under the covers. She said to Tressa, "Has he said yet why he won't get up?"

"He says it's no use."

Ma frowned. "Has anything happened that I don't know about?"

Tressa fell silent.

Ma reached down and gave Dirk's leg a push. "Get up!"

Dirk's voice was muffled under the pillow. "No."

"Get up!"

"It's no use."

"Well, we're not bringing you food up here."

"Okay with me."

"You crazy boy, what's the matter with you?"

"It's no use living."

Ma turned to Tressa. "Why does he say that?"

Again Tressa held her tongue.

Ma thought hard to herself. She folded her arms, lifting up her bosom a little. "Hmpf. Well, he's too old to lick. So I guess what we'll have to do is let him starve to death up here. Come, you better get to your milking, Tressa, or your father will get mad. You know how particular he is about milking six on six."

"Yes, and now I'll have to milk Dirk's cows too."

Both women slowly went downstairs, each with her own somber thoughts.

For two days Dirk stayed in bed and refused to talk to anyone, not even his bedmate Tane. Ma refused to let the girls bring him food.

Everybody wondered how Dirk managed it that he didn't have to go to the privy. It was Tressa who discovered he used the chamber pot under the girls' bed. Apparently he snuck into the girls' room on soft bare feet when he was sure no one downstairs would hear the floor creak over the living room. It had to be when all the menfolk were out working on the yard somewhere and when Ma and the girls were washing the milk pails and the milk separator tins.

Tressa decided to catch him. Maybe she could embarrass him back into behaving himself. She excused herself when Ma went to work on the tins. Taking off her green button shoes, Tressa snuck up the stairs on stocking feet. She was careful to set her feet on the sides of the stairs where the stairs were the least apt to creak. She hid in the linen closet at the head of the stairs.

Sure enough, first she heard Dirk's bed creak, then she heard his bare feet near the closet door, his calluses making a squeaking noise as he turned into the girls' room. She heard him kneel quietly, heard him pull the chamber pot out from under the bed as it made a light rumble across uneven floor boards.

She let him tinkle a little; and then burst out of the linen closet. "Aha! caught you."

Dirk straightened up from his humped over posture. "What!" Before he could pinch his pintle shut, a little spurt of gleaming yellow fluid flew up and broke into flying drops sparkling in the morning sun. "Tressa!" He dropped his shoulders, and then, reaiming himself, went back to peeing. "You scared me half to death."

"That's not as bad as the way you're scaring us, laying in bed there like a dead horse."

He remained intent on what was going into the pot.

"Get away from there. You have no right to use our white owl. That's for us to hoot in."

"Just a shake and I'll get out of here."

"I'm gonna tell Ma that this is how you do it."

He finished and pushed the chamber pot back under the bed and stood up. The two-day fast had given him hollow cheeks and a thinner neck.

"I'm not gonna empty that for you," Tressa said. "And I'm gonna tell the girls not to either."

He steered himself past her and reentered the boys' room and slipped back under the covers. He pulled his pillow over his head.

She followed him into his room. "I suppose you think you're gonna win out on this, don't you?"

"I've decided I don't care to live anymore. What's the use." Smothered under the pillow like he was, Dirk began to cough in rough ragged blasts.

"And I'm gonna see to it that you can't use our pot any more. We girls can get up in the night for a while if we have to, what?"

"I've decided to die."

She stared at his form shaped like a Z under the quilts. She decided she'd been upstairs long enough. Ma would get suspicious. Tressa went downstairs slowly, thoughtfully. Her wonderful nut of a brother had it bad.

An hour later Ma went upstairs. Tressa could vaguely hear her talking persuasively, could hear Dirk's occasional grumbled monotone replies.

Then they heard Ma's raised voice. "So you've been using the girls' pot! I've

233

been wondering how you managed that. I could hardly believe that I'd raised an angel who never had to go. Well, you're not using this anymore."

Dirk began to cough, loud.

A few seconds later, Ma emerged through the stair door, carrying the pot. "Tressa, you empty this, wash it, and leave it downstairs. In the closet under the stairs. We'll fix him."

When Pa was told about the pot business, he gave Ma a most peculiar look.

Tressa had long been aware that Pa and Ma sometimes had strange looks for each other. Tressa was sure it had something to do with the behavior of the children. It was most apparent in the case of Ma whenever either Dirk or she fell into a coughing spell.

The fourth day at noon, Pa went upstairs to see what he could do. Tressa and the girls could hear his deep resonant voice cutting across Dirk's fits of coughing, but they couldn't make out the words. Pa didn't sound mad; just strong.

After a while Pa came downstairs and went to the bookcase where he and Ma kept their books, Pa's set of Mark Twain and Ma's set of Charles Dickens. Pa went back and forth across the titles, finally picked *Roughing It*, and took it upstairs.

Soon Ma called upstairs. "Pa? Dinner's ready. And while you're at it, tell that lazy bum we raised we always have his plate set out for him."

There was some more baritone talk upstairs, and then Pa came down alone. Everybody was already sitting in their place around the table, Ma nearest the stove, with the huge bowl of potatoes and the big white plate of meat steaming in front of her.

Ma said, "So we're not going to have the pleasure of His Lordship's company."

Pa drew up his swivel armchair. "I guess not."

Ma said, "Pa, we've got to do something about that boy. I will not have a young man lazing around in bed in my house. I saw enough of that when I worked for Lord Sutherland. Uggh!" Ma shook as the memory of something awful came back to her. "Such goings-on! It's what you get when you let young boys put on airs."

Pa shot at her, "You know, you never did tell me what you found upstairs that day you quit at Sutherland Hall."

"It is too disgusting to discuss."

A day later there was one change. Ma found Dirk reading *Roughing It*. Dirk was almost in hysterics over the way Mark Twain told the story of the wild ride Hank Monk the stagecoach driver gave Horace Greeley, where the coach had "bounced up and down in such a terrific way that it jolted the buttons all off of Horace's coat, and finally shot his head clean through the roof of the stage," and where Horace allowed "he warn't in as much of a hurry as he was a while ago." Ma didn't like the ironic way Dirk had laughed. It wasn't healthy. Dirk was going over the edge.

Everybody became sick over what was happening. No jokes at the table. No pep on the yard. The three men, Pa, Tane, and Rolf, picked corn but came in with small loads. It began to look as though Dirk not only wanted to starve himself to death but also to take everybody else down with him. To die. No one bothered to worry anymore about where Dirk was going to the bathroom or where he was getting the water to drink.

But Tressa worried. Until she found out how he was managing the peeing.

Then she had to laugh. When Dirk was sure the womenfolk were at work on the east side of the house, and the men were out of sight of the yard, he removed the screen in the west window in the boys' room and relieved himself out of that. Tressa found out about it when she brought up a forkful of straw from the barnyard to cover the flowers under the bay window for the winter. Dirk had almost wetted on her. Tressa decided not to mention it.

Dirk began to look like an old man dying of galloping consumption. His blue eyes glared out of their sockets huge and ghastly. He was all lantern jaw and spindle shanks.

Tressa told him, "You look a fright."

With an effort Dirk held up *Roughing It* to the light from the west window. He was almost finished with the book. It wobbled in his claw hands.

"Get out of bed, you crazy nut."

Dirk read aloud from Twain: "I now come to a curious episode—the most curious, I think, that had yet accented my slothful, valueless, heedless career—"

"Oh! shut up with that book stuff. Listen to me. If you keep this up, staying in bed, you're going to get so weak your brains are going to turn to mush, and then your mind will wander and you'll spill the beans on us. And then where will we be?"

"—the town was thrown into a state of extraordinary excitement. In mining parlance the Wild West 'had struck it rich!'" Dirk let the book fall to his gaunt chest. "What?"

"You're hopeless," Tressa finally said, and left.

Tressa found Ma sitting at the head of the kitchen table. There was a strange look in Ma's eyes. There was also an odd kind of silence in the kitchen. The other girls had apparently been ordered outside.

Ma said, "Sit down a minute, Tressa. I want to talk to you."

Tressa sat down in Dirk's chair. She waited.

Ma fixed her grave gray eyes on Tressa. There was an air of watchful suspicion in Ma's manner. "Tressa, I must ask you something. And I expect you to tell me the truth. Has something happened between you and Dirk?"

"I don't know what you mean, Ma."

"The truth, please."

"Ma, I can't just tell you any old fiddley thing. It might not be what you expect to hear. At the same time I might confess something you didn't need to know."

Ma held Tressa's look.

"If you're wondering if Dirk and I are still good buddies, Ma, sure we are. You know how we're thick on each other. That's why I'm just as puzzled as you are about him. There must be a side to him I don't know about."

Ma stared at Tressa a while longer; finally let her shoulders sag. She sighed a vast sigh. "All right. You can go."

Tressa left. Her heart didn't begin to beat violently until she was well out on the yard, carrying the egg bucket, and then it really began to pound. Tressa decided she'd better be doing something useful in the next while or she'd die of a heart attack.

Two evenings later, right after everybody had taken a seat at the supper table, Ma turned around from the white-and-blue kitchen cabinet where she was cutting bread on the breadboard and threw a seething gray look at Pa. She placed

235

the bread on the table. "Pa, I'm not eating tonight unless that boy upstairs sits down here at the table with us."

Pa flared up then too. His pearl gray eyes turned to ice.

The kids all bowed their heads. Pa and Ma were about to have another staredown.

At last Pa said, "What do you propose I do about it, since it seems to be my fault when something doesn't go right around here? Sister."

"I want you and Tane and Rolf to go upstairs and dress him and bring him down here to his place at the table. Brother."

A giggle bubbled up in Tressa's belly. She fought it. She was as scared as the rest of the kids. But the giggle rose like a balloon with gas in it. Quickly she placed a hand over her mouth. That made it worse. It broke into her mouth, then slipped through her fingers. "Fffftt."

Ma glared at Tressa.

Pa glared at Tressa too. Then, after a moment, he began to laugh. Like Dirk, Pa had the gift of understanding her kind. Pa swung his eyes back to Ma. "All right. We'll get him. Tane, Rolf, come with me."

Everybody around the table waited with their eyes open wide and blue. What was coming was going to be something to remember. The steam rising from the bowl of potatoes slowly diminished.

There was the sound of bungling down the stairs. Then in a moment there came Pa holding Dirk's legs around his middle piggyback fashion with Tane holding one arm and Rolf the other. They sat Dirk in his chair. Dirk sat stiffly a moment, then let himself tip toward Tane. Tane quickly caught him and pushed him upright. Pa and Tane and Rolf sat down.

236

Dirk looked awful. His beard had grown out dark and ragged, giving him the look of a lost apostle. The collar of his blue shirt was so loose around his scrawny neck another neck could have been put in with it. He was as pale as old lard. His blue eyes were watery and pink from weakness.

"Now," Ma said. "Before we commence here, before we ask the Lord to bless this food, I want something decided."

"What is that, wife?" Pa said, brows lifted.

"I've decided Dirk should go on to school. Get an education. Make something of himself in the world. He's not a farmer. That's easy to see."

"What!" Pa cried, rising in his swivel chair.

"Can't you get along with just Tane and Rolf?"

"Yes, I guess I can. But I'd like to be in on such a decision. Let alone have the boy have something to say about it."

Ma said stoutly, "The way he moons around here, he's better off in school. It seems he can read all right. So I guess he can do schoolwork."

Tressa right away knew what that was going to mean. Dirk would slowly grow away from her. She would lose him to the fleshpots of the cities. She could feel her face turn white. She dropped her head so her hair would fall around her cheeks.

Dirk slowly tipped toward Pa.

Pa gave him a push. "Be a man, boy. Flopping back and forth here like a rooster with its head chopped off ain't going to win the election in this family."

Ana squirmed in her chair. "Well, if he can go, then I can go on to school too. If I'm going to be a missionary, I've got to go to school for it. Even college. I read that in our Episcopal church paper."

Ma held up the shining bread knife. "One at a time now, please. We'll get to you, Ana, in good time. When you've graduated from high school."

"But I want to know now if I'm going," Ana declared, clicking the handle end of her table knife down on the yellow tablecloth. "So I can pray to God about it, and can dream about it, and can get ready for it."

"Each in your own time, Ana. And now quiet you."

Mallie smiled sweetly with her thick lips. "Is Dirk gonna be our minister, Ma? Then we won't have to go all the way to Whitebone to our church." Mallie slipped off her chair and came around the table and gave Dirk a wet kiss on his cheek. "I like you, Dirk."

The kiss softened the stiff air around the table.

Geoffrey had been listening to the giants in the family around him. "I'm gonna be a lawyer when I grow up." He spoke with boy solemnity.

Pa had a wonderful smile for his youngest child. "Why, Geoffrey?"

Geoffrey sat very erect. "So we can sue those high school boys who're always teasing us when we ride by."

Ma's chin came down. "That's another thing. With Dirk going to high school in town, he can ride with the children all the way to the Little Church Grammar School and then walk those couple of blocks to the high school. That should help quiet those rapscallions down.

"That reminds me," Pa said. "One of the consistory members of the Little Church told me they feel our children shouldn't be going to their school unless we at least attend church there some. Now that's something I'm not going to do, listen to Dutch sermons—"

"Enough of that!" Ma broke in. "Besides, I'm one up on you. One of the women in their Ladies Aid told me they're now going to have American sermons every other week. The young people want it. And we can go to that."

"Oh."

Ma looked directly at Dirk. "Young man, look at me."

Dirk managed to swing his half-closed eyes in Ma's direction.

"What do you think about all this?"

Dirk looked at Tressa to see what she had to say.

Tressa looked out of the window. The sun was setting. She hoped the red sunset would give some color to her cheeks.

"Dirk?"

"Do I have to wear Tane's Sunday hand-me-downs to school?"

"We'll see to it that you get your own new suit."

Dirk tried to sit up. "Well, it looks like I'm gonna have to want to do better." He tried a wink in Tressa's direction. His eyes were so hollow he couldn't quite close his eye. "So, Hufty, it looks like you and me won't go graping any more."

Thea said, "You'll be home evenings to see her."

"It won't be the same."

Ma said, "Son, you've got to learn you can't live on just eating honey."

"I know that, Ma. But honey is sure sweet."

Ma said, "Maybe we can ask Geoffrey to ask the blessing. He's learned a new one."

Geoffrey bowed his head. "Lord, our hungry bodies need this food. May the table set before us give us strength to do our work. Forgive us our sins, in Jesus' name we ask it, Amen."

Ma had tears in her eyes. She nodded toward Pa. "Tunis, will you start serving the meat, please? I'll start the potatoes from this end."

Pa picked up the carving knife and fork and began the carving.

The moment they were through eating, Tressa got up from the table. "I've got to go out to the granary a minute."

"How come?" Ma asked.

"I don't know if that hen in the granary I heard this afternoon was laying babies or just plain eggs."

Dirk finally had to laugh.

26. Stoop Talk

1908

A summer evening after a hot day cutting oats.

Chores and dishes were done. Pa and the boys, and Tressa, were sitting on the concrete stoop on the east side of the house. Ma and the other girls were sitting just inside the screen porch.

Pa and Tane had their jackknives out and were whittling away at some ash twigs to make whistles. Dirk was leaning forward, now and then letting a handful of sand trickle through his lean fingers. Rolf was smiling white to himself with his huge teeth. Geoffrey was reading in a much-thumbed copy of *Grimm's Fairy Tales*. Tressa was watching a full moon slowly rise over the high east hills. Ma and Thea were busy with their tatting. Ana was reading in her own copy of the New Testament. And Mallie was playing with her homemade dolls, a pa and a ma.

The setting sun behind the house shone with a diffused bronze gold, giving the gray fence posts an ochre hue, touching the grass with a yellow patina, making the horizons luminate as though they were about to burst into flames.

There was no wind out. It was utterly calm. A crow could be heard complaining raucously on the other side of the river. Even the cows could be heard cropping grass as they slowly moved down the lane toward the pasture.

Tane looked up from his whittling. "I hear Stinson up at the Falls elevator has left us."

Pa brushed some shavings off his knee. "Oh?"

"Yeh. He kicked a can of nitroglycerine, thinking it was a can of maple syrup. It took the coroner's jury three hours to get his remains together."

Dirk said, "How do they know he thought it was maple syrup?"

Tane said, "Just before, he'd opened the can and saw that it was colorless. Maple syrup? They said he even dipped in a fingertip to taste it. It was sweet. After he put the lid back on the can, he gave it a kick to one side. And then, blawey! he was gone."

Dirk spilled more sand between his fingers. "That nitroglycerine must've belonged to that peddler I was reading about in the Bonnie *Review*."

"I don't remember reading that," Pa said.

"It was an item in last week's paper." Dirk turned to Ana. "You had that paper last. Where did you put it?"

Ana said through the porch screen, "I'll get it." Ana was jealous of Tressa and every chance she had she tried to win Dirk away from her. She came back after a moment and, opening the screen door, tossed it at Dirk, who caught it on the fly.

"Thanks," Dirk said. He looked at the front of it. "Yeh, this is the one. July the tenth, 1908." He opened it to the inner pages for the syndicated boilerplate news. "Here it is. 'A peddler down in Missouri was apprehended by the local constable for making fly-killing paper. It works this way. He coats the paper with a mixture of molasses and nitroglycerine. Pretty soon a fly lights on the paper, gets molasses on his legs, flies off, rubs his nose on his legs, the nitroglycerine explodes, and the fly is blown into the next world.'"

Everybody had a good laugh.

"You would spot that item," Pa said. "I never look at that inside stuff. It's usually all malarkey anyway, pumped at us from the East somewhere, to take our attention away from the real news. From politicians cheating us."

Dirk said, "Pa, we've got to have humor in this slippery world."

Pa said, "Well, maybe you're right. Mark Twain felt the same way."

Tane looked southeast toward a new farmstead across the railroad tracks. "The neighborhood is going to the dogs with all the poor trash out of Indiana buying up land around here."

Rolf laughed his huge smile. "Yeh, that Will Sisterman ain't gonna make it. Talk about dumb. In the hog world he wouldn't make it."

Tane tried out his whistle. It emitted a hoarse noise. "Just shave a little more out of this corner and I've got you."

Thea looked up from her tatting. She was almost finished making an edging on a doily. "And have you noticed the raft of kids they've got? The place is full of them. Like a barnfull of kittens."

Dirk said, "And they got such funny names. One. Two. Three. So on."

"Oh, c'mon, Dirk."

240

"S'Gods fact."

"You mean," Ma said, "they've actually got the names of numbers?"

"That's right. Mrs. Sisterman said that when she got to eleven, the kids could chose their own names. Because she said she'd never learnt to count past ten."

Pa's moustache wiggled under his nose as though it itched him. "Those Puddesters who took up that half section between us and Hack Tippett ain't gonna make it either."

Tane said, "They too dumb too?"

Pa said, "No, there's a big trouble there. Man and wife ain't speaking."

Dirk laid the *Review* to one side. He smirked to himself as if what he was thinking about couldn't be mentioned in front of the ladies.

Tane guessed Dirk was thinking something dirty. He liked to bait Dirk to get him to tell raw stories. "You better tell us, Dirk. Because I'm gonna pester you until you do."

"Oh," Dirk said, "it's nothing."

Ma said, "Down with the Devil now, Dirk."

Ana said, "I don't think it's fair that you menfolks can have jokes that we womenfolks can't."

Dirk said, "After Mallie and Geoffrey are in bed."

Tane said, "Go ahead and tell it. Those two ain't paying attention anyway. Mallie's playing getting married and Geoffrey's busy with the seven dwarfs somewhere."

Pa tried out his new whistle. He licked the mouthpiece, making it wet and blew. A sweet mellow note lifted over the yard.

Ma said, "Ain't that nice."

The sun hit the horizon behind the house and almost immediately cool air breathed down from above, touching sweaty necks. Even the concrete in the stoop began to cool off.

Rolf let go with a wonderful horselaugh. "I know the one you're thinking about, Dirk. Where Emily Puddester caught her husband come flying out of the barn with his horse out."

"What!" Pa cried.

"Dirk!" Ma warned.

Thea said, "Oh, shucks, Ma, he might as well tell us. We won't sleep all night wondering what it was."

Tane said, "His horse out?"

Ma said, "That's enough of that!"

Darkness swooped in over the eastern hills like a great black mist.

Ma said, "All right, all little children off to bed."

Mallie said, "Aw, Ma, my dollie ma is just now getting ready to kiss my dollie pa."

Pa spoke up with an indulgent growl. "Mallie."

Ma said, "Geoffrey, you too."

Mallie banged the heads of her dolls together and then got up and slowly headed for bed.

Geoffrey said, "I just got a half page more to go about the fish that swallowed a gold ring."

"Go!"

Geoffrey stood up. "There ought to be a law against little children going to bed so early."

Again Pa spoke up. "Well, there ain't yet, my boy. So off you go. March."

Geoffrey pushed out his lips. "Well, when I grow up to be a lawyer I'll fix a law in favor of little children."

Shortly after the two little ones had gone upstairs, Ma and Thea gave up on their tatting. Too dark. With a sigh, knowing that they'd been well used that day, the two left for bed. Soon Ana too closed her Bible and went to bed.

Pa said, "Nuh, Tressa, you're getting to be a bit of a tomboy, always hanging around with us men."

"Well," Tressa said, "if I'm good enough to milk your cows, I'm good enough to hear your stories. After all, some of the things that happen in the barn ain't exactly without sin either."

Dirk said, "Aw, Pa, let her be. I ain't got any secrets from her."

Pa's face and the four faces of his children could just barely be made out in the dark. "Go ahead then, Dirk. I'd kind'f like to know myself about that horse."

Dirk picked up a handful of sand and again, slowly, like he was holding an hourglass, let the sand spill out.

"Well, Stiffy and his wife, Emily, came home from church at noon, and like always, while she's getting Sunday dinner ready, he goes out to the barn to do some chores. The winter sun is out and it's warmed up a little, a good time to let the cows out for a few minutes so they can have a drink and butt each other around a little. He opens the cow door, and then opens the stanchions one by one, and the cows slowly march outside. Just about then, he notices he's got high water, so he turns and stands in a corner of the barn and unlimbers his tool and lets fly into a pile of straw."

241

Rolf let out a blast of laughter. It was as if he was reading over Dirk's shoulder what was coming next.

"Stiffy stands there emptying his petcock and thinks a little about the great sermon the minister gave that morning, about how David lusted after Bathsheba and how that was a great sin, especially since David already had a wife, and also that Bathsheba was another man's wife, and so as Stiffy is standing there draining his tank, he lets his eyes roam around inside the barn, admiring how neat he keep things, almost as neat as his wife keeps her house spick and span . . . when suddenly he notices that one of the calves has jumped out of the calf pen and that it's heading for the open door where the cows just went through. Well! he can't let that happen. You know how calves are in the winter after being holed up for months—they're rarin' to run. He'd probably be chasing it around in the yard for hours trying to catch it."

Tane let go with a choked laugh getting ready for the crack-of-the-whip in the joke.

"Stiffy don't even bother to shake the dew off his lily, but takes off for the door, trying to beat the calf to it. The calf sees him coming and lifts up its tail and lets out with a beller. Well, Stiffy really digs for it then . . . and just as the calf jumps out of the door he manages to grab it by the tail. And there they go, both sailing high outside in tandem, for all the world looking like the cow that jumped over the moon with a man hanging on."

Pa's mouth slowly fell open as Dirk progressed with his tale. Of a sudden he broke out with a loud chop of laughter. Even for Pa that was too much not to laugh at.

242 "Well! Of course you know it had to happen. Just then Emily Puddester is looking out of the kitchen window over the yard while she's peeling potatoes in the sink. She sees the flying calf and the flying man. She has to hang on to the edge of the sink to keep from falling to the floor. Her husband? With a calf? With his peter hanging out? What had he been doing with that calf just before? That was as bad as what them Israelists was commanded not to do in the deserts of the Sinai peninsula. She doesn't even bother to see what happens to Stiffy after that, that he hung on to the calf by the tail like a bulldog and finally did get it back into the barn. She didn't notice of course either that in hanging onto that calf his peter had slowly retreated back into his pants, that all that was wrong with his clothes then was that he still had his barn door open."

All the men rolled with wild laughter. And just when it looked like the laughter was about to stop, one of them would look at the other and then begin laughing all over again. They all laughed until tears showed in the corners of their eyes.

Rolf finally had to ask it. "Well, what did happen after that?"

"When Stiffy came into the house a half hour later, hungry for his wife's usual great Sunday dinner, roast pork and boiled potatoes with thick flour gravy, home-canned pole beans, applesauce, and a piece of cinnamon-flavored apple pie, hmm-yum, he found his wife, Emily, nowhere around, with the dinner still not ready. He called her and called her. Finally he went to their bedroom and found her in bed with a pillow over her head and crying a flood. Stiffy asked her what the trouble was, but she wouldn't say. When he removed the pillow from her face, he saw that she'd been crying so hard her face had turned beet red and her eyes was bloodshot. But she wouldn't say why."

"What happened finally?"

"Stiffy found out the next day. When he went out to milk the cows that Sunday night, she'd called their minister. Because around coffee time on Monday morning their minister with their strictest elder showed up on the yard. And then over the kitchen table, while having a cup of coffee, the church trial began."

"Not really."

"Sure. That's what they're saying in town. Emily accused him flat out of lying with an animal. She got out their Bible and read the verse about it, Leviticus eighteen, verse twenty-three. 'Neither shall thou lie with any beast to defile thyself therewith: neither shall any woman stand before a beast to lie down thereto: it is confusion.'"

"But didn't Stiffy explain what happened?"

"Sure he did. But a lot of good that did, after what she thought she saw."

"What a sight that must've been," Tane said.

Dirk picked up some more sand and let it drift out of his cupped hand. "Finally though, Elder Aaron Whitehead had a question. Because Reverend Converse didn't know what to say or do. Reverend Converse, you know, was brung up in Munster, Indiana, where he never saw any animals but cats and dogs. Elder Aaron Whitehead asked, 'Tell me, Stiffy, was that a bull calf or a heifer calf?' Ha. You know how dumb Stiffy can look sometimes when you ask him a surprise question. He thinks hard for a minute, and then his face lights up, and he looks over at Emily with love, and he says, 'Hey, that's right, Aaron. I swear by all that's holy that that was a bull calf.'"

"Did she forgive him then?"

"What else? Though she sure dragged her tail about it. Like I say, it was hard for her to forget what she saw."

243

"Yeh," Pa said at last, looking off into the east where the stars were rising, "that must have been some sight. Even without there not being any moon around to jump over."

Tressa licked the lips of her open mouth. She hadn't laughed much. She threw Dirk a disgusted look. Her blue eyes picked up the last light of a saffron bronze dusk in the west. "That was an awful story, Dirk."

"Well, you had your chance to go to bed with the rest of the women."

"Are you sure you didn't make that up?"

"Why, Tress, you know how much I respect the marriage vow. I wouldn't want to desecrate it with some story that wasn't true."

"I dunno now," Tressa murmured. Then Tressa slowly got to her feet and headed for bed. As she stepped past where Dirk was sitting, she gave him a little push on the shoulder to let him know that she really was disturbed over his tale about the flying calf.

27. Rolf

1910

Rolf came to love their red Hampshire hogs, and because of it he became a first-rate pig man. He knew when was the best time to breed the sows so they would bear young in late March, well past the really cold weather, and still have the young ready for the market the next winter when the price was the highest. Rolf had Pa's permission to take a team of horses and drive to the other side of Rock Falls looking for a good red Hampshire boar so there would be no inbreeding.

The rest of the family was on their honor to be careful what they said about hogs so as not to hurt Rolf's feelings. The poor fellow already had a bad enough time while at school with all the teasing he got for his strange stiff black hair sticking straight up like the bristles on a hog, for his sloping forehead with a forelock coming to a point almost between his black brush eyebrows, his little animal eyes quick and gray, his heavy lower lip, his huge white teeth set well apart like a mustang's, his receding chin so small it was as though he had no chin at all. As long as Tane and Dirk had been around at school, teasing had been at a minimum. Both Tane and Dirk were quick to defend Rolf, Tane with his powerful fists and Dirk with his cutting wit. Tane had once let one of the Tolson boys know at the Little Church catechism classes that he would just as soon kill him as not after he'd caught him ragging Rolf.

Yet for all his Neanderthal looks Rolf's sisters liked him. They knew he had the most deft hands of all the boys. They often watched him repair their shoes. He worked the awl in and out of the leather like a seamstress stitching up a hem. His work was as neat as if done in a shoe factory. They trusted him with their trinkets when those too needed fixing.

Rolf was especially tender with his younger sister Ana. Ana had a habit of sitting apart from the rest and with her high blue eyes looking with disdain at their antics. Rolf understood her. He knew they both were special. Rolf would probably never catch a girl and Ana spat fire around boys. While Rolf wasn't exactly the kind of candidate that would make a good priest or a monk, Ana though had the perfect kind of nature to make a nun. Rolf and Ana often took up each other's causes.

Ma favored Rolf just a mite more than she did any of her other children. No one resented it, however. Rolf was Rolf and he needed that extra comfort from Ma. Rolf was going to be a lonesome man someday.

Pa meanwhile tolerated Rolf's way of doing his share of the work. When Pa made Rolf his fence man as well as his hog man, Pa let the rest of the kids know that Rolf could choose his own work hours. Rolf was more on his own than any of the rest of the boys.

Rolf rarely went to town with the family on Saturday nights. When all the rest looked forward to the fun they'd have in town, Rolf was busy figuring out ways to get the fatteners to put on weight in a hurry, or how to set a corner post in the wet part of the wasteland.

When Rolf did go to town he could more than hold his own. Once when one of the meaner Tolson boys tried to pull his leg about him being so close to his hogs, making pets of them, that he was beginning to look a little like them, Rolf was quick with his retort. "Hogs is cleaner than rats if you give them a chanct. And rats is cleaner than human beings if you give then a chanct. So, take your choices."

When one of Hack Tippett's friends took exception to Rolf's remark that he thought Hack pretty dumb, Rolf was swift to retort again. "I ain't saying Hack ain't smart, see. But Hack sure ain't overly smart."

When one of the crude pool hall bums passed some gas while sitting on the bench outside the billiards palace and then laughed at what he thought was hilarious, Rolf had a flattener for him. "You know, Pence, to let a fart is not the same thing as saying, 'Let there be light.'"

When Rolf became sixteen, he had several interesting things happen to him. One came about as he was putting in a new line of fence through the wasteland. The neighbor living to the west had complained that the Freyling cattle sometimes broke through the old fencing put in by the previous owners, the Worthings. Rolf took one of the horses, the old gray Polly, hitched her to their democrat, loaded the democrat with new cedar fence posts and rolls of wire and staples, and slowly began stringing new barbwires from the end of the good fence north into the tangle of trees and wild grapevines.

One noon, looking up at the sun, he knew he would be late for the noon meal. He didn't like watches, liked to think he could read time by just glancing up at the sun. But he was so busy trying to set a proper corner post that he'd forgotten the time.

"Well," he said to himself, "I guess there's nothing for it but I'll have to scrounge up some grub for myself. Too bad I didn't take a fishhook along or I could've had me a fine river trout for dinner."

He unhitched Polly and led her down to the river for a drink.

It was while he watched Polly lipping water that his eye caught the shimmer of a purple river clam lying in the rippling ford at his feet. It gave him an idea. There was nothing so savory as a good river clam properly baked. Searching through is pockets he found several stick matches. Lucifers, as Pa called them when he lit the kitchen stove in the morning. Rolf stepped back into the edge of the wasteland and gathered up an armful of deadfall twigs. He was careful to build the little fire on the sandy beach. After the fire was going good he picked up the shining clam and dropped it into the fire. The clam opened and closed several times, as though with its tongue sticking out it was gasping for breath, and then closed up tight. A half hour later, when the clam's edges relaxed and opened up again, Rolf knew the meat in it was done.

He fished the clam out of the hot ashes with a stick. Using his jackknife he parted the clam and then cut the rubbery meat up into small pieces. Licking his thick lips, he tasted the first piece. Ah. There was nothing in the world like clam fresh baked in its own shell. Looking about he spotted several wild turnips growing on the river bank. He pulled up one of them and again with his jackknife cut the turnip into a dozen thin slices. Then he mounted a piece of clam

245

on a slice of turnip and ate them together. That was even better. Now and then when his mouth began to feel tart, he kneeled and had himself a drink from the river.

He nodded to himself. If a man had to, and there was no human habitation nearby, he could scratch up a living off the country real easy.

The wild turnip didn't set easy on his stomach and after a while he began to burp between bites. Again he kneeled down and sipped himself a long drink. He drank like the gray Polly, dipping his lips in the water.

As he scraped out the last of the meat from the clamshell with his jackknife, he was startled to see a round gleaming pellet pop out of the pocket under the joint. The pellet rolled off his blue overalls onto the sandy beach.

"I God."

He picked it up. The juicy fat from the broiled meat made the pellet glow like a big drop of milk. A pearl. It was a perfect sphere and as big as a gooseberry.

"I'm rich!"

His head sank between his shoulders. His gray animal eyes flicked back and forth as though afraid someone might have seen him find the pearl. This was something he was not going to share with the rest of the family. He'd hide it somewhere and then have it someday for an emergency. When he needed money in a big hurry.

His next thought was he should look around for more clams in the river. But then he remembered that the jeweler in Bonnie had gone pearling one summer after he'd found a pearl the size of a pea. But try as he might, the jeweler never found another one. The jeweler though did make a little money selling fresh clam meat to the butcher besides supplying his own family.

The pearl was a wonder. It picked up light from the sun like it might be a milky window. It even began to feel warm in the palm of his hand. Rolf unbuttoned the little pocket next to the watch pocket in the bib of his blue overalls, dropped in the pearl, then buttoned it up again.

He went back to fixing fences. All afternoon as he worked he glowed inside.

That evening when chores were finished, and after the family's usual gossip on the stoop, Rolf went off in the direction of the privy. He knew exactly where he would hide the pearl. He'd once noticed a small knothole in the back of the privy in which spiders liked to hide. He was sure it would make a perfect fit for his pearl. When he tried it, he found the opening into the knothole a little tight. He gave the pearl a hard push and, click, it popped inside the knothole. It filled it exactly. Perfect. He next went to the toolshed and dipped up a fingertip of tar from the tar bucket and then went back and sealed the knothole, or what he now called his jewel box. In time the dab of black tar would weather over with a tannish color, blending in with the color of the weathered surface of the wood.

For the next couple of days he didn't bother to come home for the noon meal. Instead he asked Thea to make him some sandwiches with lettuce and a pot of tea. He told Pa and Ma it was too far to drive home at noon; he was losing an hour both before and after dinner. He didn't tell them he was having fresh-baked clam along with the sandwiches and tea. He didn't care if they found out and thought it sneaky of him. There weren't enough clams to go around for the whole family.

The fifth day he went down to the river for a clam in a different place. It was where the Big Rock River drove hard straight west before it doubled off sharply to the left toward the south. It had cut deep into land sloping toward the hills on that side. He had finished his meal and had washed his face and hands when his eyes spotted it. Something gleamed in the lower layer of sand just above the water line. The sun was striking down just right to catch it.

The top eight inches of earth in the steep high bank was black. Then came orange dirt, some five feet of it, then yellow clay, two feet of it. There was some more black dirt, which was slowly changing over into gray because of age, then followed some more orange-colored material. There were a lot of stones and pebbles in the lower órange material, yellow and green and pink, with something that resembled half-petrified wood. At the very bottom part of the lower orange material was a strata of sand, about an inch thick, that glittered. It was that which had caught his eye.

He stepped along the edge of the water and knelt down. He picked up a pinch of the yellow stuff. It was soft. Hey. Wasn't gold supposed to feel like a fellow could put a dent into it with a fingernail? Gold. Now he really was rich.

Or Pa was. The law said children couldn't own property.

His gray eyes narrowed. What if he didn't tell Pa?

After some thought, Rolf knew he couldn't keep his find of gold to himself. Pa would have to know. There was more than a bushel of the stuff and that would be hard to hide.

The girls Tressa and Ana had given him a bucket to pick gooseberries in case he should find some. Well, he'd found some all right. Golden gooseberries. With a pailful of what he had found they could buy all the gooseberries in creation, tame or wild.

Gold had been found in the Big Sioux River some dozen years earlier. Several miners on their way back from the Black Hills had panned the sandbars of the Big Sioux north of Canton and had come up with a couple of hundred dollars' worth of gold dust and two button-sized nuggets. For a week there'd been a gold rush. Pa sometimes talked about it with a laugh. But no one else found any gold, no matter how thoroughly they worked the river. But it did mean that it was possible there might be occasional gold in the area.

Rolf got himself a little twig and holding the bucket up to the wall he pried and probed at the inch-thick layer of gold sand until he had a pailful.

The gold was heavy. He had to shift the pail back and forth from one hand to the other a couple of times before he could clamber back up to his democrat.

He worked on the fence the rest of the afternoon, his eyes often drifting over to the democrat where his pail of gold stood.

Once he got home he unhitched his gray, Polly, watered and fed her, took off her harness and hung it on its hooks on the wall, and then went to get his pail of wealth.

Ma saw him coming across the yard. She was hanging out some wash and her hands were red from the homemade lye soap she used. Ma looked at the way he was carrying the pail. "Well," Ma said, "it looks like you picked a whole lot of gooseberries, boy. Were they nice and ripe? Black?"

Rolf tried to act nonchalant. "Where's Pa?"

"Why?"

"Pa might want to meet King Solomon himself."

"Who?"

Rolf shagged the heavy pail up to where Ma stood and set it down in front of her. "All the gooseberries I picked turned into gold. Solid gold. Look."

Ma stared down at the glittering stuff. The falling afternoon sun gave the yellow stuff a soft mellow gold look. "Oh, my Lord. Fancy that."

Pa was in the toolshed. He'd heard Ma exclaim and came walking up with his quick steps. "What's this?"

Rolf said, "Look."

Pa stared at the shining stuff. "Where'd you get that?"

"I robbed a bank."

"What?"

Rolf laughed. "Yeh. I robbed a riverbank. Where I was fixing fence in the wasteland."

Pa reached down and took up a pinch of it. He crinched it between his fingers. "Where?"

"Where the Big Rock takes that sharp turn. It was at the bottom of that steep bank there."

"Hmm."

"It's gold, ain't it, Pa?"

Tane and Dirk and Tressa came out of the porch carrying empty milk pails and two five-gallon cans. It was milking time. They stopped to look at Rolf's find.

"If it ain't gold, what is it then, Pa?"

Pa set his feet wide apart to think better. "Tell you what. I've got to go to town tomorrow and get some salt. And Ma needs some sugar and flour. I'll take a sample of this along and show Chauncey at the bank. Ma, put a little of this in an envelope and then we'll see what we'll see. Meanwhile, Rolf, carry the rest of this into our bedroom. And then come pronto out to the barn and help us milk."

The next day when Rolf came home from fencing at four-thirty, he had several pails full of gooseberries that he'd found in the far back part of the wasteland. After he brought the gooseberries into the milk porch, he looked into the kitchen to see if Pa had come back from town.

Pa had. He was sipping tea. At his feet stood the pail of glittering stuff, which he'd gotten out of the bedroom.

Rolf knew right away there was going to be bad news. "What did they say at the bank?"

Pa set his cup down in its saucer. "Chauncey said you'd found yourself some plain ordinary fool's gold."

"Not real gold then?"

"Just a bunch of rusted iron pyrites."

"Oh."

"Sorry, son. You ain't the first one to be fooled by fool's gold. That's how come it got its name."

"What shall I do with it then?"

"Why don't you bring it out to the sandpile where Geoffrey likes to play."

Rolf nodded. No use dreaming in that direction anymore. But far back in his head he made up his mind all the more that someday, somehow, he was going to be a rich man.

He went outside with the bucket of fool's gold, out to where Geoffrey was playing under the ash tree. Rolf poured it all in a pile next to some of Geoffrey's stick animals.

"I can have all that then?" Geoffrey cried.

"Sure. Some fresh wheat straw. That's what it looks like."

"Goodie."

Rolf stumped away.

The next day he got set to put in the big corner post in the very northwest corner of the Freyling section. From Pa he'd learned how to put one in that would never move, not even if they hung another earth on it. Rolf loaded the biggest cedar post Pa'd bought at the lumberyard, a good nine feet long and ten inches thick, onto the democrat. He also took along some cement and two big stones Tane had unearthed behind the barn. Each stone was as big as a bushel basket. The democrat's springs were flat.

With a post auger and spade he dug three holes, a deep one next to the iron stake left by the surveyors, a wide one on the northwest side of the iron stake, and another wide one on the northeast side. He first set the big cedar post in its hole. Shucks. Hole wasn't deep enough. He hauled the post out and then down on his knees worked the post auger down some more, piling the dirt in a heap to one side. The first dirt out of the hole had been as black as stove soot, and of about the same consistency, but the dirt after that gradually changed in color, to brown, to yellow, back to black again for a few inches, and then to orange. The new dirt he threw out continued to be orange. He wondered if here too he might not hit another thin layer of fool's gold.

He'd dug down maybe some six more inches, widening the hole as he went, since he needed room for the cement he meant to pour in later around the bottom of the pole, when it struck him he was smelling gas.

He sat back on his heels to think about it. If it really was gas, and the bit of his auger struck a spark off a pebble down there, he'd be blown to kingdom come. He carefully and delicately pulled out the post auger.

Then he heard a noise. At first he thought it was a snake hissing at him in the deep wild grass beside him. Then he thought it was Ana, who'd snuck up on him and was trying to whistle. Ana just didn't have the lips to whistle. No matter how she tried to purse up her lips, she still sounded like a goose hissing. He flashed a look around to either side, so quick his neckbone cracked. No Ana. What in the world . . . ?

He looked down into the hole. The forenoon sun lit up the top third of the hole, but the bottom of it was hard to make out. Now the hissing seemed to be coming out of the very bottom of the hole. Was there a wolf down there that resented his accidentally probing into its den?

Again he sat back on his heels. There definitely was a very strong stink of gas, and it was coming out of the hole.

Then, suddenly, a blast of sand shot up out of the hole, up past his face like someone might have shot off a cannon down there using shrapnel. Rushing sand and pebbles rose straight up, rising, rising, up past the highest cottonwood, a good hundred feet, and then, at the very top, mushrooming out like a jet of water, spraying the tops of the trees around. There was a roar like the hoarse sound of a great blowtorch. Except that the sound was alive. Like there might be a mad dragon down there in the bowels of the earth.

"Holy k-peter!"

Polly the gray also took note of the gusher of sand. She sagged back on her rear legs, almost as if she were a dog begging, and then, whinnying strangely, she shot forward and made a sharp turn left, dragging the democrat around on

249

two wheels, and disappeared down the narrow path through the brush along the new fence he was making.

Rolf was too startled to holler after Polly. She probably wouldn't have listened anyway.

"Talk about a blowout! This has got to be the biggest one ever in this part of the country."

About then sand began to rain down on his straw hat and shoulders and hands. He ducked; then bounded to his feet and ran under the trees.

"Man! I better go tell Pa about this."

When Rolf arrived breathless on the yard, he discovered Pa and Tane and Dirk already knew about it. They'd spotted the rising jets of sand above the treetops of the wasteland. When Rolf tried to tell them what had happened, he couldn't find the words. His tongue kept trying to jump out of his mouth ahead of the words. Finally he pointed at where Polly had come to rest in front of the gate to the pasture lane. She stood with her head reared in the air and her mane sticking up.

Pa made a curt gesture. "C'mon, let's ride the democrat back out there. Maybe Rolf's made us rich after all. If not with yellow gold, then with black gold."

Dirk scoffed. "Oh, c'mon now, Pa."

"I mean it. Oil. Like Rockefeller."

"Huh," Dirk said. "Imagine us as rich as him."

Pa said, "If it does turn out to be oil, Dirk, we're sure to have enough money to send you off to college."

They all hopped aboard the democrat, with Pa taking the lines.

But Polly didn't care to go back. She's already seen too much. No matter how Pa cursed her, or slapped her butt with the lines, or the boys yelled at her, she just wasn't going to go. At last Pa gave up, jumped off the democrat, and started hurrying toward the geyser of sand. Rolf and Dirk followed him. Tane, the responsible one, stopped a moment to secure Polly, tying her hitching strap to a fence post to one side of the pasture lane.

When they arrived at the northwest corner of the Freyling section, they found the posthole still roaring and blowing sand.

All four stood staring at it, keeping well away from where the sand might fall on them. A south wind had come up and the bouncing jet of sand began to shade off to the north, spraying onto the neighbor's cornfield.

They held an arm up over their eyes to keep occasional bits of sand from getting into their eyes.

Finally Pa said, "Hell's bells and holy balls. A wind well."

"What?" Rolf cried.

"A wind well. In this case, a wind hole. I've heard about them. A fellow near that Quaker ranch east of Bonnie was digging a well when all of a sudden gas shot out and one of the well drillers fainted dead away."

Dirk raised his eyebrows. "Oh, so that's how come they named that little town near there Blow Out."

"The same. They said the wind coming out of that well hole was strong enough to burst a sheet metal cover wired down over the top well curb."

Rolf rocked back and forth on his stocky legs. "If we threw a lighted match at it, what would happen?"

Pa snorted. "We'd witness the first natural Roman candle in creation. If it didn't blow us into the next county. Can't you smell the gas around us?"

Over the roaring noise, Rolf heard the chatter of light voices. Turning, he spotted Ma and the girls Thea and Tressa and Ana and little Mallie and the boy Geoffrey coming hurrying toward them.

Ma shrilled over the roaring. "What in the world are you men doing out here?"

"Ask Rolf." Pa shouted back.

"Rolf?"

"I dunno! I was just digging a hole when all of a sudden I had me a volcano on my hands."

Ma and the girls and Geoffrey stared at the rising jumping blasting sand geyser. Ma finally said, "What are we going to do with it? Will it ruin our property?"

Pa's moustache wriggled under his nose. "Just let it blow itself out, I guess."

"When will that be?"

"Your guess is as good as mine. This is all new to me."

Thea said, "It sure is scary."

Tressa said, "It makes one realize that this earth we stand on ain't all that solid after all."

Ana's eyes took on a holy light. "Job talked about this in his book. Where it says, 'Behold, he discovered deep things out of darkness, and bringeth to light the shadow of death.'"

Sand streamed off the leaves of the highest cottonwood. If ever a thing could be called hair-raising this certainly was one. The worst part of it was the awful hoarse sound issuing out of the earth. Truly there did seem to be some kind of huge monster alive down there, outraged and furious that it had been disturbed in his sleep. Even Pa was a little scared. His eyes glowed like heated pearls and his fingertips trembled.

251

Finally their neighbor Albert Reynders to the west showed up riding one of his draft horses. The horse, a bay, still had its harness on. It was all lathered up. The bay took one look at the sand gusher and it too instantly wanted to run back home. No matter how Reynders jerked the lines and slapped the horse over its butt with them, the horse wouldn't go another inch. Finally Reynders slipped off the bay and tied it to a fence post. Then Reynders advanced cautiously along the fence, mouth open, eyes turning like boiling onions. Reynders was known as a man quiet in manner, beloved of his wife and children, honest in his dealings with the people of Bonnie. He was an elder in the Little Church.

Reynders advanced to within a few rods of the roaring hole and then, leaning down, climbed through the old fence and joined Pa and the family. Reynders stared at the geyser of glittering rushing sand and finally ejaculated, "By the roaring bulls of Bashan, what in the . . . ?"

Dirk had to smile. They'd almost heard a church elder swear.

Pa smiled sideways too. "Yeh, somebody down there is as mad as hell."

Reynders said, "Well, hell is in that direction all right."

Pa said, "It's coming out of the exact corner there. So you can't blame us if it's ruining your corn."

Reynders waved that off. "Man, does that thing stink."

"So we noticed," Pa said. Pa spotted a pipe stem sticking out of the bib of

Reynders's overalls. "Don't take that thing out and light it."

"'Course not."

Tane said, "Pa, I'm wondering if we shouldn't call the sheriff. Or somebody like that."

"What for?"

"Well, somebody important ought to see it. Maybe even the governor."

Ana said, "Maybe we should just pray."

Holding her bosom, Ma said, "I've thought of that. Though there doesn't seem to be any immediate danger."

Dirk sniffed. And sniffed. At last, snapping his fingers, he had it. "I know what that is. Methane gas. We've been studying gases in physics. When a volcano is about to pop out of the center of the earth, the first thing to show up is methane gas."

"What!" Pa cried. "You mean to say we might have a mountain grow on us here?"

"Could be."

Rolf said, "Well, what are we going to do? I'd kind of like to finish fixing the fence here."

Reynders slowly began to get hold of himself. The usual impassive expression returned to his lean handsome face. "Well, it can't hurt nothing really. Except some trees and a few hills of corn. So I suggest we all go home and wait it out. Until it blows itself out. And maybe pray a little to see if we can come to some kind of understanding as to what the good Lord has in mind for us here."

"Good idea," Pa said. "Ma?"

"I think so too," Ma said. "Children, off we go."

252 Everybody started walking home, with many a glance back over the shoulder at the phenomenon.

Rolf followed behind the others, carrying the post auger. All the other fencing tools were on the democrat that Polly had run away with.

The cattle had taken notice of the roaring hole too. They stood facing it, heads held high, eyes popped and glowing, tails tilted up. Some of the calves interpreted the event as a kind of cow picnic. They sailed around and around their mothers, tails up too, bellowing as if trying to sing some kind of school ground roundelay.

A geologist from a nearby university had a look at it. He theorized that the last glacier had dumped a great mass of dirt in the Big Rock River valley, covering an old vent from the magma. It was just possible, he said, that a minor earthquake had reopened the old blowhole. "You don't feel the earthquake in this part of the country because of all the dirt between you and the bottom rock. The dirt absorbs the shock of lesser quakes. But they're there."

Two days later the wind hole quit blowing.

Four days later Rolf went back to the hole and finished setting the corner post. He first threw some rocks down the hole and then filled in some dirt. He set the post canted slightly to the northwest to take up the pull of the two longer fence lines, the one going south as well as the one going east, and then cemented it down tight. He dropped the bushel-size stones Tane had found into the bigger holes, one to the northwest side of the cedar post and one to the northeast side. He anchored the cedar post to the great stones with several strands of heavy wire. Pa called the great stones tied to a corner post deadmen.

"A deadman under the frost line won't ever move on you." Finally Rolf hooked up all the fence wires coming to the corner post, from the south, east, north, and west, using the fence stretcher to make the four fences so tight they sang like violin strings when struck with a pincers.

The smell of gas slowly vanished.

28. Ana

1912

One morning Ma called Ana into the back bedroom. When Ma wiggled a finger at one to follow her into Pa and Ma's room something serious was afoot. Ma gestured for Ana to sit on the big blue bed while she herself pulled up a chair.

Ana waited. She was afraid Ma was going to ask her what she knew about Dirk and Tressa. Every now and then Ana couldn't resist sticking it into her brother and sister. Ana was almost insanely jealous of the way those two took to hugging each other in front of everybody. Though so far as she knew Dirk and Tressa lately no longer hugged each other when they were alone. Ana had often spied on them. Ana sensed that some kind of sin had taken place between them.

Ma said, "Let's see, you're fifteen now, aren't you?"

Ana said, "I'll be sixteen come November eleventh."

"My, my, how times flies. When I remember as if it was only yesterday when you were born."

Ana watched her mother closely. The sunlight coming through the south window of the bedroom struck her mother's face from the side. Ana was shocked to see how lined her mother's face had become.

"How are you feeling these days, Ana?"

"Fine." Out of the corner of her eye Ana also noted how the bright sunlight gleamed a heavy gold off Ma's ivory comb and mirror set on the mahogany dresser.

"Looking forward to going to high school again this fall?"

"Yes. Except they don't have Bible study there."

"I know." Ma sighed. "If we only had this farm on the Big Rock River near Whitebone, then you could take special instruction from Father Garlington."

Ana waited. Something serious was afoot all right.

Ma picked up one of the strings to her green gingham apron, toyed with it a moment, then dropped it. "Ana, are you having trouble with your periods?"

Ana stiffened. Her short back formed a shape like a question mark.

Ma went on. "I always like to be the good friend to my girls, and have them confide in me about their female problems, so . . . Your periods don't come regular, do they?"

It pinched out of Ana. "No, I guess not."

"Well, it's nothing to worry about, really. When I was your age I sometimes skipped as much as three months."

Ana let her back relax. "You did, Ma?"

"Yes. It wasn't often. Just now and then."

"Oh, Ma, I was scared to tell you. I didn't know what to think. Thea and Tressa are so regular."

"Girl, why should you be worried? You haven't been with any boys, that way, so it couldn't be anything, could it?"

"No, of course not." Ana almost spat. "I don't like boys that way, Ma. Never. I'm going to be a missionary. And if not that, a nun. You know that, Ma."

"Yes, I know." Ma sighed again. "Sometimes I think it's because you don't eat right, daughter. I notice you always skip red meat. Won't eat eggs. Just vegetables and dark bread. Not even butter."

"That's just me, Ma."

Ma picked up Ana's short slender hand. Ma's hand, though wrinkled from all the housework she'd done over the years, was still a mannered hand. "Ana, how would you like to earn some money this summer? This is the last week of June, so that means there's still two months of vacation left. Maybe you can earn enough to buy yourself some new clothes for school."

"Are we that poor, Ma?"

"No. It's just that both Pa and I think it's good for our children to go out and work for other people now and then to learn the value of a dollar. Learn what it means to earn your living."

Once more Ana sat up very straight. "You're not going to send me away?" Ana remembered a remark Pa had made to Ma one night after the folks thought all the kids had gone to bed. "You know, Clara, that girl is as busy as a bee in a tar bucket, she buzzes so about how naughty the other kids are. A real tattletale about sin. Maybe it would be good for her to go work for other people for a while to learn how good she's really got it here with her brothers and sisters." At the time Ana hadn't been sure just who Pa was talking about. But now she knew. It hurt to remember that. She loved Pa. Pa was so Christ-like around Ma. Never teased her, nor jollied her up, to hint they might do things at night in their bed. Pa never looked at Ma the way Dirk looked at Tressa on hot mornings when Thea and Tressa and Mallie lay naked. That was why she herself was always careful to have her nightgown pulled well down past her knees after Pa called the boys to get up.

255

Ma went on. "As Pa was driving home from town yesterday, Clate Bartles rolled out to the road and called to Pa to stop."

"Oh." After Clate had lost his legs in a blizzard, his sister Hettie had bought him a boy's red coaster wagon and had it rigged up so he could ride around in it on level ground. She'd had the new blacksmith in town, Booney McBroom, weld a bicycle pedal to the side of the little red wagon and then connect the pedal with a chain drive to a sprocket wheel welded to the right rear wheel. Clate worked the pedal with his right hand.

Ma went on. "Clate said Hettie needed some help in the house, she was feeling so poorly. Said he'd pay well. Board and room and a dollar a day. In two months that'd be sixty dollars for you, Ana."

Ana began to feel sick to her stomach. Several times she'd had to walk home from high school because she'd stayed after to catch up on her biology lab work, and in so doing of course had to walk past the Bartles place. She always hurried past their lane. She'd long felt that something unholy was taking place with that strange couple, a brother and a sister living together and being offish with the neighbors. Only Hettie ever left the yard and that was just to get groceries and clothes from town. They never joined the threshing rings or cornhusking bees, never went to picnics either on Decoration Day or the Fourth of July.

"What do you say, Ana?"

"Oh, Ma, do I have to?"

"Ana." Ma pronounced her name as though it were spelled Awna. Ma'd once said that the reason she'd given her the name Ana was that it was one of the first names ever given a woman in far ancient times. When Ana had protested that Eve was the first woman to have a name, Ma'd smiled and said that the pronunciation of Ana and Eve, or Ana and Eva, were not all that far apart, especially the way she pronounced it in the Old British manner. "Ana?"

"Why can't Thea go?"

"I need her here."

"What if she gets married pretty soon? Then what are you going to do?"

"We'll take care of that then."

"Or Tressa?"

"Pa needs her on the yard. When she isn't busy in the house with me."

Something flashed in Ana's memory. She remembered when Pa had suddenly asked Ma, as Pa and Ma sat drinking a cup of tea on a Sunday afternoon when again they thought they were all alone in the kitchen, "Something hasn't happened here, has it, between those two that we should know about?" and Ma had answered, after a moment's hesitation, "Not that I know of." Pa was referring to Dirk and Tressa.

"Ana, I can't sit here all day talking to you, when there's so much to do with such a big family and a whole section of land to handle."

"Then why are you sending me away?"

"Because the way Pa talked, Clate Bartles sounded like they really needed help there. And you're the only one of the girls I can let go."

"Maybe they need help in the field and one of the boys can go. Doesn't Hettie do all the field work?"

"Pa said Clate said they needed help in the house."

Ana began to hear a series of strange sounds in her head, sounds she'd heard a couple of times before. She didn't know what to make of them. She'd first heard them in her dreams while asleep, but then soon heard them while awake. "Ana Ana. Ann Ann. Uhn Uhn. Oon Oon." It was a sound that seemed to rise out of the bottom of her backbone.

"Ana? What's the matter?"

Ana blinked; and was back in the bedroom with her mother. "Nothing."

"Don't you feel well? You're sheet white."

Ana brushed her blue dress down over her short limbs.

Ma's eyes crinkled up, sharply quizzical. "You looked like you were going to have a visitation, child!"

"I did?" Ana blinked again. "Well, that's why I want to be a missionary. Or a nun. Because sometimes I think I hear Jesus calling. Direct. He himself."

Ma slowly sat up. Her grave gray eyes fixed sharply on Ana. She brushed back several straying graying auburn hairs from her high forehead.

Ana couldn't hold up to her mother's look. She didn't want her mother to think she was going crazy. She was all right. She was the way she was. There was never going to be a baby growing in her belly. She was too narrow, too tight for that. There wasn't any room for such foolishness. Ana stood up. "All right, Ma, I'll go. If they need help they need help. And if I'm going to become a missionary to the heathen, I'd better learn how to get along with the down and out. And what better way than with one's neighbors. When do I go?"

Rolf brought Ana over in the democrat. He jumped down from the spring seat and helped her down. Then he picked up her brown leather suitcase from the democrat and walked her to the door. Clate in the house saw them coming and on a homemade creeper, another invention of Hettie's for use inside the house, rolled to the door and held it open for them. The creeper was a small platform mounted on casters.

"Well, well, am I glad to see you," Clate exclaimed. Clate had let his pale white moustache grow so long the ends curled back under his ears. "I've seen you walk past here many a time on your way home, and I always thought, my, what a nice-looking girl."

Ana shivered. This man may have looked at her in lust all those times she walked past.

Clate's light blue eyes shied off. First one stump at the end of his body flopped up and down, then the other. "Come in, come in. Hettie's in bed through that door there." He pointed to what had to be the living room. "And then it's the door on the left." He offered up a hearty laugh. "On the sunny side of the house."

Ana wrinkled up her nose. What a smell in the house. Every family had its own kind of smell in the house of course. The Bartles smell wasn't the smell of a dirty mop or a dirty dishrag, because the kitchen they stood in was as immaculate as Ma's at home. It was a smell of something decayed, or old milk, even like the aged smell of the colostrum milk off a cow that had just come in. Mingled in with it was yet another smell, a mineral smell of some kind, like thinner for varnish.

257

"Go ahead," Clate urged. "Hettie will know what needs to be done."

Rolf set her suitcase down by the door. "Well, Ana, I guess I'll head on home then."

Ana turned to Rolf. How she wished she could go back with her brother. Rolf might look like a brute ape in the eyes of the world, but to her he was a wonderful brother. Rolf had always been tender with her, had never looked at her the way Dirk looked at Tressa, and had often defended her when somebody got after her. Like that time Ma had got on her hands and knees and scrubbed the floor under the kitchen table and had spotted all those black bread crusts up on the cross supports of the table next to where Ma stored the Bible. Ma had then carefully watched during dinnertime and had caught Ana. Rolf had come to Ana's defense. He had apparently seen her put the black bread crusts there, but told Ma that he'd put most of them there himself. Rolf for all his dumb looks saw just about everything. When Ma'd asked him why he of all people should do that since he had such big strong teeth to chew up the crusts, Rolf had laughed his huge laugh and said that he had tender gooms sometimes and that he was saving the crusts for their dog Shep.

Ana said, "Thanks for bringing in the suitcase, brother."

"Think nothing of it."

Clate tried to make some good-bye conversation. "How do you like the weather, Rolf?" The way Clate on his creeper looked up at Rolf showed that he felt Rolf was beneath him.

Rolf stepped down off the stoop outside. "Fine. Can't complain. It couldn't be better if you and I'd made it."

"Ha."

"Well, Mr. Bartles, see you in the funny papers."

Ana smiled. Her brother had sure shown that miserable wretch. She turned and headed into the living room.

Hettie called out, "I'm in here."

Ana entered the bedroom. There the smell was more one of fresh blood. And looking, Anna saw it. There were blood smears on the part of the sheet that showed on one side of the bed. She could also see drops of drying blood on the upper insides of the chamber pot. What in the world . . . had Hettie cut herself bad?

"Oh," Hettie said from the bed. "They sent you, Ana. Clate and I've often seen you walking by."

Ana pinched out the words. "Ma said she needed Thea more than she did me. And Tressa milks with Pa." Ana couldn't help but stare down at the woman. Hettie appeared to be even longer lying on her bed than when she was standing up. Her complexion was paler than white bread. Her eyes were really more holes than eyes, and set far back under her white brows. The freckles over her nose looked like someone had spattered drops of coffee over it.

"What are you staring at?"

"You look so poorly. And then all that blood . . . did you cut yourself?"

"Never mind about that. Change into your work dress. Your room is upstairs. The east one."

"You should see a doctor if you're bleeding bad."

Hettie's thin lips narrowed into slits. "We'll talk about it later."

Ana got her suitcase from the kitchen, found the stair door, and went up. The door to the west directly at the head of the stairs was closed. She guessed that that was where Clate slept. There was no other room downstairs in the small cottage to serve as a bedroom. Did he mount the stairs with just his arms? Ana had noted that Clate had extremely huge biceps, bulging out like loaves of bread, and a great chest, spreading out like a salt barrel.

Ana swung left and entered the east room. The sloping ceiling shot up steep from the baseboards. There was just enough headroom down the center for her to walk erect. She put her suitcase on the narrow cot on the right. And sighing, wishing the ordeal of the summer was already over, she slipped out of her good red dress and slipped into her green gingham work dress. She also changed shoes, sliding her pointed black patent leather shoes under the cot.

As she was about to start down the stairs, she noticed the peculiar varnish or shellac smell again. It was more noticeable upstairs. Smells tended to rise, like heat, and would naturally gather at the head of the stairs.

She entered Hettie's room. "What shall I do first?"

"I'd like you to help me out of bed so I can sit over there on the window seat. And then you can change the sheets and such." Hettie swung back the covers.

Ana slipped an arm under the gaunt woman's shoulders. It was with an effort that she tried not to notice the sour sweat smell of the woman. Hettie needed a bath badly. Ana helped her to her feet and then over to the seat in the window recess. The window seat was low, almost as though it had been built for a child. Maybe it had been built for Clate. It certainly wasn't built for Hettie's long legs.

Hettie said, "Bring me my bathrobe. In the closet."

Ana got it. She was startled to see, amid Hettie's dresses, a brown suit for a man hanging in the closet too. The suit jacket hadn't been buttoned up after it had been hung on its hanger and the trousers showed through. The trousers were without legs. There were also a few shirts and ties hanging in the closet. Strange. Clate must be using her closet to hang his things in. Ana then remembered that some of her brothers hung their shirts in the girls' closet at home.

Hettie said from the window seat, "Those sheets you better soak in cold water."

"I know." Ma had long ago shown her girls how to get rid of blood-stained sheets.

"And the pot you empty in the privy."

Ana had to fight off a shudder.

When Ana had finished redding up the bedroom, Hettie said, "If you'll bring me that small tub that's hanging out in the front porch, and some fresh hot water and soap, I'll give myself a bath."

Ana wondered if she should offer to help her.

"And you better lay out a fresh towel and washcloth. From the closet just outside the door there."

Ana nodded. After she made sure Hettie had everything she needed for her bath, Ana picked up the pot and headed for the privy behind the house. She held her nose to one side so she wouldn't have to look at the contents. What an awful job. Little did the folks at home know what she was going through. But if she was going to be a missionary to some wretched heathens somewhere, she'd better harden herself. What stories she'd have to tell Thea and Tressa when she went home Sunday for dinner. She pushed open the privy door, and still holding her head away, and figuring out peripherally where the privy hole was in the dim light, she let the contents of the pot slosh into the vault below. Almost immediately a wave of dead old fecal-matter odor bloomed up through the hole. Uggh.

Taking the path through the grass back to the house, Ana was surprised to see Clate out by the hog barn riding in his little red wagon. From a sitting position Clate was slopping the hogs. How strange it was to see a man with his bottom half cut off still getting around as though life were worth living.

Ana flished out the pot under the pump in the yard and then went over and placed it on the rack outside the kitchen door, where some milk pails were also set to catch the sun. Ma had taught Ana and the girls that there was nothing like sunlight to purify utensils.

Ana entered the kitchen. She noticed there were a few dishes to wash in the sink. She went at them, using water from the warm reservoir. She sudsed up the water with a bar of homemade soap and thoroughly washed the dishes, then rinsed them with more warm water and set them out to dry on a wire rack above the drain.

Hettie called, "Can you come help me?"

"Right away."

Exhausted, Hettie sat naked on the floor beside the tub of water. The water was gray, with flecks of white floating on the surface. Hettie said, "I'd hoped to get my nightgown on alone, but . . ." She smiled wryly down at her hands lying on her knees. "I'm still so weak."

Ana felt a bubble of sympathy for her. Hettie looked like a great broken crane. Ana picked up Hettie's faded blue nightgown and, doubling it up, slipped it over Hettie's head, helped her arms into the sleeves like she might help a child, and then let the nightgown slide down her body. Ana noticed that several drops of thick milk had oozed out of the nipples of Hettie's breasts. Ana also noticed that Hettie's breasts were unnaturally swollen. Further, Ana couldn't help but note Hettie's patch of white pubic hair. Its whiteness startled Ana. Except for Tressa, her sisters had blond pubic hair. Even Mallie, who was just beginning to show halved apricots for breasts, had blond fuzz inside her thighs. Ana hadn't known that women could have white hair there.

"Now help me to my feet and back into bed."

Struggling, lifting with all her might, the shorter Ana doughtily helped shag Hettie into bed. Hettie was so weak Ana had to lift her legs in bed. Ana then reached for the folded sheet at the foot end of the bed and spread it out over Hettie.

Hettie puffed. Sweat beaded out on her forehead. A vague flush spread over her cheeks. "Thanks, Ana. You're a dear."

"Oh, that's all right."

Slowly Hettie got her breath back. "I suppose now you can get dinner ready for this noon. If you'll just rustle around in the kitchen there, you'll find most everything you need. Potatoes to peel. Beans to strip of their strings. Beets to boil. And Clate's probably killed a rooster for you by now. He said he would anyway when he got up this morning. He usually boils the rooster so we can have soup out of it too." Hettie noticed a puzzled look on Ana's face. "Yes, Clate does the cooking when I'm working in the fields." Hettie shook her head. "I don't know what's going to happen to our crops this year if I don't get well in a hurry."

"Would you like me to comb your hair?"

"That would be so nice. No one's done that for me since my mother did it."

Ana swallowed down another bubble of sympathy. She wasn't going to show Hettie, or Clate, that she in the least liked working for them. It was going to be a heavy duty, not a pleasure. She got Hettie's thick-toothed ivory comb from the dresser and began combing the tangles out of Hettie's long coarse hair. Pa had once remarked that Hettie's hair had reminded him of the tail of a white horse. How right Pa was. Ana asked, "Do you want me to put it up?" Combed out neatly, Hettie's hair came down well past her hips.

"No. Clate likes me to wear it long and loose."

"Pa likes for us girls to wear our hair that way too." Ana combed and brushed gently. "Though Ma says we better pretty soon get used to putting it up in a knot. Most men like it that way."

Dinner that noon turned out to be fairly pleasant. To keep Hettie company Clate suggested they eat in her room. Ana could set out the food on a little table in front of the low window seat.

Hettie, refreshed from a morning nap, managed to make it to the window seat on her own. Clate sat beside her, all smiles. Ana sat on the hard-back chair facing them, dishing out the food, getting Clate an extra piece of mincemeat pie, bringing out the coffee.

Clate's moon-pale eyes kept shying off to one side. He would look at Hettie directly, even with adulation, but he simply would not look Ana in the eye. "Hettie, wouldn't it have been nice if we could've had a daughter like Ana here?"

A wan smile touched the corner of Hettie's thin lips. She sighed. "But God wished otherwise, I guess."

Ana's brows tightened. A daughter? Surely Clate must have meant if Hettie had got married.

Clate finished his coffee. "Well, now for the good old catnap to restore the soul." Clate flicked Ana a pale glance, then looked away. "Ana, you too. For every catnap you take when you're young, you add a month to your life in your old age."

Ana helped Hettie back to her bed and then carried the dirty dishes back to the kitchen. After she'd washed and dried them she headed for the stairs. She noted as she passed through he living room that Clate had heaved himself up onto the davenport under the bay window facing the road. Ana decided that that was where he must sleep at night. The davenport was one of those couches that could be opened up to form a bed. During the day the bedclothes would be hidden inside it. Clate sleeping there meant that the west upstairs room was used for storage.

At the head of the stairs she again noticed that peculiar smell she'd noticed on first entering the house. Most of the house smells she'd gotten used to, but this one continued to be sharp. She tried the door to the upstairs west room. It was locked. Storage room? That was odd. Why should a person want to lock a storage room? Unless they'd hidden some prized family heirlooms in it. Or their money. Pa and Tane had often wondered if Clate and Hettie Bartles didn't have some money stashed away somewhere to make ends meet. Because surely the little crops they raised on their sandhills wasn't enough to keep body and soul together. Ana tried the knob again to see if maybe she hadn't turned it hard enough, or hadn't turned it the right way. Still firmly locked.

She knelt down to peer in through the keyhole. There wasn't much to see. The blinds were drawn on the two west windows. She remembered now having noticed when she walked past coming home from school the blinds were always drawn in that room like a blind man with nictitating membranes. She stared through the keyhole until she could make out the vague outlines of what looked like a row of cradles set under the two windows. But stare as she might she couldn't make out what was in the cradles. Much mystified, she finally gave up and went to her room.

She unloosened her button black shoes and removed them. With a soft sigh she stretched out on the cot. It had a web spring and sagged in the middle. It was worse even than her bed at home with Mallie. She and Mallie were always tussling in sleep over who was going to lie in the middle of the little valley.

Tired, not really wanting to know more for the moment about the queer fish she was living with, Ana dropped off to sleep.

Later in the afternoon, after Ana had completely finished redding up even the yard around the house, with supper cooking on the stove, she fell into a surprisingly easy talk with Hettie. Hettie was beginning to feel better by the moment. Hettie had to know all about the Freyling family, from Pa on down to little Geoffrey, how big their farm was, how they got it in the first place. Finally centering back on Pa, Hettie asked if it were true that Pa had a temper.

"Oh, Pa can get pretty mad sometimes."

"Did he ever hit you, Ana?"

"Once. And I had it coming. He gave me a flip of his fingertips over the ear."

"Did it hurt?"

"I'll say it did. But I stood up to him. When the sting of it went away, after supper when we were all sitting on the cool side of the house, I went up to him and said, 'Pa, you hit me, your very own daughter.'"

Hettie had to smile. The smile for the first time pulled up the corners of her mouth. "What did your father say to that?"

"He choked up a little it seemed like, and then he burst out laughing."

"Did he ever touch you again?"

"No."

"Did he ever love you up?"

"No, not me. Though he's beginning to love up Mallie once in a while. You know, like a loving father."

"Why do you suppose he doesn't you?"

"Maybe he knows I don't like having anybody touch me. Not even Ma."

Hettie shifted her legs about under the sheet. "Ana, you're lucky in your family. That's something neither Clate nor I ever had. My mother died of the cholera when we were babies. And our father had to raise us. That was in Missouri. There was no one around for miles. And oh, was he cruel to us. You can't imagine! So we finally ran away. We followed old Indian trails, first through the woods and then across the prairies, until we came here to Bonnie. If our father, or the law, had ever caught us, it would have been the end."

Ana found herself listening intently.

"You see, our mother had inherited some gold coins from her family. When she died, our father found them. He also found her will in which she'd willed the gold coins to us, Clate and me. But he didn't tell us. We knew he had a hiding place for something in the house. So one day when he went to town for supplies, we snuck into his bedroom and found the gold coins and the handwritten will. We right away made up our minds. We grabbed the coins and the will, packed a suitcase and ran. We took Mother's last name, Bartles, and when anybody asked us who we were, that's who we said we were, Clate and Hettie Bartles. The first week we were scared to death he'd catch us. Twice in the distance we saw him coming after us, looking for us, riding his fastest horse. We always quick hid in the bushes. Thank God he didn't take a hound with him to smell us out. Finally when we crossed over into Iowa, we began to feel better."

"Aren't you afraid he still might find you?"

"No, he's dead now."

"How do you know?"

"We used to subscribe to the local paper there in Missouri. Four years ago there was a story about him dying, and that his death wish was that he might have found us. Said he wanted to forgive us. Ha!"

"Oh. But didn't one of you go down there then to claim the property? As his heirs?"

Hettie's mouth thinned out. "Both of us, without even thinking about it twice, vetoed that."

There was a knock on the door.

Hettie said, "Would you go see who that is, Ana?"

To Ana's surprise, it turned out to be one of the seniors she knew in high school, Fuzzy Griffith. He fancied himself a ladies man and dressed in a foppish manner, black sideburns, long hair, gray spats, a folded kerchief in his breast pocket. He had long slender fingers with impeccably manicured nails. His dark eyes were narrow-set like a mink's. He had a way of looking at girls as if he were mentally undressing them. He clerked in Rexroth's Mercantile in the summer. He had several times asked Ana for a date to go dancing but she'd turned him down cold.

"Hi, Ana."

"What do you want?"

"Hey, I'm here on an errand. Mrs. Bartles sent us a postcard to bring out a gallon of shellac." Fuzzy held up a glass jug filled with yellowish fluid. Behind Fuzzy his horse and buggy waited on the yard.

Shellac. Aha. That was the smell she'd been trying to identify. Hettie had been doing some woodwork finishing in the house then. Ana held out her hand. "Give it to me. Hettie doesn't feel well."

Hettie overheard them. "Let Fuzzy in. And I'll pay him for his trouble."

Fuzzy entered the house, and then the bedroom. He took one look at Hettie and his face changed. Gone was the waggish look. "Why, Mrs. Bartles, what's happened to you?"

"Nothing much, really. Just one of life's misadventures. How much do we owe you?"

"Ninety-eight cents."

"And your trouble to bring it out here?"

"No trouble at all. It's all part of our service to our customers."

Hettie reached for an old scabbed leather purse lying on the bedstand nearby. She fingered out a dollar bill and gave it to him. When Fuzzy began to dig into his pockets for the two cents change, she said, "Keep it all, please."

"Thank you very much, ma'am."

Ana followed Fuzzy to the door.

Fuzzy slipped an arm around Ana's hips and snugged her up close, at the last second cupping his hand up over her breast.

263

Ana jumped away from him. The slimy vaselined city slicker! She lashed out at him with her open hand, catching him across the cheek and in his right eye.

"Hey, you wild pussycat you!" he cried. "That hurt." His eye teared over.

"You had that coming you stinker. Oh, I know all about you. The awful things girls say about you in the girls' rest room."

"And I know all about you too," Fuzzy retorted. "You prick-teaser. Already at fifteen a dried-up old maid. Going to bed with you would be like going to bed with an ironing board. No place for babies to go in or come out."

"What a terrible thing to say!"

"We know that not even the Little Churchers would let you join their church."

Ana tried to kick him in the crotch with her pointed button shoes. She caught him instead in the right thigh.

Bent over, Fuzzy Griffiths crippled out of the door and out to his horse and rig.

Ana slammed the door and went back to Hettie.

Hettie was smiling to herself. "What was that about the Little Churchers? They wouldn't let you join their church?"

Ana flicked imaginary lint from her green apron. "Oh, it was nothing really. I'm the religious one in our family, and I thought I should go to church regular in a nearby church. We're really Episcopalian. In Whitebone."

"I see."

Ana decided not to tell that she'd been quite a puzzle to the Little Church consistory. When they told her that to join their church she'd have to first confess all her sins as well as promise to leave all her sinful ways behind her, she said she really didn't know of any sins to confess or any sinful ways to leave behind. She told them she was born already loving Jesus, and didn't have to experience a moment of conversion. She was already a member of Christ's heavenly church and only wanted to confirm it by joining his earthly church. When they insisted on trying to make her feel she was full of sin, she was shocked. And mortified, she finally withdrew her application.

Hettie said, "You don't go out with boys, do you?"

"In our family we start late with that. Why, not even Tane or Thea go out yet. We're an awfully close family. We have a lot of fun together and so really aren't all that wild to escape."

"How lucky you are."

"When I decided not to join that church, because of all the nosy questions, I had an awful time. The Devil thought he had a chance to get me then. He compassed me about like bees for a while. But I resisted him."

"That about the Devil, isn't that all in your head?"

"Sure it is. Because you think about it. But it really is mostly in your soul where you wrestle with him."

"Where is your soul? In what part of your body?"

"Oh, Miss Bartles, what an awful question to ask. Don't you believe in heaven and hell?"

"I believe in hell all right." Hettie was lying without a sheet covering her legs.

Ana happened to spot a tiny pink streak in Hettie's white nightgown. "You're still spotting."

"I am?" Hettie looked. "I guess I am." She pulled up the sheet to cover the pink tinge.

"Shall I tear up some more sheets for you?"

"No. I'll get up pretty soon and do it myself. Is supper about ready? If it is, call Clate."

Ana had to ask it. "What ails you . . . does it have something to do with your period?"

Hettie didn't say anything for a moment. At last she said, "I guess you could say that. Yes."

"Are yours regular? Like clockwork?"

"Not anymore."

"Mine never was. Once I skipped four months. I knew it couldn't be because I was going to have a baby. Because no man had touched me. Not even my brothers."

Hettie threw her a searing look, said nothing.

Ana said, "I'll call Clate." She looked at the gallon of shellac standing on the floor beside Hettie's bed. "Shall I put that under the kitchen sink?"

"No. Just leave it right there." Hettie sat up. "You know, I'm beginning to feel pretty good. I think I'll eat at the dining table tonight."

Ana smiled. "Think you can make it?"

"I'll try."

"Then I better set the table out there."

Ana called Clate. She found him slopping the hogs, doing it from his sitting position on his specially rigged coaster wagon. Ana then set the table.

When all three sat down to eat, Ana was surprised to see Hettie take the swivel chair at the head of the table and Clate the place where the woman usually sat. Hettie was the head of the house, not Clate. Mmm. Wait till she told about this at home.

They were well into the meal when another question popped into Ana's mind. She saw again those little cradles in the dimly lit west room upstairs. "Miss Bartles, did you play with dolls when you were a little girl?"

"Pa wouldn't let me have a doll. Said we were too poor. I had a little rag doll named Merry when my mother was still alive. Merry had such a wonderful wide smile. Made of red yarn. But of course when Ma died, that doll disappeared."

Clate looked up from his second helping of country sausage. "I saw what Pa did with it too. He threw it in the stove one morning when he lit the fire for his coffee." Clate shook his head sadly. "It surely made us wonder if maybe the whole world was against little children."

Ana looked down at her plate. She had eaten very little, only a little section of the sausage, a small potato, and a corner of bread with no butter or jam.

When they finished eating, Ana asked if they had a Bible. She'd like to read from it like Ma did at home.

Clate looked down at his plate.

Hettie shook her head. "Pa wiped out all religion in us. I guess you might say we're outright heathens." Hettie chuckled sardonically to herself. "If it is true that hell is a place of eternal fire, at least winters will be warm there. No blizzards."

"You can say that again," Clate murmured. "Where at least you won't be in danger of losing your legs."

Ana wanted to say, wouldn't one be covered all over with blisters in hell, but she quick bit on her tongue. She was after all only hired help and not a member of the family. At home, if someone had made such a bitter irreverent remark she would have sailed into them.

Soon Hettie retired to her bed and Clate rolled on his creeper out to the stoop to sit in the cool of the evening.

Ana did the dishes.

As Ana worked, her right button shoe for some reason squeaked on each step. Ana finally said out loud, "What's the matter, shoe? I thought we paid for you."

Hettie in her room heard the remark. She laughed. Her laugh had the sound of a hen's soft cackle. "I haven't heard that since me and Clate lived with Pa. He was always saying, 'If the shoe squeaks it hain't been paid for.' Just to make sure we realized we were church poor."

Several days later, with Hettie up and about again, Ana began to wonder of what use she was to the Bartles. There wasn't much to do. She found herself with a lot of time on her hands. She wondered a little if she wasn't actually in the way.

Ana missed being home with her family. She even missed being bawled out by the other kids because they thought her such an awful tattletale. She smiled when she remembered the reason she gave for tattling. She told on others because she thought it was her duty to point out sin. And she especially missed watching Dirk and Tressa.

Ana was lying in bed at night thinking about all that, when suddenly a hunch ruptured up in her mind. It was so unnerving that she popped upright in bed. Not really!

But the more she thought about it the more she became convinced she'd come upon the real secret.

Well, how could she open that locked door to the west room? Hettie probably kept the key in her purse downstairs. Ana thought about it some more. Actually the lock was a simple one, and the locks to all the rooms in the house were probably alike and one key would fit them all. If she could find the key to her room it might fit the lock to the west room.

Very quietly Ana raised herself out of the hollow of her cot and swung her bare feet to the floor. At home the folks often just put the key above the door, either on the inside or the outside. On tiptoe she reached up and felt along the top of the door frame on the inside. No key. Then she felt along the top of the door from on the outside. Still no key.

Hmm. Where else could they have hidden it? Or where would Hettie have hidden it, since Clate probably no longer went upstairs? Or where would she, Ana, have hidden it were she in Hettie's place? She thought hard to herself. Why, of course. Above the frame of the window. Ana softly tiptoed across her room, careful not to wake up the floorboards, and felt along the top of the window frame. Sure enough. A key. She could feel where it lay amid accumulated dust. Now to see if it would turn the bolt over.

She slid her feet on the floor across the length of her room and then across the hallway to make sure there'd be no sound of a footstep. Kneeling, she inserted the key and easily, oh so gently, turned it. The bolt moved and, when she turned the key farther, the bolt clicked. She tried the door. It opened.

It was dark in the west room. There was a half-moon out, but with the curtains drawn and the blinds rolled down there wasn't enough light to see what was really in those cradles. The smell of the shellac was strong. Stealthily she slid her feet back to her room to get her kerosene night lamp. She found a match on the dresser, scratched it alive under the edge of the top of the dresser, and lifting the glass chimney, touched the wick with the flame. In a moment the wick came alive with a low brown-edged orange flame. She blew out the match and laid the burnt end in a jewel tray on top of the dresser. Then, refitting the glass chimney back into its brass holder, she once more traversed the room and the hallway and reentered the west room. She knelt beside the cradles, holding the lamp low to get a good look.

At first she thought they were dolls in the cradles, all of them well-varnished. But they were so beautifully and cunningly made! And then it hit her. They were dead babies. All shellacked. Their faces and what could be seen of their necks shone with coats of shellac. Gently, with a prying finger, Ana lifted the doll dress of the first dead baby. Yes, it had been shellacked down the length of its poor body.

God in heaven. Hettie had had a series of stillbirths. That was why Hettie was bleeding in her bed. And instead of burying her babies out at the Hillside Cemetery, she'd stored them up in the spare bedroom.

But what man had lain with her and had strengthened her, as the Bible had it?

Maybe the truth was Clate slept with his sister. And he didn't sleep in that bed in the davenport after all. That's why that window seat downstairs was so low. Come to think of it, even Hettie's bed was built especially low. Ana had earlier spotted that the legs of the bed had been sawn off a little and then reset in their casters.

Ana's belly drew up into a tight knot.

She looked at the cradle at the end on the right, holding the lamp low over it for a close look. Oohhh! It was a new baby. Just born. And it had been freshly shellacked. That was why Hettie had ordered by postcard more shellac from Rexroth's. She had to keep shellacking it to preserve it. Like the Egyptians did their mummies. Otherwise the maggots would get started. Babies just born were without sin and had no corruption in them to eat into their flesh. Ma had often said that little babies were born rain-pure, and were little angels, and that because of the evil on earth, because of what Adam and Eve had done in the Garden of Eden, were bound to become corrupt after a while, and at death be eaten by maggots.

What an awful thing.

Ana was afraid she was going to burst apart.

Should she tell on the Bartles? In this instance was it her duty to point out this sin?

A shadow under the last baby's little chin caught her eye. It was a skin bruise. Had they killed the baby? Killed all of them? She counted them. Four.

She was going to faint. Carefully she steered the lamp down to the floor until she'd set it safely down.

When she came to, light was beginning to come into the room from her own room. Dawn was opening up all across the rim of the earth.

Barely able to think, she managed to blow out the flame in the night lamp. Then on sad feet she went back to her room.

She made up her mind. She dressed; packed her suitcase; on soft toes went downstairs. In the kitchen she found a piece of scratch paper an quickly penciled a note:

Dear Miss Bartles—

My family needs me again. You can give what you owe me to some charity.

Ana

Then she started walking.

"Everybody will expect me to get married someday. Well, I wish I could get married to myself."

29. *Stoop Talk*

1914

And the Freylings continued to live and live. Eating bumblebee honey and puckery chokecherries.

It was late July and the boys had just finished shocking the grain and the girls had just finished canning crabapples. It was hot, especially in the house, and after supper everybody hurried outside, the women settling on the cool folding chairs inside the screen porch and the men sitting on the cool concrete stoop. Tressa for once decided to sit with Ma and the girls.

Talk began slowly. Dirk was still puffing from the day's work. Around four in the afternoon he'd almost fainted. Pa had seen it and had told Dirk to go home and lie down until milking time. Sunstrokes were no fun.

The shadow of the house lengthened across the yard, finally reached into the nearby stubble field. The low sunlight mellowed the gold heads of grain in the shocks to a warm rust color. The shadows of all the fence posts crept east even as the men watched.

Pa loosened his shirt down to his belt. "We could use a breeze."

Tane slowly fanned his face with his straw hat. "I'd welcome even a horse's warm breath."

Dirk said, "Maybe it's time for a windy story."

Tressa said from behind the screen, "Your stories are always windy, Dirk."

Dirk laughed. "Well, the one I'm thinking of sure is."

Rolf was the only one whose shirt wasn't wet where the suspenders came down over the shoulders. "You better tell it, Dirk, because we know you won't rest easy in your sleep tonight unless'n you do."

Dirk picked up a couple of pebbles from between his feet. He fumbled them in his hand a moment, tossing them up a few times and managing to catch them both at the same time. "You know that slough that's down there by the Big Sioux River below Klondike?"

"Yeh?"

"Well, it seems there's a little water here and there in that saw grass. Swarms and swarms of mosquitoes rise up out of there every night, making life miserable for man and beast. Sleep's impossible near those swales." Dirk loosened the shoestrings in his heavy blucher shoes. He slipped the shoes off and wriggled his toes. His brown socks were sopping wet. "Well, it seems that Pence White-head decided one night there was no use trying to get sleep in a house full of mosquitoes, so he took his sheet and climbed up on the roof of his house."

Rolf's head reared up. "Can't mosquitoes fly that high?"

Young Geoffrey said, "Hey, yeh, Dirk."

Rolf said, "Maybe Dirk thinks their little lungs'll bust wide open. Har."

Dirk went on. "Anyway, it wasn't long before the mosquitoes found him up there. They stung him right through the sheet. Like some fellows was trying to get him with a dozen three-tine forks."

Pa nodded. "Yeh, some of them do sting like that. Reminds me of them monster mosquitoes we had along the Little Sioux."

A single late hen, white feathers taking on a golden tinge in the sinking light, pecked at the ground a dozen yards away.

Dirk tossed a pebble at her. The pebble bounced off the ground and hit her in the breast.

"Rawwk!" The hen flew up a foot and then scurried off to the chicken house.

Dirk continued. "Desperate, Pence slid down off the roof and headed for the top of the bluffs, thinking to catch a breeze there. If the breeze was strong enough there'd be no mosquitoes. He followed an old wagon trail up there in the dark and found himself a spot in some tall bluestem."

"Hey," Tane interrupted, "I think I just now felt a little whiff of a breeze off the end of my nose."

"There was a breeze up there. A good stout one too. Pence folded the sheet under him on both sides to keep the ends from flapping."

Rolf, anticipating what came next, started to laugh.

"The breeze worked and worked at that sheet. And you know how it is when you're trying to fall asleep, first you lay on one side and then the other. Pretty soon the ends came loose and started flapping. Well, it just happened that about then neighbor Aaron Tolman and his son Jonathan came down that trail in the dark. They'd been in Bonnie getting their old lady a new kitchen range."

Ma broke in. "So I'm an old lady to you, am I?"

"Oh, Ma," Dirk said, picking up more pebbles, "this is a story. It has nothing to do with you."

269

"I still don't like it."

Dirk held back a smile. "Tolman and his son spotted that white form lying in the grass. Actually, their team of mules spotted it first, and they shied off a little. Tolman and his boy didn't know what to make of it. Was it somebody laying there dead? Tolman hauled back on the lines for a better look. Just then a real strong gust of wind came along and caught the end of the sheet, and by golly—"

"You're swearing again, Dirk," May interrupted.

"—and by jiminy, the wind jerked it loose and that sheet floated off like it was alive. Then up off the ground a naked form rose and took out after the sheet. Ha-ha-ha. This so scared Tolman and his son they whipped up their mules. The mules already had their ears flopped forward and that slap on their rump was all they needed. They took off in a perfect matched gallop like they was in a potato sack race. When the Tolmans got home they told their old lady—excuse me, Ma—they told Mrs. Tolman about seeing a ghost out on the prairie. A real naked one."

Thea scoffed. "Is that really true now?"

"Well," Dirk picked up some more pebbles and jiggled them in a loosely balled fist, "well, mosquitoes can be awful bad. And I do know for a fact that Pence Whitehead has been known to wear a woman's poke bonnet while out shocking grain."

"Oh, come on now, was you there?"

"Didn't you read in the local paper the other day how Pence beat up on a fellow because the fellow whistled at him in the field?"

Rolf said, "That don't prove nothing."

Ana finally spoke up. She'd been very quiet for months. Ma had privately warned everybody not to say anything about her strange silence. They were to wait for her to get over it. "I believe in ghosts. Only they ain't ghosts."

The sun ovaled a red hole down into the horizon. The whole world, sky and hills and buildings, was suddenly bathed in bloody hues.

"Ghosts really are souls that never had a chance to live a full and happy life here on earth. When God put them into just-born babies, he meant for them to reach the fullness of their days."

A thrush sang near the river. It was a bird's sad lament summer was going.

Geoffrey asked, "Did Pence ever catch his sheet?"

Dirk pursed up his lips. "I don't know. I did hear tell though that a white sheet was seen sailing over Sioux Falls and that it got hooked on the point of the steeple of the Catholic church there. The bishop had to hire a high-line guy to climb up there and take it down. Otherwise everybody would've thought the Catholics were surrendering to all those Hardanger Lutherans around Devil's Gulch."

Pa interposed. "Now, Dirk, don't you think you're being just a little too smart with your little brother Geoffrey? Wait until he's a bit older before you stick it into him with your stretchers."

Rolf said, "What I want to know is, what happened to our poor naked Pence?"

"He didn't get any sleep that night, that's all."

Tane took off his shoes too. He wiggled his toes in the cool dusk. "That Aaron Tolman you just mentioned got into another fuss once along that same trail. Or near there anyway."

"How so?"

"Well, Tolman bought a load of hay from a farmer near Alvord, and as it was getting dark he decided to cut across a field belonging to Ole Koveland. Ole Koveland had just finished milking and was letting his cows out into the night yard when he spotted the load of hay cutting across his property. Ole thought that a little strong, so he run out there and held up his hands and stopped Tolman's team of mules. And he asked, what the heck did he think he was doing ruining a perfectly good patch of alfalfa."

Rolf broke in. "You oughta see Koveland's hands once to get the true picture of that. They're as big as a pair of badgers."

Tane next took off his damp socks. "Tolman told Koveland he could go to grass for all of him, but he was going to take the shortcut home because by then the supper his wife had made him was getting cold, and he didn't like having his wife scold him."

Tressa asked, "Why must you men always drag a woman into your stories so she can take the blame?"

"Koveland's chin set out an inch. He grabbed the cross lines between the two mules and started to turn them back to the main trail. That really got Tolman's goat. He slid down off the load of hay and grabbed Koveland by his shirtfront and headed him into the field again, the mules following. Koveland let go of the mules and took a swing at Tolman. Tolman swung back. They knocked each other down a couple of times. Tolman finally stuck his head into Koveland's middle and pushed him down and sat on him and hit him some more. Then Tolman, thinking he'd pounded some sense into Koveland, got up and climbed onto his load of hay again and started for home, still taking the shortcut. Koveland meanwhile got up and ran to his toolshed. Tolman almost made it across the field. Just as he was about to go through an open gate by the barn, Koveland showed up with a spade and began pounding Tolman's mules over their heads with it. Tolman once more jumped down and went after Koveland. Only Koveland turned out to be handy with the spade. He was like a fancy swordsman with it. Before long Koveland had stove in four of Tolman's ribs."

Cool star air breathed down on the stoop. Everybody took a long breath and stretched their limbs.

Rolf's great teeth showed white in the dark. "Well, what happened then?"

"Nothing, really. Koveland led the mules back across his alfalfa field, took them around the proper route, and brought the hay onto Tolman's yard. Then he got out his own team of horses and hauled Tolman off in his democrat to the doctor for repairs. Last I heard, Tolman was in a fair way to recovery. A month ago, though, both sued each other. But Judge Monlux acquitted both on the grounds of self-defense."

"That really didn't happen now, did it?"

"Don't you read the paper at all?" Tane said.

"Well, none of us is interested in becoming a newspaperman like Dirk."

"I like that," Dirk said. Then Dirk had a puckery tidbit to tell. "I heard Charlie Thompson had his throat cut last week in one of our saloons." Dirk smiled sideways in the dark. "When Rexroth our grocer was told about it, he was heard to remark that he regretted that the accident wasn't serious."

Thea's face was invisible inside the porch. "The one thing good I did see in our weekly blab was that Madame Schumann-Heink is going to give a recital in Sioux Falls next winter. I'd surely like to go hear that. She's the world's greatest singer."

Ma said, "Maybe we can talk Pa into taking us there. I'd like to hear her too."

Pa slowly spoke up. "That's forty miles away."

Ma said, "We could stay overnight. That way our trotters wouldn't get too tired in one day."

Rolf said, "Why don't you buy a car, Pa? One of them Elgins. They made a jump of over a hundred feet with one of them at the county fair last year and it didn't break apart. Good as new afterwards."

Pa growled to himself. "Never. I'm for progress, but not of that kind." Pa turned to where he thought Ma was sitting in the dark behind the screen. "If that Human Shank woman is gonna sing in Sioux Falls, she'll sing in Sioux City too. And there we can take the train to it. Trains I'm all for." Then Pa sneered up at the sky. "But that's as far as I'm willing to go when it comes to machines."

"Shucks," Rolf said. "When I'm so handy around engines."

Dirk said, "Rolf, maybe you can become our local saw man."

"What's that?"

"Well, I read where over t' Le Mars a fellow walks the streets his clothes covered with saws."

"Saws? What's he do that for?"

"Who knows. Maybe he's got a fixation on saws."

Rolf snorted. "Yeh, and maybe he has a guest in his upper story."

Ana drew in a sharp breath in the dark.

Pa had to laugh to himself about something. When Pa laughed it usually was about something pretty funny.

Everybody waited.

Finally Pa told it. "You know our old Spanish War vet? Jasper Cooney? Well, it seems one night he ran out of whiskey. Every bottle he had was cork dry. Not a drop in a single solitary one. He ransacked his shack by the Thunderbolt Railroad tracks there from one end to the other. No tangleleg anywhere."

Ma said, "Is this going to be one of your barn stories?"

Pa glared hot eyes at Ma. "Maybe telling some rough stories 'ud make you a little more friendly in the bedroom."

Ana said quickly, "Please, Pa." What Pa and Ma did in the bedroom was the one thing she didn't want to hear.

Pa growled some more in Ma's direction. "For all your going to church and all your reading of the Bible, you don't listen very well. Where it says in Genesis two, verse eighteen, 'And the Lord said, It is not good that the man should be alone; I will make him an help meet for him.'"

Ma snapped back. "'Lewdness is an abomination in the eyes of the Lord.'"

"Where does it say that?"

"You know I'm poor at remembering chapter numbers. But I know it's in the Bible."

"The hell it is. I've heard the Bible read often enough to know it's not in there. I'll bet my bottom dollar on it. And until you can show me where it stands in there, what I said still goes. A couple of dirty stories might help juice you up a little."

Tressa was scandalized, "Pa, now you've gone too far."

Tane cried, "What I want to know is, what happened to Jas Cooney?"

Lowering his voice, Pa went on with his story. "Jas Cooney didn't trust his buddy Arlo Green getting him a bottle."

"Why didn't he go himself if he needed a drink so bad?" Geoffrey wanted to know.

Ma said, "You see? Geoffrey has already learned all about that rough stuff."

"Because Jas Cooney is a cripple, that's why. And when he's had one too many he keeps falling down."

Tane said, "I still want to know what happened."

Pa went on. "Finally Cooney thought of something. He knew Arlo Green had a wheelbarrow and he got him to haul him over to the saloon in it."

"Not really now," Thea said. "Is that true?"

"As true as I'm sitting here."

Ma said, "What a poor way to spend a summer evening, talking about drunks and men fighting with spades and men running naked over the prairie. Maybe it's time we all caught the train again and heard us a sermon by Father Garlington in Whitebone."

After that nobody said anything for a while. Everybody in the family liked the aging Father Garlington, but they didn't like the long train ride just to go to church. They'd been hoping that occasional visits to the Little Church of the Christian Hollanders would satisfy Ma.

Ana once more had something to say. "What I don't understand about the church, both the Little Church and Ma's Episcopal church, and maybe even the Roman Catholics too, is that if you get a divorce the church will kick you out so that you're doomed to everlasting punishment in hell, but that if you murder somebody you can be forgiven and stay in the church."

"Good gravy, Ana," Dirk said, mindful of Ma's admonition to take it easy around Ana but still feeling he should say something, "is that all you've got on your mind lately, murder?"

Ana said quickly, "I was thinking about that Mrs. George Blood who shot her husband in the back of the head with a thirty-eight while he sat at the table eating breakfast."

"What's that got to do with anything?"

"Just that the church fathers don't always act fair and that they don't keep a close enough watch on their parishioners."

Dirk said, "Well, for me they're already too nosey."

Ana said, "If they'd paid attention to what she told the minister and the head elder when they made house visitation to her home, they would have been able to stop that murder."

"How would you know that?"

"I read it in your Bonnie rag. According to the paper, when they asked her why she hadn't shown up in church lately, she said she had her reasons. When they pointed out that it was serious business when she didn't take Lord's Supper, she again said she had her reasons. About then her husband pipes up and says that Mrs. Blood had been threatening him lately, that she'd said she was sick of living with him. At that her minister began to question her closely. 'Don't tell me,' the minister said, 'that you've been thinking of striking your husband, possibly with intent to kill him?' When she didn't say anything, but just looked black at Mr. Blood, her minister asked, 'Don't tell me you're also thinking of divorce?' She then said, short off, 'Divorce, no. Murder, yes.'"

Ma said, "I don't know if I can explain the church's position on that."

Ana said, "That's why I've decided for sure to become a nun. Once you're a nun, I hear, your duties are simple."

Pa shook his head. "It's like I've thought before. Ana, you sure are a pure-born all right."

273

30. Mallie

1916–1917

Mallie was born fair. And she remained fair all through childhood into girlhood. By the time she became eighteen, her blond hair had turned into a rusty gold. Her blue eyes became hazel eyes. And her sweet thick child lips, curved in lovely innocent appeal, thickened even more. Her soft lips were the first thing people noticed. When she was eight she began kissing everybody, when she got up in the morning, then impulsively at any time of the day, and certainly when she went to bed at night. Everybody in the family thought it kind of cute, and smiled about it, and welcomed the most affectionate gesture. Pretty soon they nicknamed her Kissy. And that inspired her to kiss even more.

Of the boys Dirk enjoyed the kissing the most. He had yet another nickname for her. Triplelips. She had a way of pushing out her lips with her tongue showing in the middle a little.

Dirk also soon spotted that Mallie was aware of how much he loved Tressa. Mallie showed her jealousy in a most sweet way. She'd ask Dirk if he'd kissed Tressa yet today. When it was time to go to bed, she'd go over and kiss Dirk and then ask him to kiss Tressa so she could see it. Dirk knew that behind Mallie's request was a girl-child's love for a man. Once Mallie said to him, when they were alone in the back porch where she was washing the tins of the milk separator, "When are you gonna look at me like you look at Tressa when you first get up in the morning?"

"How'd you know about that?"

"I spied on you. I pretended my eyes was closed."

Mallie once almost found out what it was Dirk was doing with Tressa. It was in the summertime when she was ten. She'd asked Ma if she couldn't go over and play with Grace and Gordon Pullman. Mallie'd become acquainted with Grace and Gordon at their country school a mile north. Ma liked the Pullmans because they had the style and manners of people she'd known in eastern Iowa. Mallie and Grace got along all right, gossiping about their dolls and exchanging doll dress patterns. But Mallie got on better with Gordon.

It happened once that the Pullmans had company when Mallie was over for a visit, cousins from New England, Oscar and Louise Batchelder. The five children played hide-and-go-seek around Pullman's stacks of oats. There were two rows of four stacks each, and the children ran many a figure eight around them as they tried to get home free to the home base. Old Man Pullman was heard to remark that those five kids playing around his pointed stacks reminded him of Indian kids playing around an encampment of tepees.

Pretty soon Gordon whispered in Mallie's ear that he knew a good place to hide where the one who was It would never find them. The good place turned out to be up in the haymow of the Pullman barn. They climbed up a wooden ladder and then settled down on some hay near a small door. The door had a crack in it and they could see the eight stacks through it and so could watch where It was.

After a while Gordon thought it might be nice to lie back and rest a bit. They'd been running so hard around the stacks that he was all tired out. When Mallie didn't right away follow his suggestion, he pulled her down alongside him.

Mallie smiled to herself. What a nut. She didn't really like Gordon all that much to be alone with him. Gordon had blond hair and light blue eyes and funny thin lips like his mother's. He was kind of a pretty boy trying to be naughty. If it had been Dirk who led her up in the haymow, maybe then she would have let herself be pinched and played with.

Sure enough, after they'd heard the kids calling several times for them, with Grace, who was It, calling the loudest and acting kind of mad, Gordon suddenly snatched at Mallie's blue cotton dress and pulled it up and then rolled himself on top of her and bounced up and down a couple times.

Mallie almost laughed out loud; and then, gently, because she felt sorry for him, because he groaned so, she slid out from under him. Mallie said, "Tain't right that we hided up here in the barn. When rule is we're supposed to stay inside the fence around the stacks."

Gordon said, "I know. But I just had to try it once. Grace never lets me see her."

"Well," Mallie said, "Grace ain't supposed to. She's your sister."

"That's why I thought maybe you would."

"Nope, never me." Mallie got up and with a private smile slid down the ladder and emerged on the far side of the barn so It wouldn't see her and then ran along the north side of the eight stacks and got home free.

Grace saw her too late. Grace snapped back her long braid of gold hair. "Shoot. Where's Gordon?"

"Hey, I'm not supposed to help you find him."

"I thought he was with you."

Mallie looked around. "I don't see him."

"Shoot, I can never catch him." Grace quick ran around the nearest stack of grain thinking he might be behind it waiting for her to drift off home base.

Pretty soon Gordon came sneaking out of the cornfield and got home safe too. He'd taken the longer route to home base on the north side of the stacks.

After that Gordon wouldn't look at Mallie. Mallie didn't care. She had Dirk at home. If she could get him away from Tressa.

When Mallie was twelve she found a nest of baby mice. She'd watched one of Pa's barn cats, the yellow one with the white breast, go stalking around the granary and had seen it leap in the air in a pounce. Then it looked around to make sure no other cat was nearby. Mallie saw that it had a poor mouse in its mouth. When the yellow cat saw Mallie, it slid away under the nearby corncrib. Mallie looked where it had pounced. There, hidden under some faded corn leaves, was a cunning cuplike nest made of corn silk. In it were four little still-blind baby mice. They were squirming, and two of them had their mouths open as though they'd just been interrupted suckling their mother.

Angry, Mallie hurried over to the corncrib and crawled under it, calling, "Here, Kitty. Here, kitty!" It was true mice were awful to have in the house, but those poor little baby mice had to have their milk. Her eyes adjusted to the

275

dusk under the corncrib and soon she spotted the yellow cat with its back hunched up. She'd cornered the cat against the rock foundation, the mouse still between its teeth. The cat wanted to snarl at her but couldn't. Its whiskers twitched up and down. Even though it was dusky under the crib, Mallie could make out the pimple tits on the mother mouse. She also made out that the mother mouse was dead.

"You darn cat."

Tears in her eyes, Mallie crawled back out from under the corncrib.

Dirk happened to be strolling by. "Hey, what's wrong with my Kissy girl?"

Mallie pointed at the ruptured mouse nest and the little ones in it. "Our yellow cat is eating their mother."

Dirk stared down at the little ones. "I think Ma would want us to get rid of them. Besides, without their mother they're going to die." Dirk lifted his heavy brown work shoe and with one powerful stomp squashed them to death.

"Dirk!"

"What's the matter? I was only helping them out of their misery."

"But maybe another mother mouse might have come along and fed them."

"Never. She wouldn't have enough milk for her own set of kits."

Mallie began to cry, She sat down on her heels.

Dirk settled beside her. He put his arms around her. "Now, now, Triplelips, no need to cry over spilt milk. That's life for you. And you better learn that that's the way it is." He hugged her; finally kissed her. "Boy," he said with surprise, "your tears ain't salty. They're sweet-like."

That made Mallie smile. That Dirk, he had a way of making things seem better than they were. She hugged him back at the same time she was still mad at him for stomping on the baby mice.

Dirk kissed her again, this time savoring her thick full innocent lips.

"Oh, kid," Mallie said, "what do we do now with those little mice? Bury them?"

"No. We'll just let nature take care of them. Come. Isn't it time for you to go get the eggs?"

"I guess so." Mallie sighed. It had felt so good to have Dirk hug her and kiss her the way he always did. "When are you going to look at me in the morning the way you look at Tressa? I'm laying there naked too."

"Never. It's enough of a sin with one of you."

Ma called worried from the house. "What's the matter out there?"

Dirk said. "Nothing. Kissy here just learned about the facts of life."

From the way Ma frowned it was plain she hoped it was the right kind of facts of life.

Dirk patted Mallie on the head. "What you should have done, kid, is to have made that cat smile. Then it would have dropped your mother mouse."

Mallie looked to one side. "It's awful hard to get a cat to smile unless'n you can rub her on her back. And she wouldn't let me get close enough."

Sometimes, when all the older kids were busy working, Mallie took to playing with Geoffrey, the youngest in the family. Geoffrey was favored by everybody. He was a good boy too. He never started fights. And often, if there was a scrabble between a couple of the kids, he had a way of making the pat remark to make everybody laugh. Once Tane teased Thea about being sweet on Oliver Tice. Oliver Tice went to the Little Church. Thea got mad and finally scratched

Tane across the cheek, almost catching her fingernail in his eye. At that Tane gave her a good jut with his elbow. And then the cats were dancing.

Geoffrey watched them awhile and then made up a little poem:

> Ain't it nice
> That Thea likes Tane.
> Thea liking Tice
> Is better than having lice.

Everybody had to laugh, including Thea and Tane.

Goeffrey pushed the humor of the moment a bit further by repeating what Ma liked to tell the girls when they talked about dating boys. Geoffrey imitated Ma's voice to the syllable, even catching the slight lingering British accent: "So you girls like to talk about going out with men, ha? All right, I suppose someday you will. We can't hope to keep you home forever. So listen carefully to me. Don't be too tame and don't be too wild. Be somewhere in between. And if you must stick out, stick out from behind."

Everybody really laughed then. At that moment they truly were one family.

Another time, when Alfred Alfredson V, who worked on the Bonnie Omaha Railroad section when he wasn't building storm cellars, dropped by in the late afternoon and was invited to stay for supper, Geoffrey pulled off something that, if any of the other kids had done it, would have made Pa go on a rampage. But Geoffrey got away with it.

Because they had company, Ma changed the seating arrangement. Usually Ma had the youngest boy sit on Pa's left at the head of the table, with the other three older boys on a bench along the right side of the table by the west window, and the three older girls along the left side of the table near the stove, with Ma and the youngest girl, Mallie, holding down the far end of the table. That evening Ma switched Geoffrey to Pa's right, bunching up the boys tight on the bench, Goeffrey, Tane, Dirk, and Rolf. Ma placed Mr. Alfredson in Goeffrey's old spot, to Pa's left.

Children were not supposed to talk no matter how old they were when there was company. Pa and Mr. Alfredson got to talking about the old days before there were railroads, how everybody mostly rode horseback to town or to go visiting. They told some jokes about it, about how a jackrabbit jumping up could spook a horse, about how hard it was to hug your girl if she was riding a frisky horse, and laughed and laughed, so hard that even Ma had to laugh though she really wasn't enjoying it. All the while during the talk and laughter, it could be seen that Geoffrey was getting shorted when the food was being passed around. Geoffrey finally managed to pick a bun from the bread plate but needed some butter. Pa and Mr. Alfredson kept piling on the jokes and stories, kept laughing, and Geoffrey kept waiting and waiting for someone to pass him the butter. Geoffrey nudged Tane to pass it, but Tane was enjoying the stories too much. Then Geoffrey looked with a lover's sweet eyes at Thea for her to pass it across the table with a boardinghouse reach, but she was too busy worrying about what to get next off the hot stove behind her.

Finally Geoffrey got that clever look in his blue boy eyes and started to mutter to himself. At first he muttered real low, so that Mallie couldn't make out what he was saying. But pretty soon the muttering became louder. "Please pass the butter. Please pass the butter. Please pass the butter."

Mallie quit eating. She worried what would happen next.

Finally Geoffrey said it real loud: "Please pass the butter! Please pass the butter!"

Then Pa heard it. Pa swiveled his eyes around at Geoffrey. Pa stared at Geoffrey to make sure he was hearing what he was hearing. Of a sudden Pa swung his right arm to swat Geoffrey one.

But Geoffrey was ready for the swat. He ducked down, and Pa's hand hit the wall above Geoffrey's head, hit it so hard it jarred loose the nail on which the picture of the Lord's Supper was hanging. The picture hung just to the right of the west window. The picture crashed to the floor, the glass in the frame breaking into flying bits.

There was a mighty silence.

Pa's mouth and Mr. Alfredson's mouth opened wide under their red-brown moustaches.

Ma's and everybody else's mouth opened too.

Geoffrey remained ducked down. He waited.

Mallie thought it a great joke on Pa. She burst out laughing. "Pa, it's a good thing we wasn't sitting in that picture with the twelve apostles or we'd all be laying on the floor with them."

"Yeh," Geoffrey said, "and don't forget the Lord, I think he fell down too."

Pa's face looked like a garden with a whirlwind chasing across it. Finally a smile snuck in under his red-brown moustache and moved up into his cheeks. "Wife, I always knew I'd hammered that nail in the wrong place. I should've sounded for the studding in that wall and then pounded the nail in. Well, live and learn." Then Pa gently touched Goeffrey on his shoulder. "You can raise your head above water now, son."

278

The whole table broke into relieved smiles.

Mr. Alfredson said, "Looks like your youngest there is going to be pretty clever."

"That he is. Probably's going to be our lawyer." Pa reached for the butter dish and gave it to Geoffrey.

Geoffrey helped himself to the butter. With a boy's straight face, he said, "Well, with everybody older'n me around here, and bigger and stronger, I've got to do something to get my share of the feed."

Pretty soon Pa and Mr. Alfredson were telling stories again. Pa really liked Mr. Alfredson.

Later the girls washed dishes and cleaned up the kitchen, while all the men went out and sat on the stoop in the cool of the evening.

When Mallie was fifteen she was chosen by Ma to stay home with Dirk on a summer Sunday when the rest of the family took the train and rode to Whitebone to go to the Episcopalian church. Ma had almost picked Tressa, but at the last minute for her own mysterious reasons she decided against that.

Mallie was happy. Her brother Dirk was so handsome and had such winning ways. She liked being touched by him. She was aware that Tress always gave her an odd look whenever Dirk hugged her up.

Mallie had just finished washing the separator tins and the milk pails when Dirk stepped into the back porch.

Mallie looked up with a warm smile. "Got your yard chores finished?"

"Yep. You?"

"I just need to put these pails on the drying rack outside."

"Good. I'm gonna sneak something in the kitchen."

"Better be careful. Ma can always spot when something's been moved in her cabinet."

"I know. I know. But I'll be real careful."

"What're you gonna make?"

"A wonderful potcher of sweets."

"Like what?"

"Just watch."

Dirk selected a deep soup bowl and began pouring in various ingredients: golden raisins, shredded white coconut, tiny slices of green citron, crisp corn-flakes, four heaping tablespoons of brown sugar, and a thick flow of dark wild honey. Over it all he poured some fresh yellow cream. "Mmm! Don't that look good?"

"Can I have a taste?"

"Sure. But only a taste. Or else I might as well make you a bowlful."

Mallie had watched how, after he'd taken a handful of raisins out of a green box, he'd shaken up what was left of the contents to make the box seem as full as before. He'd done the same with the other ingredients. Mallie had smiled to herself to see how careful he'd been to place the boxes in exactly the same spot he'd found them.

Dirk said, "Tell you what. I might consider giving you more spoonfuls—pro-vided I get a nice triplelip kiss for each one."

Mallie laughed. She looked down at the opulent mix of sweets. "In that case there won't be any left for you. Because I have more kisses than you have spoonfuls."

279

"Hey, I wonder if that's what they mean by spooning." He slipped an arm around her and gently cupped her breast. "Ha?"

His warm hand on her breast made her belly suddenly feel warm inside. Mallie smiled. "Then it's a kiss for a spoonful?"

"It sure is. Up to three."

Playfully she jerked out of his embrace. "Then I won't play."

Dirk had thickened to the game. He reached for her and drew her against his side again. He placed a hand firmly on her breast. "Come. The first kiss then."

Slowly Mallie let her face be turned up and with a mischievous smile let his lips touch hers.

Dirk prolonged the kiss, pressing his lips hard on hers, pulling her body around to fit against his. His thin lips were lost in her thick lips.

Mallie could feel a bump growing against her belly. She began to melt inside. She wondered if lately, in the hot mornings, he'd taken to looking at her naked like he always looked at Tressa.

A bell tinkled in the other room.

Both jumped backward, mouth open.

Then Dirk heaved a sigh. And laughed. "I still ain't got used to that darned telephone." A brown telephone had recently been hung on the wall by the front door. "That someone miles away can suddenly bust in on you without first get-ting invited."

Earlier that spring there'd been some abrupt changes in the life of the Frey-lings. First, the state highway department had decided to upgrade the Iowa por-tion of the old King's Trail. The King's Trail ran from Winnipeg to New Orleans.

Two highway crews worked at the project, one coming up from Sioux Center and the other coming down from the state line above Rock Falls. The improved highway continued to parallel the Bonnie Omaha Railroad. The two crews met at the banks of the Big Rock River at the north end of the Freyling section. Almost immediately afterward the dust began to fly. Horsebackers and spanking buggies and dashing carriages came rippling by, and whooshing steam-engine cars and pop-popping gasoline cars chased after each other. Ma and Thea went into a state over it—all that dust sifting into the house, onto the window ledges, into the white curtains, even into the clothes hanging on the clothesline behind the house. If that was progress they were against it heart and soul.

Second, the telephone came through. It paralleled the telegraph line. The telephone poles stalked along the west side of the highway and the telegraph poles the east side of the railroad. Of course everybody living within a mile of the telephone line was asked to join the exchange. Pa and Ma were against it. But Thea was for it. It was her one way of staying in touch with Oliver Tice. And Dirk and Ana said they needed it for their schoolwork. If they had a problem in one of their lessons they could call their friends to see how they'd worked it out.

There was one definite benefit that came along with the widened highway and the new telephone. Pa and Ma got two big fat checks for right-of-ways.

Rolf wanted Pa to buy that Elgin car he always favored; and if not that car then the new Luverne motor made up in Whitebone. Both Pa and Ma vetoed that. The unexpected money was going to be used to send to college whoever wanted to go beyond the twelfth grade.

The bell tinkled again. Four shorts.

"That's our ring," Mallie exclaimed.

"It sure is." Dirk hurried into the other room. The rosy hue of arousal quickly drained out of his cheeks. "I wonder who wants us now?" He lifted the black receiver from its nickel hook. "Hello? Hello?" He listened intently, swinging his glance around at Mallie who'd followed him. "Hello? What?"

Mallie waited.

"Oh. It's you, Ma. What's the matter there in Whitebone? . . . You say Pa thinks Tane forgot to hang the cream down in the well? It'll turn sour . . . Okay, I'll go look." Dirk was much relieved it wasn't something else. "Say, Ma, this is kinda fun. I never talked long distance before. Where you calling from, the church? . . . Oh, the parsonage. All right. Good-bye." Dirk hung the receiver on its hook. "Wow."

Mallie was more than glad that the telephone had interrupted what was going on in the kitchen.

Dirk said, "I better go quick check the cream. Okay?"

Mallie nodded. She wandered back into the kitchen while he hurried outdoors toward the well.

When Dirk came back, he tried to pick up wher they'd left off. "The cream was down there all right. Let's see now, how many kisses do you want to give me?"

"I've decided I don't want any of your sweet slumgullion. Too rich. Plus the feeling I've been helping you steal is bound to give me a stomachache."

"Me stealing in our own house?"

"Ma'd think so if she caught you."

Dirk slipped an arm around her again. "Well, Kissy, do we trade or not?"

She pushed herself away from him, hard. "No."

"Lady, you know what? You got fists in your tits."

"Hey! I don't like such rough talk."

"When I thought yours would be more soft—"

"Like Tressa's?"

Dirk grimaced, wrinkles working up around his blue eyes. Then he sat down in his chair and picked up his spoon.

Mallie sensed that sometime somewhere something had passed between Dirk and Tressa. "Dirk, did you ever do it with Tress?"

He threw her a sliding look. Then, closing his eyes, he began to spoon up his sweet slumgullion.

When Mallie was eighteen and a senior at the Bonnie High School, she took a class in art. It turned out she was very gifted at sketching, and was particularly good at making up color combinations. Her teacher, Grace Gibson, a tall lovely spinster with a sad lost look in her eyes, suggested Mallie might be good at painting roses on plates. It wasn't long before Mallie was held up as one of the more gifted students in high school.

Then Mallie got an idea for a project. Sister Thea continued to be serious about Oliver Tice and planned to marry him the next year. What could be nicer than to make her a present of a set of eight dinner plates, all of them decorated with painted roses?

Mallie asked Ma for the money to buy the set.

Ma looked surprised. "Where'd you get that idea?"

"Miss Gibson put me next to it."

Ma's gray eyes turned reflective. "Isn't that funny. My mother painted plates too. She was very good at it." Ma shook her head. "Oh, how I regret that some of those family heirlooms couldn't have been saved. It would have been so nice if I could have even just one of those beautiful rose plates of Mother's."

"You will help me then, Ma?"

"Of course I'll help you buy them. And I tell you what. We'll get some plates they didn't finish firing. And after you've painted on the roses, we'll have some enamel fired on. That way the roses will never wear off."

Mallie finished the eight place settings in February. She was wondering how she could sneak them into the house, when the president of the country solved the problem for her. On April 6, 1917, Woodrow Wilson declared war on Germany.

The whole family went into a state of shock. Pa was especially upset. "That damned president! I never did trust him. People voted him into office because he promised to keep our boys out of that horrible war in Europe. And now here that turncoat suddenly declares war! He sure didn't turn out to be a man of his word."

Dirk said, "But we can't be having German submarines sinking our ships, Pa."

"We have no business bringing supplies to Great Britain in the first place. That's her war, not ours."

"But we speak the same language, Pa. And we have history in common. And our governments are much alike."

"Bullshit. Old Alfredson is right. This is a war to save the rich. The rich have a lot of money invested in British trade."

"We've got to save democracy."

"England is a democracy with a king? A monarch? And a country we had to fight to get our freedom? Are you forgetting the Revolutionary War?"

They were eating supper and the food became cold on everybody's plate.

Ma didn't have much to say. But it could be seen she was troubled. She was proud to be of direct British descent.

Thea spoke slowly. "Yes, and I suppose Oliver will be one of the first ones called up. He's single with no family to support."

Pa bent a sharp eye on Thea. "He's Dutch, isn't he?"

"A Dutch couple adopted him when he was fourteen. His American parents choked to death from diphtheria. And now even his Dutch parents have passed on."

"Well, I'll say this for the Dutch. I've had my sour thoughts about how the Dutch immigrants are taking over this part of the country, pushing out the British around Le Mars, and then all the other first settlers nearby. But hurray for the Hollander. He's never thought much of the British either. So you can bet your life that some of them ain't going to be too anxious to save Lloyd George's chestnuts." Pa had been heard to mutter several times about how the Hollander outworked, outbred, and outvoted everybody. They worked harder than any other immigrant, they had bigger families, they helped keep each other from going under financially. They worshipped God and the Almighty Dollar . . . all because back in the Old Country they had to fight for their lives keeping those dikes from breaking down under the pounding of the North Sea. "I for one ain't gonna call them slackers. At least they're men of their word."

Thea brightened. "Then it is all right if I marry Oliver Tice?"

"Well . . ."

"I know you've been sort of against it, Pa. But I really love him."

"Then have him!"

"And I want to marry him before he's called up. I at least want to share that with him before he falls on the battlefield." Tears showed in the corners of Thea's blue eyes. "Poor fellow, he's had it tough so far in life."

All the children around the table stared at Thea. So she was going to fly the family coop. The first one. Their eyes glowed with wonder and envy.

Mallie asked, "When will you set the date?"

"He's coming tomorrow. If the weather's all right."

Dirk chuckled to himself. "That Oliver. He's so pigeon-toed it's a miracle he don't trip over himself."

Thea snapped, "He isn't that pigeon-toed."

"Two more inches turned in and you could sell him for an eggbeater."

Later on upstairs in the girls' bedroom, Mallie and Thea fell to talking about the wedding. Thea decided that her three sisters, Tressa and Ana and Mallie, would be her bridesmaids. And if Oliver couldn't find a man to stand up with him, maybe Tane could be the best man.

Mallie had to know. "Are you afraid of that first night?"

"No."

"Then you and Oliver have done it?"

"Heaven's no! We don't do those things in our family."

Mallie let her glace fall.

Thea asked suddenly, "Would you?"

"I don't know. I think Tressa might."

"Oh, her."

"But Ana wouldn't."

Thea had to laugh. "Ana? If she ever got married . . . and she never will . . . but if she ever did, she'd have to be raped to have children."

Mallie laughed too. "Ana is a strange one all right. But maybe the Lord has some special job in mind for her that no one else can do. There has to be a reason why the Lord had her born."

Thea nodded. "Just like there was to be a reason why Rolf was born to us."

"Yes."

Pink color came and went in Thea's cheeks. She bounced up and down on her bed. "It's going to feel funny leaving the family." She giggled. "But I am twenty-nine and if I'm ever going to get married it's about time. Or I'd become an old maid like Ana's gonna be."

Ana had come quietly up the stairs and stepped through the door. "I heard that!" Her eyes burned a cold light blue. "I'm not going to become an old maid. As a bride of Christ I'm going to be a missionary to the Indians."

"I'm sorry, Ana," Thea said.

"Oh, it's all right. In fact, I'm glad you're going to make the jump. Like sledding down the hill for the first time in that bread pan. Because that'll give me an excuse to leave too. I'm going to see the reverend at the Little Church next Sunday about taking up my life's mission."

Mallie sighed. "Well, there goes our family. Tane'll next find a girl and then we'll explode all over the country. Like prairie chickens chased out of their nest by a fox."

There was a rustling noise in the clothes closet. Then the closet door opened and Tressa stepped out. "Yeh, I heard you two talking too."

There was a moment when all four mouth hung open; and then all four laughed and laughed. They fell into each other's arms; finally tumbled together on Thea's and Ana's bed. They had a good cry.

Tressa said, "I think Dirk is thinking of leaving too. If he can get a job working for a newspaper."

"Ohh. So."

"He hasn't said anything yet because he hated to think he was going to be the first to start breaking up the family."

Again all four girls looked at each other with wide eyes.

Mallie finally said it. "Pretty soon Pa and Ma are going to be home alone here with just me and Geoffrey."

Thea murmured, "Yes, and the way Geoffrey's taken to reading books, he isn't going to want to stay home either. One can look at him and you know he wasn't meant to be a farmer."

"He isn't even gonna stay home as long as we did."

Thea mused down at her long slim hands. "Until now, we sure have been a bunch of homebodies, haven't we? Late bloomers. A houseful of old maids and strong-headed bachelors. It's like it was in our blood to be that way."

Tressa said, "Mostly though it's because we have too much fun to leave. There just aren't any men around as good and as lively as our brothers."

"And I suppose our brothers feel the same way about us."

"Except for letting some of us go on to school, Pa and Ma weren't much for encouraging us to go out with boys."

Mallie laughed. "Oh, come on, admit it, none of us is much of a prairie rose."

"Yeh, I noticed there haven't been many bees buzzing around us."

All four girls sighed. The bed creaked under them.

"The Lord's will," Ana whispered.

Oliver Tice was drafted. But none of the Freyling boys were. It was exactly as Thea had predicted—Oliver was single with no family. And the reason why none of the Freyling boys were drafted was that the draft board decided they were needed to help their father run a whole section of land, produce food which was needed for the war effort.

Oliver had two weeks to get ready to go. Thea and he decided to get married immediately and live in a boarding room in Rocks Falls those two weeks. Mother and the girls went into a wild flurry to get the wedding dress ready.

The whole family took the Bonnie Omaha train to Whitebone, where Father Garlington married Thea and Oliver in the Episcopalian church. Then they caught the train back to Rock Falls. Pa talked Earl Van Valkenburg the conductor into waiting a half hour at the Rock Falls depot so they could wish Thea and Oliver well as they set off on foot to their boardinghouse.

Oliver was an easygoing smiler. He let Thea fuss over him, straightening out his tie, combing his cowlick down, brushing lint off his lapel, taking it all with a musing good-humored look in his pale blue eyes. Some of his friends showed up at the wedding, having taken the train too, from Rocks Falls to Whitebone and back. All were baseball players and in their eyes he was a hero. They teased Oliver about his big curve, that it was no wonder he'd chosen Thea for wife with all her great curves. They teased him about his pigeon-toed pitching stance, claiming that batters were so busy watching to see if his left toe would catch inside his right leg when he wound up that they forgot to look for the ball. Even Pa had to laugh at their joking, though he thought baseball a boy's game and not for grown-ups.

Mallie wasn't quite sure when she should give the rose-painted plates to Thea since Thea didn't intend to take up housekeeping in her own home right away. Mallie finally settled on giving Thea two of the plates just as Thea and Oliver were to start walking to their temporary home in the boardinghouse.

Mallie said, "Now don't open the package until you're up in your room. And then, remember, it's from the rest of us stay-at-home girls."

31. Thea

Together, holding hands, each carrying a valise, they walked up the stairs in the rooming house. Oliver took each stair with an Indian turned-in-toe and Thea caught each stair with a white lady's turned-out toe. Oliver found their room, No. 4, at the far end of the hall. He set down his valise, as she did hers, and with a heavy key opened the door. Then with his easy musing smile he picked her up and carried her inside. She was almost as tall as he was, but he carried her easily. For a slim man he was wonderfully strong. He set her down in the middle of the room. Then he got both valises and closed the door.

It was like her eyes were almost drowning, like she could only see out of the upper halves of her eyes. She saw the top of the single window and the top of the bedstead and the top of the mirror over the dresser. She was vaguely aware that the bedspread was white and the walls gray. She shivered. It would soon happen. After all these years. She had never touched herself. What chance had there been for that in a house crawling with brothers and sisters? If she had been given the chore of getting the eggs, on the yard and up in the haymow, then perhaps she might have had some privacy for self-exploration.

They stood smiling at each other.

He crooked his head to one side, a sliver of blond hair sliding down his forehead. "Thea, I'm pretty green at all this. What do we do next?"

"Then you're innocent too?"

"I am."

"Truly?"

"Yes."

Thea smiled. Then she started to laugh, and finally became silly with it. "In that case, neither one of us will know if the other one is doing it wrong."

"I guess not."

"I suppose we should undress for this."

"If you say so. Unless you'd like a wedding dinner first."

"Oh," she cried. "Perfect. Of course we should have our wedding dinner first. Let's go downtown and find ourselves the best cafe."

With a soft smile he felt of his pocket. "I think the old billbook can stand it."

She took his arm and led him out in the hallway again. "Better lock the door. I don't want anybody stealing Mallie's present. At least not until I know what it is."

He nodded and locked the door and dropped the key in the side pocket of his dark blue jacket. Then he checked to see if his red tie was still in place.

As they passed the Marriette Hotel, Thea spotted a sign in the window: HOME COOKING AT THE MARRIETTE. ALL YOU CAN EAT FOR A DOLLAR.

Oliver paused with her. "Shall we try that?"

"Hotel food is bound to be better than cafe food. Especially in a town where there's two trains and two main highways. Drummers will make sure of that."

The dining room in the Marriette had high light from tall windows. The curtains and the tablecloths were a sharp red. The waitress, obviously a farm girl, plump, high-waisted, spotted right away that they were newlyweds. "Would you like our little private dining room? It's for small parties."

Oliver looked at his bride. "Thea?"

Thea pinched his arm. "Of course."

The little room was also done up in vivid red. Even the backs of the chairs had been draped with red slipcovers.

Both ordered smoked ham with raisins, sweet yams with butter, canned snap beans, scarlet beets, and spicy mincemeat pie. They finished with a cup of tea and a slice of lemon. It was all elegant. The plump waitress was almost as much in a dither as Thea. Thea and Oliver didn't have much to say. They sat smiling at each other, he with his baseball pitcher's smile, she with her Freyling farm smile.

Over their second cup of tea, Thea finally had something to say. "I suppose when this war is over you'll want to live here in Rock Falls? Instead of Bonnie?"

Oliver tipped his head to one side. With his fingers he combed his shining blond hair out of his eyes. "The county highway department says they need a maintenance man to run a blade up and down the King's Trail. From Rock Falls to the Lakewood corner and back. The guy that does it now is getting on in years and wants to retire. He says I can buy his team. The county furnishes the big blade."

Thea's eyes opened. It was the longest speech she'd ever heard Oliver make. "I thought maybe you were thinking of running a hardware store."

"I was. But this just came up last week and I didn't get a chance to talk to you about it."

"Wouldn't you rather run a hardware store?"

"That takes capital. Which at the moment I don't have. Though I do have enough saved up to buy the horses and the harnesses."

"You'd have to have a barn for them."

He nodded. "I got my eye on a cottage on the edge of town. It goes with ten acres. It's too small to make a living off it as a farmer, and too big just to have it to live on if you have a business in town."

"Maybe you can save enough money grading the highway so that later on you can buy out the hardware man."

"Maybe."

"You won't mind grading in bad weather?"

"I like outdoor life. I guess that's why I like to play baseball in old pastures."

Thea pushed at him a little. "Don't tell me you also thought of making a living pitching baseball?"

"No." He smiled down at his right hand. "I've got a little rheumatism in my fingers. Pretty soon I won't be able to throw that big roundhouse curve. Besides, I'm not really that good."

Thea sipped the last of her tea. "Well. And here I was looking forward to being a businessman's wife in the county seat."

Oliver's feet moved restlessly under the table, finally crossed at the ankles. "Let's wait until I'm back from the wars and see what's up. Who knows, maybe everybody'll be broke by then and we can pick up a hardware store for a song."

Thea winked back tears. Of course they would have to wait until the boys came marching home. Yes. She wanted to lean across the table and give him a big fat kiss. It would be terrible if she never saw him again. She'd seen several pictures of German and English boys all shot to pieces, their bodies horribly mangled by cannonballs hurled from great guns miles behind the front. She'd read about young men, the very flower of their countries, being gassed and coughing themselves to death. It seemed impossible that anything so horrible as that could touch the body of this sweet smiling man sitting across from her.

Thea remembered the very first time she'd spotted him at church. She and Ana and Tane had driven to the Little Church in Pa's black shining buggy, and just as they drove on the churchyard she'd seen this young blond boy ambling from the church barn to the big front door of the church. She'd laughed out loud at the way his turned-in toes always just missed catching in the cuff of his brown trousers. Then the next moment her heart had gone out to the shambling fellow. It wasn't that he was pathetic exactly, as that he had such an abashed look about him.

They got up to go. Oliver shambled over to the cash register and pulled out his billbook and laid down a five-dollar bill. The girl who'd served them gave him three dollars in change.

Oliver looked down at the change in his hand. He threw a glance at Thea and then with a smile he handed the three dollars back to the girl. "Your tip."

"Thanks!"

Thea took Oliver's offered arm. She gave it an appreciative pinch.

Slowly they walked back to their room. The early May evening air was dreamy with the aroma of lilac blossoms. Children playing in the backyards cried in happy glee that winter was over at last. The devastating war in that far-off place, Europe, meant little or nothing to them. Cricket song from the bushes along the sidewalk became so thick ears cracked with it.

Again they climbed the stairs, his toes in, hers out. Again Oliver opened the door and, just for the fun of it, once more carried her over the threshold.

He got a match out of his pocket and lit the gas jet high on the wall.

"Oh," she said quickly, "let's keep it dusk in here. That always was the nicest part of the day in our home. In the summer we all sat out on the stoop and talked until the stars came out as thick as knots in a hairnet. And in the winter we all sat around the kitchen table drinking hot tea with lemon and honey."

"Lucky you." He turned off the gas jet.

They undressed on opposite sides of the bed, backs to each other. Both undressed from the top down, and when they were bare to the hip slipped on their night garment, she in her nightgown and he in his nightshirt. Each then with a sort of silly self-conscious grin, making a strange sound like puppies seeking comfort, turned and crept under the quilts. The sheets were cool and crisp. The air emitted from the pillows when their heads pressed down smelled of white rain-washed geese.

He waited.

She could feel him smiling his sunny smile in the dusk. She knew his summer-white forelock would be hanging down over his blond brows. It so endeared him to her. Finally she pushed her hand across the cool sheet and, fingertips fumbling a little, touched him. It was his hip she touched. His arms

287

were folded over his chest. She could just see him—hands crossed at the wrist and feet crossed at the ankles. The fingers of his right hand would be set to throw the big outdrop and his toes would be turned in, forming a fish tail.

He whispered. "What do we do next?"

Thea laughed funny. "I once asked Ma what she and Pa did that first night."

"What did she say?"

"Well, it seems Pa was a real greenhorn too." Thea laughed another scattered laugh. "He didn't seem to know where things were. There didn't seem to be any place for it, he said."

"Your Pa?"

"Yes. Finally Ma told him, 'Just push it in and hope for the best. I can bear it. Someday I'll have to bear children through that small place. And that'll surely be much worse.'"

Oliver fell silent. He lay very still.

She gave his hip a little push. "Did I say the wrong thing?"

"No. I was just thinkin'."

What a sweet shy man he was.

Oliver said, "You're lucky you had such a pa and ma."

"I suppose I am." She turned on her side toward him and pushed her hand across his belly. She was stunned when her fingers encountered a considerable stalk of flesh. It jumped as he jumped. "You sweet darling," she said. "Let's not let that go to waste. Come. Those cocky roosters Ma's got shouldn't be the only ones to have fun."

288

32. Geoffrey

1919

Geoffrey happened to be in the house when the phone rang: four shorts. Geoffrey took the receiver off the hook. "Hello?"

"Geoff?"

"Speaking."

"This is Thea." Thea was having trouble talking.

"What's the matter, Sis?"

"Oliver's just come back on the train."

"Hey. Then he got home just in time for Easter."

"You remember I told you Oliver was in the hospital? In France?"

"Yes?"

"Well, it was worse than he wrote."

"How so?"

"Oh, Geoffrey, you wouldn't recognize him."

"Did he get shot up bad?"

Thea sobbed a moment. "He got gassed."

Geoffrey remembered the horror stories of how both sides began to gas each other when the battle lines became stalemated. "He'll be all right though?"

"Oh, I hope so. My poor Oliver."

"Maybe I better come up, Thea."

"Oh would you, Geoffrey? I know Pa and Ma and the rest are busy getting the crops planted."

"They are pretty busy at that." Geoffrey hadn't gone out with Pa and Tane and Rolf disking and sowing that Saturday because he'd had to prepare for an important debate. He was on the Bonnie High School debating team. "Look, my school's going to cross horns with the Rock Falls debating team next week Tuesday. Why don't I catch the train Monday morning and come a day early?"

"That'd be wonderful. You're a sweetheart of a brother." Thea started to cry again and finally, not being able to say more, hung up.

Geoffrey hung up too and sat down in Pa's rocker. Geoffrey remembered how happy the family had been last fall when in November 1918 Armistice had finally been declared in Europe and the Great War was over.

In fact, the country celebrated twice because there'd been a false armistice. In early October on a Saturday night Rock Falls had gone hog-wild to celebrate the great victory in Europe, lighting bonfires on the high hills around town. Several bonfires had also been lighted on the street corners in town, and somehow, no one remembered just how, the old Bonnie Omaha Railroad water tank burned to the ground. The editor of the Rock Falls *Record* was very happy about it:

The job on the water tank was a complete one; and an eyesore to the public, which had been allowed to stand for 25 years, was removed pretty effectively. The fire whistle was blown until the arms of the blowers ached, and the fire bell, church bells, and school bells added to the din.

When the real armistice was finally declared the next month in November, Rock Falls went even more berserk. It started at 2:30 A.M., in the dark. Mayor Carpenter had arranged with the Sioux Falls daily paper, the *Argus-Leader*, to let him know when the peace document was finally signed. When word finally came, the fire whistle at the light plant was turned loose and remained loose. Once more bonfires were lighted everywhere. Again all the bells in town were pulled. A stuffed dummy of the Kaiser was hung from a telephone wire and everyone joined in the glad refrain: "The hell with the Kaiser!" Nobody wanted to work that day so Mayor Carpenter declared it a holiday.

The Rock Falls *Record* reported:

> During the day the fire bell was rung until it cracked and sounded like a busted kettle, and the old cannon, a relic of the War of the Rebellion, was dragged out and fired repeatedly, the gunners directing the cannonballs into the high bank across the Big Rock River and, retrieving them, using them over and over. In the evening a big crowd gathered at the corner of Main and Story street and listened to speeches by Judge Hutchison, E. C. Roach, and Professor Wilson. Finally, a funeral service for the stuffed dummy of the Kaiser was held and Professor Wilson delivered the funeral address. It was all hugely enjoyed by the big crowd present. Then a parade headed by a mob of pallbearers carried the "remains" of the Kaiser in a basket to its last resting place, where it was cremated to the accompaniment of great cheering. It had been planned to have a big pavement dance in the evening, and also a dance in the Armory, but an orchestra could not be secured for love nor money, not even for good old-fashioned patriotic hate. There were too many towns in the same fix as Rock Falls— they all wanted to celebrate.

Geoffrey was still sitting in deep thought when the front door opened and Mallie stepped in. "Mallie! For godsake, how did you get here?"

Mallie gave him her wonderful thick smile. She'd chosen to go to the University of Iowa in Iowa City for her bachelor's degree. "I caught a ride with Reverend Colegrove's son. Mike." Reverend Colegrove was the Congregational minister in Bonnie. "We drove all night."

"All night? You don't look tired." Mallie was wearing a light green dress and it gave her hazel eyes a hint of the color of early spring grass. There were roses in her cheeks. "You had some fun with Mike on the way over."

Mallie laughed. "None of your business." She set her suitcase down and came around the table and gave Geoffrey a warm hug and a pursed-out kiss on his cheek. "You look glum. What's the trouble?"

"Thea just called."

Mallie drew up a chair. "What's the matter with her?"

"Oliver Tice has come back and I guess he's not in very good shape. He was gassed."

Mallie turned pale. "What! That's awful. Poor Thea."

Geoffrey nodded. He'd read an article in the *Harper's* magazine in which a doctor stated there wasn't much hope for badly gassed soldiers. They would die a slow death. "That's why I've decided to go up a day early Monday and visit her. I have to debate in Rock Falls on Tuesday anyway."

"Oh dear." Mallie combed back her wavy auburn hair. "I'd planned to spend

Easter break here with the family. Have some more of our wonderful stoop talks. I was so homesick for them. But if Thea needs us . . . maybe I should instead go visit her." Mallie's wavy hair wouldn't stay in place and she gave it a vigorous push back. "Listen. Why don't we both catch the old Bonnie Omaha tomorrow on Sunday morning instead?"

"If you want to."

It was raining when Geoffrey and Mallie ran out of the house to flag down the train, but by the time they arrived in Rock Falls the sun had come out. In town the grass around some of the houses had just turned a delicate green.

They walked out to the place Thea had bought while Oliver was at war, the ten acres he'd wanted. It was on the south end of town near the graveyard. The one-story rambler-style house sat on the northwest corner of the acreage, across the street from the last houses on that end of town. Thea had repainted the house a deep cream with green-trimmed windows and doors.

Thea saw them coming and came out on the front steps. "You came today instead! And you brought Mallie with you! How sweet of you." Thea rushed down and embraced both at the same time, fiercely. "Come in, come in! I was just about to make some dinner."

The house inside was neat and shining: white ironed curtains at all the windows, gleaming yellow linoleum in the kitchen, well-brushed brown mohair furniture in the sitting room. Thea had perfumed the air with sachet power, but it hadn't helped to overcome the odor of decaying flesh. Both Geoffrey and Mallie reacted to it with wrinkled brows. Both made it a point not to pull up their noses.

Thea called ahead to a room in back. "Oliver? Guess who's come to visit us." When there was no reply, Thea went on. "Geoffrey and Mallie. They've come for Sunday dinner."

Still no reply.

Thea led the way into the back bedroom. There the smell of bad flesh dominated the perfume in the air even more.

Geoffrey and Mallie looked down at the figure lying on the white bedspread.

Oliver had put on his brown khaki fatigues, including his rolled-on leggings. From his hips to his chest his belly lay sunken. The collar of his tan shirt appeared to be several sizes too large. The veins and tendons of his gaunt neck showed like a tangle of clothesline ropes. Worst was his face. It was a shock to look at it. His cheeks and forehead resembled the bled and scraped hide of a slab of bacon. His lips had the dull purple color of a very sick man.

Mallie spoke first. "Welcome home, soldier. Nice to see you again."

Oliver tried to smile. His faded eyes took on a momentary blue color. "How come you're here?" His voice made a noise as though someone were crumpling up some stiff paper. "I heard you were in Iowa City."

"Spring vacation."

Oliver's veined eyes swung to Geoffrey. "And you?"

Geoffrey told him about the debate.

A hint of his old smile touched the corners of Oliver's discolored lips. "Can you throw curves in a debate?"

"Lots of 'em. The ins and outs of things."

"Any fadeaways?"

"Well, we have rebuttals."

Oliver's white blond brows came together. "Did you take a course in debating?"

Geoffrey nodded.

"What good will debating do you when you have to go out into the world to make your living?"

"I'm going to take up law."

Oliver shifted his eyes to Thea. "What a family. A farmer, a newspaper man, a missionary. And now here a coming lawyer."

Mallie laughed. "And I've decided to become a nurse."

"Why a nurse? Not that most of them ain't wonderful."

"I don't know. I always felt sorry for helpless creatures."

Oliver tried to smile. "If your sister Thea wasn't so purty, I'd think of asking you to be my nurse."

"I can at least practice on you."

Oliver's eyes swung back to Geoffrey. "Really, why law for you?"

"I don't always want to suck the hind tit. As the youngest in my family, I had to use my wits to get my share of love and food at the family board. Manipulate my brothers and sisters."

Oliver rolled his head on his pillow. "I hadn't thought of it that way before. I wonder, are most lawyers the youngest in the family?"

Mallie said, "Now there's a subject for a term paper."

Thea said, "I'll leave you two with him while I go get dinner ready." She hurried off to the kitchen.

Geoffrey and Mallie joshed Oliver a while. Presently Mallie left to help Thea set the table.

292

Geoffrey wanted to ask about the war, but he'd learned reading newspapers that families were warned not to ask returning war veterans too many questions. If the veteran wanted to talk about it, fine. But the best was to bring up subjects involving peacetime life. Watching Oliver, Geoffrey felt sorry for Thea that she would have to spend the rest of her life with an invalid. Thea deserved better. If ever a woman was meant to be a mother of many children, Thea was one. She would have made a better mother than even Ma. In fact, as the oldest daughter, Thea had already served as a wonderful second mother in the Freyling family, just as Tane the oldest son had served as a good second father.

Oliver said, "Funny, in a big family like yours, that some of you didn't take up baseball. You almost had enough kids to make up a team."

"Maybe if Pa'd played ball as a boy we might have. No, we were too busy working that big section of land. Six hundred forty acres is a lot of ground to cover year round."

"You didn't play any games at all then? After supper when the work was all done?"

"We had too much fun telling stories on the stoop. On the cool side of the house. Some of those stretchers . . . man."

"I would have given anything to have had a family like that."

"Maybe you can still have it. Your own, I mean."

"Not a chance of a moth in hell. I'm all burnt out."

Geoffrey asked, "Where's your privy? I was so busy getting here I didn't take time to go."

"Out back. Through the kitchen there."

"Thanks."

When Geoffrey came back from the privy, taking the narrow boardwalk to the kitchen steps, he heard Thea crying in the kitchen, with Mallie comforting her. Geoffrey paused outside.

Mallie was saying, "Are you sure it's no use?"

"Yes. And I so wanted a child from him. We tried so hard before he left. And now that he's back, he can't."

"You've tried? Really?"

Thea blew her nose. "Yes."

"What seems to be the trouble?"

"He says he can't deliver that shot any more."

"Goodness. That war talk."

"He's too tired or something. That's what being gassed does to one."

"Are you sure it isn't something else?"

"Mallie, whatever do you mean?"

"I mean, are you sure he didn't pick up something from some Lisette somewhere?"

"You mean . . . ?"

"Thea, men can get awful horny on their furloughs."

"Not my Oliver Tice."

"Because he's too fine?"

"Mallie, don't you like Oliver?"

"I love him like a brother. But I've learned a lot since I started going to school at Iowa City, working my way through as a practical nurse at the University Hospital."

293

"What a difference between you and Ana."

"That snow girl. She's cold all the way through."

There was a sound of hissing steam.

Thea let out a gasp. "The soup's boiling over. I forgot all about it."

Geoffrey then mounted the steps and entered the kitchen. "Aha. It's like Ma always says. Too many cooks spoil the broth."

Thea blushed. "Sorry about that."

Mallie said, "Do we have to help Oliver to the table?"

There was a rasping laugh from the bedroom. "No, I can still bring my snout to the trough on my own." Next followed the sound of slippers touching the floor. In a moment, Oliver shuffled in, bent at the hips, head bobbing on top of a lean neck, Adam's apple protruding. He plopped down with a bony noise in the armchair at the head of the table. The short trip from bed to board made him puff as though he'd just run the mile.

Thea said, "Oliver and I have made it a custom to have silent prayer at family worship." She closed her eyes and lowered her head.

Geoffrey watched Oliver and Mallie close their eyes too, and then somewhat reluctantly followed suit. At home he sometimes didn't join in with family worship. Already as a young man he was convinced that many people faked piety and he didn't want any part of that.

A long sigh from Thea came as a signal that silent prayer was over. By the end of the praying Oliver had pretty well got his breath back.

The meal was wonderful: beef broth with grains of barley, baked potato with fresh butter from the farm, roast pork savored with basil leaves, boiled cabbage, home-canned peas, all finished off with hot apple pie and wild bergamot tea. The meal was served on Mallie's gift—the rose-painted plates. Everybody ate smackingly, even Oliver.

Geoffrey said, "I see you didn't lose your appetite in France, Oliver."

"Oh, I always ate good. But I always stayed skinny. If I'd been born a horse, they'd've called me a hay burner for all the good grub did me."

"Then you were in luck when they made you a cook in the army."

"I'll say. But as you can see, it still didn't do much good. I kept losing weight even before the gas attack."

"Was that pretty awful?" Geoffrey was aware of Thea's warning frown. But he had to know. "I mean, did it come as a surprise to the Americans?"

"Oh, we'd heard rumors about the Germans planning to use gas." Oliver coughed. Some food not completely chewed showed at the corners of his dark lips. With a pale tongue he licked the crumbs back into his mouth. "Yeh, it was pretty awful. We almost choked to death through the first attack. We tried to strain the stuff out by wearing a handkerchief over out noses."

"How long before you got gas masks?"

"That's the funny thing about it. We got them the very next day. So you see, our brass knew about it. Scuttlebutt had it that we even tested our masks against our own gas."

Thea changed the subject. "You should see the pancakes Oliver makes. Maybe tomorrow he can make you some."

Mallie smiled. "I look forward to it."

294

Thea went on. "He makes them with water, no milk, and they come out real thick and fluffy."

Oliver worked his lips, "Oh, they ain't all that good. It was just that milk was hard to get at the front and we cooks had to make do."

Later, Thea took Mallie out to her garden plot. Thea'd already spaded up part of it. The warm sunny weather made Thea anxious to get in the lettuce and radish seed as well as the onion sets.

Oliver worked up a little smile as through the kitchen window he watched Thea and Mallie sprinkle and pat the seeds into the dark black soil. "My wife sort of interrupted us, didn't she?"

"That's all right," Geoffrey said.

"Well." Oliver raised a gaunt hand to scratch his thinning white hair. "I don't mind talking about it. Thea doesn't want to hear it, so I sit here with it all bottled up in me." Oliver puffed. "Maybe we ought to retire to my boudoir, eh?" Oliver raised himself erect from his armchair mostly with his arms. Bent, he shuffled back into the bedroom.

Geoffrey followed him. Geoffrey was tempted to take Oliver's arm and help him, but held off, knowing that Oliver was too proud to admit he couldn't get around on his own.

Oliver slowly settled on the bed and slowly lay down. He puffed. He coughed. Finally he managed a wobbly smile. "Take a load off your feet, Geoff." When Geoffrey made a move to take a hard-back chair, Oliver added, "No, no, take the one Thea always sits in. That Morris chair. She often sits in it in the evening to read to me."

"Thanks." Geoffrey settled in the long soft chair.

Breath caught, Oliver said, "Now, where were we?"

"You were telling about how our brass even tested our gas masks against our own gas."

"Oh, yes." Oliver's eyes half-closed in reverie. "Maybe I ought to start from the beginning."

33. Oliver

Oliver caught the train in Rock Falls and took it to Bonnie. In Bonnie he transferred to the Cannonball and rode to Sioux City. There he was inducted into the army and then put on another train from Denver with a bunch of country boys.

The bunch turned out to be a bit rowdy. They were sure that once they landed in Europe they'd run those Huns out of France in a week and the next week would march on Berlin and capture it and then the war would be over and they could return to the good old U.S. of A. genuwine first-class heroes. There wouldn't be a girl in all of America who could resist them. They could have their pick of the beauties.

They rode in a cattle car. Through the criblike bars they watched the flat countryside go by. Theirs was a special train and it often had to wait on a siding for the regular passenger and freight trains to go by.

The second day they stopped at the edge of a small village near a grocery store. They spotted boxes of oranges in the showcase windows. With a rousing shout, they piled off the cattle car and invaded the little country store. While two of them kept the proprietor busy arguing over the price of some licorice, the rest filled their pockets with oranges.

A lean crabby man in slick clothes entered the store leading a bulldog. The lean man spotted what they were doing and began to yell his head off. "Thieves! Thieves! Police! Where's the police?"

The boys laughed at him and kept on filling their pockets.

The lean man then lowered his voice and said, "Sic 'em Spice." And with a great wide growl Spice charged.

A farm boy, used to dogs, made a certain coaxing sound at the same time that he patted his knee. The patting sound was exactly like the sound of a bitch slapping her tail on the floor while nursing her young. Spice stopped. The farm boy gently reached down and picked Spice up by the collar.

All the boys cheered, and then, pockets full, with the farm boy cuddling Spice up in his arms, they ran for their cattle car. In a moment their engine started puffing and they were off.

A half hour later, at the next stop, some officers of the law boarded the train and picked up the bulldog. It turned out that the handsome tan dog belonged to the banker of the little village. Nothing was said about stealing oranges and the dog—boys going off to war were allowed a few high jinks.

They got their uniforms in Denver. The quartermaster didn't bother to ask for their sizes. He had stacks and stacks of uniforms piled behind him and just threw them at the men and let them sort them out. The fellows traded uniforms until just about everybody got a fairly good fit. It was the same for shoes.

Then it was on to San Antone. There they started drilling. Life became hard. Some of the fellows defected, but were soon caught in the nearby hills, hauled back, thrown in the guardhouse overnight, and threatened with court-martial.

Oliver was sure the infantry was headed for the front lines in France. He told of his fears in letters to Thea. "What a joke life is. Here my name means 'olive leaf,' but a lot of good that does. Peace. Ha!"

A censor read one of Oliver's letters with a sour mind and reported what he'd read to Oliver's captain. The captain called Oliver in and read the riot act to him. And then the captain, seeing what an abashed and gentle fellow Oliver was, lowered his voice and wondered out loud if maybe Oliver might not like to be a cook. Cooks were never sent to the front.

Oliver instantly seized on that. "How do I get to be cook? Volunteer?" It was like noticing a batter's weakness of stepping in the bucket just as he is about to swing and right away taking advantage of it by throwing him a big hook low and away.

"Right. You volunteer. And then you take an exam. You know how to bake cold-water buns?"

"Not yet."

"Find out then. If you can bake 'em, you're in."

Oliver got a four-hour leave and looked up the best baker in town. From him he learned how to make a cold-water bun. Then he was in. From then on he no longer had to drill with the men. He cooked.

One day he accidentally cut his hand on a tin can. The tin was dirty and he got blood poisoning. He was sent to a hospital. When he managed to fight off the blood poisoning, the docs told him not to use the hand for a while. While his hand was healing he took a lot of walks through old San Antone.

He got a little tired of having his incoming mail looked at by the censor, so he decided to rent a box in the big downtown post office. He didn't want anyone to know how much Thea missed him.

One day the military police picked him up just as he was leaving the post office. He was reading a letter from Thea as he came down the front steps.

They questioned him. "Your name?"

"Oliver Tice."

"Nationality?"

"American. Why are you arresting me?"

"We have reason to believe you're a spy."

"For who?"

"Who else but Germany?"

"Oh, for godsakes."

"Where were you born?"

"Rock Falls."

"Where is that?"

"In northwest Iowa."

"How far is that from where you live now?"

"About a mile. I was born on a farm and now live in town. As you know, with my wife, Thea."

"What kind of farm?"

"Corn. Oats. Cattle. Hogs."

"What do you do for fun?"

"Play baseball."

"Oh. What position do you play?"

"Pitcher."

"Any good?"

"Wal, last Fourth of July, on a windy day, I struck out eighteen men. I had to pitch into the wind, and man, did I have a curve."

"You're awfully pigeon-toed for an athlete."

Oliver had to laugh. "Yeh. The guys all say the reason I get by is that everybody batting against me is waiting for me to trip over myself as I deliver the ball. By the time they see I don't, the ball is by them."

Silence.

"You guys really think I'm a spy?"

"You can go. But listen. No more mail here at the downtown post office. From now on you mail your letters at the camp and you get your letters at the camp. Understood?"

"Yep. But Thea ain't gonna like it."

One day Oliver was given permission to take a hike out in the country. He'd been cooking inside so much he'd turned pale. His superior officer thought he needed some sun to pick up a little color. Oliver hiked out to where some cactus grew seven miles away and finally decided to sit on a stone overlooking a gully and rest awhile.

He sat alone for an hour, catching his breath, thinking about how much he missed sweet Thea, picking up pebbles underfoot and throwing them at objects around, a mesquite bush, a dried white buffalo skull, a skittering bush rat . . . when one of the pebbles bouncing along hit something soft, hardly making any sound at all. That caught his attention. Fixing his eyes on what looked like an old rag, he soon made out that the rag seemed to be moving, as though under it was something breathing.

Curious, he stood up for a better look, and made out a pair of toes sticking up. What. A dead body? The rag was bluish, faded somewhat, so it couldn't be a U.S. soldier. He stepped closer and made out a second pair of toes.

Hey. He then remembered that the U.S. Army had caught some German infiltrators on the American soil (they'd been put ashore by U-boat submarines in the night) and imprisoned them in a barricaded encampment near San Antone. Those toes belonged to a couple of those German prisoners. They must've escaped.

Well. No red-blooded American was going to let a couple of Huns go scampering around on American soil. A country grin, the one he sometimes had when facing a tough batter, moved under Oliver's nose. Looking around, he spotted a piece of weathered wood with a big knot in it. He picked it up and with his strong fingers broke off the crumbly portions until he'd shaped it into looking like an Army revolver. He shoved it into the right pocket of his khaki jacket and made as though he were armed. Then he approached the toes with cautious step.

Sure enough. Two German prisoners. They apparently had seen him coming and had ducked down in a depression where, when it rained heavily, a freshet sometimes ran.

His leather soles made soft crunching noises on the sand and stiff clay. He stood over them. He saw two young blond faces, skin baked red, eyes closed tight.

"All right, you Boches, up on your feet."

The eyes opened blue and afraid.

"Blutwursts, up, up on your feet." Oliver gestured with the hand in his pocket, suggesting he was about to shoot them. He had played baseball against a team of East Frisians living near Yellow Smoke who spoke Plattdeutsch. "Aufstehen!"

The two boys popped up from the ground like two jack-in-the-boxes. Their hands shot straight up in the air. Both cried, "Kamerad! Kamerad!"

The sun burned down on their faces. It was obvious they were feverish. They were also very thin, even gaunt, which meant they'd been wandering around in the desert for some days without food, maybe even without water.

"Wasser? Flesch?"

"Ja. Ja."

Oliver pointed with his left hand in the direction of his camp while with his right hand he again gestured as though he might shoot them. "Marsch!"

They fell in ahead of Oliver. They went along some hundred steps very briskly; then, because of weakness, began to stumble. Oliver saw they were so badly burned by the sun that even the backs of their neck had begun to peel.

After about a mile both of the young Germans looked like they might collapse. Oliver decided to rest them. Quite grim-lipped, he made up his mind he was going to bring them into camp alive, if only to show his commanding officer, and those two military policemen, that he was a loyal American. "Halt." He pointed to a long boulder the size of a kitchen stove. "Setzen sie!"

They sat down, puffing.

He let them rest some fifteen minutes, then gestured them up on their feet again, pointing toward his camp, which was still hidden behind some low sandy hills. "Marsch!"

Walking them a half mile, then resting them, he managed to bring them to the last hill overlooking the Army campground.

The two Germans took one look at the encampment and thought of running.

"Nein! Nein!" Oliver growled, lifting his right hand while it was still in his jacket pocket, making as if he were aiming at their bellies. "Nein! Vorwarts!"

Weak, trembling in fright, they shuffled forward.

Camp guards spotted them and came running.

The first guard said, "What the hell? Germans?"

"Yep," Oliver said. "Dyed-in-the-wool Huns."

A sergeant came running up. His heavy face looked even more German than Oliver's captives. "Where in Christ's name did you find them?"

Oliver told him.

"Well I'll be dogbit by a cat." As more guards came running up, the sergeant ordered them to seize the Germans and drag them into camp. He gestured for Oliver to follow him.

The Germans were led into the commanding officer's tent. The C.O. leaped to his feet when he spotted the faded blue prison garb. "There they are. We just got word two of 'em had escaped the prison camp west of here. Who caught them?"

The sergeant pointed to Oliver.

"You? One of our cooks? How did that happen? Did they smell your cold-water buns?"

Oliver allowed himself a grin. "Naw. My sergeant thought I needed some sun, I'm inside so much. So I took a walk. Found them buddied up in a small wash. Like a pair of spoons in a tableware chest."

"Good work, bean jockey. I'll put you up for a medal."

The medal never came, of course. They were all too busy drilling.

Within a few weeks Oliver's unit was shipped to Detroit, where they joined several other units to form a battalion. While there a cloudburst fell during the night and the dyke surrounding the camp burst and they all were choused up out of their bunks to run for their lives. They managed to grab their blue duffel bags and their soaked socks and shoes and escape.

After their officers had completed paperwork, they were next shipped to Long Island, where they were processed aboard an old wheeler steamboat. The niggers were housed down in the hold and the lower deck, while the white boys slept in the first-class cabins and up on the top deck.

They all talked about their chances of making it safely across the Big Pond. U-boats were sneaking around them underwater. A kind of fever seethed in the units and it wasn't long before influenza broke out.

Oliver was one of the last to come down with the flu. Already all around him, both upstairs and down in the hold, men both white and black were dying like flies sprayed with sheep dip. Every hour a bugler blew the military funeral rites as dead bodies, encased in canvas sacks, were let slip into the sea forever.

Oliver might have joined his comrades in Davy Jones's locker had it not been for Old Man Wright. Wright was a small wizened cowboy from western Siouxland; really a biscuit-shooter cookie from a roundup crew. He had taught Oliver how to make sourdough buns with water, flour, spook, and a pinch of salt. Wright took care of Oliver like a father. He gave Oliver whiskey, stolen from an officer's cabin, and extra blankets, taken from the quartermaster's stock. Wright cradled him, and loved him up, and talked to him about the mademoiselles they'd soon yentz in France. Wright felt of him all night long to see how he was, if his fever was going up or coming down.

Two mornings later Oliver suddenly felt better.

Crossing the choppy English Channel during the night, their boat banged into another ship. There was an awful cracking noise. Officers hit the deck in bare feet and roared out orders. The captains of the two ships swore great heavenly oaths at each other in the dark; then snarling around, swore at their helmsmen and the nightwatch.

The wildest time occurred down in the hold. There was room for only one man at a time to come up through the hatch, yet all the niggers made it in two minutes flat. It made Old Wright laugh. "They boiled out of there like black rats."

But the ships didn't sink and no one was hurt, except the pride of the captains, and soon everyone lay down again to get such sleep as they could on a rocking ship.

Landing at Le Havre in France, the boys marched down the gangplank single file and then out on the plank pier. They strode along in pairs between two lines of cheering Frenchmen, old men, women, and children, happy that relief had come at last.

Old Man Wright heard a French soldier, home on leave from the front, make a derogatory remark about the American soldier. The battle-scarred French veteran didn't think the Yankee doughboy looked like much of a fighter. "Pooder-puffs." Wright took it personally. He stepped out of the marching line, knocked the French soldier down with one looping cowboy punch. "Toot sweet, Froggie, that'll show you."

Five days later Oliver's unit found themselves just a mile behind the front near Verdun. The first night they suffered through a long bombardment. The Germans were using their Big Bertha long-range guns. Great falling shells walked toward their barracks; finally found them. They were tumbled out of their bunks, like field mice out of a nest by a farmer's plow.

After that it was quiet for a month on their front. Both Oliver and Old Wright tried to get fat on their own cooking. Their jokes slowly changed from sour ones to happy ones.

Old Wright liked to make up ditties and then sing them at the top of his cracking voice. One of them became a favorite in the barracks:

> Don't yentz your aunts
> your blue boar johnny,
> for if you do,
> old Aunt Lu
> will pinch our money
> right out of your pants.

The next spring came hell. One morning a soft breeze from the northeast flowed out of the German lines, crossed no-man's-land, and breathed over the American front. The soft breeze smelled sweet, and the khaki-clad soldiers sleeping in the trenches smiled in their dreams. Then within minutes everybody started coughing. Coughing. Coughing.

A sergeant, ducking down, came raging through the zigzag trenches. "We're being gassed!" he sputtered. "Everybody wet your handkerchiefs and cover your mouth and nose." The last place he gave the order was in the barracks where the cooks lay sleeping. Already they were sniffling and clearing their throats in dream. Because they were awakened late, Oliver and Old Man Wright got it the worst. The very next day they were sent to an Army hospital behind the lines.

Even after they felt better, Oliver and Old Wright could still taste and smell the sweetness coming out of their lungs. It got so bad they couldn't eat honey or take sugar in their coffee. Both learned that there was nothing so sickening as having the aroma of sweetness around one all day and all night long.

Two months later they went back to the front, still coughing, still tasting acidic nectar even when they took their coffee black.

Four months later, Old Man Wright died when an artery burst in his lungs. He drowned in his own blood.

A week later, Oliver Tice was sent to a U.S. Army hospital in the south of France. He stayed there until the next February, 1919, and then was discharged with honor. He went home with his lungs still giving off the odor of sweet decay.

34. *Stoop Talk*

1920,

Except for Thea, they were all home for a few weeks that summer.

Ma and Ana swayed in their rockers on the creaking porch behind the screens. Tressa and Mallie sat with the menfolks on the stoop. Pa sat next to Mallie. Tane and Dirk and Rolf sat on the north end of the concrete stoop. And Geoffrey sat on a log off to one side.

It was so hot that everybody puffed a little. That July afternoon the temperature had gone up to 105 degrees. With the sun blazing down like a blast furnace and no wind out, Pa told the boys to unharness the horses and slap them on the rump and sent them out into the night yard, and then added that he and the boys should find a cool spot somewhere and rest.

The sun sank behind the house. Shadows off the house and the toolshed moved slowly eastward into the oats field. The oats were dead ripe, ready to crinkle and fall over on the least breath of wind. The oat heads shone a stippled coarsegold in the evening citron light.

Ma and Ana tried to cool their faces with Japanese fans. Pa sometimes pushed out his lower lip and puffed a breath up through his moustache and over his face.

The sound of a motor came to them from the north before they could see what it was. Soon the automobile crossed the rattling bridge over the Big Rock River and then they could make out a plume of glittering dust where the sun caught it. The car came on fast.

Tane said, "Man, is he hell-a-kiting it."

Pa said, "Wonder if that's our new doctor."

Rolf said, "It has to be. He's the only one that's got a fast car around here." Rolf stood up for a better look.

Dirk said, "Or it could be our local rumrunner."

Pa said, "You mean Manly?"

Dirk said, "The same. I heard the other day they've got a route worked out all the way from Canada to Bonnie. And Manly takes care of the run between Trosky and here in his super-charged car."

The car flashed past going south to Bonnie. It was a blue Buick with a shining nickel radiator. With the plume of dust following, it resembled the passing of a comet.

Pa said, "Where did you hear that about his route?"

Dirk said, "The boys in the pool hall were talking about it." Dirk laughed to himself. "They tell a good story about Manly when he'd just started his run last February. He was coming down from his drop in Trosky when he got stuck in the snow north of Whitebone. Well, he knew that if the sheriff caught him there, the sheriff was sure to search his Buick and find the hooch. So he quick unloaded it and buried it in a snowbank. Sure enough, the sheriff did come out when someone called in to say there was a car stuck in a snowbank. But of course, by then, Manly was clean and the sheriff couldn't pinch him."

Tane said, "What happened to the hooch?"

Dirk laughed some more, a wry sound in his throat. "I guess when Manly went back to look for it, he couldn't find it. The snowbanks blowing off the Blue Mounds there all looked alike. And he didn't dare hang around too long. Well, this spring, the road gang found the cache. They knew if they brought it into town, the sheriff would confiscate it. So they sat down on the blades of their road graders and had themselves a toot. One old-timer claims the road gang got so drunk they made a new road across some farmer's field. When the county commissioners called them in to give them hell, they argued they was only making a shortcut to town for the farmer."

"Ha. I bet that went over."

"I think some guys got fired."

Rolf said, "I wonder what those horses thought when they found themselves pulling those graders through the cornfield."

Geoffrey piped up. "Can horses think?"

Tane snorted. "Think? Of course they can. When you drive out to the field they got slowpoke feet. But at noon, when you're headed back for the yard, they run like they're in a race . . . in a hurry to get at the corn and hay in their mangers."

Dirk said, "You're right there. Reminds me of that one summer when we kids was still all going to catechism at the Little Church on Saturdays. When we drove Old Bess in front of our democrat. Pa, you remember that time when you asked us to find Old Man Alfredson and ask him if he'd dig us a new cistern?"

"Yeh, I remember."

"After catechism we drove to his stone house by the church there. His old lady—"

Pa broke in. "I don't like it when you kids call a man's wife 'his old lady.'"

"Okay, Pa."

"I know you think you're grown up and all, but you still better show respect for your elders."

Ma chimed in too. "That's right, children. I hope none of you speaks of me as being your father's 'old lady.'"

"'Course not, Ma."

Pa grumbled some more. "Hereafter, when you kids speak of Mr. Alfredson, or any of those others like Mr. Rexroth, be heavy on that 'mister.'"

All the children fell silent.

The sun sank. Crickets woke up weak in the heat. A cow in the night yard bellowed for her calf.

Tane lifted a ham and let fly with a little tune. Without half-trying he made it sound impertinent. Tane jerked up his blond head, pretended he was as surprised, and shocked, as the rest. Then he leaned a finger at Geoffrey. "Quick! There he goes! Catch him!" Tane's blue eyes opened elaborately. "Ohh, shucks. You wasn't quick enough. He got away." Tane let his shoulders fall in gentle regret.

Geoffrey acted as if he hadn't heard. He continued to muse to himself.

Ana spoke from her rocker. "That wasn't vary edifying, Tane. I'm ashamed to be known as your sister."

Rolf said, "I wanna hear what kind of a story Dirk made out of our runaway."

"Runaway?" Pa exclaimed.

Dirk frowned. "Rolf, Pa was never to know about that. Remember how we all promised never to mention it?"

Ma said, "I knew something had happened that time. So many of you came home with scratches and bruises."

Pa said, "You kids said you got that because of a scuffle with the Engleking kids on the gravel barnyard at church there."

"Well, we had that too," Dirk said.

"What did happen?" Pa demanded.

Dirk took up the story again. "When we asked Mrs. Alfredson where we could find her husband, she told us he was busy reliming the cistern on the Holmes place. You know, that half section east of the water tower there? So we drove toward there. Well, Old Bess first thought we was going home, but when we headed her up Main Street going east past the tower, she was so disgusted she started to trot in one place. We found Mr. Alfredson all right and gave him the message. Then we turned around and headed for town again. Old Bess still thought we wasn't going anywhere, surely not home, so she dragged her feet even more. She started to walk in one place."

A wet laugh burst out of Rolf. "I remember that. I even jumped off the democrat and picked up a couple of clods and threw 'em at her. But it didn't help."

304

Dirk went on "We was going up the Holmes lane toward Main Street again when I happened to spot some kids sitting up on the platform high on the water tower. The sun was glancing off something shiny in their hands, and then I saw they had BB guns and were shooting at pigeons on top of the water tower. Then they saw us coming, and one of the kids just for the fun of it aimed at Old Bess. I heard the k-thung of his air rifle and then the whizz of the BB just as it hit Old Bess in the belly. Boy, did she perk up. Her head came straight up like we'd checkreined her too high. She popped her tail and then raised it stylish. Another kid up there got the same idea and he cranked in a BB and fired. Again there was that k-thung sound. This time the BB caught Old Bess in the delicate part under her raised tail."

Rolf's great teeth shone in the falling dusk. "Har! I remember that."

"Old Bess took off like a man shot out of a cannon. Like she thought there was some honey hay waiting for her at the far end of Main Street. She took off so hard, the lines slid out of my hands and I fell over backwards. All us kids fell over backwards, Rolf, Ana, Tressa, Mallie, and me. And—"

"Hey," Rolf said. "Not me. I'd just jumped off and thrown some clods."

"Oh, yeh. That's right. Anyway, Old Bess kept going so fast down Main Street, past little Jackie Van Valkenburg's house, past the banker's big house, that we never could get our balance back no matter how we tried. That's how strong the wind of her runaway was. When she hit the corner of Highmire's Hardware, by the flagpole there, she recognized where she was. She took a right so sharp that the democrat rose up on two wheels and we all tumbled out like colored marbles spilling out of a busted pouch. I rolled up against the side of the First National Bank, and Ana hit a hitching post, and Mallie bounced up against Old Lady Prousty out shopping, and Tressa landed in the gutter. I tell you it was a wonderful mess of flying legs and underpants."

"Yeh," Rolf said, "and I came running down the hill after youse all hollering my head off for Old Bess to stop."

Everybody on the stoop and in the porch had a good laugh.

"So that's what really happened," Ma said.

"Sure. When Old Bess disappeared around the curve north out of town, we were sure we had to walk all the way home. But when we come to Clate Bartles's place, walking, there Old Bess was, practically eating out of Clate's hand. He'd rolled out on the road in his coaster wagon and stopped her. She'd probably run out of breath by then, going so fast, and so was ready to call it quits. By that time too our bumps didn't hurt so bad any more, and so we climbed aboard and headed home. Old Bess went along at a right merry clip because she knew that her manger would be full of a dozen ears of corn and some fresh alfalfa hay."

Tane nodded. "Yeh, when a horse remembers that full manger in the barn, there's no stopping him."

Ana asked, snippish, "Why must a horse always be a him? Old Bess was a her, wasn't she?"

Tane ignored Ana. He passed another cheeky blip of aromatic gas. "Another country heard from."

"Tane!" Ma scolded.

"Well, Ma, that's what you get for serving onions for supper. When you boil them slow in skim milk I can't say no to them."

Ma rocked agitated. "To think I raised you all these years, thirty-four of 'em, and now you've begun to pull off these naughty stunts."

305

Tane smiled quietly to himself. He knew something. "I always had trouble with gas, Ma. You remember the time when Miss Fikes sent home a note from school about that?"

"Yes," Ma sighed, waving her fan, "I remember."

"That was in the wintertime, when you always served so much johnnycake. With melted lard instead of butter. And Karo syrup. It always tasted like more and I always ate too much. And for me, eating a lot of johnnycake makes for a lot of farts—"

"Must you tell that?" Ma exclaimed. "And use that awful word?"

"—that ain't called for. It's all right as long as a fella is home on the yard, but in the school . . . the winders are hard to handle. It was the day before the Christmas program, almost at noon, when a bad one came along I knew I couldn't handle. I tried to pinch it back twice, but when that didn't work, I tried to pass it as quiet as a mouse. But of course, quiet or not, it stunk to beat the band."

Rolf leaned back getting ready to laugh at what was surely coming next.

Pa chewed on the ends of his moustache to hide that he too was about to burst out laughing.

The sun sank in the west in a blush of rose glory. A breath of cool air plumed down off the purple hills to the east.

"Well, it wasn't long before some other johnnycake winders came along, and the smell of them drifted across the aisle. First Gordon Pullman pulled up his nose at me. And then his sister Grace did. Man, did I feel ashamed."

"Well, good for you," Ana managed to say.

"Finally Gordon leaned over when Miss Fikes wasn't looking and whispered under his speller, 'Pinch 'em a little just as you let 'em and they won't smell so bad.'"

"I don't believe he said that," Tressa said. "He's too polite."

"He did, though. Even Grace heard what he whispered and she didn't think anything was out of the way. Didn't giggle or anything. Anyway, I thought there might be something to what Gordon said, so the next time I felt a bad one coming I tried it. I pinched it a little."

Mallie spoke up. "Must we go through this whole sorry recital of someone's rectal problems?"

"Shut up, nurse," Rolf said. "I want to hear what happened to that pinched-in one."

Tane lifted a ham again as if to entertain them with another tune; then resettled himself to show he hadn't meant to after all. "What I heard next almost shocked me out of a year's growth. My sitter made a noise like a mouse being stepped on. Well, Grace all of a sudden had to laugh. She covered her mouth with her hand, but the laugh still squirted through her fingers. And then Gordon laughed. He laughed so hard he slipped out of his seat and fell to the floor."

Tressa said, "The Pullmans wouldn't've."

Tane said, "Dirk, you was there."

Dirk said, "They did all right. Just like he says." Dirk, remembering, bent over his knees in laughter. He coughed wet several times.

Tane went on. "Miss Fikes stepped over. 'What goes on here?' she asked. 'Nothing,' I said. 'Are you sure?' 'Sure.' 'Gordon Pullman, will you tell the rest of us what you're laughing about?' Gordon couldn't tell her because he couldn't stop laughing. About then Miss Fikes smelled what the problem was and she colored up and changed the subject. And that was the end of that."

"Thank God," Ma said. "And I hope that's the end of your story."

Pa cleared his throat. He brushed out his brown moustache with thumb and forefinger. "So, Geoff, you're still going after that law degree."

Geoffrey rose out of his musing. "Yes."

"Hmm. Well, maybe you can represent your mother when I sue her for loss of conjugal rights."

Ma sucked in a breath. So did Ana.

Tressa said, sadly, "Oh, Dad."

Rolf said, "What's conjugal rights?"

Mallie said, "The right to sexual intercourse between husband and wife."

Rolf looked askance at Pa. "I thought you two would be done with that by now."

Ana said, "I feel ashamed to hear all this."

Tane said, "Go off to bed then, Ana. You ain't nailed to the floor, are you?"

Mallie said, "I'm shocked too, Ma."

Ma said, "Don't feel shocked because of me. It's your father who's making the complaint. Get after him."

Ana said, "It's even hard to think where we might have come from. All because of something you two did with each other."

Tane said, "That's because you're on the way to becoming an old maid."

"Missionary," Ana said. "And that's a whole lot different."

"Time to go to bed," Pa said, looking at his watch. "Tomorrow is another day of hard work."

Geoffrey said, "It's too nice to go to bed so early."

"Well, son, that's the way it is on a farm in summer."

"There ought to be a law against it. Really, so early."

Dirk coughed again, deep, bringing up phlegm.

The coughing caught on with Tressa. She too hacked up phlegm.

Pa looked at both of them. "Well, I notice that what a monkey sees a monkey does."

Ma had sat up very straight. She snapped, "Tunis, our children are not monkeys."

All the children saw a fight coming on and they looked down at their hands. A nervous smile pulled at the corners of their lips.

Tane reared up his head and looked around at all the horizons, as though at last the time had come to make an announcement. "Now that you're all here, except Thea, I might as well come out with it. I'm getting married this winter."

There was a long silence.

The sunken sun shot up a last ray of light at a ribbon of cloud high overhead, turning it from silver to a soft scarlet.

"What!" Ma said, finally.

"Who would want to marry you?" Ana cried. "With your filthy habits."

Tane laughed down at the ground. "Snort all you want to, Ana, but there it is. I'm getting married. About time too."

"To who?" Ma asked quietly.

"Yes," Pa said. "We never see you go out with anybody."

"You'll find out soon enough."

Dirk said, "I think I know."

Tane stared at Dirk in the dusk. "How would you know?"

Dirk said, "When I was still home, I used to wonder what you did after we all went to bed, when you took the lantern and said you were going to check the animals to see if they were all right. Sometimes you came in a couple of hours later. So one night I followed you outside. You doused the lantern, and then in the moonlight you walked over to our old schoolhouse."

"I thought someone was follerin' me once. You son of a gun."

"I saw you kissin' the Pullman's hired girl. Arva Tolliver."

"Her? Why, she's almost a foot taller than you," Ana exclaimed. "And what a name to bear. Arva."

"So what?" Tane retorted. "We like each other. We get along like two peas in a pod."

"You've been sneaking out at night to see a girl?" Pa said.

"Sure. You didn't think I was going to wind up being a bachelor, did you?"

"I was hoping you'd go on being my hired man for a while."

"Nosiree. I don't intend to keep following that trade forever."

Pa said, "If you leave, I may have to give up this farm."

"Aw, Pa," Tane said, "now don't you stand in my way with that kind of talk. After all, you still got Rolf."

Rolf said, "I don't intend to keep up that trade forever either. I got my eye on my own girl."

"You!" Ana cried. "Who'd marry you?"

Rolf said, "You might be surprised."

Ma said, "Tane, you don't have to get married, do you?"

Again Tane reared his head around at all the horizons. "You mean, did I knock her up?"

"You don't have to say it that way," Ma said.

"No, I don't have to get married. Arva won't let me get in her pants. Tell jokes, yes. Laugh, yes. Spoon, no."

"Well, good for her," Ana said. "Now I feel better about it."

Tane said, "If the girl can't be as she should be, then she'll have to be as she can."

Ma asked, "Where is she from?"

"Rock Falls," Tane said. "She takes the train down and gets off at Lakewood. Then she walks from there."

"What are her folks like?"

"They own that first farm south of Rock Falls."

"What's their religion?"

"Baptist. They believe in immersion in the river."

"We'll have to meet them."

"You will, come our wedding day."

"Any other children?"

"Two boys. One's gonna stay home and help the old man. And the other's gonna become a minister."

"Sounds like a good Christian family at that," Ana put in.

Tane glared at her in the near dark. "Thanks. But I don't need your okay."

Pa shook his head. "That you had to go sneaking around to find yourself a girl, that I don't like."

Ma said, "I don't like it either."

Tane said, "I was starting to get headaches, Pa, that's why I took that long walk one night. And so ran into her. She was doing the same thing because of headaches."

"Oh," Pa said.

Ma said, "My goodness, boy, how often did you do this?"

"Oh, altogether maybe a dozen times."

"And you think you know enough about her to marry her after only seeing her that much?"

"Ma, didn't you tell me once that you just took one look at Pa at Lord Sutherland's house and you knew you'd found your man?"

Ma fell silent.

Dirk coughed some more. He ratched up a big glob of phlegm; finally spat it out on the ground.

Ma got to her feet. "Better go to bed, Dirk. In fact, we all better go to bed."

Pa got to his feet too. "Right. Another day of hard work tomorrow."

Mallie rose easily to her feet, and with a big warm smile went over and sat down on Tane's knees and put her arms around him and gave him a thick kiss. "Oh, Tane, I hope you have a happy life with Arva. You deserve it."

"I will."

35. Tane

1920–1921

Tane didn't tell the bunch the other reason why he took the lantern to check the animals. A fellow couldn't very well play with himself with all his brothers sleeping in the same room. If that was what he wanted to do.

Tane didn't like how he felt afterwards, didn't like how he was changing, so one night he blew out his lantern, set it on the ground, and took a walk. The moon was full and as yellow as the yolk of a goose egg, there wasn't even the least breath of a breeze out, and all the fields were jumping with growth. The oats was about to turn into silver-gold, the corn was breast high and cracking softly in the moonlight, it was growing so fast, and the peonies in Ma's garden scented the yard with a woman's sweet perfume.

It wasn't any fun walking toward town. That way lay the farms of the miserable Hack Tippett and the outlandish Clate Bartles. Tane leaned around and headed north toward the abandoned schoolhouse, where once some boys in play had tried to crucify him.

As Taned walked, he muttered to himself, "I can't keep this up, or the first thing you know, I'm gonna go sex crazy. At the same time, I don't want to become one of the deadpecker boys."

It was wonderful out walking in the moonlight. Crickets and night animals were all out making their special noises. He found himself bouncing along on each step all the way to the schoolhouse.

Wild grass and wildflowers had shot up in the schoolyard, so thick it was like striding through sticky syrup a foot deep. The earthy perfumes were so heady he had to clear his nose several times.

The front steps had sunk in on one side, causing a crack, out of which grew stinkweed. The door was nailed shut, but all the windows had been knocked out by vandals. In the muted light what little white paint was left gave the building the look of a Hansel and Gretel cottage. What great times he'd had with his brothers and sisters in that hoary old shack.

Puffing a little from the brisk long walk, Tane settled on the top step. The step felt cool to his seat. What a great night to be out. Too bad a farmer had to work so hard that at night when the moon was out he had to sleep. It truly was a waste.

He got to thinking about how nice it would be if some angel girl came walking down the road, and would see him, and then with a smile would come over and sit beside him, and then pretty soon she would slip her arm around him and kiss him on the cheek. It would be only in dream, of course, before he'd ever see some girl do that.

For some crazy reason that he didn't understand, a ditty rose to mind. He'd heard one of the men working on the railroad section singing it when they were putting in new ties:

> Sioux City and Sioux Falls
> are two big cities
> where all the pretty girls
> have great big titties.

He smiled to himself.

There were more verses, more raunchy. It was the kind of song that drove Ma wild.

He was sure Ma would never understand a man's needs when it came to having a woman. Pa might, but Pa wouldn't talk about it. The way Ma kept putting Pa off when he tried to touch her, or put his arm around her, was enough to frost the balls off a brass monkey.

He wondered what Dirk and Rolf and Geoffrey did about their need to womanize. Probably snuck off on the farm somewhere to take care of it. Or what the girls were doing for their man needs.

Sometimes he caught the hint of something going on between Dirk and Tressa. He knew that Dirk had often looked at their sisters when they lay naked on their beds on warm summer mornings. He himself had looked several times, if only to find out where the important things lay, but then later on had resolutely turned his head away when he headed downstairs in the morning. It only made his craving worse to look at them. Besides, it was a sin. He murmured aloud, "I couldn't do it, I tell you that right now."

A voice said behind him, "What couldn't you do?"

At first he was sure he'd heard the words in his head, and not out on that old schoolyard. But then his eyes pulled his head around for a look to make sure. There she was. A girl. Just like he'd wished for a little while ago. An angel girl. Slowly he got to his feet. "What? Where'd you come from?"

She smiled at him. She was taller than he was. "I'm a snowflake and I floated down."

"I don't see any snow clouds. Besides, this is summer."

"A person doesn't always need a cloud for it to snow, does one?"

"No, I guess not. That's what makes snow rainbows."

She had brown eyes and brown hair and a round face. "I've never heard of snow rainbows. Are there such things?"

"There is now, I guess." Quite nervous, he looked her up and down. What a fine muscular girl she was. What a mother she'd make. Pups out of her would make champions. "Really, where did you come from? Because just a minute ago I was daydreaming to myself about an angel girl that might come walking down the road."

"You were? You did?"

He nodded. "And here you are. It's hard to believe." He shook his head as if to clear his eyes. "Who would have ever thought that at this time of night, when all decent folk are sound asleep, all the better to work tomorrow . . . that a fellow like me and a girl like you should happen to meet in an old schoolyard. And in the moonlight yet." He laughed a wild laugh. "No, it didn't happen, it ain't happening, because it couldn't happen."

Her long brown flowing hair lay fluffed over her shoulder. It could be seen that during the day she usually put up her hair because the kinks and knots of braids still showed in it. "You're the oldest Freyling boy, not?"

"I am. Tane."

"Well, I'm Arva Tolliver. Hired girl for the Pullmans." She pointed to the farm up on the hill to the east.

"How come you're out walking? That I do it once in a while, that's to be expected. Because of the way I sometimes feel. But you?"

"What do you mean, the way you sometimes feel?"

"Well, so tied down to one spot on earth. To the same family all my life. Maybe that's what's wrong with me. I already should be out in the world on my own."

"Why don't we sit down?"

"Good idea." Tane settled down on the steps with her.

"I heard the Pullmans talking about your family. They said some of you Freyling kids are doing real well. Out in the world."

Tane leaned down and plucked a spear of grass. He chewed on it. "That's true. Thea got married. And Dirk's a newspaperman in Bonnie. And Ana is studying to be a missionary to the Indians. And Mallie is taking up nursing so she can become a physical therapist, whatever that is. And Geoffrey says he's going to the University of Minnesota law school next year."

"It all sounds okay to me."

Tane shook his head. "But we're still all too close. We all have an awful time leaving home." He waved his arms around. "I feel like I'm living in a closet. And I've got to get out or I'll rot inside. Become like a piece of musty timber."

"Leave, then," she said.

"I'm thinkin' on it. If I find me the right gal, I'm gonnn do it too." He wriggled his nose. "What bout you?"

311

"I left home to work for the Pullmans because I couldn't stand seeing my life go by either, cooking and cleaning after my father and mother and my two brothers. Farming and farming. Getting the eggs and making the beds and having my periods and still no babies. Never any picnics. Or kisses."

Kisses?

She faced him. "You like going to church though, don't you?"

"You mean, really, and not just a churchgoer?"

"What else?"

Tane lifted a shoulder.

"You do believe Christ is our Savior?"

Tane lifted the other shoulder. He didn't want to offend her by saying the wrong thing. In the back of his head a voice said: "Here's the one girl you ought to marry."

"Christ came down to earth, you know, to die for all our sins and have them forgiven, so that we might go to heaven. So if you don't believe on him, you're going to go to hell."

"You're sure about that now?"

She said gravely, arms folded around her large breasts, "I am."

Tane cocked his head first to one side, then the other. "Oh, the hell with it. I'm not going to argue about it. I'll just go ahead and believe Christ is the son of God."

A laugh spurted from between her lips. Then, not liking the swearing, she frowned. "I don't know if God is going to like that kind of confession of faith."

He laughed momentarily too; then sobered over. "I know. It's just that I'm a little short-winded when it comes to thinking. I've got to get off that home place, much as I love my pa and ma. Got to get away."

"Well then, just up and leave."

"Heh. Where would I go? I haven't got any money. No car. Not even a horse and buggy of my own."

"Yes, the Pullmans were talking about that. That you folks still don't have a car. The Pullmans kind of approved that."

"Well, we kids don't. Rolf has wanted a car for a long time. He already knows how to run gas engines." Tane set his elbows on his knees, chin in his hands, looking out over the pearl-soft landscape. "You know, I think I'm gonna have a talk with Pa and Ma. They've given money to Dirk and Ana and Mallie and Geoffrey so they could go to school. And what have I got out of it? Just room and board and clothes. I guess I don't squeak enough."

"The squeaking wheel gets the grease."

"Right." Tane nodded.

"Mind you now, I don't want to cause trouble in your fine family, I'm just sorta asking, but, what would you really like to do?"

"I'd like to get married and have kids. I'd like to own a farm of my own."

Her brown eyes leveled on him. "Who'll inherit your big farm when your father and mother retire?"

"I hain't thought that far ahead."

"Well, who will?"

Tane looked down at his hands, then looked at Arva. "Well, the way things are shaping up now, it looks like Rolf and me are to be the only farmers in the family."

"Then it's either Rolf or you."

Tane nodded. He looked steadily at Arva. He was pleased to notice how at ease he felt around her. It was like being with his sisters. Most women made him feel like a clodhopper. "I think, though, before I begin to dream about taking over the Freyling section, I'd first rather strike out on my own. Just to show I can do it. Like Pa once did."

"Times are different now though. You won't be able to find any more free land to homestead."

"Well, then I'll try owning a smaller piece of land. And work to beat all creation until I own it free and clear." He nodded vigorously. "Here I am, going on thirty-four this fall, and all I've got for all I've done for the family is a swat on my butt for each year of my life."

Arva looked puzzled. "A swat on your butt?"

Tane laughed. "In our family, every time you get a birthday, the rest of the kids gang up on you and give you a love tap on your butt for every year you've lived."

She choked back a laugh. "You mean, you kids still do that?"

"No, no. We quit that when we got to thirteen. I think Ma was afraid we boys would get too many free feels of our sisters."

Arva laughed heartily. "I'm afraid your family was run a whole lot different from mine. We were never allowed such jolly fun. And I've made up my mind that when I have my own kids, I'm going to allow them a lot of fun. And I'm going to be part of it."

Her remark set very well with him. He stood up. He'd found his woman all right. "Well, I think I'll call it a day and head for hay."

Two nights later they met again about the same time. The moon had waned a little and the farm land and the high hills to the east and the dark line of trees along the river had a misty edge to them.

Arva's first question was, "Did you talk to your folks about striking out on your own?"

"No. Not yet. I thought I'd think on it some more. One of the things you learn as a farmer is never to hurry about going deeper into debt."

"Oh." She seemed disappointed.

"But I have a question to ask you. You sounded like you wasn't too hot about being a farmer's wife. What do you want to become?"

"If it's the right man, I don't mind what he does." She looked out over the subdued moonlit night. "I have thought of working in a store someday. That way I'd finally meet a lot of people. Maybe even someday meet my man."

"Arva, how old are you?"

"I'm twenty-five. Almost an old maid."

"There's nine years difference between us. If I went after you they'd accuse me of robbing the cradle."

"Oh, after a person is twenty-one, it don't make much difference who you marry, old or young."

He liked that. "Stand up once."

"Why?"

"Stand up once."

Slowly she got to her feet. The soft moonlight falling on her blue dress made it seem as green as the tall grass around them.

He stepped up close and with his right hand touched the top of his head and then moved his hand level across to her eyebrows. "Yep. Just as I thought. You're a good three inches taller than me."

She dropped her chin. "You don't know how often I've cursed that. I know I shouldn't. It's what the Lord gave me and I should be happy with my lot. But I'm not. I'll probably never find a man who won't mind how tall I am. Even if I clerk a hundred years in a store."

He stood first on one leg, then the other. He looked up at the sky first one way, then the other. "I don't mind how tall you are. In fact, I kind'f like it. You'll make a great mother and a better wife."

"You really think that? Really?"

He laughed. "Tell you. To get that business of you wanting to clerk a little out of your blood—quit your job at the Pullmans' right now and take a job at the Lakewood store up the road there." He pointed northeast to a grain elevator and a depot and a country store showing over the river trees. "In the meantime, I'll work on my end of it."

She seemed to swell in front of him. Her breasts touched him. Then, impulsively, she took his face in her large hands and kissed him, firmly, even a little wet. "Tane."

Her large breasts warmed him in two places. He kissed her back. He became so thick with it he thought he'd burst out of his overalls. He was very powerful and in a moment his power bore her down to the grass. At first she submitted

313

her limbs to him, but when his hand reached up under her dress and pulled down her bloomers, she reacted, almost violently.

"Not so fast, buster!" She pushed his hand down so hard she threw it to one side. "What do you think I am, just a cow that can be jumped on?"

He fell slack.

"I promised my God I wouldn't do it with a man until after I got married."

"Oh."

She sat up in the thick grass. "Heh. Really. You're no better than a bull. I've watched them in Pa's pasture. He sniffs her and then he jumps her bones. Heh."

"I'm sorry."

A rush of compassion suffused her round face. "Oh, Tane," she said. She kissed him lightly on the cheek. "It's all right. I kind of like to see that in a man. It's just that I want that man to remember I have human bein' feelings too."

"I know. Ma would agree with you."

"She sounds like a nice lady."

"That's exactly what she is. A lady."

"Let's sit on those steps again. Down here in the grass is too much of a temptation."

He blinked, shook his head. "Let me get this straight. You mean, you're tempted too?"

"Of course."

"Truly now?"

"Every bit as much as you. But a woman's got just a pinch more sense. At least until she gets married."

He got up and reached out a hand to help her up beside him on the steps. "You just said, 'until she gets married.' I take it then that if I was to askt you to marry me you'd marry me?"

"Why don't you try me?"

He was about to dive in the deepest part of the river. "All right. How about you and me getting hitched?"

"That's not the way I expected a man to ask me."

"How then?"

"What you just said now sounds more like you're making a joke out of it."

"You mean, you want to hear the real word?"

She held up a hand. "Stop right now. The way you're stalling around, it sounds like you don't really want me. That maybe I'm too big for you."

"You're bein' so tall don't faze me the least bit."

She waited, smiling.

"And I ain't stalling. It's just that it's the first time for me and I'm scairt."

"Why should you be scairt?"

"Ain't you?"

"I'm scairt you ain't gonna ask me."

He swallowed. The swallowing made a clicking sound.

"Tane, I tell you what let's do. Let's make a trade. I'll accept it that you're a little too old for me if you'll accept that I'm a mite too tall for you."

"Fair enough."

"Well?"

"Arva, will you marry me?"

"I will."

"A kiss to seal it?"

"Sure. If you don't try to jump my bones again."

"I'll be a gentleman about it." Just before he leaned forward, he added, "One thing you better know too. I'm just as green about all this as you."

"I know. And that's real nice."

They were married the next February in her Baptist church in Rock Falls. Ma dragged her feet about the Baptist church but at last managed to smile about it because she'd come to like Arva. Pa hated it that his best hand was leaving; and he made Tane promise that when the Freylings ran behind in field work Tane would come over and help catch up. Pa had helped Tane find a quarter to rent just east of the schoolhouse. It was also a good place for Arva, since she had to walk only a short ways to the Lakewood General Store, where she took a job as store clerk.

Just before they left on the train for a honeymoon in the Black Hills, Tane pulled Pa to one side. "Pa, I know how things go in the pasture. But how do things go in the bedroom?"

Over the years Pa's face had gradually formed into a set scowl. A smile tried to show through the mask. "Boy, I had no one to ask with your mother."

"But what do I do? Arva's held me off so far."

"Do what comes naturally. Bulls are born knowing how."

"I've already caught Hail Columbia for trying it that way."

The smile grew on Pa's face, cracking wrinkles under each light pearl eye and moving down into his graying brown moustache. "Your train is about to leave. You better hurry."

315

"That's just what I'm not supposed to do."

"Just don't forget that 'morning after' story I told you."

They found a log cabin for rent in the dark forest several miles from Rapid City. It was up a gorge with a running stream of very cold water. Late February snow crowned the granite peaks about them. Both liked the old-style place.

After Arva made them a supper of wieners and buns and a cup of tea, with the sun down early behind the high west horizon, they got ready for bed. They had only a thick white candle for a light. She blew out the candle and then, side by side, they undressed. In the dark she draped her clothes on one log chair and he threw his clothes on another log chair. The smell of pine resin was sharp in the cabin. She climbed in bed first, moving against the wall; then, trembling, he climbed in next.

They lay silently together a while. Below their cabin the cold waters of the brook splashed over a riff of rocks. A night bird, strange to them, squawked loudly.

After a while he reached in a kiss. She kissed him back. He slipped an arm under her and hugged her. She hugged him back. He kissed her again; then rolled on top of her.

"Here, here, there you go again. Not so fast." She pushed him off.

"I don't get it," he said, voice muffled in her hair. "I thought we were married now."

"We are. But why must you be in such a hurry? Can't you play a little? You know. Have fun."

"You mean tickling and such?"

She gave him a push. "Not tickling really."

Tane became a little angry. "Okay, you take over then. You act the man."

"Not like a man. I mean like a lover."

"You show me then. How you think it should go."

She lay still beside him. She sighed. "Oh, dear. This is not going the way I thought it would."

"How did you think it would go?"

"Well, you'd kiss me a little, then hold me close awhile, then kiss me some more. And then you'd play with my . . . my . . . "

"Titties?"

"There you go again. Can't you say 'bosom'?"

"Yeh. Go on."

"And then keep hugging me and then you'd let your hands play over me and then . . ."

"Show me how you'd do it if you were the man and I was the woman."

She started to laugh. "You silly goof you. I will not pretend I'm the man."

Tane withdrew his arm from under her and folded his arms over his chest. "Then it looks like we won't have any kids after all. Grow old together complaining about how come we never had kids."

The log cabin cracked around them. The fire in the black range slowly sank away and heat from it no longer breathed toward them.

"Both your folks and my folks will say, neither one of us was any good. You see that sometimes in churches, couples who have no kids."

Arva wriggled beside him. "You funny man you."

"That's just what they're gonna say about me if we don't have."

"Oh, Tane, you can sometimes be so funny." She snuggled up against him and ran a hand over his chest. The movement pulled the blankets off him.

He pulled the blankets back up.

She ran her hand back and forth across his chest. She nuzzled her head against his.

"Well, I will say this," Tane said smiling up into the dark, "you are a warm stove in bed."

"Tane, Tane."

"Though the truth is the stove ain't gonna stay warm forever."

"Why won't it?" she whispered.

"When you get a regular stove in bed with you, you've now and then got to put a log in it."

She lay still for a moment. He could feel her face beginning to smile. Then she burst out laughing. "You are the strange one all right." She began to wrestle with him, trying to roll him back and forth. She grabbed him by the shoulders to get a better hold. Presently the bedclothes slid off them. Soon too his nightshirt worked up and her hand landed on the side of his bare hip.

"Hey," he cried, "you got cold hands."

"I have, huh." She ran her hand across his belly. And in so doing she fumbled upon his firm member. She stopped.

He waited. He trembled.

She whispered, "You do have a big log there."

He trembled.

"I think," she said, "I think the stove is ready for some firewood."

"No," he said. "No, you didn't believe in affections before marriage. And now that we are married the funny thing is I don't after."

"Then you must not love me in Christ."

"I guess not."

She fumbled with him some more.

"Whew! Really, you sure do have cold hands."

"Why don't you throw in that log? That'll warm us up all over."

So Tane kissed her a little, and hugged her close, and kissed her some more, and played with her bosom, and kissed her, and then reached down between her thighs, and moaned a little when he felt how wet she was.

"Now!" she whispered hoarsely.

He rose over her slowly. "Now what?"

She had her arms around him. She patted his buttocks. "Just do it. It's gotta go in there."

He did.

"Ow. Oh, it's all right, Tane. My husband."

Afterward, noting the cold air in the cabin touching them, they slid apart.

Arva kissed him, and then she said, "Maybe you better light the candle."

"How so?"

"I feel something running. We don't want to soil the sheets."

He lighted the thick white candle.

She sat up and looked. "Oh, dear," she said with a smile. "Now you can see for yourself I was a virgin when you married me. I'm bleeding."

Tane was aghast. "Was I still too rough?"

"No, my husband. You were wonderful. Get me a pan of water. And a couple of washcloths." She had to laugh for joy. "And take it out of that black kettle on the range there. I want the water warm."

Arva bled most of the night. Tane brought her kettle after kettle of warm water until the bleeding was stanched.

"I really didn't hurt you, hon?"

"No. I didn't notice it anyway." She laughed some more. "You're gonna make a wonderful husband."

"I hope so."

"Don't worry. Everything's gonna be all right." She nodded to herself as she remembered something. "Your mother was telling me a little that the same thing happened to her and your father. Your father ran all night bringing her pans of water."

"She told you that?"

"Yes. I couldn't very well go to my own mother to ask her what to expect, she's so strict. So I asked your mother."

"Ha." Tane remembered that he too had asked his father what to expect.

The next morning they awoke at about the same time. It was very cold in the cabin. They were snuggled tight together, so close it was hard to tell whose arms were whose.

Tane glanced over at their clothes, her petticoat on one log chair and his pants on the other log chair. A smile moved into his lips. He was remembering that Pa had told him not to forget that "morning after" story. Tane lifted an arm

317

out from under the warm quilts and pointed. "Now then, Arva. There they hang, the petticoat and the pants. Which do you mean to wear from this day forth?"

She laughed under the quilts. "Well, if I have to get up first to start the fire, then I'm putting on the pants."

He thought that over for several moments. Then he bounded out of bed, shivering in the cold, and climbed into his trousers.

She peeked out from under the quilts. "What a brave man you are. While you're up and getting the fire started, put on the coffee too, will you?"

"I will. But you're making the pancakes." Pa's story hadn't worked out the way he'd planned.

When Tane and Arva got home, Ma called a conference on a Sunday when the whole family could be present. It was held after dinner, after the table had been cleared and tea had been served. A later afternoon sun shone through the two west windows, silhouetting the boys sitting in front of the windows and highlighting the faces of the girls across the table. Arva was also present, but Oliver couldn't make it.

"Well now," Ma began, a quiet smile pulling at the corners of her thin lips, "I thought probably that you should hear what Pa and I have been talking about lately."

All eyes swung from Ma to Pa.

Pa fingered his moustache, said nothing.

Ma went on. "Here we've been helping Dirk, and Ana, and Mallie to go on to college. Geoffrey is next. Meanwhile, Thea has gone on to marry Oliver with no help from us. And now Tane, our eldest, who has been with us the longest, has gotten married. Pa and I thought it was time we gave them both some help too to get started in life. After all, both Tane and Thea have labored long and hard for us, with no recompense, except for board, room, and clothes. And that is hardly fair. Later on, when the rest of you are ready to get married, we'll think of helping you too. Not, Pa?"

Pa's full lips pursed up. "You're running this show."

Ma looked down at her hands. Her fingers over the years had thickened at the knuckles, their tips alongside the nails had become somewhat frayed. Then Ma raised her graying head and gave Pa a loving glance, a glance that seemed to rise out of an old time. "Do you remember, Tunis, when all we had here on this place was the log cabin that is now our back porch?" She pointed through the north kitchen door. "When you were living here alone, and you'd come back from Wanata and you saw smoke rising from the chimney out there and you thought a claim jumper had taken over and you got out your gun to chase him off—only to find that it was me? That I had followed you here from Le Mars where I'd met you in Lord Sutherland's mansion?"

Pa began to smile under his moustache.

"Well, after we agreed I could stay with you for the night instead of sending me off to town—"

"What!" Dirk cried. "Ma? You stayed overnight here in that front porch and you still weren't married?"

Ma took the question firmly in stride. "Yes, that's right. We made an agreement I could stay. But the agreement included that he and I would sleep in separate beds until we got married—if we got married."

Tane and the other children had never heard that part of the story. All were astounded. Tane murmured, "Will wonders never cease."

Ma smiled, the tiny creases of age working into her pink cheeks. "Remember too, Tunis, how I showed you the cache of food I found under one of the one-legged beds? Tins of food? Pork and beans? Pears?"

Pa nodded.

"What the previous owners, the Worthing family, had put there in the cache, deep in the earth so it wouldn't freeze while they were gone during the winter months? This place was a sort of Eden for them during the summers. A summer home."

Tane threw a look at Arva. She sat beside him at the family board with a wonderful waiting smile on her lips. It could be seen she liked being part of that white-winged blackbird family.

Ma went on. "How we ate of those beans and pears?"

Pa nodded.

"What I didn't tell you though, Pa, was that I found something else in this place. Come." Ma got up and motioned for everybody to follow her into the back porch. She knelt before the old fireplace, which they rarely used. Sometimes when it was thirty below they built a fire in it to take off the chill so they could separate the milk and wash clothes.

She knelt to the right of the fireplace and traced the outline of what looked like several cracks in one of the logs. Everybody watched closely, some of them leaning forward from the hips. "Watch," Ma said. She caught the edge of one of the cracks, and with a fingernail began prying at it. The thin edge didn't move. Ma next pried at it with two fingernails. At last it came, spilling old dust. It turned out to be a little door.

319

"Well, I declare!" Pa exclaimed.

"Yes, Tunis."

"You've known about this all these years?"

"Yes, Pa."

"How come you didn't tell me, for godsakes? When it was my property in the first place? Before I married you?"

"I had my reasons," Ma said firmly. She reached into the little cavity behind the door and pulled out two things, a brown leather-bound diary with gold trim and a pearl necklace. The pearls glowed in the evening dusk as though each one had a tiny candle lighted in it.

"Hell's bells," Pa whispered.

Tane noticed that Pa was also looking deeper into the cavity. Tane followed the look. A pearl-handled .38 lay in the back of the cavity.

Ma closed the little door and stood up with the diary and the pearls in hand. "Actually, all these years I was sure the diary writer, Betsy Worthing, would someday show up asking for the pearls and the diary. She probably always meant to, but somehow never got around to it, and finally died. And here it is."

Dirk held out a hand for the diary. "Can I see that?"

"No, you cannot," Ma said.

"Why not?"

"I think her secrets should die with her."

"Oho," Dirk said, "secrets, eh? All the more reason why I want to see it. Make a good news story for the Bonnie *Review*."

"All the more reason why I don't want you to see it."

Geoffrey spoke up. "Besides, Dirk, before you use that in a news story, you better make sure the diarist's nearest of kin are also dead. Any one of them can sue you."

"Wait a minute," Dirk said. "When Pa bought the property, didn't he own everything he had and found on it?"

Pa said, "It probably all depends on how the deed of sale reads. What we'll do is go to the First National Bank and look up the deed. I put it in a lockbox there." Pa next looked at the pearls. "Can I see them, wife?"

Ma handed them over.

Pa examined them in the light. The pearls had almost the exact color of his eyes. He weighed them, jiggling them a little in his hand. He looked at Ma. "And you think if we sell these, that'll make quite a sum of money? Enough to give Tane and Thea their portion of an inheritance?"

"It'll help."

"Hm." Pa stared up at the log ceiling. "Well, what we'll do is the fair and right thing. There's a good lawyer in town, Timmons. The only honest one I know of around here. We'll have him investigate to see if these are really ours."

Ma took the pearls from him. "I'll do it. Because at the same time I personally want to make sure that the diary gets into his hands without being read by anyone else here."

Dirk was miffed. "But you read it."

Ma shrugged. "Well, I found it. And naturally I looked. And having looked, I now want to make sure nobody but me, and Timmons, knows what's in it."

Tressa shook her auburn curls. "What could be so awful in it that we shouldn't know about it?"

Ma said, "I ain't gonna say. Except that I may remark that there were four people involved. Betsy the diarist, and three brothers, James, Joseph, and Robert."

Dirk expelled a soft breath. "Oh."

Ma caught at Dirk with a swift searching glance. Then she added, "I don't think we want it known that this place was once the scene of a scandal. Everybody will be driving out here to have a look at it. And in the end it will reflect on all of us. It is better left untold."

Dirk's lips came down at the corners. "I can go to the courthouse in Rock Falls and look up the recording of the deed. All such records are open to the public."

Ma said, "You won't find in those records what's in this diary."

"We'll see," Dirk said. "I'll get old Jensen to help me. Maybe he'll know some old-timer around her who'll remember the facts."

"Or the gossip," Ma snapped. She held the diary to her bosom as if it were something she herself had written.

Two months later, Ma called another conference of the whole family for Sunday tea. After they were all seated around the long table in the kitchen area, and tea was poured, and each had tried a sip of the steaming brew, Ma looked at Tane and Arva and Thea with a smile.

"Well," she began, "Mr. Timmons has found out that all four people, Betsy, James, Joseph, and Robert Worthing are dead. And none of them had any issue. Nor is there any record that they had distant relatives who might still be alive or who might have issue. Mr. Timmons also conferred with Mr. Boughers, who sold Pa the section in the first place. Mr. Boughers is in the old people's home in Rock Falls. Timmons said Boughers still had a good clear mind. Timmons said he was careful not to let Boughers know why he was asking about the old sale and what it included. So Boughers never mentioned anything about a secret cache. Boughers still had some letters from this Betsy. But the letters didn't mention it either. It probably means that Betsy never told anybody the secret."

Everybody took a sip of tea.

"So the diary is ours. Timmons suggested that we send it to the Iowa Historical Society and have it sealed until some later date. Pa agrees that this is a good idea. Not, Pa?"

Pa nodded. His lips moved under his speckled moustache. "Ma also decided that I could read it." Pa looked in on himself. "Which I've now done."

Tane said, "So we can't then, huh?"

"No," Ma said.

Tane said, "Pa, what did you think of the diary?"

"Strange doings by strange people."

"Oh."

"Something I hope hain't infested our land."

Ma went on. "I also had the pearls assessed. By our local jeweler. He in turn had them evaluated by a jeweler in Sioux City. It seems the pearls are priceless. Because it was such a long string, they come to almost seven hundred dollars."

"Whew!"

Pa drummed a single finger on the table. "Get to the real point, Ma."

Ma smiled. "Yes, Tunis and I noticed an odd lump in the binding of the diary. I showed it to Timmons. Timmons get out his penknife and very carefully pried open the bottom curl of the binding and there it was. You'll never guess."

321

"Some more pearls?" Tressa wondered.

"Close. Name another jewel."

"Not a diamond?"

Ma nodded. "That's exactly what it was. A ten-carat diamond. Of a good clarity grade."

Dirk's eyes opened high blue. "I wonder what that was all about, that she should have hidden a diamond in the binding."

Ma said, "We'll never know. We had the diamond evaluated too. And that came to three thousand dollars." Ma sipped the rest of her tea. "So we have, after paying the lawyer for his time, thirty-five hundred dollars. Pa and I have decided to give both Thea and Tane a thousand dollars each as a wedding gift. That should give them both a good start in life."

Tane had trouble believing it all. He looked at Arva and then leaned over and took her hand.

Thea started to cry. "What Oliver couldn't have done with that."

Ma looked over at Pa. "You've got your checkbook handy?"

"I have." Pa drew out a black leather checkbook and pen and began writing two checks.

Ma said, "And we've also decided we should catch up with the times. Pa ordered us a new Ford at Wickett's Garage."

Rolf stared, dark hair bristling up like the flourished mane of a horse. "At last! At last we're joining the rest of civilization." It was such a funny remark for their beloved throwback to make, everybody let go with a great laugh.

Tane held out his cup for more tea. "In that case, I think Arva and me will use part of our wedding gift to buy us a new Ford too. Certainly a good second-hand one. So we can get around better."

Arva said, "After we furnish our house, Tane."

Tane nodded. "Our horse and buggy are pretty nobby, but it takes us too long to get anywhere."

36. *Dirk*

1921–1922

The Bonnie *Review* was a four-page paper, with the two inner pages boilerplate, syndicated material sent up from Sioux City. The front page and the back page were left for local news and ads.

Setting up stories and news items was slow work. It took the patience of Job to pick out the type from the cases and form them into sentences. Sometimes Dirk was tempted to dump all the cases of type onto the oiled floor. Old Man Jensen often had to remonstrate with Dirk for his hurry-scurry way of wanting to do his work. "Take it easy, bo. The day will come when you'll be able to set a string at the cases as fast as me."

Old Man Jensen mused aloud as he formed a column of type in his catchall metal holder. "Let's see now. *D* and then an *r* and then a period for Dr. *M* and then an *a* and then an *r* and then a *y* for Mary. *W* and an *a* and an *l* and a *k* and an *e* and an *r* for Walker." Finished, the paragraph read:

> Dr. Mary Walker was remonstrated for wearing trousers. She replied indignantly that she would wear them—or nothing. We hope, in her case, she will stick with the pants.

Jensen proofread it and then inserted it into the form on the stone. "There. That should liven up the front page of our rag." He threw a sidelong glance at Dirk. "If we can come up with one astonisher per issue, we'll make it." Old Jensen was referring to the matter of getting enough income out of the paper for the two of them. He knew Dirk had it in him to be a good newsman, but competition from the county newspaper in Rock Falls, which got most of the legal notices, had hurt.

Dirk liked to read the exchange papers. He also read back issues, all the way to the early 1900s, and had many a laugh at the diatribes that various editors in those days hurled at one another. He tried his hand at writing a few himself. When he was satisfied he'd caught the spirit of them, he submitted a few to Old Jensen.

Jensen read them and snorted. "You didn't aim this at anybody."

"I know. But I personally ain't mad at anybody."

"Tell you what. We won't aim them at any editor. But instead we'll take some old-fashioned potshots at people we think generally need a little bracing up."

The first one Dirk came up with made Jensen laugh:

> The ease with which prisoners escape the Hello city jail, it would be wise for the city fathers there to hustle around and sell it for a chicken coop.

When the mayor of Hello wrote an indignant letter, challenging them to print his letter intact, Jensen with a smile did print it all; and added a footnote in amelioration, saying: "We've long known that in general the Hello boys are hustlers and good mixers and will do their part in winning success for their fair city."

A couple of weeks later, Dirk came up with another stinger for their readers:

We have noticed that the prayer of every selfish man is, "Lord, forgive us our debts," while he, the selfish man, makes everybody who owes him pay to the uttermost farthing.

That little shaft drew the ire of a minister in Rock Falls, a Dr. Berthold Bloomer, who complained of their use of the word "farthing," saying it was a biblical word and that it had no place in an article condemning the banking profession.

Dirk waited a few weeks and then let the good minister have it:

Dr. Bloomer delivered a very fine discourse at the schoolhouse here last Sunday, he having come down from the great city of Rock Falls for that very purpose. The only fault to be found was that the discourse was read. No minister should deliver a sermon unless it be offhand. Most people would rather read a sermon at home by themselves than go any distance to hear someone read it.

Dirk didn't like the way some women dressed and one day he composed the following:

Notwithstanding the fact that the recent tornado near Ireton blew the feathers off the poultry, we have yet to hear of a single woman losing her false hair; the moral of which is, that chickens should use hairpins when venturing out in a tornado.

Miss Mable Molenar, owner of the local millinery, resented the squib and wrote to say that it wasn't any more silly for a woman to add a strand or two of false hair to build up a modish coiffure than it was for the London barristers to wear a wig in the British court.

Dirk wasn't finished with Dr. Bloomer, and he arranged for a friend to pick up some back bulletins in Dr. Bloomer's church. From them Dirk culled the following:

"Thursday at 5 P.M. there will be a meeting of the Little Mothers Club. All wishing to become little mothers will please meet with the minister in his study."

"This being Easter Sunday, we will ask Mrs. Brown to come forward and lay an egg on the altar."

"Wednesday, the Ladies Literary Society will meet and Mrs. Johnson will sing 'Put Me in My Little Bed' accompanied by the pastor."

"Thursday at 5 P.M. there will be an ice cream social. All ladies giving milk, please come early."

Dirk soon found other things to lampoon, and he did it as though the time was a decade ago:

NEW ROAD RULES—Upon seeing an approaching team of horses, the motorist must pull up at the side of the road and cover his machine with a horse blanket. The limit of speed on the country roads this year will be a secret and the penalty for violation will be $15.00 for every mile in excess of that secret limit. On all country roads at night the motorist must send up a red rocket every 11 minutes for the road to clear; he can then proceed carefully, blowing his horn and shooting Roman candles.

A week later Dirk let go with yet another wry dig:

Hallowe'en night passed off remarkably quiet in our pious little burg, considering that the next morning no bulls were found bellowing on top of the Farmers Co-operative Elevator, and no women were heard to scream in the night that they'd fallen into the vault after the privies had been tipped over.

The use of the word "pious" drew the ire of the local minister of the Little Church, who said in his letter that "to be pious was to be known as one who was a Chosen One of the Lord" and that if any more blasphemous remarks were to appear in the Bonnie *Review*, he, for one, was going to preach from the pulpit to tell all his parishioners to cancel their subscriptions.

Old Jensen reviewed the good reverend's letter through his spectacles and finally came up with a scorcher:

If there's anyone out there who's anxious to see a wonderful ass braying in his highest glory, he should attend a service at the local Little Church.

The little squib caused an uproar on Main street. Some of the businessmen in town were upset about the way the Little Churchers, many of them of Dutch descent, were taking over the farms in the area as well as the businesses in town. Dirk remembered that his father had often railed about the same thing. Because of their Lowlands background in Europe, the Little Churchers could make corn and oats grow in swales that the average American farmer left to the frogs and bulrushes. When the old man of such a family retired from the farm, the farm was assigned to either the oldest son or the oldest daughter and her husband. The old man, or the old lady if she was the survivor, then went out 325 and bought farms for the rest of the children, and bought them in neighboring counties. Even when the price was raised over the going rate per acre, the Little Churchers bought it anyway. "We'll just work a little harder for a couple of years to make up the difference," the Little Churchers said. "Be a little tighter with our money. And pray to God for his bountiful help." People of New England and Western Reserve descent were convinced they would soon be overrun by the pious invaders.

Other Bonnie businessmen, however, for the moment welcomed the business the Little Churchers brought to their stores. The Little Churchers paid cash, were neat in their appearance, kept their yards square and precisely cut, kept up their buildings with repair and paint.

Thus when Jensen's barb appeared in the Bonnie *Review*, the old-liners smiled in their easy chairs of an evening, but the Little Churchers went into a boil and almost in mass had their subscriptions canceled.

Both Jensen and Dirk were shocked.

But the paper survived because the county commissioners, most of them old-timers, agreed with Jensen's ideas about the Little Churchers and voted to give him more of the legal advertisements.

Dirk soon made merry with other topics. What with automobiles being relatively new to the area, some of the drivers had trouble negotiating corners in the metropolis of Bonnie.

One day there was a horrible collision at the flagpole in the center of town, where the old King's Trail crossed Main Street. An old Dutchman of West Frisian descent who'd just bought a brand-new Ford, shiny black with glistening windows, hit a black Velie driven by an old German of East Frisian descent. Marshall Colt, who didn't care much for either kind of Frisian, happened to be standing nearby in the entrance to the First National Bank. Only trouble was, he had his back turned to the accident, and so couldn't be sure who was guilty of reckless driving. He gathered up his paunch and waddled over. He inspected the wrecked portions of the two cars and then checked the condition of the drivers. Both drivers were relatively unhurt, bumped noses and bruised egos. Looking at the bent fenders and the broken glass of the headlights, Marshall Colt couldn't make out who had the right of way. Not even to the inch.

Dirk was setting up a new string at the cases when he heard the crash. He ran outside and arrived on the scene just in time to hear Marshall Colt begin his interrogation. Dirk swore to the doubting Jensen that the following was exactly what he'd heard Marshall Colt ask:

> "Now, gentlemen, what I want to know is, which of your two cars hit the other one first?"

Dirk had fun too with a story dealing with a good Bonnie citizen stealing wood from his neighbor in the dead of the night when all good citizens should've been asleep. John Hollander, strangely enough of ancient English descent, was sure that his next-door neighbor August Borden, formerly a citizen of the Netherlands, was the culprit. Hollander hated having bad feelings with a next-door neighbor, but he hated even more having his wood disappear. He had, all alone, gone down to the Big Rock River and cut down dying ash trees, had sawn them into lengths and then carted them home, had split the wood in his backyard, and then had piled the wood against the west wall of his carriage house. Finally, grim-lipped, he went down to the hardware store and bought a stick of dynamite, drilled a hole with an augur into one of the chunks, packed in the dynamite, and placed the chunk on top of the pile where the thief was most apt to steal it. Sure enough, two nights later, the dynamite blew up the stove in August Borden's house. The explosion blasted out all the kitchen windows and ripped off the back door. There was no more wood missing after that.

Dirk had the most fun reporting on a society item. It was Mrs. Lillian Hill's turn to host the local bridge club. The game of bridge was then the latest rage in the social whirl. Mrs. Hill went out of her way to serve a shrimp salad from a buffet. Shrimp was one of the very newest dishes then in vogue in Siouxland. Dirk wrote:

> Just a few minutes before the luncheon was to begin, Mrs. Hill made a quick trip out to the kitchen to make sure everything was in order. To her horror she found their cat with four feet firmly planted on the table and with its mouth going a mile a minute on the shrimp.
>
> With a gasp, Mrs. Hill snatched the cat off the table by its tail and booted poor pussy out the back door. Then Mrs. Hill went to the table and carefully picked off the top layer of shrimp and flung it out the door after the cat. Nobody would be the wiser. Only she would feel some nausea during the shrimp course.
>
> All went as planned. The ladies arrived. The ladies ate. The ladies played cards.
>
> It was just after Mrs. Hill had bid three no-trump that she smiled to herself that no one had spotted the faint nausea she was experiencing. At the same time she couldn't resist looking out of the window to see where their dratted cat might be.
>
> There on her lawn lay her cat. The way it lay sprawled out, as if it had stiffened in horrible convulsions, it surely had to be dead from poisoning.

Mrs. Hill broke out in a mortal sweat. Her stomach knotted up. They were all going to die if she didn't act fast.

There was only one thing to do. Mrs. Hill did it. She stood up. With a voice that broke on every other word, she told the dear ladies that they had just eaten poisoned shrimp. When the ladies looked at her bewildered, and full of wonder as to how she knew that, she finally told them why she was sure they'd eaten poisoned shrimp. She pointed to the dead cat outdoors.

Little bridge was played the next few minutes. Several of the ladies began to feel sick. One of them fainted dead away. In her fainted state, the woman wriggled and jerked and foamed at the mouth as though she had the fits.

At that point, the rest of the women rose from their chairs, ran out to their cars, and drove to the hospital. To Mrs. Hill fell the sad burden of carrying the fainted woman out to the car. At the hospital the ladies, holding their stomachs, crying, gasping, eyes rolling in pain, stood in line and each of them had her stomach pumped out, shrimp, cake, and tea.

Then the party, still gagging slightly from the pump tube, gamely returned to the home of the hostess and resumed the interrupted bridge game.

Conversation was at a minimum. Strained.

The front doorbell rang. Mrs. Hill rose and answered it.

At the door was her next-door neighbor Mrs. Rockwell. Mrs. Rockwell was crying, and sighing, and her face was full of apology.

"What seems to be the trouble?" Mrs. Hill asked, wondering if her neighbor had picked up one of the poisoned shrimp thrown out after the cat.

"It's taken me two hours to get up the nerve to come here," Mrs. Rockwell said, "but I must tell you that I ran over your cat with my car. In your driveway."

One morning Dirk looked up from where he was writing a news item in longhand before going to the cases with it, when he saw out through the showcase window his father driving up in his new shining black Ford. In the front seat with Pa was Tressa. Pa had hold of the steering wheel as though he were holding down the horns of a bull. His pearl eyes were bulged out, as were his neck muscles. Rolf most generally did the driving for the family, but sometimes Pa felt he should go to town to run the family errands—Rolf was too valuable a hand on the farm to be let off work. Pa'd had trouble learning to operate the tricky shifting of the new car and often had difficulty stopping in time. He sometimes overshot the mark a few yards. It was true again that morning. His thin front wheels bumped against the high curb, then mounted the curb and rolled onto the new concrete sidewalk.

Dirk went outside. "Well, Pa, I see you almost managed to pull up all your horses in time this morning."

Pa grunted as both he and Tressa stepped out of the car. "Henry Ford deliberately made that clutch a mess so we poor souls would have a lot of accidents."

Dirk looked at Tressa, a quip ready on his tongue, until he saw her face. She'd been crying. "Hey, what's louse with you?"

Tressa had put on a new town dress, a blue checked gingham that came halfway down her calves, and new stockings and new blue shoes. She carried a blue purse. "Can you take off a few minutes?"

"You bet."

"Can we go to the Corner Cafe?"

"Sure." Dirk glanced at Pa. "You going to join us?"

"No." Pa glanced toward the First National Bank. "I'm gonna share a little chin music with Chauncey." Pa threw Tressa a heavy glance, reset his old frazzled straw hat on his head, then set off toward the bank. Pa walked with his usual stong muscular stride. Dirk had to laugh about Pa's straw hat. New and shiny in April, in a few short months, having suffered salty sweat, sudden thunderstorms, hot winds, and been used occasionally to whack a cow over the butt, Pa's straw hat resembled a wookpecker's nest.

Dirk took Tressa's arm as they started to walk down toward the Corner Cafe. The street was empty, no cars or buggies, nobody out walking. Dirk held the cafe door open for her and followed her inside. The smells of morning cooking were still in the air, bacon and eggs and coffee and toast and American fries. He led her to the far corner table, an old-fashioned glass-and-wire affair with wire chairs. After he helped her to her seat, he took a chair across the table from her with his back to the door.

Dale Hodges, proprietor, had a coin smile for them. "What'll it be this morning for you and your lady?"

"How about a dish of ice cream? Okay, Tress?"

"Anything is all right with me."

"Coming up." Hodges was a slim dandy, with slicked-back blond hair, dime gray eyes, quick cardshark fingers. There was a rumor in town that he and his buddy Aaron Phipps had robbed Old Shoester, Wilhelm Terpen, and then had beaten him up to within an inch of his life.

Well into their ice creams, Dirk finally said, "Well, are you going to tell me?"

A tear fell into Tressa's vanilla ice cream. She continued to take little spoonfuls and presently lipped up the tear.

Dirk's belly began to feel tight. Lips closed, he sucked on his tongue. Tressa was about to tell him something he wasn't going to like.

Tressa got out her handkerchief and dried her cheeks. "I came to town because I thought I'd better be the first to tell you I'm getting married."

Dirk dropped his spoon. It clattered on the glass-topped table and fell to the floor. When he reached down for the spoon he could feel his face whiten. It was like her words had skinned his face.

"We're getting married in August. At home. We thought it would be nice to have an outdoor wedding near those lilac bushes Ma loves so."

"Good God, I didn't know you were dating anybody. Who's the fellow?"

"Wallie Starnes."

"Him! That pious prick from the Little Church?"

"Wallie loves me."

"Ha." Dirk's blood boiled. He felt such a jealousy he wanted to strangle Tressa. "When did this all take place? Because I never saw you out with anybody. And I get around in this old burg."

"Now that we've got a car I've been going to church Sundays with Rolf at the Little Church."

"Yeh?"

"Ana's been going too."

"Ana was born without a womb."

"That's not a nice thing to say about your sister."

"Well, no one's ever going to date her. Or whisper sweet nothings in her ear. That'd be water thrown at a goose."

"Anyway, Dirk, Sunday nights we three went to catachism. Pretty soon Wallie Starnes got up enough nerve to ask if he couldn't drive me home."

"Yeh, him and that overdecorated Chevie of his. Red steering wheel. It's a wonder he hasn't strung some red celluloid rings from the dashboard to the radiator cap."

"Be careful what you say. He's going to be your brother-in-law."

"Him with that honker of a nose."

"Dirk."

Dirk shivered. Live without Tressa? "Now what am I supposed to do? You know I love you."

"That was back then when we were little children and we didn't know no better."

"So that's how you've settled that in your mind."

"Well, we were just little children then. When what we did didn't really mean all that much."

"You mean, what children do doesn't count?"

"Well, yes."

Dirk leaned toward her. His eyes yearned into hers. "You know that you and I love each other more than ever."

Tressa faced up to him. "Not any more. I love Wallie."

"Bullshit. Or, I should say, cowshit."

"Don't make it any harder for me, Dirk. Let me go."

"In the meantime, like I said before, what must I do, gnaw off my balls?"

"Not so loud. Dale Hodges can hear us."

"So what? He won't dare say anything. He knows I'm still investigating what happened to Old Shoester."

"You'll come to my wedding of course."

"Guess again."

"If you don't, then Ma will sure know something."

"I think she already guesses."

"I don't think so, Dirk. She trusts me."

"You hope." Dirk pushed his dish of ice cream to one side, unfinished. He felt a vomit coming on. "By God, I guess I'm gonna have to marry my right hand after all."

"Dirk, don't say such awful things."

"Wallie Starnes." Dirk sneered. "Isn't he the son of that principal of the Christian School in Amen? That beef bladder stuffed with rotten eggs?"

"What a mean tongue you have." Tressa finished her ice cream and pushed her dish to one side.

Dirk grimaced until his ears hurt. "You're going to live the life of a martyr with that Wallie fellow, mark my words."

"What makes you think that?"

"Old Man Starnes runs that school like a tyrant. No mercy. With his big belly hanging out, he still whips kids. And his son is bound to follow in his father's footsteps."

"Well, anyway, Dirk, I'm still going to marry Wallie Starnes. And I felt that you should be the first to know. At least you have that from me."

"Thanks a lot."

Tressa got to her feet. "I better go. I have to look for goods to make my wedding dress and veil."

"I suppose you're gonna wear white."

"What color do you recommend?"

"At least the red-winged blackbird is honest."

329

"Dirk!"

"I one day saw one of those birds where the red on its wings looked exactly like the letter *I*."

Tressa stared at him. Slowly she turned white. Then she slapped him across the mouth.

Dirk remained sitting. He clapped his hands over his ears.

37. Tressa

1922–1923

Dirk showed up for the wedding after all. He hadn't dared to stay away.

The choice of the day, a Saturday in early June, turned out to be perfect. The night before it had been chilly and so the day remained cool. The sun hung an hour high over the line of river trees. It shone warm on all the faces and enriched the grass with finite shadows. The purple and white lilacs were in full bloom. Perfume drifted off them like heat waves. The luscious aroma made everybody happy, even giddy. Promises were made all over the lawn to be friends forever.

Tressa the bride had a wide and sisterly smile for everyone. Wallie Starnes beamed, his thin-lipped smile forming a crescent moon under his pelican nose.

Right after the last vow was made, the bride and her parents, and the groom and his parents, and the Reverend Young from the Little Church with his stiff leg, formed a receiving line on the grass. Neighbors came by to shake hands, congratulating the bride and groom and laughing with the parents of both. Several families from the Little Church came along too.

Wallie's father, potbelly Principal Starnes, strutted in the midst of his family like he was the only big burgher in the area. He had even more of a honker of a nose than Wallie, and wiggled it back and forth importantly, all the while smiling cock-a-hoop. Beside him stood his skinny wife, nervous, legs clapped tight together. Wallie was the oldest of the Starnes children. After him came six sisters, with faces as flat as white saucers and noses as big as saltshakers, and at the far end of the family were three more boys, their blond hair slicked back with tallow into a swallowtail point. Like their mother, all the Starnes children stood in the shadow of their father as quiet as quail chicks.

The Freylings stood in a bunch too, bride and groom, Pa and Ma, Tane and wife Arva, Thea, Dirk, Rolf, Ana, Mallie, and Geoffrey. Oliver Tice was by now far too ill to travel at all.

Tressa was pleased to see how jolly her family was as compared to the Starnes family. The Freylings joshed around like they might be sitting on the stoop of a hot summer evening.

Tressa had worried a little that Dirk might show up sarcastic and drunk. There'd been a rumor the past week that he'd visited the home of rumrunner Manly. But Dirk had driven onto the yard in his car, a second-hand Chevie, with his old superior smile and intimate wink of the old days, dressed in a black suit, black bow tie, white shirt, and black patent-leather shoes. Even during the wedding service Dirk smiled as though no one could have been happier for his sister.

Refreshments were served on card tables set up on the long wide concrete stoop. Soon everybody was sipping coffee. Not to waste a crumb they nibbled at their slices of cake from the side. Talk became as heady as the lilac perfume.

Wallie's black car, glinting with polish, the nickel over the radiator gleaming like a bar of silver, was ready to go. Someone had taken chalk and written over the side of the front door: JUST MARRIED. From the rear tire trailed a daisy chain.

Wallie touched Tressa's elbow. "Ready to go?"

"Just a minute. I want to see Dirk a second."

"Can't it wait?"

"No." Tressa smiled up at Wallie. She tried not to look at Wallie's nose, remembering what Dirk has said about it. She was sure that in time she'd get used to it.

Tressa wove her way through the crowd, finally found Dirk telling a story to Tane and Rolf about rumrunner Manly. She heard Dirk say that the reason Manly hadn't got caught in a chase in Minnesota was that he'd put a supercharged racing motor in the chassis of his old Buick.

Dirk caught sight of her. "Well, sis, ready for your honeymoon?"

Tressa took him by the arm and led him to one side. "Thank you for coming, Dirk."

"I wouldn't have missed it for the world."

"It was still very nice of you."

"Then you did wonder if I might not show up with my nose."

Tressa pinched his arm. "Please, no stingers."

"Sorry."

"We'll remain friends?"

"Forever."

"I mean as brother and sister."

"Of course."

"And you'll keep putting out the paper, Dirk?"

"Maybe."

"Dirk! You're not thinking of leaving?"

"Funny thing is, I am."

"Where will you go?"

"Oh, I've got a hen on a nest."

"Please don't leave because of what I'm doing."

"I'm not." Dirk gave her a twisted smile. "Did you and Wallie buy that Triggs house after all?"

"We did. Ma gave us our thousand dollars too."

"Huh. And what did Mister Bulge Belly give his son for a wedding present?"

Tressa winced. "Wallie thinks we can make do. He just finished barber school in Sioux Falls. And I hope the first of the year or so to clerk in Rexroth's store."

"Barber, eh? Bonnie can use another barber. The one we got, old Ellingwood Kay, talks your ear off about all the girls he missed hosing. And his haircuts lately make you look like a plucked chicken."

"Oh, Dirk, you always exaggerate so."

"Me? I'm a hard-nosed newshawk. Only the facts."

Tressa laughed. "Someday you'll find a wife you'll deserve. Who'll understand your stingers."

"Me get married? Neh. I think I'll go it alone."

"Patience, Dirk. There'll be someone for you someday."

Dirk shook his head. "By the time I find her, she'll have to understand that I'll be making a right hand out of her."

"Oh, Dirk, what a mean thing to say. She might be a princess. A queen even."

Dirk's nose came up in a sneer. "I don't believe in miracles any more."

Tressa pinched his arm gently. "Anyway, please don't take a drink."

"Yeh. You don't know how lucky you are. I almost came to your wedding stone-blind drunk on a bottle of linseed oil."

"When you say you have a hen on a nest, what do you mean?"

"I have a play afoot."

"You're still talking riddles."

"You'll find out soon enough."

Wallie came stomping over. Now that he was married he'd suddenly taken on the strutting airs of his important father. "C'mon, Tress."

Tressa woke up to what was wanted of her. "Ready whenever you are."

Wallie gave Dirk a hard look. "Good thing you're just her brother or I'd be jealous."

Tressa quick took Wallie's arm, before Dirk could mouth a quip. "I still have to throw the bridal wreath away."

It was soon done. And as luck would have it, Ana caught the wreath. And caught it reluctantly. When she saw it was going to sail to earth, she quick grabbed it up. To let a bridal wreath fall to earth meant bad luck for the bride who threw it.

Ana looked at the wreath in her hands; and then, face pinching up into wrinkles of distaste, she quick handed it to Mallie. "Here, this is more for you. Let's just say it bounced off me into your hands."

Mallie took it with a laugh. "Thanks. I don't know if I'm the next to get married in our family, but someday maybe."

Wallie led Tressa to his fancy black Chevy. He opened the door for her on the passenger side, helped her in, and closed the door with an emphatic slam.

Geoffrey came running out of the house with a little sack in hand. He began throwing rice at Tressa and Wallie. "Many happy returns," he cried.

"Here, gimme some of that," Rolf said. He cupped his hands to let Geoffrey pour in some of the white grains. Then he too flung rice after the couple.

Wallie stepped on the starter. The engine fired on the first revolution. He honked the horn, tilted up his big nose, and they were off, dust and gravel sprettling up from the rear wheels, spraying the lawn where Rolf and Geoffrey stood.

"Bye. And good luck."

"Bye."

At first their honeymoon in the Black Hills was lovely, much better than Tressa had expected. Wallie was bossy, but he was kind. The first night he didn't bother her, just held her close all night, and in the morning he let her sleep while he made breakfast. The second night he touched her but did not make her his own. The same for the third night.

The fourth night was to be their last night. Tressa hoped that Wallie was thinking of saving the best for last. By the fourth night Tressa was ready and welling with desire. To her great surprise, that last night, instead of holding her in his arms as a beginning, he plopped his pillow upright against the head of the bed, and sitting high, announced he had something to say about their married life.

"Yes, my husband?"

"You know how I believe in Christ?"

"Yes, my husband."

"And in the Biblical injunction to be fruitful and multiply?"

"Yes, my husband."

"How with that injunction goes another Christian law?"

Tressa waited, wondering what in the world he had in mind.

"That there shall be no sex unless we have children in mind when we couple."

Tressa's head slowly came up off the pillow. "What?"

"Since I don't think it's a good idea to have a baby before the year is up, until June next year, we shouldn't couple during our honeymoon."

"But, husband, what after all is a honeymoon for but a time to make love."

"No! It's a sin if we do it not intending to have children."

"Ohh."

"So. All we're going to do is hold each other warmly in Christian love, cuddling and kissing, but no more. That way nobody can point the finger at us that we did it before we got married."

"Oh."

"I hope this is all right with you."

Tressa sat up then too. "Well, I'm surprised! Especially after the way you courted me! Hot breath. Hands everywhere on me like an octopus in Lover's Lane. Panting and gasping. I respected you nevertheless for holding back always at the last minute. But this! I never expected this from you."

"I could neck you hot and heavy so long as we weren't married because I knew you'd stop me, being the noble girl you are. But now that we're married, and we're alone in this bed here, far from home and church, the temptation is almost too much. Nobody to watch us. So we have to watch ourselves all the more. And I pray God that he may give you even more strength to resist temptation. We must not have flesh fun for fun's sake."

Tressa continued to have trouble believing what she was hearing. After the thrilling flush of love she'd once had with Dirk, when they were children, was she now going to have an old man's tormentive kind of love with an overly pious groom? It was enough to make even Mother Mary laugh out loud exasperated.

"What do you say to that, wife?"

Tressa couldn't resist a Dirk stinger. "In the eyes of God, there is no marriage until after it is consummated. So I'm still not your wife."

That stumped Wallie Starnes.

A little laugh escaped Tressa. "If I told this to Dirk, he'd laugh his head off."

Wallie cleared his throat. "Maybe he'd be glad."

"I don't understand."

"That his sister hadn't been violated yet."

"Then in your eyes the act of love is a violation?"

"Isn't it to you if it isn't done with children in mind?"

"No. I think it is a gift of God to enjoy as we decide."

Wallie shook his head, so vigorously the bed shook. "Ho! Have you got a lot to learn yet about being a partner in Christ with me."

Tressa groaned. "You're all wet about that." Then she laughed softly to herself. The truth was she was all wet expecting love. Aloud she said, "The girls in your church told me you were a good catch. And that they were real jealous."

"Who?"

"That'd be telling."

Wallie Starnes sniffed to himself, still sitting up in a tight bundle at the head of the bed.

To herself Tressa whispered, "Please, God, this is not happening to me. Please, God, don't let this be true."

Wallie finally spoke up. "I suppose you're mad at me now."

Tressa whispered some more to herself. "That's what I get for being impatient about getting married. Almost thirty years old and worrying I was going to wind up an old maid. So that I went out to trap Wallie. Making a tender trap of myself. Oh, how I wish now I'd led him on when he was hot to have me in Lover's Lane."

"Aren't you?"

"No, Wallie. Not mad. Just a little sad."

"Hmpf. The way some people's kids are brought up."

"Your father and mother, with all those children, do you think they always waited to do it until they thought it was time to make another baby?"

Wallie seized her by the shoulders and shook her, so violently her head snapped back and forth like a rag doll in the mouth of an angry dog. "Don't you talk like that about my father and mother!"

"Wallie," she whimpered, hurt.

"My father and mother are noble Christians! They don't do a thing but what they don't first pray to the Lord for guidance. You hear? You hear?"

"Please, you're hurting me, Wallie, your own wife."

He let her go. "Oh." He was still so taken with wrath he shook as though he had a bad case of the chills. "Just leave my parents out of it. I love them very much. They're great Christians. None better."

"Then you can leave my brother Dirk out of it too."

"Hmpf."

She lay in silence. Her neck hurt.

He sat crouched up, sullen.

Slowly she turned away from him, nestled her head in her pillow, and rolled her under shoulder back and forth until she found a comfortable spot in the bed.

Wallie slowly simmered down. He sniffed several times through his big nose. "Well," he said finally, "I suppose we should try to sleep. But first, I've got to take this up with my Lord. I've sinned in getting angry with you. And I must ask for His forgiveness."

Tressa thought: "And not ask me for mine?"

"Prayer helps me an awful lot when I lose my temper. Christ always helps me handle it." Wallie slid out of the sheets and kneeled beside their honeymoon bed. He folded his hands and in the dark presented his face to the heavens. "Father in heaven, look down upon this thy humble servant kneeling here in this strange place, about to go to sleep in innocence with his chosen bride. Forgive him for having touched this bride in wrath. I am sorry. I am asking her for

335

her forgiveness too with this prayer as well as asking for Thy forgiveness. Be with us in the night to come. Keep us from evil. Bless our hearts together. May we live in peace and love all our lives. In Jesus' name we ask it, Amen."

Tressa felt torn inside. She wanted to believe in Wallie's God but she wasn't sure she wanted to live in the peace and love he wanted for all their lives.

Wallie crept into bed, drew up the sheets to his chin, nuzzled his head down on his pillow, and let out a huge sigh of satisfaction. He had done his duty as a God-fearing husband.

Tressa rolled over on her back. She stared up at the log ceiling in the dark. After a while she whispered, more to herself than to her husband, "I wonder why we ever came here in the first place on what's supposed to be a honeymoon."

"Why, Tressa," Wallie said, "to get acquainted with each other while we're far away from our families. Get a chance to know each other."

"I'm not sure I wanted to know what I've just learned."

"Pray, Tressa, pray and it'll be given to you. I'm sure the Lord will do this for you. Otherwise I wouldn't have chosen you for a wife."

"Hehht!" Tressa almost spat on the bed covers, she was suddenly so out of patience with what she'd done—marry the pious clod lying beside her. If Dirk knew what was happening . . . Godd.

The next morning Tressa persuaded Wallie they should end the charade of a honeymoon. "We both better get back to our jobs. Especially since we still have to pay off the mortgage on the old Trigg house."

336

It wasn't long before Wallie began to have a lot of customers in his barbershop. He not only gave good haircuts, he did them fast. All the males in town began to have a better-groomed look about them. Even men from other towns drove in to get haircuts. Often they took their wives along, and those wives went shopping while the old man was in the Starnes Barbershop. Main Street decided Wallie was a welcome addition to the business community.

Some two months after their honeymoon Tressa happened to walk past the windows of the Bonnie *Review*. She hadn't seen Dirk once since the wedding and she quite naturally looked to see if he were in sight, busy getting out the paper. Instead of Dirk she saw a stranger standing at the cases, fingers nimbly selecting different letters.

Wondering if Dirk might be ill, she stopped and entered the printshop. She saw Old Jensen busy at the stone, making up a form. "Mr. Jensen?"

"Yes?" Jensen lifted his chin, tightening up the pink wattles under it.

"Where's my brother Dirk?"

"Haven't you heard? I thought you knew."

"Heard what?"

"Why, that he's left us. He resigned to take a job with the *Eastside Argus* in Minneapolis."

Tressa could feel her face blanch. "Why, he never told me he was thinking of going there."

Jensen stared at her over his glasses.

Tressa mused to herself. "He did say something about having a hen on a nest somewhere."

"That's where the nest is."

"Thanks." Tressa left. Back on the sidewalk, she found herself short of breath. Dirk gone?

She walked down to the corner, crossed the street, stopped to have a drink of cool water at the town fountain near Highmire's Hardware. Dirk in Minneapolis? That huge place? Where all kinds of strange women lived?

Her belly hurt. Her best heart person gone forever. Her husband a prude in bed. There was nothing to live for. Just work, work, both in the house and at Rexroth's store. Pay off the mortgage. Pile up money at the First National Bank. Go to church twice on Sunday and listen to sermons that had nothing to do with her life.

Usually before she began work for the day in Rexroth's, she'd walk one door down to wave at Wallie cutting hair in his shop. She still liked Wallie and hoped he'd change; she meant to do her duty as a good wife by being cheerful for him each day. But that day, after hearing that Dirk was gone, she couldn't smile at him. Sadly she entered the front door of Rexroth's and trailed slowly down an aisle toward the back where the help hung their coats and put on the store smock for the day.

Rexroth appeared suddenly at her side. He blinked brown eyes at her from behind glinting spectacles. His heavy arms were folded over his portly body. He held his square head sideways at her. "Somebody's dauber is down today," he said, trying to be cheerful. "We won't catch any fish with you looking like that."

Tressa couldn't resist making a sassy remark. "I didn't know women had daubers."

"Maybe I meant dobbers then," Rexroth said, still smiling warm and friendly.

Tressa tried to smile back, and put on her store smock.

337

A month went by. Looking at the calendar one Wednesday morning, Tressa noted that it was exactly three months to the day since she'd gotten married. She wondered if Wallie remembered the date.

That same evening everybody came to town to do their midweek shopping. The winter goods had come in and mothers had to find school clothes for their children.

When Tressa came home at ten she saw that Wallie had made a quick supper for himself and then had gone back to his barbershop, leaving the kitchen a mess. Tressa first cleaned up the sink and the counters, then had herself a cup of tea and a cheese sandwich.

What a life. She was so sick of Wallie's endless talk about his great father that she had to fight off an impulse to vomit. Every night just before he went to sleep Wallie had to tell her yet another story about his pa. Sometimes it sounded like Wallie really believed the sun could not rise or set without Pa's permission. Principal Starnes was more of a watchdog over the Amen Little Church congregation than even its minister.

Once a barren couple in the Amen church by the name of Mr. and Mrs. Benjamin James decided to adopt a baby. They went to an orphanage in Sioux City and picked out a smiling little fellow about a year old. Mrs. James chose him mostly because he had such cute ears. The ears stuck out a little and gave the otherwise round face of the little fellow the look of a friendly imp.

When the couple went to the Amen church consistory to get permission to have the child baptized, they ran into opposition from Principal Starnes. He'd appeared specially to object. Did they know if the orphan was born "a covenant child," possibly from the womb of an erring though "covenant mother"? Benjamin James said he didn't know and Mrs. James said she didn't want to know.

"What? We can't let a noncovenant child into our midst. It would be like deliberately putting a rotten apple in a barrel of perfectly good apples."

"I don't care," Mrs. James said. "The little tyke has such cute ears and I'm going to keep him. We've waited so long, too long, for a baby, and I'm not going to give him up now. Besides, I love him already."

"But the smell of sin is about him," Principal Starnes protested.

Benjamin James pitched in for his wife. He smiled. "Aw, maybe all you're smelling in his pantsful."

"Nevertheless," Principal Starnes said.

Finally the consistory voted on it. The tally was: six elders and six deacons in favor of accepting the child into the church.

Principal Starnes went around for a week exclaiming to all and sundry: "Those monkey ears got that kid into the covenant!"

Tressa, sound asleep, was awakened by Wallie clearing his throat sharply. In the dim light of the night lamp she made out that he'd undressed and was standing naked at the end of the bed looking down at her. The look on his face made her sit up with a snap. "Wallie? Couldn't you find your nightshirt?"

His face was thick with it. "Tonight's the night."

"I don't get you."

"Remember?" Even his nose seemed larger and longer. "We got married three months ago today."

"I know. I thought of it myself this morning."

"Nine months from now when we have our baby nobody can point the finger at us." His member was standing straight up, red, almost reaching up to his belly button.

"My God, Wallie, what are you up to?"

He strode around to her side of the bed, threw back the covers, grabbed hold of the hem of her white nightgown and jerked that up over her head, and then dropped down on her. He was panting. There was a rutting whinny in his throat, a sound she'd once heard when she'd seen cats mating.

"Wallie!" she shrieked.

With his knee he pried open her legs. Then, with his sharp nose poking into her neck, he outraged her. It was over in a moment. Six quick ripping thrusts and then a vast groan and he was done. He draped limply over her.

She gathered up her strength and in utter disgust threw him over on his side of the bed. "You beast you. Ulk! You're no better than a darned bull."

He lay still, breath slowly returning to normal.

Tressa got out of bed and ran to the kitchen. They still didn't have an inside bathroom like banker Chauncey had, so she had to make do with a pan and some warm water from the reservoir in the stove. She scrubbed her private parts. She didn't have a water bottle with a douche syringe or she would have used that. She didn't want a baby to come out of what had just happened to her.

When she went back on bare feet and slid into bed again, Wallie turned his beak toward her. "Thanks, dear wife."

"Thanks? My God. For what?"

He was soon asleep. Little mezzo-soprano snores began tootling out of his high triangular beak.

The next day, around noon when she went home for lunch, she began to look in a warmer light at what had happened in bed the night before. It had hurt, yes, but perhaps that one taste of her might have awakened him enough to ask for more. The next time she would hold him back a little, until she was ripe for it. She wanted to have some fun out of it too.

Sure enough that night after he mowed the lawn and she'd already gone to bed, he came in, undressed, and stark naked came around to her side of the bed and threw back the sheet.

She was ready for him just as he let himself drop, and dodged to his side of the bed. She fought him off. He said nothing. Just rut-ratched that strange wild gutteral cry as he tried to divide her with his knee. When at last she found herself enjoying the wrestling, even groaning in pleasure a little, she let him in. Eight thrusts and he was done. It was a little better.

But she was still furious with him. "I thought you said that you only believed in coupling to produce young, not to enjoy it."

"I do."

"Then how come two nights in a row?"

"To make sure. There's about five days there where I've got to make sure to catch you. So I've got to fill you with seed those five days."

She shivered. Counting the days back she saw that he'd picked the exact middle of her twenty-eight days. The damned schemer. That big noodle of his had some guile in it after all. She also remembered how his semen had run down her leg that morning. At first she'd thought it was her period.

The fifth night she fought him off long enough, put up such a battle, that Wallie almost forgot what he'd had in mind, and his ardor had fallen a little. And once he was inside her it took longer, at least a couple dozen thrusts.

Two weeks later, waking from sleep, she was pleased to find something trickling down her inner thigh. She got up and went to the kitchen. Yes. Her period had come. All that grunting and rutting and wrestling had been for nothing. At least so far as she was concerned. Maybe he had enjoyed it but mostly she had not.

Two weeks later, again late on a Wednesday night, she was awakened by that strange whinnying sound at the foot of their bed. And there he stood, red-faced, rampant; ready, as Arva with a laugh had once put it, to jump her bones. With a huge sigh, resigned, Tressa threw back the sheet for him and drew her nightgown over her head. She at least wanted a baby out of the marriage. Maybe in having children life might not be so bad with Wallie after all.

Her acquiescence startled him. It took away some of his power. He strained and grunted and tried and finally managed to couple with her. It lasted long enough so that she actually found a mite of pleasure in it. Again there were those five days of servicing her.

She never did conceive. A whole year of the monthly servicing went by. No pregnancy.

Finally the act palled on him. "Trouble with you is, you're no good."

"How do you figure that?"

"Well, you didn't take."

"Maybe it takes more patience. And real love."

"My father tells me that he only had to make one connection and Mother was with child."

She flared out at him. "Did you talk to your father about what we do in the privacy of our bedroom?"

He blushed. "Yes, I did." He threw up a stubby arm. "Well, I had to talk to someone."

"Maybe your father that one time was the better lover."

Wallie became angry and stomped out of the house.

After that Wallie's prayers at family table worship became fervent, even frothy at times.

Later that summer, partly in rebellion, partly because she wanted to be in style, Tressa had her hair bobbed. She'd seen a picture of what bobbed hair looked like in the Sioux City *Journal*. Mallie wielded the scissors.

Wallie Starnes was shocked. But he said nothing.

38. *Rolf*

1924–1925

When Rolf hit the age of thirty in October, he suddenly took an interest in girls. He watched pairs of girls parading up and down Main Street on Saturday nights, wondering which one might be a good one to take out. He watched the girls after catechism on Sunday nights as they marched from their church to Main Street and back, wondering which one might say yes to his offer to take them home. No one girl seemed quite right; at least not one Ma or his sisters would approve of.

Late in November, when the corn was out and the hard work for the year was over, on a Saturday, he happened to be driving three miles east of home, going to a farm sale to see if there was a good boar to be had. Pa hadn't been too happy with the one they'd put in with the sows. Pa thought they had a dead-pecker boar and if they didn't hurry up and replace him they'd have no crop of little pigs in the spring.

A grass fire in a roadside ditch caught his eye. When he saw that a brisk wind was spreading it toward the acre on which stood a white wooden country schoolhouse, he stepped on the gas. Even small grass fires could be dangerous. Just as he pulled up he spotted, through the ragged flames and shooting smoke, the figure of a young woman trying to fight the fire. With one hand she was holding her gray skirt tight to her knees and with the other hand she was flailing at the creeping line of flames with a wet sack. Every time she whacked down at the earth, some of the fire was smudged out, but the line on either side of her kept searing slowly but surely toward the wooden steps of the schoolhouse.

Rolf jumped out of his old Ford and scrambled down through the ditch and then, with a high leap over the swirling smoke and flames, landed beside her. "Here! Gimme that." He took the sack from her. "You go get some more water."

Startled, her light blue eyes squinched together against the stinking smoke. "Who—?"

"Get some more water!"

She stared at his straight-up hair and big lips, blinked twice, then ran to pick up a pail standing nearby and hurry to the school pump. She pumped vigorously, slim body lashing up and down. Pail full, she came slopping back with it.

Rolf dunked the smoking burlap sack in the pail, deep, thoroughly until it was sloshing wet, then went after the moving line of flames, flailing, slapping, whacking. It didn't take him long to douse the line of fire to the west. Bounding back, he again dunked the sack in the pail, then went after the line of fire off to the east, once again slamming the wet sack onto the moving searing edge of flames. Finished, he turned, only to find that there were still several little live sparks left along the black line, with here and there even a tiny flame. With his heavy-soled shoes he stomped them all out.

"There!" he said. "I guess we got 'em all."

She let out a great sigh. "Yes, thank God." She brushed back her blond hair. She too like Tressa had bobbed her hair. Leaning forward, it'd slide down over her eyes. "I don't know what I'd have done if you hadn't come along."

"You'd have lost your schoolhouse," he said.

"Yes, I guess I would've."

He looked at the smudge of soot on her cheeks. "You all right?"

"I think so."

He looked around at the wide black patch of burnt grass. "How did it start?"

She couldn't help but look at his bristle hair. "I saw a man toss his cigar out of his car as he went by. I just then happened to look up from my desk."

He smiled down at her. "I see. Catching up on your paperwork on a Saturday."

"Yes."

"Good thing then you did work today."

"It surely was." She couldn't keep her eyes off his strange face. "I didn't catch your name."

"I'm Rolf Freyling. And you?"

"I'm Greta Browne."

"Well, Greta, glad to meetcha."

She smiled funny at him.

"What church do you go to?"

"Presbyterian."

"Hum. Bonnie don't have such a church."

"I know. I belong to the one in Rock Falls. And since I don't have a car, I don't go very often."

"Oh. You're religious though?"

"I like to think so."

"How about me picking you up Sunday mornings and taking you to church?"

She had to laugh. "Really! You don't waste time." Her laugh was nervous. She was almost silly with it. She kept staring at his roach of wild dark hair. "Would you really drive me to church?"

"Sure. I don't often see a woman like you. My mother would think you okay. So would my sisters."

"Well, I don't know them but thanks anyway."

"You ain't heard of the Freylings? We live just three miles west of here. On that old Worthing section. The Bonnie Railroad cuts through one corner of it."

"I'm a stranger around here."

"Where do you live? So I'll know where to pick you up tomorrow morning."

"Already tomorrow?"

"Well, might as well start tomorrow as any other Sunday."

"Whew!" She brushed back her blond hair again. "Are you Freylings all that fast?"

"Only Dirk is. And I'm not really fast. Though I know you gotta pound that iron when it's finally red hot."

She looked him up and down. "I'll think about it."

"I'll be there tomorrow morning with bells on. Just tell me where you live."

A sigh seized her chest and lifted it. "Very well, if you must. I live over there." She pointed to a farmyard up on the rise to the east. The house was hidden by a thick grove of willows and cottonwoods.

"Thanks. You'll be seeing me."

When Rolf drove over to pick her up the next morning, he found her waiting for him on the front porch. On high heels she came down off the steps and down a concrete walk. In her green dress she swished through the white house-yard gate. He held the car door open for her on the passenger side. He took her gently by the elbow and helped her in. Then he went around and got under the wheel.

"All set?" he asked.

She looked just past his big nose as though she didn't want to embarrass him by staring directly at his strange face. "All set."

Everything went off swell. He was the perfect gentleman. She was pleased with the way he listened attentively to the entire sermon. "Before you can approach the throne of God and expect help, you must . . . and I repeat it . . . you must confess all your sins, and you must have them all forgiven, before He will deign to help you."

On the way home Greta asked, "What did you think of the sermon?"

"There was one word I didn't catch. What's 'deign' mean?"

"It means to condescend. To unbend and be kind to the lowly."

Rolf kept his eye on the road. Occasional dust wisped up behind the rear window of the old Ford. "You went to college then. 'Course I might've guessed that. Being you're a teacher."

"I did. Our church has a college in Missouri. Both my sister Fannie and I went there."

"She older? Or younger?"

"Older."

"She teaching too?"

"No. She likes housework better. She took a job as housekeeper for a retired farmer in Rock Falls."

"You gotta be careful with them old coots."

She laughed, bending forward, nose almost touching her knees. "You surely have a humorous way of talking."

"I have? Hum." He aimed his Ford past an oncoming car. They whisked through the cloud of following dust. "I just say what comes to my mind. If you want humor, real humor, you should listen to my brother Dirk. Now he's real funny."

"Where did you go to college?"

"I didn't. But I read a lot. Farm journals. Books on agriculture. So on."

"Well, that's at least something."

"No, I just went through the eighth grade. And then I took up farming with my dad. Some of us Freylings went to college and some of us stayed home. It takes a lot of hands to run a whole section." Rolf smiled large-lipped. "I'm really not smart enough to sit on my ass and make a living."

Her blue eyes opened. They took on the green reflecting up from her dress.

"But I figure, college or no, one man is as good as another, and equally better. I know enough not to carry guts to a bear."

A laugh blipped out of her before she could catch herself. "I'm sure you do. And you also know how to fight grass fires."

"Thanks." He took a left at the Lakewood Corner and headed east toward her boarding place. "Though truth to tell, after we got that fire doused, I sure felt like taking a header in the crik. I'll stink of that weedy smoke for a week."

"So will I." She kept looking just past the end of his nose. "What do you have in mind doing some day?"

"Me? Hum. I guess farm. Though I don't plan on staying on the old place forever. Someday Pa's gonna retire and I suppose Tane and Arva will take over the old homestead. Tane is the oldest in our family. And I sure as heck ain't gonna work for my brother either." The old Ford rattled over a little wooden creek bridge. "No, I plan on getting married someday and owning my own farm. And maybe I might go after making my first million."

"You mean, be a financier of some sort? How will you do that as a farmer?"

"There are ways. Play the futures on the grain market. And buy up land where the taxes are past due and unpaid." He saw her eyes narrow in admiration at the way he talked so importantly. "With the help of ringing dollars, if you're in the right place at the right time, you can turn over whole empires." He pursed his lips up into hard tubers. "Nothing makes me smile more than when I hear some city highbinder squeal like a stuck pig—after one of us peasants sticks it to him."

"Turn here," she said.

"Oh, yeh." He'd almost overshot her lane. "Sorry."

"That's all right. I sometimes forget where I am too."

He took her to church through November and December.

On New Year's Eve a party was held at Old Will Haber's, where Fannie worked. Some of Old Will's seventy-year-old cronies were there and some of Fannie's friends. It was an odd mix. The old gents and their wives laughed at jokes that meant little or nothing to Fannie and her peers and Fannie and her gang laughed at jokes that sailed over the heads of Old Will and his bunch.

Rolf sturdily refused to drink wine like the rest did. Instead he drank a lot of coffee. It wasn't long before he had to visit the toilet. Old Will had one of those modern wonders, a bathroom installed inside the house. While admiring the white enamel fixtures and thinking to himself that when he got his farm he was sure going to have one built in his house for the queen, Rolf was startled to hear Greta say outside the bathroom door: "I know he looks like a Neanderthal. With that sloping forehead, and that wild horsetail hair, and those thick lips, and the way he walks with a slight humpneck. But he's so gentle. Oh, so very gentle."

"Yes," Fannie said, "all you have to do is look at his hands to know that. I just love those long fingers of his."

"Then you approve of him?"

"Oh, yes. After all, beggars can't be choosers. With those false teeth of yours."

"I know." Greta sighed. "Every time my date learns I have false teeth because I once had pyorrhea of the gums, he doesn't call on me again."

Rolf stiffened. Greta had false teeth? He hadn't noticed. Well. That meant they both had a defect.

Fannie said, "You're lucky. I'm still looking for my permanent one. With me it's my body odor that sends them running."

Greta said, "We poor Browne women."

"Meanwhile, don't let him get away."

"I won't. You should see the skin on his body. As soft and as smooth as a baby's. Strange that that should go with those heavy brows of his."

"When the lights are out, just feel his skin and forget the rest."

Greta giggled. "That's just what I'm gonna do." She sighed again. "I've sometimes wondered what sort of children we might have."

"Is it that far along with you two then?"

"Oh, we haven't done it yet. We're saving that for our wedding night."

Fannie said, "I wonder who's in the bathroom, taking so long? They must be sick or something in there."

"Yes, I wonder too."

"Can you hold it a minute longer? Because I better see if my cheese sandwiches are toasted proper in the oven. Come help me."

"I guess I can. Otherwise I'll just go outside and sit in the grass out back."

The two sisters laughed, and then their voices faded into the general commotoin of the party.

Rolf buttoned up. So Greta was thinking of marriage already. Well. He hadn't even dared hope she'd say yes to a proposal. Rolf gathered up his heavy shoulders to think. By gummy. Tonight on the way home he'd pop the question to her. He went over to the mirror. He got out his hair brush and pulled it harshly through his stiff bristly hair again and again, hoping to make it look like a descent pompadour. But the more he brushed it back, the more his hair resembled the bristles of a mad boar. As he brushed his hair, he also worked at thinning his lips, as though he might be thinking of something important. But the more he thinned his lips, the more he resembled a Ubangi. Finally he gave up and folded up the hairbrush and dropped it into a side pocket of his blue jacket. He straightened his red tie, snugging it up neat and tight into the collar of his white linen shirt. So she was already thinking of the night when they would do it, their wedding night. Well, so was he. He thought: "This coming year the bird is going to be mine. I'll be able to crow over my hen like Tane does over his Arva."

345

Later, on the way home with Greta at two in the morning, Rolf abruptly turned off the King's Trail highway and drove up an old rutted road leading to the river. Rolf knew that very few people used that country road, only fisherman and farmers. No one would think of looking for them there that late at night.

"Where are we going?" Greta asked. She sounded both scared and excited.

"You'll see."

"Shouldn't we be getting home? It's awfully late."

He drove until the road petered out into a wall of elderberry bushes. He backed the car around until it faced out, then shut off the motor. "I have something I wanna say to you."

She smiled silly at her hands in her lap. "With the motor off it's going to get cold in here if we sit here very long."

"By that time I'll have had my say." Very gently he lay a hand over her fumbling hands. "Greta, I'll open the ball by sayin' I want to marry you."

"Ohh."

"How old are you, Greta?"

"I'm thirty-one."

"I thought maybe you'd be twenty-nine."

"Thank you. But I'm thirty-one. Does that bother you?"

"Not at all. That makes us even."

"How so?"

"Well, you bein' one year older than me makes up for this throwback face of mine. Which reminds me. What's a Neanderthal?"

"Oh, Rolf. Then it was you in the bathroom."

"Yeh. What's a Neanderthal?"

"They were a gentle people who lived on earth before our kind of people did. They were a little humpbacked but they actually had bigger brains."

"Oh." Rolf rolled that over on his tongue. "Well, I long ago got used to looking at myself in the mirror. Suppose I had got mad about the way I looked? What could I have done about it? Nothing. I'm Rolf and that's it."

"Then you also heard I have false teeth."

"Yeh. But thank God you didn't die from pyorrhea."

Greta withdrew her hands from under his hand and lifted them to his face. "Rolf, I really don't mind how you look. What's important is what kind of man you are."

"Thank you. You see, I also knew I was smarter'n most men. Even as a farmer I am. Just stick with me, gal, and you'll sit in silk underwear for the rest of your life."

"Oh, Rolf, you're such a card, the way you talk."

Rolf looked at her soberly. "Now, I don't mean to get rich dishonest."

"I know that, Rolf."

"I'm not so money crazy that I'd kiss a dog's ass for a nickel."

A snort exploded out of Greta's nose. "You're a strange one, the way you talk. When you say such things . . . it's funny, but when you say such things it sounds all right. So open and honest."

"I'm high to get all that's coming to me in an honest way because I think that's the best way to go."

She kissed him on the cheek. It was a dry kiss.

Rolf took her face in his hands, deftly, and slowly planted a kiss on her lips. He kissed down, hard, until he felt something give way inside her mouth. Her false teeth. Then gently, so very sweetly, he gave her a light kiss on her chin.

Impulsively she hugged him. "Oh, Rolf, sometimes I'm so afraid of you just when I like you the most."

"We'll do all right, don't worry. I've already got my eye on a piece of land where the very pasture grass drips butter."

"Where's that?"

"Right here where we're sitting." With his head he gestured to the north of the car. "They're gonna hold a sheriff's sale here next week and I'm gonna bid on it. I've already talked to Pa and Ma about my inheritance, like the one Tane and Arva got, and I think I can swing it. Course, I'll have to let the bank in on it with me, but Chauncey ain't gonna be that bad of a partner."

"Oh, Rolf, are you sure it's a good piece of land?"

"I already walked over it. Most of it is bottomland, kind of wet. But with some drainage tiles I think I can make it pay."

"Where did you ever learn about that?"

"From that farm journal I take. And from those Hollanders in Sioux Center. They know all about lowlands in their old country. It'll be the clear deal."

"What will you do for machinery and horses and cows?"

"Buy them on time."

"But that's such a big gamble."

"No, not if I raise hogs it won't be. Raising hogs is gonna be the coming thing. And I have good luck with hogs, as Pa will tell you. That's because I understand them. And they understand me." He drew her up close in a warm manner. "You see, it all has to do with keeping it clean around them. Hogs are cleaner than human beings if you give them a chanct. Why, even rats are clean if you give them a chanct. Cleaner than hogs. So take your choices."

Greta laughed right out loud. "You know, if I was told when I was going to college that someday I'd be sitting in a car near some bushes along a river with a farm boy talking about hogs and rats . . . I would have said whoever told me that, that they were crazy. Yet here I am. And liking it."

He chucked her up close in a good hug.

"Rolf, maybe I better tell you I got some money saved up."

"How much?"

"Two thousand dollars."

He turned that through his mind. "Naw, we ain't gonna touch that buying this farm. You better keep that in the bank to earn interest. For emergencies. I'll make us enough for both of us."

"You're a sweet man, Rolf."

"Hum. Well, I suppose it's time to take you home. Before we get into trouble."

"Yes, I guess it is, Rolf. I hope they haven't locked the door."

The next evening, after everybody had retired for the day, Rolf headed for the privy with a lantern. He found the dried bit of tar plugging the small knothole he'd once spotted. He got out his jackknife and very carefully pried out the pearl he'd long ago hidden in the knothole. He rubbed the pea-sized pearl until it shone in the lantern light. It still picked up light like it might be a milky window. Again it began to feel warm in his hand.

Two days later he drove to town and had the jeweler set the pearl in a gold ring. And a week later he slipped the ring on Greta's left ring finger.

They were married in February in the Presbyterian church in Rock Falls. Everybody except Dirk attended the wedding. Rolf's sisters were especially moved that their strange Rolf had really pulled it off, found himself a wife. And a wife who was educated! They were crying and smiling all through the ceremony, as well as afterward at the reception in the basement of the church. Ma too was crying, at the same time that she occasionally fell silent thinking her own secret thoughts. Ma had borne the darkmoon boy and so would know things about him the rest of the family would never understand. Pa sat biting the ends of his salt-and-pepper moustache. Meanwhile the boys joked about first-night rights, which automatically gave Tane first chance, with Geoffrey last. No one mentioned Dirk, not even Tressa. In their eyes he was lost to the big cities.

Ana's reaction to the wedding was more than a little curious. She was alternately affectionate with and hostile to Greta. From her sometimes silly and sometimes snippish remarks it could be made out that she'd always hoped that Rolf, like her, would remain single, have no interest in the opposite sex. On the one hand she told Greta she hoped they'd have many children; on the other she said there was nothing so satisfying as bringing the message of Christ Jesus to the heathen Oglala Sioux in the western Dakotas, which she hoped to do someday.

Like the other Freyling children ahead of him, Rolf took Greta on a honeymoon to the Black Hills. Even in the winter it was the thing to do.

Rolf turned out to be a courteous lover. He saw the tight look around Greta's eyes as they undressed for bed, he on one side slipping into his nightshirt and she on the other side into her nightgown. He let her slide into bed and pull the quilts up to her chin, and then said, "You know, wife, I got me an idea."

"Yes?"

"Why don't we agree that the first night we won't do it. But just take it easy. Turn out the light and talk in the dark. There's nothing like talking in the dark with someone you like. My brothers and I always did it, and sometimes we had the most wonderful talks. You see, you can't see the other fellow's face, nor he yours, so you only listen to the voice, and because neither one can see the other, that voice is gonna talk true. But we can lay here close together, touching each other all night. Then after tonight, we can take our chances."

Tears swelled up in the corners of her eyes. "Oh, what a thoughtful husband. Yes, yes, let's just cuddle tonight." She lifted her arms to draw him into bed.

Even the second night they went to bed as though they might be chaste brother and sister. It was toward morning that they both woke up at the same time. She'd kept pushing her seat into his lap, spoon within spoon, and it was then that they'd finally consummated their marriage. She'd felt a lump in his lap and reached around to see what it was. His fist? She let out a little yelp when she felt what it really was. She jerked back her hand. Until then she'd had absolutely no idea what a man's private parts might look like. For all she knew a man was always hanging down, like the cross of Calvary. After a while her hand drifted back to the lump. She had to know more. Soon she turned over to face him. And then was ready for him.

39. *Ana*

1926

Ana dumbfounded the consistory of the Little Church in Bonnie. She'd again attended one of their meetings to say she wanted to join their church. She'd been baptized an Episcopalian, a baptism they were willing to accept, but they still weren't sure what to make of her statement that she didn't need to make a confession of her sins. She'd always been a child of God. She was already saved.

It was evening, and dark outside, and the single light bulb hanging over the long table illuminated fourteen faces: Reverend Tiller at the head, six elders down the right side, six deacons down the left side, and Ana at the foot near the door.

Reverend Tiller was a good man, stocky, with a head of brown hair just barely tinged with gray, full pink lips, and light blue eyes. "But Miss Freyling, we are all prone to sin, you know, no matter who we are. So how can you say that you have no confession to make because you're already saved. Being examined for membership in our church is a very serious business."

"I know it is, Reverend. But my heart has always been the Lord's. I don't have to confess that I ever doubted Him. I have been His night and day. Both in my open prayers and in my secret thoughts."

"Are you saying that you've never sinned?"

"Not that I'm aware of." Ana had dressed carefully for the examination, wearing a long green dress that came down well over her knees. She wore her long blond hair in a Grecian knot on top of her head. She hated lipstick and rouge and mascara, preferring instead to wash her face in cold rainwater. Sometimes she used a small scrub brush on her cheeks.

"Never?" Reverend Tiller challenged, eyes turning a chilly gray.

"No."

"Would your brothers and sisters agree to that?"

"My sisters have sometimes called me a liar tattletale."

"And why was that?"

"I sometimes told on the others because I thought it was my duty to point out sin."

"Why liar tattletale? Being a tattletale as a little girl is one thing. But a liar tattletale?"

"They said I made up things about them that weren't true."

"Were they right?"

"No. They'd sometimes forget that they'd done something bad."

"And you wouldn't have forgotten if you'd done something bad?"

"Reverend, I have a very strong conscience."

349

"Mm. I see."

Elder Highmire sat at Reverend Tiller's immediate right. He was the most powerful lay member of the church. Some had even called him a tyrant. He had a brush of shock-white hair, with brows so thick they had to be barbered. "What sort of sins did you catch your brothers and sisters at?"

Ana sat straighter. She hadn't thought that she'd be asked to confess her family's sins. "Oh, little things."

"Like what?"

"Oh, they'd sometimes reach across the meat plate for the biggest steak."

"And?"

"Oh, the boys would sometimes break wind when we all sat around visiting on the stoop."

"And?"

"Oh, sometimes cut corners in their work."

Reverend Tiller broke in. "Nothing more serious?"

"Well, sometimes Dirk would play favorites with Tressa."

"So you were jealous."

Jealous? Ana could feel herself becoming angry. "Reverend, are you trying to make me feel sinful, so that I'll have something to confess after all?"

"No, no. We examine all candidates for membership in our church very carefully. We do this so that later on, once you are a member, you will likewise examine your conscience just before you partake of the Lord's Supper."

Ana tried to keep her lips from thinning. "Reverend, may I say something?"

"Of course. Go ahead."

"Reverend, I can truthfully say that all my life I've considered myself truly a woman of God. I don't need to change my mind to leave sin behind."

Deacon Abt spoke up from across the table on Reverend Tiller's left. He too had a lot of hair, graying. "I see that you are a very pretty thing and that in the eyes of a young man you might be highly desirable."

Ana waited, eyes wide. She almost knew word for word what was coming next.

"Have you ever noticed a young man lusting after you?"

"I don't look for that so I don't see it."

"I see. What about the Ten Commandments . . . before you came here this evening, did you go over them carefully to see which one of them you might have broken?"

"Yes."

"You've always honored your father and mother?"

"Oh, yes."

"You've never coveted a neighbor's son?"

"Never."

"Or your neighbor's husband?"

"Dear God, no!" Ana thought of what she'd found in that spare room at the Hettie and Clate Bartles place. She had to work at not shuddering over that awful memory.

"And the seventh commandment, thou shalt not commit adultery, you've examined yourself in connection with that?"

"Sir, that would be the last thing I'd think of."

"We all know you Freylings are a little slow getting married. But you, you haven't considered marriage at all?"

Reverend Tiller held up a hand. "Now, now, that's enough in that line."

Ana said, "It's all right, Reverend. Mother has often said we probably all have latebloomer blood in us."

Every man around the long pine table was smoking a cigar, and slowly the room began to fill with smoke. Ana could just barely make out the dark brown wainscoting around the lower half of the room and the lighter tan wallpaper above it. The tobacco smoke of many meetings had stained everything darker in the room. The strong odor of an oily sweeping compound as well as the smell of peppermints lingered in the place. And laced through it all was that man smell she'd come to loathe. She'd just barely learned to tolerate the yeasty smell of her brothers, but that same smell from other men always made her lips thin into a tight line under her nose.

A smile softened Reverend Tiller's ruddy face. "Ana, how old are you?"

"Twenty-nine. I'll be thirty in November."

"And when did you graduate from college?"

"When I was twenty-two."

"What have you been doing the last seven years?"

"I've been in mission work. With the Mexican beet workers in Minnesota. With the Navajo in New Mexico."

"The Navajo? Then you're acquainted with our mission in Rehoboth?"

"Yes. It was in part the influence of your missionary there that convinced me I should try again to join your church."

"Oh? Who was that?"

"Reverend Flens Greydanus."

"Oh, yes. He has preached here to raise funds for that worthy mission."

"That's what he told me."

351

Reverend Tiller looked at the burning end of his cigar, flicked off an inch of gray ash into a tray, lipped the wet end of the cigar, and took a deep puff. He blew out a perfect smoke ring. He mused upon the rising expanding ring. "Your mother had you baptized in the Episcopalian church. Why aren't you inclined to join your own church?"

"I don't care for all their folderol. Colored windows. Vestments and endless rituals. Their sermons are much too short to bring out the full range of God's truth of a thing."

"You don't like their *Book of Common Prayer?*"

"Not really."

"Hm. I found it quite poetic, and I've often wished our church had religious writers of like quality."

Ana said quietly, "Well, I don't read poetry much."

The heavy elder sitting immdiately at Ana's left had a question. He raised his left hand. An Old Country ring gleamed on a finger. His strong voice seemed to come more from his belly than from under his long brown moustache. "You've really never thought of marriage then?"

"No."

"Your sister Tressa has and she seems to be content."

"Content! Ha."

"Don't you consider yourself a normal woman then?"

"Of course I do."

Reverend Tiller raised a hand. "Uhh, that line of questioning, John . . ." Reverend Tiller paused. He smiled at Ana. "I don't know if you know the distinguished elder on your left there, but that's John Engleking. Also sometimes known as Big John."

"I know of the Englekings," Ana said evenly. There were Englekings everywhere around Bonnie.

Reverend Tiller looked at Big John Engleking again. "What did you have in mind with those questions?"

"Well," Big John grumped, "I just wanted to know if she was regular. Like most normal girls."

Ana seethed inside. She almost spat at Big John Engleking. "That's none of your business. That's purely a private matter for a lady." Ana knew that her lack of regularity was odd. She had often thought she wasn't normal because her periods came so infrequently. She skipped sometimes as much as nine months.

Reverend Tiller whacked the old pine table with the flat of his left hand. "Miss Freyling is right." He glanced up and down the length of the table. "More questions anyone?"

Elder Highmore had one more. "Do you know of anything at all you should tell us? Consult your conscience carefully now. Anything at all that has bothered you?"

Ana thought again of Hettie and Clate Bartles. Should she tell them about those dead bodies of just-born infants she'd discovered in that west room in the Bartles home? The Bartles weren't members of the Little Church so there was little the consistory could do about it. It was more a matter for the sheriff. Perhaps she had sinned in not telling the law. Though if the babies were born dead it really was the Bartleses' own business. It was a sticky question.

"Ana?"

352

Ana thinned her lips even more. "No."

"Good."

Big John Engleking directed a pair of glittering blue eyes at her. "Suppose we deny your request to join our church, and suppose the church, even after we've accepted you, decides not to employ you as one of our missionaries—what will you do then?"

Ana wiggled on her hard chair. "Much as I don't care for the idolatry of the Roman Catholic church, I might take instruction from them and then join that church."

"Rather than your mother's Episcopalian church?"

"Yes. Because then I'll give up being a missionary and instead become a nun."

"If you did become a missionary for our church, would you go where our synod sent you?"

"Yes. Though I hope they'd agree to send me to the Oglala Sioux Indian."

"Why them, for godsakes?"

"I met some Sioux Indians in Minneapolis, and what I learned about them made me feel bad about what the white people did to them."

"Why not let them become Americans, like the rest of us?"

Ana shook her head. "It isn't that simple."

"Not?"

"No. They were here first. They worked out their religion with this land, and now we're asking them to give up their land and their religion both."

"But isn't our religion the one true religion? And if that's so, then don't they gotta change?"

"What I want to do is to show them that their name for God, Wakantanka, is like our name for God, Jehovah. It's the same God. Their language is different from ours so their name for God is bound to be different. Once I've convinced them of that, I next want to show them that they lack a true Savior. There is already a hint in their religion that they are on the way to understanding that. They hold a yearly sundance, where certain men undergo piercing—thrusting a little stick through either side of the muscles on their chest—then tie themselves with long leather thongs to a sundance pole and dance all day long facing the sun while leaning away from the pole—until they pull out the little sticks. Or faint away. So instead of one man being pierced through the hands and hung on a cross for all mankind, they have it that each generation and each man in that generation undergoes a piercing and a suffering while hanging from a pole."

"Oh," Elder Engleking grunted.

Reverend Tiller cocked his head to one side. His ruddy face had turned grave in thought. "That's a very original approach, Miss Freyling. I don't think anyone in our church has quite thought of it that way." He drummed his fingers on the pine table. "You are aware though, aren't you, that our church does not have a mission for the Indians in the Dakotas?"

"Yes. That's why I thought your church would be interested in having me establish such a mission amongst the Sioux. Why have one for the Indian in faraway New Mexico when you can have one for the Indian next door in the Dakotas?"

Elder Engleking growled, "If you was a man thinking of setting up such a mission, maybe we might think of it. But you, a woman? Hardly."

"Why not?"

"Well, those Indian men would never listen to you. Worse yet, they'd think our religion was a religion for women, not for men. How are you going to get around that?"

Ana made a show of teeth as she gritted them tight together. "They'll soon learn that I can be as brave as any man of theirs. Also I learned from my Indian friends in the Twin Cities that they have societies for manly-hearted women. In the old days they let such women lead them in their hunts and their wars. And sit in their councils. Wakantanka had specifically chosen these women as leaders. Like Joan of Arc. Like Jael of biblical times."

Reverend Tiller's blue eyes opened very wide. "You really have looked into all this, haven't you?"

"Yes. And I have prayed often for guidance in this matter."

"What will you do—and we must ask this again—if, after we agree you can join our church, the church decides not to establish a mission to the Oglala?"

"Pray to God that they may change their mind."

"But if they don't?"

"Go where the synod asks me to go."

Silence.

Ana asked, "Hasn't my sister Tressa shown that she can be a good member of the Little Church?"

Reverend Tiller again tapped the end of his cigar on the edge of the ashtray. An inch-long piece of gray ash fell off. "Gentlemen, I think we've heard enough. Miss Freyling, if you'll step outside a moment, I think we're ready to vote on it."

Ten minutes later, Elder Engleking opened the outside door of the church and called to Ana where she was waiting under the trees out front. He was smiling. "Could you come in now?"

Heart beating hard—she could feel her breasts shake—Ana let herself be ushered into the consistory room.

Reverend Tiller was also smiling. "Have a chair, Miss Freyling."

"Can I stand to hear your decision?"

"You may." Reverend Tiller waited until heavy John Engleking had seated himself. Old Engleking had a way of sitting down that was peculiar to his great girth. His hand reached down between his thighs to find a corner of the chair and then he let down his hams. When his chair quit creaking, Reverend Tiller went on. "We have decided unanimously that you can join our church. Can you make it next Sunday?"

Ana quelled an impulse to jump up and down. "Yes."

"Good. Congratulations. And now you can go, as we have other church matters to consider."

"Thank you very much. And with God's help, and your prayers, I shall not disappoint you."

"With God's help."

Ana dreamed out through the wide church doors. When she reached the bottom step outside, she suddenly did leap up in joy. Once. She'd finally found what she truly wanted to do. Life was truly miraculous after all. Her tongue became stuck to the roof of her mouth.

On the way home, driving up the old King's Trail, Ana spotted a light in the Bartles house.

She let up on the footfeed. Leaning over the steering wheel, she whispered to herself, "You know, I really ought to look in on those people. Pa and Ma never talk about them anymore. Maybe there was a proper explanation for those dead babies up in that west room. Maybe they weren't Clate's babies after all, but some other man's."

She turned into the Bartles lane.

She walked up the path, through the gate, and then up the stoop to the kitchen. She knocked.

The light in the living room moved into the kitchen, and then the door opened. It was Hettie, a small brass kerosene lamp illuminating her face from the side. Hettie had aged into a handsome person, more male than female. Her hair now really was as white as the white tail of a gray horse, her brows white wisps over glittering blue eyes. "Well! Ana! How nice to see you."

Ana smiled. "It's been a long time."

"Yes, hasn't it." There was a numinous air about Hettie. "Come in. Clate will be happy to see you."

Entering the tiny living room, Ana spotted Clate sitting on the low window seat. Clate had a wide smile for her. He held out a hand and Ana went over and shook it.

"Sit down, sit down," Hettie said, drawing up a chair for Ana.

Smiling tightly, Ana settled down. Part of her wanted to reach out and hug poor crippled Clate, while another part of her picked both Clate and Hettie apart, remembering what they'd done. Clate too had aged but in his case he had aged into ugliness. His already huge torso had ballooned out grotesquely. He looked like a pink hot-water bottle bloated out with too much water, in his cheeks, the bags under his eyes, the wattles under his chin. Even his fingers were fat and swollen.

"How have you been, Ana?" Clate asked.

"Fine."

"I thought maybe you'd be married by now."

"No. Not me. I'm not the marrying kind, I guess."

"So good-looking."

"Well, the Lord likes to have good-looking people working for his cause too, you know. Can't have only the ugly ones working as his missionaries."

Hettie said, "Is that what you want to be?"

"Yes. There are more than enough people having families and raising crops."

"Curious. That's what we've come to think too."

Ana instantly seized on the meaning of that remark. Perhaps they did abort those little babies after all.

Hettie mused on. The unholy look in the circles of her eyes opened even more. "Remember the last time you helped out here, when I had that miscarriage? That's when we came to the same decision. We were broken-hearted that once again I'd lost a child. Oh, how we wanted a child as a blessing in our old age. But it wasn't to be."

"Ahh . . ." Ana swallowed hard. She made up her mind she was now old enough to ask tough questions. She no longer had to shut up in the presence of her elders. "Ahh . . . I've always wanted to ask you . . . did you have a lover to father all those babies?"

Hettie and Clate stared at Ana; then finally both looked down. Hettie said in a low voice, "All those babies . . . then you looked in that room upstairs?"

Ana swallowed noisily. "I have to say, yes, I did. I had no right to look in that room . . . but I just had to know."

Hettie said, "I was pretty sure you did. But Clate said, Naw, Ana wouldn't do a thing like that."

Ana said, "It was wrong of me."

Hettie said shortly, "Well, in answer to your question, yes, I did have a lover of course. But who he was, that shall forever remain a secret."

"From Clate too?"

Hettie spoke even more slowly. "Well, from Clate I have no secrets. What I meant was, no one outside this house will ever find out from me."

Ana thought: "She still hasn't answered my question." After more thought, Ana decided to let the matter rest. It still really was none of her business. Let bygones be bygones. It had all happened such a long time ago. Ana asked, "You two have never found Christ, have you?"

"No."

"How can you be happy without Him?"

Clate shrugged. The shrug gave his shoulders an odd rolling action, as if it were more water put into motion than fatty tissue. "Het and I have been content with our lot. What we had in the past was like the first fruits of June. What we have now is like the husks of October."

"You have regrets then?"

"No. Not one."

Hettie nodded in agreement.

"Well," Ana said, getting to her feet, "I thought I'd just stop by and say hello. I come by here so often and never call on you, and I thought tonight for once I'm going to do it."

"I'm glad you did."

"Goodnight."

"'Night."

As her headlights picked out the rest of the way home, Ana murmured to herself, "One never knows, does one."

40. *Mallie*

1926–1927

When Mallie learned there was a position open as physical therapist at the Siouxland Hospital in Sioux Falls, she immediaely drove over and applied. To her great delight she was hired the same day.

Mallie rented an apartment on Summit Avenue some ten blocks from work. She had the lower floor, with the landlady living on the top floor. The landlady, an old widow named Ella Grey, said the reason she lived upstairs even with her bad legs was that she couldn't stand having people making noises on a floor above her. Ella Grey turned out to be an indulgent woman. She never complained about the modern records Mallie sometimes played. She liked music. Mallie's bedroom windows opened on some lilac bushes. The kitchen and the dining area had a half-dozen windows with white curtains. There was an airy quality about the apartment. Mallie looked forward to many happy days in her new situation.

She had some trouble at first with the doctors at the Siouxland Hospital. It was mostly due to a misunderstanding as to what it meant to be a registered nurse in physical therapy. Old-line doctors tended to think of it as a "laying on of the hands" nonsense, a form of sybaritic massage. Mallie had to explain that a massage under medical supervision dilated the various capillary beds, both superficial and deep, and determined the redistribution of blood in many parts of the body. A gradual increase in the exercise of an atrophied muscle could restore that muscle. What finally convinced the medical staff were the results. Mallie seemed to know what she was doing.

Mallie soon became aware of a young doctor named Gary Lyman. Gary was a lanky fellow, thin biceps, long feet, brooding brown eyes, and a diffident manner. Most everyone on the staff considered him a brilliant diagnostician. But he didn't socialize much and there was considerable speculation as to why he hadn't married. He took a lot of walks in his spare time. He had a curious way of taking short steps so that while he looked like he was streaking along he actually wasn't covering much ground. When the weather was warm and pleasant he got on his bicycle and pedaled far out into the country.

It happened that Mallie noticed she was picking up weight so she bought herself a bicycle too. She also took long rides out in the country. One evening in June she caught up with Dr. Gary Lyman on a lonely road north of Sioux Falls along the Big Sioux River. He'd run into some spilled roofing nails and had a flat tire.

Mallie pulled up and stood on one foot, with her other leg still over the frame of the bike. "Tough luck, I see."

Gary looked up, brown eyes frowning. "Yeh. Some carpenter must have dumped out the back end of his pickup here. Look at all those rusty nails."

"I wouldn't have seen them either. They're the same color as the gravel."

"Yeh." He began to look through his leather bicycle kit. "Shoot. I don't have any rubber patches. You wouldn't have some with you there in your kit?"

"Let's have a look." Already she'd begun to think that this accidental meeting could be the beginning of something interesting. She liked diffident men who took short steps. Men who came on strong and horsey disturbed her. "Ah. Here we are. A half dozen patches. Help yourself."

"Good."

Mallie watched Gary as he removed the tire and took out the inner tube and dressed the tube. What lovely long hands he had. So sure-fingered. No wonder some of the staff thought he'd also make a fine surgeon, something he'd rejected out of hand. He wasn't savage enough, he said, to cut people up and run the operating room like a dictator.

"Can I help you?" Mallie asked.

He smiled. "No, thanks. For once it looks as though I can manage." He glanced briefly at her. "My older brother thinks I'm helpless around machines." He finished putting a red rubber patch on the gray tube. "There." He pushed the inner tube into the casing and then fitted both around the rim of the wheel again. "Now to pump her up." He glanced in apology at Mallie. "No pun intended."

She laughed. "No pun noticed."

The sun began to sink into the trees on the far side of the Big Sioux. It cast slanting saffron light across the pasture grasses.

"Well," he said, tire pumped up hard enough, "all set to roll again." He looked west at the sun. "I suppose we better head back into town before it gets dark."

"I suppose so."

Together they turned around and headed south. They pedaled up the incline onto Summit Avenue. They coursed together through the reaching shadows of the houses.

They came to her house first. She pulled up.

Mallie said, "How about some lemonade?"

Gary said, "No, I think I'll just head on home. I took some files on my patients home with me. Kind of puzzled me when I looked at them today, so I thought I'd brood on them a bit before I went to bed."

"Lemonade will clear your head."

He laughed at her, lips turned down at the corners.

She remembered that he'd been the only one of the young doctors to agree with the old-line doctors that physical therapy was a medical frill. "Or better yet, maybe I should demonstrate one of my better massages."

"I'm not much for touching, I'm sorry to say."

"Well, it's your neck, not mine." She gave him her most winning triplelips smile.

His brooding sensitive brown eyes settled on her lips. "Oh, well, what the heck, why not?" He rolled his bike up the walk with her. They kicked out the stand on their bikes and sat them on the porch. She held the door open for him.

What happened then surprised her. After she'd served them each a tall glass of lemonade, ice cubes clinking, with a chocolate-studded cookie, sitting across from each other by the picture window, he began to look at her with thickened eyes. He took a sip of his drink, nibbled off a bit of the cookie, then said, "Sit on my lap."

"Oh," she said. Maybe he wasn't so diffident after all. She set her glass and cookie to one side, and slowly and gracefully went over and settled on his lap.

He set down his drink and cookie too.

Soon he whispered, "What wonderful lips you have."

"You smell so good," she whispered back.

In a moment he was drawing her down on the floor. "Mallie, Mallie."

"Hey, just a minute." She was still a virgin and wasn't sure she wanted to part with her virtue just then. "Boy, are you a fast worker."

"I'm sorry." A little-boy look shaped his red lips into an abashed pout. "It's been so long."

"It's all right."

He got up off the floor awkwardly. He couldn't look at her. "Maybe I better go."

"Finish your lemonade and cookie first." Then she added, with a short laugh to make him feel at ease, "I know I'm not going to eat your cookie." She patted her stomach. "Have to watch that spare tire, you know." She got to her feet too.

He glanced briefly at her waist. "Oh, you don't have any trouble with that, do you? All the exercising you do with your patients?"

"I have a farm girl's appetite."

"Well," he said, "I'll go now. Thanks for the refreshment."

"You're welcome."

It took a month of carefully graded smiles before he spoke to her again in the hallway of the hospital.

He asked, "Been bicycling lately?"

"Every evening."

"Well, I've been too busy."

"How about tonight?" she said.

"Oh . . ."

"You like squash? I was home to our farm last weekend and got me some."

"I love squash. It's good for what ails men."

"Good. Why don't you come by with your bike and then I'll put the squash in the oven and when we come back we'll have it."

Once again, after they'd eaten, he abruptly asked her to sit on his lap; and then, after a few moments, lifted her down to the floor. Since it had taken a while to get him into her house again she decided to let him have his will with her. She thought she was a little in love with him.

Far back in the cave of her mind she wondered how Gary would fit in with her family, especially the men, Pa and the boys. Gary was like most of them. Pa was like a commander. Also Pa had eight children so he knew what to do around a woman. Tane was earthy. Dirk was a lover boy, very witty and self-assured. Rolf was the Old Adam of the tribe. And Geoffrey, sweet bright Geoff, was the epitome of an educated Siouxlander—well mannered and an ardent ladies' man. Well, perhaps it was best, healthy, for her to like a man different from the men in her family.

"You have wonderful lips," he whispered.

"I love your long fingers."

"Kissy."

She laughed thickly. "That's what my brothers used to call me when I was little."

His hands moved under her dress. She reached for him to let him know she wanted to touch him at the same time. Her motion seemed to cool his ardor. His arms relaxed around her. His lump softened; almost disappeared. Finally he got to his knees and stood up. "I better go. Thanks for the wonderful squash."

Mallie reached up a hand from where she lay on the floor, thighs exposed. "Don't go yet." Here she was ready and willing and wet; and he was pulling this fade-out on her again? "Please?"

He murmured something; couldn't look at her.

"What's wrong? What did I do wrong?"

"Maybe it's wrong for members of the same staff to know each other this way."

"Are you nuts? That's our business."

"I better go."

She got to her feet. With an emphatic jerk she drew her dress down tight over her hips. She couldn't resist shifting blame onto him. "Is there something the matter with you?"

"Me? Of course not. No!"

"To use a crude term, are you a queer?"

He let out a cry; then rushed outdoors.

Through the window she watched him mount his bike and pedal off furiously.

"Too bad, too bad," she whispered. "He had such wonderful long fingers. And long feet."

360

After that when she saw him in the hospital hallway she made a point of ignoring him. Dressed in her white starched uniform she made herself appear cold.

For the next several months she went bicycling alone. Sometimes she talked to herself. "He called me Kissy. I'm gonna miss that. In my mind it tied him to my brothers."

That November, her assistant, Tracy Tidwell, had some hot gossip for her. Tracy had the build of a fullback, with smoldering blue eyes and very thick lips, and with the hint of a moustache under her nose. "Dr. Lyman got married over the weekend."

Mallie looked up slowly from the clipboard she held. "Oh?"

"Yes. Eldon Clarke says it was to a real hot pussy."

"Eldon would know." Eldon Clarke was a male nurse on their floor with a reputation for being a skirt chaser. "Funny, I saw Gary this morning. They didn't go on a honeymoon then."

"They plan to go on one in January. I guess he couldn't wait to get married until then."

"Well, good luck to him." What a surprise that woman was going to have. Mallie felt hurt. So she wasn't juicy enough to harden him to the game of love.

Tracy spotted the regret in Mallie's manner. "You're lucky. He wasn't your kind anyway."

"Thanks."

"Why don't you make a play for Eldon Clarke?"

"Well, he has been eyeing me up."

"You could do worse. I'd make a play for him myself, but he's told me he don't like girls with moustaches."

"Oh, come on now. That's easily fixed these days. Go visit a dermatologist. They're good at depilation."

"Somehow the idea of using sulfide to remove hair doesn't appeal to me. Probably leave a big red welt under my nose."

A couple weeks later Mallie did give Eldon Clarke her smile. Two days later she had him over for a herring dinner.

Eldon was bald on top but the rest of him was almost as hairy as a chimpanzee. Somehow the baldness and the black hairy arms went with the way he spelled his name, Clarke with an *e*.

After Mallie had the table set and the food steaming in the center of it, Eldon helped her into her chair, all gallantly done. He touched her hair. "You're so lovely," he said, "Rusty gold curls. And those hazel eyes, they're sexy enough to wake up the pope."

She laughed, looking down.

"I mean that, Mallie. The ends of your curls, the way they frizz up . . . well, they help me see you naked."

"Hey, I like that."

"It's true, though. They do."

They'd barely finished eating and were having a glass of wine when he set his tapered glass to one side and got to his feet and then pulled her to her feet. "Let's go to bed. I want to be nice to you."

"Wow," she said, "you don't fuss around, do you?"

"Isn't that why you invited me over? All nurses like it."

"I didn't invite you over. You invited yourself."

"After you smiled at me."

Slowly she pushed him away. "Can't we finish our wine first?"

"No." He took her glass from her hand and set it on the table. "Come." He began to pull her into the bedroom. "Where's the light switch? Oh, hell, we don't need light. We know where everything is."

She tried to fight him off. But he had hands everywhere. When he unbuttoned her blouse, she buttoned it up again. When he unhooked the top of her skirt, she hooked it back up. When he reached under her dress and pulled down her silk pants, she pulled them back up. Finally, enraged and engorged, he began to rip off her clothes. And somehow, while all this was going on—she never did figure out how he managed it—he'd dropped his own trousers and underwear. He had her mostly naked when he managed to part her legs with his knee.

"C'mon, you know you want it."

"Not this way."

"Don't be a ballbreaker."

"What!"

"Yeh. One of them castrater women."

"I am not!"

"How come you're still a virgin then at thirty?"

"I just haven't met the right man, that's all. I'm picky."

"Ah, you probably like your brothers too much."

"What's that supposed to mean?"

"Well? What else is one to think of a family where no one gets married before thirty."

"What do you know about my family?"

"Oh, I have ways of finding out."

"You'd better leave."

"C'mon, you know you can't resist me."

"Not this way, I said."

He growled in her ear. And snorted. Made strange rutting noises.

"I want to be in love first," she cried.

"That comes afterwards," he snarled.

Curiously, part of her kind of liked the growling and the strange rutting sounds. It reminded her of the time she saw a stallion mounting one of Pa's mares. She remembered how Pa and the man who brought the stallion over stood with their hands in their pockets.

"God, you're tight."

She gave up. If only somehow she could put into Gary's testicles what this Eldon had too muich of; and somehow have Gary's gentleness and Eldon's hairiness all put in one body. Well, she could think of Gary while Eldon deflowered her. She let her legs relax.

Ow. It hurt at first. Lord, Eldon was big. After a while she thought she could feel him all the way up to her lungs. Once inside, Eldon seemed to take it easier. He rode her in an easy gallop. Sometimes he paused, as if to enjoy looking at some flower he'd spotted off to one side of a path. Then he'd ride on.

Finally Eldon Clarke did a strange thing. "May I finish?" he asked. He spoke very tenderly.

"Sure."

In a moment he was back to being the rutting stallion again. He snort-grunted in her ear. Some kind of paroxysm grabbed him in the belly and he thrust far up under her mount of love and then he really seemed to reach all the way into her lungs. And he moaned as though he were a Beethoven playing the final movement of a sonata. A great pleasure seemed to seize him. And then he fell limp upon her belly.

She envied him the convulsion of ecstasy.

She saw him a half dozen times after that. Each time it was the same old story. He didn't want to visit any first; just head straight for her bed. Also, there was always that wild rutting, and then the lovely easy ride, and finally the concluding wild convulsive topping off.

One evening he barged in on her without calling first. She had just removed her stiff white nurse's gown and was in her housecoat. She was tired. That day she'd had to help several old women get started with their crutches. One of the women was heavy and Mallie'd had to practically carry her from one end of the long hallway to the other. The last thing she wanted was Eldon Clarke around.

Mallie pulled up her housecoat tight. "What do you want?"

The sharpness of her voice slowed him down. "Hey," he said. "What's the matter, don't you love me?"

"Love you?"

"Well, yeh. After all we've had together we should start being a little in love with each other."

"A little is right."

"No, really, Mallie. I think I've fallen in love with you. That's the way real love works. First physical attraction and then spiritual attraction."

"You? Spiritual attraction?" She laughed right out loud, tipping back her head.

"Haven't you slowly been liking me more and more?"

She stepped past him and opened the door. "Get out."

"What?"

"Get out. I've just now decided I don't ever want to see you again. You beast."

He stepped back. Gone was the dominant look. He pleaded with her. "But I've fallen in love with you, Kissy. You're so luscious and wonderful and full of lips. And you're sweet too."

"Where did you learn that name for me?"

"Gary told me about you. How much he loved you too."

"Fat chance he did that, the wimp."

"He said the reason he didn't go on with you was that he didn't feel he was up to you. You were too good for him."

"He didn't really say that."

"Yes, he did. And now he's kind of sorry. He's in the groove and all that with his wife, but he realizes he really loved you."

Mallie wanted to hit Eldon, hit all men. "Get out. And you can tell that Gary that he can go stick it."

Eldon backed another step. "Why, Mallie Freyling, you really did love him, didn't you?"

Mallie looked around for something to throw at him. She spotted the iron on the ironing board near the stove. There was always some ironing to do when one was a nurse or a therapist. She jumped over and grabbed the iron and hurled it at him. She missed. The iron crashed against the door.

"Hesus Hristus!" Eldon jumped outside and disappeared behind the lilac bushes. 363

"Goddamn men and their horny hands."

She went into the bathroom and removed her clothes. She looked at herself, standing naked, in the full-length mirror on the back of the door. "Curly auburn hair, crap. Hazel eyes, crap. Triple lips, crap. You can have them. If that's all I am to men, give me skinny hips and boyish lips any time."

Mallie didn't date anybody for several months. When she learned Eldon Clarke was badmouthing her at the hospital, she really hardened her heart against men. Eldon told some of the interns she was an easy make. Two of the interns tried to date her, and when she wondered out loud about their sudden interest in her, Tracy Tidwell told her about Eldon's stories.

Mallie said, "The son of a bitch."

"You can say that again."

Mallie became further disgusted with her life at the hospital when she learned that Eldon and Tracy began dating. Tracy became very secretive, and there was a look on her face that she'd been surprised to discover something wonderfully new about herself.

One evening, after a hot shower, Mallie sat down to read the Sioux Falls evening paper. The first thing to catch her eye, on the front page, was a story about a certain Don Van Acker who was accused to conning a miser out of part of his savings. The reporter writing the story couldn't help but reveal admiration for the way Van Acker had worked the rich old coot.

Don Van Acker was an accountant working for the Frontier Bank in Sioux Falls, and one day he happened to come across a bank statement about to be sent out to John Meester. Old John was worth millions. It struck Don Van Acker that here was a guy who could help him out. Don was an only child. After his father, Maurice Van Acker, died in a car accident, Don had become his mother's only support. Everything went well until his mother became ill with tuberculosis. Don wasn't earning enough to pay for her stay in a sanatorium. He asked the president of the bank for a loan, but the president frowned, and hemmed and hawed, and finally said no, because Don had no security to offer. His mother's house was a ramshackle affair, hardly worth burning.

Don finally came up with an idea. He deliberately made an error in making out the monthly statement of Meester's interest earnings; and then, using that as an excuse, drove out to see old John Meester. Meester also lived in an old shack, on the north end of Summit.

Old John took one look at the statement and started ranting and raving and swearing to high heaven about them big-city crooks and double-dealing bankers.

Don let him roar for a while. And then, when the swearing died down, Don told him he personally would make sure that the error would be corrected and that he would send out a new statement.

Old John had some manners and after a bit thanked Don for taking the trouble to drive over to help straighten out the mistake. He offered Don a cup of coffee.

Don accepted.

Gradually Don laid it out. How after his father died, Mom began to fail, at last came down with galloping consumption. How the county relief people wouldn't help her because she owned a farm, a quarter section of bottom land along the Big Sioux River, which they told her she would have to sell to pay for her stay in a Black Hills sanatorium, that the truth was she had promised her husband before he died that she would never sell the place, that she would make sure their only son, Don, would inherit it.

Old John asked one question. "How much does she need?"

"For a year's stay at the sanatorium? Five thousand dollars."

"Mmm. That much."

"Well, I've got a letter of delegation here"—Don drew an important-looking paper, folded, out of his jacket pocket, which he'd made out beforehand—"which states that after I inherit the farm I can pay back the principal plus accrued interest to whoever loans me the money."

"But I'll have to have in hand the deed to your mother's quarter."

"But this letter of delegation is even more binding than the deed."

"You're sure now?"

"I swear on it in the name of my mother."

"Well, you look like a good kid." Old John shook his head sadly. "I never had a kid of my own. Okay." He pursed his thin lips until they almost touched his potato nose. "But I'll want the legal limit in interest. Eight percent."

"That's all right. And if I possibly can, I'll try to meet the interest out of my salary at the bank."

"I also want a statement in the agreement that if you can't make the yearly interest payments, it applies against the quarter, that once the loan plus the accrued interest are worth more than the assessed value of the quarter, then I can foreclose on it."

"Agreed."

Then to Don Van Acker's great surprise, Old John dug out a gallon pickle jar full of old bills and laid out on the table five thousand dollars in cash. "Now," Old John said, "let's you and me draw up a paper on this."

Don somehow managed to keep his eyes from bugging out. He had a question to ask. "How come you didn't put that money"—Don pointed at the money on the table as well as what was left in the pickle jar—"out on interest?"

"I don't really trust banks. And in case they go kaput on me, I've at least got this for backup money."

"Aren't you afraid of being robbed some night?"

"No one knows I've got that money here. Except you now."

"It's safe with me."

"It better be."

That night, money in hand, Don Van Acker went straight to a roving poker game out in the country. Playing for money was against the law, yet Don knew a friend who ran a poker ring that moved from farmhouse to farmhouse. Don was sure that with his slick fingers he could double the five thousand, and then would return the original sum to Old John Meester. But by four o'clock the next morning Don had lost every penny of it. Shrewd cunning farmhands cleaned him out.

That same night, Old John Meester got to thinking. That letter of delegation, now, it looked powerful enough, sure, but a question kept nagging Old John— why hadn't Don Van Acker gone to his own bank for a loan of five thousand dollars if his mother's quarter section was such good security? The more he thought about it the more sure Old John was that he'd been fleeced. There was little sleep for him that night.

365

The next morning Old John walked down to the courthouse and checked the records in the recorder's office. There was no quarter section owned by a Mrs. Maurice Van Acker. There was a ramshackle house in her name but even that wasn't clear. There was an outstanding mortgage on it by Don Van Acker's bank, the Frontier.

In a rage, John Meester went down to the sheriff's office and reported what he'd learned. The sheriff took him to the county attorney's office, and shortly thereafter a warrant was issued for the arrest of Don Van Acker for criminal fraud.

In the trial that followed, Don Van Acker was found guilty and sent to the state penitentiary in Sioux Falls. Because it was his first offense, his sentence was for six months, along with his promise to make restitution of the five thousand he'd conned out of John Meester. With interest.

Mallie found herself fascinated by the account. In her family such things as criminal fraud had never been mentioned or discussed. She wondered what kind of fellow this Don Van Acker was to have such warped values. What especially caught her eye was that from his picture in the paper he looked a lot like her brother Dirk. Don Van Acker had that same warm artful look of a witty person, someone who liked to tease and who bent the language a little to have fun. Don Van Acker also had the same hollow cheeks and the same way of holding his hand cockily to one side.

A couple of weeks went by and then Mallie read in the paper that there'd been a fight in the penitentiary involving Don Van Acker. He'd been badly beat up by other inmates. When asked why, he wouldn't say. "I'm no squealer." He was laid up with a badly wrenched shoulder and elbow, a cracked shin, and a badly sprained ankle.

Two more weeks went by and then the Siouxland Hospital got a call from the penitentiary asking if they could send over a physical therapist. The warden was worried that Don Van Acker might sue the state penitentiary for negligence. Don Van Acker had let it be known that if he left the pen a cripple he'd hire a lawyer.

Still curious about this Dirk look-alike, Mallie offered to go. She called the warden and he arranged for her to see Van Acker at four P.M. for an hour-long session.

Mallie parked her red Buick coupe in the lot across the road from the penitentiary. To the south, at the foot of a very high hill, lay the commercial section of Sioux Falls, first the smokestacks of a packing company, then the stockyards full of bawling cattle and squealing hogs, and beyond that the plain houses of workers. Over on the right, sparkling in the falling sunlight, tumbled the falls of the Big Sioux River. The sliding and crashing yellow water sparkled in vivid contrast to the pink rocks on either side. Water also rushed down a race attached to a flour mill. Beyond the falls rose the towers of downtown Sioux Falls. Still farther west, silhouetted sharply against the blue horizon, pricked the spearing steeple of the Roman Catholic church.

Mallie took the walk up to the front door of the penitentiary. She couldn't help but admire the structure, with its purple Sioux quartzite masonry, especially the white stones used to dress the frames of the doors and windows.

She gave her name to the control desk and was promptly ushered by a guard through a clanging door of steel bars, down a narrow stairway, then along a narrow concrete-block passage painted gray, finally into a visiting room. A mattress on a steel table had been provided.

The guard said, "Wait here. He'll be along in a minute."

Soon the door behind her opened and another guard ushered in a lanky fellow, Don Van Acker. Mallie got to her feet. In real life Van Acker looked even more like her brother Dirk than he did in the photograph. There were several differences though: Van Acker was a couple of inches taller than Dirk, and his hair was much darker. The height and the hair gave Van Acker a more dominating look. Where Dirk used his winning manner to get his way, Van Acker appeared to be one of those who could also use his commanding air to get it.

"Well," Mallie said, "let's see you walk over to the table there so I can get some idea of what our problems are."

"Okay, lady." Van Acker, dressed in gray prison garb, using a wooden crutch, limped over to the table. He swung himself up on the table.

"You do have a stiff ankle there," Mallie said. "But that looks like in time it'll be okay. Let's see what the problem is with your shoulder."

"The first guard had taken a chair near the door. Short and squat, inclined to be fat, he didn't appeared to be very happy with his work. He had a look of contempt for Van Acker. It was apparent he thought Van Acker a phony.

Mallie gently massaged Van Acker's shoulder and elbow. Both cracked under her ministrations. Mallie turned to the guard. "Did the prison physician take any X rays?"

"Yeh."

"I wonder, could you get them for me?"

The guard got to his feet and opened the door and called down the corridor. "Jackson, the bone bimbo here says she needs Van Acker's X rays. Bring them up." Then the guard took his chair again.

Presently the X rays came. Mallie held them up one at a time against a hanging light bulb. "Well, you're lucky. No real breaks that I can see."

"That's what the doc said." Von Acker had the voice of a vaseline-smooth radio announcer, New York style. He lay meekly under her hands.

"Now, can you bend your elbow like this?" Mallie bent her own elbow to show him how she wanted it done.

He tried; and flinched. It was obvious it gave him pain.

"Well, we'll slowly sneak up on that sore elbow. I want you to try bending it twice a day. Like this. See? No oftener. Because we want some healing to take place between exercises. Slowly. Understand?"

He nodded.

"Now let's try your shoulder. Can you roll your arm around like this?"

He tried; and again grimaced, a deep wrinkle from the corners of his lips working back under his ears.

Mallie nodded. He'd really been hurt.

She worked with him for a half hour. She set a date to see him in a couple of days, and once again instructed him on how to work the sore joints by himself.

She couldn't resist asking a question. "What else are you doing here? To fill in the time?"

"Thinking back on what a damn fool I was."

The guard behind them grunted.

Mallie turned on the guard. His grunt had angered her. "Isn't this a correctional institution?"

"Why?"

"If it is, that comment was hardly called for."

The fat guard had a thin slit for lips, drawn down at the corners. "You're put in here to pay for your crimes."

"Do you like being a guard?"

The guard bristled. He seemed to swell up through his shoulders. "Hey, I don't have to answer your questions. Are you through with him?"

"For now, yes." Mallie turned and smiled at Don Van Acker to let him know she felt sorry for him. "I'll be back in three days. Let's see how well you do by yourself. Okay?"

Van Acker nodded. For a second he had a little sick smile for her, a smile she'd once seen on Dirk's face when in the presence of the whole family he'd tried to wish Tressa well on her honeymoon. "I'll try."

"Good."

She saw him three more times before she was satisfied that his elbow and his shoulder would heal without surgery. She complimented him on the healing ability of his body.

Van Acker wagged his head to one side. "If only Ma'd had that."

"She'll probably be all right."

"No, she won't. She died yesterday."

"Not really!"

"Yeh. And the warden says he won't let me to go to her funeral."

"When is her funeral."

"Day after tomorrow."

"You want me to talk to the warden?"

"No. I asked him once and around here once is enough. Besides, I'm working hard on having a record of good behavior. There's a chance they might cut my sentence."

"If you say so."

A smile of a bitter sort drew back into his hollow cheeks. "Also, I want them to feel guilty that they didn't let me go to the funeral of my mother."

"Oh."

Two days later, Mallie took off and went to Mrs. Maurice Van Acker's funeral. There were only a dozen people in the huge Episcopal church. None were relatives; only neighbors. When Mallie viewed the face of Mrs. Van Acker she could see that Don resembled her. The service was lovely, Mallie thought, and it brought back memories of the times when her own mother had hustled the whole family aboard the Bonnie Omaha to attend Episcopal services in Whitebone.

Father Isham had the cultivated voice of one who might have once preached in the Anglican church in England:

"We brought nothing into this world, and it is certain we can carry nothing out.

"Let me know mine end, and the number of my days, that I may be certified how long
    I have to live.

"For man walketh in a vain shadow, and disquieted himself in vain; he heapeth up
    riches, and cannot tell who shall gather them.

"O spare me a little, that I may recover my strength, before I go hence and be no more
    seen."

368

Mallie waited several days before she told Van Acker she'd gone to his mother's funeral.

"You did? Why?"

"Just curious about you, I guess."

They were visiting through a grill, with Van Acker sitting on the prisoner side and she on the visitor side. There was a strong smell of kerosene insecticide about.

He looked down at his hands a moment. When he glanced up, a look of pleasure had opened his face. In the corners of his eyes, though, there lurked another expression, furtive, as if he'd just then thought of another scheme to get money.

Mallie caught the second look but let it pass. "What are you going to do when you get out?"

"Start over. And I mean, start over."

"Here in Sioux Falls?"

"No, I'm heading for Denver. I've got a pal there who took accounting with me in college."

A sinking feeling spread through her belly. She'd been hoping a little that after he got out she might date him. She watched his slim hands fumble in each other. He had such flowing fingers. It gave her a thrill to think he might stroke her breasts with them. She had to admit she liked him. She had asked the warden how Don Van Acker was doing and was told he was an exemplary prisoner. The warden liked it that Van Acker hadn't squealed on the men who'd beat him up. The warden was even thinking of making him a trustee. Van Acker was trustworthy and so could be allowed special privileges.

Van Acker spotted regret in her manner. "Of course, I'm first gonna have to take care of what's left of Ma's estate. Sell the house and pay back John Meester his five thousand bucks. That'll take a little time."

"Where will you stay?"

"I don't know. Can't stay in our house because the bank has rented it out."

She smiled at him. She let her tongue show. "If you want, you can stay with me." What she heard herself say surprised her.

"You would?"

She looked him over point for point. For the first time she had a good look at his eyes. They were bold eyes; not at all evasive like one might expect in a con man. She noticed for the first time they were black-blue and not blue like her brother Dirk's. There was a curious shine to them, especially in the corners, like he might have a fever, or like he might be burning angry about something. It wasn't a slippery shininess so much as it was a lickerish shininess. "Sure," she said. "If you want."

His sallow face bloomed. "That's wonderful. At last I got something to live for. The minute I get out. Oh, boy!"

Voices arose in the back of her head. Far back. One voice had the cold inflection of an objective commentator; the other voice had the loving accents of the dreamer.

. . . . Commentator said; "He's a crook."

Dreamer said, "But I love his wonderful hands."

Commentator said, "You're about to make another mistake. Like you did with two other men. You have a fatal tendency to pick crappy men."

Dreamer said, "Don just made a mistake, is all. He realizes it and is sorry for it. Even the warden says that."

Commentator said, "So it's Don already, is it?"

Dreamer said, "How can anyone resist those penitent eyes?"

Commentator said, "One good look at the corners of those dark eyes and you know he's slippery."

Dreamer said, "Everybody should be allowed to make one mistake."

Commentator said, "He's a spoiled mama's boy."

Dreamer said, "I have a soft spot in my heart for him."

Commentator said, "You remember that little verse Gordon Pullman, our neighbor boy, used to sing at our country school?

> When I met him I liked him,
> When I liked him I loved him,
> When I loved him I let him,
> When I let him I lost him."

Dreamer said, "There but for the grace of God goes Dirk."

Commentator said, "I'm not sure I'd use Dirk as a model. Dirk's shirttail isn't exactly clean either."

Dreamer said, "I'm afraid it's too late" . . . .

Don said sharply, "Hey, are you listening to me? Or what?"

"What? Oh. I was just thinking about something."

"Like you was gone to a far country somewhere."

"What did you say again?"

"I said, the minute I know when I get out, will you come and get me then?"

"I guess so. Sure."

That night, waking up in bed around two in the morning, that time when dreams and ghosts emerge, Mallie repunched her pillow and asked herself: "How come you fell for a handsome con man?"

The back of her head, her interior commentator, thought it knew. She was the youngest of four sisters. The other three girls had gotten way ahead of her. It wasn't either that her sisters were mean to her. She'd actually grown up in a happy family. It was just that Thea and Tressa and Ana were older, and had learned how to get what they wanted. The same thing was true of course of brother Geoffrey, the youngest in the family. The older brothers Tane and Dirk and Rolf by luck of chronology had gotten there first.

Mallie remembered how Geoffrey had once brought the point home at the family table, before the older ones had left home. Ma'd always set the platter of meat in front of Pa. Pa was to help himself first, and of course that meant he got the biggest piece of meat because it faced him, the way Ma had set down the meat platter. The rule in the family was, Don't be impolite by turning the plate half around to get at the biggest piece. A person had to take what was in front of one. Naturally, by the time the meat platter arrived in front of Mallie and Geoffrey only he smallest pieces were left. Mallie often fixed it so that, of the two pieces left, Geoffrey got the larger one. That day Ma served pork chops.

370 Just after the blessing, as Pa was about to pick up the meat plate, Geoffrey raised his hand.

Pa lowered an eye at Geoffrey. "What is it, son?"

"I'd like to ask an important question."

"Fire and fall back."

"I'm not only the youngest in the family, I'm also the littlest, not?"

"That's right."

"And I've got the most to catch up if I'm to grow up to be as big as Tane."

"Right."

"The same is true of Mallie if she is to grow up to be as big as Thea."

"What do you have in mind, son?"

"Well, if I have the most to catch up, I should get the biggest pork chop. And Mallie the next biggest."

Pa gave it all deep thought. Ma was smiling a little, waiting for what Pa'd say to their clever youngster. All the kids waited too, mouths slightly parted. They knew it would be just. Finally Pa said, "You got a point, boy." And Pa turned the meat platter half around and took the smallest pork chop. Everybody around the table sat a moment in shock. What especially got them was that Geoffrey didn't say, "You see?" or act vain or too proud. Geoffrey took it as a matter of course.

The only trouble was, Geoffrey's protest worked for just the one meal.

Interior Commentator had more to say. "Mallie, the reason you probably fell for this jerk is that for once, this time, you're sitting ahead of Don Van Acker at the table of life, like you once were with Geoffrey, and you can choose to give him the biggest piece of meat of those pieces still left to you. You can have the luxury of being kind and loving to a lesser person. Also, it's a kind of a victory over Tressa, and even Thea, where you can have a Dirk-like person as your best buddy. Watch out. You deserve better."

A month later, after a dozen more visits, Don told Mallie his sentence had been commuted to three months, that he was free to go the coming Monday.

"Really?" Mallie exclaimed.

"Yeh. You're coming to get me then?"

Mallie examined her heart. She waited for Commentator to speak up. When it didn't she decided it was because it didn't have anything more to say. She felt a surge of joy. Glory be. She was going to have a man in her house at last. One who needed her. Patients who needed to have their muscles brought back from near atrophy were one thing; but a man in the house who needed to have his self-respect restored, let alone his joints, was another and far more satisfying thing. "What time?"

"Warden says to be ready to go at ten."

Mallie had the feeling she was smiling at him like she might be a sister to a little brother. "I think maybe I can get off."

"Well, Jesus, if you can't, I'll have to take a taxi. Can you lend me ten bucks?"

She laughed out loud. "Seeing as how I'm the boss of the physical therapy unit at the Siouxland Hospital, I think I can let myself off."

"Oh," Don said. "Good." His dark black eyes began to glow at her. "Man, will it be good to get out of this bughouse." Quickly he added, looking over his shoulder, "Not that they haven't been good to me."

"I'll see you at ten then."

When she pulled up in her red Buick coupe, Don was waiting for her, dressed in a dapper blue suit and red tie, raincoat caught over an arm, suitcase set between his feet. His black eyes glowed with joy. Gone was the odd sheen in the corners. The moment he saw her, he waved a hand, then picked up his suitcase and ran toward her.

"It's happening!" he cried as he jumped into her car, throwing the suitcase in back, folding the tan raincoat in his lap. He looked handsome dressed up. He would look good alongside her brothers when the family had its next clan meeting.

"Yes, it is." She put the car in gear and they rolled out of the curving drive. She glanced over her left shoulder to make sure no cars were coming down the street, then headed toward Minnesota Avenue.

"Wow! Wow!" Don kept exclaiming, looking at the houses and the trees going by. "Man, you'll never know how good it is to be out. And all because of one lousy damn-fool notion I had. Never again. Never again. Because I don't ever want to be attacked again by a bunch of cornholers."

"Is that what happened when you got beat up?"

"Yeh." A grimace twisted up off his lips and moved across his face.

"Really! I didn't know that went on in the pen."

"Hraa! The place is full of sodomists. Even the guard. Buggers, all of 'em."

"Not the guard!"

"Lady, it was a guard who let those five cornholers into my cell in the first place."

"Oh, Lord!" It was such an awful thought it made her neck muscles pull up, convulsively, making her ears crack. "Did they get you?"

"No! I fought hard. And yelled so loud the guard finally had to act like those five had just then got in with me accidentally, and then he put on a show as if he was against them, even whacking them over their backs. Which made them mad. To the point where they said they'd get him someday. Of course about then the warden showed up."

"Oh," Mallie breathed. "No wonder the warden was worried about a lawsuit."

"You bet!" Don said vehemently.

"You're still not thinking of suing?"

"No. No, I'm done with all that. I don't ever want to think of that limbo joint again."

"You called it a bughouse too. Were there bugs in there?"

"Bedbugs and roaches. Besides the buggers."

Mallie shivered. "Bugs I've always hated."

"You and me both."

Mallie pulled up in front of her apartment. "Well, here's where I live."

Don looked at the big white box of a house and at the green lawn. "Looks like a palace to me."

"Come with me."

Don picked his suitcase off the back seat and went up the walk with her. Riding in the open car had messed up his black hair and he tried to comb it back in place with his fingertips. He threw several furtive looks around, at the neighbor's house, up and down the street.

Mallie said in a soft voice, "Nobody along this street cares who you are."

"I wish I could believe that."

"Relax. You're with me." She held the door open. After he'd stepped inside, she closed the door firmly behind them. "Tell you what. I have one room I'm using as a sort of storage room. It isn't big, but it has a window. And I've put down a thick pad and some sheets on it for your bed." She led the way to the extra room and opened the door. "Here you are. A room all your own."

He looked in. He hesitated. "Uhh, it's nice all right. For the time being." He couldn't quite look her in the eye.

"What's the matter?"

He set down his suitcase and in soft deference touched her elbow. A smile, which he meant to be winning, drew his lips back at the corners. "I'd kinda hoped that . . ."

"You might sleep with me?"

"Yeh."

It was what she'd thought of too. But she couldn't let him think she was easy. It was already tough enough that he'd once been her patient. Oh, dear.

"Come on," he urged, taking her elbow, "it's been so long."

"Who was it before?" she challenged.

"That's the funny thing," he said. "There's been nobody."

"Never?"

"Well, you know. Once after a high school prom I had too much to drink. When I never drank because of Mom. We were with another couple and they were doing it in the front seat, and my date whispered in my ear, 'Why don't we?' So I tried it too."

Again she challenged him, archly. "Tried?" She could feel her breasts softening, even warming toward him.

"Well . . ."

She fell back on medical terminology. "There was no penetration?"

"God," he said, "you nurses. You sure know how to put the shotgun questions."

"Did she cry out?"

His dark eyes shifted off. "Yeh, she did that all right."

She placed a hand over his hand where it held her by the elbow. "Sorry. If you'd turned out to be a virgin I don't know what I would've thought."

"Then it's all right?"

"What is?"

"Oh, Mallie, I'd like to sleep on a good bed. And with you. Really, it's been . . ." He bored a lover's look into her eyes. "I don't want to sleep on the floor. I'm out and free now, remember?"

She bowed her head. "All right." She turned and entered her room. "You can set your suitcase there. And I think there's still some room for your clothes in my closet."

He swelled up like a suddenly happy boy. He set his suitcase down. "Let's undress. I want to see you naked. I can hang up my clothes later."

"Such a rush."

"Mallie, if you really do like me, and I think you do, don't toy with me. Let's undress." He began to unbutton her white nurse's smock. "And you unbutton me."

She laughed. "I'll do my own."

He shivered. "I'm so nervous." A laugh of lust broke from him. He had trouble finding his own buttons.

When she got down to her slip, she said, with a sidelong look at him. "I'll keep this on. You should have to rip something off me."

Odd sounds burbled from him. His fingers fluttered. He said, half-choked, "Then it's true. That you girls like to be raped a little."

"I just want to have it that I didn't give in all the way. Was completely shameless. After all, I was raised in a wonderful family."

"You know, I love that in you. Oh, Mallie, I've always so wanted a true and regular woman."

"Thank God," she said. With her white slip coming halfway down her thighs, she flipped back the quilt and sheet and knelt into bed, sliding over to the far side.

He stepped out of his shorts and lay down beside her. He rolled on his side, facing her. He had the delicacy to hold back. He looked at her, from her toes to where tufts of blond hair rose from her mount of love, to where her breasts were hidden under her silk slip. "I'm having trouble believing this."

"So am I." She swallowed back a chuckle for fear he'd take it wrong. "So am I."

He kissed her. It was a soft kiss, just barely catching the corner of her lips. There was a little sound of separate skins sticking together for a moment. He looked into her eyes. Her eyes had already received him. He saw the look and kissed her full on. He slipped an arm around her middle. He was considerate. It was only after their lips had opened a little that he finally allowed the top of his hand to touch the underside of her breasts through the slip. She was very aware of it. She regretted a little she hadn't undressed all the way just to be nice to him. She gave him her two full lips and the edge of her tongue. Triplelips, her brothers called her. How lovely to be called that by one's loving brothers. Especially by Dirk. Oh! this Don Van Acker resembled Dirk so. Don inserted his two thin lips between her lips. They held. It was then she knew she loved him. She loved him with her belly and the points of her breasts. When would he ever touch her nipples?

Slowly his hand slid down and began to pull up her slip. She broke away then and helped him remove it. She could feel herself color up. It was out of yearning. She threw him a swift glance. His eyes were closed. He was lost in her. His face was that of an angel. He touched her. In a moment she knew he truly loved her too. He loved her with a full heart.

Suddenly she said a silly thing. It went back to when she and Geoffrey were plumming one day. She'd fallen halfway down through the plum tree, and Geoffrey, trying to help her, also fell halfway down. They were hooked on the plum tree prickles. "Oh, kid, what do we do now?"

The goosey question seemed to release Don. He rose over her and divided her with a knee and drove down. It seemed to her it was too swift. What she'd said inflamed him at the same time that it weakened him. He had to reach under her to help himself into her.

Too swift. He rode seven waves in and groaned as he reached deep into her and then lay heavy on her.

She was disappointed. But she held him close. She thought she understood.

"I'm sorry," he whispered.

"It's all right."

"Too much in a hurry."

"It's all right, love."

"It's been my trouble all my life. Be rich too quick."

She comforted him. She loved the way his lips touched her neck as he whispered. She moved under him to hold him better. Almost instantly after her movement she could feel him harden into her again. This time it was firmer, and longer, and more wonderful. She began to lift her hips under him, pulling him down into her. She began to groan.

He woke up then. "God, I must've been really hard up to be ready so soon again."

"Yes." She began to float upward. She was rising like a kite. She'd never before been lifted up that high. She yearned to rise higher. It was like he was letting out the string to her kite in rhythmic releases. At last she knew how a bird felt.

But she got only to a certain height, and then there was no more string. She yearned for more string. She began to moan. The moan became a cry. More.

But there was no more. And after a while, after he once again made a rutting sound in her ear, and fell slack upon her, heavy, she let up. It was no use. It would not come to her.

They fell asleep with him still lying on her.

An hour later she awoke with a start. He had rolled off her and was lying on his side, knees up against her hip, head under one of the pillows. He was crying in his sleep. She rose on an elbow. She could just make out the corner of his lips past the edge of the pillow. He looked so sad. A little boy who'd been spanked. She thought of reaching in a kiss under the edge of the pillow but was afraid of waking him up.

She elbowed herself up out of bed. She got out her varicolored housecoat, yellow and pink and green, slipped into it, and barefooted it out to the kitchen. She closed the door gently, careful not to let the latch click.

Smiling, thighs stiffish, she made them dinner. Living alone she'd rarely ever made herself a fancy meal. She usually had plain dishes of meat, potatoes, lettuce, fruit, milk. But for that wonderful lover lying in her bed she'd make a special meal. She'd garnish the entrees with parsley.

The steaks were ready and the potatoes were about done when he stepped into the kitchen, rubbing his eyes. He'd slipped into his blue shorts and white jersey. He rubbed his eyes with his knuckles. "Wow, did I sleep a hole in the day."

"You certainly did."

"What woke me up was the wonderful smell of those steaks." He looked at the neatly laid-out place settings on her small dining table, the American design of the knife handles, the bone white plates, the tall spindle glasses. "Wow. I hardly deserve all this."

"Nothing's too good for our hero."

"Can I pull up a chair?"

"Please do."

He sat down slowly. He stared at the steady burning little flame on a single white candle. "You're too good for me."

"Don't run yourself down. There are always enough people around ready and willing to do that for you."

"I know." He twitched on his chair. "Maybe I better wash up and comb my hair. And at least put on a shirt."

"Do that," she said. "Dinner should be ready in about five minutes. Then I'll be ready to pour this wine. I've put it in the freezer compartment to chill it."

He shook his head. "I don't drink."

"Not? Not even on a special occasion?"

"Not even then."

She was pleased to hear it. She removed the slender bottle of wine from the freezer and set it in the cupboard again. "How about tea though?"

"Tea is fine." Smiling, he shook his head. "I have trouble believing all this." He sighed. Twice. "Where's the bathroom?"

"First door on the right past my bedroom."

When he returned, hair combed back neatly, eyes bright, shirt and trousers and shoes on, she had turned on her little radio. KSOO had just then started playing a recording of Gershwin's *Rhapsody in Blue.*

"Oh, God," he said. "No music please."

"You don't like music?"

"No, I don't. It drives me wild. It just catches across my nerves raw."

"For heaven's sake. The man doesn't like wine and he doesn't like music." She went over and turned off the radio. She was disappointed. She'd hoped that the good dinner and the burning candle and the good music would put them both in a true loving mood. She thought that a couple of hours of rich romantic dawdling over a private dinner would mellow and excite her enough to help her climb up through that hole in heaven. She'd had a vague glimpse of it and wanted it. Already she'd had more fun with a man than she'd ever had before.

Dinner flowed along fine. Slowly Don relaxed. He began to tell stories about his father. He cried several times when he realized once more he'd never see his father or mother again. He regretted that he was their only child. For relatives there was a distant male cousin in Las Vegas but he'd never seen him or heard from him.

Don helped her with the dishes afterward. She was pleased to see how handy he was with the dish towel, how he could polish up a glass until it shone and made pinching noises.

They went to bed at ten. They meant to make love again but fell asleep laughing about a story Don told about his father. His father had fallen into the Big Sioux River while fishing and all he'd said was, "Ma'll say I sure wet my pants this time."

Dawn was just blooming into the bedroom windows when they awakened. They lay luxuriating a moment, he for his reasons and she for hers. And then they turned thick-lipped and thick-eyed to each other. And again, in a rush he was upon her. Soon both were crying out, he as he coasted into a haven and she still trying to get past a barrier reef.

Then they had breakfast.

After a last cup of coffee, Don became all business. He shaved his swarthy chin, put on a clean shirt and red tie, and was off for what he called work. He was going to arrange, somehow, to pay off his indebtedness to miser John Meester. He was out to get rid of that shadow in his life as soon as possible.

They had a happy time the next two weeks. Mallie had to smile to herself at a certain private knowledge. Not a morning went by at work but what she had to visit the bathroom to dab up with a piece of toilet paper the semen running down the inside of her thigh. She was proud of Don for the eggwhite trickle. She hoped she'd become pregnant. With the other two men she'd used a contraceptive method taught her by her knowing nurse friends, a halved lemon placed like a suction cup over the mouth of the uterus. But even if this Don Van Acker didn't want to marry her, she wanted his baby. She was willing to have the baby out of wedlock and raise it by herself.

One evening she came home to find Don sitting in her favorite spot, the Morris easy chair, and listening to country music over KSOO. He presented her with a mixed look. One side of his face seemed to be all smiles, while the other side expressed caution.

She decided to address the smiling side first. "For heaven's sake, Don, you're home early. And you're listening to music. The next thing, you'll be drinking wine."

"I might."

"What's up?"

"Well, I've got two potatoes to peel with you. One potato I'm sure you're gonna like and the other maybe."

She kicked off her flat-heeled white shoes and loosened her white nurse's smock. She settled in a hard-back chair across from him. It was cloudy out, and to relieve the darkness in the house, Don had put on a bridge lamp beside his chair. She managed to smile despite a tired feeling. "Try me."

"Well, with the bank's help I finally sold the old homestead. And after the mortgage was satisfied, I took the money and also paid off John Meester. I even got enough for Mother's house to pay him the accrued interest. And! I still had four hundred and twenty-five dollars left over." He got out his billfold from his back pocket and opened it and flipped through some crisp new bills. "Isn't that wonderful?"

"Don! It sure is."

"My debt to society is paid."

"And to Mister Meester."

For the moment his whole face was all smiles.

"And the other? The maybe potato?"

"Well . . ." He popped up out of the easy chair and began to pace back and forth. His brown wingtip oxfords creaked on each step. "I've decided I've got to get out of this burg. I want to go live in Denver with an old pal. I guess I mentioned once before that I took accounting with him in college."

"And who's that?"

Don's dark eyes shied off. They glistered in the corners. "Tiny Bean."

"Tiny?" She couldn't resist sticking it into him a little. "With that name, is he some kind of wimp?"

A laugh burbled out of him. "Wait'll you see him."

She rebuttoned her white smock. "Tiny can't be his real name."

"His real name is Timothy. He's got a great idea for making a lot of money in a hurry."

"Like how?"

"Hey, you don't like the idea of me going to Denver."

Of course she didn't. She'd fallen in love with him. Should she tell him she loved him enough to put the harness on him, marriage, and so hold him? "Well, if you're not going to miss me, go."

"Hey, I haven't finished yet what I was going to say."

"Oh?"

"I thought you could come with me and we'd start life over in Denver."

"I didn't know I needed to."

"Christ, woman, let's not get catty now."

"Can you blame me? You want me to quit a perfectly good job? A wonderful job even? One I pioneered in that hospital and in this area? I was the first to set up a physical therapy department anywhere in Siouxland."

"I see."

"You're asking a lot, hon."

He plumped himself down in the Morris chair again. "I suppose I am. And here I was already dreaming of a wonderful life for the two of us together in mile-high Denver."

Mallie recognized the familiar tag line, mile-high, that a Denver radio announcer used to help identify his station. "Can't you wait a little? So I can think it over? You know, this is awful sudden."

"I know it is. But then you'll go?"

"Are you hungry?"

"After a day like today, you bet."

She made them a simple supper of meat, potatoes, lettuce, canned pears, and tea.

They'd finished the dishes, with him drying as usual, making the glasses squinch until they shone, when he said, "I can pay for the gas out there now, you know."

"And we'll drive in my red Buick?"

"Well, yeh." He sniffed. "Or do you want me to buy a cheap jalopy with what little money I got?"

"Of course not." She felt sick. Her belly loved him. She also loved her job. "Give me a couple of weeks to think about it."

"Christ, Mallie!"

"I'm sorry, that's the way it is. In my family we made it a rule to sleep on it at least one night."

"Damn your family."

Mallie bristled. "I have a wonderful family and don't you dare say anything mean about them."

He let his shoulders sag. "I'm sorry. I was out of line on that one."

"Can't you wait just a couple of weeks? We don't want to have it that the day after we're on the road I'm suddenly sorry I left Sioux Falls, do we?"

"No, I guess not. All right." He pouted; then tried to hide it. "I'll find something to do in the meantime."

Two weeks later she came home with a kind of a smile on her face. "Well, I did it. I quit my job." She didn't add that the manager of the hospital had been angry with her and had told her not ever to come back looking for work with them should she change her mind.

"Hurray, then we can go!" He leaped up out of the Morris chair. He danced around her. Then he embraced her, and lifted her up, and finally kissed her. "Wow."

She had to laugh.

"Come," he said, "let's celebrate." He started to lead her to her bed.

"You mean . . . celebrate that way?"

"Of course. What better way is there? We can always find time to eat later." He made a soft ruckling sound in her ear. "Come."

His request coming just then was so strange she hoped it would help her climb the beanstalk into heaven. He was rough taking off her nurse's uniform but tender with his touches.

But it was not to be. The possibility of their having a happy evening was gone. But at eight she made a special supper anyway. And despite his protests she served herself several glasses of wine. She wanted to get something out of the deflated day.

In the morning he was in a hurry to get going. But she had to make arrangements with her landlady to store her things in the basement, pay up the rent for the rest of the month, pay her utility bills. It was noon before they were ready to go. It was all he could do to hide his impatience. His smile was forced.

She was aware that the housewives living to either side of her and across the street were watching them load up her red Buick. She had a good idea what they were thinking. She mentioned it to Don.

"The hell with 'em. They're just jealous of all the fun we're going to have. See new country."

"I think they know we never got married." She didn't add that they undoubtedly also knew who he was.

"Eff 'em."

Finally they were all packed up.

She said, "I suppose you'll want to drive."

"Sure, if it's all right with you."

"All right. We can take turns."

True to his word, when they came upon a Standard Oil station, he pulled in and bought the gas and oil. He didn't seem to begrudge the money he had to shell out.

They took Highway 77 south down through Sioux City and into Nebraska. At Fremont they picked up Highway 30 going West.

It was June and the sun didn't go down until after eight. Dusk was just browning over when they hit Gothenburg. He had driven all the way not wanting to give up the wheel; mostly, she was sure, because he feared that when she took over she'd turn around and head back for Sioux Falls.

She said, "Don't you think it's time we stopped and had a bite? And maybe look us up a cabin for the night?"

He gave his head a bossy waggle. "I thought we'd drive on through the night."

"I thought we were going to take turns."

"We will. We will."

"Gets awful boring sitting here looking out at this flat land. Flat. Flat."

"Pretty soon," he said, "you'll see something wonderful. Mountain peaks like storm clouds rising out of the horizon."

"Fat chance of that if we're gonna drive all night."

"All right." He almost snapped at her. "We do need gas. And while they fill up, we can grab a bite." He turned into another Standard station.

Stiff in the hips, they walked up Main Street. In Barney's Restaurant, Gothenburg's best, they both ordered a hamburger and a malted milk.

Again Don was as good as his word. He paid for the eats.

As they headed back toward their car, Mallie spotted some handsome-looking white cabins a block from Highway 30. "I still think we should get a bed instead of driving on to Denver yet tonight."

He jumped up; made a complete spin on his toetips, he was so exasperated with her. "Man, you sure want to get me into bed."

"Tonight I'd just like to rest. I'm not used to riding all day long in a car."

"Arrh. The hell with it then. We'll get us a room." He threw back his head and sniffed the air. "Maybe you're right. I want to be fresh when I hit Tiny's apartment. He's always a mile ahead of me in mile-high Denver when it comes to schemes. He's a genius with figures."

An hour later, almost asleep in a white cabin, Mallie asked, "What sort of schemes?"

"How much money did you take with you?"

"Why?" She wrinkled her nose at the smell of insecticide in the otherwise neat cabin.

"Well, my four hundred plus ain't going to last forever. And if we're gonna share life together . . ."

"A hundred dollars."

"Hmm. That's hardly going to be enough for what I had in mind."

"I've got my checkbook with me." Too late she realized she was a fool for telling him that."

"Huh. How much money you got in the bank? If we get married I should know about that, shouldn't I, hon?"

"Oh, some five thousand dollars." She had the five thousand in a savings account at the Sioux Falls First National Bank.

He made a sound with his lips as though he were grimacing in satisfaction.

"That should give us enough backing if we need it."

"What is this scheme you've got in mind with Tiny?"

He chuckled, and then turning on his side, slid an arm under her neck and drew her to him. "All in good time, darling." He hugged her. "Come, come to papa."

The riding in the car had jostled awake her desires. She wanted to as much as he did. But. "Oh, Don, I don't want to remember a time with you laced with the smell of insecticide."

"You got a point there."

She felt his knob against her hip. "I see you got a point too." She had to laugh. "Be kind of a shame to let it go to waste now, wouldn't it?"

"It sure would."

He was awake at dawn. He hustled her out of bed. "Time's a-wasting."

"Well, me, I've got more time than money." It was a remark her father often made.

"A couple of weeks from now you'll change your tune."

She swung out of bed. She felt all beat up. "My God," she said as she watched him flish around getting ready to go, "after all that's happened and after only a few hours sleep, you actually look refreshed."

"Naturally."

She shook her head. "Maybe someday when my body gives me the glory you men get, then maybe I'll feel the same. All I feel like now is like a handful of wool that couldn't make it through the spinning wheel."

"C'mon, c'mon. There's still enough gas in the car to drive hard a couple of hours. In the cool morning. Then we'll stop somewhere and have us bacon and eggs."

"Uggh."

At Big Springs they picked up Route 138 and started to head southwest. An hour later, with Mallie at last behind the wheel and Don asleep beside her, his head on a pillow against the door and his black hair flying like old moss trailing in a running stream of water and his mouth open like an oxygen-thirsty guppy's, Mallie suddenly saw, as their red Buick lifted over a slight rise in the land, what looked like a whole set of white-tipped alligator teeth rising out of the land. As she drove on, wind lifting her gold-red hair, she watched the white-tipped teeth become great thrusts of rocks covered with snow. She looked at Don, wondering if she should wake him so he could enjoy the sight with her, but with a wiggle of her head to herself she decided to let him sleep. She smiled to herself when she thought how easy it would be to casually turn the car around and head back for Sioux Falls. She could just imagine what he'd say when he woke up and, looking back, see the Rocky Mountains receding behind them and not increasing in size ahead of them.

She watched the mountains lift. She kept exclaiming softly to herself at their growing majesty. Sight of them almost made up for the gnawing sick feeling she had in her belly about leaving her job and her family behind, about riding across the country with a . . . yes . . . a con man.

Route 6 took them through Hillrose and Brush.

The mountains kept rising in front of them. Mallie began to feel exhilarated. It was all going to turn out all right. It was going to be worth it. She had a wonderful lover in the car with her. He would bring her heaven at last. They would find a good home. With his inventive mind, he'd find a way to make a good living. She could just see the children they'd have. And oh, she so wanted a child by him. And yes, what fun it was going to be to show her father and mother and her brothers and sisters her wonderful firstborn.

"Now ain't that pretty?" Don said beside her.

She jumped a little at the wheel. She flashed a look at him. He'd awakened and was watching the mountains coming toward them too. "Ho! you scared me."

"Sorry."

"And they aren't just pretty. They're . . . Well, even the word beautiful, or magnificent, or—"

"Gorgeous."

"—or radiant, isn't quite right." She glanced at him again, keeping an eye on the road at the same time. "I hate that word 'gorgeous.' Everybody is saying it these days. About the silliest things."

He laughed at her. "You're not much for catching on when a person is just having a little fun."

"No, I'm not. And thank God."

"Well, okay."

Don took over the wheel on the outskirts of Denver. Mallie was surprised with how much he knew about the city, what streets to take, where the shortcuts were to get to the south side, where Tiny lived.

It was dusk when they pulled up in front of a yellow clapboard bungalow. A black nickel-trimmed Packard stood in the drive. The door to the garage was open as though the Packard had just been rolled out. Mallie noted the address: 2500 South York. It was a middle-class neighborhood with neat yards, houses kept up, flowers along the walks. With the mountains in sight to the west it looked like a lovely place to live. Mallie hoped they could get a house like it soon.

Don got out of the car. "I'll go up and see if he's home." He shut the car door and then stretched. He strolled slowly up the walk, whistling, looking at the flowers and the aspen trees on either side of the walk. He glanced back and threw Mallie a reassuring smile. Great things were ahead. He climbed the steps and rang the bell.

Mallie brushed down her blue dress. She hoped she wasn't too much of a mess from riding in an open car. She leaned over and looked at herself in the rearview mirror. She was surprised to see how the wind coming over the windshield had sculpted her gold-red hair into a fine-looking head. Combing it out probably wouldn't improve it any. She decided to meet Don's friend just as she was.

After a moment, Don stuck his head out of the door and waved for her to come in. He held the door open for her and ushered her into a dusky room.

The blinds were drawn and it took Mallie a moment to make out objects. Gradually she made out plush easy chairs and a bookcase, finally the faces of Don and another man.

Don introduced her to the other face. "Mallie, this is my wonderful genius buddy Tiny Bean."

Tiny with a groan got up out of his chair. He turned out to be a huge zeppelin of a man, with a big pumpkin of a head and fat pouches under his eyes. Even the coloring of his cheeks was that of a ripe pumpkin. "Ha-do."

Mallie worked up a smile for the strange man. "Don's told me a lot about you."

"Let's hope it was complimentary." Tiny had a soft voice. It was almost the purr of a contented tomcat. Had he gone in for the ministry he would have had hundreds in his congregation. "Sit down, please."

Mallie looked around the room expecting to see Tiny's wife.

Tiny read her look. "I'm sorry, but Darcie isn't feeling well."

The nurse in Mallie became alert.

Again Tiny read her look. "I'm afraid it's pretty bad with Darcie, Mrs. Van Acker. She has some kind of disease that's eating up her nervous system."

Mallie was quick to correct Tiny. "I'm still not Mrs. Van Acker." Mallie flicked a hard look at Don.

"I'm sorry. What should I call you then?"

"Just Mallie is all right." She added, "And if you must be formal, call me Miss Freyling."

Tiny nodded, chin settling down into three fat folds. "All right, Mallie."

"I'm sorry to hear about your wife. I suppose her doctor has recommended certain exercises to keep up her muscle tone?"

Don broke in, "Mallie here is into physical therapy."

Tiny smiled. "So you wrote me."

Mallie read Tiny's unctuous smile. He was a bender. He'd bend the facts and his smile one way so as not to hurt one's feelings too much, and yet under pressure bend them another way to make sure he got what he wanted. Under that ballooning fat lived a hard money man. Mallie said, "Don keeps talking about some plan to make money in a hurry."

Tiny let his smile linger on his heavy lips, at the same time that he shot a vivid blue glance at Don. "You haven't told her then?"

Don sat up very straight in his chair. "As a matter of fact, no, I haven't." Don cast up a soft laugh toward Mallie. "It's best to let sleeping dogs lie as long as possible."

Mallie stiffened.

Tiny said, "I can tell her though?"

Don said easily, "Sure, go ahead. I've nothing to hide from my future wife."

Tiny heaved a sigh, and in doing so, three folds over his stomach swelled out and then settled back. He looked like a huge accordion being played by invisible hands. "As you can probably guess, Miss Freyling, I need money bad. For special medical help for my poor Darcie. I've known for a long time now how to beat the gambling casinos. It's a dead cinch the way I work it. But I've been reluctant to use it, preferring instead to make my living the regular American way as an accountant and statistician."

Mallie's eyes narrowed.

"But I finally decided the time had come to use my plan. Once. Make a killing and then get out." He waved a wide hand. "Oh, it's legitimate legally and all that. It just is that a man doesn't want to make a living at using such schemes. If he does it long enough he'd turn into a crook."

"This scheme of yours . . . ?"

"Yes." Tiny smiled to himself. It was a smile to lull a snake. "I've worked out a way to beat the percentages in blackjack. It's somewhat complicated, but in essence you memorize the cards that go into the discard pile at the same time that you are aware of the number of ten-point cards still left to play. As well as know the averages of how often those left to play will fall on the table."

Don said, "Tiny has a memory like a camera. He can remember a hand played like it was a picture."

Tiny allowed himself a little smile. "And then statistically you work out how often the ones and the twos and the threes will fall."

Mallie waited.

"And then, of course, there are those four aces. Which can be counted as either a one or an eleven."

Don sat forward. His eyes glittered. "Tell her what you do when you lose the first showdowns."

Tiny said, "Don't blink an eyelash and keep on playing. Because I know, from statistics, that you're going to win over the long haul if you stay in the game with totals of nineteen or over. Eighteen or less, you're going to lose your shirt. And of course, the more cards that fall into the discard pile, the more sure you can be of your nineteen and over. And when you get down to the last deal of a deck, and you know exactly what's gone into discard, you can even gamble on winning with an eighteen. Sometimes even a seventeen. It's a sure lock."

Mallie began to feel even more sick about having left her good job in Sioux Falls.

Tiny said, "Don, you brought some money?"

"Yeh." Don's eyes couldn't hold steady on Tiny.

"How much?"

"Well, I got about three hundred with me."

Tiny showed disappointment. "That all? I thought you said over the phone you had about five thousand. I'll need that for leverage. To fall back on in the beginning. Until I catch on to the run of the cards."

Don squirmed.

Mallie slowly swung her eyes on Don. "Did you sneak out there in Gothenburg and call Tiny to tell him about that five thousand of mine?"

"Well . . ." Then Don tried to bluff her. "I sure did. Ain't we in it together for better or for worse now?"

"But legally we're still not married."

"You're not gonna let me down now? After bucking me up while I was in the pen?"

She wanted to say, "I wish now I'd never met you." Instead she finally eased off her hard look. "Most of that money is in a savings account."

"Lord," Tiny said with a sad look at Don. "Darcie is going to be disappointed."

Mallie said, "Darcie approves of you trying to make extra money that way?"

Tiny lowered his head. "Darcie has now reached that stage where she's willing to let me try anything to help her."

"Her doctors have told you that they can help her?"

"We've been to the Mayo Clinic in Rochester."

"Oh."

Don got to his feet and began to pace back and forth. Finally he stopped in front of Mallie and burned silverish eyes at her. "I can't let Tiny down. Besides letting myself down."

Mallie held up to his burning look. "And me?"

Don leaned down and almost touched her nose with his nose. "I want to get that money back I lost in that Meester business. Plus more. And when I get enough back, I want to buy back my mother's house. That property is still really mine and I shall always consider it mine."

"Well, it was your own darn foolishness that got you into that mess in the first place."

"I know that. And I want to make up for that too. Clean the slate for myself. I won't rest easy until I've squared myself with my own conscience."

In the back of her head Mallie could see her brother Dirk sneer at this dead-ringer of his.

Don's voice slid down a whole octave and became a soft catching purr. "You can telegraph your bank, can't you, to send you the money out of your savings account?"

Mallie's mouth went dry. She thought, "My God, I'm a fool for even listening to him, let alone thinking of doing it."

"Mallie? Honey?"

"No."

Tiny sat like a fat stone Buddha. Slowly he fixed his implacable lizard eyes on Mallie. "You needn't worry. I have never lost yet. So long as I can start out with enough money to rebound from possible early losses."

Mallie stared back at Tiny.

Silence.

Mallie's belly yearned for Don. He was so full of seed.

Don abruptly slapped her, first across one cheek, then the other. He had long soft hands and it was like a boy slapping her.

384

"What did you do that for?" Mallie cried.

Tiny watched them both.

Don said, "I'm trying to let you know that this is all terribly serious. Mallie?"

Mallie stirred. "First, can I see how you do it? With real cards?"

"You mean," Tiny said, "you want me to play against Don?"

"Yes. Let Don play the part of the dealer."

Tiny thought it over. "Well, Don already knows my method. So it's going to be hard to beat him."

"I still want to see it. If you can best him, I'll let you have the money. But I want a written statement from you and Don that when you make all that money I get double my investment."

"You got it."

Tiny heaved himself up out of his plush chair and slowly swung his heavy legs into a rolling motion. He entered a side room, came back with a card table and a fresh pack of cards. "Don, will you get those two folding chairs around the corner in there?"

"Sure thing."

Soon they were at it, Don shuffled the cards. His hands were magic with them. The cards fluttered like fifty-two bird wings inside his cage-set hands. He'd shuffled cards thousands of times before. Once he even opened his hands and let the cards glissade from the lifted hand to the bottom hand, with every card falling into place, into a neat compact pack.

Tiny said, "Let's get on with it, Don. Cut out the fancy-dan stuff."

Don got down to business. He shuffled the cards thoroughly; then set the deck down for Tiny to cut.

Tiny touched the deck to say he declined to cut.

Don dealt. A ten of clubs to Tiny, a hidden card for himself. Then a three of hearts to Tiny and a four of spades up for himself.

"Hit me," Tiny said.

Don dealt Tiny a six of diamonds.

"That's it," Tiny said. He had his nineteen.

Don lifted the edge of his hidden card; studied to himself a moment; then thumbed off a five of clubs for himself. Don pursed out his lips, still studying what he had.

Mallie leaned in to see what Don had under. It was a ten-spot. He had his nineteen too.

Don asked, "You're staying then, Tiny?"

"I'm pat."

Don turned over his ace of spades. "Dealer takes the tie."

Don dealt again. Tiny was dealt a king of hearts and a five of spades and a three of diamonds. Eighteen. Don'd dealt himself a hidden card and a seven of spades.

"Still pat, Tiny?"

Tiny thumped his stack of three with a long finger.

Don pursed his lips some more; finally dealt himself another card. An eight of clubs. Don swore. He was about to throw his three cards into the discard when Tiny said, "Show the under card, please. I've got to know what's been played." Don showed it. A ten of diamonds. Total of twenty-five. Four over twenty-one.

So it went. Slowly but surely, no matter how Don the dealer played, and despite his knowing Tiny's method, Tiny got the upper hand. They played an hour and Tiny slowly piled up a thousand points.

Finally Tiny orbed his fat-lidded eyes around at Mallie. "Satisfied?"

Mallie licked her lips. "It does look pretty good at that."

Don fluttered the deck of cards from one hand to the other. "It's the clear dope, Mal, old girl." He leaned against her and snuck a kiss under her chin. "And I know."

Mallie caught on to something. "You were a dealer once, weren't you, Don?"

"Who, me?"

"Weren't you?"

Tiny shrugged his shoulders. His shirt was so tight on him it looked as though it'd give way at the armpit. "Suppose he was, what has that got to do with anything?"

"I want to know how good he is at gambling. If I'm gonna let him gamble with my money."

"It'll be my method we'll use. And mostly my memory."

"But he'll play some too?"

"Yeh. Where I push the odds, I'm gonna let him pick up the slack bet."

Don dropped the cards back into their carton. "Well, what say, Mal, ol' gal?"

"Where's that paper I want you two to sign?"

Don wasn't so sure they should have such a paper between them, but Tiny didn't mind. He went to his desk and typed out an agreement, signed it with a flourish, then handed it to Don. Don made a face as he signed it. Then Mallie signed it.

Don leaped up and did a couplete pirouette in the air. "Wonderful. I promise you, darling, that we'll double your money easy. You'll never regret it. Never."

"And you'll get my job back too?"

"Job . . . ? Job . . . ? Well, sure. After I get my mother's house back." Don rubbed his hands. "And now to find you a room somewhere."

"You're not going to take me with you to Las Vegas?"

"No."

"Why not?"

"We need to concentrate on the game." Don said. "With you along I'd be thinking about going to bed with you while I'm playing. And that might be just enough to wreck our game plan." Don gave her a gallant's winning smile. "You're too much of a temptation."

Mallie squinched up her eyes. "Well then, Tiny, instead of getting a room for me, can't I stay here in your house and take care of Darcie?"

"We already have a nurse for that. Besides, Darcie doesn't want anybody to see her. Only me and the nurse."

"Is it that awful?"

"It's that awful."

Don said, "One thing more, Mallie. We have to use your car to drive to Las Vegas."

Mallie bristled up then. That was too much. "Nosiree! You guys will have to use Tiny's Packard out there."

"But—"

"You can forget the whole thing then! I still haven't wired the bank for that five thousand yet, you know."

"Oh."

"I'm not going to be stuck in a room somewhere so I can't get around."

386

"Okay, okay."

Don found her a room two blocks away. It had a private entrance that gave on a backyard full of honeysuckle bushes.

Meanwhile Mallie, with a dry tongue, wired for the money.

Don said, "We'll be back in a couple of days."

"Let's hope so."

Don and Tiny left almost immediately.

The first while Mallie slept most of the time. It took her a couple of days to catch up on the lack of sleep. She ate at a hamburger joint on the corner. The third day, not hearing from the boys, she decided that as long as she was that close to the mountains she should have a good look at them. She drove up to Squaw Pass and pulled into a lookout point. She made several snowballs and smiled to herself. Here it was June and she was going to throw a snowball at a noisy chipmunk. She sat a long while looking east toward the hazy distant prairie horizon beyond Denver; then turned and looked up at the white peaks around her. It would be lovely to live in Denver if she could now and then drive up into the heights of the mountains. She would miss Sioux Falls and the rolling country around it, and her family, and the wonderful old homestead, but there was something to be said for having both worlds, the prairies and the mountains. It was too bad Denver wasn't the capital of the country. With Denver the capital, the song "America the Beautiful" would make the perfect national anthem.

A week later, late at night, a knock on the door awakened her. It was a heavy knock, and she right away knew who it was. It wasn't Don Van Acker. She got up and turned on a light and opened up. "Hello, Tiny."

Tiny looked beat. The pouches under his eyes resembled dried prunes.

"You lost it all," Mallie said.

"Yes."

"Where's Don?"

"I don't know. When our last dollar disappeared, Don let out a terrible yip, got to his feet, jumped up once, and disappeared too."

"Poor Don."

"Yeh."

"What happened with your sure-fire method?"

"Somebody else must've tried it on them. Because they were ready for us at every turn. At first they let Don place pick-up-the-slack bets. But after a while they told him his money wasn't any good."

A breath slowly filled her chest, deep. Then she shuddered, once. "I guess I knew all along that was going to happen." She brushed a tear out of the corner of her eye. "There was no sign of him afterwards?"

"None. He'd beat me to our room, grabbed up his clothes and suitcase, and vamoosed."

"I guess that piece of paper between us doesn't mean much any more."

Tiny got out his billfold. "I'll give you what I got left."

"Keep it. Darcie's gonna want that at least."

Tiny's shoulders sagged until the points of the shoulder pads of his jacket stuck out. "Yeh, now I've got to go and tell her."

"Good luck."

"What are you going to do?" Tiny asked.

"No use dreamin' in Don's direction anymore."

"No, I guess not."

"Thank God that I insisted he couldn't have my car. Or he'd have run off with that too."

"Yeh. And in the meantime?" Tiny persisted.

"Drive back home, of course, and see if my job is still there. And if my apartment still hasn't been rented out."

"I'm sorry."

"Forget it."

Tiny turned hugely and melded away into the dark.

Mallie swung around on her toes and reentered her room. She got out her purse and counted her money. Land o' Goshen. A stricture of fear grabbed her. After she paid her rent by check, there'd be less than a hundred dollars, hardly enough to get her back to Sioux Falls. She'd have to eat sparingly and hope her red Buick didn't have any breakdowns.

The next morning she packed and was on her way. The day was bright and open and high blue. It was a day for romance and fun and great expectancy that shortly something wonderful was going to happen. But she felt sodden and dead.

She skipped breakfast to save money.

At Ogallala she stopped for gas and coffee. Even with an extra spoon of sugar the coffee tasted like it had been made from burnt carrots. To have at least something that tasted good she bought a candy bar. That was fine until in the last bite she hit a piece of walnut shell. Crack! She could feel a piece of her upper right molar break off. A moment later she felt both the piece of shell and the broken bit of tooth with her tongue. She tongued them out into a teaspoon. That was going to cost her.

An hour farther down the road she developed a toothache. It was in the upper right molar.

It soon got so she didn't dare to take a breath through her opened lips. The raw broken edge of the tooth hurt too much.

By the time she reached Gothenburg the tooth hurt so fierce it affected her sight. It was also getting dark and time to think of finding a room. But she couldn't stay in that town, remembering the night she and Don had spent together in a handsome white though stinky cabin.

She drove on to Willow Island. There she found an old woman who had a back room for rent. The room was a couple of blocks away from Highway 30. In it she could be sure the pounding truck traffic wouldn't keep her awake.

The molar hurt worse by the hour.

Finally at two in the morning she woke up the landlady to ask if she didn't have some oil of cloves. The landlady did. Mallie wrapped some cotton around the end of a toothpick and daubed it into the little bottle of oil of cloves. Then she carefully, mouth wide open before a mirror, touched the brown-stained cotton into the broken corner of her molar.

"Ohh. Oee. That stings."

The landlady, a gaunt drawn old crone, finally managed a smile. "It's gotta hurt if you're gonna kill the pain."

"I suppose."

"You better go see a dentist about that right away."

"I intend to do just that when I get home tomorrow."

"If you can last that long."

Mallie slept for about an hour and then the cracked tooth began to pound in her jaw and head with every beat of her heart. She'd had a good look at the part of the tooth that had broken off and it hadn't looked rotten or decayed to her. It meant the enamel and dentin had broken away from the pulp chamber, leaving the nerve in the raw break exposed.

Somehow she steeled herself into catching several pinched-in naps the rest of the night.

By morning she knew she'd never be able to drive home. Her right eye was almost swollen shut and the left eye wasn't much better.

She drove the five miles back to Gothenburg and looked up a dentist, a Dr. Dale Martinson.

The receptionist was about to turn Mallie away when it happened that Dr. Martinson overheard Mallie through the transom and came out for a moment. "I'm busy making a partial plate, so I can put you in my other chair and take a peek betweentimes while the plaster is hardening."

Dr. Martinson turned out to be a short fellow with graying hair and a bemused smile on his blond face. He had slender fingers that smelled of soap. He got out a probe and a tiny mirror on a handle and had a look. "You say this just happened?"

"Last night."

"Then I think we can save the tooth. If you're willing to wait, I'll get at it as I can. Meanwhile, let's deaden the nerve in your upper jaw."

It took two hours before he finally managed to fix the tooth with a gold cap. Though slender, his fingers were strong, and he was inclined to be somewhat rough. But he was a sure and patient worker. He worked so long in her mouth, and she held it open so long as wide as she could, that she felt like a boa constrictor that had had tried to swallow a calf, leaving its jaw unhinged.

"How much?"

"I've got to have fifty dollars for that."

Mallie turned white. That would leave her with less than five dollars to drive home on. She'd have to skip eating altogether if she was going to have enough gas. She dug out five tens from her purse and handed them to the receptionist.

Dr. Martinson had a softening smile for her. "You're probably going to be breathing through your mouth a lot on the way home, so you better take some of these pain pills with you."

"I can't afford them."

"They're on the house."

Mallie took the little round white pillbox. "Thanks."

"And if your tooth still hurts, go see your own dentist in Sioux Falls. And if he wants to check with me, my address and telephone number is on that box."

"All right."

The tooth did hurt after about an hour. She tried to ride it out but when she got to Fremont she couldn't stand it any longer. She stopped at a filling station for a drink of water and took one of the pain pills.

She also got some gas with the money she had left.

She studied the map, running her finger up along Highway 77, through the Omaha Indian Reservation, through Homer, Sioux City, Elk Point, Beresford, adding up the miles. It came to some 150 miles plus, a long ways to go with what gas she had.

Belly empty and gnawing at her, gold-capped tooth still aching all the way up into her right eye socket, sphincters tight as she worried about having enough gas, she headed straight north up 77.

Some twenty miles south of Sioux Falls she saw that she would have enough gas. She relaxed some.

She drove straight to her former home. By great luck her landlady had not yet found a renter and was very happy to have Mallie back.

Mallie moved her bed up from the basement, put on some fresh sheets, and exhausted and sore all over, even more sore at the world, went to sleep.

The next morning she moved the rest of her things up from the basement. Then she went to the neighborhood grocery and charged some food. Then, with a sad heart, she looked for a job. She was too proud to go back to the Siouxland Hospital to see if her old boss would take her back, not after how he'd raged at her for quitting suddenly the way she did. She tried the McKennan Hospital run by the Roman Catholic church. They were sympathetic but hadn't advanced enough to think of starting up their own physical therapy section.

She tried doctors' offices. No luck.

She put an ad in the paper to say she was prepared to do private nursing. No luck.

Sometimes she fantasized having Don return to her door saying he was sorry and could they try over. She longed for his lovemaking. But having him come back for even a one-night stand could be like swallowing a shotglass of gall sweetened with a spoon of honey.

Finally, desperate, she took to reading want ads in the paper. She read where a taxicab company needed drivers. She went down for a driving test. They liked her driving, liked her knowledge of the city and her looks, and hired her.

After a half year she got to know every street and every alley in Sioux Falls.

A year later, her former boss at the Siouxland Hospital died in a car accident, and the new hospital manager invited her back to run the physical therapy unit again.

41 Geoffrey

1929–1930

Geoffrey, in his law office in Whitebone, finished the dictation for the day and sent his secretary Adela Sharples back to her desk out front.

Geoffrey took a couple of minutes to think to himself before the first client would show up. Earlier he'd taken off his shoes and had pulled out the bottom drawer of his desk and placed his socked feet in it. It was a habit that cool-dressed Miss Sharples frowned at. He always made it a point to put his shoes back on before the clients came in.

Some things his father had said earlier bothered him.

. . . . Geoffrey had driven down from Whitebone to see the folks for Sunday supper, and it was while they were sipping tea that Pa said, "Me and Christ, we died on the cross for nothing. It's no use anymore."

Pa was referring to what had happened to him while bindering oats. Pa was rethreading the binder needle out in the middle of the oats field, wetting the broken end of the twine string with his tongue, rolling the string to a point, and then trying to insert it into the eye, when a scudding rabbit startled the four horses and they took a step forward. Then the horses, heads still reared high, luckily stopped. But they'd moved forward just enough to make the bullwheel turn the gears in the binder and force the bundle-making needle through the center of Pa's left hand.

There Pa was, pinned. There was no way for him to free himself unless someone came by. The reins to the horses were out of reach of his free hand. He was too far away for his voice to carry to the house, where Ma was busy making dinner. He knew Tane would come by in a couple of hours, at dinner time. Tane would have finished shocking his own crop of oats by then. He and Tane worked the two farms together, the old homestead and Tane's quarter section, instead of each having to hire a hand.

Pa had a good look at the hand and saw that it wasn't bleeding. The punched-in needle sat too snug in the wound. The needle was about the size of a goose's head and neck and he could see that the needle had bent the bones somewhat in the metacarpus. Pa gave his hand a jerk to pull the needle back, but the pain was so fierce he almost fainted. That wouldn't work; the machine was still in gear. And there was no way he could get his hand all the way past the point of the needle where it rested against the shuttle.

Then Pa noticed that the toolbox, located under the steel spring seat, was only a few feet away through the machine. Very carefully, so as not to stir his pinned-down left hand, he turned his body half around and then with his right hand reached down through the chains and gears and just barely managed to open the lid to the toolbox and dig out a wrench. Grim-lipped, eyes gimlets, he set the wrench and managed to loosen all the nuts around the needle and then remove the heavy needle with his left hand still stuck in it.

"Whew! That was a close shave. If something had started up those horses again, I'd've been a dead duck."

One-handed, he unhitched the horses and drove them home, all the while carrying the needle caught through his hand. Ma was upset and wanted to call Tane's Arva and have her drive Pa to town. Ma hadn't learned to drive a car yet. But Pa was bullheaded and said he could drive their car one-handed. Dr. Chalmers greased the needle with salve and with a sudden jerk removed it from his hand. Pa's first words were, "Now I know how little Tane felt when they nailed him to the cross. Let alone Christ."

Still sipping his tea, Geoffrey shuddered as he remembered Pa's telling of it. But what bothered Geoffrey most was the remark, "It's no use anymore!" It was of a kind with some other remarks of Pa's. "Three score and ten is long enough." "My ears are beginning to look big and old and wrinkled." "Yep, I've had enough."

After supper Pa and Geoffrey had gone out to sit on the stoop. They talked about this and that for a while, then Pa picked it up again. "Yeh, pretty soon Ma'll say it's time for me to go to bed and for you to get on home. But what fun has bed been for me these last years? I long ago lost my bed rights. And lately my dreams have turned muzzy. Ain't clear any more. Time to move on."

Geoffrey protested. "Aw, Pa, c'mon, take a look at yourself. You're still a young man the way you work."

392

"Ha!" Pa said. "Tell that to Old Frans Haber. He should've had you for a son. When Old Franz was fifty he overheard his son Jack say, 'When a man reaches fifty he ain't of much use to us anymore and one might just as well shoot him as not.' Jack was thirty at the time. Well, when Jack reached fifty himself, Old Franz, who was by that time a grampa several times over, walked over early one morning to Jack's house and woke up Jack and handed him a shotgun, and said, 'Help yourself.'"

"Oh, Pa."

Pa went on. "I'm almost seventy, you know, and any day now Tane is bound to walk over and hand me a shotgun and tell me to shoot myself."

Geoffrey had to smile at the story as well as at the way Pa had shifted the ages around to fit his own case. "Pa, Tane loves you and would never think of it. We all love you."

"But I can tell. He's waiting for me to pass on so he can take over the old place."

"Pa!"

"As the oldest son he has that right."

"But Rolf took up farming too."

"But Rolf didn't just stop at farming."

"Pa, you take all that stuff too serious."

"Yeh, I'm a smart fellow all right. With my hide raw and salt on it" . . . .

Geoffrey, knowing it was time to see the first client of the day, stirred in his swivel chair. He shook his head. Pa had always had a strange withdrawn air about him, as if he were having dark thoughts he couldn't reveal. Lately that air had deepened. Pa's burning eyes were deeper set than ever and often his moustache moved as if he were chewing on the inside of his upper lip. It was true that his ears were quite wrinkled, but, shucks, wrinkles had shown up on all the Freylings, especially around the eyes. Though curiously enough, Ma still appeared to have the youngest skin of them all.

Miss Sharples tapped a fingernail on the door and then poked her head in. She wore her straight hair in a long flow of black to her shoulders. "Mr. Bately is here. You know, about his daughter Grace."

"Oh, yes."

Miss Sharples's black eyes looked down at where Geoffrey's feet still rested in the lower drawer.

Geoffrey said, "Go ahead, say it."

Miss Sharples continued to look with disapproval at his socked feet and where they rested. He had a long slim foot.

Geoffrey flared up inside. "Dammit all, speak your mind, woman. I'm tired of getting all those wordless black looks of yours."

"You'll be angry with me if I did."

"Say it!"

"Well, all right. Mr. Freyling, I hate to be so critical, but really, if one didn't know you, one'd say you were uncouth, with your feet like that in a drawer."

Geoffrey let his nose move once. "Uncouth, eh?"

"Yes, I'm sorry. But really, that's what that bad habit of yours is."

"Oh, shit, Miss Sharples, I'm as couth as you any day."

"Ulp!" Miss Sharples's black eyes closed over and she withdrew her head. 393

Geoffrey smiled. "That should put her in her place for a while. Just because she plays the organ in the Episcopal Church doesn't mean she knows how to train me to be a good lawyer." With a groan he removed his feet from the drawer and slipped on his brown oxfords again. The truth was, Geoffrey liked Miss Sharples. Adela had class, in her slim erect carriage, in her choice of clothes; today, for example, a black velvet blouse and a blue-grey plaid dress.

He picked up the Bately file, which Miss Sharples had earlier set out for him. He paged through a little of it and then laid it down. He shook his head. He looked around his office. There were rows upon rows of red and gray and brown volumes of law books. He noticed that his diploma from the University of Minnesota Law School as well as his state bar document were both hanging crooked again. Those damned trucks crashing down Main Street always shook them askew. He got up and straightened them level. He liked things kept neat and precise. He glanced at his blond oak desk. Everything was in order there: pad, pen holder, boxes for incoming and outgoing mail. Ashtray for visitors; he himself didn't smoke.

There was a knock on the door.

"Come in."

Mr. Jack Bately leaned in. One look and a person could tell he was a re-formed drunk. His face, once a flushed purple, was now a faded slack gray. His blue eyes had partially recovered their old color. He wore patched overalls, though clean.

"Have a chair, Jack."

"Thanks."

Geoffrey picked up the Bately file again. He looked at the first couple of pages, accurate notes taken over the phone by Miss Sharples, and then looked at Bately again. "I see here that you wish me to make out a complaint for your daughter Grace against our deputy sheriff and a local dentist."

"Yeh. For spaying her." Bately's voice was remarkably crisp. Outrage had aroused the old tough in him.

"So you say. What's your evidence?"

"She told me."

"Any witnesses?"

"There was a nurse present."

"Oh? That's the first I know of that. Who's the nurse?"

"Essa Dawson."

"Her? I'm surprised."

"I'm not. She almost runs a whorehouse."

"Almost?"

A sneer curled up the corners of Bately's gray lips. "She boarded my daughter in one of her back rooms. Along with that Flescher girl."

Geoffrey spotted a piece of lint on the sleeve of his gray jacket. He flicked it off. "Why isn't your daughter here to make the complaint herself? She's of legal age, isn't she?"

"Grace is twenty-five. But she's scared shitless of that deputy sheriff. You know how rough Bart Rauch is."

"Is she afraid of the dentist too?" Geoffrey glanced down at the top paper of the file. "Peter Toth?"

"No, dammit all, she loves him. She asked him to give her a baby, and I guess that started off the whole shebang. He got scared. He already has six kids with his wife. He wanted to keep Grace for a little on the side now and then. As did that roughneck Rauch."

Geoffrey sat up straighter. Aha. A big case. One that would cause an uproar in the old burg of Whitebone. He read a little further. "You told my secretary that the dentist Peter Toth actually did the so-called spaying."

"That's right."

"Hmm. I suppose though if we were to haul Essa Dawson into court she'd deny everything."

"She sure would."

"What about this other girl who boards with nurse Dawson? This Lida Flescher girl? Was she operated on too?"

"You bet. She was the first. When it worked safe on her, Toth figured he could easy try it on Grace too."

Geoffrey pursed his lips in and out. He studied Bately with grave eyes. Bately didn't have much of a reputation in town. And Mrs. Bately was a mop woman at the First National Bank who'd kicked daughter Grace out of the house for being a tramp. The two older Batelys wouldn't make very good witnesses; whereas Rauch and Toth were considered upstanding citizens.

"Do you get along well enough with your former wife that she'd make a good witness?"

"No, worse luck. She said I had bad blood in me and that I'd passed it on to Grace."

"Hmm. Their lawyers will probably subpoena her and then the dolls will really dance."

Bately's weathered eyes hardened. "If she does show up in court, and if she don't mind her mouth, I'll get her later."

"Meaning what?"

"I'll stick her."

"Kill her?"

"You bet."

"Have you said that to anybody else?"

"Think I'm a fool?"

Geoffrey picked up his black pen and began to doodle in the corner of his blue desk pad. "Are you working these days?"

"Yes. Winters I help fill the icehouse with ice from the river. Summers I help the city keep the park by the river neat. I pick up paper and bottles and such."

"Enough to make a living?"

"Hardly."

"When's the last time you had a drink?"

"I went on my last toot exactly a year ago yesterday."

"And you've stayed off the tiger milk ever since?"

"No more shakes for me. Spilling coffee all over."

Geoffrey studied to himself. Toth and Rauch had underestimated the Batelys. Toth was a dapper fellow, a good dentist, liked by most everybody, especially women. But Rauch was known for playing fast and loose with the law. Geoffrey felt a little sorry for Toth. Toth actually was a nice guy. Though there were raunchy stories about him, namely that he was said to have seduced women in his dentist's chair while they were sedated. But Geoffrey didn't feel sorry for Rauch. Rauch was a son of a bitch. Geoffrey liked girls himself, and had had relations with two women in Whitebone. Whitebone was known for its comely women, women who, though one could not call them loose, were at least smiling dates. But sex with women by the dozen—no.

"Where is your daughter now?"

"I've got her hid."

"Where?"

"I have a brother in Sutherland. She's keeping house for him while his wife recovers from a 'pendix operation."

"I tell you. Your daughter Grace has got to bring the action herself. She's over twenty-one. Ask her to come in and see me soon."

"You bet."

"In the meantime, button your lip. No talkee."

"You got it. I'm gonna get those two sonsabitches even if I finally have to kill them."

"Now, now, none of that kind of wild talk." Geoffrey frowned. "Do you own a gun?"

"Yip."

"You better bring that in when Grace comes to see me. I want it here in my desk. You understand?"

Bately fell silent.

"Understand?"

Bately got to his feet. "Gotcha."

Geoffrey nodded him out.

His next client, Bill Boer, clumsy and knobby, wanted to fix his wife, Drentha. She'd run away, which he thought was probably a good thing, since she was no good. But what was bad about it, Drentha had taken to charging all kinds of expensive clothes in his name, as well as board and room. Bill Boer was a devout Christian and couldn't give her a divorce. He wanted something done legally to keep her from sucking any more money out of him. She was working as a waitress in the Rapids Cafe and she could pay for her own bills.

After some hemming and hawing, Bill Boer finally agreed to let Geoffrey draw up a notice for the Whitebone *Press:*

> To whom it may concern:
>   My wife, Drentha Lutt Boer, having left my bed and board without cause or provocation, all persons are forbidden to harbor or trust her on my account, as I will not pay any of her debts nor pay for anything she charges in my name.
>
> William Boer

Geoffrey wanted to make it sound more legal. But Bill Boer had found a squib in the Bonnie *Review* that was more to his liking as a model, and Geoffrey let him have his way. The notice as it now read sounded like Bill Boer.

So it went all day long. Except for the Bately thing there wasn't anything really challenging. Geoffrey sometimes wondered if maybe his sister Mallie wasn't right. She said he was too good, too bright, for a small place like Whitebone. Whitebone had only five thousand people; what could he expect in the way of challenges in a burg like that? She wanted him to move to Sioux Falls, where he'd meet brighter people, run into more complicated cases, have a chance to really mature into a big person.

396

"You're far too smart for Whitebone, Geoff. And pretty soon country juries are going to lean against you, on the grounds that the peewee lawyers there should win once in a while too. Especially if the case is a toss-up."

Geoffrey only smiled. He liked the leisurely pace of a small town. As for being too smart, well, he knew if he ever got into a case where he had to argue in district court against imported city lawyers, it would be his turn to have the jury lean in his direction.

"And another thing, dear brother. It's time you thought of getting another secretary. Nobody really likes her. She's so snooty. Even if God were a woman, Miss Sharples would still be able to find fault with Her works."

"But I like her."

"Softy. You have to think of your law practice first, not your sentimental old heart."

"That would mean sending her back to Mount Curve in Minneapolis. When she quite deliberately chose to live here where things are simple and open. She's turned her back on all that high-society mink stuff."

"Geoff, you should have a quietly pleasant woman out front to greet the local small-town public."

"Miss Sharples isn't snooty."

But Mallie had a point. Only the other week one of the lawyers around the corner had remarked, as the two of them stood talking together on the street and watched Miss Sharples walk past them on her way to the post office to get the morning mail, "My goodness, Geoffrey, the way she walks. Your secretary's got such a proper behind. It sticks out like a bustle."

Mallie went on. "And I know just the one, too, who'd make a perfect receptionist and secretary."

Geoffrey had heard enough on the subject. "All right. Silence in the court-room. Judge Freyling has spoken."

The last client left around four o'clock. Geoffrey picked up the phone. "Miss Sharples?"

"Yes, Mr. Freyling."

"Could you come in here a minute?"

"Yes, Mr. Freyling."

Miss Sharples came in carrying her stenographer's notebook. "Another letter to dictate?"

"No. Not that. Sit down."

Miss Sharples sat down chastely on a chair facing his desk. A girdle kept her from relaxing.

"Miss Sharples, did I hear you say your landlady went to school with Essa Dawson?"

"Yes."

"Do you remember if your landlady ever said anything about her, like, was Essa smart in school? Popular?"

"Oh, she was popular all right." Miss Sharples smiled to herself. "My land-lady said the boys hung around her like bees around a honeysuckle bush."

"But she didn't get married."

"No. She always said she was never going to get married. She'd get from the men what she wanted but she'd stay single. Terribly independent."

"That house she runs. That's sort of a halfway house, isn't it? For patients who can't afford to be in a hospital but who need to be near a doctor?"

"That's right."

397

"Do you think she's running a whorehouse in the back part of her house there?"

"Oh, not that exactly. Just a call girl sort of place."

"What kind of a witness do you think she'd make in court?"

"She's full of snappy comebacks."

"One of those who has to have the last word."

"That's right, Mr. Freyling."

"Is she a bulldyke?"

"A what, Mr. Freyling?"

"A lesbian. Surely you know what they are."

Miss Sharples turned pink. "No, I don't think she is. In fact, I know she's not."

"How do you know that?"

"Deputy Raunch sometimes cohabits with her too."

"How do you know that?"

"I have my suspicions."

"Facts, Miss Sharples."

"I think if you were to question Mr. Rauch about that in court he'd lie so obviously everybody would know he was lying."

"Facts, Miss Sharples."

"Well, Mr. Rauch has also asked me to sleep with him."

"Oho."

"He's sex crazy."

Geoffrey wished he could be more at ease with Adela Sharples. Instead of being balky around her, such as putting his shoeless feet in his lower desk drawer, or seeking to shock her with a dirty word now and then, he longed to have an easy, even laughing, relationship with her, like he had with his sisters. The two women lovers he'd had so far in Whitebone, well, he hadn't loved them; just liked them. The two women in the beginning had gone out with him to have a good time, both dancing and in bed; but after a couple of months both lovers turned serious, finally said they'd like to marry him. It had been a sticky business; how to extricate himself without hurting them. It took months; to the point where he was depressed. The problem with them really was they'd never make good deep friends like his sisters were for him.

Behind that proper front of Miss Sharples, that classy composure of hers, she had to have some kind of deep warmth.

He thought: "What I ought to do is ask her if she's ever had a man."

Miss Sharples broke in on his ruminations. "Will that be all, Mr. Freyling?"

"Yes." He'd been leaning back in his swivel chair. He leveled grave blue eyes at her. Then he sat forward. "Uhh, no. I'd like to ask you something." He thought: "She isn't going to like this, but I'd just kinda like to know." He cleared his throat; tried but couldn't quite look her in the eye. "How come you never married?"

She straightened up ever so little. She gave him a distant smile. "I've worked for you a full year now, and so far we've never been very confidential with each other. I believe it best we continue our relationship that way. My family has always believed that one should never mix business with sex."

"Sex? Well, I didn't know that my question involved that. I was just thinking to myself, Does that secretary of mine, this Miss Adela Sharples, ever have any fun?"

398

She pinkened again. "That slipped out. I meant pleasure. Also, that's really none of your business."

"I suppose not. You're always so formal, I got to wondering if I couldn't get you to be a little more at ease with me. So that . . ."

"So that I'd present a more amiable front for your clients?"

Good Lord. Had she overheard his sister Mallie talking about her? "Miss Sharples . . . don't worry. You're doing just fine in that department. Every lawyer in the area here, especially here in Whitebone, is jealous of me that I have such a competent secretary."

Her face softened. "Oh."

"My hope is that you in turn aren't disappointed in me as your boss."

She glanced down at his feet. "Only when you take off your shoes in the office, Mr. Freyling."

"Oh, say, about that I do have a question to ask you. Tell me truly now . . . do my feet stink? When I played a little basketball in high school I was very careful not to get athlete's foot."

Her classic straight nose twitched. "No, your feet do not smell. It's just that in public it might be considered a bit uncouth."

"Oh, shit, Miss Sharples."

"Will that be all?"

"Yes, Miss Sharples."

. . . . Geoffrey recalled the morning he hired Adela Sharples. He'd put an ad in the Whitebone *Press* that he needed a secretary-receptionist. It ran three weeks before it brought a response. He was out front trying to handle phone calls at the same time that he did some legal typing when the door opened and a tall young woman stepped in. She was wearing a stylish dark blue suit, jacket and dress, with a white blouse and a soft red necktie. She stood like an athlete. Her black eyes seemed to pick at everything in his front reception room. Finally she looked directly at him. The look seemed to get a perfect fix on him.

He stood up. "Can I help you?"

She opened her purse and took out a newspaper clipping. It was his ad. "Maybe I can help you."

"Oh." He smiled. "You've come to be interviewed for the secretary-receptionist job."

"Yes."

"Let's go to my inner office." He ushered her into his book-lined room. "Have a chair." He went around and sat down in his own chair. "Do you have a work summary of some kind? Where you've worked before?"

"I've never had a job before."

"What?" He looked at her expensive clothes again.

"No."

"Can you type? Take shorthand?"

"No."

"Well, what makes you think you might be qualified to be a legal secretary?"

"The legal profession sounds interesting. Also, my cousin Frank Chandler is in law."

Geoffrey's ears pricked up. "Are you from Saint Paul?"

"No, Minneapolis. My people live on Mount Curve."

"But you're related to the Chandlers of the famous Chandler firm in Saint Paul?"

"Yes."

"Well, that changes things. You've at least got it in the blood."

She gave him a shy cryptic smile. "But that won't count for much, will it, if I can't type and take dictation?"

"No, it won't."

She smiled shyly some more. "Well, I decided that if you would bear with me for a few weeks, at least let me be your receptionist at first, I could take a crash course in both dictation and typing at the nearest college. In the evening."

He liked that. Here was a woman with backbone. "May I ask you something?"

"Yes?"

"Were you ever in sports of any kind?"

"I play tennis. And I've done some horseback riding. Professional, even. Right after I left Vassar."

Ah. That accounted for that erect posture and that winner of a seat.

She slipped the ad back in her purse. "You've probably had a lot of applicants who can take dictation and who can type."

"To be frank, not one."

"Oh. Then perhaps . . . ?"

"Yes. Let's give it a try. At the end of the month we'll talk again."

"I'm glad."

He pursed his lips. He allowed himself a smile that he meant to be waggish. "How in the world did a Mount Curve girl hear about this job down here in lowly Whitebone?"

She grimaced. For a second it didn't become her. "I was hoping that could remain a deep dark secret. Someday, when I'm six sheets to the wind, I may tell you about it."

"You, six sheets to the wind?"

"You might be surprised, Mr. Freyling." She stood up. "Then I'm hired?"

"Yes, you are."

"Can I start work right now?"

"Right now?"

"Yes."

"Of course. Come with me. I'll show you what I want out front as a receptionist" . . . .

Miss Sharples burst into his office without knocking. She was visibly disturbed. "Sorry to break in on your thoughts like this, but have you heard the news about Bert Rauch?"

Geoffrey had been about to call her in to take the morning's dictation. He'd come into his office through the back door, something he often did to avoid clients waiting to pounce on him out front. "What about Rauch?"

"I just saw the sheriff take the corner on two wheels going west. So I stepped out a moment and asked the cop standing on the corner what was up." She took in a great breath. "Bert Rauch hung himself in his garage last night."

Geoffrey jerked erect in his swivel chair. "He did?"

"His wife found him."

"How would the cop know that so quick?"

"Our other cop took the call. And he called the sheriff and the coroner."

"Hmm. Well, Miss Sharples, that sure changes the complexion of the Bately case."

"It certainly does, Mr. Freyling."

"See if you can get hold of Mr. Bately for me, will you? We've got to get his daughter up here right away to issue a complaint before our dentist Toth skips the country."

"All right, Mr. Freyling."

A half hour went by. Geoffrey finally got his thoughts in order for the day, mostly concerning two other cases he was working on. He picked up the phone. "Miss Sharples, any luck getting Mr. Bately?"

"No. His landlady says he's gone to Sutherland."

"To get his daughter presumably. Mmm. Why don't you come in here and we'll get at the correspondence."

"Yes, Mr. Freyling."

Geoffrey made short work of his dictation. "That'll be all, Miss Sharples. Any clients out front?"

"No."

"Ha. They're probably too busy gossiping about the Rauch hanging to be thinking of their complaints. At least the hanging did us some little good. Because this is the suing-est area! Instead of being called Siouxland it should be called Sueland. People here sue on the least excuse. Over the most miserable little miserly things! I keep trying to talk 'em out of it, but then they blink their eyes, and go around the corner and bother Kalmer. Who in turn again tries to talk them out of it and then they go see Klein. And Klein finally takes 'em on because he's got a junky legal mind. And of course, later on, he finally hauls one of our clients into court and there we still are, dealing with those fribbly mouseshit cases." Geoffrey had once again tried to shock her. "I'm sorry. But all that suing does get me down sometimes." He shook his head. "How often haven't you heard people around here say, 'There ought to be a law against that!' Not 'for' something; but 'against' something. It shows you people just simply do not understand what true democracy means. The average person is in favor of free speech, free press, sure, so long as he is doing the talking and the writing. But when the other fellow is in favor of it, then it's time to sue him."

Miss Sharples said quietly, "Will that be all?"

"Yes." Geoffrey swung his chair half around. "Though wait a minute. I think I'll take off tomorrow and go down and see my father. There's something going on down there I don't like. In the meantime, you come to work as usual, handle all calls, and postpone where you have to. And if you get time, would you try to ferret out all the information you can as to just why Rauch committed suicide? Get the police report as well as the coroner's report? And if Rauch's wife makes a statement, get that too. I'm interested in any hint that will implicate our ladies' man Toth."

"Yes, Mr. Freyling." Miss Sharples stood up, started for the door; then hesitated and cast a backward glance at him. She opened her lips. Then, whatever it was she had in mind to say, she bit it back. She closed the door quietly.

Geoffrey rocked back and forth in his swivel chair. "I think what I'm gonna do about Pa is recommend that he retire. And let Tane take over the farm. Like Pa's already mentioned. Pretty soon Tane's kids will be old enough to help Tane run the section. Like Pa did with us a long time ago."

401

Geoffrey had just bought himself a new gray-blue Model A Ford and on the least excuse got in it and drove around to look at the sights. Going to Pa's house was going to be another good excuse to go riding in it.

The King's Trail went down the same valley with the Big Rock River. It was September. The forenoon sky was as clear as a drop of dew. The north wind was so good to breathe it made the nose widen like a rabbit's.

He took the two corners of the correction line between Minnesota and Iowa on two wheels, scaring some white chickens from Minnesota across the road into Iowa, making the eyes of a young girl pop as she looked up from weeding her garden. He soared up over the Illinois Central Railroad pass like a floating swallow and came down on the other side like a heavy bluejay.

In Rock Falls he had to slow down to fifteen miles an hour. The town's traffic laws were old-fashioned. He remembered reading in the Leonhard County paper that the old ladies in Rock Falls got after the mayor and the town council about the young bucks from other nearby towns speeding through their fair city. The ladies became so vocal about it they made the council pass the fifteen-mile-an-hour law.

Three miles south of Rock Falls, Geoffrey took the K.T. Highway a mile west, then once again headed south across rolling and slow-sloping land. All the oat fields had already been plowed black and lay in vivid contrast to the soft tasseled gold of the cornfields and the old greens of late summer pastures. It was all a lovely country. He should have taken Adela Sharples with him. With her keen eye for art, she would have been the perfect person to enjoy the neat classic farmland rectangles, black and gold and green. Someday he would take her with him, if anything to let Ma know he had a good eye for women. Ma would like her; so would Thea and Tressa. And to heck with Mallie and her opinion. Mallie was jealous. And a little bitter after what had happened to her and her jailbird.

As for Ana? God only knew what she'd say about Adela. Poor Ana. She was lost to the best things of life. She'd started out being short on touching. And then something had happened to her when she'd worked for the Bartleses. It had queered her forever. It was sometimes said of a sulky girl that she might be cured of her offishness if one took her out in a buggy with a seat just barely wide enough for two—but not Ana. The funny thing was, Adela would be more apt to understand Ana than Ana understand Adela.

His softly humming gray-blue Model A lofted itself up over the Weatherly hill and then swanned down toward the grove of the Siouxland Home for orphan boys. Through the trees along the Big Rock River beyond, he could just make out the abandoned country schoolhouse where he and his older brothers and sisters had started school.

He crossed the new steel-and-concrete bridge over the river. He missed the old plank bridge and its wondrous clattering roar when a vehicle crossed it too fast.

He took the slow turn southwest toward Bonnie just where the highway and the railroad together entered the north end of Pa's section of land. Looking ahead, he saw that Pa still had not threshed his grain. Pa's stand of some twenty grain stacks looked like a small village of Indian tepees. Swinging a look to his left, Geoffrey saw that Tane living up on the table just above the first riverbank hadn't threshed either. Tane had eight stacks of grain. It meant there had been a bumper crop in the Big Rock River valley and that the threshers were late in getting around to the last stacks.

Geoffrey slowed down the last mile. Vivid memories of the old days whelmed up and his attention wandered. He had trouble keeping to his side of the road. What great times they'd all had on what everybody now referred to as the Freyling section. Pa should be happy that he'd pioneered that portion of the river valley and had started up a worthy family dynasty. Why should Pa let fly with remarks that showed that deep inside he wasn't very happy? Pa had never known a sick day in his life. At sixty-eight he was still as tough as a forty-year-old. His red-brown hair and his moustache were only now turning grayish. Pa looked like he might live forever. Provided, of course, he remained optimistic. Pa had also become a thorough reader and a good reasoner, as the editor of the Bonnie *Review* had remarked in an editorial about another pioneer. So why shouldn't Pa enjoy life, for godsakes? Pa was a king among pioneers. He had the true Siouxland step—something one couldn't say about most men.

Geoffrey took the turn into Pa's lane in low gear. It made his heart pound in his throat to see the old yard again. His eyes misted over. As always, it was a neat yard, mowed around the house and out toward the barn, no clutter of paper or broken boards anywhere, fences tight, buildings freshly painted, the roofs tight against the weather.

Pa was walking ahead of him down the lane reading the headlines of the Sioux City *Journal*. Pa'd just got the mail. Pa heard him coming and stepped to one side to let him by.

Geoffrey pulled up near the front stoop. He got out slowly. He turned and smiled.

Pa came stepping toward him in his familiarly slightly pigeon-toed walk. Pa's glowing grave eyes kept wanting to look down at the headlines. "What can I do for you that don't take too long?"

Geoffrey started to laugh. "Oh, Pa, you can be so funny sometimes."

"Well?"

"Pa! It's me, your youngest, Geoffrey."

"I can see."

"What's eating you, Pa?"

"Nothing you should bother yourself about."

Geoffrey looked at his wristwatch. It was ten o'clock. "Ma got the coffee ready?"

"Ma ain't home."

"Where'd she go?"

"She walked over to Tane's to see the grandkids."

"Walking?" So Ma still hadn't learned to drive a car. "You didn't bring her?"

"Nope. She wanted to walk it. She can be awful balky, you know."

"Pa, it sounds like you really don't care to see me today."

"I'm not sure I care to see anybody."

"Boy, has somebody got the grumps. No wonder Ma took to walking over to Tane's." Geoffrey cocked his head to one side. "You two not talking again?"

"I got the best wife in the world. She always hits me with the soft end of the broom."

"Haha." That was better. "How's the hand?"

Pa waggled his left hand, flexed it several times, then balled it up into a tight fist. The star-shaped scar on the back of Pa's hand showed up a sharp white. "Fine. I had better luck than Christ. His holes didn't get a chance to heal."

"If they had, life for us would have turned out a whole lot different."

"Ha. You're right there. We'd have all grown up heathens. Worshiping Wodan on Wednesday instead of Jehovah on Sunday."

"And we'd have had Baldur as our Christ and Loki as our Satan."

Just then the new Freyling dog, a brown collie named Shep (as his predecessor had been), came loping around the side of the barn. Shep spotted the car, then Geoffrey. Shep gave a leap, and then came bounding toward Geoffrey. Shep was so excited to see his pal Geoffrey, he made several casts around him in riotous joy. Finally, moaning in pleasure, almost breaking out into speech, Shep reached up and licked Geoffrey's fingertips delicately.

Geoffrey noticed the hair under Shep's belly was sopping wet. "Where you been? Huh? Huh?"

Pa snorted. "Probably out topping off Haber's bitch."

"What's wrong with that?"

"Nothing. Just that he's lucky."

"Pa, if Shep was the boss here, he would long ago have invited me in for coffee and cake."

Pa let down at that. "You're right. I guess I got up on the wrong side of the bed this morning." Again Pa snorted. "Though I must say the wrong side was not on your mother's side."

"Kind of funny talk in front of your son, Pa."

403

"Aren't we finally both old enough to talk about such things without winking?"

"I guess we are."

"Surely by now you know what it means to a man to sleep with a woman. I hear stories about you, you know. Thank God you ain't a pansy."

Geoffrey opened the screen door. "Shall I lead the way into the house? Or what?"

"Come on. I'll make you a cup of coffee."

They sat at the kitchen table, the coffee perking to one side on the stove, and Shep, wagging his tail, lying against Geoffrey's feet. Geoffrey for old times' sake sat in his old place while Pa sat at the head of the table in his worn oak swivel chair.

Geoffrey tapped a finger on the newspaper lying between them. "What was so all-fired interesting in the headlines you hardly had time for me?"

Pa turned the paper over and pointed at two lines in bold capitals at the bottom of the front page. "This."

Geoffrey held the paper up to the light coming in through the west windows behind him. Oho. A rich financier had jumped out of a window in his office on Wall Street. Suicide. Geoffrey flicked a look at Pa. But Pa's face was as impassive as the cover of an algebra textbook. "Well?"

"Take a look at the financial section next."

"Oh, Pa, that part of the paper has always remained a mystery to me."

"It hasn't to your brother Rolf."

"How do you know that?"

"He's gotten rid of everything he'd bought on margin."

"Why that?"

"Because of why that financier, what's his name, Trevor-Sachs, jumped out of the window."

"You mean, the stock market's going to collapse?"

"That's what Rolf says."

"Yeh, that Rolf is doing all right." Geoffrey sighed. "In his case I guess we're going to have to say it was possible to make a silk purse out of a sow's ear."

"Yeh. Or a whistle out of a pig's tail." Pa shook a finger at Geoffrey. "But don't say 'sow' around your ma. She don't like that word. And she does have a soft spot in her heart for her throwback."

"Boy, Pa, you sure got the sours today."

"I know it. And I'm sorry." Pa reached for the coffeepot and poured them each a cup, then passed the cream and sugar. Pa helped himself. "You must've come out here today for a reason."

"You were saying the other day about the oldest son having the right to take over the family farm when the old folks pass on?"

"Yeh?"

Geoffrey tested the steaming brew. Ah, still good. Pa knew how to make coffee with hair on it. "I don't think Tane is going to get any argument from the rest of us on that. He's more of a farmer than me, that's for sure. And Dirk too. And I don't think Rolf ever expected to inherit it."

"No, Rolf's so busy buying up tax-delinquent properties and then restoring them that he wouldn't care to just run this farm. Besides, he's richer than all of us put together, so he don't need it."

Geoffrey sipped some more coffee. "Thea's husband, Oliver, is never going to farm again. And Wallie Starnes is no farmer. Ana ain't the marrying kind, so she won't want it. And we know Mallie is never going to want it." Geoffrey sighed. "It's beginning to look like poor Mallie too is never going to marry. So, like I say, Tane is the one."

"Get to the point."

"Pa, I'd like to recommend that you and Ma move to town and let Tane take it over this winter. So his kids can remember this place as their place, and not that farm of his up on the table there."

"Yeh, I've thought of that." Pa took several swallows of coffee. "You know, it's beginning to look like Tane is the only one to give me grandchildren. Thea ain't gonna have any. Dirk ain't the marrying kind either. And Tressa's husband, Wallie Sternes, is a deadbeat in bed."

"Who told you that?"

"Arva blurted it out one day. Tressa had been talking to her."

"Poor Tressa."

"And Rolf's wife let drop to Tressa that Rolf's seed is slow." Pa gave the table a whack with the flat of his hand. "Man, I sure hatched me a funny bunch of turtles."

"How in the world would Greta know that?" Geoffrey let fly with a short laugh. "Did she look?"

Pa allowed himself a laugh too. "Greta so wanted babies she had both herself and Rolf examined at the Mayo Clinic. They can afford to go to the Mayo, you know. She was all right but he wasn't. I guess they looked at his seed under a microscope."

"God's peace!" Geoffrey exclaimed. He'd recently learned the meaning of his name and sometimes liked to use the phrase as an expletive.

"Yeh." Pa poured both Geoffrey and himself a second cup of coffee. "Ana of course has sewed herself shut. And like you say, there's poor Mallie."

"And me." Geoffrey spilled some cream and sugar in his second coffee. "I'm gonna have kids too, Pa."

"Let's hope so."

"I think I got my eye on one now."

That odd otherworldly look in Pa's grave eyes slowly retreated. "I don't suppose we can meet her sometime?"

"Yeh, I wisht I'd taken her along with me today." Geoffrey looked down at his long slender fingers, at his precisely manicured nails. "She would have enjoyed seeing the country on the way down."

"Where's she from?"

"You won't like to hear that, Pa."

"Try me."

"She's a Mount Curve girl. Minneapolis."

"Ha. Your mother will like that. You know of course Ma comes from some sort of royal line that went broke."

"I remember Ma talking about it when we were just kids."

"It's true. When I first saw her she was cooking for Lord Sutherland. Near Le Mars. But she hated him. And she hated her job. Because she felt she'd been meant for better things. The Shortridges were once bigwigs in Yarmouth. And before that they came out of Dumfriesshire. Monocle and all."

"Yes, I heard all that before. But you, now, Pa?"

"I came out of the real aristocracy. If I can believe old Alfred Alfredson. Before Alfredson died he told me the Frisians were 'the real people' of the Old

Country. And I guess that's what my real father and mother were. Frisians." The wild gray disembodied look in pa's eyes continued to retreat. "According to my foster father, Old Dirk Freyling, my real father's name was Alfredson. Me and that mason were probably second cousins or something. But I never talked to Alfredson about it. Why go into all that? We're Americans. And in our case, I like to think we're prairie aristocrats. We clean up after ourselves as we go. Neat. No loose ends. We know how to use the old corncob without help from any maid-in-waiting." For a second Pa's eyes blazed wild and whitish again. "And that's just what I'm gonna do."

"Do?" Geoffrey sensed that Pa had been thinking about something dark and terrible.

"By the way, your British mother believes in primogeniture too."

"Oho. Then you and Ma have been talking you might retire."

Pa allowed himself a snort of a laugh. "No, not really. Anyway, I've just now decided I will retire. Sometimes it helps to talk out loud to another pair of ears besides your own." Pa mused to himself with a drawn smile. "Then Tane can take care of paying for the hired man."

"You hired a man?"

"Yeh. Shortly after I almost got crucified on my own binder. On a farm where you're around machinery you should always have two men present."

"Good thinking. Any more coffee in that perker?"

"You bet." Pa poured out the last of the coffee from the shining nickel pot.

Later, Geoffrey asked, "Who's making out your will, Pa?"

"Not you. The other kids might not like it if their own brother did it. No, I'll drive up to Rock Falls one day and see a lawyer there. Be good to have it made out in the county seat."

"Good. And do it soon." Geoffrey finished his third coffee and pushed the cup aside. "Well, I better get back. There's something I want to get done yet today."

"Sure you don't want to stay and share some soup and sliced cold ham with me? Sorry that all I can offer you is what the icebox serves up."

"No. I took the morning off to drop by here for a cup of coffee. But oh, boy, every time I take off like this, that work sure piles up on the old desk."

"I take it you're doing pretty well."

"Better than I ever expected. And you, Pa, you've done pretty well too over the years, haven't you?"

"Yip. Not only is the farm free and clear, but I've got a nice chunk in the bank. Drawing interest. When I make out that will, I think I can give a fair shake to all you kids. Besides Tane."

"When I asked you about your will, I didn't mean I think you're at death's door. You look like you're going to live another twenty years, easy."

"Twenty years? Ha. Fat chance of that, especially if I retire to town with your mother. For years now she's tried to cut my tail off right behind my ears."

"Oh, come on now, Pa." To himself, Geoffrey thought: "I just wonder if Pa and Ma's not getting along had something to do with us kids being slow to get married." Aloud he said, "In many ways you and Ma are a remarkable couple. Look at what you two did here in this valley, turning this wild land into a productive farm."

"You'll never know, son, you'll never know. Until you get married yourself someday." Then Pa quickly added, "Though of course you may have better luck in the drawers."

"You mean, better luck in the draw, don't you?"

Pa's pink lips drew down deep under his speckled moustache. "No, I meant drawers."

"Pa, really now, aren't you getting a little old for that sort of thing?"

"For coupling with a woman? Never."

"Anyway, I know you. You'll find something to do in town."

Pa shook his head. "No, I'll slowly dry up like an old piece of leather. And that's not for me. I want to go out with my flag flying. A man's a fool to want to live beyond the biblical three score and ten if he doesn't have love." Pa threw Geoffrey a glittering white-gray look. "Just wait until you hit sixty-eight, boy."

"Okay." Geoffrey still had trouble understanding that a man that old might want to fornicate.

Both stood up at the same time and walked outside.

They were surprised to see that a huge anvil cloud had arisen in the southwest. Just as they stepped down off the stoop the shadow of its front edge moved over the yard. They stepped around the side of the house for a better look.

Pa said, "That looks like it might be a bad one. On the underside of it there, that's a mean white sky. Falling streaks of gray usually mean hail."

They stared at the oncoming thunderhead for a minute. Both watched the edge of the cloud move past the chimney on the house to determine its exact drift.

Finally Pa said, "That bank is just gonna miss our farm."

"Yeh," Geoffrey agreed. "It's going to stay on the other side of the river."

"That river with its wasteland back there often does that for us."

There was a quick knick of a sound coming out of the middle of the garden behind them; then a tremendous bolt of lightning, jagged and brilliant, stabbed straight down into the earth.

407

"Holy balls," Pa said. "If that'd been a bull up there he sure would have stuck it to the good old earth that time."

Geoffrey said, "I better get going, Pa. Get ahead of that shower before it crosses the highway."

Pa softened. "Come again, son."

"I will."

Geoffrey got into his new gray-blue car, started the motor, and with a wave of the hand was off.

Geoffrey managed to just slip ahead of the rain. Only a few big drops pinged on the hood of the car.

Driving along, Geoffrey brooded over his father's gloom. He cocked his head one way, then the other. "Anyway, except maybe for Tane, Pa can still lick the rest of us."

Geoffrey drove slowly through Rock Falls, then headed on toward Whitebone.

"But something is eating him. And it isn't just that Ma's no longer interested in sex."

Geoffrey drove past the sandpits south of Whitebone. He smiled to himself. "You know, maybe I too will still want to divide a woman when I get to be sixty-nine. Like pa, I like my women split."

When Geoffrey stepped in through the front door of his office, Miss Sharples looked up, then stood up. For a second there was a look about her as though on impulse she was about to embrace him; then very quickly suppressed the urge. He refixed his eyes on her but by then the hint of the hug she had for him had vanished.

"Anything new?"

"Yes." Miss Sharples looked at a pad. "Peter Toth suddenly left town this morning."

"Oho. So he'd rather pull out than pull teeth."

"And his wife called here, crying, very bitter, saying that the law and old-maid gossip are responsible for chasing her husband away."

"Hey. Why did she call here?"

"She wants you to represent him. And her."

"No can do, now that Bately got here first."

"That's what I told her. And then she really started to cry over the phone."

"Too bad. Any hint of where Toth might have gone?"

"None."

"Well, it's all right. If we need him, we'll find him. Bately been in?"

"No."

"In any case, we can't do anything about Toth until Bately shows up with his daughter Grace."

"I guess not." Looking down at his feet, she gave him an impish smile. "Time to pull out the old drawer, eh?"

He returned the impish smile. "Did you say, pull off the old drawers?"

With a toss of her dark proud head, a toss vigorous enough to shake her winner of a seat, she said, "Is that the next outrageous thing you're going to do in the privacy of your office?"

He chuckled. "Now there's something the local Whiteboners could learn from Mount Curve. Change their underwear a little more often. The way some of my clients stink up the joint here, heh, it's enough to make me want to wear a clothespin on my nose."

"I always get first dibs on that while they wait to see you."

"Maybe we ought to install a ventilating fan."

"I wouldn't object to it."

Geoffrey went into his office. And he did take off his shoes. Just as he was about to plant his feet in the bottom drawer of his desk, he was surprised to see that someone, surely Miss Sharples, had placed a small pink pillow in it. She'd also neatly pinned a pink sachet to the pillow. The musk perfume from it wafted up at him.

A short laugh burst from him. Then his chin set down and his eyes glowed. Well, well. Miss Adela Sharples had a sense of humor. Of the kind he liked. A secretary in a million.

His phone rang. He picked up the black receiver.

It was Miss Sharples. "Mister Scrivener is on the line."

"I'll take it." Geoffrey waited a moment, and when he heard a click, he said, "Freyling here. What can I do for you, James?" James Scrivener was the oldest lawyer in town. He was slow in court, slow in his office, but oh, was he sly. He often won cases against Twin City lawyers, mostly because they worked intermittently on a case, while Old Scrivener worked at it full-time, night and day, until the case came up in court. Bright lawyers were often not a match for small-town knaves.

Scrivener's rough old voice crackled over the phone. "I got a contractor who may go belly up."

"Yes?"

"It's Joe Bolt."

One of Geoffrey's clients had been taken to the cleaners by Bolt. The gall of that contractor still made Geoffrey angry. "Yes?"

"I think the First National Bank is going to foreclose on him. He has a sizable loan with them."

Geoffrey took his feet out of the bottom drawer and sat up straight. "Yes?"

"Do you know who's going to represent the bank?"

Aha. That question meant that the First National was thinking of asking attorney Freyling to represent them. And sly old coot James Scrivener was going to spike that move with a friendly call, during which call the younger lawyer would be asked for some advice on how to handle a possible legal maneuver where some aspect of banking was involved, and the moment the younger lawyer offered that advice, no matter how trivial, he was subject to the old law of conflict of interest. The old bald-headed bastard. Any time an older lawyer asked a younger lawyer for advice about a case one had better sense danger afoot. Geoffrey said into the black mouthpiece, "I take it then you intend to represent Joe Bolt?"

"Well, yeh, I was thinking of it."

"He's in your office there now?"

Silence. Too blunt a question. It also involved James Scrivener's honor. What there was of it.

Before Geoffrey could stop himself, he said, "Strike that, your honor." Geoffey offered up a laugh to ease things over the phone.

Scrivener cleared his throat of a gob of spittle. "You might like to know I subpoenaed Bolt once, but then later on, thinking about it, I kicked it over."

"Oh."

"So that'll tell you."

"Bolt sounds like bad news to me."

"Well, somebody's got to defend him. And I guess I was chosen."

"Sorry I can't help you about who's going to be the new counsel for the bank. Because I don't know."

"They haven't come to you then yet?"

"Isn't there a statutory year of redemption on a mortgage?"

Old Scrivener sighed over the phone. "There's a bill in the legislature about that, but it still ain't law."

"The trouble with your client is, he's never bothered to understand something about the American business world—that the leisurely seller sells to a knowing and able buyer under normal conditions."

Scrivener became snappish. "Thanks for the instruction, young feller."

"Sorry. I was just speaking in general terms."

"I know you were. But tip me off, will you?"

"Sorry, but I never heard that. See you in the judge's chambers sometime." Geoffrey hung up.

Soon the phone rang again out front. He heard Miss Sharples answer it. In a moment she tapped on his door, poked her head in. Her dark eyes were wide with pain.

409

"Now what awful calamity hangs over our head?"

"That was long distance from my father."

"Oh. Sorry. In the lawyer business a person has to have a built-in case of paranoia to keep his sanity."

The remark was lost on her. "My mother just died."

He stared at her. Was he going to lose her now? Would her father demand that she come live with him?

"If I hurry I can still catch the evening train for the Cities."

"Take my car." If she took his car that would be one way of making sure she'd come back. At least to deliver it.

"If I have your permission to go, I can still quick make it on the train."

"Of course. Go. I'll manage somehow. I did before."

"Thanks." She turned to go.

"Adela, in case I need you, where can I get hold of you?"

She gave him her father's Mount Curve telephone number. Walnut 4797. Then she was gone.

He felt deflated. It was as if half the life of his office had left. She'd become his right-hand man all right. The evening coming up was going to be a dead one. The thought of her not being in town somewhere made him feel sad.

He went home early to his apartment over the Whitebone Bakery on Main Street. The smell of fresh-baked bread and fresh apple turnovers from below was almost too much. The hollow feeling in his belly spread through his whole system until at last he came down with a severe headache.

He turned on the radio, looking for a station playing classical music. When he found it, he discovered that too was too much.

"The way I'm carrying on, a man would almost think I was in love or something."

At dusk he couldn't stand the silence in his apartment. He slipped into his shoes and jacket and went downstairs and turned east up Main Street. The evening sky behind him glowed a light purple while the eastern sky ahead of him was already sparkling with myriads of stars. There was no traffic. Everyone was home eating supper.

He stopped on the bridge over the Big Rock River. Light from a white globe above bounced on the rippling water. The speckling light reminded him of fireflies.

"When Adela comes back, I'm going to take her walking out here so we can watch the running water together. There's something about a flowing river that's romantic. Somewhere in our heredity there's got to be a passage in time where we lived on or near busy water."

He strolled on. He took a path down the side of the highway into the city park. He wove his way around and through picnic tables under the ash trees. Vague illumination from the lamp over the bridge gave him just enough light to find his way. Frogs roared from the rushes along the river ahead.

"Those frogs could use a soprano."

Soon he found himself standing at one end of a dam. Water backed up from it reflected an undulating Milky Way. The reflected misty starlight moved like a slowly waving gray shawl.

A passenger train came pounding in from the east and crossed the trestle south of him. The engine hooted twice and then began to slow for the White-bone station. All the flying-coach windows were alive with yellow light, sil-houetting passengers, some sitting, some walking down the aisle.

He wondered what sort of family circle Adela found herself in that very moment. He tried to imagine what life was like on Mount Curve.

"Living alone like I do, working with some of these sorry folk here, by sundown a man is ready to make a whore out of his mother."

It became very dark out.

Soon he was strolling back across the bridge. He tried to whistle a tune. He could carry a tune singing, but his lips weren't made for whistling.

Coming back up Main Street, he saw Bill's Tavern was still open. He looked in through the windows; spotted several workmen he knew, each having a mug of beer. Most were wearing bib overalls and smiled out of swarthy unshaven faces. Lucky devils. At least they were having companionship with someone.

It was time he got married. For one thing Pa wanted more grandchildren.

But Geoffrey was afraid to ask Adela Sharples to marry him. She came from such a different background. It was true she had already taken a big step away from her kind, but to ask her to take yet another big step was probably asking too much.

Adela was gone for ten days. During that time there were several developments.

Jack Bately came in to say that his daughter Grace had disappeared. Bately had gone down to Sutherland to get her, only to find she'd skipped town the day before. She hadn't left a single hint where she might have gone. Bately had next driven to Sioux City on the chance someone there might have seen her. He'd even visited a Sioux City whorehouse to see if a madam he knew could tell him something. Not a trace. Gone.

Geoffrey shook his head. "That ends that case I guess. Toth can come back home if he wants."

Jack Bately swore. "One thing is for sure though. Bart Rauch can't come back. The son of a bitch."

The First National Bank did approach Geoffrey to ask if he wouldn't represent them in the Joe Bolt matter. Geoffrey turned them down. He was in no mood to crush Old Scrivener.

Within the hour after the president of the First National had seen Geoffrey, the phone rang. Even before he picked up the receiver, Geoffrey knew it would be Scrivener. "Yes?"

"Scrivener here."

Geoffrey couldn't resist it. A touch of mockery curled along his full lips. He remembered the funny question his father had thrown at him several weeks before. "Well, James, what can I do for you that don't take too long?"

There was a shocked silence on the other end of the line. Finally Old Scrivener said, "Thanks for the snub, you little shitepoke."

"Don't mention it. And no, I didn't take on the First National offer."

"Oh." Old Scrivener swallowed loud enough for it to make a clicking sound over the phone. "Any hint where they might go next?"

"No. But I do have a question, James."

"Shoot."

"What makes you so goddam anxious to save Joe Bolt's knots?"

"Under the Constitution every man has a right to counsel."

"Okay."

The third development involved one of his brothers. Rolf showed up one day all unannounced, just barged into Geoffrey's inner sanctum without so much as even a clearing of his throat. It was the typical stunt of an older brother not respecting the rights of a younger brother, as though the older brother still considered the younger brother a snotnose. It made Geoffrey hot.

What made it especially galling was Rolf's dress. He wore patched overalls smelling of hog turds, dirt-encrusted brown work shoes, and a faded blue shirt out at the elbows. It was also obvious Rolf hadn't shaved that morning.

Once before Rolf had shown up in his overalls, with the front of them unbuttoned, so that Geoffrey had to remind him his horse was about to pop out. Afterward Adela Sharples had come in with her nose slightly flared, and Geoffrey, terribly embarrassed, had had to tell her that that was his brother. He went on to say, though, that if he wanted to, Rolf could be the neatest of all the Freyling boys, that his sisters said he had the most delicate touch.

Rolf pulled up an armchair. "What's this I hear about you not making out Pa's will?"

"Where did you hear that?"

"I got it out of Tane."

"So?"

"Well, you should make out that will. That way we kids can have some say about how it'll read when Pa has gone to his eternal roost."

"So you think I'll make Pa be fair to all of you."

Rolf houghed up a laugh. "Well, one thing, as a brother you won't charge much for your legal services. Most lawyers charge you the earth."

"That's exactly why I don't want to help Pa write his will. I couldn't make a living if all my cases came from my relatives."

"And since as the youngest in the family you've always been worried about who gets what as his fair share, I figured—"

"Hold it. I don't want to hear any more, Rolf."

"What I want to know is, and I meant to askt you this before, do you think Pa's gonna give the section to Tane?"

"You know of course Ma believes in primogeniture."

"That's what has me worried, Geoff."

"But, Rolf, Ma has always been wonderful to you. Has favored you even."

"I know. But I deserve that section ahead of Tane. Look at all the inventions I made for Pa on that farm."

"I'm surprised, Rolf. With all the money you've made buying up taxdelinquent farms and playing the stock exchange, I didn't think you were interested in the section any more."

"That reminds me. You're sitting on the inside of the law here in this county, why don't you tip me off when you hear of a good piece of land being sold for back taxes?"

"Rolf!"

"Geoff, I've made up my mind to be a millionaire, and I need that farm. And with the help of good ringing dollars, I'm gonna do it."

"What does Greta think about all this?"

Rolf waved her off. "What's she got to do with it? She's as cold as a dog's nose."

Geoffrey finally said, "Was that all you came for?"

Rolf caught on. He turned a little red. He got to his feet. "Anyways, it stuck in my craw that maybe Tane would get the section and I thought maybe you being an officer of the court you'd see things done fair and square."

"So long, Rolf."

Adela Sharples came back to work on Tuesday morning. The first frost of the season had touched the valley. Water in the bird baths had tinkles of ice in it. There was also a coolness, if not ice, in Adela's lustrous ebony eyes.

"Good to see you, Miss Sharples."

"And you, Mr. Freyling."

Geoffrey told her about the development in the Bately case.

Her nose came up out of her sadness just a little. "Perhaps it is just as well."

He looked at her in frank appraisal. His blue eyes held level with her dark liquid eyes. They looked at each other for seconds. It wasn't a staredown. It seemed to him that for those moments they were looking into the very center of each other's brains. And looking deep into her, it came over him that if there once might have been a chance for him with her, it was now gone. The loss of her mother had been a hard blow. He was almost sure, looking at her, that she was thinking of asking for a long leave of absence, if not of quitting the job.

Finally she dropped her eyes. She moved the pad around on her crossed knees to let him know she was ready to take dictation.

He sighed. "Quite a few letters have piled up, so let's get at it." He picked up a file and paged through it. Then he began.

Miss Sharples remained cool and distant all through the winter of 1929–30. From hints she dropped, Geoffrey knew she was in correspondence with her father. Her father was distraught and begged her to come home and help him adjust to the loss of his wife, her mother. He even pled that he needed her to help him make financial decisions. Luckily he'd had the foresight to unload all stock bought on margin and so was able to ride out the Great Stock Market Crash in the fall of 1929. But she resisted her father's pleas. As an only child she inherited two-thirds of her mother's estate, the other third going to her father. She was often at the bank making arrangements for a transfer of funds from her father's bank to a bank of her own choosing.

Then one April day in 1930 she came into his inner sanctum with a wry smile. "I see Dad took my advice."

"How so?"

"He's found himself a second wife. I now have a stepmother." Mockery touched her ebony eyes. "Tyrone Sharples went to the Caribbean to get himself some much-needed sunning. And wound up sinning."

"You mean?"

"Yes, I guess that's what happened." She sighed. "Poor Dad. But he did sound happy over the phone."

"You sound relieved."

"I am." She looked up, pencil ready. "What do we have today?"

His heart began to pound. He instantly sensed that now the moment had come for him to make his move. "All right. Take the following letter." A smile crept over his face as he thought about the clever thing he was going to do. He dictated:

Miss Adela Sharples
320 West Main
Whitebone

Dear Miss Sharples:
Will you marry me?

Sincerely yours,
Geoffrey Freyling

He looked down at his pink fingernails. "After you have typed that, bring it in for my signature, if you will."

"Is that all?"

"For today, yes."

Miss Sharples got to her feet and, very erect, her winner of a seat even more winning, left for her typewriter out front.

Geoffrey had to smile, at the same time that he was aware that his heart was beating like a hovering hummingbird's. He tried to imagine her thoughts.

Some ten minutes later she knocked on his door.

"Yes?"

Miss Sharples opened the door. "That's a serious letter?"

"It was."

"Thanks, Mr. Freyling."

A moment later her typewriter rattled briefly. Then, silence.

Again there was a knock on the door.

"Yes?"

Miss Sharples came in, stepped toward his desk, and handed him a typed letter with an addressed envelope. "For your signature."

He managed not to tremble as he signed it with a flourish.

She took the letter, folded it, slipped it into its envelope, and went back out front.

Again after a moment her typewriter rattled briefly. And once more she entered his office and handed him a sealed envelope addressed to him. "Very fast return mail today, Mr. Freyling."

"So I see."

"Was there anything else?"

"No."

"Thank you." And with an impersonal smile she left for her desk out front again.

He rocked back and forth several times in his swivel chair. He cursed that it squeaked. He didn't want Miss Sharples to know what his reaction to her reply might be. His fingers trembled so much the letter almost fell out of his hand.

"Well, dare to be a Daniel," he finally whispered and, picking up his silver letter opener, slit open the envelope. He pulled out the sheet. It read:

Mr. Geoffrey Freyling
127 East Main
Whitebone

Dear Mr. Freyling:
Yes, I will marry you.

Sincerely yours,
Adela Sharples

He almost collapsed. He took several quick breaths. He puffed. "God's peace." He stepped around his desk and opened his door. "Miss Sharples, would you come into my office a moment?"

"Of course." She got up and with her stately seat stepped ahead of him into his inner office.

He closed the door behind him. His brain felt like it was hanging over a hole as deep as a country well and his feet felt mushy in his shoes. His heart beat up loud and noisily in the back of his nose. There were even several skipped beats. "Will you take a kiss, Miss Sharples?"

She stepped forward and reached up a light touch of lips to his lips. There was a sound of dry skin wisping on dry skin.

"Will you take a hug?"

"Oh, yes, Geoffrey. Yes, yes. Yes, God, yes!" She threw her arms around him and gave him a hug to make him gasp. "I thought you'd never get around to this."

"My darling. Oh, Adela, I didn't know if I dared. But, oh, I so wanted to all these days."

She kissed him until wet inner lips found wet inner lips. "Let's hope now that the return male can continue to be fast. Pun, Geoffrey."

"Yes. Yes."

To his mother's delight, Geoffrey and Adela were married in the Whitebone Episcopalian Church.

Pa only smiled sardonically.

415

42. Tunis

1931

Tunis was at the wheel as he and Clara drove over to Tane and Arva's for Sunday dinner. In two days, Tuesday, February 10, he would be seventy years old.

Tunis didn't feel seventy. He felt fifty. Nights he was still occasionally awakened by an old friend. Also he could more than keep up with their hired hand Saul Pollen. Saul Pollen had recently emigrated from Fryslân. The only one in the family who could still outwork Tunis was Tane. But there was one sign of aging. Tunis's forearm under the rusty fuzz had begun to look like a fish from which the scales had been scraped.

The morning was very clear and cold. The sun glanced off the snow sharply and eyes had to narrow to gimlet points to keep from watering over.

Clara watched the way Tunis drove their new green Chevrolet. "It does look easy at that." Tunis had been after her that she should learn to drive a car.

"It's very simple."

"I'll think about it." She brushed the fox fur of her coat smooth over the knee.

Tunis crooked his head toward her. "You never know when I may have an accident again. Like the time that binder needle was rammed through my hand. And then where will you be? Saul still can't drive either."

"We now got the telephone."

"Sure. But while an ambulance is coming out to get me, you could already have me in a doctor's office in town."

They turned the corner past the deserted schoolhouse, where the orphanage boys in play had once tried to crucify Tane.

Clara threw Tunis a fleeting look. "Why are you getting after me so hard? All I hear is, learn to drive, learn to drive. It's almost as if you know you're going to get hurt again in the next couple of days."

Tunis grimaced. He hadn't really wanted to go to Tane's for Sunday dinner. With what he'd planned for Tuesday, it was hardly the fitting thing to do.

Tunis took a left at the next corner and rolled past where Lakewood used to be. A fire had destroyed the general grocery store, the house of the proprietor, and the nearby elevator. Only the old Bonnie Omaha depot was left. There were no plans to rebuild the town. With improved roads everywhere in the county, farmers could now drive easily to Rock Falls or Bonnie for their supplies. Tane had been thinking of buying up the town site acreage and tying it onto his own quarter. One of the reasons why Tunis had finally agreed to go have dinner with Tane was to talk him out of buying it.

They rolled onto Tane's yard.

Tunis was pleased to see how neat Tane kept his place. Straight paths ran through the snowbanks from the white house to the red buildings, barn, hog house, chicken coop, cattle shed. Tunis noticed that Tane had just turned the cows out for a couple of hours so they could drink at the water tank and get some sun on their hides. The horses were working on a mushroom-shaped straw pile. One of the geldings noticed their car coming into the yard and lifted his nose in the air. The horse had a nose shaped exactly like one of Clara's hard loaves of bread.

Tunis pulled up in front of the house and shut off the engine. Neither he nor Clara had liked Tane's house. It was more of a shack onto which two lean-tos had been nailed. Both felt sorry for Arva that she'd had to make do with the dumpty structure.

Two little blond faces showed up at the kitchen window. Ah, the grandchildren, Tyson and Clairabel. Almost instantly the glass pane steamed over with their breaths.

Clara's face broke into a wide smile. It was when she smiled over their grandchildren that she almost looked young again. "Those two sure make life worth living," she whispered.

"That they do," Tunis agreed. "It does go on, doesn't it?"

They walked up the straight path through the foot-deep snow. The kitchen door opened, and both Tane and Arva stood smiling big white teeth. Arva had filled out and now bulked larger than broad Tane. Little Tyson and Clairabel next showed up, filling the gap between their father and mother.

Tane said, "Look who's showed up with their bells on."

Tunis went along with the sally. He glanced back at his new Chevie. "With all forty horses jingling away."

Arva looked at Clara. "Ma, that coat becomes you. Good-looking."

Clara pretended it wasn't much. With her gloves still on she fingered the fur edges. "Yes, Pa turned foolish on me when we went shopping at a late winter sale at Brockway's in Rock Falls."

"Come in, come in," Tane cried. "Let's not let the weather in. I'm not all that anxious to heat up the whole of Leonhard County."

Inside, Pa and Clara took off their coats and Arva hung them up on black hooks behind the door. The house was filled with the good family smells of roast pork and boiled cabbage and baked potatoes.

Tane said, "Take a load off your feet."

Arva said, "You might as well sit right down at the table, as dinner's ready. In the kitchen here. Pa, you sit there by the window with Clairabel, and Ma, you sit here with Tyson."

Tunis and Clara pulled up chairs and sat down.

Tunis couldn't resist smiling at his little granddaughter sitting next to him. Clairabel had skin so light it was almost transparent. A hint of blue showed in the skin over her forehead. Her large eyes had the exact color of African violets. Just for the heck of it, Tunis caught her pug nose between the knuckles of his forefinger and long finger, gently, and gave it a little tug; and then, as he released her nose, quickly thrust his thumb up between the knuckles of the two fingers. "Got your nose! See?"

Her puzzled look took on the shape of a frown. She almost believed him. She looked at the wiggling thumb between his knuckles, then felt of her nose to see if it was really gone. "Did not," she said, "You're teasing, Grampa."

Tunis hadn't felt like laughter, but at her reaction he had to let go for a moment. "You're a sweetheart."

Arva put the last of the steaming bowls and pot on the table. "Yes, sometimes she can be."

Clara mock-protested. "You mean to tell us our little granddaughter sometimes isn't a sweetheart?"

Arva sat down. "Yes, I'm afraid they're both a little spoiled."

Clara smiled at both children in turn, indulgently, yet with a hint of strictness in her manner. "Gramma finds that hard to believe."

Tunis also had a good smile for Tyson. The boy had the long fingers and big feet of Arva and the shoulders of Tane. He was going to be a big one. Like his sister, he had light gold hair with a hint of red in it. He had a stubborn cowlick that persisted in sticking out no matter how often Arva wetted it down. It looked like a butterfly had lighted on his head. "What are you going to become someday, boy?"

"An engineer on a train."

"How come that?"

Tane pulled up his armchair at the head of the table. "Tyson likes to watch the Bonnie Omaha go puffing by."

Tunis said, "Watch while you can, boy. I hear they're thinking of abandoning the old Bonnie Omaha." Tunis found he had trouble looking Tane in the eye, and he concentrated on the children. He hoped Tane hadn't noticed.

Arva looked across the table at Tane. "Well?"

418   "Yeh," Tane said. "Let's grace a little." He closed his eyes and lowered his forehead into his folded hands. "Lord God in heaven, in the noon hour of this thy Sabbath day, we come to thee to ask thy blessings on this food, on our work, on our lives. We ask this in Jesus' name. Amen."

The little children followed, first Tyson, then Clairabel: "Bless this food, Amen."

Tunis wasn't sure prayers were heard, but he warned himself to keep smiling; not too much, but just right and usual.

Food was passed. Gravy was spilled over potatoes. Meat was cut into small pieces for the children. The noon sun shone bright through the kitchen window. All six faces pinkened over.

Clairabel said, "Grampa, your moustache sure grows good."

Tunis chuckled. "Yeh, my moustache grows good all right. And it don't need any rain either."

Tyson asked, "Does it need manure though?"

Clara couldn't resist sticking it into Tunis. "No, boy, but Grampa could use a little soap in it now and then."

Tunis fixed her with one of his light blue glares. "Is that how come you don't like kissing?"

Tane quickly broke in. "Let's have none of that hard-up-husband talk, Pa."

Tunis nodded. "You're right. Sorry."

Clara looked like she wanted to make a further mean remark but somehow managed to bite it back.

Tunis looked at the little darlings. "You two have been good duckies, haven't you?"

Both Tyson and Clairabel gave him large-eyed looks.

Tunis asked Arva, "Any temper tantrums in those two?"

"No," Arva said, "no, I can't say that there have been."

Tunis nodded. Maybe that had been bred out of the Freyling line. Tunis didn't know which one of those two little tykes he loved most. He remembered the time when Tyson was two years old and had come to visit them on a Sunday and stood in his lap inside his arms and talked to him in his private infant language, a whole long spiel of soft talk, almost a series of whispers, all of it sounding as though the boy knew exactly what he was saying. The boy was talking to him man-to-man. Confidentially. Very seriously. And Tunis remembered the time when Clairabel also at two had climbed up on his lap, and stared at him, and read him, and finally said, "I want to marry you, Grampa." He'd half-shook his head at her, and said, "But why would you want to do that?" Archly, cocking her white head to one side, she said, "'Cause you ain't got anybody to hug you like I can."

Arva and Clara talked about how expensive children's clothes had become at Brockway's. Both agreed it was far cheaper to make the children's clothes at home.

Tunis's eyes filmed over. He hoped the two grandchildren would have a good life despite what he had in mind to do in a few days. Just so they didn't get too close as brother and sister. It still bothered Tunis that he'd once overheard Tressa say to Dirk, "If only you weren't my brother." Tunis hadn't dared to think through what that might have meant at the time. It was something he hadn't wanted to know. In general he agreed with Clara's scheme, her precaution, not to allow her children to mingle with the world until they were fully grown.

In fact, Clara's precaution with the children was all of a piece with her denial of his bedroom rights. She really was, for all her daring when they first met, a conservative woman. That damned British blue blood.

Tunis found himself staring at Clara, not so much to see her sitting there in her dark purple Sunday dress, as to see her as a woman. Why, in God's name, as a woman hadn't she let him have some fun once she was forty-five and there was little further danger of her getting knocked up? If anything, at forty-five, she should have been able to relax, and laugh catchingly, and have great fun with a man. Let go and enjoy coupling. It couldn't be that she was just being stubborn. Though that could be part of the problem. It had to be that she had the soul of a nun. If so, no wonder they'd produced Ana, their odd neuter child.

Tunis switched his eyes to his plate. He deftly cut his slice of roast into small pieces. He picked up one of the pieces with his fork and then, with his knife, loaded on a catch of mashed potato and ate up.

Out of the corner of his eye he noted that Tane had just then cut himself a piece of roast too, then knifed on a potch of mashed potato and eaten it. Exactly like himself. A moment later Tunis saw little Tyson follow suit. Except that in Tyson's case a portion of the mashed potato slid off his fork just as he lifted it to his mouth.

Arva and Clara continued to talk about child raising, how wonderful it was when the children were at last housebroke.

Tunis's mind jumped back to the time when he'd visited his children's teacher, Velda Fikes, to see her about Tane's being crucified by the neighbor orphanage boys. Velda Fikes'd had such wonderful large lips. Luscious even. Looking back he now knew he'd made a mistake. Clara had forbidden him any further coupling about then. He should have put his arm around Velda, and kissed her, and had her right there on the oily schoolroom floor. Velda never did find a man, so far as he knew. There was no question in his mind that that time she would have divided for him. And would have done it with him again and again. That should have been his outlet. And had there been a child, well, so what? It would have shown Clara she'd not done her wifely duty by him. Velda was too hearty a woman not to have wanted a lover.

Velda Fikes was gone now. And there were no other women around he might approach with his needs. All that was left now, as he'd decided earlier, was to find some whore in a distant town and pay for what he needed.

He flicked a glance at Clara. Ah. She too was lost, wrapt up in some private reverie. He wondered what it might be. She was staring at their little grandchildren as though she were trying to see them grow up. There was a tiny pinched look in the corners of her eyes. What in the world could she be worried about in them?

It wasn't either that today he regarded the matrimonial vow sacred that he didn't step out on Clara. It was more that he'd let himself fall into a rut and didn't have the ambition to crawl out of it and assert his rights as a man.

Nor did it have anything to do with being fair. If it was fair for him to have a lover on the side, then it would have to be fair for her to take on a lover too.

He crooked his head as he considered the idea of Clara having a lover. Ridiculous. She'd dried up inside.

When they finished eating, Arva got out the Bible and read about Job's tribulations, when the Lord, at the provocation of Satan, took everything away from Job to test him. That irked Tunis. Not the story of Job so much as that it wasn't Tane who did the reading. Slowly but surely the women were taking over. Tunis hardened his heart against the reading and closed his eyes. He didn't let a word sink in. Then Tane gave a word of thanks to the bountiful Lord.

420

The children slid off their chairs and crawled under the table to play with their blocks. They were making a city with cars and trains.

A wave of nostalgia for the old days arose in Tunis like a change of weather coming in. He missed the cob fires in the kitchen range in the morning, missed the complaints of farmers that hunters were lapping over into Iowa from South Dakota and shooting up their cows thinking they were deer, of ads in the paper listing ten-cent whiskey and fifteen-cent cigars and five-cent lager beer. He didn't drink, but he missed men talking about buying a silver pitcher filled with rye whiskey.

In those days one woke up thinking about fly nets for horses, and whips, and lap robes for the buggy. Living along the Big Rock River was like living in paradise; there was skating in the winter and plumming in the summer. Not to forget clamming and the chance to find a valuable pearl. It was even kind of wonderful to have an honest-to-God dirt-hole privy, where a man could realize his mortality and his close relation to Mother Nature—unlike today's toilets where one's droppings were flushed away so quickly one didn't get a chance to smell if one were still healthy inside or not. It was the women who were changing everything. Damn. Lord deliver us all from bluestockings and bloomers and strong-minded women generally.

Tunis blinked; and realized that Tane had been trying to get his attention. "What did you say?"

"I said, could you come out to the barn with me a minute?"

"Sure." Tunis got to his feet. "Let's go."

Tunis slipped into his dressy blue-black checkered mackinaw and Tane his sheepskin, and then both men went outside. Tunis followed Tane down a path through the foot-deep snow. The sun bounced white off the glittering surface. Hens cackled triumphantly in the chicken house. A horse whinnied out by the straw pile.

Tane led the way into the barn. "There's a cow here I'm having trouble with." He opened the cow door to the barnyard. "Come help me round them up. They've been out long enough now."

Stepping carefully to avoid the cow piles, Tunis helped to chouse the red-and-white Shorthorn cows inside.

Tane closed both the bottom and the top doors, then slipped in between the cows to lock the stanchions.

Tunis stood to one side, watching. It pleased him again to see how tidy Tane kept his barn. There was even a good hearty smell to the gutter behind the cows. Tane had become a first-rate farmer. It was time for him to take over a larger farm.

Tane said, "My end cow there, Switcher, has a bad tit. Looks like I let her out too long last week and it got frostbit. I was wondering how I should treat that. Or should I call the vet? Would you take a look?"

Pushing the end cow against the wall and the cow next to her away, Tunis stepped over the gutter and sat down on his heels and had a look. Switcher had unusually long fat tits. The nearest front tit had an ulcerous wound on it. It was the kind that wasn't going to form a crust.

"What do you think, Pa?"

"I'd cauterize it. That's what the vet would do."

"But I don't have his kind of instruments."

"Got a blowtorch?"

"Yes."

"Get me that. And a piece of stiff wire."

Tane left for his toolshed.

Tunis stood back from Switcher. She knew something was the matter, with him standing behind her, and she began to move her butt first one way then the other, switching her tail nervously, trying to look at him past the stanchion.

Tane soon came back carrying the blowtorch, several pieces of stiff wire, a pair of pliers, a nippers, a pail of warm water from the house, and a bar of tar soap. He had trouble hanging on to all of it at the same time.

Tunis humphed. "Now that's what I call a lazy man's load."

Tane protested. "I thought I was doing pretty good carrying it all at the same time."

"Only a lazy man would think of saving steps by carrying it all at once. Much simpler to make two trips. Or you could have asked me to come along and help."

"Didn't right away think of the hot water. But I thought it would be a good idea to wash the whole bag and four tits first."

Tunis took the blowtorch and lit it with a match. In a moment it was flaming with a low roaring rush.

Tane washed Switcher's bag and tits. "Stand still, you nervous old hen you. It's a miracle you ever got bred, the way you switch your ass back and forth. If Arva'd done that we'd never've had kids."

Soon the sore tit was clean. Tunis took the pliers and with it picked up one of the pieces of stiff wire and held it in the rushing flame. In a moment the end of the wire turned red hot, then white hot. Quickly settling on his heels again, Tunis took hold of the tit and swiftly passed the white hot end over the suppurating wound. There was a sizzling sound as of a weiner being roasted, a smell of burnt meat—and then Switcher erupted with a ceiling-high kick, both heels flying.

Tane jumped back. And laughed. "Wow. If she hadn't been tied down by her stanchion, she'd have kicked herself over the moon."

Tunis jumped back too, and smiled.

"What a ride she'd have given the old bull if he'd been aboard her just then."

Tunis shut off the blowtorch. "That should do her. Now when you milk her, just strip her at the very end of the tit there until it heals over above it."

"Right." Tane began to pick up the various tools.

"So you ain't in favor of me buying that piece of old Lakewood?"

Tunis wiggled his moustache. "Can you pay for it?"

"Nope. I was gonna put some on the pump."

"What? Get a mortgage?"

"Oh, Pa, such a little debt ain't gonna amount to a hill of beans. I can pay that off within a year." Tane rocked back and forth on his feet and started to laugh at what he was going to say next. "I could do like my neighbor DeBoer once pulled on me. For a joke, of course. He owed me for some seed oats I sold him. He says, 'Tane, here's my check. And if that's no good, I'll make you out another one just like it.'"

Tunis allowed himself a chuckle.

The two of them carried the tools back to the toolshed.

Tunis shivered and buttoned up his mackinaw. "It's colder out then I thought."

"Yeh, the north end of a south wind is generally cold. Especially in winter." Tane shivered too. "The way the wind blew yesterday somebody must've hung himself."

Tunis drew himself up even more erect. "Well, at least you've got those two wonderful kids to raise."

"Huh. They're on their good behavior because Gramma and Grampa are here. But you should see them other times. Might as well tie a knot in a dog's tail as to ask them to behave. Those two fight something terrible sometimes. The other day they got to fighting over an old sheet Arva gave them to play tent with. Before they got through with it, that sheet was torn to fladders."

"Well, in your day you kids weren't all that well behaved either. You and Dirk used to go at it pretty good."

"No, Pa, not like those two. The other day we was eating supper when all of a sudden Clairabel set up a squawk that Tyson had a bigger piece of meat than she did. So finally, in fairness, I cut a little chunk off Tyson's piece and give it to her. Then of course Tyson wouldn't eat. So we had both of them squawking like I was a thief in a henhouse. Finally Arva sent Tyson to his room in punishment. He wouldn't go, and hung around bawling his head off. So I snapped at Arva that if she was gonna be fair, she better sent Clairabel to her room too. That got us to shouting at each other. Pretty soon those two kids actually was laughing to themselves. That made me so mad I sent them both to their rooms. At that point Arva said I could go to my room, and she would eat alone in peace."

422

"You didn't go!"

"No, of course not. We sat there cooking like a couple of boiling teakettles. The kids meanwhile were yanking their heads off in their rooms. Arva says then, 'I don't like to hear children crying.' And I says, 'Neither do I.' So we got the kids, and we each made up to them, and asked 'em if we couldn't have a make-up kiss, and they kissed us, and we went back to eating."

Tunis shook his head. "Good thing I didn't see that."

"Why, what was the matter with that?"

"Well, far be it from me to give you advice on how to raise kids."

"You don't think we done right then?"

"I ain't gonna say."

"C'mon, speak up. You raised eight. I still only got two. C'mon."

"Well, for one thing, never, but never, argue in front of the kids. About anything. And surely not about how you should punish them."

Tane looked down at the path in the snow. "Yeh, come to think of it, we kids never did hear you two argue about how you should punish us. You and Ma was like a two-headed bull. Though you did argue some about your bed rights."

"That last is where we made a mistake. At least I did."

"Oh, I dunno, Pa. It taught me not to expect too much from Arva."

"Another thing, Tane. Once you send a kid to his room in punishment, for godsakes let him cry himself out a little before you feel sorry for him. Let him sit there a while in silence to think over why he was sent there. Besides, crying is good for his lungs. And then go get 'im. Otherwise sending him to his room isn't gonna mean a thing. He'll have won out and he'll think the less of you for it."

"But I hate the sound of crying, Pa."

423

"Who doesn't? Rather that than a spoiled brat."

Tane had a little smile for his father. "How'd you get so smart, Pa?"

"I wasn't the first one to think of that. It's as old as the Garden of Eden."

"Yeh. That Cain could've used a good kick high up under his balls."

Tunis said, "Tyson and Clairabel don't pound each other though, do they?"

"No, not that I noticed."

"Otherwise no sign of a bad temper?"

"No."

"Like they might grow up someday wanting to murder somebody?"

"Hey, no. Why do you ask?"

Tunis shrugged. "Just wondering."

"You mean they might have inherited that from Ma?"

"No."

"Or you with those blazing cougar eyes sometimes?"

Tunis said shortly, "We better go in and join the women." Then in turn he offered a little smile. "Before I lose my temper."

Tane said, "I always did figure that a feller who could lose his temper just like that"—Tane snapped his fingers—"had to have a screw loose somewhere. And that my kids don't have."

"Or a screw missing maybe."

"Ha. Yeh."

Later, when they were in the house having a cup of tea over the kitchen table, Tane raised a hand. "Say, Pa, I saw in the paper they're thinking of bringing back Daylight Saving again." Tane pounded the table and his face purpled over.

"Now by Christ and by God, that I'm ag'in."

Tunis remembered when Daylight Saving had been in force during the Great War, 1917 to 1919, to save fuel for both the stove and the lamp, since it got people up an hour earlier and to bed an hour earlier. But farmers everywhere were against it and went into a rage over it, and finally Congress repealed the law. Tunis himself hadn't minded much.

Tane pounded the table again, hard enough to make the sugar flounce up in the sugar bowl. "My cows won't like it. And pretty soon when my tykes grow up they'll have to walk to school in the morning while it's still dark."

"Why won't your cows like it?"

"Why, Pa, you know cows got a clock in 'em. Throw them off that and you'll dry 'em up. Remember how you used to make us milk six on six, each cow in her time slot in turn? On the dot?"

Tunis nodded. "I wonder, though, did Adam have a clock in the Garden of Eden?"

Tane rushed on. "Besides, God ain't gonna like it that we tamper with his time."

"I suppose you think God carries a watch around on him? Like some railroad conductor?"

Tane's light blue eyes rolled up and around. "Well, I guess I ain't never thought on it like that."

"Man, not God, made the clock. So man made time."

Tane lowered his head. "Well, I guess there ain't much we farmers can do about it anyway. Congress is full of windbags, and there ain't much you can do against whirlwinds with a pitchfork."

424

It was time to go home. The little grandchildren ran up and gave both Tunis and Clara wet smooches. Tunis returned the puppy nuzzlings with moustache kisses.

"Bye."

"Bye-bye."

"Don't forget where we live now."

The sun was almost down over the gold-tinted snow as Tunis took a left after they'd passed the old country schoolhouse.

Clara asked, "What were you and Tane doing so long in the barn?"

"We had to cauterize a tit."

"Oh."

"There was no dirty man talk."

"I didn't say there was."

"But you women always wonder what we men talk about, don't you?"

Clara sniffed. "Don't you men wonder what we women talk about?"

"It ain't gonna be dirty woman talk, worse luck."

Clara refolded the fur coat over her short knees. "Tane didn't happen to talk to you about us retiring to town?"

"No, he didn't." Tunis turned into their lane. He saw their stump-legged hired hand Saul starting for the cow barn carrying a milk can and a couple of milk pails. "Don't worry about it, lady. Time will tell. It's all gonna fall into place and you will finally get your way."

The next night, Monday, they'd had a supper of sorts, cold meat, bread, a slice of cake, and tea, when there was a knock on the back door.

Tunis said from his armchair at the head of the table, "I don't want any company no matter who it is."

"Even if it's one of the children?"

"That's different. They're family."

"It's probably one of them. They're the only ones who come in that way." Clara got up and opened the door into the back porch, then the outside door. "For heaven's sake.. Malena!"

Tunis groaned. The Tippetts. Of all people to come visit them on the last night. He was about to tell Clara to send them on their way, when Malena, then Hack, came shambling into the kitchen. Clara tried to block their way, but Malena, leading Hack like he might be an old blind horse, pushed past her anyway.

Clara rolled up her eyes at Tunis to say she was sorry, and then closed the door. She didn't want that kind of company either.

Tunis threw one look at the pair, then swung his eyes back to his plate in front of him. He'd give them a strong hint to leave, get out.

Clara finally said, "Well, you might as well sit down a minute. Would you like some tea?"

Malena led Hack to a chair and set him down. Then she sat down next to him. "Don't mind if I do."

Clara brought out some cups and saucers and put more water on the stove.

Tunis finally lifted his eyes from his plate. He burned a look into both of the Tippetts. And looking, he was quite astounded by what he saw. Hack sat with his head hung forward, mouth open a little and drooling, and poached brown eyes staring unseeing. Hack had gone blind! And demented. While Malena, usually the weak one, had aged into a hard wiry blotchy witch. Her once pale blue eyes had changed into a pair of luminous hailstones.

425

Clara asked, "Is there something we can do for you?"

"Maybe not," Malena began. "Maybe it's already too late." Her whiney voice had coarsened into a rough voice.

"How so?"

Malena threw a despairing look at her husband. "Well, as you know, like you people, our kids have all flown the coop. And that was all right, because while we loved them, we often wished they'd go out into the world and fight their own way through it. Like we had to do. But then all of a sudden last fall my Hack here took a turn for the worse. Just when we were having it wonderful. We had the corn out, horse manure piled around the house to make it snug for winter, and such. And we could play pickle-in-the-middle all we wanted to all day long and all night long, because there was no one around to catch us at it, and we didn't have to worry about no more babies. Just could have all the fun we wanted to and not have to worry about a thing." Malena let go with a deep long sigh.

Tunis flashed a look at Clara. The very thing he wanted Clara to have with him. Well, well. His regard for Malena went up a thousand percent.

Clara was disgusted at what she'd just heard.

Malena wrung her hands. "And Hack began to slip real fast. He couldn't make it as a man in bed. Then he couldn't make it out to the barn to milk the cows and chores. And I had to do it. Finally he got so bad I didn't dare leave him in the house alone. It got to be a mess."

Tunis's stomach began to revolt at what he was hearing. "So?"

"Well, I've been trying to talk him into moving into town with me. So we can rent out the place for this year before it's too late to get a renter. But that's the one thing he's got left in him. To say he won't go. He won't budge. And I thought maybe you people could help me talk him into moving into town."

It was Clara's turn to flash a look at Tunis.

Tunis ignored Clara's look. He stared at old Hack Tippett. There sat the very reason why he was going to do tomorrow what he had to do. Tunis remembered his foster father Dirk Freyling's last helpless days, remembered how he, Tunis Freyling, had sworn at the time that he was going to end it all before he got that senile: "I want to go out while I can still go full blast. With my sweet tooth still shiny. They're never going to put me up at the poor farm."

Malena continued to list all of her troubles she had with Hack. Her harsh voice slowly slipped into her old whining ways.

Clara clucked sympathetically.

Tunis had had enough. He cleared his throat loudly. It was time for them to go. But Malena was so deep in her lament that she didn't hear him.

Clara threw Tunis a deep frown.

Tunis ignored Clara. He got to his feet and started to undress in front of the company.

There was an eye-widening silence.

When Tunis got down to his woolen winter underwear, Clara let out a cry. "Tunis, not here!"

"Why not?" Tunis snarled. "This is my own house and I didn't ask for this company, this of all nights."

"Of all nights?" Clara echoed. "Whatever do you mean? It isn't proper for a person to undress in front of company. As though you even do this in front of me! In our bedroom!"

Tunis finished unbuttoning and slipped his shoulders out, and then slid the underwear down past his hips and over his knees. With arrogant aplomb he stepped out of it. He stood stark naked in front of them. It was a bit chilly in the kitchen but he fought off an impulse to shiver.

"Tunis!" Clara shrieked. "That's scandalous."

Malena stared. And stared. She looked Tunis up and down, slowly from his shoulders, to his narrow waist, to his knees, finally at his privates. Then gradually as she stared at his privates a lustful gleam came into her almost white eyes.

What? Malena desired him? He needed a woman but not that bad. "Good night," Tunis said shortly, and picking up his underwear and other clothes, stomped off to bed.

It took Clara an hour to get rid of the Tippetts.

They were in bed trying to compose themselves for sleep, Tunis on his side, Clara on hers, backs to each other, when Tunis had a visitor in bed with him. For godsakes. It had been a long, long time since the presence of Clara in bed with him caused him to be aroused.

He listened to see if Clara was sleeping. She was.

What a waste.

The more he thought about it the madder he got. After they were dead they couldn't; so why not now while still alive? By God, what a devil of a note it was to have been cheated out of his jollies ever since she started carrying Geoffrey their youngest.

He smoldered: "Got a half a notion to roll her on her back and climb aboard. Even if I am going to do what I have in mind tomorrow. Just to show her what an awful thing she's done to me all these years. Not even her sweet Jesus would let her get away with that."

He heard the alarm clock tick on the chair on his side of the bed. He became even more swollen.

His body made an involuntary jerk.

"For godsakes," he thought to himself. "I've sure got it bad, haven't I?"

Then he made up his mind. He lifted himself up and drew his nightshirt well up his chest, rolled over on his right side, placed his hand on her hip, and rolled her toward him, making her lie flat on her back. To his surprise, he found that her hip was bare. Somehow, in getting into bed, and turning about in her sleep, her nightgown had worked up over her hips.

Clara murmured. She was slow to wake up. He rose over her, and with his knee parted her legs, and thrust down at her.

When Clara finally made out what was happening to her, she convulsed into a tight ball, her legs coming up in the air at the same time that she tried to push him away. "Tunis! Are you crazy? You beast you, trying it anyway after all this time? You must be possessed by the Devil himself."

He managed to set his forehead down on the pillow next to her ear. His teeth gnashed together.

"You sex maniac you! Get off!"

Slowly by sheer weight and power he lowered down between her legs. He was too busy holding down her clawing hands to help himself into her. His visitor almost found its way into her mount of love on its own. He could already tell she was as dry as a stiff chamois skin. It would hurt both of them if he got in.

"Ow! Tunis! You really must be sex crazy with all this nutsy lust in you. Think of the hired man upstairs."

"That's what you get for denying us fun all these years."

"Oww!"

"Am I really hurting you?"

"You beast you. This is rape!" With a final mighty effort, she pushed, heaved, and somehow miraculously managed to tip him over on his side, all the while screaming a high shrill yell.

Tunis was about to spill piled-up seed, but now, frustrated in that, instead exploded into murderous rage. He made a grab for her throat with both hands. When he finally managed to encircle her neck he squeezed for all he was worth to shut off her shrilling. Goddam her stingy hide!

The clock in the parlor beyond their bedroom struck ten, slowly: bongh, bongh.

A voice in the back of his head woke up. "Hey, Tunis! Remember that grain hand you killed in Wanata? Long ago?"

Clara for lack of air began to shudder in his grip. Her legs began to kick out wildly like the legs of a mouse caught in a trap.

The voice continued. "Better let her go. Or is it your intention to take her along with you?"

Abruptly he relaxed his grip. Then he swung away and rose out of bed, nightshirt falling back to his knees.

Clara, in bed, sucked and sucked for breath.

He stalked out of the bedroom, through the parlor, into the living room, then on into the kitchen. He plumped himself down in his swivel armchair at the head of the table. His visitor sat bobbing in his lap.

427

Clara finally managed to croak sounds. She started to yell and carry on again. There were sounds coming from their bedroom which could only mean she'd gotten up and was throwing clothes and shoes and perfume bottles around.

It hit him that Clara was packing a suitcase and was thinking of leaving.

A smile worked under his moustache. At the same time the visitor in his lap subsided. Well, if anyone was going to pull out that night, it was going to be him. He'd intended to leave the next morning anyway. Might as well make it tonight. And he'd walk it as he'd also originally planned. He'd leave her their new Chevie so she'd have to learn to drive.

He got up and stalked back to the bedroom. He found she'd lighted the night lamp on her side of the bed and was actually packing a bag. She sensed him coming into the bedroom but didn't look around at him.

He said, gruffly, "Stop. Back in bed with you. I'm the one who'd better leave." He stooped over the bed and emptied out her bag on the floor, dresses, underwear, stockings, perfume, hairpins tumbling out. "You hear me!" He grabbed her by the shoulders and threw her back on the bed. "Get under those quilts! It's cold in here." He lifted her legs and then covered her. "And now to blow out the lamp. It would now be unseemly for you to see me naked. I can find my clothes in the dark. I've been hanging them up in the same place for more than forty years."

Clara whimpered. The sound was like that of a pet dog that had been commanded to shut up.

Tunis dressed rapidly in his Sunday best: new underwear, white linen shirt, black silk socks, red tie, blue serge suit, black oxfords. He found his pocketbook and slipped it into his back pants pocket. He grabbed up his shaving kit and turned for the door.

428

"Good riddance! You dirty old goat you," she grated.

"That's exactly the problem. That I was a lusty old goat and you didn't catch on. Why, it's got so bad lately that even a knothole in the barn has started to look interesting." He snorted to himself. "If it'd had fur around it I just might have tried to rape it."

"Och!"

"You're damned lucky I never went after your daughters."

"Ohh! That I have to listen to this. Me, Clara Shortridge!"

"With my hormones I should long ago have looked me up a bouncy whore."

"Get out! Leave!"

"That's just what I'm doing, lady."

"Well, then! I'm glad you're dragging your valuables out of here. I'm so sick of you. So sick of you always exposing yourself to me here in the bedroom."

"So long. See you in hell."

Quietly he stepped out through the parlor. In the living room he got his fur cap and blue-black mackinaw and slipped into them. He stepped into his four-buckle dress rubber boots. Then, nodding to himself with a grim smile, he went to their back porch. He found the flashlight they always kept on a little shelf behind the back door for night emergencies on the yard, clicked it on, and went over to the little door Clara had found in the wall next to the old fireplace. He opened the little door with a fingernail, flashed the light in, picked up the pearl-handled .38 pistol, slipped it in the side pocket of his suit jacket, and then closed the little door. He flicked off the flashlight and put it back in place behind the back door. He reentered the main part of the house again.

Ready to go, he took one last deep smell of the house, nodded to himself, and stepped outside. He closed the door softly behind him. Looking up, he saw a half-moon was out, giving off enough light for him to follow the highway to town.

The county grader had come along the day before to blade the snow to either side of the road. It made walking easy.

Tunis thought of the many times he'd taken that stretch to town: the time when he'd first arrived back in 1885, the time of the awful snowstorm when Clate Bartles had lost his legs, the time several years ago when their car wouldn't start and he'd been too proud to call either Tane or Rolf to give him a ride to town. Tunis thought too of the many times his children had had to walk to school in Bonnie. Well, this would be his last time.

He had no regrets. There wasn't the least doubt in his mind that he was doing the right thing. Sight of the helpless Hack Tippet had only made him all the more sure he was right. Go out when one's sweet tooth was still sharp.

It was 4:30 when he turned the corner past the First National Bank and headed west down Main Street. Good. He had plenty of time before the train from the north came through. The town was dead. Six street lights were on, three on each side. The blinds in the showcase windows on the stores were down, giving the stores the look of blind horses.

For the final time he strolled past Rexroth's store, the harness shop, the billiard hall, past Roy Wickett's garage, past a grain elevator. The old livery stable was gone. Tunis remembered the time when Lonnie Brandon shot Jack Church as Jack was standing between two chestnut bays. Tunis had immediately pounced on Lonnie and had held him down in the dry powdery horse manure in the dusky alley until Ockie, the proprietor of the livery stable, could call the marshall. Though it had happened more than forty years ago it was still as vivid to him as if it had happened only yesterday.

Also vivid was the memory of the pretty chambermaid who'd come into his room in the Bonnie Hotel the first day he arrived in town. She was blond, cuddly like a kewpie doll, dimpled round pink cheeks, and oh, such thick lips. She'd let drop the hint that if he wanted anything special from her he could find her in the maid's room, 301. Lord, if only he could visit with such a fat-lipped maid now. Well, shortly that too would be taken care of.

He ambled down the slope toward the Cannonball Railroad. He stepped into the depot. Lights were on, but there was no sign of the agent. The place smelled of fresh tobacco smoke. It meant the agent was up and about somewhere. The telegraph receiver in the lighted office rattled away irregularly.

Tunis settled on one of the green wooden benches and with a sigh leaned against its curved back. He glanced around at the neat interior: shining brass spittoons, dark green walls, oiled wooden floor, nickel ashtrays. Besides the smell of tobacco smoke there was another odor he couldn't right away identify. He took in several deep breaths, savoring the air. Then it hit him. The agent was having a wake-up cup of coffee.

Tunis checked his pocketbook. Counting the bills, twenties and tens and fives, he found he had a little over two hundred dollars with him. Good. He'd blow it all.

Presently the station agent, Tub Lawson, came downstairs from the rooms above where he and his family lived. Tub was a nickname given him in irony by the Bonnie men. Tub was so skinny that some of the boys at the poolhall said

429

they could count the outline of at least six vertebrae through his vest. Tub spotted Tunis instantly. "Hi. I see you got up before the birds."

Tunis got to his feet and approached the ticket window. He glanced briefly at Tub through the brass grill. "Ticket to Sioux City."

"That'll be thirty-two dollars round-trip."

"I just want a one-way."

"Oh?"

"One-way, please."

"It's none of my business, but how will you get back?"

"I've got a ride." Tunis didn't add his next thought: "A ride back to where I came from."

"Okay. Sixteen dollars." Tub made out the ticket.

Tunis paid him and stuffed the ticket in the breast pocket of his suit jacket and sat down on the green bench again. He could feel Tub staring at him. To divert Tub, Tunis asked, "Train on time today?"

Tub glanced over his shoulder where the telegraph key was clicking. "Last I heard it was. Should be pulling out of Alvord right now."

"Thanks."

After a few minutes Tub spoke again. "How's the wife?"

"Fine."

"Give her my regards."

Tunis nodded. He pushed his fur cap back from his forehead. With his elbow he made sure the pistol was still in place in his side pocket.

"My wife thinks a lot of her. Says she is one of the most sensible and cultured women around."

430 "Thanks."

Coffee loosened Tub's tongue. "And all those kids you two raised. Man, they sure are a credit to this community. We often talk about it uptown."

"That coffee you just made, got any more of it?"

"Sure thing. Had breakfast?"

"Not yet."

"Would you like a sticky pecan roll with?"

"I wouldn't throw it out to the dog."

"Cream and sugar?"

"A spoon of each."

"Coming up."

In a few minutes Tub came downstairs carrying a steaming mug of coffee and a sticky brown roll on a paper napkin.

"Thanks. Looks good."

"Don't mention it."

Tunis sipped the coffee. It tasted even better than it looked. And the roll tasted like more.

When Tunis finished, Tub started up talk again. "You know, that Rolf of yours, what a character."

"Mmm."

"People uptown say he's the richest man around."

"Could be."

"He don't look smart. Except when you look into his eyes. Then you know you're looking into the eyes of an old Yankee trader."

Tunis thought: "You're not so dumb yourself." Tub like himself was a reader, both of eyes and of books, one of the few around.

Tub started to say something else when he was interrupted by a long whistle to the north. "There she is. Whistling at the railroad crossing by Mulder's there."

Tunis got to his feet. He looked at his wristwatch. 4:58. It was on time all right. In two minutes it would pull up into the station.

Tub came around through a side door and then led the way out onto the platform. He grabbed hold of the handle of a heavy red-wheeled baggage wagon and started to tug it to the point where the baggage car would pull up.

"Good luck in Sioux City."

"I may need it."

The high owling eye of the great black pluming engine grew larger and larger, and then in a moment loomed up over Tunis, the great shoulders of the cab bulging out to either side, the clanking drive shaft slowly braking the big wheels. The locomotive pulled up in a hissing stop.

A conductor wearing dark blue stepped down between the second and third green passenger cars. He set a little metal step down below the stationary steps. " 'Board!"

Tunis nodded at the conductor and mounted the steps.

"Car on the right," the conductor said behind him.

Tunis pushed his way through folding doors and entered. Some dozen passengers sat scattered through the car, most of them sitting next to a window. Sweet smoke from expensive cigars hung in the air. There was also the acrid sulfur smell of coal smoke from the engine ahead. Tunis removed his mackinaw and took a seat on the right side next to a window. He'd barely folded the mackinaw over the seat next to him and leaned back when the engine hooted hauntingly up ahead and then the car under him lurched forward with an anguished groan of iron. In a minute the train was rolling swiftly out of town. The engine whistled for the crossing south of Bonnie; then the steam engine began to double its power, blasting huge balls of smoke upward, as it started to climb up toward Chokecherry Corner.

431

After a while the conductor came scowling by. He took Tunis's ticket, punched it, tore it in half, gave the punched half back to Tunis. He gave Tunis an ice-edged look, glanced up at the baggage rack above. "Traveling light, I see." He had a nose like a hound.

"I might have a trunk up front in the baggage car."

"You might. Though I didn't see Tub load it on."

"You working for the Pinkertons?"

"You worried I might be?"

"Holy hell, man, I don't care who you work for. I'm going to Sioux City to have me a high old time."

"Suit yourself." The conductor moved on.

Tunis looked out the window. In the light of a sinking orange moon, he could make out an occasional grove. In some of the houses the master was awake, with the light on in the kitchen. The farmer was probably making himself an early cup of coffee.

The Cannonball stopped briefly at Chokecherry Corner for the connecting mail from Hello.

It also stopped at Sioux Center, some ten minutes, for mail and passengers. A young couple, just married, entered Tunis's car. Tunis smiled shortly to himself. They had the same Frisian look he remembered seeing that time he'd stayed overnight in the upstairs rooms over Meademan's Cafe. He wondered if the Sioux Center folk still spoke with an accent. He thought of Alfred Alfredson, the Frisian who'd made a cyclone cellar for him. Old Alfred hadn't had an accent. Both the white-blond bride and groom had round open faces and pure blue eyes and firm fingers. They were so in love their shining eyes were locked on each other as they found a seat with their hands feeling around behind them.

Of a sudden Tunis remembered his first days of love with Clara. He could even smell the musk of it again. She'd been the first to kiss him on their wedding night, had been the one to say, "Don't you want to try it?" He could still feel the tightness of her along with the sweet wet silk of her mount of love. Tears started in his eyes. How wonderful it had been way back then. How happy she'd been that she'd bled to prove she was a virgin. How happy she'd been that he'd also turned out to be a virgin that night. Damn. Why hadn't she let him be a man with her after Geoffrey came along? Doing it with one's sweet wife, while having all those juicy memories together over the years, would have been a glory. Would have been a triumph over chaos. A good piece of music one could not play often enough.

Did Clara in memory ever think of those good times? If she did, she never let on about it. Because of her fear of pregnancy, and because of the kind of people she'd been raised by, she'd probably slowly but surely let the memory of it frost over.

Too bad. Too bad.

Tunis got out his handkerchief and wiped his eyes. He noticed out of the corner of his eye that the two Sioux Center lovers had spotted him crying. He resisted an impulse to turn to them and warn them that if they wanted to stay together that both, husband and wife, had better keep up with each other when it came to sex. They might get along on all other matters, but, if they didn't get along as lovers, the marriage would slowly unravel. If neither cared much for sex, fine. In fact, maybe so much the better. But if one of them loved it, wife or man, and the other didn't, good-bye heaven on earth.

The train stopped some ten minutes in Le Mars. A single passenger, a heavy man, came aboard and settled in the seat ahead of Tunis. The man had eyes like worn dimes. Either a banker or an undertaker. The man carefully placed a briefcase on the seat beside him, then kept his hand on it as though afraid someone might snatch it from him.

The train started up.

Tunis watched the lights of Le Mars blur past his window.

Tunis recalled the first time he saw Clara. It was at Lord Sutherland's mansion southeast of Le Mars. He'd liked her instantly. She was the first woman in his life to catch his eye. Thinking on it, he also saw that if he'd have looked more carefully at her he'd have spotted what she became—a strict bossy woman who didn't care much what a man's bed rights might be. Her fury at all the immorality at Lord Sutherland's establishment should have told him that.

Tunis got to wondering what the old British town of Le Mars might be like now. Were there any British left? Clara had never wanted to go back and visit it.

Tunis had to know. He tapped the fellow ahead of him on the shoulder. "Pardon me, but—"

432

The fellow jumped; then whirled around. "What?"

"Sorry. Didn't mean to scare you. But I was through here once before and was wondering if there were any British left around Le Mars."

"Oh." The man collected his wits. He pushed out his string-thin lips in thought exactly like Chauncey the banker back in Bonnie did it. "No, they've mostly either died out or went back to England."

"I suppose it's mostly Frisians and Dutch around here now."

"And Germans. Though most of those Germans are East Frisians."

"Same thing then."

"Yeh. I guess so." The man's dime eyes softened with interest. They picked at Tunis as he wondered what kind of business Tunis might be in. After a moment his eyes narrowed. "Come to think of it, there is one of those Britishers left in town. George Hotham. Bachelor. His father was a second son of the Hotham family in England. Nobility, I hear. His father married an imported German girl and had George by her." The man shook his head in a smiling way. "George Hotham never did a tap of work in his whole life. Just lives off the remittance the Hotham family in England sends him. I hear George is still listed in *Burke's Peerage* in England."

Tunis's eyes opened. "Really." Tunis thought: "Maybe I should have taken Clara here after all. She could have visited with this George Hotham. It might have made her softer, full of good memories about her ancestry."

"Yeh, only last week I was visiting with him in Vander Meer's Bakery. He was having a cup of coffee and a Danish roll. Handsome fellow. Got that English look. Long nose. Stand-offish eyes. I asked him how come he hadn't got married. Wasn't there danger of his branch of the Hotham clan dying out? Know what he said? He said, with his nose lifted, 'Oh, I'm still looking.'"

Tunis smiled. He remembered how Lord Sutherland had talked with his nose in the air too.

"Funny town, Le Mars. Never saw such a mix in your life. Always something lively, if not wild, going on. As conservative as King George the Third himself. And yet the farmers around, when they feel the pinch too long, they'll break out and block roads. As you may have seen in the papers, the farmers around here are in a boil. When your farmer begins to organize, it's probably already too late."

"I heard about that. Times have been tough for the farmer. If the farmer's a renter. Even those who own their farm and have a mortgage against it got it tough."

The fellow turned farther around in his seat to face Tunis. "Yes, but you know who's got it the worst?"

"No?"

"The banker."

"Then you are a banker."

"How did you guess?"

"Just something in the way you came aboard."

"Well, I've been lucky. I've still got my bank." He frowned to himself. "Maybe it's not luck at that. I was hard-headed with loans. I made sure I had at least fifty cents in the bank for every dollar I loaned out. So I didn't go belly up." He thinned down his lips to a slit line. "How about you?"

"I own a whole section of land. Bought it cheap from a homesteader. And I made sure I never bought anything but what I could pay cash for it."

433

"That's the way to go. The only way to go." The man held out a hand over the back of his rattan seat. "I'm Mark Bilsborough."

Tunis took the hand slowly. "I'm Tunis Freyling."

"It's a pleasure to meet your kind, sir."

"I remember when I came through Le Mars that time, there was a couple of British clubs. The House of Lords and the House of Commons. They still around?"

"No. Gone long ago. Even the Prairie Club."

"That's too bad. They had class. Which it wouldn't hurt our country to have."

"Just like it's kind of classy for us to still have some Hotham blood in town." Bilsborough held his head to one side. "Somehow we got to get George Hotham married so that that line continues here. My wife would sure like that."

Tunis smiled under his moustache. Well now, Clara's British blood was being continued through her eight children and her two grandchildren.

Bilsborough saw the abstracted look that came over Tunis's face, fell silent himself; at last turned around and sank into his own private reveries.

The engine whistled for all the railroad crossings, long haunting wails, as though some great turtledove were sounding off. The heavy wheels under the coach k-thunged k-thunged across the joints of the iron rails. The coach rolled a little from side to side and creaked in the frame overhead and in the floor.

Soon it began to lighten up outside. The moon had sunk out of sight, but dawn was blushing up in the east.

Tunis went back to reliving those early days with Clara. What a joy it had been to open up the virgin prairie sod of their section of land, with Clara riding his shoulders to help him hold down the heavy breaking plow, with Clara helping him with the yard chores after she'd finished her own and still no children in the house, with Clara telling him about the booming of the prairie chicken cocks. He had loved their talks in the dark at night. But he had loved most the thought that soon, soon, she'd receive him into her very heart and soul. And then, and then, after they were married, he had known what would be coming each night, she opening her arms and pulling him tight into her. He remembered the nights they'd awaken at about the same time, around three in the morning, and they'd kiss suddenly hot with sweet lust, and then at his moment of hesitation, wondering if she were ready for him at last, she'd say, "What shall it be tonight? You climb the mountain? Or shall we side-by-side it with my leg over you?"

He shuddered. And awoke to the fact of riding in a train going to Sioux City. And also woke to the fact that he was aroused. Well, at least he knew that still worked. So much the better for what he had in mind.

The train whistled again, and just as it did so the sun popped over the low hills on the east side of the Floyd River. It was going to be a clear February day.

"Tenth of the month. My birthday." His moustache moved under his nose, the top edge of it tickling his nostrils. "Three score and ten at last."

He tried to visualize what Clara might be thinking at that very moment. She probably hadn't slept a wink after he left in the dark. She'd probably wait until noon, and then, if she didn't hear from him, she'd call up Tane to ask if Pa were there. He began to smile as he thought of their consternation at the end of the day with still no word from him. What was going to be even worse was the moment they read the paper on the morning of the eleventh.

434

The edge of the city began to roll past: huge grain elevators, a viaduct over a dozen railroads, houses of the poorer class of people, filling stations along Highway 75. A foot of fresh snow lay chalkwhite over the roofs and yards. The sun bloomed over it all in soft pink-gold, making even the more tawdry dwellings seem liveable.

With a friendly smile, Tunis turned to the newlyweds across the aisle. "Pardon me, but may I ask you a question?"

The bride smiled sweetly. "Sure." The groom wasn't sure he liked it.

"I came through Sioux Center once long ago. And I'm kind'f curious to know if the place is still mostly Dutch. What's your name?"

The blond bride pinched her groom's arm in pride. "It's Sueverkruebbe."

"Come again?"

The groom allowed himself a self-conscious smile. "Sueverkruebbe."

"Lord, that is Dutch."

The bride laughed, and nudged her bashful husband. "But I'm not Dutch."

"What are you then?"

"My parents are Frisians. Clevering. They used to spell it with an *a* at the end."

The groom glanced down at his bride. "Remember what Old Vander Meer the baker said? When you asked him if he was of Frisian descent?"

"Oh, that," she said laughing.

"He said," the groom went on, "'gelukkig niet.'"

Tunis said, "What's that mean?"

"'Luckily not,'" the groom said. "Then Old Vander Meer went on to tell about how stiff-necked those Frisians were. Couldn't reason with them at all. Old Vander Meer was afraid they'd never become civilized. Like a good Hollander is. So stubborn they are."

435

The bride gave her husband a push. "You! We Frisians are not stubborn. Or stiff-necked. We're people who stand fast. *Stânfestich. Stânfries.*"

"Ha," the groom said.

Banker Bilsborough turned around in his seat ahead. "I couldn't help but overhear what you two said. Both of you, Holland or Frisian, are welcome to do your business at my bank. You people are the salt of the earth. Here we are, in the middle of a terrible depression, and yet by God there ain't one of you that's applied for relief. Your church sees to it that if somebody goes hungry, or is out of a job, they get work of some kind somewhere."

The groom sobered over. "That's mostly true, sir. But don't forget that some of the Frisians are grumbling about what's happening. In the Old Country many Frisians are Christian Socialists."

"Oh."

The engine ahead let go with several short hoots, and the train began to slow down.

The Sueverkruebbes brightened. "Here at last."

Their coach pulled up with a groaning wrench of iron on iron, even jerked back a little.

Tunis let the banker and the newlyweds get off ahead of him. Then he too stepped down on the little iron stair set out by the conductor. He felt of his hip pocket to make sure his pocketbook was still in place. He next checked the side pocket of his suit jacket to make sure the .38 too was safe.

The Sueverkruebbes walked ahead of him. When they got to the end of the station platform, the bride turned and gave Tunis a warm smile. "Are you going to the Smokey Bear Hotel too?"

"That a good place to stay?"

"They have a special for newlyweds."

Tunis crooked his head at her. By golly, that young woman was flirting with him. Was he still attractive to young girls? Tunis flicked a look at the young husband. Ha. The groom also sensed her flirting. He frowned darkly down at her. Tunis then scowled a little to reassure him. Maybe she was just feeling bighearted because in a little while she'd be giving her all to her man. Tunis slowed his walk.

"They have singles for men like you too, you know," the bride said.

"Thanks. I'll see."

The bride smiled some more and nodded, and then her husband took her firmly by the arm and they hurried off to their bridal suite.

Tunis saw a yellow taxicab at the end of the platform with the driver sitting on the dirt-blotched hood of the engine.

"Ride?"

Tunis said, "Well, I don't know. Ah, maybe you can tell me something. What I'm really looking for is a place where I can hole up for a couple of days with a bottle and a woman."

"Then it's the Smokey Bear for you." The taxi driver's heavy dark chin came up. "There's a madam there, Rhea Redwell, and she has some rooms up on the top floor." The driver snickered to himself. "Where she thinks she can run a safe joint because the fat cops don't care to climb that high."

"No elevator then."

436

"Nope. It's an old-fashioned place. Like it was in the nineties. But it's sure kept up nice and neat."

"That's for me then."

"You won't need a ride then?"

"Nope, I'll walk it. That old I ain't yet."

Tunis saw the Sueverkruebbes walking ahead of him a couple of blocks. He continued to follow them slowly.

Yellow sunlight whelmed over the snow-decked city with a dazzling winter wash. It gave the great packinghouse along the Missouri River a glittering sheen of luminescence. Black hissing engines shunted boxcars back and forth. A steamboat hooted piercingly from the great river.

Just as the Sueverkruebbes turned into the Smokey Bear Hotel, the bride looked over her shoulder once more, blond hair lashing up. Out of sight of her husband she gave Tunis a quick little wave of the hand.

"I'll be damned if I still don't have it with the young women," Tunis murmured.

The Smokey Bear Hotel turned out to be four stories high. The old-style ornate front had been repainted a bright white, with the pillars painted gold. Tunis stepped inside. As he did so he saw the heels of the newlyweds going up a wide curving stairwell on the right. Ignoring the desk clerk, Tunis followed them up, on the assumption that the madam upstairs would be registering her own guests. He walked up slowly, not wanting to catch up with the young couple. On the third floor, as he made the turn in the stairwell, he heard the bride laughing with silver joy as her husband tickled the key into their door.

Tunis made sure they were safely into their room and then went up to the fourth floor.

He was surprised to see a huge blue policeman standing outside a set of double doors.

"This where Rhea Redwell lives?"

The blue cop's gray eyes examined him up and down. "She does."

"Can I go in?"

"This your first time here?"

"Yep." Tunis wondered if the cop could see the slight bulge of the pistol inside his mackinaw.

"Who told you about Rhea Redwell?"

"Oh, Madam Redwell is famous out our way."

"Where's that?"

"Rock Falls," Tunis lied.

The huge blue cop slowly relaxed. "Yeh, we do have some fellows in from there. Go ahead."

Tunis pushed through the double doors.

Tunis was astonished by the opulence inside. There were various hues of purple, shading off from near blue to near red: chairs, carpeting, drapes over the windows, flowered wallpaper, lampshades.

A plump woman with a jolly smile got up from a fat easy chair. "Good day, sir." She had frizzed bobbed blond hair, dyed with a touch of red, wide eyes that looked like they'd been touched up with blue enamel, full rosy cheeks. She had a considerable bosom.

In her dolled-up way she was good-looking. But she wasn't his type. Tunis has something else in mind. "Mmm."

"Would you like me to call out the girls?"

"Oh, I like young girls, but I was thinking of something else."

"You a sheepherder?"

"Sheepherder?"

"Yes. Sheepherders from the West River part of South Dakota always have special requests."

"Such as?"

"You're not a sheepherder dressed up in his Sunday best?"

"No."

"You don't look like a man who's worn that suit every day."

"I haven't. I own a farm north of here."

"Ah. That's better. Because this morning I wouldn't know what girl to call for a sheepherder."

"What's so damned different about a sheepherder?"

She winked. "You never heard the story about the sheepherder and his favorite ewe?"

Good Lord, Tunis thought, she's gonna tell me a dirty story. "No."

"Well. The end of the summer grazing season has come, and it's time to cull out the young stuff for breeding the next season and to send the older sheep off to the market. This sheepherder watches the men load the old stuff up a chute into a boxcar. Pretty soon a big fat ewe goes waddling up the chute. The sheepherder looks at the old ewe and tears come into his eyes. That old ewe had been the bellwether for his flock all summer long. Then he's overheard to mutter to himself, 'If that ewe coulda cooked I'd have married her.'" Madam Redwell let go with a finishing merry laugh.

"Ha."

"Ain't that funny to you?"

"My tastes don't run in that line."

Madam Rhea Redwell became all business. "What did you have in mind then, if you don't want one of my girls?"

"I'd kind of like to be with a good woman who's decided she'd like one more good time before she dries up and becomes an old maid. For once I'd like to enjoy every minute of a whole night with such a woman in bed. Relax and smile and enjoy."

Madam Redwell's metallic eyes slowly became points of blue light. "And after that?"

"I'll see when I get there."

"You still married to a wife who's shut the door on you?"

"You got it."

"You're not thinking of blowing your brains out afterwards?"

"Hell's bells, woman, I'm not that much of a saphead."

"Because I won't have a mess of blood and brains in my house. Let alone a bunch of newshawks poking around in here."

Tunis stuck to the main point. "Then you don't know a woman in town like that? I'll pay you well for your room and meals. And a bottle of apricot brandy."

Madam Redwell's chin sank into fleshy dewlaps.

The pistol in Tunis's side pocket began to feel warm.

"How old are you?" she asked.

"Seventy. Just today too. I thought I'd go out and celebrate my three score and ten the right way."

Slowly she shook her head. "Why don't you just go home and sit on a stump somewhere and enjoy the memories of the good times you used to have with your wife."

"Memories don't help a hard-on much. It wants the real stuff."

"You poor bedeviled men."

Tunis coughed up a harsh laugh. "It's still nice to have that left though."

Madam Redwell thought to herself some more. "Tell you what. I have a friend in town who's never married. Now and then she likes to have a fling with a man. Though she's pretty careful who she chooses. She's in her fifties and so doesn't have to worry about having children any more. Can just relax and have fun."

"I'd really like something younger. Something like thirty-five or forty."

"Wait'll you see her. She looks like she's only thirty. Never had children."

"All right, let's see her."

"I'll call her. She's never taken on a man here. She may not like meeting a man in my establishment. Would you go to her home? It's beautiful."

Tunis gave that idea some thought. He really couldn't. Not for what he had in mind afterward. "Call her and see if she'll come here."

Madam Redwell got up and picked up the receiver of a wall telephone. She belled central and gave them the number 56328. She turned her back on Tunis and looked out of the window toward the Missouri River. "Velda? Rhea here . . . I just had a curious request . . . I've got a handsome man here who won't visit with my girls. Says he wants a good woman who wants one more good time . . . Oh, yes, very handsome and built like Frank Gotch the wrestler . . . Farmer from up north of here. But seems to be quite well-to-do . . . Yes, I do like his looks. It's obvious he don't want me . . . He'd rather you'd come up here . . . Well, it won't hurt to have dinner with him. With a little wine. Oh, that's right, he likes apricot brandy. And then as things go along you can make up your own mind . . . How much? I'll ask him." Madam Redwell covered the black mouthpiece. "Would you be willing to pay her a C-spot?"

A hundred dollars? He had about two hundred dollars with him. Well, why not. Blow the works on a last good-bye. "Sure. If it turns out good, maybe I'll give her even more. All I ask is that there be no rod in there when I start to put mine in."

Madam Redwell at first flinched; then laughed at the rough slang. She turned to the phone. "He says that's fine . . . No, he doesn't look like one of those whip-me boys. All right. See you soon then." She hung up.

Tunis asked, "What's this dame do for work otherwise?"

"Works part-time in a library. And is a substitute teacher in our grade school system."

"What'd you say her name was?"

"Velda Fikes."

Tunis stiffened. "What!"

"You know her?"

"My children had a schoolteacher by the name of Velda Fikes."

"Well," Madam Redwell smiled, "maybe it'll turn out you're old friends then. Makes it all the better."

With a name like that there could be only one Velda Fikes.

"Have you had breakfast? It'll be a couple hours before she's here."

"No, I haven't."

439

"Take off your mackinaw and boots. Now. What would be your heart's desire?"

"It's been some time since I had pancakes with steak. And plenty of maple syrup and butter."

"Coffee too?"

"You bet. With cream and sugar."

"Come with me."

Walking stoutly, Madam Redwell led the way down a long hall to an apartment in back. Tunis followed her carrying his mackinaw, fur hat, and buckle boots. The rooms in back had none of the purple opulence of the rooms out front. The walls were mostly done in quiet light blue flowered wallpaper and natural maple wood. Even the natural quarter-oak flooring was treated with dull varnish.

Breakfast turned out to be wonderful. And the coffee was just right, dark and strong, which with cream and sugar made it taste especially good. Tunis soon started to feel at ease. He began to look forward to meeting Velda Fikes. If it turned out to be the same Velda from Le Mars.

Madam Redwell was full of talk. She told a little about city politics, about how much she had to pay under the table to the chief of police, how even the mayor and the alderman often came to sample her girls.

When Tunis finished the last swallow of coffee, she got to her feet. "Now to show you your suite. Come." She led the way down yet another wing in back and opened the door into a little apartment. "Here you and Velda will have all the privacy you'll want."

The little apartment was furnished much the same as the big apartment, maple woodwork and beige easy chairs. The windows opened on the Missouri River and the shores of Nebraska beyond.

Madam Redwell opened a door to one side. "And here's the casting couch. There isn't a bed in all of Sioux City as big. It'll take you all night to work your way across it."

It was a huge bed. It almost filled the room. Madam Redwell had decked it out with a shining white silk bedspread and a dozen little fluffy white pillows.

"The bathroom is through that door. So you and Velda will have absolute privacy."

Tunis nodded. He set his buckle boots to one side and hung up his mackinaw and fur hat. There'd have to be a slight change in plans for what he had in mind to do after he was through with Velda. But it was all right though. There had to be another way of handling it.

"Why don't you take off your jacket and shoes and relax until Velda comes."

"Thanks. That's just what I'll do."

"And that'll be fifty dollars for this little suite. Dinner, supper, and breakfast tomorrow included."

Tunis paid her.

About an hour later, the door to the suite opened slowly and a head poked in. It was Velda Fikes.

Tunis slowly got to his feet. Quickly he slipped into his suit jacket. He didn't button it to make sure the bulge of the .38 wouldn't show. "Long time no see."

Velda Fikes closed the door behind her. "Why . . . it's Mr. Freyling!"

"Yes."

"For heaven's sakes." She turned very red. It became her, made her look like she really still might be only in her middle thirties.

"It's all right," he said. "I'm blushing a little myself. Under my moustache."

"I suppose now you won't think much of me." She puffed, holding her full bosom in her arms. "I don't do this very often. In fact, I think this is only the—"

"Shhh!" he said, placing a finger to his lips. "I don't want to hear about it."

"But it's true though."

"Of course it is. I believe you."

Still breathing heavily, she settled down on the far edge of the big bed. "I never got married, you know. And, well . . . I sometimes get very lonesome. And I've always liked men."

Tunis smiled at her. She was still very attractive. Her blond hair, done up in a knot in back, had some gray in it. A few wrinkles around her wide blue eyes softened the oxlike expression of them, even gave them the grave look of a thoughtful woman of class. And her large mouth still had the kind of thick lips a man longed to kiss. The collar of her mink fur coat drawn up around her face made her look especially flowerlike. He said, "I know that."

She sighed. She looked down at the white bedspread. With her long fingers she began to play with the fringe of silk tassels.

He stepped around the bed and held out his hand. "Glad to see you again."

She looked up at him. A pleading look had crept into the corners of her large blue eyes. Slowly she held our her hand. "Yes. Just so you don't get the wrong impression."

"Don't worry. What you don't know is that I've often thought about you. You remember the Sunday in the fall when you went down to the schoolhouse to correct some papers? And you'd lit the stove and I spotted the smoke? And I thought you might be a bum who'd camped in the schoolhouse overnight? And I went over to check?"

"I remember."

"I almost walked around your desk that day to pick you up and lay you on the floor right then and there."

"Yes. I saw that in your eyes."

"But you were afraid too. And I saw that so I didn't."

"Oh, I wasn't afraid of what would happen on the floor. I was afraid of something else."

"You were?"

"You had such blazing eyes. Wild. Just like the first time when you came thundering in through the door angry about what happened to your cute little boy Tane. That crucifixion of his behind the schoolhouse."

Tunis looked down at his hands. "I've had my troubles with my hot temper."

"It's scary."

"I don't mean it to be."

"I know you don't. Some people are born hot-blooded, and that they can't help."

"Yes, and for the rest of your life you have to fight it every day." Tunis shook his head. "Sometimes when things didn't go quite right I used to get so mad, I wanted to break everything around me. Beat up on bulls even. And worse yet, you're scared you might have passed that fault on to your children."

Velda's eyes narrowed reflectively. "I didn't notice temper in either Tane or Thea. In fact, Tane was wonderfully even-tempered the way he took what happened to his hand." She shook her head. "You don't know how mortified I was to have had that happen on my school grounds. I didn't sleep well for weeks after that." She looked at Tunis beseechingly. "You said then that you were afraid that Tane would be taunted about being crucified for the rest of his life. Did that happen?"

441

"No, it didn't." Tunis settled on the bed near her. He chuckled to himself. "Maybe the neighbors and their kids were afraid of me. If so, maybe the threat of me having a bad temper was of some good after all."

The deep blush had slowly receded from her cheeks. She looked at him level-eyed. "Really, it is so strange to be seeing you again." A self-conscious laugh rippled from her. "I must confess that while you were scary to me, I also found you attractive."

"You did?"

"Yes. There were times afterwards when I wished you had picked me up and laid me on the floor that day."

"Holy balls." He swallowed. "Excuse me."

She threw her head back and laughed. "There's that explosion in you again."

"I'm sorry."

"It's all right." She placed her hand on his. "You really are very charming. Masterful."

He nibbled at his moustache. "I wish Clara could hear you say that. Man, man."

"You were already having troubles with her when we met, weren't you?"

"Right after Geoffrey was born she shut the door."

"You mean, to your bedroom?"

"No, I mean to her body."

She gave him a deep blue look. "You do have a most wonderfully blunt way of talking." She shook her head in commiseration. "Then all that time since then there's been nobody?"

"Yes. Like a damn fool I've been faithful."

"I wish I might have had a husband like you."

"We would have done all right." Again he took her hand in his. "Now tell me about you. After the school closed down, where did you go? I never heard around town."

"I packed up and took the Cannonball to Le Mars. Where my people used to live. I'd heard that a lawyer there had been trying to find me. So I called on him. It turns out that the Fikes family in England, the rich branch of them, had been sending money to my father's address even after he'd died. I don't think I ever told anybody in Bonnie, but he was one of the British pups sent over by his family, a second son who might cause trouble for the estate. My father was a remittance man."

"Hey. Clara was of that same kind of blood. Though her people came a generation earlier. To eastern Iowa."

"Anyway, when I looked up the lawyer, I found out that I was a person of some wealth."

"Really!"

"So I took the money and came on here to Sioux City and bought myself a house on a bluff overlooking the Big Sioux River."

"Good God. Besides being a good looker you were also rich? And you never found yourself a man? Seems to me that would be too much for any man to pass up."

442

"I was picky. As a teacher I'd learned to run my own life. When you run a school you learn how to be the boss."

Slowly they warmed to each other.

She asked, "Have you ever thought of divorce?"

"What for?"

"Well, start over with another woman."

"At my age? Don't be silly. One little bump upstairs here"—he touched his forehead—"and I'm a vegetable. And I'd rot away into senility. Into dumb blind stupidity. Like a rooster with his head chopped off. No, I'm not going to let that happen to me. I'm going out with my steam up and with my whistle blowing full blast. I've got it all figured out."

She pinched his hand. "You shouldn't have such gloomy thoughts. You're a handsome strong man. You look like you still might be only forty or so." She gave his hand another fond pinch. She laughed as though to indulge him, her large lips opening away from her very white teeth. "You're not thinking of committing suicide now, are you?"

For a second he couldn't look her in the eye. Quickly, with an effort, he redirected his glance at her, and made it hold, firmly, even blazing a little.

"Looking at you, I know you still have a lot to give. For your grandchildren. For your friends. Look up, not down."

His glance settled on her large lips. They were still lovely, without wrinkles or cracks. His shoulders jerked of themselves. He could feel nervousness coming on. "I wonder . . . may I kiss you? Please?"

She held back. "Maybe you better not." She rose to her feet. "Instead I better go. Somehow, this isn't right."

"Why not?"

"I know you as a friend. Now if you were a stranger . . ."

"You'd rather with a stranger than an old friend? With those kind of rules ain't that a little odd?"

"I know it sounds funny, but that's how I feel, Mr. Freyling. If we—"

"Please call me Tunis, Velda."

"Tunis, then. If we make it under these circumstances, where you expected some kind of call girl to come to you and instead I came . . . Don't you see that cheapens me?"

"But with a stranger doesn't it cheapen you?"

Velda's eyes closed and slowly she shook her head.

"You want me to call up some other girl then?"

She opened her eyes. "Girl?"

"I want someone young in spirit for my final blast."

"And you consider me young in spirit?"

He stood up. "Please, woman, take off your coat and stay awhile. You can at least stay for dinner. And if after that you still feel you've gotta go, well then, so be it. We've never really had a chance to have a good talk. There was always something to keep us from it."

"I know."

He stepped closer and took hold of her dark mink coat at the shoulders to help her out of it. "Please, Velda."

"No promises then. I may still go home after dinner."

"Fine." Temper that had almost erupted into anger now became a wide smile. "Maybe all I really need is a good talk with a good woman. And not lay with a woman."

She let down her shoulders. "All right." She let him take her coat. Then she sat down on the edge of the bed and started to take off her galoshes.

Quickly he knelt in front of her. "Here, let me help you." He finished removing her boots, her shoes coming off with them. "There." Velda had a very slim foot. Tunis shook his head to himself. Compared to her, Clara had a short stubby foot. He stroked Velda's feet gently, first the left one and then the right, over the arch and then up the instep.

"Oh," she whispered. "How lovely."

He smiled under his moustache.

"You're not one of those men who has a fetish for feet, are you?"

"I like the whole woman." He let go of her feet.

"Flatterer. You are a charmer."

Two easy chairs faced a bay window overlooking the Missouri River. He said, "Why don't we go sit over there until Lady Redwell brings us dinner." He took his watch out of a vest pocket and looked at it. "It'll be an hour yet."

"Good idea." On stocking feet she stepped toward the easy chair on the right. In her powder blue suit, slim, she moved with a slow swinging of stylish legs.

They reminisced about Adam Erdman and his orphanage across the river from the old schoolhouse, about the Pullmans, where she'd boarded, about the latest news in Bonnie. He told her about that strange couple, brother and sister, Clate and Hettie.

443

"You mean," she gasped, eyes widening a big white-encircled blue, "incest?"

"I wouldn't put it past them. Both of them had a mind of their own and didn't give a rip what others thought."

She held her head to one side. "Actually though, in small towns like that, it's really the only way to survive."

A black man brought them their dinner on a cart: T-bone steaks, baked potatoes, creamed beets, snap beans, light dry red wine, brandied cherries for dessert, and a pot of tea. The black man also set out a flat bottle of apricot brandy and two small glasses. They had the dinner set on a table to the right of the bay window, in the far corner. Tunis helped her into her chair, took the chair across from her.

They ate with relish.

They were savoring and eating the dark purple syrupy cherries when she said, "One thing I've decided."

"What's that?" He was worried she might leave shortly. He had begun to fall in love with her a little.

"If I stay, I'm not taking your money. It's going to be for the fun of it between two old friends."

His heart pounded in his ears. Good.

"I still feel kind of stupid though," she added. "That I had to mention money at all."

"But just think though that if money hadn't been part of it, you wouldn't have come."

"You have a wonderful way of looking at the brighter side of things." She looked him over point for point. "Look at you. Graying auburn hair a little curly. Pearl gray eyes. Clean white shirt. Light gray socks. So well got up."

"Like some hick hired man who's blown his first check at Wolf and Bernstein."

They sat talking and smiling, and drinking tea, and then sipping apricot brandy for a couple of hours.

The sun sank bright and big in the west. It shone through the bay window with a wide throw of gold light.

Finally she said, "I suppose we ought to clear the table onto the cart and roll it out into the hall. Because, heavens, it'll soon be supper time."

He nodded. He helped her set things on the cart. He rolled the cart out into the hallway.

When he returned to the room he found her standing at the bay window looking out at the snow-coated city. He walked up behind her and slipped his arms around her, and when she didn't seem to mind he nuzzled nose and moustache into her neck.

"Oh," she said, shivering, "that tickles."

He kissed her under the ear. She had a lovely smell. It was more her smell than that of a perfume.

She said, "A woman might like a little fun too now and then, you know. Like a man might when he dallies with a girl on the side."

"Don't worry about it."

"But I do worry about it. I want you to respect me."

"Shh."

"Like I said, I've always liked men."

"Then you should've married."

"The right one never showed up."

"Velda, please."

"Women sometimes just for the heck of it have one-night stands too."

"Shh, now." He turned her about and kissed her on the lips. Her soft full lips gave way under his pressure and opened a little.

The big round gold sun bounced on the horizon across the Missouri and then dropped out of sight. Within moments darkness rushed overhead going west.

She withdrew her lips. "Just so you understand. I want this to be wonderful for you."

"For both of us," he said. He took her firmly about the waist and drew her toward the bed. It had become very dark in the room and he found his way with his toes. They settled down together.

"I should probably remove this dress," she whispered.

"And me my jacket."

They stood up. He helped her unhook her dress in back and then she stepped out of it. He took off his blue serge jacket, careful to place it just right on a nearby chair so the pistol wouldn't show in the side pocket.

He began to feel very thick. With swollen tongue, he whispered. "Please take everything off."

"Should I?"

"Please. And I will too."

"All right."

As he undressed, he heard the rustle of her silks slipping to the floor. He watched her flip back the bedcovers with a practiced gesture. Then she kneeled into the huge bed, and he got in, and both pulled up the sheet and quilt.

They lay quietly for a few minutes, hip to hip.

A steam engine whistled in the stockyards west of them, long and lonesome.

They turned to each other, mouth seeking mouth, hands seeking the yearning part of the other's body. He found her swollen and wet; she found him swollen and firm.

He was lost in the luscious moment. He was still a man with a woman.

It was all as though it had happened many times before with them. It was all a sweet tumbling together, and then she was receiving him.

"I want your seed," she whispered, "your seed."

He could hardly believe it, after so long, home and warm in a woman again. He remembered, fleetingly, a poem by Bobby Burns, where a lass from the Scottish hills had two go-ups for Bobby's go-down. To Tunis's surprise Velda soon cried out; and a little later, soon, she cried out yet again. And then he, Tunis Freyling, orphan, lately a landowner, became a royal creature too, and also cried out.

Later, they had supper in bed, and another little glass of apricot brandy.

And then there was more sweet tumbling.

"Your seed," she whispered. "I want your seed."

He tried to remember as he slowly sank away into sleep, his cheek on her high full white breast, if Clara, in her most ardent moments, had ever had as many urgent go-ups for him as this woman did. It was all a wonder. In his most

445

dream-run reveries he'd hardly expected that the moment would have swallowed him as though an earth had parted and he'd fallen into it.

"I'm so dizzy," Velda whispered, as she too fell asleep.

The next morning, long before dawn, they went down their new road once more.

Then she said, sitting up in bed, catching the vague light on her wristwatch, "I must be going, love. Today's my day at the library. At the checkout counter."

"All right."

She dressed swiftly in the dark, somehow managing to find her clothes. Fur collar drawn up around her face, she leaned over him in bed and kissed him. "Until next time then."

After she'd gone, he lay very still in bed for a while.

He thought of waiting for breakfast, but then finally decided that was silly. He didn't need a full stomach for where he was going. He dressed.

He found some stationary in a desk drawer and, getting out his fountain pen, wrote a note for Mrs. Rhea Redwell:

Thanks for everything. Here's the rest of the money that Velda wouldn't take. Maybe someday you and Velda can have a dinner on me at some fancy place. I've been well repaid.

Tunis Freyling

He slipped the letter in an envelope along with all the money he had left.

He felt of his left jacket pocket to make sure he had the pistol. He didn't have the heart to make a mess in Rhea's swell apartment where he'd had one of the last good times in his life with a lovely woman. Also, he didn't want to mar the honeymoon night of that young couple from Sioux Center who were sleeping in the same building.

He slipped into his overshoes and coat, put on his fur cap, and careful not to make any noise going downstairs, stepped outside.

He walked across the stockyards out to the long bridge over the Missouri River. Dawn was just opening a dull maroon along the eastern horizon.

He walked out to the center of the bridge. There was no traffic. Except for the river water licking at the fingers of ice reaching out from both shores, it was utterly silent.

He thought: "Well, at least while I was alive I didn't lose my temper on my kids. Though I almost did on Clara two nights ago. I had her by the throat like I did that tramp."

He thought: "So I guess it was only a matter of time before I turned that crazy wild rage on myself."

He swung both legs over the railing. Then, hanging on with one hand as he leaned over the running tan water, he reached his other hand into his pocket, pulled out the .38, and held it to his temple.

"I'm sorry," he whispered, "but it had to be. There was no other way of getting around it."

Then he pulled the trigger—whoom!—and dropped into the river below. And was gone.

BOOK THREE

43. Clara

1931

She heard Tunis close the front door.

Her breathing leveled out.

"Good riddance!" she said again in the dark.

The air in the bedroom was cold. She pulled the quilts up over her exposed shoulders and drew up the ends of the pillow to her cheeks.

"That he should have finally tried to choke me."

The quilts and the pillow tight around her began to warm her. The thickness in her throat and in her fingertips subsided.

She couldn't imagine where he'd go, all dressed up like that. Probably to the hotel in town. But she couldn't be bothered with that now. It was a relief to have him out of the house. With Saul Pollen upstairs she felt safe.

She nuzzled her head deeper into her pillow, and shifted first to one side on a hip, then the other, crossed and uncrossed her feet at the ankle; and slowly drifted off to sleep.

She dreamt.

. . . . Tunis was taking a bath in the next room, Lord Sutherland's library. She could hear water spilling as Tunis poured some down his back. She thought it might be nice to offer to wash Tunis's back. Most people couldn't reach all the way around and give the top of their backbone a good scrubbing. She thought him just right for her. But to make sure she had to see him naked. It surprised her that she should think that way. She hated musty old Lord Sutherland. Dirty old goat. And she couldn't stand those horsey British pups of his with all their leering talk and their fingers always sneaking up under the hired girls' dresses. She got a pan of warm water from the reservoir in the kitchen range, and some woman's sweet smelling soap, and a fresh washrag, and on stealthy toetips so Lord Sutherland wouldn't hear her pushed into the library. She had an apologetic smile all ready for Tunis. And then she saw something she didn't understand right away. What? Tunis had turned into Siamese twins? A boy and a girl attached at the hips? Where had they come from so quick? Out of one of Mark Twain's books? She stared. The two were actually trying to make connection with their valuables. But couldn't quite make it. And they smiled softly and sadly at each other as they gave up. Clara was suddenly so angry she threw the basin of warm water at them. The water splashed over everything, including Lord Sutherland's red leather sets of English classics. A single yellow drop flew back at her and hit her in the eye; and she woke up . . .

She found herself puffing and her heart beating violently. The drop of water in her eye became a tear that slowly began to form a rivulet down her cheek.

Darn Tunis.

She wiped the tear off her cheek with a corner of the sheet. She sat up. Lordy. It was already light outside. Glancing at the clock she saw it was almost six-thirty. She'd overslept.

Then she remembered Tunis had left in the night and there was really no reason to get up right away. Hired hand Saul Pollen would already long ago have been up and gone milking their three cows and feeding the hogs. He and Tunis came into the house around seven-thirty for breakfast. She had an hour yet. She lay down again and covered herself with the quilts.

The first thing she was going to do that morning was to ask Saul to drive her to town. She'd read in the Bonnie paper that a new house was for sale next to the banker's red house in the Silk Stocking block. She had enough money left over from the sale of the pearls to make a down payment. Tunis wouldn't be able to say no to the house. Surely he would finally go along with her desire to live their last days in town. And let Tane and Arva take over the old homestead.

She got up. Making sure the blinds were drawn, she slipped into her winter long johns, then put on her white cotton shift and her green housedress. Last she stepped into her black button shoes. They were worn over the toe and the heel was tippy. Button shoes had gone out of style and these would be the last pair for her. When she'd had them repaired by Old Shoester in town he'd shaken his head at them and said he wouldn't touch them if she brought them in again.

450

As she stepped into the kitchen a thought struck her. It had taken Tunis more than a few minutes to finish dressing. He hadn't checked the little secret cache by the fireplace, had he? There was nothing more really to take out of there, except the diary and the revolver. Just to make sure, she looked.

The diary was still there. But the gun was gone.

Now what in the world would he want a gun for? Sell it? When he had plenty of pocket money? Shoot somebody? Who was he mad at?

She ran through the names of all the people they knew. There wasn't one he hated. The Tippetts he merely despised. Boughers the realtor was long dead. There was no one. Except herself. And he couldn't very well shoot her if he had gone away.

She thought of calling Tane to tell him a little of what had happened. But after some thought decided not to. Should Tunis come back after a day or so . . . well, no use waking sleeping dogs. Tane and Arva had their own husband-and-wife troubles.

But why that gun?

That noon at dinner Clara asked hired hand Saul Pollen, "What did you have planned for this afternoon?"

Saul helped himself to some more potatoes and a thick slice of prime beef. "I better tune up the Fordson tractor."

"Could it wait a day?"

"Sure."

"It's such nice weather out, I thought we should go to town. This is the time of the year you better hustle off to town when you get a nice day, to get in your supplies against a blizzard."

Saul's big round blond face opened in a smile. Saul had eyes of the sea; one could look into them and never spot a horizon. Centuries of seafaring by his ancestors had built in him a curious silence. He loved cars. Automobiles were ships on the prairie for him. "What time?"

"Oh, in a half hour."

"Goot. I put on my new overalls."

When Saul had brought the new green Chevie around and she'd got in, Clara said, "One thing. I've decided I want to learn to drive this contraption. Now, every time you do something, tell me why you do it."

"Hokay, Missus."

Clara watched carefully as Saul worked the clutch, the gearshift, the foot-feed. She asked him to explain why one had to shift from low into intermediate and then into high. She watched how he handled the wheel as he aimed the car down the old King's Trail toward Bonnie. Driving didn't seem all that complicated.

As they rolled into town, Saul asked, "I suppose Tunis will be back in a couple of days. After he helps Rolf buy another section of land."

"Never mind," Clara said shortly.

"Where shall I park the Chevie then?"

"By the First National Bank. I need to see Chauncey. I should be through in an hour. Then I'll go over to Tillman's Mercantile. Where you can pick up the groceries."

"Hokay, Missus."

Chauncey's Scotch face drew down at the corners of his thin mouth. "So you want to put down some money on the Berg house. Tunis never mentioned it."

"I know. He's dragging his feet. But it's my money I'm putting down as an option on the place. And once Tunis sees that I really want to move to town, and want that house—it is after all almost new—he'll come around."

Chauncey pursed his lips some more until the upper lip almost touched the end of his long nose. "Well, it's your money. And it is a good house. The Anderson boys built it and they're the best carpenters around."

"So I thought."

"Tunis didn't come to town with you?"

"No. I had our hired man drive me."

"Hmm."

Just as she was about to step into Tillman's Mercantile, she ran into Tub Lawson, the stationmaster.

"Mr. Lawson."

Tub's tired blue eyes widened. "So. Hear you're planning on driving to Sioux City."

"Sioux City? Not that I know of."

"I see."

Clara fixed Tub with a sharp look. "What makes you say that?"

"Oh, nothing."

"Why?"

"Ohh . . . your husband bought a one-way ticket to Sioux City this morning. So I thought maybe you was planning on getting him."

One-way? So that's where Tunis went. Clara forced a smile to her lips. "Well, I'm learning to drive our Chevie, so I can get him if necessary."

"Mmm."

The rest of the day, riding home, making dinner, washing dishes, having learned where Tunis went, Clara began to fume to herself. She remembered that, even back in the days when she cooked for Lord Sutherland, Sioux City was known as the best whorehouse town in Siouxland. After what he'd tried with her the night before, wife rape, Tunis may very well have gone to see a floozy. The church was right. Concupiscence was one of the more deadly sins. If he really did go look one of them up, then she was all the more sure that she'd been right to resist him. Dirtying himself with a soiled woman!

She fell asleep troubled. She slept a good couple of hours, when a dream in which she was attacked by a cougar awakened her. Right after the cougar had managed to split her legs, it leaned down and bit her in the right breast. That popped her out of sleep. Her breast hurt as if something had actually bitten it.

She sat up and massaged her breast gently, until the sting of the dream bite subsided.

Several days of dry weather came along. Though sunny the temperature remained below freezing and the barren pasture west of the house became iron dry. To the open-mouthed astonishment of hired hand Saul, Clara came out of the house one morning well bundled up and went straight to the little white garage. She opened the doors and hooked them back, then went inside and started up the car. It ran rough for a minute, but having learned that if one were patient it would level out she waited quietly. She studied the gearshift, the clutch, the footfeed, and the instruments on the dashboard. When the irregular revolutions subsided, she pushed in the clutch, shoved the gear into reverse, goosed up the motor a trifle, and backed out. It worked. Smooth as pouring warm syrup. Well. She turned the wheel over; stopped; and then headed out through the open gate into the dry pasture.

She first drove a couple of long turns in the pasture in low gear. She stopped; started; stopped.

Next she shifted from low to intermediate, and to her pleasure discovered she hadn't crashed the gears like Tunis sometimes did, or Tane did with his car. And once she'd learned how to shift while the car was rolling, she moved the gear up to high. She began to smile and her arms relaxed. Shucks. Tunis and Tane, and now Saul, had made driving seem so important and hard to do. But it really wasn't all that complicated after all.

She made some dozen figure eights on the frozen pasture grass. She stopped; started; sped up; braked; stopped. She aimed the left front wheel for a single standing dead bull thistle, and after several tries at it began to flatten it every time. She then knew she could keep the car going down the tracks on the right-hand side of the gravel road.

When she had convinced herself that she could drive, she eased the wheel over and headed for the yard. She saw Saul come running out of the corn crib to watch her negotiate the turn through the gate and then into the garage. She smiled to herself when she saw his look of concern that she might enter the garage too fast and come through the back side.

She made a perfect stop in the garage, the hood of the green Chevie a yard from the far wall.

452

"Yes, Saul, I no longer need you to lean on, should I have to go to town. Or to church. Or to Sioux City to get my renegade husband."

She shut off the motor and got out and pocketed the keys. From now on she'd keep the keys in her purse.

Three days went by. Then four. Five. And still no Tunis. When she went to bed at night she began to wonder what she should do. Tell the sheriff? Hardly. He'd make a news item out of it.

She tried not to think about what Tunis might be doing that very moment. Every time her mind began to fantasize how it might be for her husband with a strange woman, she'd inadvertently let out a groan, and with a burning, even searing effort force her mind onto something more mundane, clothes to wash next Monday, how she'd move to town, what she should discard or give to the kids.

Every hour that went by she became more and more torn between two thoughts: bitterness that Tunis was being an old fool with a floozy; wonderment that maybe something had happened to him, mugged and shot, murdered by thugs in the red-light district, run over by a truck.

On the sixth day Tane came over. Clara was ironing in the kitchen when he suddenly appeared in the door.

"Hi, Ma."

"Tane."

"Where's Pa?"

"Oh, around somewhere. Why?"

"I was going to make some plans about how we'd go about planting together this spring."

"That's nice."

"Anyway, where is the old bear?"

Clara set the iron on its end on the nearby kitchen range and then settled down in her usual seat at the table. "Son, I don't know what to say."

Tane's innocent blue eyes opened. "Say? You two been fighting?"

"You could say that."

"I thought you might. When Pa was over the other day, I got to mentioning how Arva and me sometimes show our horns. And I sorta caught on by the advice he was handing out you two maybe were."

Clara began to puff. "You guessed right."

"Well, where is he? In a huff go sleep in the haymow?"

"If it was only that simple."

Tane stiffened. Then he slowly pulled out Pa's chair and in turn settled down in it at the head of the table. "What do you mean?"

"I don't know where he is."

"You better tell me what happened."

Clara picked at a flower design in the yellow tablecloth. "Well, we argued during the night, and then the next thing I knew, in the dark, he put on his best suit and walked out. Just went."

"You mean, up the road somewhere?"

"I guess so."

"Did he dress for the weather at all?"

"Oh yes, that. But I don't know where . . ." Clara paused. How could she lie to her most loyal son? The one who would inherit the homestead the moment she moved to town? "Well, I do know in what direction he went." She told about meeting Tub Lawson in the grocery store.

Tane whistled. "Sioux City and Sioux Falls are two big cities—"

Clara bristled. "No more of that, please."

Tane said, "We better call Geoffrey. He was mentioning something about Pa feeling down. Maybe he'll know what to do. Where to look in Sioux City. He's used to cities."

"Probably we should at that." Clara was still angry with Tunis. "Though if my husband did what I think he did, then he can go lump it."

Tane got to his feet. "I'll call Geoffrey."

"What did Geoffrey say about Pa being down?"

"It wasn't what Geoffrey said so much as the way he looked when Pa's name came up. Later on I got it out of my brother. That Pa had said, 'Me and Christ, we died on the cross for nothing. It's no use anymore.'"

Clara began to feel sick to her stomach. Had Tunis taken his life in Sioux City? He had always had that healthy pink look.

Tane held his head to one side. "I just now remember he said a funny thing to me last summer when we was haying. I'd been kiddin' him about not going to church more often with you. Right away he riled up. His eyes blazed like a madman's. And he said, 'Her God ain't the only God I have to worry about.' Boy, did I shut up after that."

"I know what you mean. Talking to an angry man is like talking to somebody who's been drinking."

454   Tane rang the operator and gave her Geoffrey's office number in Whitebone. While he waited for Geoffrey to come on the line, he muttered to himself, "I hope Geoff don't take that silk stocking wife of his along."

"You don't like her?" Ma asked, surprised.

"No. She stands around like she's sure she farts perfume."

"Tane, I will not have you talk that way in my presence. Besides, I think Adela is a lovely woman for him. She's Episcopalian. Has good manners."

"Yeh."

"It is what I'd hoped I'd brought all my children up to have."

Tane stiffened erect as a voice began to tickle in his ear. "Geoff? Tane here. I'm at Ma's . . . Well, we was wonderin' if you could come down here. We got a conundrum on our hands . . . Of course it's important or I wouldn't be calling you long distance . . . Well, suit yourself. But remember what you hinted about Pa's saying he was down? Well, Pa walked away from home early the other morning and Ma just found out from Tub in town that Pa went to Sioux City. Pa bought a one-way ticket . . . Okay, I'll be here when you get here." Tane hung up.

"He's coming then?"

Tane went back to Pa's swivel chair and sat down. He cracked his knuckles, showing the big white knot on the back of his right hand where the orphan boys had once tried to crucify him. "Yeh."

44. Geoffrey

1931

Geoffrey hung up the phone, got up, and went out front where wife Adela sat at her desk. Her black hair flowed down in long waves to her shoulders. "Adela, I have to go see Ma. Something mysterious going on down there. Could you call the judge and say I'd like to postpone the hearing we had set for today?"

Her lustrous black eyes softened. "Serious?"

"I'm afraid so."

"See you late tonight then."

"Hope so."

He put on his gray woolen coat, clapped on his gray hat, stepped into his black galoshes, and went out to his gray-blue Ford. The motor caught on the first revolution and soon he was heading down Highway 75.

In his mind he heard Pa muttering again as they sat on the stoop: "Yeh, pretty soon Ma'll say it's time for me to go to bed, and for you to get on home. But what fun has bed been for me these last years? I long ago lost my bed rights. And lately my dreams have turned muzzy. Ain't clear anymore. Time to move on." And later on, Pa had said, "Yeh, I'm a smart fellow all right. With my hide raw and salt on it."

When Geoffrey drove onto Ma's yard, he found Tane talking to Saul Pollen.

Tane stumped over. He rocked back and forth on his heavy legs as he scowled at Geoffrey's car. "Riding around in one of Henry's tin cans I see."

Geoffrey slid out of his car. "Yes. Runs cheap."

"Ha. A Ford will dime you to death."

"Ma in the house?"

"Yep. Waiting in the kitchen."

Geoffrey found Ma sitting in her usual seat, the second in command when the family was all at home.

"Yes, son," Ma said.

Geoffrey sought out his old spot at the family table, while Tane took Pa's swivel chair.

Ma said, "Sorry you had to come down under such odd circumstances."

"Tell me."

Ma told all she knew.

Geoffrey sat awhile in thought. He drummed his fingers on the table. The family clock tocked in the other room. Finally he looked up at Tane. "You'd be too busy to go to Sioux City with me?"

Tane lifted his shoulders as if to say there was nothing he could do about that. "And then there's the kids. You at least don't have that to hobble you."

Geoffrey looked at Ma. "Wanna go with me?"

Ma's eyes took on a hostile glint. "Not to Sioux City and what they got there."

Geoffrey gave the table a whack with the flat of his pale hand. "All right, I'll go alone."

Tane said, "You know the law better than we do."

"Yeh," Geoffrey murmured, "I know the law all right. I think I'll drive down. That way I won't have to depend on taxis."

In Sioux City Geoffrey drove straight to the police station.

A heavyset sergeant in blue at the front desk gave him a bland look. "Who are you?"

Geoffrey introduced himself as a lawyer from Whitebone.

"Looking for a runaway daughter?"

"No. Looking for my father. He may have been mugged in the red-light district."

"Well, we don't have any cathouses in Sioux City."

The smart ass. "Got any hotels where a lot of widows stay?"

"Them neither."

"Thanks. And when you come to Whitebone and want a favor done, be sure to look me up."

Geoffrey stepped outside. There was a threat of snow in the air. The low gray clouds were thick enough to keep him from making out where the sun was. He watched the traffic go by. The faces of the drivers had the tight wrinkled look from the long winter.

456   A cattle truck bumped by. One of the steers let out a strangled bellow at the same time that a car horn sounded—both were basso but violently out of tune with each other.

The cattle truck gave him an idea. Pa had several times gone along with a Bonnie trucker when he took his fatteners to the market. Pa would know the stockyards best. Geoffrey got into his Ford and drove over. Just opening the car window helped him find it. As he looked for a place to park, he spotted the Cannonball depot. That would be where Pa got off the train. Geoffrey pulled over.

Going up the street toward the depot, he noticed the Smokey Bear Hotel a few blocks away. That gave him a further idea. Pa probably headed for the first likely place to stay.

An old man desk clerk looked up at Geoffrey. The old clerk had a heavily waxed ropelike moustache. "Room for you, sir?"

"Well, maybe. Uhh, actually, I'm looking for an elderly fellow. To see if he might have stayed here. Heh, maybe he's still here." Geoffrey gave Pa's name and described him as he might look with his Sunday clothes on.

The desk clerk got out the register and flipped back a few pages. "Nobody here by that name last week, sir."

"Do you . . . this is going to be a funny question . . . do you have any widows staying here? Or single women?"

"Sir!"

"You're so near the stockyards this hotel might be a likely place."

"Sir!"

"Only asking. It's important that I find him. His life might be at stake."

"Sorry."

"Suppose I'd taken a taxi over. Would the driver give this address as a place where I might have a lot of fun over a weekend?"

"If you had your own wife with you, yes."

"But suppose a couple wasn't married?"

The ropey points of the clerk gray moustache jiggled. "If they look over twenty-one and they say they are married, that's good enough for me."

Geoffrey stared at the old fuff of a clerk. Something about the man's responses didn't ring right. There probably were rooms for call girls somewhere in the building. "Well, anyway, I think I'll stay in town over night. Got a room for me?"

The clerk turned the register around for Geoffrey to sign in.

Geoffrey got out his own fountain pen. "Up on the fourth floor? I'd like a high room overlooking the great Missouri."

"No, not on the fourth floor."

"I was born along a river. So I'm kind of a river nut."

"Sorry."

"What's up there on the fourth floor? Private residence?"

"Yes. A lady has made the Smokey Bear her home for many years."

"Got a room on the third floor then?"

"No. All filled up. But I do have one on the first floor."

Geoffrey signed in. He was given a key to room 111. Geoffrey said, "I parked my car down the street a ways. Can I bring it up to your parking lot behind the hotel here?"

"Help yourself."

After he'd parked his car in the hotel lot and had gone to his room, Geoffrey sat down on an old hard bed. There was a smell in the room as though the janitor had used straight kerosene to kill bugs.

First things first. He put a call through to Whitebone to let good wife Adela know where he was.

Next he paged through the Sioux City telephone book, mostly at random, to see if he could spot the name of some woman who might be living on the fourth floor of the hotel. He went through the *A*'s and the *B*'s, and then just for the heck of it went to the back of the book and paged through *Y* to *Z*. He often read the daily paper that way.

He hit upon the *R*'s and found it. Rhea Redwell. Same address as the number out front of the hotel. She was the one.

He washed up in the basin, combed his hair in the mirror on the medicine cabinet, and then headed for the back stairwell where the red arrows for the fire escape were located.

On the fourth floor a huge blue policeman stood in front of a double set of doors. "Yes?"

Geoffrey made sure the top button of his suit jacket was neatly secure. "I'm looking for a Rhea Redwell. This where she lives?"

"Your first time here?"

"Yes."

"Your business with her?"

Geoffrey made sure his inward smile didn't show. He'd hit the jackpot. "I was told this was a good place to have a nice quiet drink with a friend."

457

"Who told you about her?"

"A friend of mine from Bonnie. That's near Rock Falls. A man of about sixty or so."

"Oh. I remember him. You can go in."

Again the jackpot. That had to be Pa.

Geoffrey pushed through the double doors. He was surprised by the tasseled overstuffed look of the big room. The garish purples hurt the eye. Adela would blanch if she saw it. Adela's tastes were actually quite simple for all her wealthy bringing up.

A jolly woman a bit overweight got to her feet and approached him with a welcome smile. She liked it that he was young. "What can I do for you?"

"Well, I'm not really looking for a companion for the night so much—"

"You a process server?"

"Oh, lord, no."

"Well?" She touched back her crimped blond bobbed hair.

"I've already rented a room downstairs. I . . . uh . . . it's more that I'm looking for someone." Geoffrey decided to be frank with the woman. "You see, it's my father. Tunis Freyling. He got mad at my mother and walked out on her. We know he took a train to Sioux City. A one-way ticket. So naturally we're a little concerned. That one-way ticket might mean something serious."

The jolly woman's light blue eyes turned blank. They fixed on Geoffrey's nose without showing any emotion whatever. But behind the eyes Geoffrey was aware that several animals were wrestling. "Yes, a Mr. Freyling was here all right. But I didn't notice anything out of the way. He seemed in good spirits to me."

458

"He saw a woman here then?"

"If you're thinking a prostitute, no."

"But some lady though?"

"Yes, he saw a lady. It turned out to be someone he knew from the old days."

Geoffrey straightened up. "An old friend? A woman?"

"Yes." Rhea Redwell allowed herself a little smile. "I suppose you'd like to know who?"

"It would help."

"Velda Fikes."

"My God! Really? She taught my brothers and sisters."

"So you see it was a lady."

Geoffrey was dumbfounded. He remembered the talk about her. Had Pa kept in touch with her all these years? Written her in secret? Now and then called her long distance? Geoffrey's belly hurt. So that's how Pa took care of his sex life after Ma had shut the door on him. Poor man. And poor Ma. "Could I have her telephone number?"

"No, you may not. She'd be horribly embarrassed that a son of his would know what happened. You see, she never expected to see him either."

"Oh."

"I guess they'd both liked each other back then, but did nothing about it."

"But I'd still like to talk to Miss Fikes. To see if he dropped any hints about where he might go next."

"I talked to her afters. She didn't mention any hints."

"Her number, please. It's very important."

"No." Rhea Redwell lightly brushed back her permanent wave. "You see, she came into some money. And now lives the life of a lady of fashion. It'd just be too awkward."

"I can look it up in the telephone book."

"You won't find it there. Her number isn't listed."

"A lady of fashion. How come she hangs around here then?"

"Sir!"

"Can I see the room he stayed in? He might have left something behind. A scrap of paper. Anything."

"I cleaned the room myself." Her nickel eyes twitched. "He left nothing behind. But come. You can have a look."

In the room what caught Geoffrey's eye was the view of the grand Missouri River. Pa had seen that. Pa liked grand prospects. Geoffrey looked the room over. It was pin-neat. No chance of a stray scrap of paper left behind. Geoffrey murmured to himself. "I don't know where to look next." He fixed Rhea Redwell with a scratching look. "No hint in his manner that behind it all he wasn't happy?"

"Nothing." She took a step toward Geoffrey. It could be seen she'd decided he was all right. A fine son. "Are you thinking that maybe he . . . ?"

Geoffrey nodded. "At the time I didn't really pay any attention to it. Only later on I caught at it."

"I'm sorry I can't help you."

"I'm sorry too. Thanks for all your trouble."

Geoffrey went back to his room to think.

After an hour Geoffrey put on his overcoat and headed outdoors. The sight of the Missouri from the fourth floor made him want to see it. Looking to the west, he soon made out through the factory smoke the tops of the cantilever towers of a great bridge. 459

He stepped onto the end of the long bridge and took the catwalk along the right side. Only a few cars and one booming truck came along. When he got to the middle of the bridge, he stopped and looked down at the sliding yellow water. Points of ice reached out from both banks and also spread out from the concrete support under him. If Pa had jumped from the bridge, he would have done it from the other railing, going with the current. Geoffrey stepped across the bridge.

He leaned over the rusty iron railing and looked down. He willed with all his might to evoke from somewhere what might have happened at that very spot. He'd read in the Sioux City *Journal* that suicides often jumped from that very place; and always from the south railing. He tried to imagine what Pa's thinking might have been as he leaned over the railing. What secrets. What inner turmoils. What troubling darks.

But Geoffrey couldn't see it. It wasn't in him to think death, to think suicide. Not with a wife like Adela. Not with the profession of law to pursue. He had a great life coming ahead.

He let go of the railing and saw that some of the rust had come off and soiled his gray gloves. He flaffed his hands to get rid of the brown stains.

He finally agreed with Rhea Redwell that it would be too embarrassing for everybody concerned for him to seek out Velda Fikes. For now. But if Pa didn't show up in a couple of weeks, he'd come back to Sioux City and find her.

A week later the phone rang in Geoffrey's office. Adela answered it; then buzzed Geoffrey.

"Hello."

"Son?" It was Ma. "Geoffrey?"

"Yes, Ma."

"You got a letter here from Sioux City."

"Who's it from?"

"It doesn't say. Just has your name on it in my care. Shall I open it?"

"Uhh . . . no. I'll come down this evening. Otherwise any news about Pa?"

"None. And I think we ought to call a family meeting. Shall I ring everybody and have them come over tonight too?"

"Do that." Geoffrey hung up. He sat a moment in thought; then took his feet out of the desk drawer and slipped on his tan oxfords and went out front. "Ma thinks we ought to have a family meeting. I'd ask you to go along . . ."

Adela shook her dark head gravely. "Oh, I wouldn't want to intrude into what is really a family matter."

"Ma says there's a letter for me from Sioux City."

"Ah. Sounds interesting."

"So I thought."

After dinner, Geoffrey got into his car and headed for the old homestead.

They were all there when he arrived: Tane, Thea, Dirk, Tressa, Rolf, Ana, and Mallie. Thea had caught the Bonnie Omaha from Rock Falls. Dirk had driven down from the Twin Cities. Ana happened to have come home from her mission work, and on the last leg of her journey had caught a ride with Mallie in Sioux Falls. All the rest came from nearby.

They gathered around the family table in the big kitchen taking their usual places. Strangely empty was Pa's swivel chair at the head of the table.

Everyone waited for Ma to begin.

Ma's face was puffy. The skin over her cheeks was tight and pale. Ma had her big purse in front of her. At last, after a swift look around at the faces of her eight children, she reached into the black leather purse and drew out a white envelope. "Would you pass this on to Geoffrey? It was mailed to him."

Geoffrey looked at the address. The handwriting was formal, of the kind a teacher might use when writing out a lesson on a blackboard. Geoffrey knew instantly it was from Velda Fikes. He turned the letter over, catching himself examining it to see if Ma had maybe steamed it open. But the seal was flat, not rumpled. He trusted Ma, but mothers had a way of taking the law into their own hands when it came to wanting to ferret out the secrets of their children.

Geoffrey ran his finger under the flap and softly tore the envelope open. He felt Mallie leaning toward him, as if to read the contents of the letter with him. Not wanting to hurt her feelings, yet knowing that perhaps no one but he should know what was in the letter, he turned slightly, as though to get better light from the single big light bulb over the table, unfolded the single sheet, and began reading silently to himself:

Dear Geoffrey:

Rhea Redwell called me this evening to tell me about your visit and your concern about your father. She said you hinted he might have done something sad. Let me tell you that he seemed in very good spirits: making witty remarks, telling jokes and stories, very jolly. To my mind there isn't the slightest possibility that he might have done hurt to himself. I enjoyed my visit with him very much—talking about the old days, talking about you children, about life. You had a wonderful father, you know, and I always admired him very much.

I'm sorry that I can't be of much help in finding where he might have gone. There wasn't any suggestion that he might be running off somewhere. My feeling is that he should soon return to the old homestead.

Best wishes,
Velda Fikes

Geoffrey read the letter a second time, then folded it up and replaced it in the envelope. He slipped the envelope into his inside jacket pocket.

Rolf's bristly head shot forward. "Wull, ain't you gonna tell us what it says? I ain't got all night. Time is money."

"No."

"Why not?" Mallie exclaimed.

"It turns out to be a private letter to me."

"Who from, for godsakes?"

"An old friend."

Dirk's lips curled back, sardonic. "Friend? Or friend friend?"

Geoffrey backed in his chair a little. "I don't care to discuss it."

Rolf hit the table with his fist. "Dummed lawyers. They always got secrets." He fixed his animal eyes on Geoffrey. "You put your lawyer tricks ahead of your family?"

"Being a lawyer has nothing to do with it."

Ma spoke up. "Can I see it, Geoffrey?"

Geoffrey slowly turned to his mother. "Sorry, Ma."

"I see."

461

Tane, who'd always sat at Pa's right in the order of the oldest son first, began to wiggle in his chair. "What I want to know is, what are we going to do? Call the sheriff and have the law start looking for him?"

Ana perked up. She'd sat through it all as tense as a virgin aunt worried that she might be assaulted by dirty talk. "And have it get in the papers? Never. Pa'll show up and then it'll all be over with."

Rolf shook his lunging head. "But what if he met with foul play? Stabbed in the back and robbed? It happens in them godless cities."

Tane's left hand lay near where Pa's right hand often lay on the table. "Well, we better decide something pretty soon. Ma wants to move to town. I guess that's what they had their fight about. Right, Ma?"

Ma nodded. Her lips thinned out. "I think Pa'd pretty well made up his mind that he and I should move to town yet this spring. And for Tane to take over the farm."

Tane jerked erect. "Really, Ma?"

Rolf reared up. "How come not me?"

Dirk almost sneered. Like the rest of them, he'd always tried to be considerate when it came to Rolf, though as the years went by Rolf's avarice, "got to strike while the iron is hot," "got to make dough when the market is ripe," had got under his skin. "Good God, Rolf, ain't you rich enough yet?"

Rolf said, "Well, I'm gonna get it while the gettin' is good. That's my motto. 'Course, Tane would farm this old section good. I know that. It's just that I want to make sure I'm not missing out on anything."

Thea shook her head in a thoughtful way. "Boys, boys. You're quarreling here like you think Father is dead."

Silence.

Tressa was sitting sideways so she wouldn't have to look at Dirk. "I trust Pa. He's tough. He'll come home all right. He's been too wonderful a father not to."

Mallie cried a little. "If something's happened to him . . ."

Thea said, "Pa'll be back when he cools down."

Ma grimaced. The corners of her lips cut into her cheeks. "Geoffrey already knows this, but I think the rest of you should know it too. Pa took a gun with him."

Silence.

Ana closed her eyes. "What gun?"

Ma mentioned again the secret compartment next to the old fireplace, now part of their back porch, where she'd found the string of pearls and a diary. "What you didn't notice was that there was also a pearl-handled revolver in there."

"So Pa took that?"

"Yes."

Geoffrey fixed Ma with a direct look. "What made you wonder if Pa took the gun, Ma?"

Ma shrugged.

"Did you sense something about him that made you check the cache again?"

"He was so angry. You kids may not always have noticed it, but he had a terrible temper. Somehow around you he managed to control it. But it was there. And I was always scared of it."

Dirk sat up, alert. "So he took the gun, did he?"

Tressa finally looked at Dirk. "What wild notion are you thinking now?"

"Nothing."

Tane pushed out his full red lips. "Newsmen always like to find a body when there ain't one around."

Rolf peered out of the cave of his head. "Ma, do you know if Pa made out a will?"

"Rolf!" Thea cried.

"Did he, Ma?"

Dirk almost had to laugh. "Rolf, you sure know in what direction to point your nose, don't you?"

"Did he, Ma?"

Ma said, "I don't know. I've looked everywhere for it in the house too."

Rolf swung his sunken-back eyes at Geoffrey. "You're our family legal beagle—did he make one out with you?"

Geoffrey shook his head.

Rolf blundered on like a merciless bill collector. "That means then that if Pa is dead, Ma gets one third of his estate, and the rest is shared by his kids. Us."

Geoffrey spoke slowly. "That's right."

Thea got to her feet. "I don't know if I want to hear what's coming next."

Rolf growled, "Sit down!"

Tane wyed his head toward Rolf. He was a little afraid of Rolf. "What you gettin' at?"

"Wal, I picked up already that both Pa and Ma want you to take over the old homestead—"

"Picked up? We've all known—"

"—and if you're gonna do that, you gotta pay the rest of us kids all some money, each our share of the remainin' two-thirds."

Thea said, "God forbid that we have to think this far, but if we have to, Tane can have my share. He's sure to do right by the old place."

Ana said, "Tane can have my share too. I won't need it for my mission work." Mallie said, "And mine too."

Rolf couldn't believe what he was hearing. "Holy smokes! The way you guys are throwing money away, a person'd think you was all Rockefellers."

Tressa said, "Wallie wouldn't appreciate me giving up my share either, but I'm going to do it anyway."

Rolf next stared at Dirk. "And I suppose . . . ?"

Dirk laughed softly. "Yep. If Tress can, I can."

Tane held up a hand. "Hey! First of all, Pa ain't left us for sure yet. Next, maybe I don't agree with all this giving away stuff. Maybe I can be proud too. So this is the way I want it to go. If and when I take over the homestead, I want to buy it on time. I'll sell my quarter by Lakewood and give you all that. Then all of you can make out a mortgage to me for the rest. That means, less my eighth share in it, I'll be paying for three-quarters of this section. Right now land ain't all that expensive—"

Rolf broke in. "But in five years, when good times come again, this land will triple in price. Take my word for it, I know. Real estate is my business."

Tane went on, holding a shoulder against Rolf. "About a hundred dollars an acre. And interest is the lowest it's been in years. About five percent. So I think I can handle it. And that should be fair for everybody."

Ma finally raised a hand. "Well, now, we aren't sure yet just what happened to Pa, are we? In any case, I've already made up my mind I no longer want to live here. I want to live in town. And since Pa in effect walked out on me, with no hint he was coming back, that's just what I'm gonna do. Move to town. I've had enough of this place. And even if Pa shows up again, he's going to have to live with me in town." Ma's chin came down like a general's. She'd made up her mind what the battle plan should be. "With that in mind, starting tomorrow, I'm going to call Mike Trout the mover and have him take Pa's stuff as well as mine into the new house." Ma saw the look of surprise on everybody's face. "Yes, I've already put in motion buying a house in town." She mentioned the Berg house in the Silk Stocking district. She swung a penetrating look at Tane. "That's a word to the wise. You can start planting your crops on the old homestead."

Tane drew in a huge breath; slowly let it out. He whacked the table with the flat of his hand. "Good, then. Because when I get up from this table, I'm heading straight for Hy Snapp. He made me a fine offer for my quarter. Soon's he pays me, I'll turn it over to you, Geoffrey, and then you can figure out how to distribute it to everybody here." Tane lifted expectant eyes at Geoffrey. "Thinkin', a course, that you're gonna handle our family legal affairs. For your usual legal fee."

Rolf said, "He really ought to do it for nothing."

"Why?" Geoffrey wondered.

"As a labor of love," Rolf said.

463

Tressa moved her hand back and forth in front of her as though she were wiping the table clean. She began to cry.

Thea saw Tressa's tears and began to run tears too.

Soon Ana and Mallie's faces also mottled over.

But the boys looked down and fumbled their hands in each other.

Ma sat unyielding.

And then at last, Tressa, who'd started all the crying, broke out with a low keening wail.

464

45. Clara

1931

She was sorry she hadn't steamed open the letter addressed to Geoffrey. The mask that came down over Geoffrey's face as he silently read the letter told her it was about Tunis. The handwriting on the outside was that of a fancy woman. It burned her that Tunis might have had relations with a high-toned woman. What a pity it was that she'd married such a bull of a man. If only he could have been a model husband.

"Well, no use holding my breath over that anymore. What's done is done. And I'm going to live in town."

But before she called Mike Trout the drayman, she had to have a look at the Worthing diary again. She never did send it on to the Iowa Historical Society as she once promised attorney Timmons. Once the brown leather diary with its gold trim got into the society's hands, the whole world could learn about what had once happened on the place.

Clara read it slowly. Betsy Worthing, the diarist, had written about the shame in a stilted manner so that at first glance it didn't look all that awful. But any woman reading it would know. Betsy had been married to James, but she'd also loved the other brothers, Joseph and Robert. Several times she'd written that when husband James was gone on a trip, Joseph, and then Robert, had also been sweet to her. And that being "sweet to me" were the same words she used when referring to those times when James cohabited with her. That's what happened when there weren't enough women around. Lord Sutherland and his horsey boys and their imported maids proved that.

Awful stuff.

Clara stared out of the kitchen window over the frozen snow-dusted land. A thought snapped in her head, and then, nodding to herself, Clara got up from her chair and went over to the range and lifted one of the lids and dropped the brown leather diary with its gold trim into the titted flames. She didn't even bother to watch it burn. She fitted the lid into place.

"Betsy," she whispered, "now may your bones rest in peace. No one will ever know once I die."

Then she went to the phone and called the drayman.

With Saul Pollen helping Mike Trout, she moved everything, including Tunis's things, to the new house on upper Main Street. She put Tunis's clothes in the spare bedroom and his garden tools in the garage. When and if he came back, he surely wouldn't think of sleeping in the same bed with her.

She liked the new house. The Bergs had recently painted the outside a warm cream and the window trim a soft green. Thank God the Bergs had also had the sense not to stain the woodwork and the floors. The oak everywhere had been coated with a clear varnish so that the swirling grain showed through. The kitchen had city water with faucets. The toilet also had a seat with water. The house was somewhat large but that she didn't mind. It reminded her of her father's spacious home in Welton, Iowa, as well as Lord Sutherland's mansion near Le Mars.

When Saul finished helping Trout move her in, he went back to the homestead to help Tane and Arva move in from their quarter section.

It took Clara two weeks to get herself settled in comfortably.

Every evening when she went to bed she stood awhile in the enclosed entrance to her house and looked down the street toward downtown. She wasn't sure how she'd feel should she see Tunis come walking up the street from the depot. And if he finally knocked on the door, she wasn't sure just what she'd say.

When she at last settled into her pillow and composed herself for sleep, she lay awhile hating Tunis with all her heart. That he should have turned out to be such an old goat. Concupiscence was such a bother.

Later, heartbeat back to normal, she'd lament a little that it was beginning to look like she'd never get all her girls in white. Married. Thea and Tressa were married. But there was no hope that martyr-bound Ana would ever attract a man. And Mallie was beginning to live a little like a wild woman.

She reviewed the boys too. Tane was the only one who was set. Dirk, like Mallie, was living the life of a wild one too. It was beginning to look as though Rolf and Greta would never have children. Greta had confessed to her once that they were trying but nothing worked. As for Geoffrey, the youngest, it was hard to tell what he and his reserved wife would decide to do. Adela came from a rich family and the rich always seemed to have a way of having only one or two children. If any.

On the fifteenth of March Clara woke up knowing that Tunis was never coming back. A dream had convinced her something dark had happened to him.

. . . . In the dream, she was worshiping in the Episcopal church in Whitebone, when suddenly, above her, in the apse, a glory opened; and as the glory slowly formed into a courtroom, with a resplendent judge wearing shining black, there, in front of the great judge, stood Tunis. A clerk to one side was reading from a document: "The petitioner, one known as Tunis Freyling, hereby requests the court for permission to enter the kingdom of heaven. What is the wish of the court?" The great judge's terrible eyes, burning like a pair of gas jets, fixed themselves on Tunis. Tunis quivered. The great judge said in a powerful sepulchral voice: "The petition is denied. And the sinner is consigned to hell. There to burn in the flames of our wrath forever." The great judge pointed with a long finger. The fingernail at the end of the finger shot out a beam of light as though from a pencil flashlight. "That way, sinner!" Tunis shivered; sank to his knees; cried out, "Forgive me, O Lord, forgive me. I knew not what I was doing." The great judge slowly shook his grave gray head. "Ignorance is no excuse in the eyes of heaven's justice. Go!". . . .

The aftereffects of the nightmare lingered for hours. It was as though a lightning bolt had struck near her, close enough to leave her nervous system buzzing. Even her lips felt thick as though frostbitten.

466

When April first rolled around, Clara finally decided she herself had to do something to find out what had happened to her husband. She was sick of seeing, and feeling, the eyes of people uptown wondering what awful scandal had happened in the Freyling family. Some people actually turned away when she approached them. Chauncey the banker looked at her sometimes as if she were a criminal.

She packed a suitcase, put on gray traveling clothes, got out her blue rain-coat, walked down to the Cannonball depot, and bought a ticket to Sioux City from Tub Lawson. Round-trip.

She disembarked in the Sioux City main depot. She walked out across the flagstones onto the street side. It was a soft April day. The south wind was laden with the smells of the sea.

Where to next?

She spotted a yellow taxicab at the curb. Ah. That's what Tunis would have seen too. But what directions would he gave given? Ask the driver to take him to a house of ill repute? According to modern novels, taxi drivers were very know-ing about city life, more even than policemen.

The taxi driver saw her looking in his direction. He got out and called over the hood of his engine. "Taxi, ma'am?"

Setting her low heels sturdily down on the brick approach, she strode toward him. "Yes." She got in as he held the door open for her.

He slid into the driver's seat and picked up a clipboard. "Where to?"

"Ah, first a question." She pinched her nervous lips into a thin line. "I'm looking for a friend. It's kind of embarrassing. A lady friend of mine who disap-peared into the underworld here, became . . . how shall I say it? . . . a lady for hire."

"You mean a whore."

"Sir!"

"A hooker then."

"That I don't like either."

The driver turned and looked at her over the back of his seat. He had blood-shot eyes. But they were hard, like rusty ball bearings. His rough voice took on the edge of sarcasm. "Oh, you mean, a daughter of joy."

"I suppose one could say that." She swallowed bile. "She would have gone to a fairly nice place."

"A fairly nice place."

"Yes."

"Well, there's Madam Redwell over at the Smokey Bear. She has a few gals there." The driver looked at her neck and then at the backs of her hands as though examining them wrinkle for wrinkle. "How old would your friend be?"

"Oh, fifty or so."

"Well, Madam Redwell has nothing but young stuff there. Jailbait, really. So that wouldn't be it. And then there's that fleabag, the Overland Hotel. Buggy."

"Oh, she wouldn't have gone to that."

"That leaves the Orchid."

"What a name for a . . ."

"Yeh." He resettled in his seat. "Okay, will that be it?"

"Let's try the Orchid."

The Orchid turned out to be a flophouse for transients, mostly grain hands in the summer and out-of-work hired hands in the winter. At the moment, between seasons, the place was almost empty. And the desk clerk was astounded, so it seemed, to learn that a taxi driver had told Clara that he also harbored a house of pleasure. His pale ropey face became taut with anger.

"Who are you? Some kind of do-gooder?"

"I'm merely looking for a lost friend."

"Well, if it's a woman friend you're looking for, you better look somewhere else." He turned his back on her. He snapped on a dark mahogany radio, opening up the volume until ears cracked with Grand Ole Opry music.

Clara gave up. Carrying her suitcase, she slowly trudged outside. Looking up, she was surprised to see her taxi driver still out front. Again pinching her lips tight, she approached him. "Maybe you better take me to this Madam Redwell you mentioned. That seems to be the only one left."

"It's your dollar, lady."

When the driver dropped her off at the Smokey Bear Hotel, he had a word of advice. "Don't ask at the desk where you can find Madam Redwell. They're still pretending they don't have a cathouse there. She's up on the fourth floor. Just go in and take the stairs to the fourth floor."

"Thanks."

Madam Redwell's high forehead under her high pompadour wrinkled up when Clara showed up at her door. "Yes?" she said crisply.

"Ahh, I'm hoping you can help me find someone."

"Yes?"

"I was told a friend of mine . . . that you might know where she is." Clara knew it was a wild shot in the dark but she had to try.

"A woman?"

"Yes. She'd be about fifty. Good-looking blond. You'd probably use her for older men. Men of, say, from fifty on up. To seventy, even."

"Use her? What do you think this is?"

Clara stiffened to the task. "Don't your girls service men?" Clara tried to look past Mrs. Redwell into the opulent furnishings behind her to see if there were any girls lolling about. There weren't. "Also, I'm looking for a man who might be with her."

A slow deep breath lifted Madam Redwell's heavy breasts. Madam Redwell's eyes became cold icicles. She saw what she had on her hands. An angry wife out to nail an errant husband. "I don't know who you are. And I don't want to hear who you are. Case closed. Good-bye."

Clara stood her ground. "Though seventy, he'd look like fifty. Well set-up. Graying rusty hair and moustache. Gray eyes that burn right through you. There'd be a look about him that if you crossed him he'd turn on you and be dangerous."

Madam Redwell blinked. It was obvious from the blink that she'd seen such a man. Madam Redwell's chin slowly set down and her eyes became even more icy. She stepped around Clara and held the door open for her.

Clara decided to be specific. "I'm looking for a man named Tunis Freyling."

"Your husband?"

"Yes. He just suddenly up and left me. I myself wouldn't get too worked up over that, but we have children. Eight of them."

"Lucky you." Madam Redwell opened the door even farther.

"Naturally they're all worried what might have happened to their father."

"If he was a good father, I suppose they would."

"I mean to find out for them."

"Your son Geoffrey didn't find him then?"

Aha. "My husband didn't mention where he might be going after he left here?"

"You can leave now, please."

"Not even a hint at all?"

Madam Redwell swung around on her heels. "Jackman? Come out here a minute."

A section of the purple-padded wall opened and a giant of a black man stepped into the room. "Yes, ma'am?"

"Would you show Mrs. Freyling the way out, please?"

Sight of the huge black man made Clara stagger back a step. He had a great white smile. But his eyes were small and feral. Clara said, "If you won't give me any information, I can have the law on you."

"Try me."

Clara considered to herself. If Geoffrey, having been here, had decided he couldn't do anything legally, perhaps she couldn't either. "All right," she said firmly, "all right. I'll go." And turning on her heels, very erect, Clara left the commodious opulent room.

She took the steps slowly downstairs. "Tunis was here then," she whispered. "At least we know he was alive till here." She picked up her suitcase where she'd placed it behind a palm. "Hard telling where he went from here." She walked across the lobby and out through the front door. She looked up at the pale sky. "I just wonder if maybe he didn't go look up his old home by Wanata. Like a fire engine horse always runs back to its stall."

469

She got out her ticket from her purse. The return train to Bonnie was due to leave in an hour.

"Better I should go back home. I'm not up to visiting Wanata just now. Where I've never been." She spotted a yellow taxicab heading her way and flagged it down. "If after a month Tunis doesn't show up, maybe Geoffrey and I can drive out to Wanata. In the meantime, thank God I had the sense to move to town so Tane could take over the home place."

When the Cannonball engine whistled for the stop at Le Mars, she suddenly got the notion that it would be fun to stop in Le Mars and see what might have happened to the British living there. To Lord Sutherland and his scalawags. Might as well get something out of the trip. No sooner thought of than done. She got up and looked for the conductor.

"I wonder. This ticket of mine is for a return to Bonnie. Could I stop over here in Le Mars without having to buy another ticket?"

"Certainly. Give it here and I'll fix it up for you."

In the Le Mars depot she asked for directions to the Regent Hotel, where many years before Lord Sutherland had dropped her off.

"That's been torn down, lady. It's a parking lot now."

"I suppose those dens of iniquity, the House of Lords and the House of Commons, are both gone too."

"Never heard of them."

"And the Prairie Club?"

"Never heard of that either."

"Pity. Even though I hated saloons." She ran her tongue along the edge of her upper lip. "Then all the English pups, the remittance men, have gone back to England?"

"Lady, I don't know what you're talking about."

"That's answer enough." Even after all that time, she still hated those horsey young gallants lying in the opened legs of her girl help at Lord Sutherland's. Strangely enough though, she also felt a tiny sting of nostalgia for those days.

An old man sitting on a bench inside the depot spoke up. He had a great head of white hair and was smoking a low-slung pipe. "Lady, I couldn't help overhearing you. There's still one of them pups left. A son of one of them."

"Who's that?"

"George P. Hotham. He lives in a cottage alone just a couple blocks away."

"Hotham. Yes, I remember Lord Sutherland talking about a gentleman named Hotham. Didn't he marry one of the German maids who came over to work?"

"Right."

"I remember Lord Sutherland saying he was one of the more honorable of the second sons to come over. So he never went back?"

"No. The first son of the Hotham line in England outlived our second-son Hotham. And when our second-son Hotham finally died, the Hotham estate in England still kept sending his son, this George P. Hotham, remittance money. Our George never worked a day in his life. Like he might be royalty."

"Did he ever marry?"

"No. Just lives alone. Walks over to the Le Mars Cafe for his meals. Sits around in the pool hall mostly. Smiles to himself a lot. A high-class loafer. Just carries on his father's habits."

"Thanks."

Clara wondered if it might not be interesting to visit this George P. Hotham, if only to refresh her memory of what her father used to tell about Old England.

She looked up the only hotel in town, the Le Mars, and rented a room and stashed her suitcase.

Twenty minutes later she went up a brick walk toward a squat cottage in the middle of a large lot. The grass in the yard lay dead and yellowish gray. Rose vines climbing over an arbor hung broken and budless. It meant the main rose stem had died. The cottage was painted with what looked like ocher paint, with green window trim. She went up the stoop and worked the knocker on the door.

After a minute the door opened a crack and a man with dark hair and a long thin-ridged nose, with a face resembling the philosopher Bertrand Russell, peered out at her. "Yes?"

Clara found herself nervous. "I'm Clara Shortridge." She allowed herself a little laugh to suggest she should be forgiven presumption. "Well, actually, I'm married and my name now is Clara Shortridge Freyling."

"Yes?"

"Well, my father was a second son. Cecil Shortridge from Yarmouth. He settled with my mother in Welton, Iowa. But he lost everything. And died. So I took the train to here in Le Mars and cooked for Lord Sutherland."

"Ah, yes, Sutherland."

"It's all so long ago. But I just thought it would be nice to talk about England with someone who would have heard about it from his father too." She gave him her best smile. She hadn't smiled that way in years. "Could I come in? For just a bit?"

"Of course." He opened the door and waved her inside. He was only an inch or so taller than she, and very slender, with fingers neatly manicured. He had on a pair of brown trousers, a tan shirt without a tie, a brown vest, a faded purple dressing gown, and a pair of scuffed brown leather slippers. His feet were narrow and long. The smell in the house was typical of a bachelor's nest: lingering smell of socks not washed often enough, trousers that hadn't been cleaned and pressed in a while, even the penetrating smell of decayed meat that had been roasted anyway. He pointed to a walnut rocker for her to sit in while he seated himself in a brown plush chair. A radio sat perched on a small stand on his left and a low-slung pipe rested on a nickel ashtray. "You were saying?"

"I loved my father and I miss him talking about the Old Country."

"Ah. Yes." His nose came up a little and a twinkle showed in the corners of his brown glimmering eyes. "Your father was a second son too, was he?"

"Yes. And wasn't yours?"

"Yes."

"Didn't your father ever wish to go back to England? Mine did."

"No. No. He had it good here. As the Amerricans say."

"And you? Didn't you ever think of looking up your relatives in England?"

"No. No." He crooked his head at her. "Would you mind terribly if I smoked my pipe?"

"Not at all. That would remind me all the more of my father." She watched Hotham fill his pipe from a stained leather pouch. His gestures filled her eyes with tears. They were exactly like Father's. Same slow elegant way of packing in the tobacco. She watched him light up, sucking and sucking on the flame of the match until the top of the packed-in tobacco seethed a dull red.

"Do you smoke? I'm sorry I don't have cigarettes for my lady guests."

"Oh, Lord, no. Thanks."

He smiled thinly to himself. "I see by the papers that in certain circles ladies are beginning to smoke. Even in public in Amerrica."

"So I've noted."

"Equal rights and all such."

"Yes." Her eyes kept working the room as she talked. She spotted a bookcase. In it she recognized leatherbound volumes of Charles Dickens, William Makepeace Thackeray, and John Richard Green. "My father had some of those books too. But when our remittance ran out, and he failed in work, he had to sell them."

Hotham puffed on his heavy briar pipe. "Someday I may have to sell these myself."

"You mean . . . ?"

"Yes, the family may cut me off. You see, since the Great War the family fortune has dwindled. Investments overseas failed. Business in England went bankrupt. That sort of thing."

"Too bad."

"I never thought it would happen, as our family had extensive holdings."

"Then you've kept in touch?"

"Oh, yes. I always acknowledge each bank draft sent." He placed his pipe on the ashtray stand, and as he got to his feet indulged himself in a mild groan. He went to the bookcase, leaned down, and pulled out a fat book. "What did you say your father's name was? Shortridge?"

"Yes."

"If he was a second son, his family should be listed in here. *Burke's Peerage.*" His slender pale fingers flipped through the pages. "Ah, yes. Here it is." He carried the open book to Clara. "Care to have a look?"

"I surely would. I knew our family was in *Burke's,* but I never saw the book itself." Clara took the tome and looked at the opened page. Sure enough. Cecil Shortridge, second son born to Lester Shortridge, Yarmouth, House of Short-ridge. She lifted the book to sniff deep into its pages, as she'd seen Tunis do when he'd bought the set of Mark Twain. The smell of the aged page did smell definitely of another country.

Hotham smiled upon seeing Clara sniff into the book. He was seeing a true lover of books. He sat down in his chair again. "You say you're still married?"

"Yes." She next looked up the Hothams. She was surprised to see the long entry, almost six columns. She ran her finger down the columns, until she ran across the entry about the man sitting in front of her. "George P. Hotham, Le Mar, Iowa, USA. No issue." Le Mars was misspelled. She looked at the two words. "No issue," again. She smiled at Hotham. "Mr. Hotham, aren't you a little concerned that your branch of the family line is going to die out?"

"You mean?"

"Hadn't you given thought earlier about getting married? Like your father, marrying some German girl and carrying on the line in America?" Clara found herself caught up in a sweet glow of memory about the old days as Father and Mother has once described them. Stopping to see this true son of Britain, polite, with elegant gestures, had been a wonderful idea. Comforting. Making up a little for what Tunis the American had done to her.

"Oh, uhh, I've given it some thought. It's still not too late."

"I beg your pardon?" Clara stared at the fellow. He had to be well into his fifties.

"I'm still looking," he said with a lift of his high long nose. "I've noticed lately some very pretty Holland girls on the streets. The Hollanders have pretty much pushed out the British, you know. As you Americans say, if you can't beat them, join them."

Clara stared some more. That's what she got for asking that silly question. Slowly she stiffened. Why the dirty old goat. He was no better than Tunis.

He caught her look. He smiled. Then, as if a king, and it was time to dismiss a suppliant, he lifted a heavy gold watch out of a vest pocket and checked the time. Next he took a key hanging at the end of the gold chain and inserted it into the thick watch and slowly began winding it up. "Time for my sleeping draught, you know. I always take long naps in the afternoon."

46. *Thea*

1932

Thea knew her wonderful tough old father was never coming back. Just as she knew her husband, Oliver Tice, didn't have long to live.

Oliver slowly thinned away. He'd never had much to say and in his last days fell silent. He couldn't get up to do his duty in the bathroom, and Thea found herself carrying him to the seat. Each time she carefully set him upright. "He's as light as a pheasant," she thought. And he puffed like a pheasant, little pushes of air with his narrow scaly tongue. He couldn't eat much so he didn't have to do number two very often. His number one was always dribbling a little.

The worst was Oliver's terrible wracking cough. Little flags of lung tissue, like the coating on boiled milk left to cool, floated up into Oliver's mouth, sometimes so thick he accidently swallowed some of them before he could spit them out. And blood? It came up in coagulated lumps resembling chicken livers. Thea found herself soaking pillowcases and sheets in cold water to get rid of the bloodstains. Dr. Cottam shook his head at all the stuff coming out of Oliver's chest. Dr. Cottam warned Thea that some night, when his coughing was at its worst, the effects of the German gas would eat through the walls of an artery and then he'd spring a big leak. Die of hemorrhaging. 473

The blue in Oliver's eyes faded away to watery gray. His face shriveled up until he resembled a head shrunk by headhunters. He sipped water constantly to keep his lips moist.

Thea suffered it all because she loved him. She remembered the sweetness of their first lovemaking. She remembered the sacrifice he'd made for his country. She remembered his quaint pigeon-toed walk.

But then one day, after carrying him to the toilet seat, she found that once he was seated he could no longer pee without help. His penis had almost rotted away. She thought, for a fleeting moment, of deserting him. That rotted penis was too much.

Geoffrey happened to stop by on his way to see Ma again about Pa's disappearance.

"Why, Sis, you've been crying."

Thea was washing dishes in the kitchen. As she worked, she looked out of the window at the glowing lilacs along the edge of their garden. She swallowed and swallowed. She dried her hands on a towel. "You'd cry too if your husband came home from the wars with his pecker mostly rotted off."

"Thea! My God."

"It's true."

Geoffrey put an arm around her. "That's terrible. May I see him?"

"He stinks in there."

"I still want to see him."

Geoffrey wasn't able to take much of it either. After he'd said hello and tried to say lamely that he thought Oliver looked better, something that was so obviously a lie that even Oliver had to crack a smile, Geoffrey took Thea gently by the arm and led her back into the kitchen. Geoffrey asked, "What do the doctors say?"

"Dr. Cottam says there's no hope whatsoever. And Oliver's disability compensation isn't enough to pay for the trips to the Veterans Hospital in Sioux Falls."

"Maybe I should take him there now and then."

"No use." She fell on Geoffrey's shoulder. "Oh, my brother, why does it all have to end so horrid? Pa's disappeared. Probably jackrolled and killed in Sioux City. And my wonderful sweetie husband, he has to die a miserable death." She sobbed in jerks.

"Thea."

"I must've had my head in a cake to have married him just as he was going off to a terrible war. Much as I loved him."

"Oh, Thea. Remember the great curve he used to throw in baseball? How you used to brag about it even when you didn't know what a curve was?"

She pushed Geoffrey away. "I did too know. The ball started out like this and then went this way. Like the ball was being pulled down and away by a long rubber band."

"Bear up, Sis. Somehow you've got to see your way through this."

"But what am I going to do if he dies?"

"Find yourself work somewhere."

"Me? At my age? Into my forties?"

"Dear God, Sis, you haven't aged a hair."

"Maybe it seems not. But it's not because I didn't grieve enough."

"Won't you be getting widow's pension from the War Department?"

"What an awful thought. When Oliver and I had planned on having many babies." She started to cry again. "Too late for babies now. I quit having my periods last winter."

"I'm sorry, Thea."

"Once my flower invited bees. But now all I have left is dried-up hips for them. And I mean that two ways."

"I better go see Ma about Pa. Bye."

Three weeks later Oliver Tice died in Thea's arms as she was carrying him to the bathroom. He didn't die of a massive hemorrhage. In fact he hadn't coughed blood for several days. It was as if there were no more lung tissue left to raise. Oliver Tice just simply seemed to recede and sink away into the marrow of his shrunken bones. His intestinal tract relaxed and before she could reach the toilet seat he did number one and number two out of the end of his abbreviated nightshirt. She looked at the wizened creature in her arms and at the mess on the shiny white terrazzo floor. She had expected she'd cry when he finally went, but instead she found herself hardening everywhere under her skin. Even her heartbeat leveled off and her lips began to shape the grimace of thankful release.

At the graveside, with her whole family attending except Pa, along with two of Oliver's brothers, she accepted the folded American flag from the American

Legion. She almost threw it into the grave after Oliver. Much good it would ever do her. As for the honor of being the widow of war dead, she thought it hardly better than having to eat a bowl of ashes soaked in milk and honey.

Afterward, Geoffrey and Adela were the only ones to linger in her living room. Thea made another pot of tea and set it out to steep on the maple coffee table. Geoffrey sat looking down at his city hands. Adela had a guarded smile. When the tea was ready, Thea poured. Each took a spoon of sugar along with a squeeze from a halved lemon; no cream.

Adela was dressed in quiet gray. She had a way of appearing elegant in cheap clothes bought at a clearance sale. Her black critical eyes were for once kindly. She wore her long black hair brushed back from her forehead and combed impeccably smooth down to her shoulders. "Thea, why don't you come live with us in Whitebone? I'm sure you can find some kind of job there. Meet new people."

Thea said bitterly, "You mean, meet new men."

"Well, yes, that too. But I was thinking of just plain sociability." Adela ran a smoothing hand over her stomach. "And then too you can join the Episcopal church."

Thea nodded. Church in Whitebone would be nice. Inwardly she commented to herself that Adela had to be pregnant to be touching her stomach so often with that loving gesture. It made Thea jealous. Mad at life. What had she done to God to deserve a lonely childless fate?

Adela said, "You can stay with us until you find a job. Not, Geoffrey?"

"Of course," Geoffrey said.

"I dunno," Thea said. "I might not make such good company. You want to remember that I'm at the radical age now. Where I might do something silly one day and something old-fashioned the next."

Adela said, "I do know of one job that's open in Whitebone. I think."

Geoffrey looked up surprised. "A job in Whitebone? In the middle of this terrible depression we're having?"

"At the Palace Theater. Hilary Jessup's wife died last fall. He's been using high school kids to take tickets and sell popcorn, but it hasn't worked out very well."

Geoffrey shook his head. "My sister wouldn't want to do something like that."

"Well," Adela said, "I just thought it would be a nice way to meet people. Like I did in your front office. She could do that until she found something she really liked."

Geoffrey wasn't convinced.

Thea finally said, "I'll think about it. But first I better go through Oliver's things and give them to the Salvation Army." She sat a moment in slow breathing silence. A gray feeling began to spread in her belly. "This is the worst fix I've ever been in." Then the gloomy mopes bloomed in her head; and of a sudden they so seized her that she had to turn aside and weep. "Oh, that we could've had one child. At least. Even an imbecile."

"Shh," Adela whispered.

"So that I could at least sometimes look at a facial feature of Oliver's carried on."

"Now," Adela whispered.

Thea stood up. "Maybe you two better go. I'd like to be alone now."

It took Thea a week to clean out Oliver's things. She gave away his suits and overalls and shoes and overcoat. She kept their garden tools. She also kept his khaki uniform and pictures taken of him just before he left for boot camp. And she kept his baseball glove, along with a scuffed-up baseball. Maybe Tane's boy, Tyson, would someday turn out to be a pitcher. Though she had some doubt about that. The boy's fingers were stubby and thick like his father's, when Oliver's fingers had been long and slender.

She remembered something about Oliver's fingers. Supple and pliant. Once, as they were about to make love, as he was playing with her breasts, he laughed into her neck. "You know, sweet love, your little puppyheads are about the size of a National League baseball."

She pushed his hand away. "Well, you better not try throwing a curve with them."

"Not my big outdrop?"

"What do you mean by that? Outdrop. If you don't like 'em sagging a little, the heck with you."

"Oh, they ain't saggin' any. They're still a nice white harvest apple." He'd cupped her up again. "The only thing wrong with them is they don't have any seams. Can't throw much of a curve with a smooth billiard ball."

"Oh, so now you're going to play billiards with them."

"Sure. A little snooker. While you're busy watching me aiming my cue ball at your round puppyheads, I'll be sneaking the eight ball into the middle pocket."

"You crazy nut."

476 A month later, in July, she got into Oliver's old tin lizzie and drove up to White-bone. She parked near the Palace Theater and went directly to the side door that opened on the staircase going up to the apartment where Hilary Jessup lived.

Hilary Jessup, a tall lank of a man with a slight pot, with thin hard lips and life-narrowed eyes, took one look at Thea and hired her on the spot. Thea had beauty. She had stance. And she looked like someone who would take no non-sense from rowdy patrons.

47. Stoop Talk

1933

It was the Fourth of July, and again at Ma's request they all gathered at the old homestead. Tane and Arva were the hosts for the picnic supper. Thea came down with Geoffrey and Adela from Whitebone. Dirk drove down alone from the Cities. Tressa came with husband Wallie Starnes. Rolf drove over with his wife, Greta. Ana caught the train from Pine Ridge to Sioux Falls, and from there rode in with Mallie.

Arva and Tressa prepared most of the supper. Ma sat on the old long porch in her old rocker. Her two grandchildren, Tyson and Clairabell, played in the sandbox just south of the porch under the ash trees.

All the boys were careful not to sit where Pa used to sit on the concrete stoop. Tane was now the head man there, but he too made it a point to sit in his own old place.

There had been no news of what might have happened to Pa. He was still listed as a "missing person" at the sheriff's office. Pa's mysterious disappearance was a shadow and a doubt that hung over all their lives.

The family couldn't do anything either about dividing up the property until they knew what had happened to Pa. If he didn't show up after seven years they could then take steps to declare him legally dead. But who would be the first to want to do that? In the meantime, Tane paid the taxes on the estate.

Curiously it was stringy Ana who had the first stoop tale to tell. She spoke of the strange Indian ways of the Oglala Sioux at Pine Ridge. In particular she talked about the *yuwipi*, those eerie little spirits about a foot tall who'd show up in a darkened tepee to cure an ailing person.

"They look like long candles flying around. Except that the whole candle is flaming."

Dirk was skeptical. "You've seen them yourself then?"

"Yes. I went to see one of the Oglala healing rituals. I didn't want to believe it myself. But since the Oglalas like me, they decided to prove it to me that the *yuwipi* really are there."

"That's hard to take there, Ana girl."

"Well, I not only saw them, I felt them."

"Felt them?"

"Yes. I started to ask a question in the dark . . . you know how we Freylings are, you have to show us . . . but before I could finish my question, I got a box over the ears."

Dirk snorted. "One of those old bucks sitting behind you probably did that."
"You cynic."

Tane picked up a handful of gravel at his feet and slowly let it pour out of his fist like an hourglass. "How do you like working with those Indians, Ana?"

"I've come to love them. They're heathens, and the men still have the awful practice of skewering their flesh at those forbidden sundances back in the hills, but they're wonderfully loving with each other, especially with their children. And those who've turned to Christ are even more faithful churchgoers than the whites are around here."

"You haven't fallen in love with some brave, have you?"

"What? No!"

Rolf really hadn't been listening. He lifted his high nose and started to laugh, almost like a donkey. "Women may put on that they're so well behaved and all. Go to church regular and so on. But Bill Gibson was telling me the other day about something that happened when he was a kid living in Yellow Smoke. A high-toned Scottish lady, Old Mrs. McInerny, was riding along in a buggy down Main Street when she tells her young niece who's driving the horse to stop a minute. The old lady steps down out of the buggy and, right there on the main drag, lifts up her long dress and squats there and passes her water. Right there on the gravel! Later on the old Scottish lady rewarded her young driver with a tumbler of chokecherry jelly. The young lady driver took it and didn't say a word. Didn't even thank her. I guess the young girl didn't approve of that watering job on a dusty street. Well, Old Lady McInerny got real mad when the tumbler wasn't returned afterwards."

Ana shook her head at her brother. "You boys. I guess you'll never grow up." Ana glanced over at where Adela was sitting beside Geoffrey. "I hope you've learned to excuse the barnyard manners of my brothers."

478

Adela smiled graciously. "I'm enjoying it all. My family never did anything like this."

Rolf turned to his wife, Greta. "See, I told you top-shelf folk don't have as much fun as we do. Just plain old brother-and-sister funs is scarcer among them than brains is in a fly."

Greta sighed and looked down at her hands, then rolled her eyes at the dimming sky. "Maybe you're right, Rolf."

Dirk noticed something Thea was doing. "Are you knitting woolen mittens there? In the middle of the summer?"

"I am. Gifts for Christmas."

Dirk looked at her wickedly. "Well, just put it down that I don't want a pair."

"Why not?"

"Take a look at what you're doing. None of us boys has fingers six inches long."

Thea held up the mitten she was knitting. "For gosh sakes." But when she saw Dirk was right, she blushed in the falling light. "I guess I wasn't paying attention to my knitting, as they say."

Tane and Rolf held up their hands and wiggled their fingers a little as if to measure them.

Thea reddened even more.

Dirk smiled. "You know what they say about how long a guy is, don't you? No? You take the tip of your long finger, like so, and fold it down onto the muscle below your thumb, like so. Then you stick your finger out and measure from the spot you touched to the finger tip."

Tane and Rolf promptly folded the tips of their long fingers down and then made measurement with their eyes. Even Geoffrey did it.

Ma was scandalized. "You boys are no better than your father."

Arva turned her head away when she felt a smile coming on.

Ma sought to change the subject. "One thing I can thank God for. And that's mostly because when I breastfed you children I always held you close and warm in my arms, and loved you up, and played chubby-chubby-chin with you all. And your father loved you up too, and tossed you all up in the air, and caught you, and played with you like you might be puppies."

Tane said, "I remember Pa throwing us in the air, all right. Boy, was that fun. I was never scairt to climb a tree."

Ma said, "And none of you became a fussy eater either, not even little baby Geoffrey. And that's because both Pa and I encouraged our little babies to try new food, by smacking our lips when we'd taste it first, and by going, 'Umm-umm, is this good.'"

Ana said, "Now, Ma, you're starting to make me feel guilty that I don't have any kids."

Tane said, "Maybe Pa did take his own life, like they hint in town. But what would he do that for anyway?"

Dirk picked up some gravel at his feet and bounced the gravel in his cupped fingers. "We all know Pa had an awful temper. He tried not to let us see it, but you knew he had it. All you had to do was to take a look at those light blue mad eyes of his when a cow at milking time would kick up and then land with one foot in his bucket. Man, man."

Geoffrey offered, "Maybe he took it out on himself finally."

Tane nodded. "Pa had strange ways all right. Remember that time when Gordon Pullman came home with us from school once? And Pa visited with him a couple of minutes, and then asked Thea to find him an overall so he could help us milk? Then Pa took Gordon with us to the barn and pointed out the cow he could milk? The one we was going to dry up?"

Dirk laughed, remembering. "Yeh, Pa was never much impressed by fancy clothes or fancy titles. The Pullmans might be big shots around here, but that meant nothing to Pa. He was a king himself if it came to that."

Talk on the stoop loosened tongues more and more. There was gentle teasing, and gentle sarcasm, and gentle advice, and gentle digs. Yet through it all, each person's private life, each person's real self, was cunningly withheld. There was both much openness and much secrecy.

"Yeh," Tane said, "I remember one time though I got Pa one back. I was taking it easy, sitting on a barrel going through a pile of corn for seed ears, when all of a sudden Pa came in the corn crib. He looked at me and snorted, and said, 'A man on his feet is worth two on his seat.' Quick as a cat's tongue, I snapped back, 'Yeh, but not while he's milking a cow.'"

"Speaking of cows," Rolf said, "I guess I never told you about my old tom bull who had curly hair on his forehead. No? Well, when I tried to get rid of him at my neighbor's sale, nobody would bid for him."

"Why not?"

"Seems everybody around here thinks curly hair in that place means he'll be no good. Too much a chance his seed wouldn't be any good. He passes on that fault."

"Oh, come on now."

"S'fact. And it turns out they were right after a while. You know how I always used to tie a cow in heat in her stanchion to make it easier for the bull to put the blocks to her? Well, when I led him in to do his job—"

"My gosh, Rolf," Tane broke in, "we heard that story before."

"—he went over and smelled her all right, but when he took to jumping her bones, by gar if his tool didn't come out limp and he missed her and his wad shot past her hips and hit the stanchion next to her head with a big splat. His tool slid out of him like he was pouring cold syrup."

Greta shivered nervously. "That's the way Rolf is, Tane. You know that."

"What's wrong with what I said?" Rolf asked. "Don't we always say what we're really thinking here on the judgment seat of our family stoop?"

"But not so cob rough, Rolf," Dirk said.

"But it's only stoop talk," Rolf said.

Ana spat. "Stupid talk, you mean."

Rolf ignored Ana. He turned to Dirk. "Boy, you should talk, with all your scalawag tricks with those Minneapolis floozies."

Ana was finally so disgusted she got up and went into the house.

Thea thought to change the subject too. "Reverend Havens told of a funny thing that happened in church the other week." She was speaking of the Episcopal church in Whitebone. "He said he heard a sound like somebody was playing the organ in church next door to the parsonage. So he got up to investigate. The organ was playing all right, but there was nobody at the console. The keys were working by themselves like the keys of a player piano."

Dirk snickered. "Probably a short in the electrical controls. When the church cooled down the short started arcing."

"You would think of that," Thea scolded. "I'll have you know our organ needs someone to pump in the air to play it."

Dirk said, "Anyway, there's a couple of questions I'd like to ask your church."

"Like what?"

"Noah is supposed to have led two of a kind aboard his ark, and that's where all living creatures came from. What did he do in the case of the amoeba, which divides to propagate itself instead of by coupling?"

"In that case he probably only took one aboard."

"And what about when a person prays to God in heaven? Where's heaven, when every twenty-four hours the earth turns once? When you say, 'Up there in heaven,' depending on whether it's night or day, your nose can be pointing at any one point of three-hundred and sixty degrees, not?"

"I don't understand what you're getting at."

"Well, when a Chinaman prays to God his nose will be pointing in the opposite direction from yours when you pray to God on this side of the earth."

"I never thought of that. That is a puzzle."

Ana had quietly returned to the porch. "Really, Dirk, what kind of people do you have truck with there in the Cities that you get such outlandish ideas?"

"Mostly I get that from just listening to your ministers. That's why I don't believe in organized religion."

"Then I guess you're bound for hellfire."

"I respect the Quakers, though. They don't have ministers and so don't have to pay that salary. When the Friends hold church, they all shut up until one of them finally feels something so deep he has to get up and speak his mind and heart."

"But you're not even a Quaker."

"I know. I guess it's set pretty deep into me to doubt any church. Especially the pastors. There's a story I heard when I worked here on our local gossip sheet. One of the parishioners at the Congregational church had trouble getting his pastor to visit them out on their farm. Not even for supper. So one time after church let out, as his pastor was shaking everybody's hand, our parishioner says to him, 'You know, I've seen hard times, a lot of them, but I have yet to see my own beloved pastor cross the threshold of my home.' The pastor didn't like hearing that, what with everybody on the steps outside listening, so he said, 'My dear brother in Christ, you must remember that we shepherds are sent out to find the really lost sheep of the house of God.' The parishioner snapped back, 'Yes, and if I'd have been a fat lost sheep you'd long ago have found me.'"

"You and your godless stories. They don't prove anything. They only make fun of the things I hold dear."

Geoffrey didn't like the touchy direction the talk was taking. "Remember how we used to stop at Fraser's Drugstore and have a dish of ice cream? And sit on those rickety wire chairs at a round glass table? One time when Mallie here and I was there, we happened to see something pretty funny. Those two girls who work at the First National Bank came in for a dish of ice cream. Tina Holt and Liz Stalling. Tina was chewing gum a mile a minute. When her ice cream came, she snuck the gum out of her mouth and stuck it under the seat of her wire chair. When they finished their ice creams, talking away, Tina reached under her seat and took back her gum. She chewed a few times and then let out a shriek. It'd dawned on her that it was the wrong gum. The gum she took back was Sen-Sen flavored, while hers'd been spearmint flavored."

481

Mallie remembered and laughed. "But why must you boys always tell stories that are aimed at women? Don't any of you men ever do anything foolish?"

Rolf said, "Well, I know of one against the men. And Greta"—Rolf gave his wife a look—"I know you won't like this story, so close your ears. My neighbor Billie Alfredson told me this. 'Rolf,' he says, 'you won't believe this, but my hired man couldn't pass a kidney stone the other week. It got stuck halfway down his tool. And this is the part you won't believe. That nut took and lay his peter on an anvil and with a hammer crushed that kidney stone right inside his tool there and broke it up into little pieces, and so passed it on.'"

That was too much for Geoffrey. With a look at wife Adela, he jumped up and started to pace back and forth on the long concrete stoop. "God in heaven, Rolf!"

But the bent to shock the womenfolks was on. Tane had another one. "Lawyer Timmons in town got the feeling that someone was peeking into his office through a keyhole while he was at work. So he bought a syringe and filled it with water spiked with pepper. So later, when he heard a noise on the other side of his office door, he squirted some of that peppered water through the keyhole. That night when he came home, he heard his wife complain that she'd gotten a chip of wood in her eyes while chopping wood."

Mallie said, "You men peek too sometimes. I remember one summer, when it was so hot we girls slept naked, I saw Dirk sneak a look at us."

"Well," Tane said, "I never did. No, Arva, I never did."

"Me neither," Rolf said.

Geoffrey shrugged. "Well, I was too little then to know what it might mean to sneak a look in there."

When Dirk said nothing, Mallie said, "See? Silence means consent."

Ma was visibly disturbed. "Dirk? Dirk? I wouldn't want it known that that happened in my house."

Dirk picked up another handful of gravel and jounced it a little in his hand. "Aw, Ma, that was so long ago I don't really remember no more."

Tane said, "Don Hawke was telling me a funny one the other day. You know that filling station at the far west end of Main Street there? That Peter Weeks runs? Well, he run a wire from his station through the deep grass into the two-holer privy he has there. Then he hooked a loudspeaker to the wire and set it under the holes. When a lady went in there one day while her hubby was buying gas, Weeks had his helper Hack Brown say over the loudspeaker after he figured she'd just sat down, 'Lady, will you please use the other hole? We're painting under this one.'"

"You darn men," Thea said. "Now let me tell you a wonderful saving story about a noble woman. About that pioneer woman who was captured by the Indians and tied up and put on a pile of logs to be burnt. Right in the middle of the flames and smoke, she started singing hymns. 'Though your sins be as scarlet, they shall be as white as snow.' And, 'We'll meet each other there, and the Savior's likeness bear.' The Indians were stunned. 'She's singing the white man's death chant,' they said. They motioned for her to sing some more. So she sang and sang all the hymns she knew. She kept singing until her husband came with some neighbors and chased the Indians off and saved her."

482

"A likely story," Dirk muttered to himself.

Ana gnashed her teeth. "You men think you're so smart. And so much better than we women. What about Dale Dodge and his gang of ruffians? Who caught Mrs. Chauncey's pet dog and poured kerosene on its tail and set it on fire? And then sat back and laughed at the poor dog's misery as it went howling down Main Street?"

Dirk agreed that was pretty awful. "But they had a reason of a kind though, you know. Chauncey's bank foreclosed on Old Man Dodge."

"I don't care what the reason was. It was cruel and inhumane. And then to sit back and laugh at it yet."

Mallie said, "Oh, for the good old days when we didn't have to think about such awful things, because we didn't know about them. And all we had was our little sins. Remember how none of us liked those hard black crusts when the bread was baked too long? How we'd eat out the white part and then when nobody was looking we'd sneak those black crusts under the table on that support under there? Right where Ma would place the Bible after she'd read a portion after a meal?" Mallie laughed, and the rest joined her. "Ma would never have found out about it, but one time Rolf and Tane got to wrestling on the kitchen floor, and bumped into one of the table legs, and lo and behold, there went the black crusts all over the floor. And Ma got down on her knees and crawled under the table to have a look for herself?"

Ma laughed too. "That reminds me. I brought some Holland rusks along with me from town. Who'd like a rusk with butter and sugar on it, served with some green tea?"

Every hand went up. It was one of Ma's old-time favorite treats on a Sunday after church.

While Ma and Arva prepared the treat, Geoffrey had a story. "I got an interesting case coming up. It seems Mrs. Cooper took her time crossing the street just as our Bonnie Omaha train pulled into Whitebone. She's always doing the same thing with cars on the theory that the pedestrian has the right of way at all times. She thinks we should get rid of all cars, even the old horse and buggy, and everybody should walk instead. What she didn't understand is that a train can hardly be braked as quick as a car. Engineer James Suddaby recognized who it was too late. He slammed on the brakes, but the cowcatcher caught Mrs. Cooper anyway and flipped her over a fence into Brenda Stickney's asparagus bed. Man alive! Mrs. Cooper came around that fence just steaming mad. And did she give Suddaby a piece of her mind! She used language so strong that Suddaby decided to countersue her for rough language when she brought in a complaint for damages."

Adela had something to offer. "The way you dictated that case to me, husband, didn't she say that James Suddaby was a mean-hearted Beelzebub riding a vicious Behemoth?"

"Ha. That she did."

Ana had another instance of how great women could sometimes be. "Didn't Rena Engleking show real spunk that time she jumped into the river to save her drowning child when she got caught by a cloudburst coming down the valley? Right in the middle of all those whirlpools and tumbling trees?"

Dirk nodded. "Yeh, I remember that story." He laughed. "But I remember too that when she got back on the bank of the river and looked downstream, she fainted dead away when she saw her false curls floating off."

"Oh! Why did you have to spoil my story? Couldn't you have left well enough alone?"

Ma and Arva brought out the treat, giving each a plate with a rusk and a cup of tea.

Rolf sniffed at his rusk. "I suppose you smeared this with bull butter, huh? Instead some genuwine farm-produced butter?"

"Bull butter?"

"You know. Oleomargarine."

Ma snapped, "I suppose next you're gonna complain about the sugar? Eat what the pot gives up."

Dirk had to make one more gibe at religion. "Once when I went to your Little Church here in Bonnie, Ana, I had to laugh at the way your preacher roared about all the homebrew beer certain members of the congregation were making for themselves. How it was against the law because of the high alcoholic content. How wine was all right to use at the Lord's Supper, but not beer in one's home when it was as strong as rotgut whiskey . . . oh, he was frothing at the mouth to a fare-thee-well . . . when an elder sitting there right under the preacher's nose burped. Real loud."

"You can't condemn the church because of one rotten apple. The exception proves the rule."

"Not with me it don't."

The whistle of a train sounded north up the valley.

Everybody turned to look. Watching the Bonnie Omaha go by was always a

483

pleasure. They'd seen it come and go most of their lives, yet it was still something to enjoy, to speculate about what kind of people might be riding in the single passenger car, what kind of produce it might be hauling in its freight cars.

First to appear was the bubbling plume of smoke showing over the tops of the trees along the Big Rock River, then the tall black smokestack, and then the bold round nose of the engine with the moustachelike cowcatcher beneath it.

"Say," Geoffrey said, "is the rumor true that the Omaha people are thinking of retiring our Bonnie train? Something about company retrenchment."

Wallie Starnes had been silent most of the evening. He knew he wasn't liked too well by the family. But finally he couldn't resist putting in his two bits' worth. "See, Tressa? I told you something like that was going to happen, the way they've let things run down. Ties rotting all up and down the line. Boxcars needing paint."

Tane said, "Wallie's right. Just look now at the way that engine comes wobbling down the line. Swaying back and forth like a woman with a bustle on a dance floor."

Dirk said, "Wouldn't it be something if the old Bonnie Omaha jumped the track?"

"Remember that penny we put on the tracks once to see how much it'd flatten out when the train ran over it?"

The Bonnie Omaha whistled again as it approached the crossing near the old country schoolhouse. The short white plume of its whistling joined the rolling voluminous stream of black smoke coming out of its tall stack.

Tane looked at his pocket watch. "An hour late."

484

Wallie Starnes's nose pushed forward. "It's trying to make up for lost time on those rotting ties."

Geoffrey said, "I remember one time when I was getting up the cows, when Pa put them out to pasture in the alfalfa there, I happened to see a poor snail on one of the iron tracks. While I was looking at it, wondering what kind of thoughts it might have, how it probably figured the six-inch-high rail was the Himalayan mountains, how the puddle of pee I'd just peed was the Atlantic Ocean—when I heard the Bonnie Omaha out there by our schoolhouse. Well, I wondered a little too long whether I should help the snail and put it down in a safe place. The next thing I knew the train had whooshed by. When I looked afterwards where the snail had been, I couldn't even find a wet spot. Gone. Totally gone."

Wallie Starnes waggled his wise nose. "You know what people in Rock Falls say about our train, don't you? They call it 'a streak of rust.'"

"Yeh," Dirk said, "or 'a string of rusty tin cans.'"

Tane said, "That's because those Rock Fallers are jealous of Bonnie."

Then, even as they watched, the nose of the engine swung very wide in one of its swayings—and all of a sudden the engine jumped the track, leaning so far over it looked like it might tip on its side. The deep sway passed on to the coal car, and then on to the single freight car, and then on to the passenger car.

Everybody leaped to their feet. "Holy smokes!"

The little children, Tyson and Clairabel, who'd been playing train and town in the sandbox, came running up. Tyson's eyes became as big as a pair of shooter marbles.

Tane was torn between laughter and rage. "Look at that thing running around in my alfalfa field there."

Dirk started to slap his thighs. "Old Suddaby's decided to take a little side tour on the prairies."

The cowcatcher continued to kick up clouds of earth and vegetation.

Rolf houghed up a guffaw. "Like an old boar, with its snout rooting around in the dirt. Man, is he making the dirt fly."

Then, nose deep into the earth, the engine's rear end raised, lifting the coal car with it; and stopped; and then slowly settled back to earth.

All four Freyling men reached around for their hats and caps and set sail for the scene of the disaster. Wallie Starnes knew he wasn't welcome and stayed with the womenfolk. The four men hurried across the highway, then ran up the railroad track. They stumbled sometimes as their shoes broke into the rotted ties.

Arriving on the scene, they found the mastodon steam engine puffing and hissing. Its cowcatcher was covered with dirt and alfalfa roots. Engineer James Suddaby and fireman Lou Thompson and conductor Earl Van Valkenburg stood with soured mouths some thirty feet away. All three had pushed back their caps and were scratching their hair. Some of the coal in the coal car had piled over into the engine's cab. A terrified woman in the passenger car stood with her face pressed against a window pane.

The three railroad men stared at the four Freyling sons and the Freylings stared back at the train men.

Tane finally said, "What the hell . . . are you guys trying to make a new shortcut to Bonnie?"

"Well," Suddaby said, "something like that."

Tane said, "Suddaby, this is gonna cost you. Tearing up my alfalfa field. I'm gonna lose at least a ton of hay here. Maybe even two, 'cause it's gonna take all summer for the alfalfa to grow back. And some of it I'm gonna have to reseed. And that'll take even longer."

485

Rolf put in, "What about the fence they tore down?"

"Yeh," Tane said, "what about that? I can't put any cattle in here at the end of summer, or they'll run from here to Sioux City."

Conductor Van Valkenburg in his blue uniform slowly collected his wits. He was a handsome man. He pulled his blue conductor's cap down over his forehead. "Don't worry about the fence. The railroad bosses will send down some men to fix that. Along with the wreck crew and their crane."

Tane looked at all the thrown dirt from the deep gouge the cowcatcher had made. "By gar, a dying calf in its last struggle could not have tore up the ground more."

Fireman Thompson couldn't help but laugh a little. "C'mon, Tane, it ain't all that bad."

A shrewd look came over Tane's face. "That reminds me. Is it true they're gonna shut down the Bonnie Omaha? If they are, you can forget fixing the fence. Because I'll buy the right-of-way."

Conductor Van Valkenburg's face turned bland. "I wouldn't know about that. We're not told about such things."

"Aha," Geoffrey murmured to himself. In an aside to Tane, he said, "That means he does know that's just what they're gonna do."

"I see," Tane said in a low voice.

Cars on the nearby King's Trail highway began to stop. People all agog emerged for a better look. Some of the men began to laugh uproariously.

Conductor Van Valkenburg said, "Tane, can we use the phone up at your house? We better report this in pronto."

"Sure, help yourself." Tane studied the huge breathing iron engine. "That thing won't take off again, will it?"

Engineer Suddaby shook his head. "No. Just take a look at those drivers. They're broke."

"By golly, yeh." Tane scratched his head. "How long will it take to clean up this mess?"

"Two days. One day for the wreck crew to get down here, and one day to repair the track and to lift it all back on. They do it real fast because the mail and the freight has got to get through."

Tane's eyes screwed up into gimlets. "I suppose you'll be laying fresh ties?"

"That's up to the crew and the bosses."

Tane nodded. "Well, there's nothing more we can do here. C'mon, lets get you to the telephone."

When they trooped into the porch, Arva stopped the men. She was looking at their shoes. "Watch your feet. I don't want all that fresh dirt in my house. You too, Mr. Van Valkenburg."

After conductor Van Valkenburg had made his call and had left, the family settled back on the stoop and porch. The sun had just set and it cast a radiant crimson ambience over the flat prairie and on the hills across the highway and railway. In the distance smoke continued to lift from the stack of the steam engine, black turning to purple to blue to pink.

Ana began wondering out loud. "I wonder what you're gonna do about going to church in Whitebone, Ma, if they're really gonna shut down the Bonnie Omaha."

Ma's lips worked. "Maybe I should join your church, Ana. Think the Little Churchers will welcome me?"

"Oh, I think so."

Dirk shook his head. "With the cloud of Pa's disappearance hanging over our heads, I wonder."

Ma decided she'd had enough of that. She smiled down at where Tane was sitting. "Son, I forgot to thank you for bringing me that load of chicken manure for my garden. Like it's been said before about the virtues of chicken manure, the flowers grew so fast the petals shot right off them."

48. *Tane*

1935

Tane finally bought himself a one-row corn picker. It took five horses to pull the heavy machine and the horses had to be changed every few hours. He bought it because it took too long for him and hired hand Saul Pollen to pick all the corn by hand. In fact the previous year they didn't get all the corn picked before the first big snowfall. The final forty acres had to be picked the next March before they could begin the regular spring work in the fields.

But Tane missed the old way of picking by hand. Tane had fat short fingers, perfect for snapping an ear out of its husk. There weren't many around who could match his huge loads at the end of the day. Sometimes in one day he picked three loads of fifty bushels each, each load taking three hours. The best Saul could do was to come in with two loads of thirty-six bushels each.

In the evenings, as they milked the cows, Saul often urged Tane to go out for the county corn-picking championship. Maybe even the state championship. "I'd bet on you if you did."

"Nah. What would it prove?" Tane paused to tip a tit sideways and squirt milk at their white-and-chocolate cat. He hit the cat on the nose, and the cat, blinking, trying to wipe its eyes clear with one paw and then the other, and licking both paws in the process, at last lifted its pink mouth open just right to take in the full stream.

"Well, it would take people's mind off what might have happened to your dad."

It was true. Tane had gotten pretty sick of having to answer the question, "Hear from your father yet?" He heard it uptown, heard it across the fence talking with a neighbor, heard it from Arva, who in turn was sick of hearing it from her friends.

Once even Sheriff Rexwinkel had dropped down from Rock Falls to ask a few questions. Holding up his booze belly, the sheriff waddled over to where Tane was fixing a hitch on a wagon. Brown eyes looking in all directions at once, Sheriff Rexwinkel asked, "How do you like running your dad's farm?" Of course Tane told him it was good doings, something that had been in the family plans all along. The sheriff next asked if his dad liked living in town. Tane said, "That's something you're going to have to ask him yourself." With a deep humph that raised his belly an inch, the sheriff trundled back to his car.

Tane remembered the old days when he was just a shaver and corn was first cut and set up in shocks, and then he and Pa and Ma would take a wagon and gather up the corn from each shock, using a pick instead of a hook. Those were the days when Pa had been so very jolly, exaggerating the fun they were having, telling Ma, when they came home with a full load of corn, that while she was making supper he'd go out and kill a horse to feed the hogs, hit the horse in the head and cut open the belly so the hogs could feed the easier. "That'd be a good way to get rid of that misfit Kang. I knew at the time we bred Old Pet with that coarse stud we'd get a bad colt. Clumsy, blockheaded, wrongheaded, with a bung so wide his tail didn't begin to cover it." Tane remembered how, when one of their horses got the sleeping sickness, Pa had taken a board and placed it against the forehead of the prostrate horse and hit it several times with a heavy hammer; and, miracle of miracles, the horse had recovered.

Early in July driving drying winds came out of the south. They parched the hay fields so badly Tane had trouble cutting it. At supper Tane told Arva, "I swear, that alfalfa was so short we had to lather it with horse slobber to mow it."

The only moisture they got was when hail as big as white onions crackled on the roof in late July.

Two weeks later another cloud passed overhead. After it had vanished into the northeast skies, Tane shook his head. "She tried to rain around four o'clock. But that earth was so hot, and so dry, like a stove, the raindrops turned to steam before they hit the ground, and then that wind from the south carried it away."

Just when he thought of putting down a well to make sure the stock had enough drinking water, it began to rain again. The rain came too late to help the oats and the corn but it did turn the pasture green.

Like his neighbors, Tane took his wife and children to town after the rain. The rain-touched countryside smelled like candy. Tyson and Clairabel were all excited. They were each going to have an ice cream cone at last. Arva smiled at her grocery list, a long one, and got a promise from Tane that when he finished his business with the blacksmith he would help her carry out everything to their car.

Main Street, freshly paved with concrete, smelled like a bakery floor that had just been scrubbed with soap. Everyone had a wisecrack with an upbeat snap in it. Tane was thankful that no one, not one, mentioned his father. They didn't even look as if they might be thinking of it. Rain had a way of wiping the slate clean for a few days.

Tane had put on his new overalls, new oxfords, a white shirt, and a jacket from his gray town suit. He went walking down the street with his thumbs hooked in his suspenders.

John Semple, who ran a flourishing harness shop, couldn't help but smile a little as Tane walked by. "You know, Tane," he called after him, "you're like the gophers. When it rains you show up in town like you just got drowned out of your hole."

Tane stopped to stare at Semple. Semple was one of those old men who fancied bright colors. "You know, John, you remind me of the days when if a man brought horses to a sale, he always put his best horse blanket on his oldest horse."

Down at the Farmers Elevator beside the Bonnie Omaha tracks he ran into Don Hawke. Hawke he liked. Hawke always gave the accurate weight on any load of grain or corn brought in. His scale was even more accurate than the town scale at the end of Main Street. Hawke was a well set-up man with a thoughtful mien. "Tell me, Tane, how are the crops out your way?"

"I'll be lucky to get back chicken feed."

Hawke nodded. "Bad year for all of us. Except for a couple of townships north of Wodan. They had two good showers of rain at the right time. Oats went thirty bushels to the acre. And it looks like their corn will do even better."

"Lucky them."

"Yes, and Rex Moad over there will have the added benefit of having the annual Leonhard County corn-picking contest held in one of his fields."

"Someday I ought to have that contest held on that bottom land of mine north of my barn. That's some of the best land in the whole county. No gravel under it. Just solid black dirt five feet down. I know from the holes I sometimes have to auger for a corner post. And the deadman to anchor it."

Hawke looked at Tane's hands. "You've never gone out for that contest, have you?"

"I've thought about it."

"Why don't you try it? And help put Bonnie on the map? I know last year's champion, Ben Haber, is worried you might come out for it. I guess he's seen you pick."

"Yeh. He and I picked out at Lou Lonergan's one fall when Lou broke his leg. We'd come in with about the same size loads every day." Tane allowed himself an indulgent smile. Ben Haber didn't really have a smooth motion in the way he went at it. There was a jerk in his motion as he snapped the ear out of its husk. Tane himself had learned from Pa to do it all in one motion: grab the ear with the mittened left hand, come across the side of the ear with the hook on his right thumb, have the mittened left hand gather up what leaves were left, then, right after the hook had raked across the ear, have the right-hand fingers under the hook catch the bare ear, deftly snap the ear free of its stem, and all in one motion, without looking, toss the ear in the air toward the bangboard on the wagon. "'Course, Don, I took it easy around Haber. There was no rush. We was getting eight cents a bushel and making money hands over fist."

Hawke had to laugh. "I guess picking corn you do make money hands over fist."

Tane made the gesture of a man snapping an ear out of a husk and tossing it up against a bangboard. "You know, I just might try it this fall. Nothing much else to do. 'Cepting chase the wife into the bedroom. Where she don't wanna go in the daytime." Tane shook his head to himself. "Funny about women. Once they're married, they don't wanna play around in the daytime. It's all got to be done at night. With the lights out. Like they're sort of sneaking it past the eyes of the Lord."

Hawke eyed Tane with a quizzical smiling look. "I know what you mean."

"I guess I'll never understand women. The moment breakfast is over they shoo you out of the house. Ain't you got something to do in the toolshed? Or in the barn? Ain't you got some field work to do? And it's always said sarcastic. They just don't want you underfoot. I really own the house, you know, but I don't in the daytime. Even Ma and my sisters was that way when we was all still living t' home."

Hawke nodded. "True of me here in town too."

"Those women are as bad as Indian squaws, who owned the tepee and the food supply."

Another farmer came into the office of the elevator and Hawke had to leave off talking to Tane.

Tane helped Arva with the groceries. He watched Tyson and Clairabel licking their ice cream cones.

489

Arva saw Tane's eyes. "I probably shoulda bought you a cone too."

"Naw. I was just remembering how I used to turn the folks' ice cream freezer and afters got to lick the dasher."

Fall came and still no word as to what might have happened to Pa. Pa had just simply disappeared. Tane and Arva, about to go to sleep at night, enjoying their nightly talk in the dark, speculated Pa might have bought another train ticket in Sioux City, after his night at Madam Redwell, and gone on to Arizona. Or perhaps even to sunny California. Or Mexico, even, where Ambrose Bierce had vanished. That Bierce idea was Dirk's. Dirk was pretty well posted from all the reading he did as a newsman. Arva said sleepily that she was sure Pa was still alive somewhere. "He enjoyed the grandchildren too much to want to hurt himself." Tane agreed out loud, but inwardly wasn't so sure. He'd heard Pa make some pretty dark remarks.

Early in September Tane decided to enter his name in the county cornhusking contest.

He began to practice on his nubbin corn. He felt that if he could rip out the three-inch-long nubbin corn with ease, it would be a snap to break out the big ears in Rex Moad's fat fields. Also, picking the nubbins when they were still green strengthened his wrists. From the small loads he only managed, though, it was hard to make out if he was picking fast enough.

Picking the last couple dozen nubbin ears, Tane began to notice a soreness in his left wrist. At first he was afraid he'd sprained it. When he finished the load, he took off his husking mitten and discovered a boil had started up on the outer point of his wrist.

"Dammit, if that ain't cleared up by contest day, it ain't gonna be good."

When he showed the boil to Arva after supper, she said, "I bet you didn't dope up your hands and wrists with arnica before you started out on those tough nubbins."

"No, I didn't. I forgot. I got a corn-picking machine now, you know."

She shook her head and quietly went to the cabinet and got a can filled with flaxseed.

Tane was surprised. "Where did you get that?"

"At your friend Hawke's elevator. To set my hair, I boil a little of it until it turns pasty and then I put it in my hair. Later on, a person combs out the paste and there's your hair, nice natural waves." She poured a handful into a small pan of water and set it on the stove. "This will make the perfect poultice."

"Better than an unsalted piece of bacon? Pa always said that raw fat had a natural way of sticking to the core of the boil, and then when you pulled the strip of bacon fat away the core came with it."

"My people would liefer use a flaxseed poultice."

After the flax had boiled awhile and turned to a sticky mess, she got an empty salt sack and poured the mess into it. Then she laid it over the inflamed risen boil.

"There ain't no white head showing yet," Tane said, looking down at his thickened wrist.

"This poultice will bring it to a head real quick."

The day of the contest, October 24, opened bright and clear and cool. There'd been a light frost during the night, as well as a deep freeze a week earlier, and Tane knew that an ear would break off its stem like a candle out of its holder.

With the children in school, and hired hand Saul Pollen to watch the yard, Arva decided to go along. She scolded Tane when he put on his husking clothes: a pair of stained overalls, the front of the pantlegs painted with red barn paint; a special painted sleeve for the left arm, which led the way through the harsh corn leaves as he grabbed for ears; and an old sweat-ringed cap. "What?" Arva cried. "You're going in those bum clothes? What will people think with that paint all over you?"

"Corn leaf edges cut like broken glass."

"But it looks so hicky."

"Well, I am a hick. And proud of it."

"C'mon, Tane. Please." She picked a hair from his shoulder and dropped it in the bedroom wastepaper basket. "And another thing, husband dear. You got the funny nervous habit of being too ready to pitch into things. Especially in front of people."

"I'm not taking these clothes off. And hey, ain't you gonna take me as I am after all these years?"

"Sure I am. But you make a funny motion with your head as though you want everybody to know that what you're gonna do next is gonna be easy to do. In front of people. You don't do it when you're home with me and the kids."

Tane's chin thrust up. "I can guttle down if I wanna in front of people. That's easy to learn off."

"Anyway, let me look at that wrist of yours. See if it needs a new dressing."

"It'll be all right."

"Does it hurt?"

"Not when I milked this morning."

"Then maybe it's gone down. Here, let me look at it."

491

Tane hated to have anyone fuss over him. He liked to think there never was anything wrong with him. But when Arva took hold of his arm firmly, he gave in. He watched her untie the knot she'd made in the linen bandage. "Not so fast now," he warned. "If you go slow enough the core might just come up with the poultice."

Arva unwound the bandage slowly. When she lifted the poultice, there was nothing on it but a few blood stains and streaks of yellow-purplish matter. The boil looked like a miniature volcano with a white lava dome in the center.

"Darn," Tane said.

"Wait," Arva said. She took the wrist in her hands.

"Don't pinch it out, for godsakes."

"Just watch." She drew down on the skin on both sides of the wrist, slowly, firmly. The hole widened, and bled a little; and then the white core emerged like a dead grubworm.

"Aha!" Tane cried. "We got it. And now I can really pick corn, by golly."

"Yes. But we're going to have to bandage it good, though. But first some per-oxide." She got a small dark bottle, uncorked it, and poured some clear fluid over the hollow little volcano. In an instant, the fluid, and the blood and matter, fizzed up in a large foam of bubbles.

"Boy!" Tane exclaimed. "Look at that stuff work. It bites real good too."

"The biting helps purify it."

When they arrived on Rex Moad's yard, quite a crowd of onlookers had already shown up, mostly farmers dressed in new overalls and their wives in bonnets and fall coats. Among them were a few city dudes, a banker, a storekeeper, a produce man.

Moad kept a neat yard. The grass was mowed around the house and the summer kitchen and the milk shed. No weeds around the corn crib and chicken house and machine shed. Strangely all the buildings were painted a light green with white window trim. Nor were there any manure piles in the barnyard or the hog yard. One look at Mr. and Mrs. Rex Moad and one knew why they were first class. They were just a little better dressed than the average farmer: new yard boots, no patches on their clothes, new cotton gloves. They carried themselves well: not like big shots but like people who paid their bills on time despite the terrible drought around.

The prairie north of the Moad grove spread out as level as a black stovetop all the way to Wodan. But to the west, within a mile, the land fell away rumpled and gradually formed into hugh bluffs and hills, sloping down to the Big Sioux River. Looking carefully one could see the top of the National Ski Jump structure across from Canton. Rex Moad and his family had the best of two Siouxland worlds: perfect flat land with no runoff and rolling hills to look at out of their bay window.

Tane said, "One thing I want to make sure about is get me a good running tractor to pull my wagon and a good driver. I don't want to be halfway across and have something go wrong."

The driver assigned to him was, of all people, thoughtful Don Hawke, who'd volunteered his time when it was discovered there weren't enough drivers around. The tractor was a good one, a new Fordson.

Tane spotted Ben Haber talking to his driver. Ben had a receding forehead and a weak chin. His face had a raw look, mouth open, nostrils wide, as though he might have asthma. His lower lip was usually wet with a drop of spittle.

"Hey, Ben, I see they gave you an old broken-down putt-putt. Where did they find that, in the town dump?"

"Yeh, and the worst is, my driver ain't never driv it before."

"Got your excuse ready in case you lose, ha?" Tane remembered it'd been one of Ben's tricks to make a rival think he'd have an easy time beating him. A person had to nail Ben to the cross, then he'd play fair. "Well, I got my excuse ready too."

"Ho. What's that?"

Tane lifted his left arm and drew back his painted sleeve. "Got a boil. The core only came out just this morning."

"That might bleed like a stuck hog you bump it too often."

"We'll see."

Soon the county officials of the championship cornhusking association showed up. Ten men from the county had registered for the contest, and each man was assigned four rows of corn a quarter of a mile long. Twelve rows between the sets of four had been picked earlier and leveled with disks and harrows to make for easy walking for the spectators.

The contest master announced the rules. Once the starting gun was fired they had eighty minutes in which to pick their load. Since each man had his own four rows he could pick leaners. When the gun was fired again, each man had to stop on the instant. He could finish the ear he had his hands on, but no more. The loads would then be weighed. Meantime, two men carrying sacks would follow each picker and collect the ears he'd missed. A husker didn't have to pick a small ear less than three inches long. Any ear longer than that and not picked would be deducted from the total weight of his load. Two other men would also go through the whole load afterward to remove the husks, and the weight of that too would be deducted.

"May the best man win!"

Exactly at one o'clock, in the sharp glancing skittering sunlight, the gun was fired—and before even the echo came back from the barns behind the pickers, ears were already cracking against the bangboards.

Tane found himself picking the third set of four rows from the yard side. Next to him in set four was Ben Haber. Ben's first ear hit the bangboard ahead of Tane's.

Tane counseled himself to pick steady in the beginning, with an easy flow of hands. He didn't want anyone to get too far ahead of him; yet knew he should keep a reserve for the last twenty minutes or so. Start too fast, and a man's fingers might begin to cramp up.

Everything was going just right. The corn ears broke out easy. They weren't too fat—fat ears would have given long-fingered Haber an edge—nor too small to discourage a man into thinking it would take forever to build up a load. Moad's brand of corn had a minimum of husks, which made for clean picking. Tane remembered how Pa used to get after his boys when they came in with what he called dirty loads, loads in which the yellow ears were almost hidden under a fluff of white husks. Once Pa made absent-minded Dirk pick over some ten bushels of his load to make the point about clean picking habits.

At the same time, Tane also counseled himself not to bother stopping if it looked like an ear was not going to emerge from its cocoon with a stray husk left on. To stop and strip it of that last husk would cost him several other ears.

The fleeting memory of Pa's orders about picking clean suddenly made him lonesome for Pa. How wonderful it would have been to have Pa walking behind him, with Ma, watching him pick his way to glory. Several tears started in the corners of his eyes.

Eyes always an ear ahead of his flashing yellow-mittened hands, Tane swooped along his two rows. The extra thumb on his husker mittens flapped loose like empty weiner casings. His eyes were continually measuring the different distances between the oncoming ears, some high on the stalk, some low, some on a leaning stalk, some fallen to the ground. Tane decided early on not to bother with a fallen ear if it looked like it might be a nubbin. Or a smutty ear. Sometimes cocoons of husks were filled with huge white bulb of smut. When a husking hook tore through one of those white bulbs, out would burst irritating black smoke-dust that flew up around one's eyes.

Occasionally he heard Arva talking low a dozen steps behind him as she walked with the two gleaners picking up after him. She mentioned that Tane had a boil on his wrist, which might start bleeding, and then Tane would have to quit. The two gleaners said nothing.

Often there were cheers around the other nine wagons. The loudest came from Ben Haber's four rows.

Tane smiled to himself. His wrists felt strong. Thank God he'd toughened them by picking his nubbin corn. His head sparked inside like a living room with a sunlit bay window, thoughts riding and falling like glinting moats.

As he snapped at an ear leaning away from the farther row, he threw a quick look Haber's way. If both sets of four rows of corn had the same number of ears, and if

493

Haber was picking as clean as he was, Haber was about a minute ahead of him.

Tane continued to smile. He knew he had it in him to finish with a real burst of speed. It was all falling into place.

There was always an ear hitting the bangboard, another ear already rising toward the bangboard, and an ear popping out of its cocoon.

Some sixty minutes into the contest, Tane and Haber came to the end of their first two rows at the same time. They were the first to make the turn back to the yard.

For the next ten minutes the sound in their area resembled two fellows working a pair of kettledrums in perfect time. Bang bang. Bang bang.

Arva came up close. "Can't you go a little faster?"

"Get"—bang—"back"—bang. "You'll throw me off." Bang. "Get!" Bang. "Sorry."

Don Hawke spoke over the purr of the Fordson tractor. "Wrist holding out okay?"

"Don't worry." Bang. Bang.

Don Hawke next spoke to Arva. "Actually, I think our man is already ahead of Haber. He's picking cleaner. I see a lot of white over there on Haber's wagon."

Bang. Bang. Bang.

Tane called, "How many minutes yet to go?"

"Five."

Tane nodded. And then he put the sock to it. He felt good. The few glimpses he had of his left wrist told him the boil hadn't bled enough to show through the cotton mitten. He couldn't even feel where it was exactly. He closed his ears to all sounds except for the crackling of fallen stalks underfoot and the purring of the Fordson and the bang-bang-bang-bang. He saw his hands whirling like the blades of an eggbeater.

Crack!

That was the gun to stop all picking. Tane's last ear sailed toward the bangboard. Tane had picked up another ear from the ground, but decided not to husk it. "One more ear ain't gonna make all that much difference."

Tane looked around. He saw Arva smiling at him. He saw dimples in Don Hawke's cheeks.

While the gleaners went through his load on the yard, after its gross weight had been determined, and the other gleaners following after him were busy weighing their findings, Tane and Hawke and Haber and all the other pickers went over to a picnic table that had been set up near the corn crib and had themselves warm doughnuts and hot coffee. There was a lot of talk about what a great day it had been for the event, sun, no wind, not too cold, just right. About how lucky Moad and his neighbors had been to get those two summer showers at just the right time. Otherwise, hard-luck stories of bad crops, no rain, gaunt cattle and horses, abounded.

Tane heard hardly any of it. He kept an eye on the weighers and the judges.

He also took off his mittens and had a good look at his left wrist. He was surprised to see that the little hole of the volcano had almost closed over. No blood and no matter showed up in the bandage.

At last tubby Sheriff Rexwinkel got on a barrel and called through a loud-speaker horn. "Here are the results." It was obvious Rexwinkel had some misgivings about the name he was about to announce. "The winner is . . . Tane

494

Freyling." Rexwinkel stated Tane's total: 1,320 pounds of corn, after deductions a net of 1,248.42 pounds, or 17.83 bushels. "Second place goes to last year's winner, Ben Haber." Haber had a total of 1,304 pounds, net 1,214.42, or 16.02 bushels. "Congratulations."

Arva ran up and gave Tane a big hug, so hard his cap fell off. "I told you!"

Don Hawke came over too. "It was that last spurt that did it, Tane."

"I suppose."

"You were about ten feet ahead of him at the end there."

Tane shifted back and forth from one foot to the other. "Well, I owe it all to my dad. He taught me everything."

Don Hawke noted the momentary look of pain in Tane's eyes. "Yes."

Arva looked at her wristwatch. "Maybe we better head home, Father. The kids will be there ahead of us."

Tane nodded. "Let's go then."

Every now and then, as their green Ford rose and fell over the shallow sloping valleys between Wodan and Bonnie, Tane would slap the steering wheel and exclaim, "By golly, I did it! I did it. I really didn't know I was that fast."

Arva smiled. "Let's not get the big head now. Be a bad example for Tyson."

Tane sobered over. "Yeh, I better watch that. That kid thinks pretty well of himself already. And that's because he's so naturally smart. I'm afraid when he grows up he ain't gonna want to stay on the old homestead and carry on the line."

"Let's wait until he's through college."

"By gum, wife, if he goes to college, he's going to that farm campus in Ames. Maybe they can bend him the right way at that school."

495

That night, after they'd lain in bed awhile, still talking about the great win, Arva finally moved to his side of the bed and fitted her hip against his belly as he lay on his right side. She wiggled a couple of times, drew his face around to hers and kissed him, and snuggled even tighter against him. "Maybe it's time we tried for another baby," she whispered.

"You think so, huh?"

"Unless'n a course that little nubbin of yours—"

"Nubbin? Hey. I'll show you, lady. Wiggle your sit-upon a couple of more times and I'll have the biggest ear of corn in the county ready for you. With the husks pulled back and clean."

She laughed in the dark. "You!"

There was rearranging of limbs under the quilts, some struggling as both pulled up their clothes, he his nightshirt and she her nightgown.

"Umm," she murmured, giggling, "no wonder you're the champion."

49. Rolf

1936

After Rolf bought his twelfth farm, cash on the barrelhead and nothing on the pump, he decided he was too busy being a landlord to farm himself. Also he had a hunch that the drought the coming year was going to be worse than it had been in 1935. He rented out the farm they'd been living on and moved to town in Bonnie. They bought the old Boughers house across the street from Ma in the Silk Stocking district. Rolf took some kidding from his brothers about whether or not Greta would now start wearing silk underwear. But Rolf just rolled his head and said she could darn well go on wearing cotton shifts. Rolf continued to say that with the help of good ringing dollars he was going to make of himself a millionaire a couple times over before he was through.

Dirk picked up on the word "through." "Yeh, and when you die, who's going to inherit all that wealth?"

"Never mind. I've already got somebody in mind."

It took Rolf a while to pick his various renters. "I won't make out a lease with a man until I see how he eats at my table. And then I wanna see how he sits with me in my two-holer. That way I've got him watched coming and going when it comes to manners. Also, I've got to know what he's gonna do about the manure piles on the place. You gotta think of the manure piles as a gold mine, where daily deposits are made. It's kind of a bank on the farm, from which you can make withdrawals when you need them. If the renter don't like my conditions, he can go take a header in the crik. 'Cause you see, the man who can stand abuse can generally stand prosperity. It's the same way with my hired men. Twice I had to fire a hired hand, and when they went down the lane with their time, they was talking to themselves. My theory is, hired hands are cheaper than horses."

One morning, after they'd lived in town for several months, at breakfast, Rolf abruptly set his cup of coffee in its saucer with a clatter and said, "Greta, I guess we now know we probably ain't gonna have any babies."

Greta slowly let her tapioca eyes close. "I guess not."

Rolf rubbed his chin. His freshly shaven face looked like a scraped slab of bacon. "I know I ain't gonna go see that seed expert in Sioux Falls again." Rolf shivered. "What a fellow has to go through to come up with his own seed for them to look at it in a microscope . . . heh!"

Greta's pale eyes opened. "I don't know."

"Better that you didn't. You women got your secret workings too and I don't wanna know about them either." He gave her a monkey smile. "But you been a good wife, though, hon."

"Thanks for that at least."

"Uhh . . . would you pass the lumber?"

Greta passed him a porcelain holder full of toothpicks.

"Thanks." He began to pick his teeth thoughtfully. "I was also thinking . . ." He pointed at an advertisement in *Wallace's Farmer*, "I was also thinking we might apply to one of them adoption agencies."

Greta's eyes brightened, for a moment resembling peeled gooseberries. "Oh, Rolf, could we?"

"Of course. And we'd be good parents too."

"Sure we would, Rolf."

Rolf studied his wife. It pleased him to see a healthy flush, pink skin, emerge on her cheeks. She'd become rather flat to him in bed. And as for himself, he didn't see much use in coupling anymore as long as his seed was dead. "Inactive," the seed doctor said. The doctor had let him have a peek at his sperm in the microscope. The sperm lay still, like they'd lined up at a trough and then had fallen asleep. "Anyway, let's think about it the next while. And if it still seems like a good idee, well, then let's go visit one of them agencies. I see there's one in Sioux City. Not too far away."

"Oh, Rolf." Greta started to cry. Then she got up and came around the table and embraced him and kissed him on his slick hard cheek.

"It was written up in the Sioux City *Journal* last month that the Siouxland Agency there picks some of the best orphans around. They're real picky. So we'd get a good one there."

"All right, Rolf."

"It's probably because a lot of free-spending blood has showed up in Sioux City. Coming out of all that bastard British pup blood down there."

"Just so it's healthy. We'll make a good boy out of it."

497

"Boy, eh? Not a girl?"

"I want to please you, Rolf."

"Humph." Rolf scratched his stiff cheek with a finger-nail. "Greta, you been a good girl. I swear, I was mad at you all last winter on the farm because of the way you was deviling me to buy you a new sewing machine. Well, hon, now that we've retired to what the town sports call the Silk Stocking district here, I guess you can have one of them newfangled stitchers. So why don't you go down to Rexroth's and buy yourself one. And tell 'em to charge it to me."

"Today?"

"Sure, why not? If it's a good idee, then it's a good idee right away."

She hugged and kissed him again.

"Well, shall we grace a little, before we each go our way?"

"You mean, give thanks, don't you?"

"Oh, yeah. I forgot which end of the meal we was on. Those kisses threw me off."

"Rolf!"

Rolf offered a simple thanks to the Lord.

Greta asked as they rose from the table, "What's your schedule today, husband?"

"Uhh . . . that renter I got on the old Wishart place needs a little jacking up. I've been wondering what was wrong with that family. They always look so poorly when you see them uptown Saturday nights. But I finally figured it out. They eat weak pigs."

"I don't understand."

"They don't feed the pigs proper. All they feed 'em is slop from their table and some skim milk. And that ain't good enough. Also they don't let the pigs run in the grass. Pigs'll eat a lot of grass if you give 'em half a chanct. There's nothing so smart and so cunning as a fat red pig running in green grass." Rolf pursed his thick tuber lips. "So I'm gonna bring 'em some feed free, for one time only, to show 'em what they should feed their pigs. Since they like pork so much. Once they eat good pigs they'll be full of gimp and gumption again."

"What time will you be back? So I can plan dinner."

"Oh, it won't take too long. But I've been invited to sit in on a chamber of commerce meeting this noon at lunch in the Bonnie Hotel."

"Then you won't be here for dinner?"

"Nope. But I'll be here for supper though." Rolf smiled at the thought of the noon meeting coming up. "What some of us got planned for this old burg will make New York howl. The boys along our Main Street are hustlers and good mixers and will all do their part in winning success for good old Bonnie."

A couple of days later, as he was putting their car away in the garage, Rolf was astounded to see some fresh black mounds, wet and shining, in the green lawn behind their house. What? Pocket gophers in town? Rolf looked south out past the garage, across the backyard of a neighbor, and then snapped his fingers. "I know where you buggers came from. Cooper's pasture out there." Cooper wasn't much of a farmer, was a bit lazy. Cooper's yard was always a mess, he was slow to get after that new scourge of the farms, the Canada thistle, slow to mow the hemp weeds in the ditches leading to his yard, and now slow to get after the pocket gophers.

498

"If it ain't one thing it's another. I got an old lady who complains the day away, in a house that's always smelling of tar soap and camphor balls. And now I got these devils of the night who work in the dark." He grimaced ferociously. "Well, I'll soon fix them."

Before Fraser's Drugstore closed, Rolf went down and bought a box of Paris green. Next he sailed over to Don Hawke's Farmers Elevator and bought a little bag of wheat.

"What are you going to do with that?" Don Hawke asked.

"Pocket gophers."

"Ah. But I'd be careful with that Paris green."

"How so?"

"If a dog smells a dead gopher in the ground, he's liable to dig it up and eat it. And that'll kill the dog. Then you're gonna have an angry neighbor on your hands."

"I'll take that chanct. I ain't gonna have my lawn all dug up and bumpy because of those devils of the night."

Rolf told Greta what he'd bought so she'd be careful not to get it mixed in with their food, then down in the basement he dumped the wheat and the Paris green in a pail and poured water over the mixture. "By morning that'll be soaked sufficient."

The next afternoon he went to work with a probe he'd once made out of an old box wagon rod. From his experience on Pa's farm, he knew the pocket gophers didn't dig a connecting runnel straight across from mound to mound, but very cleverly ran the runnel a foot off to one side. He poked his steel probe into the grass until it suddenly dropped down easy. The runnel was almost exactly a foot to the right of the black mound.

"Aha. So that's where he's got it."

Very patiently he worked the probe around a little to widen the hole. He was careful not to crumble dirt down below into the runnel. The pocket gopher might get suspicious. When it came to their particular kind of work they knew more about it than he did. When he had worked the hole an inch wide, he got his wheat soaked in poison and poured some down into it, several handfuls. Then, still working carefully and patiently, he balled up some of the dirt from the mound and pressed it into the top of the hole to close it. If the pocket gopher sensed light coming into his world, he always promptly and swiftly filled that part of his runnel with dirt.

"Got yuh now."

Next he took a shovel and scooped up the dozen little mounds of dirt and carried it all to where Greta had been trying to get some peonies to grow out front. "Old Boughers didn't cover the yellow clay with enough black dirt in the first place."

That night he lay smiling to himself. Pretty soon, while he slept the sleep of a good husband, warm in his bed, with his wife lying warm beside him, those damned devilish pocket gophers would be nibbling at the poison-tinctured grain. And by morning be dead.

"What are you smiling about?" Greta asked.

Rolf stiffened. What the devil? How did Greta know he was smiling in the dark? For all her college education he often thought her a dumb soul when it came to the ordinary things of life. But she could also surprise, sometimes stun, him with the way she could read his mind.

"Rolf?"

"How did you know I was smiling?"

"I could hear it. Your lips moving made a soft crepitating noise."

"'Crepitating'? That's a lot of crap. Them college words, they don't hold with me."

"Well, I knew you were smiling. And it made me wonder a little bit because I don't feel like smiling much."

"Didn't you get your sewing machine?"

"Sure, but that isn't everything."

"Don't you have it a lot easier, now that we've moved to town, where you can take your own time, away from all that yard dirt? And the smell of working manure piles?"

Slowly Greta started to stiffen beside him. And then her body began to jerk as she began to cry.

"What in blazes is wrong now?"

"You wouldn't believe it if I told you."

"Don't tell me we got one in the oven after all?"

"Of course not, you silly man. In the oven!"

"Well then, what is it? You can tell me in the dark. People can often talk about bad things in the dark when they can't in daylight."

Greta sighed. And sighed again. "Well, it's my sister Fannie."

"What about her?"

"Maybe I shouldn't tell you."

Rolf thought of the cunning red pigs he once raised. They knew when to be silent and when to run. So he waited.

She sighed again. And then spilled it all out. "You knew, didn't you, that Fannie quit her job with Old Will Haber?"

"That's old news, wife."

"And that she then went to work as housekeeper for Wallie Moon?"

"She did?" Rolf knew Wallie Moon. Moon was known in the Allard Pool Hall in Rock Falls as a dirty old fool. Any man with a name like Moon was bound to be a bit touched. "What did she do that for? That's the second old coot she's gone to work for."

"He offered her a lot of money if she'd be his housekeeper and take care of him in his old age. And she felt sorry for him."

"What if she runs into a young man who wants her?"

"I guess it's too late for that."

"What!"

Greta let fly with several little gusts of breath, half sob, half sigh.

"Well?"

"Well, Fannie is going to have a baby."

"Who's the lucky father?"

"That's just it. It's Wallie Moon."

"C'mon! That's impossible. He's way too old for that kind of thing. He must be in his eighties."

"Don't forget your father and his continuing complaint about his bed rights with your mother."

Rolf popped bolt upright in bed. Darn. That Greta of his, she might have trouble looking him in the eye with those weak chicken eyes of hers, but by gum behind those eyes lived a weasel with teeth as sharp as needles. He shivered, trying to imagine young Fannie coupling with that wrinkled old coot Moon with all those pink wattles under his chin. How awful. God must've been looking the other way when that happened.

"Fannie says that compared to the young bucks she's gone out with, he's a great lover. Tender and kind and considerate."

"Puh!"

"She says it wouldn't have happened, but she started having nice dreams about him, and that told her he was a good man. So when he touched her one day, she turned to butter."

"God! That that old bastard should have the nerve to touch her. What'd he do, grab her by the haunch?"

"Rolf, now."

"God! That that old bag of gas should knock up a young girl. And your sister yet. God! Imagine the gossip we're gonna run into up and down Main Street."

"Judge not that ye be not judged."

"Well, I'm not an old man yet for that to fit me."

Greta sat up in bed too and reached around and plumped up her pillow several times, then leaned against it. "This isn't the first time something like this has happened. There was Old David in the Bible and what he did to young Bathsheba. In fact, what he did to her is even worse. After all, he was the king and as a king he had to set a good example for his people."

"What! You're gonna put that old fart Moon and your sister Fannie ahead of Old David and Bathsheba?"

"Not really ahead of them. Just as an example that such things do happen even in the best of families."

"God."

"Remember now, husband. Someday that little child is going to be either your little nephew or your little niece."

Rolf's nose twitched up and down. "I suppose they plan on marrying."

Again Greta heaved a huge sigh. "That's already been done. They went up to Whitebone and got married there yesterday."

Holy bulls."

"Yes. And holy cows."

A long silence in the dark.

Rolf found himself thinking about those pocket gophers out there under his lawn in the backyard. About now they were probably nibbling on the poisoned grain. He hoped they'd eat themselves a bellyful. Finally, sighing a deep sigh himself, he fluffed up his pillow several times, slid down in bed, and composed himself for sleep.

In a moment Greta slid down in bed too.

Rolf was almost asleep, when he felt Greta stirring beside him like a lazy cat stretching itself.

"Husband?"

"Yes?"

"Maybe you'll think me silly, but couldn't we try once again? I'm kinda jealous of my sister Fannie."

Rolf reawakened fully. Say. Greta wasn't all that dead in bed after all. He found himself slowly risen. "Maybe there's one pocket gopher left alive around here, huh?"

"Pocket?"

For weeks afterward it stuck in Rolf's craw what Old Wallie Moon had done to his sister-in-law Fannie.

What finally got him off the painful subject were several bulletins from the U.S. Department of Agriculture dealing with soil conservation practices. He had long noticed that the best soil, black humus on the surface, was being washed off the land on the hills, that when the wind blew hard in the winter it whipped off the best soil even when the land lay perfectly flat.

He went down to see Don Hawke about it.

"I've been advocating soil contouring for years, Rolf. That you do your plowing in the spring."

"How much difference do you think it'll make when it comes to making money?"

"Well, all you have to do is take one look at Geer Engleking's yellow hills northeast of town here. Those hills used to be covered by a good foot of black dirt."

Rolf nodded. "Yeh. It's worthless land now. Same way with those hills that that cripple Clate Bartles and his sister Hettie farm."

Don Hawke had to smile. "I'm a little surprised, Rolf, that you should be interested in soil conservation, you being known as the hard man for the dollar."

"Ha. That's exactly the reason why. I want to get all that's coming to me, and I can see already that that's the best way to get it. Makes sense. All a person can raise on those yellow pimple hills is cockleburs."

Greta had a request to make one evening during supper. "Fannie's asked us over for dinner next Sunday. We can go, can't we? She is my dear sister, you know, and I'd like to be close to her while she's carrying the baby."

"Would you pass the shakers, please?"

Greta handed him the salt and pepper. "Fannie and I were always so close when we was kids."

Rolf held up his fork. "So that's why you laid out the table with these fancy tools. To soften me up."

Greta countered. "Why should we save our best things for those who aren't going to come after us? I think we should enjoy having them ourselves sometimes." Greta's weak gray-blue eyes slowly firmed up into sharp blue-gray eyes. "We can go, can't we?"

"Oh, heck, how I hate to shoot the breeze with that old slobberchops." Rolf sneered. "I can just see me watching Fannie cleaning off Wallie Moon's chin after every mouthful."

"Well, Rolf husband, it isn't everybody lucky enough to have learned the Freyling manners."

Rolf was also thinking about a Wallie Moon story. For weeks everybody in Rock Falls had been laughing about it. Moon couldn't read or write, but he was a first-rate handyman. There wasn't a thing in the house or out on the yard, town or country, he couldn't fix: plumbing, electric wiring, soldering or welding, repairing old chairs, painting, getting stubborn engines to start. He ran a shop he called Wallie the Handyman. As such he was in competition with Fritz the Fixer. One evening the two old coots got to bragging over a beer at Pete's Place as to who had the most guts. One dare led to another, until finally Fritz made the ultimate challenge. "I'll bet you five bucks you don't dare to take a crap right out in front of the Rock Theater just when the first movie lets out at nine o'clock." "You're on," Moon bawled. Both put up a five-spot with Pete the barkeep. And by golly that's just what Moon did. In the middle of the outgoing rush, Moon turned his back on the theater entrance, dropped his pants, and slowly lowered a perfectly tooled turd to the sidewalk. He'd mooned the world proper. Of course word had got around about what might be coming up and a considerable crowd had gathered in front of the theater as well as across the street to witness the event. The town marshall also got wind of it, and he promptly walked over and arrested Old Moon for disorderly conduct, exposure of private parts, and conduct unbecoming a citizen of Rock Falls. Moon sat in jail for only an hour, when the town mayor set him free. The mayor didn't want the reporter from the Rock Falls *Banner* to make a big fuss over it in his sheet to the embarrassment of the town. The story never got printed because the editor of the *Banner* agreed with the mayor. The editor was more than a little aware of the rivalry among the three towns of Rock Falls, Whitebone, and Bonnie. Fans from all three towns usually jeered at each other at baseball games. Unmercifully.

Rolf finally agreed to accept the invitation to Sunday dinner at the Moons.

502

"But don't be surprised if I don't say much. That dirty old coot."

"Let's see what you're like when you are in your eighties."

Dinner at Fannie's turned out to be fairly pleasant after all. Rolf and Greta weren't in the house more than hour when Moon had a question to ask Rolf.

"Do you know anything about how to get rid of mice?" Moon waggled his head, stirring up the pink wattles under his chin. Moon had almost no chin, his wattles had fallen so. It hurt the eye to compare his wrinkled neck with Fannie's smooth girlish neck. "I've tried everything."

Rolf grudged him a word. "In the house here?"

"No, not in the house. Out in my shop back there."

Rolf threw a glance at the yellow cat sitting near the door. "What about that set of whiskers?"

"That's Fannie's cat and she won't work the shop. She's a good mouser in the house but not out there."

Fannie smiled down at her cat. "Tuff is a high-class cat and it's beneath him to catch shop mice." Fannie had already begun to show. Even her round comely face had become swollen a little. Her eyes had a troubled look as though she had resigned herself to being scorned by people for having fornicated with a very old man. Her naturally soft voice was even more tired-sounding than Greta's.

Rolf said, "Well, lock old Tuff in there overnight."

Moon said, "He runs away. Goes out through that cat door I got there for him. And I got to have that swinging free so he can go in and out 'cause I don't want any overnight cat shit in my shop."

Rolf scratched his bristle-stiff hair and remembered something Pa had once done. "Tell you what. Find yourself a female cat that's about to have kits. Lock her in your shop until she has her kits. With a sandbox. Once the kits are crawling around a little they'll want to stay in your shop. And their old lady will stay because she'll want to stay with her brood."

"Hey, that might work." Moon's eyes opened wide and sharp blue. For an old bustard he had very young eyes.

Greta mouthed a small piece of meat loaf. "You mean kittens, don't you?"

"What's wrong with kits?"

"Foxes have kits."

"Kits or kittens, I still mean little pussycats."

Moon held his old head sideways, pink wattles hanging on a slant. "We called 'em kits too." Moon had an astonishingly thick mat of rope-colored hair. From his eyes on up he was still a handsome man.

Rolf pursed up his lips in a sour grimace.

So the dinner went off very well. When Greta and Rolf left through the Moon front door, all four were smiling as though they'd been chums for years.

Two months later calamity struck. Fannie died while having her baby, breech, and Wallie Moon in shock died of a heart attack.

Right after the double funeral Greta pounced. She took the little baby boy home with her. An old-maid nurse from the Rock Falls hospital tried to claim it; she'd fallen in love with it as it lay in the hospital nursery. So insistent was Greta that she should have it, had a right to have it because she was Fannie's

503

nearest relative, that the sad nurse gave way.

Rolf was a little shocked. He was for having the baby, but he wasn't sure he liked the show of fierce possession by his wife, Greta. She now had something she could be boss over and he was fearful that it would soon extend to him.

Rolf thought the baby a homely mutt. It had Wallie Moon's expression around its nose. It didn't look in the least like Fannie or her father or mother.

But as the months went by, the baby's face very subtly began to take on the male version of Fannie's face. The one thing that caught Rolf's eye was the baby's strong back. The first day the baby was home with them he could already lift his head. Soon his little arms and hands began to show strength.

Rolf had to laugh as he played with the baby in his lap in the evenings. "By golly, wife, more and more he's beginning to look like Tane."

"Maybe we should name him Tane," Greta offered.

"Naw." Rolf held out two forefingers for the baby to grasp with its two little squirrel hands. "If we name him anything, let's name him after his grandpa. There should be at least one Tunis in the world."

Presently the little fellow began to cry.

Greta came over and picked him up. "Aha. He's filled his pants." She got a fresh diaper and began to clean him. "Tunis is all right. But he really has no Tunis blood in him."

"Mmm."

"How about naming him Wallace?"

"After Wallie Moon? Never. Besides, naming him that would also make Tressa's husband, Wallie Starnes, think we named the boy after him. And that I couldn't take. Starnes is a prick. Poor Tress. He's letting her wither on the vine. Bosses her around like she's a slave. My sister!"

"But the Moon family name has died out now that Wallie is gone."

"What about our line?"

"The Freyling line is going on. There's Tane's children. And Geoffrey and Adela have two boys."

"That's true." Rolf watched with pleasure as Greta powdered and safety-pinned a diaper on the baby. The good wife had taken to being a mother like she'd already had a half dozen. It was in her blood like the return of the river-bank swallows in the spring. The little tyke began to murmur contentment.

"How about Walter? Then we'd name him after both Wallie Moon and my favorite uncle."

That struck Rolf just right. "Good. Walter it is. Walter Freyling. Sounds like it's going to be the name of an important man someday."

"We'll name him Walter Moon Freyling," Greta said firmly. "Okay?"

Rolf lifted his shoulders. "Well, all right. Just so we don't mention the Moon part very often."

50. Tressa

1936

Tressa had nothing to do once she had the breakfast dishes washed and the kitchen dusted—until it was time to put the supper on the stove at four. Wallie Starnes was so busy in his barbershop during the noon hour that he couldn't take the time to eat dinner at home. He was out to make his first million too. So he took his lunch with him and at noon gobbled down a beef sandwich in between haircuts. Sallie Meyer, just out of high school, a fatty flirt, brought him coffee from the Corner Cafe in a thermos bottle to help him down the thick sandwiches.

All the while Tressa coughed a lot and took treatments for asthma.

After Tressa quit her job at Rexroth's, she did some work for the Lord by calling on the poor of the Little Church. She brought them packets of food contributed by members of the church. She also went to the Ladies Aid. But after a couple of years of doing good, she got sick of it. There was a rebel in her that wanted to get out. She next tried clerking in Tillman's Mercantile. That Wallie didn't like at all. He said Tillman told dirty stories. He said Tillman questioned Reverend Tiller's sermons too closely. He said that Tillman believed in Higher Criticism and that was against Christ. Reverend Tiller had been anointed to be their intercessor as well as their guardian and it was the duty of all parishioners to accept his word as though it verily was the word of God himself.

To get Wallie off her back, Tressa quit Tillman and went to work for Nelson Foxx, the local butcher. Nelson was a heavy man, fattish, which he tried to hide by wearing a broad belt hiked up tight. But the tight belt made him look like a bale of hay with the baling wire wound too snug. He also had a heavy red face, little veins showing in his cheeks, suggesting he might have some heart problems. He wore a white canvas smock over tan trousers and a tan shirt. But it was his tiny glinting eyes that attracted Tressa. They were always narrowed, forming creases on either side of them so that the *x*'s in his name, Foxx, fit him perfectly.

Tressa worked for him when he was busiest serving customers, from ten until two. Sometimes he had to leave the store to get more meat, either from a farmer who'd just butchered, or else meat he himself butchered in back in the killing room.

Tressa soon learned that Nelson had wandering hands. He had deft fingers, and when he let them linger on her elbows as he passed her behind the counter it made her feel tingly inside her thighs. It made her wonder a little why a touch on the elbow should show up as a quiver there. It reminded her of that time with Dirk when they were home alone and they were milking the cows and she

505

couldn't stand it any longer and suggested they climb up into the haymow. She still shook her head sometimes when she thought of that time. Where had she gotten the daring not only to think of it but to want to do it? There had to be something in her that was bold, even hoydenish. Perhaps a Christian was only a heathen dressed up in a thick coat of whitewash.

How she missed Dirk. She hadn't seen him since the last stoop talk. She wondered what he was doing in the Twin Cities. From Ma she'd learned Dirk had taken a new job as an abstractor for *New Medicine*. Apparently he had never found a woman good enough to marry. But she was sure he was having women. She knew Dirk.

Dirk, Dirk.

She thought it ironic that while she wanted it and couldn't get it with Wallie, Ana could get all she wanted and didn't want it. That is, if one could believe Ana's stories about the dusky men of Pine Ridge knocking on her door at night.

Tressa thought: "I should have married Dirk. If that had been possible. Deep down we belonged to each other. We should have run away to Montana. Or farther north to the mountains in Canada. Never told a soul. Lived as man and wife." If the Egyptian royalty could marry brother and sister and not have idiots for babies, then surely she and Dirk could marry and have normal children. Pa and Ma came from different peoples. The first generation of kids would have at least been all right.

Tressa wondered what Nelson Foxx saw in her. He was married to a lively woman who was active in the Bonnie Boosters as well as in the Congregational church. Wasn't Mrs. Foxx good to Nelson? Maybe Mrs. Foxx was the counterpart to her own husband, Wallie. Oh, how mixed up couples could be sometimes. The wrong ones married each other. A dried-prune man should live with a dried-prune woman. And a horny man should live with a juicy woman.

Once, when she finished work at two, after Nelson had made another pass at her, she walked home and went directly to the bathroom and examined herself in the full-length mirror tacked to the inside of the door. She saw the beginning of tiny wrinkles as well as a fuzzy moustache on her upper lip. She saw the start of crinkles around her blue eyes. She next lowered her blouse and then her shift to examine her breasts. They too were shrinking. What they needed was a good jollying up by a strong man's hand. And every night.

"First thing you know they're going to shrink to nothing more than a couple of flat bladders."

She lowered her shift to her hips. She stroked her shallow belly button and the pattycake mound below it.

"Still no baby. Still no baby. Well, what can one expect from a husband who doesn't want to couple more than thirteen times a year?"

She tried to imagine what it might be like to be pregnant, to feel a little soul coming to life under one's stomach, to feel it struggling to get out and join the living.

That same night, waking at two because of a coughing spell, hearing her husband snoring his strange tootle beside her, she let the thought pop out that Dirk should have made her pregnant that time they coupled in the haymow. There would have been an awful scandal. But she would have had her baby.

"And it would have been a great baby," She murmured. Anything she and Dirk had was bound to be wonderful.

"Hmm?" Wallie Starnes mumbled. "Did you say something?"

Tressa quickly pretended the slow deep breathing of one asleep.

"Hmm?" He stirred around a little, found a better way to nuzzle down into his pillow. "Hmm?"

Wouldn't it be wonderful if all of a sudden Wallie forgot all his rules and climbed aboard her saddle and made her pregnant? Right now was the perfect time because she was ovulating. She could always tell when an egg was coming down. It was when she felt flushed over he whole body. A part of her felt as though it were opening up to receive something.

Slowly Wallie Starnes sank away into sleep and soon the sound of his tootling filled their bedroom again.

"Here I am, forty-four, in the terrible dry summer of 1936, with my periods not very regular any more, and still as barren as the Dust Bowl. If you're ever coming, Dirk, you better hurry up or it'll be too late."

The very next Saturday, Nelson Foxx asked if she would help him tend the store until closing time at nine. Other stores up and down Main Street stayed open until the last customer left, even into the early hours of Sunday morning, a sacrilege in the eyes of all local ministers, but Nelson let it be known he was finished for the week at nine sharp.

"But I never work past two otherwise," Tressa protested. "And Wallie and I was planning to go visit Rolf and Greta and their little boy, Walter."

"C'mon, Wallie always stays open past midnight like the rest of them."

"Well, I was going to go to Rolf's anyway. Have supper with Ma and then the two of us go visit little Walter."

"Look. I need you. Next week the threshing season starts and I'll need a lot of extra meat for that. I thought I'd butcher all day today so that the meat'll be fresh. While you tend the front."

"Well . . ."

He was careful to keep his distance. "Tress, I need you. Okay?" He spoke like a captain who wouldn't take no for an answer.

Tressa agreed. But she didn't tell Wallie. By the time he found out about it, it would be too late.

Except for supper, she worked right on through from ten in the morning until nine at night. All the while, between customers, or when she went to the bathroom, or when she stepped into the frigid freezer to get a certain piece of meat where for a second or so she lost her breath, the air was so lung-shrinking cold, she brooded over how she really felt about Nelson Foxx. She liked his gentle deft fingers, and she was always taken by his piercing gimlet X-eyes, but the shaking jellylike flab over his belly disgusted her. She tried to imagine his flab lying on her lean belly. What a sight that would be.

She decided she had to be terribly man-hungry to consider coupling with Nelson at all. Horny, as her brothers would put it. Or, hard up. Though that last more fit a man. And it was more than just wanting a baby. It was wanting and needing intimacy with a ma's body. Skin touching skin.

Promptly at nine o'clock Nelson locked the front door, pulled down the shades in both the showcase windows and on the front door, and removed his white blood-stained apron.

Tressa followed suit. She folded up her neat white canvas apron and placed it in its drawer.

Nelson slipped a heavy arm around her. His masterful fingers gripped her

507

hip. "Come in back with me a minute. There's something I want to show you."

"I better go home." A phlegm-breaking cough broke from her lungs. She stepped free of his circling arm.

"Come. You won't believe this."

"Can't you just tell me about it?"

"No. You gotta see it to believe it."

"Well, all right." She let herself be ushered into the killing room.

Carcasses of hogs, steers, sheep hung from hooks along the west wall. Hissing pipes circled the big freezer. A butcher's chopping block stood in the center.

"Well?"

Nelson pointed to a pale bloodless flap of what looked like a bladder on the chopping block. "Look in that and tell me what you see."

"What is it?"

"The stomach of a young hog. Look in it."

Squeamish, she did take a look. For godsakes. In the middle of a handful of half-masticated kernels of yellow corn lay a man's Waltham watch. It's gold cover, brightened by the action of stomach acid, shone like a little sun in the bright electric light. "How in the world . . . How come that hog didn't pass that?"

"Too big to pass through the bunghole of the stomach. And it just kept tumbling around and around in there."

"But how did it get in there in the first place?"

"Probably fell in the feed trough while someone was pouring corn. Fell out of his vest pocket. And the hog in his gluttony gobbled it down."

"I'll bet someone looked and looked for that watch, never knowing where it really went."

"Yep." Nelson shyly slipped his hand around her hip again.

"It probably happened on a Sunday noon right after church when the man quick went out to feed the hogs a minute. Just before Sunday dinner. Because that's really a Sunday watch."

"Something like that." Nelson drew her close.

Tressa squirmed. Yet it felt wonderful to have a man put his arm around her. "Have you opened it yet to see if there's a name engraved in there?"

"Nope. I thought I'd wait until you were with." He removed his arm from her hip and picked up the watch. With a thick thumbnail he pried open the gleaming front cover. The inside was even more shiny. Across the inside of the cover was an engraved name: *Ezra Pence.*

"Why, we know him. He farms that quarter south of the sandpits." Tressa wished the touch of that warm hand could have continued. "Ain't Pence going to be surprised when you tell him what you found."

"He surely is." Nelson wound the watch a little and held it to his ear. "Runs." He smiled thickly and placed the watch on a nearby shelf. "I'll call him tomorrow."

Tressa smiled. What was happening to her?

He placed his arm around her again, and when she didn't protest, or shiver, he slid his hand up over her breast.

The thick hand with its delicate fingers felt so dear. She placed her hand over his hand on her breast.

"Tress."

Her eyes closed and she let her head rest on his great chest.

508

He took her hand and tickled the palm of it.

"Yes," she said, knowing what it meant, remembering from childhood when kids at school, giggling, tickled each other's palms, thinking it daring, and yet despite their avid curiosity really being innocent.

Gently, for all his size, he bent her slowly back over the chopping block and, standing between her knees, took her.

51. Dirk

1937–1938

At first Dirk liked working for *New Medicine*. For once he was challenged to be accurate. Very accurate. One poorly turned phrase about some new medical technique could mean the death of the Lord only knew how many patients out there in the sticks.

In a way his job as abstractor was simple. In the morning he first checked in at his *New Medicine* office on 20 West Tenth Street, second floor, window overlooking the parking lot east of the red marble Hennessey County Library; then, picking up his general assignment from tendon-skinny Ruth Rudge, the managing editor, he took the stairs down, walked southeast up Tenth, took a left northeast up Nicollet to the Medical Arts Building, entered an ornate medicine-smelling lobby, took the elevator to the very top floor, the twentieth, and entered the Hennessey County Medical Library.

Elsie Alspaugh was the head librarian. After Elsie learned that at forty-six Dirk was still single, and after she found out he still chased women, she always had a specially sweet smile for him. She was forty, voluptuous tending to fat, had thick lips suggesting she might be wonderful, and had glowing brown eyes.

"Morning," she said brightly.

"Mornin'." A viscid cough broke in his throat.

"Grouch."

"Well, I feel grouchy."

"Too bad. But there are remedies for that, you know."

He'd been tempted to date her. But he knew he'd be wise to first break free of his sticky relationship with Bebe Nicolaus. When he dated two women at the same time his Bible Belt conscience got in the way.

Elsie asked, "What's it going to be today?"

"Kettering Institute. Menninger Clinic. And some reports in the *Journal of the American Medical Association.*"

"You know were *JAMA* is. And I'll dig out the reports of K.I. and M.C."

"Done. Same cubbyhole?"

"Right."

He steered his way through shelves and shelves of medical reports and found his usual desk at a tall window. It overlooked Minneapolis to the south, a lovely sweep of trees so thick that after the third block away it was hard to make out homes below. The seeming green forest was broken up only by three rather large lakes, Nokomis, Harriet, and Calhoun.

He found nothing particular to note in *JAMA*. Nor was there anything in the Menninger Clinic annals. But he found something of interest in the Kettering report.

He had to read the medical report several times to catch the central point. The writing was so polysyllabic that what the doctors tried to say slipped like an elusive drop of mercury between their choice of words. Dirk had to read between the lines, and make an educated guess as to the doctors' original intention, to find the real point. But finally he understood the report and patiently, in longhand, wrote a brief abstract:

In treating early syphilis, Roosevelt Donaldson, M.D., and associates, found that by combining bismuth, arsenic, and artificially induced fever and using them as a control, they could evaluate the efficacy of various methods. They tested 23 patients at the Kettering Institute for Medical Research who were being treated with arsenobenzene in combination with mercury. Seventeen patients indicated strong positive reactions.

When Dirk looked up he found Elsie leering at him out of the near aisle in the book stacks. He asked. "Find something for me?"

She laughed self-consciously. "Yes." She handed him a medical magazine with a slip in the middle to mark an article. "It's probably not for your magazine, but maybe you can use it for yourself. It has to do with asthma."

"Oh." He often coughed sitting in the middle of all those dusty records.

She laughed some more, lips open. "It says asthma is sex-related."

"How so?"

"Read it and you'll see."

He cocked his head at her. "Maybe instead of reading it I should just check out the sex part."

"That's the point of it."

Again he felt warmth for her. "You never married, did you?"

"Nope. Never found the right one."

"What are you doing tonight?"

Her large bosom quaked slightly. "Nothing that I know of." She let her eyes close. "Would you like to come over for tea and dessert?"

"I'd love it. Where do you live?"

"I have an apartment in the Arcola."

"Why, that's just three blocks from here."

"Right."

"What time shall I come?"

"Sevenish?"

"Seven then."

Elsie retreated behind the stacks, blushing.

Just to make sure he'd be up to it with Elsie, Dirk decided he'd first better call Bebe Nicolaus and get her off his conscience. When he got back to his desk in *New Medicine* he dialed Bebe's number. He found her home.

"Hi, Bebe."

"Hi." Her voice was flat, noncommittal.

"Remember what we sort of agreed to try last time?"

"Yes."

"Maybe we should do that."

"Meaning what?"

Dirk was startled by Bebe's directness. "That we probably should break it off. It isn't going to work."

Silence.

"Bebe?"

"I guess I knew it from the beginning."

"Anyway, I'm too old for you."

"That's not the reason. You never really liked me as much as I liked you."

It was true. "I'm sorry, Bebe."

"No more than me."

"So long."

"Bye."

Relieved, he hung up the phone. Now having reduced his women to one, he might be able to be a man with Elsie.

He remembered the first time he met Bebe.

. . . . Bebe was a journalism student at the University of Minnesota. At the time he was a reporter for the *Eastside Argus*.

Late one afternoon Bebe knocked on his door at 1814 Fourth Street, S.E., to interview him for a class report. They'd talked a while, she sitting on the nearby window seat and he on a couch. She was short but lithe, with pale hair and very light blue eyes. She had Slavic cheekbones and a strong chin. Her mouth was small but her lips were full and pink.

When she'd finished going through her list of questions she sat a moment, more lost in self-contemplation than wondering what to say next. She was a dreamer.

Dirk couldn't help it. He slowly got up and went over and sat beside her. He smiled at her, and kept smiling at her until she turned her eyes to him and began smiling back. Gently he leaned to kiss her. She kissed him back, gently. Soon they were hugging each other warmly. When he slipped his hand inside her step-ins, she held his hand back. Not strongly but just enough to let him know she wasn't quite ready for that.

"Bebe, can I see you sometime?"

She smiled at him vaguely.

"May I?"

"Well, Mother works at the Walgreen's Drugstore Saturdays. You could come then."

"Not at night? On a regular date?"

"Mother wouldn't like for me to see an older man."

"She got a thing about that then?"

Bebe nodded. "You see, I'm the result of one of those things."

"Ah." He loved the lazy curve of her small thick mouth. "Well, then, maybe you can come here to my apartment on Monday. That's my day off."

"Oh, no! That I can't do."

"Well, you came here today to interview me."

"But the next time I come here it'll be different. No, you come see me at my mother's home. I'll feel better about it."

She gave him her address. It was a large apartment house some four blocks from Dinkytown and not too far from the university campus.

At ten the next Saturday he rang her bell in the lobby. When a buzzer sounded, he quickly opened the main door and stepped into the lower hall. He climbed three floors to her number, 417 B. She opened the door, quite nervous in her manner.

"What's the matter?"

"Nothing."

"Your mother home?"

"No. She went to work all right." She pointed to an armchair for him and took a seat opposite him on a brown couch.

They smiled at each other.

A clock struck, first some chimes, then the hour.

He got up and settled beside her. Slowly he slipped an arm around her. Her smile and her sloe eyes suggested slowness. He tilted up her chin and kissed the corners of her thick lips. After a moment there was a slight kiss back.

She said, "You wouldn't know this, but I've seen you more often than you might guess."

"Really?"

"I've seen you at the symphony. And I've seen you at the University Theater. And you like to get malteds at Bridgeman's."

"Well." He became aware of an interesting smell in the apartment, a smell of musty eiderdown, one her mother might have taken with her from the Old Country.

Bebe went on. "I kept hoping I'd meet you sometime. Then when I learned you were a newspaperman, I asked my professor if I could interview you."

"So that's how."

She smiled down at her stubby hands.

He took both her hands and kissed her fingers.

She said, "We better go in back to my room." She rose to her feet with the motion of a languorous kitten, locked the apartment door, and led him down a hallway into a bedroom. She used the bathroom first and then he used it.

When he came out, she was already naked, lying on top of the opened sheets. He couldn't help but look at her lovely body in detail, short-coupled, full breasts, sloping flat belly, and a second set of short fat lips almost hidden in a patch of pubic hair.

He stretched out beside her. He'd go slowly with her. He crossed his hands behind his head in his pillow, elbows out to either side. He wondered a little how they could have come so far so fast.

It was as if she could read his mind. "I never do this."

"Never?"

"Yes." She turned her head to look at him. Her blond hair bunched up around her eyes. She tucked her hair aside. "I guess I just fell for you when I saw you and I knew if you ever asked I'd do whatever you wanted."

That checked him. My God. This was dangerous going. If he went ahead with it he might wreck her life. He couldn't say if it was possible for him to fall in love with her. She was wonderful. But.

"What do I do next?" she asked.

"You really've never had a man?"

"No."

"A virgin then?"

"I think so."

"You think so?"

"I've had myself."

He swallowed. He wetted his lips. My God, another Tressa. He suppressed a tremble.

"Does that count?" she asked.

513

"If it does, then even day-old babies have lost it."

She said, "You're so different. I've never run into anybody like you."

He felt tender toward her. He also wanted to grab her and take her.

"What kind of people do you come from, Mr. Freyling, that you should look like you do?"

Ah. If she only knew.

"You look like you're always a winner. That smile. Do you ever lose?"

"Oh, God, yes."

"You're no stranger to me," she went on, "like I said. But I am to you. So how can you so quick?"

He rolled on his side facing her. "More talk like that, young lady, and nothing will happen."

"I was just wondering, is all. I like to know."

He smiled at her and touched her cheek. "Already the habit of a good journalist."

An undulation started at the back of her head and moved down her body, lifting her teacup breasts. She looked down the length of his body, finally settled on his rising tower. Her little smile became even more wonderfully lazy. "So that's how it is."

"Is it all right?"

"It's wonderful. God surely knew what he was doing when he arranged it that way."

"That's what I always thought. I could never understand those super Christians who teach you it is acky-bad."

"That's my mother."

He cupped her chin. "How come you didn't take to that Bible Belt law?"

"Maybe I'm too young to know I haven't."

Warmth from both their bodies rose around them. Their eyes became sleepy with desire. He fondled her. Then he found he could no longer resist those short fat lips. For that one brief moment at least he wanted to lose his heart in her.

When their breathing leveled off, he asked, "Did you?"

"At first I thought maybe I might. But then I lost it."

"Next time maybe."

She waited for him to kiss her again, but when he didn't, wasn't even thankful, she withdrew ever so slightly.

He visited her twice more on a Saturday, but she finally decided that was too dangerous. Her mother sometimes came home early when there wasn't much business at the drugstore.

Then Bebe began to visit him at his apartment.

There wasn't a chance it would go better there. It was as if she needed the aura of her mother around to make it work. Several times Dirk and Bebe just talked, had a cup of tea, and then she left. She kept saying she loved him, loved him, but that made it all the worse for him. After a time he knew they should break off. He could no longer be a man with her. He still hadn't found the woman who'd help him forget Tressa. . . .

Managing editor Ruth Rudge knocked on Dirk's open door and stepped inside. "Busy?"

"Some."

"Got that abstract ready? I've got a hole left for it in makeup." She kept stretching on her toes, tensing up the tendons in her neck, trying to make the muscles around her mouth purse up so that she'd look the part of a tough editor. There was an air about her suggesting that she wasn't going to live long. She was either fretting herself to death with the way she let her job get her down or she already had a cancer secretly eating away at her. She looked at the sheet of paper in his typewriter. He had just finished typing up the longhand version of the abstract written in the Medical Arts Building. "That it, Dirk?"

"Yes."

She pulled it out of the typewriter and read a few lines; then frowned.

"No good?"

"The stuff is there, the detail we want." She frowned again, looked at her watch, and said, "I guess I got time to ding it up a little."

Dirk bowed his head. Damn. There she went again. He and Ruth Rudge had never agreed on how the abstracts should read. She'd been sucked in by the way the medico boys wrote. While he thought they wrote almost as badly as government lawyers.

Ruth Rudge, still frowning, left for her desk across the hall.

An hour later, just before going out to lunch, he poked his head into her office. Despite all its neatness, there was a sour unhappy smell in her office. "Did you get it in?"

"What? Oh. Yes. I managed to get it shaped up."

"Out of curiosity, could I see it?"

"I already sent it down."

"Guess I'll have to wait until the proof comes back." Luckily he had the handwritten version of the copy she'd pulled out of his typewriter and could later compare it with the one she'd sent down to the linotypists.

After lunch the phone rang on his desk. He picked up the black receiver. "Yes?"

"Darling, I've missed you." It was a man's wet voice.

For godsakes. "Who?"

"Ohm." There came the sound of somebody very embarrassed. "Sorry. Wrong number." The wet fellow hung up.

Dirk raised his brows at the ceiling. That call had come through the receptionist's desk. Who did the receptionist think she was ringing?

About a minute later, Algernon Berry, advertising manager for *New Medicine*, stood in Dirk's doorway. He was a slender man with pliant fingers. There was a continual quizzical look around his soft brown dog eyes. "Did you just get an odd call just now?"

"I sure did."

"Och! That damned bitch out front." Algernon was referring to Dodie Dodgson, the receptionist. "She's been trying to embarrass me for months." Algernon plucked a white handkerchief from the breast pocket of his blue blazer and blew his nose. "What did the caller say?"

"He called me his darling and said he'd missed me."

Algernon blinked. "Didn't the fellow realize you were a man?"

For some time Dirk had suspected Algernon Berry was different. Dirk had heard some of the doctors on the board of directors of the magazine muttering

515

about it. But Algernon was successful in getting lucrative advertising, enriching the owners, the Goldstone family. Dirk said, "I think he expected to be talking to a man."

"Oh, dear."

Dirk decided to stick it into him. "It intrigued me the way he pronounced your name."

"Ohh, dearr."

Dirk leaned back in his swivel chair, waiting to see if Algernon would admit it. Dirk didn't care all that much what kind of a sex a person practiced, but he did want Algernon to know that he wasn't an ignorant country hick. "Sounded like a charming fellow."

Algernon cocked his head sideways at Dirk. His wide smile formed into two wrinkles. "You never married, did you?"

"No."

"Why not, if I may presume to ask?"

"Never found the right one."

"Yes, yes, that's always the problem, isn't it?"

"I've had a lot of women in my time, but . . ."

"Always successful with them?"

"So far, every one. I surely like that gash."

"Ulp." Again Algernon cleared his nose on both sides with his pure white handkerchief. "Sorry if the call disturbed your thoughts." Algernon turned abruptly; but instead of heading for his office, shot out to the front desk angry.

Dirk smiled to himself. He was almost tempted to steal out into the hallway to eavesdrop on what Algernon might have to say to haughty Dodie Dodgson.

516

The copy boy came in with the proofs for next month's issue and threw a set on Dirk's desk.

Dirk flipped through the long sheets until he found his abstract. One look and he groaned. Ruth Rudge had not only dinged it up, she'd wrecked it. It was so bad he had trouble reading it; in fact, had to read it out loud for it to make a mite of sense:

SEROLOGICAL STUDIES IN EARLY SYPHILIS
With the purpose of evaluating quantitative serologic determinations as a measure of the efficacy of various methods of treatment of early syphilis, Roosevelt Donaldson, M.D., and associates, of the Kettering Institute for Medical Research . . .

He groaned again, very loud. In twenty-eight words she'd managed to use the preposition "of" six times. That was like diluting a shot of whiskey with six jiggers of branch water. If he hadn't known what he'd written in the first place, from the longhand version he'd saved, he'd have had an awful time to make any sense at all out of what she'd written. Or rewritten. Goddam her polysyllablic hide. She had really let Dr. Rowley Simpson, editor, and his board of fellow M.D.'s change her from a one-time good newshen for the *Minneapolis Chronicle* to thicket-wordy medical mimic. He had half a notion to go in and see Ruth Rudge and resign on the grounds that working for *New Medicine* was destroying him as a journalist. But Ruth was only the managing editor. If he was going to quit he'd have to see Rowley Simpson, M.D.

He sat a while cussing to himself; finally decided not to be too precipitate (Lord! the place was infecting the very style of his thinking) and wait until tomorrow.

At five he drove to his apartment in Dinkytown and had himself a supper of salad, canned green beans, a baked sweet potato, and a thick pork chop. Then he had himself a troubled nap until six-thirty.

He arrived at the Arcola apartments a few minutes after seven. The moment he stepped into the dark vestibule, he knew it wasn't going to last with Elsie Alspaugh either. That smell of American fried potatoes and that odor of kerosene-laced insecticide. At least the manager of his own apartment house knew how to keep the hallways smelling sweet and clean.

Elsie had been waiting for him. She stood in the doorway of her apartment. "You made it."

"Sure."

"C'min. Here, let me take your coat." She led him into her living room and pointed for him to sit on the light blue davenport facing a glass-topped coffee table. "Have a seat." She'd already set out a tea service.

He settled in the far corner of the plush davenport. He sniffed the air. Inside her rooms the smell wasn't bad. She'd scented the place with some kind of lilac spray.

She brought out a large blue teapot. Steam slowly wisped up out of the spout. "Well," she said, "good to see you." The blue teapot went well with her blue silk dress.

"Here too."

"Have a good day at the office?"

"No!"

"Oh. Somebody's mad at somebody."

"I surely am. Poor Ruth Rudge. She thinks the sun rises and sets in her boss's behind."   517

"You mean Dr. Rowley Simpson?" Elsie giggled.

"Yes. That arrogant show-off. A child's vanity not yet dead in a grown man."

"That's pretty strong talk. If it ever gets back to him . . ."

"He'll fire me? Well, I'd welcome it. I'm sick down to my very bones, yeh, my balls, with *New Medicine*."

"Such language!"

"You prefer I said testicles?"

"You don't have much shame in you, do you?"

"Try me on Sunday when I'm sitting next to my mother in church."

She tested the tea. It was sufficiently steeped, and she poured them each a cup. "You never married, did you?"

"My God, is it that obvious? You're the second one to ask me that question today."

"Who was the other one?"

"We better not go into that." Dirk dropped three cubes of sugar in his tea, then stirred the brew. "And you?"

"Oh, I was married once."

"What happened?"

She closed her eyes. "We just didn't have anything in common. Except sex. I was a reader and liked library work, and he was a baseball nut and liked driving trucks. And liked pretty waitresses on the road. So that I never knew what bug he was going to bring home with him." She shook her head to herself. "Though I must say, he had the good touch on both the footfeed and the horny woman."

"So you broke up. Then what?"

"Oh, I lived alone for a while. Then I got lonesome and a friend of mine came to live with me."

"You didn't marry the new friend?"

"Oh, it was a nurse friend. She'd been married too. And it'd turned sour on her like mine did."

Dirk nodded. Men bachelors sometimes also lived together until they found the right woman. He sipped his tea. It was green tea and it tasted exactly like the tea Ma made. Several waves of memories washed through his brain. Tears almost came.

"We got along just fine," Elsie continued, brown eyes misting over in recollection. "When either one of us had a caller, we made sure the other didn't interfere." Elsie sipped her tea. "After a while, though, it came over us that actually we had more fun together than with outsiders." Elsie began the rattle on as though a teakettle in her had come to boil. "We sometimes gave each other a hug when we heard good news. Or when one of us was sorrowing over a loss. But then one evening, right after we did the dishes, she happened to hug me differently. It felt so good to be touched, it had been such a long time, that I hugged her back in the same way. So then she suggested we sleep together. In the same bed. So . . . we did."

Dirk hid his surprise. "But you're both receivers, not penetrators."

Her eyes opened. "You know, I hadn't ever thought of it that way."

"That's because you don't think like a man. When a man thinks of sex, he's thinking, I got to get into that woman and plant my seed. Not receive it."

Worry about what she'd been saying slowly narrowed her eyes. "Of course after a while it came over me what we were doing. When here I liked men best." She shook her head. "What's come over me to tell you all this?"

He shrugged. All kinds of women for some reason liked to spill their beans when around him.

"It's that confident smile of yours, I suppose. Like you know everything and haven't ever been surprised. That you're kind of a winner around women and yet don't take advantage of them. A true gentleman."

He suppressed a snort. What she meant was that he was a bull of a man who was willing to wait until she gave him the signal to make his move. He let his eyes rove around the room. They were sitting in the cone of illumination of the only light in the room. Beyond the cone he made out two tan sofas facing each other by a picture window, heirloom pictures on the grand piano in a far corner, and a huge green fern whose fronds almost reached the floor. It was all opulent like her figure. His eyes came to rest on her heavy bosom. It hit him that she wasn't wearing a brassiere. Could her breasts be that full and ride that high without support? He asked, "Where is she now?"

"She's living in Dinkytown just off University"

"Oh, where I live."

A flash of jealousy sharpened her eyes. "Thank God, she's finally found her real man."

"And now you're looking for yours."

She drew up her shoulders coyly, and in so doing the folds of her blue dress opened, exposing the upper slopes of her breasts. They were voluptuous beauties. "I guess so. Like her, I too want a baby before it's too late."

"I know what you mean. I'd like one too. I think I'd make a good father."

"Well, then maybe . . ."

"Though it would have to be with the right woman. I'm not getting married with just anybody." He thought of his beautiful sister Tressa. Elsie certainly wasn't in Tressa's class. Nor was any other woman he'd ever met. An old story. "I guess I've been too picky."

"Haha. That's been me too. I want the right to be able to live up to my full potential."

If only Tressa had dreamed of doing the same.

"More tea?"

"Please."

They sipped. They smiled at each other.

Dirk said, "May I please kiss you?"

"Why, yes." Elsie set her cup down and stood up.

Dirk had wanted to kneel beside her and embrace her and then kiss her, but on her standing up he got to his feet too. For the first time he noticed her wide very thick lips, much like his sister Mallie's. He kissed Elsie gently. There was a motion in her that suggested she'd expected him to open her lips with his tongue, but when he didn't she played demure. He broke off and smiled at her. "Lovely."

She closed her eyes.

He kissed her again, this time ardently, and she instantly opened her lips to him. Triple-lips, just like Mallie. He thought of pushing her down on the davenport. She read his thought and shook a little. "Why don't we . . . ?"

"Yes," he said. "I'd like it if you'd lie on me."

He thought of how her breasts would feel, one on each side of his nose.

She led the way to her bedroom in back. She turned on a bed lamp. Its weak light just barely silhouetted a large bed and a dresser and a vanity and black-edged pictures on the walls. She sat down on the foot end of the bed.

519

He settled beside her, tremulous. A wonderful thing was about to happen. Slowly he slid his hand around her back and over the slope of her breast. She was a hefty one all right.

She smiled thickly at him. "I better take off my dress before it gets all wrinkled. I just ironed it before you came." She stood up and, crossing her arms and taking hold of her blue dress at the hem, pulled the dress up over her head. She deftly wafted the dress over a near chair. "Maybe my slip too?"

"If you want."

She crooked her head at him. "No, that you can take off. You ought to have to fight for it a little."

Fight for it? She'd already raced ahead of him, she was so horny.

She settled beside him, smiling.

"Maybe I ought to remove my jacket and trousers. I just had them cleaned and pressed too."

"Maybe you should."

He stood up and slipped out of his dark blue jacket and folded it over another chair. He next stepped out of his trousers, and waving them up until the trouser legs flowed neatly together, draped the trousers over his jacket. "My tie too," he said.

She helped him unbutton his shirt. Their fingers twined together.

He cupped her chin and sought out her eyes. In the dusky light her eyes flashed like washed black cherries. He kissed her nose, and then her chin, and last the near corner of her lips. She shivered under his touches. To himself he wondered: "When she and this woman friend of hers made love, what did they do? What was there to do for them? Except kiss? Maybe they used a two-way dildo."

She waited until his tongue touched her teeth; then opened up and became wildly passionate. Her tongue seemed to fill out.

He pressed her back on the bed. Then, to lift their feet off the floor, both undulated toward the pillows until they could lie stretched out. They kissed. He helped her remove her silk step-ins. He slid up her slip. He cupped her breasts. They were firm and wonderfully large. She would make an ample mother. He wondered if her woman lover had large breasts too? He rather guessed her woman lover was lean like a man.

She fumbled with his shorts. He helped her push them down. She fumbled with him. She cried out a soft "ohh." One thing had to be said for her affair with another woman; she'd learned how to touch gently and deftly.

He wondered what she was exclaiming about. Craning his head in the dim light, he looked down at her hand. Actually he was only half-risen. Even as he kissed her and held her titties, even as he kissed and suckled her mother breasts as his hand sought out her mount of love, he examined how he was really feeling about her. His hand slid down and she jerked under it. So that's what they did. At least that.

"Darling!" she whispered sharply.

He thought: "I don't know if I want to get into that." He noted that his fellow was falling into a tumble of soft plums.

She began to pinch him vigorously, trying to get him to respond, to enlarge.

But it was no use. She shouldn't have told him about her woman lover. He was still too much of a Bible Belt boy to accept that. Perhaps that too was all right. He'd had a good dozen women since coming to the Twin Cities, and that probably was a wrong, but at least when it came to sophisticated sex he was still a country greenhorn. He smiled to himself when he thought about the colorful word "greenhorn" and the raunchy word "horny."

Then, thinking about her opulent flesh, he felt he should have her at least once, just to have experienced penetrating such rich flesh. He clasped her passionately, and whispered, almost desperately, "Oh, when I'm around you, oh, I want to do something wild."

She paused in her ministrations. She thought over what he'd just said. Her black eyes opened and her smile became knowing and wise. "You were saying?"

"Something."

"You were saying 'real wild'?"

He knew instantly what she meant. He was to also make love to her the way a woman might. As foreplay. His mind reached down to his loins and he saw he'd retreated completely.

She began to work him harder and harder.

Presently, shrugging in his mind, he reached down and removed her urgent hand. "It's no use, Elsie."

She hated to give up. "Perhaps if we just rest awhile. Think of something else."

"No."

"Shall I get us some wine?"

"That won't help. Besides, I don't drink."

"Let's get under the quilts and just rest. Maybe fall asleep—that'll help."

"No." The thought of her being a Minneapolis Sappho was just too much. Dirk wondered how Sappho's husband had taken Sappho's half-and-half tastes. Sappho wrote wondrous poetry, but to have stumbled in on Sappho while she was hugging a young girl must have been traumatic. And what must her husband have thought when he came upon a poem of Sappho's left carelessly on her ivory-topped vanity:

> Mother darling, I cannot work the loom,
> for sweet Kypris has almost crushed me,
> broken me with her love for a slender boy.

Dirk shivered. He remembered what a man he'd been when as a slender boy he'd climbed into heaven, into the haymow, with sister Tressa. He recalled the look of wondrous admiration in Tressa's eyes when she saw his rampant manhood. She'd been so full of love and pride for him.

Elsie felt him slowly cooling beside her. She whispered, harshly urgent, "Please don't leave me. Please. You're my one chance."

"For me it'll have to be with someone else." He sat up a little sad. "I know who it'll be with too. And I better go look her up."

"Who? Who?"

"You've read Wordsworth?"

"In college, yes."

"Did you know about him and his sister Dorothy? That she went out and took walks, and when she came back she told William what she'd seen, and so vividly, that William then wrote it up in poems?"

Elsie's eyes quirked open in wondering question.

"It's true, Elsie. That is, if one can trust William's biographers. And William's friends."

521

"So?"

"Well, after she left to live her own life, his poetry turned lifeless. Dead. It was only when they were together that they were a poet."

"Couldn't she go on writing the poems then?"

"Dorothy's writings were lifeless too. She was only the seer and he was only the maker."

"What's all that got to do with the price of our potatoes?"

He was tempted to be as open with her about Tressa as she'd been with him about her woman lover. Confession trembled at the end of his tongue. Then a sly smile moved over his face, lifting his lips at the corners, and he bit it all back. Only two people knew about Tressa and himself, and it was going to stay that way. At least so far as he was concerned. And he was sure that Tressa's tongue would remain silent too. Good thing they weren't Roman Catholics or they'd be spilling their beans to a priest in confession.

Dirk gave Elsie a few dry kisses and then he got up and put on his tie and trousers and jacket again. He snugged up his tie carefully. Then he looked down at her, trying not to look at her triangle and her luscious bosom, directing his look at her vivid flashing eyes. "I'm sorry. But I think I'm going to look up this other woman."

Elsie stuck her tongue out at him. Twice. It came out to a vibrating point, thick and purple.

"Thanks."

As he got into his car, he thought: "Thank God, as the Bible has it, I did not go in unto her and strengthen her. And unlike Onan, I didn't even have to spill it upon the ground. Or on the sheet."

He drove across Minneapolis, crossed the Mississippi on the Third Avenue bridge, headed down University into Dinkytown. The windows in the houses on either side of the street were dark. The good Nordic folk always went to bed early. In Dinkytown, though, some students were still up studying or drinking beer. Bridgeman's ice cream parlor was just closing down.

Going down Fourth Street he almost hit two drunks, a boy and a girl. He had to jerk his wheel hard right and bump up onto the curb the miss them. He backed down off the curb and stopped and got out.

"Hey, you jacks, what the hell you doing walking down the middle of the street?"

The girl, a lovely thing with long silken platinum hair, drew up one side of her slim body at Dirk. "Sir, I'll have you know I'm no Jack."

"Well, Jill then. Jack and Jill. You're damn lucky I wasn't drunk like you or I'd have run you down like a pair of deer."

The boy, dark-haired, too thin to be an athlete of any kind, wavered on his feet. "T'hell wid yuh."

Dirk went over and took them each by the arm. "Where do you live?"

The girl said, "House on th' corner there."

"Come," Dirk said. "I'll walk you there." Still holding them by the arm, he guided them down the sidewalk.

A police car pulled up. The policeman stepped out, holstering his billy club. "What's wrong here?"

"Nothing," Dirk said. "I'm just helping them get home safely. Over there." Dirk pointed.

"That your car?"

"Yes. I pulled up so I wouldn't hit them. They were walking down the middle of the street. But they'll be all right now."

The policeman, also young, pursed up his lips. "Good. But you shouldn't leave your car with the engine running like that. It could easily be stolen."

Dirk smiled his winning smile. "I know. But I was watching my car out of the back of my head."

The young officer nodded. "Okay."

Dirk helped the young couple up the steps of the house, opened the door for them, and ushered them inside. "Will you be all right now?"

"Ulp," the skinny boy said.

"Shure," the lovely blond girl said.

Dirk noted as he walked back to the car that the young officer still stood beside his patrol car to make sure all was in order before he left.

Dirk continued on home and parked his car in back of his apartment. The people upstairs, the Quists, had long ago gone to bed. They usually retired at eight and got up at five. A quiet couple, they never bothered him. Dirk was sure that they wondered sometimes about all the girls who visited him, but they said nothing. It made him wonder a little if maybe they hadn't been a bit wild too in their youth. Or else they had children who'd sown some wild oats. Occasionally a person ran into an old couple who remembered the days of their youth.

He slid into his cool sheets happy to have the day end at last. And what a day it had been. He worried a little he might not be able to fall asleep right away.

But moments after he'd nuzzled down the back of his head into the clean starched pillow he was gone. Dreamless.

The next morning, making himself a breakfast of warm oatmeal, on orange, and a cup of coffee, he shook his head when he remembered that he'd been unable with Elsie, that desire had failed him.

He mused to himself as he helped himself to a second cup of coffee. He thought again about all the parties he'd gone to the past year. "God knows I carefully checked out all the eligible girls at those parties. They weren't bad. But they weren't the right ones either. Not even Hettie Hasland."

. . . . Some of the parties were challenging. Especially those with the do-gooder crowd.

Bruce and Betty Lanning were social workers dealing with people of French descent, people who'd come down from Canada with the métis. Betty was impulsive and sexy, while Bruce always had a moderate smile for one no matter what was said in argument. Even if Bruce didn't agree at all, he managed to continue smiling and his blue eyes twinkled. Dirk had heard they'd joined the Communist party, but from their remarks he couldn't be sure.

Mark Gilmore and his girlfriend, Chris Allison, were a handsome couple, better looking even than models on Madison Avenue. They too were said to be Reds. The only time Dirk had wondered about them came when Mark Gilmore read left-wing passages from John Dos Passos's *U.S.A.* Each time Mark finished a particularly lively portion, Chris would smile all around at the faces and pronounce, "Amen."

Remus Baker, a bachelor, was generally considered the "brain" of the social-minded "friends." His demeanor was mild, with a soft-edged approach to problems. But there was a hint of a good mind in his glowing brown eyes. After Bruce and Betty, and Mark and Chris, had pretty well torn a subject apart, Remus with his soft smile would quietly put things together again, in perspective, always with a long look down past corridors of history.

People often wondered why Remus Baker had never married. He would have made a perfect accommodating husband. What they didn't know, especially the women, was that he'd been a captain in the army, and right after the Great War his unit had been sent secretly to Vladivostok in an attempt to overthrow the new Communist regime in Russia. He'd been somewhat of a rebel as a captain and had often sided with his men instead of the officers above him in the chain of command. The secret U.S. Army rarely ran into women and the result was that some of the soldiers were accused of sodomy. Remus Baker defended them. "All they were guilty of," he argued, "was that they'd been caught leaning against a mule." The experience made a left-winger out of Remus. When rumors of his defense of the sodomite soldiers spread around the Twin Cities, Remus Baker promptly married Edna Markers, professor of education at the University of Minnesota. The marriage appeared to be a good one, though probably a back-to-back one, and all his friends smiled relieved.

One Saturday there was a knock on Dirk's door. Groaning, he got up from his easy chair and set aside the book he was reading, *War and Peace.* "Let's hope it's not a woman. I'm just not up to one today. Even if she steps in here stark baby naked."

It turned out to be Remus Baker. "Busy?"

523

Dirk waved him inside. "Not really. Reading Tolstoy."

Remus's eyes opened a brilliant brown. "Ah, he's all right. Too bad he wasn't born after the Revolution. What a novel he might not have written about that event."

"Or it might have wrecked him as an artist."

"But it might also have given him an even deeper social vision."

Dirk shook his head. "Have a seat. Cup of coffee?"

"No coffee. I'm too high to start with."

Dirk sat down opposite Remus. Smiling to one side, Dirk said, "Political systems, philosophic systems, may come and go, but a good novel or a good play or a good epic lasts forever."

"And in the meantime, of course, the proletariat can starve to death."

"Not necessarily. After a great work of art has been produced, each succeeding generation can take out of it such comfort and joy as fits their time. If it's a very good work of art, it will give comfort and joy ad infinitum."

Remus fixed hard brown eyes on Dirk. "Such as?"

"*Iliad. Odyssey. Oedipus Rex. Don Quixote.*"

"Those are exceptions."

"Those are mountain peaks. Natural too."

"But meanwhile the poor keep on starving."

"But in your Socialist world everybody is going to be a well-fed pig. You hope."

"There'll be Socialist art."

Dirk sneered. "Of dubious value. Name one masterpiece."

"That's neither here nor there. We've only just started. Since 1917. Give us time."

Dirk heard a voice say in the back of his head: "This fellow has got to be a member of the party the way he talks. And he's trying to convert me. And all the others are members too!"

Remus instantly spotted that Dirk was having some misgivings about their talk, about him. Remus came up with one of his warmest smiles. "You know, Dirk, I've heard you talk so sympathetically about the underprivileged . . . really, you're more one of us than you might think."

Dirk thought: "That's what you think. If you only knew where I came from. We Freylings from Siouxland ain't much for joining anything. We're much too close a family."

Remus next smiled at the waving branches of an elm outside the windows. "Well, at least you're not against us."

Dirk said, "Did the bunch take a vote on me and send you over?"

Remus leaned forward. "There's something else I want to discuss with you. Have you ever met a woman named Hettie Hasland?"

"No."

Remus looked down at his soft hands. "There's something tragic afoot with her and Mark Gilmore. She's in love with Mark and has been thinking of taking her own life."

"Hey, I thought Mark and Chris were happy together. That there was no other problem there."

Remus shook his head. "There was a Farm-Labor party convention in Duluth last year. And both Mark and Hetty happened to be delegates. Well, one thing led to another, and finally over a beer, Hetty told Mark she'd long admired him, had been in love with him. And Mark, ah well, you know what a Lancelot he is—so damned handsome the women fall all over him, all the time. And it finally got to him."

Dirk thought: "So Remus even looked into the chance Gilmore might like him." Aloud he said, "What's this got to do with me?"

"Well, the girls tell me they think you're neat. And that you might be just right for Hettie. Date her."

"Hettie a member?"

Remus blinked. "That's really not important. But she is in general of our persuasion."

"And the bunch is worried she might blurt it out about them?"

"We want her to be happy. We all like her."

"How come she's never with the bunch when I'm there?"

"She used to be. Always. But now she stays home nights. Goes from work to her rooms in the Saint Peter Hotel in Saint Paul."

"What's she do?"

"She's an X-ray technician at the University Hospital."

"And I'm just to call her up cold?"

"No, I thought you could come for dinner with Edna and me. We'll invite her too. And then the two of you can look each other over. And if you take to each other . . ."

The male squirrel in Dirk, ever on the ready to catch the female squirrel when she might be receptive, sat up. Dirk wasn't all that excited about taking another man's leavings; but who knew, maybe this Hettie was the one he had been looking for to erase the memory of Tressa.

Dinner at the Bakers turned out to be a rather stiff affair. Edna Markers, who'd kept her name professionally, behaved like a typical doctor of philosophy, quite concerned about academic decorum. Dirk was tempted to let drop certain four-letter words in his share of the dialogue, and he would have without hesitation if it hadn't been for Hettie Hasland. He'd liked her the moment they were introduced.

Hettie was quite short, barely five feet tall, fine-featured, with everything there in proper proportion. She had a wonderfully warm smile, and it was only in moments of repose, between sallies by Dirk and Remus, that a sad expression edged into the corners of her small bud lips. She was wearing a creamy flow-ered dress, quite long, to her calves. Her brown sun-edged hair was combed back with one side caught in a glittering clasp, and her gray eyes resembled marbles carved from ivory. Every now and then she glanced up briefly at Dirk sitting across from her. It was hard to make out what she was thinking.

Over dessert, sweet sliced pears, Edna Markers relaxed a little. "Did you see the story about X-ray technicians in the paper yesterday?"

Hettie's thin brown brows came up. "You mean, the excerpt taken from the *New England Journal of Medicine*? About exposure?"

"The very one."

Hettie allowed herself a sad smile. "I don't really worry about that. If it turns out to be true that we technicians do not have the same life expectancy as the average person . . . well, so be it. I've resigned myself to it."

Remus cocked his brown eyes at her. "Why don't you protest? Demand safer working conditions? Write your state representative?"

"I suppose I should, but . . ."

Edna gave her husband Remus a cool look. "Why must you always inject politics in our dinner talk? Can't we just talk generally?"

"Yes, dear."

Dirk was quick to catch the meaning of the look exchanged between Remus and Edna. Their marriage was a back-to-back arrangement all right. They were using their marriage to cover up their true sexual proclivities. If true, then Edna had her girlfriends. Dirk smiled down at the remaining sliced pear in his dessert dish. "I have a question to ask."

"Fire," Remus said.

Dirk smiled disarmingly at Edna. "Do you happen to know Elsie Alspaugh?"

The single flicker in Edna's eyes reminded Dirk of a chicken's eye. Edna said, "No, I'm sorry, I do not."

Dirk continued to smile. "I just wondered." Edna's formal "I do not" instead of the usual "I don't" told him she did know Elsie. Hmm. Well, there was sometimes no accounting for people's tastes. He himself hardly had the right to point the finger.

Later, as they were about to leave, at the front door, Dirk turned to Hettie. "Got your car here?"

"I came over on the streetcar."

"Can I drive you home?"

"Oh, I don't mind the streetcar."

"Suit yourself. But riding with me beats standing on a corner waiting for a streetcar."

Remus watched them with a bemused alpha smile. He took Hettie's elbow. "Oh, why don't you take advantage of Dirk's offer. Then we'll know you got home safe."

Hettie's eyes sparkled. "You're sure about that now? With him?"

"Why not?"

Dirk decided he could as well use his own masterful way. He took Hettie's other elbow. "Come. My car is just around the corner. It won't take but a minute to bring you to your door."

"Well, all right."

Dirk took University Avenue through Prospect Park into Saint Paul. The front of the Montgomery Ward building was all lit up like it might be the week of the state fair. They passed a streetcar headed for downtown Saint Paul. Several autos were being unloaded in front of the shining brass doors of the Saint Peter Hotel. Dirk took a right at the next corner and parked on a side street.

Hettie broke the silence between them. "And now I have a question to ask you."

"As the cowboys say, and to fill in after the word Remus used, 'Fire and fall back.'"

"What was that all about with Edna and Elsie Alspaugh?"

He thought to himself a moment. He wondered how frank he dared to be with Hettie. If she didn't mind being frank then perhaps other things might develop. "What do you think of the marriage between Remus and Edna?"

She looked at her hands folded in her lap. "It seems to be working in its rather odd way."

"Yeh. So long as they're both looking for a piggyback pair in stud poker."

"I wondered about that too."

So she knew. Dirk played his fingers around and over the steering wheel. Somehow he had to get Hettie to invite him in for a nightcap or something.

Hettie had to laugh. "I come from a small town near Blue Wing. Almost a hundred souls. And it seems so very strange to be living here in the Twin Cities, in charge of the X-ray department at the university, knowing some wonderful bright friends, friends no one in my hometown could imagine their like. Eggheads."

"You mean the bunch?"

"Yes. Though lately I haven't been seeing much of them."

Because of Mark. "Who do you see now then?"

"No one."

"Living in a room in this old hotel, doesn't it make you feel like some sort of drummer?"

"It's true. Though I do have several nice rooms in it."

"But that can hardly be a home when you have to walk through a lobby with leather chairs full of old geezers."

"Oh, it's not that bad. Really. And it's real cheap."

"Hard to believe."

"Why don't you come in a minute and see my rooms for yourself?"

Ah, made it. "You bet."

She lived on the very top floor. She snapped on the overhead light, and he saw right away it wasn't all that bad. She had the place lined with books. And out the window to the southeast spread a spectacular view. From the nearby streetlights the curling Mississippi River could be made out, coming up from Fort Snelling and twisting through downtown Saint Paul. A tugboat was slowly nosing a coal barge up the river, the whorlings of its screw in back kicking up phosphorescent froth.

527

"No wonder," he whispered.

"Yes."

"This has got to be the best prospect in the state."

"That's what I think."

He stood admiring it some more. After a moment she sidled up to him, touching her shoulder against his upper arm.

The red male squirrel in him poked up its nose. It surprised him that she should be that ready. After knowing so many women, they still could startle him when they showed sexual interest in him. He still couldn't read their minds beforehand. Slowly he slipped an arm around her, letting it cup over her hip.

They stood warming up each other.

Finally she turned. "It's been so long. And you seem to be a sensitive understanding man. And, I like you already. Though I hadn't expected to. I only went to that dinner because Remus asked me. Specially. He's been most kind."

Dirk wondered if she'd slept with Remus. Or what. He decided not to ask her. It was their business, not his. His business was from this moment on.

He looked over her shoulder and in the dim light coming from a single lamp made out the silhouette of her bed. Surprisingly it was an extraordinarily big bed.

She sensed where he was looking. "Yes, this was part of the penthouse for a madam once. Many a man from the blue-blood families used to dally up here. The big royal bed was left in this room, thank God. It makes me think of pastures back home. Lots of room to roam in."

He nodded. For a stallion and a mare. "How did you happen to find these rooms?"

"We social workers are privy to a lot of valuable information."

He turned them both and slow-stepped her toward the big bed. He lifted her chin and kissed her lightly, just barely brushing her lips with his. After a moment she yearned up to him, pushing her lips hard onto his. He began to fumble over her.

She broke away and hid her face a moment, then turned and said, "We should probably remove our dresses."

Dresses? Who had she been with? Edna? "Yes," he said, "and me my jacket and tie."

"At least." She laughed lightly. She said again, "It's been so long. And you're so nice. I just love your smell."

His smell? When he hadn't showered before going out to dinner? Maybe this Hettie was more earthy than the bunch gave her credit for. Maybe that was why Mark had had his way with her in just three short days at a convention.

She released herself and slowly took off her dress and slip and stockings. Though she was in her middle thirties, naked her body seemed very young, even perfect. She opened up the bed on the far side and crept between the sheets.

He undressed and opened the bed on his side and slipped in beside her.

They lay facing each other, smiling a little.

She whispered, "I already know you're not coming back, you know."

He was startled. The same thought had come to him. "Now how would you know that?"

528

"It's all right. It's time I broke out of my Puritan mold again. Life keeps unrolling. The ball of yarn you're given at birth gets smaller and smaller as the days go by."

He took his time. She was so lovely and smart. And so small. Like a child just barely nubile. He owed her nothing. Yet he was going to be tender and gentle with her.

They were about to begin when she whispered, "You have a condom of course?"

"Do we need that?"

"You're not coming back, remember? And I'm not going to have the baby alone.

"Oh." He hated being interrupted at the moment of love's entrance. Sometimes the little tower just wouldn't come back.

"It's the fourteenth day for me."

"All right."

"Thank you."

The little tower stayed with him; soon all was well, and he heard the bobolink sing.

They talked in the dark, leisurely, laughing sometimes. When she brought up how much she loved Dos Passos's *U.S.A.*, Dirk knew she still was in love with Mark Gilmore. Where Chris Allison said, "Amen," Hettie said, "Selah."

He made a discovery. "Say, the condom broke."

She nuzzled against him. "It's all right. We won't worry about it."

"But you just said you were in your fourteenth day."

"Shh. Don't worry."

He considered. Well, the damage was done. Some hundred million little arrow-shaped creatures were already hunting Princess Ove inside her. Another fifty million wouldn't improve the odds much.

The next time they both heard the bobolink sing.

Early in the morning, when he said good-bye, she said good night. They kissed some more and then she quietly closed the door and he took the elevator down.

And in bed at last he slept like a dead-tired soldier. . . .

As he finished the last of his second cup of coffee, it hit him with a rush what he should do. The conviction was so deep in him that he noticed that his jaw muscles, especially those over his temples, were hard and bulging.

When Dirk walked in through the door of *New Medicine,* he asked receptionist Dodie Dodgson if Rowley Simpson happened to be in.

"Yes." With a perky laugh, she said, "Who shall I say is calling?"

"Hippocrates."

"Being the smart ass today, eh?" Dodie always sat high in the typist chair. There was an ever-watchful air about her.

"Dodie, are you still working as an undercover agent for the FBI?"

Dodie's face stiffened. "I beg your pardon."

Dirk gave her a mixed grimace. "But first something out of my office." He stepped into his cubicle, searched and found the handwritten copy of his original abstract and then the proof of Ruth Rudge's rewritten version of it. He went back out front.

Dodie said, "I guess you can go in. He's alone in there. And mad about something."

"Good. That'll put us on an equal footing."

"Gutsy, aren't you?"

Dirk knocked and stepped into Rowley Simpson's office. Dirk had often wondered how *New Medicine* could afford such an ornate office for their medical editor. What wasn't satin-varnished mahogany wood was purple plush velvet. It was a commodious room, big enough to hold a meeting for a couple dozen people. Leather-bound medical books shone in bookcases along the wall, interspersed with portraits of famous doctors, among them Sir William Osler. Rowley Simpson, M.D., sat ensconced in a purple plush swivel chair behind an enormous steel desk. The desk was bare except for a blotter and a telephone. In front of the desk were two big purple plush chairs to seat visitors. Along the window seat was an inch-thick glass coffee table. Tucked in a far corner was a black leather sofa covered on one end with flashy pillows, red and blue and purple and green.

Simpson was seated back to the door, looking through a wide window toward green Loring Park. When Simpson heard the door click shut behind him, he turned slowly in his chair and fixed black eyes on Dirk. "And to what do I owe the pleasure of your company?" His voice was slightly high-pitched, arrogant. His black hair had thinned over his forehead, enough so that his heavy black brows seemed to have thickened some. His lips were cut flat across his face. A jutting chin kept him from being handsome.

Dirk glanced at the leather sofa in the dusky corner. "I'd heard that movie moguls had casting couches in their offices, but never doctors."

"The headaches this place gives me dictate that I take a nap now and then."

Dirk nodded. "I could use a casting couch in my little office. Because this place gives me a headache too, sometimes. In fact, many times."

"Oh? How so?"

Dirk handed over the handwritten copy of his abstract and its proof.

"Thanks. Have a seat."

Dirk settled in the deep easy chair to the left of the good doctor. "The first there is my version and the second is the doctored version."

Simpson swung back and forth a little in his huge soft swivel chair as he read them both. "Well, I'll be damned. Ruth did this?"

Dirk nodded.

"Ruth's version is the more medical sounding."

Dirk nodded again. "Ruth probably means well, but I think she's too influenced by you doctors and your private jargon."

"You know of course that not many people have the gift of words. And doctors when they go to college and medical school never get a chance to take a course in medical writing."

"I gathered as much."

Simpson fixed his hard black eyes on Dirk. "Got any suggestions how we might get around that?"

"You were right to hire former newspaper people to help you put out *New Medicine.* Because they know how to write a simple declarative sentence."

"And?"

"You shouldn't let the board lean so hard on your managing editor."

"You really mean me, don't you?"

"Well, you too, yes."

530

"Hmm." Simpson read both versions carefully again. "It just happens that work on syphilis is one of my specialties. And I have to say that your version is not only the easiest to read, it is also the more accurate."

Dirk hadn't expected to hear that. "Thanks."

Simpson growled to himself several times. "You don't know this, but the reason I haven't done anything about Ruth is that I just don't have the heart to fire her. She's been treated for cancer, and is at present in a state of remission. Only she and I and her doctor, and now you, know this. As the days have gone by, she's become more and more tense, worried it might come back, and she's become overly conscientious in trying to be accurate. I didn't sleep much last night thinking about it. Wondering what I should do."

Dirk thought, "So that's why you're mad this morning."

Simpson's haggard face softened. "One of these days Ruth herself will know she should quit. Go home and relax. Do just part-time work. And when she does, I'll keep her on her present salary. She deserves it. But then, when and if she does, I've got to find a replacement." Simpson paused dramatically. "And I know just who I want too."

"Not Algernon Berry."

"Good God, no!" Simpson scraped out the bottom of his throat saying it. "He gets the ads for us. But he's going to do no more for us."

Dirk waited. It really didn't make all that much difference to him who Simpson had in mind.

"I mean you."

Dirk straightened up. "What! For godsakes not me."

"Why not?"

"Haha. I came in here just now to quit today."

"You what?"

"Quit. You know. Leave."

"But why?"

"I've made up my mind I no longer want to live in the Twin Cities. I've had it up to here. Both at work with you and socially at home."

"Even if I offer you a job here as managing editor with a raise over what Ruth got?"

"Ruth only got a woman's wage. So a raise over her's isn't going to be all that much."

"I'll raise it a third more than she's getting."

"No. I'm going back to Bonnie." Dirk had to laugh a little. "Funny thing is, this whole interview has taken a turn I didn't expect. But nevertheless, I've had it."

"Can't handle city life, huh?"

"Sure I can handle it. But I'm not going to let working here wreck me as a simple newspaperman. And I'm not interested in writing the great American novel either. Or the great American epic à la Homer. I just want to have fun running a weekly newspaper in a small town somewhere. And make it so different, and so original, with my own kind of nutsy humor, that people living in the nearby areas will want to subscribe to it too. I like the slow coffee-drinking pace of small towns."

Simpson fixed Dirk with unbelieving eyes. "You're not married, are you?"

"No. But I will be shortly. I've got her all picked out."

"I'll double Ruth's salary."

"No. No. You see, there's something else going on here too for me. I've worked here long enough to have picked up a bad habit."

"And what's that?"

"I'm starting to look at people like a doctor does."

"For example?"

"Oh, I've seen you guys at parties. You smile, and you say hello, and shake hands—all the while a voice in the back of your head is saying, 'Ah, florid complexion. Hypertension. High blood pressure. Probably dead at sixty.' Or, 'Sallow. Sour-faced. Probably got a cancer eating at him.' 'That woman coughs a lot. Flushed face. Probably got T.B.'"

"What's wrong with that?"

"Ah, I don't want to go around looking at life from the ass hole side of it."

"Ha!"

"In a small town a person can easy-does-it with that kind of interior commentary. You love people and only later, reluctantly, do you think such blue thoughts."

Simpson rocked in his swivel chair. "But we do need doctors, don't we?"

"Sure. But I don't necessarily have to think like one. I don't like to be one who was born under the sign of Saturn. A melancholic."

"Hey, hey. That's not a doctor. That's an artist. Or a painter. A sculptor. A poet. An eccentric. Bordering on madness."

"I've never known an artist. So I can't make any comment on that."

"Tell you what. I'll double Ruth's salary and give you some stock in the New Medicine Enterprises. It's going to be very valuable property someday."

"I'm not even close to being tempted. But thank you for the offer." A laugh

531

rose to Dirk's lips. "Like I say, this session with you has taken a turn I never expected. Really. I thought maybe you and I would have one hell of an argument. In fact, I kinda looked forward to insulting you. Telling you off. But instead . . ."

"Yeh. I've had that happen to me. So little do we really know about each other."

Dirk got to his feet. "So little are we observant in the first place."

"Yeh." Simpson got to his feet too.

They shook hands. The doctor had a firm warm handshake. It was the kind of handshake that made one trust him as a doctor.

Out in the hallway again, Dodie Dodgson looked up. "Well. No bloody nose I see."

Dirk slowly let himself smile. "No. Not at all. In fact, for the first time I found myself liking the good doctor. Too bad too, since I'm leaving this joint."

"Oh, no."

Dirk nodded. "Could you have my final check made out to me by two this afternoon? There's some things I've got to take care of in my office first. And lunch. And after that, at two, I'll be on my way."

"Will do." Her face wrinkled up in disappointment. There was a hint in the way her lips shaped at the corners that she'd once hoped he might have shown some interest in her.

The look was not lost on Dirk. "Sorry. But that's the way it's gotta be. At long last I've finally got up my guts to do what I should have done in the first place. And damn the consequences. Even if it is against Jesus Christ."

"Some lucky woman somewhere?"

"That's right."

Dirk left the Twin Cities around five. At two he'd cashed his last *New Medicine* check, then withdrew all his money at the First National Bank and went to a Ford dealer and traded in his old Ford for a new blue-gray Mercury, and finally packed his clothes and such books as he wanted to keep. Beside him on the car seat lay his red *Wordsworth Poems*. The volume bristled with slips of paper for bookmarks.

As he emerged from under the viaduct south of Shakopee and rose toward a sunlit tableland spreading out to Jordan, he recited aloud a favorite passage from Wordsworth:

> "There was a time when meadow, grove, and stream,
> The earth, and every common sight,
>   To me did seem
>   Apparelled in celestial light,
> The glory and the freshness of a dream. . . .
> Our birth is but a sleep and a forgetting:
> The Soul that rises with us, our life's Star,
>   Hath had elsewhere its setting,
>   And cometh from afar:
>   Not in entire forgetfulness,
>   And not in utter nakedness,
> But trailing clouds of glory do we come

From God, who is our home:
Heaven lies about us in our infancy!
Shades of the prison-house begin to close
    Upon the growing Boy,
But He beholds the light, and whence it flows,
    He sees it in his joy;
The Youth, who daily farther from the east
    Must travel, still is Nature's Priest,
    And by his vision splendid
    Is on his way attended. . . ."

Dirk could just see Old Will sitting at his oak desk next to a window, looking out over the path leading down to an English lake and wondering what to write next; when, suddenly seeing sister Dorothy come strolling back to the house from one of her walks over the moor, hair shiny with dew and falling to her shoulders, her stride willowly, Old Will, young again and in love with his sister, seizing his pen and dipping it in his inkwell—Dirk could just see Old Will begin writing. For there, there came Will's sister "trailing clouds of glory," her head full of the poetry he'd soon transcribe onto paper.

Dirk could also just see Dorothy. Clear-eyed and beautiful. Dorothy must've resembled Tressa. Dirk had often seen Tressa walking just that way as she came up from the barn, or emerging from a patch of weeds behind the corn crib carrying a basket of fresh eggs, a wondering parted-lip smile on her pure pink face. Seeing that artless look a man just had to go over and kiss her, and treasure her, and lift her to the stars.

Dirk had often wondered too about the way a girl, a woman, walked. They didn't have to be concerned about where they wore their pudenda, stuffed into the top of the left trouser leg or the top of the right trouser leg. They could just stride forth with both trouser legs equally free and roomy. In fact, a woman should be more able to stride or run straight off from the hips than a man since she had no impediment hanging in the way.

Rolling through Belle Plaine, he recalled again that heaventime up in the haymow. He saw once more how he'd hugged Tressa from behind, held her firm young breasts full in his hands, the yeasty smell of just-poured milk rising in their faces, filling his hand with the wonder of her valley of wet delight, taking her curved offer, smelling the dried wild-rose blossoms in the compacted alfalfa hay.

They should not have done it. It was wrong. But they had done it. Out of grave child love. And now there was no possible way they could ever undo what had happened.

"So why not live it out?" He said aloud. "A great love far outweighs taboo." He pounded the new-smelling steering wheel. "And godblessit"—he almost said "goddammit"—"I want to live for a little while with the only woman I ever loved."

He arrived at Tressa's door at eleven o'clock. A light was still on in her kitchen. Standing on his toes, looking over some bridal wreath bushes, he saw Tressa's hands in the kitchen sink. He raised himself even higher to see if Wallie Starnes was still up. Wallie was nowhere in sight.

533

Without knocking he quietly stepped into the kitchen. "Hello, Hufty."

"Dirk!" Tressa exclaimed in a harsh whisper. Quickly she held a finger to her lips. "Wallie's asleep."

"So I guessed," he whispered back.

"My! you scared me."

He laughed. He noticed how young she still looked. There was an air about her suggesting that not too long ago some man had fulfilled her. He hoped it wasn't true. "Listen," he went on whispering, "listen, I've come to get you. Do you think you can slip into your bedroom and quietly pack some clothes without waking Wallie?"

"Wallie sleeps like a dying frog, he makes so much noise snoring. But what in the world you got in mind?"

He stood close to her. He trembled like some young boy wondering if he dared to kiss a girl for the first time. He longed to take her in his arms. She still had her hands in the sink water, and slowly he approached her from behind and, as he'd done once before, slipped his hands cuppingly around her waist and then up around her breasts. He was surprised there still was a yeasty smell about her.

"Dirk!" She looked out the window into the darkness. "Somebody will see us."

"Get your clothes. You and I are eloping."

"For goodness sakes, Dirk."

"You still love me, don't you?"

"Of course I love you. Like a sister should love a brother."

"No more than that?"

"Oh, Dirk, that was so long ago."

He drew her firmly against him. How he loved her. "Get your clothes. We're going."

"What about all your girlfriends? Won't they be heartbroken?"

"That's exactly what I've been all my life. Heartbroken. So have you. All because as kids we didn't have the guts to run off somewhere and just disappear."

"But where will we go? If we do go."

"It can't be the Bad Lands. Though it would be hard to find us there. But there's no town in it big enough to support a weekly newspaper."

Tressa turned in his arms. "Oh, Dirk, I've so often dreamed you'd show up in the night like this and come and get me."

"Then you'll really go?"

"Yes. I have to get out of this town. I just can't stand working on Main Street anymore. Or go to church feeling the way I do. Every Sunday I'm a worse hypocrite."

Dirk let go with a great sigh. "Get your clothes then."

"No. Let's just go this way. I might wake him up and that would be awful now. I'll just grab my new blue spring coat out in the hall and go."

"All right."

Excited, their breathing labored, sometimes coughing a little, they set out for the wilds.

52. Mallie

1941

Mallie had just got home from work and had hung up her sweater, when the phone rang on the little stand by the radio. "Mallie?" It was Geoffrey. There was an urgent note in his voice.

"Something the matter?"

"Could you come over right away?"

Oh, dear. She'd been looking forward to an evening of taking it easy, having a light supper, and listening to a mystery hour on the radio. But she loved her brother Geoffrey and his wife, Adela, and she loved especially their two little boys, Tyrone and Vincent. Adela had had the two children within a year and a half so that they'd grow up together, help raise each other; and then Adela had said she'd have no more. She once whispered to Mallie, though, that she wasn't going to cheat or deny Geoffrey of his bed rights, a phrase that Pa had sometimes used.

"Did you hear me, Mallie?"

"Yes, I heard you. Is it really important?"

"Very. Ma broke her leg."

"I'll be right over."

"Do that. Meantime, I'll get hold of Thea so she'll be ready to go along."

Mallie quickly made herself a thick sandwich of lettuce and cold beef. She took a big bite and then slipped into her sweater and went out to her new Chevie. She finished eating the sandwich on the way over, going east out of Sioux Falls on Highway 16 to Whitebone.

Geoffrey and Adela lived in the old stately Lavery house on Estey Street. There were three floors: living area on the first floor, bedrooms on the second floor, and a dance hall with an ornate bar on the third floor. The front door was a huge oak affair, with tall narrow side windows and an old-style brass knocker. Inside, the furniture wasn't new, but it was elegant, things Adela had brought down from her father's house on Mount Curve, things his second wife didn't fancy. There was an air of moneyed ease in the hallway and in the living room.

The moment Mallie stepped inside, the two little boys, six and seven, came running up and began hugging her, each taking a leg, raising her green dress a little. They hugged so hard, and came onto her so hard, all three almost fell to the floor. Both boys were dressed in neat blue coveralls and new brown shoes.

"Hey, hey." Mallie laughed.

Geoffrey, then Adela and Thea, came out of the library. Geoffrey had a grave smile for her, as did Thea, while Adela's face was noncommittal. Geoffrey, who was now forty, was beginning to show gray is his rusty blond hair. There were also high thin lines beginning to work back and down from his eyes. But Thea always surprised one by how young she looked despite the tragedy in her life. She would probably always look twenty years younger than her real age. Adela was well groomed and she too would always look young.

Tyrone looked up at all the tall ones surrounding him. Blue eyes big, just dying to tell what he knew, Tyrone said, "Gramma's hurted herself."

Geoffrey ruffled up Tyrone's light gold hair. He smiled gravely with love, down at his oldest. "Yes, Gramma broke her right leg. Thighbone."

Mallie asked, "How did that happen?"

"She had an accident," Geoffrey said. "Seems she went outside in her nightgown during the night and fell over the shoe cleaner. She called to her neighbors and luckily the town marshall happened by and found her." Geoffrey shook his head. "Really! What's going on with us Freylings? What with Pa vanishing without a trace. And then Dirk and Tressa disappearing. The crazy fools."

"And still no word of them either? Like Pa?"

"Not a word. I've twice talked to Dirk's boss at *New Medicine,* and all he can tell me is that Dirk resigned. And all his landlady can tell me is that he came home with a new car one day, packed up some of his possessions, giving the rest to the Goodwill people, and left with no forwarding address. And Tressa? Well, Wallie Starnes says when he went to bed she was busy cleaning up the kitchen. When he awoke around three, alone in bed, he got up and couldn't find her. He thinks she left of her own free will because her spring coat in the hall was gone. He says he vaguely remembers hearing her talk to some man. Though he isn't sure but what he might have dreamt that."

Mallie shook her head. "It sure is funny." When little blond Vincent tugged at her hand, she looked down at him.

"Yes, honeyboy, what is it?"

Vincent looked like he might be Tyrone's twin. "Gramma hurted herself."

"Yes, honey."

Geoffrey brushed back his graying forelock. "Anyway, I guess all that sad stuff started working on Ma, and over the last months she started having nightmares, and then finally took to walking in her sleep. That must have been how she got outside. It's just a good thing the town marshall came by."

"Dear God."

"Pa's disappearance she took awful hard. But Dirk and Tressa's disappearance really threw her. She's got the real Siouxland blues now."

Mallie nodded. "Well, are we all going down, our two little boys too?"

Geoffrey frowned. "No, I don't think so. Adela says she'll stay here with them until we get back."

"Well, let's go then. We can all ride in my new car."

"No," Geoffrey said. "Listen, I'm thinking of buying a new car too. A black Packard in town here. They tell me I can give it a trial run to see if I really want it. So let's take the Packard."

"Did you get in touch with the others?"

"Tane and Rolf are already there. And Ana we couldn't locate. She's mixed up in a lawsuit out in Pine Ridge with the BIA."

"Lawsuit? Our Ana?"

"Yes. And for her to be fighting in the one she's in"—Geoffrey shook his head in bewilderment—"is damned peculiar. You know what kind of fanatic Christian she is. Well, here she's fighting the Bureau of Indian Affairs to make them let the Oglala Sioux worship in their own heathen manner. Piercing the skin at the sundance ceremony."

Mallie nodded. "I know. The last time I saw her she talked like she's got that piercing mixed up with Christ being nailed on the cross."

Thea said, "Maybe it's good Ana couldn't come. I don't think Tane would appreciate her theory about piercing being like Christ getting crucified."

Geoffrey said, "She wanted me to represent the Oglalas. But I don't know. A lawyer should really never, if possible, get involved with family when it comes to lawsuits. Can't think objectively."

Adela smiled at Mallie. "I urged Geoffrey to go take it though. Every lawyer should once in his life fight the government. If only to make sure there is still a sense of justice in the land."

Geoffrey said, "Well, let's go. I'll call the garage to bring that Packard around."

Mallie sat in back with sister Thea. Every now and then the two sisters touched hands. Riding in the back seat of the black Packard was a luxury. It was like riding in a long boat on smooth waters. The smell of fresh leather was strong in the car. Mallie kept looking out of the left window in back and Thea out of the right. It was always a lovely thing to be riding down the Big Rock River Valley in the summertime. The sloping grainfields were turning to gold and the cornfields had just tasseled out.

Geoffrey said over his shoulder, as they crossed the river near Lakewood, "Ma shouldn't really be living alone like that."

Mallie said, "Too bad she didn't get married again."

Geoffrey said, "Ma? Never. She still thinks Pa will come back someday. Tane and I had an awful time getting her to ask the court to declare him dead, so Tane could rightfully buy up the old homestead. What finally convinced her to go ahead with it was when we told her if Tane owned the section there'd be less chance of him being drafted to go help fight Hitler."

"You Freyling boys were all lucky not to be drafted."

"Yep. Too old, except for me."

"I never did get straight why you weren't."

"Oh, I'm still one-D and can still get called up."

The long black Packard swooped over the last rise in the land, and below lay Bonnie on a slope, with beyond it thick groves of trees along the Big Rock River. The sun was just setting on the west hills, a huge ball of irregularly wound red yarn bouncing a few times on the brown land.

As they pulled up in front of Ma's house they found Tane and Rolf sitting on the front steps waiting for them. The two brothers got to their feet as Mallie and Thea and Geoffrey stepped out of the car.

Rolf said, "Well, the stylish Freylings, at last."

Tane had his usual wide smile. "What held you guys up? That fancy rig break down on you?"

"What!" Geoffrey said. "Packards last forever."

Rolf shook his head. "Here I am, rich, and yet I never once thought of buying me a Rockefeller Packard."

"I haven't bought it yet."

Tane rocked back and forth on his feet. "Well, you better come in. We just sent the nurse home. But she'll be back later when we leave."

Tane ushered them into Ma's bedroom. Light from two small lamps gave the large bedroom a homey touch. The soft illumination made Ma seem ten years younger. Her round face was smooth and pink. Only her grave gray eyes betrayed her age. And her grief. And her last hurt, the broken thighbone. Most remarkable of all, there wasn't a bit of gray in her bun of auburn hair.

Thea and Mallie sat on the only two chairs and the three boys stood lined up behind them. All five stared at Ma.

Ma looked at each face in turn. "No one's seen Dirk or Tressa?"

"Nope."

"They still haven't got in touch with you, Geoffrey?"

"No."

Ma fingered the edge of the white silk bedspread. "When Tressa was last here she coughed a lot."

No one said a word.

"Who saw Dirk last?"

Geoffrey finally said, "I guess I did. When I was in Minneapolis on a case."

"How did he look?"

"Hmm. Fine."

"Did you notice him coughing a lot?"

"Nnn, yeh. Like usual. With his asthma, you know."

"Maybe they both went to Arizona. That's supposed to be a good place for asthma. Since they both suffered from it so."

"Yes, Ma."

Mallie could feel herself breaking apart. Poor Ma. It was wrong that she lived alone. "How did it really happen, Ma?"

"Like I told Geoffrey already. I woke up outdoors with my leg cracked. And when I called out for help to the neighbors, the marshall happened by and he got the doctor. Afters, I had an awful headache from that nightmare I had."

Mallie wasn't sure she wanted to know about the nightmare. The Lord only knew what went on in Mother's mind. "Does your leg hurt now?"

Ma said, "It was such a funny nightmare. Dirk was chasing Tressa with a club and Pa was chasing after Dirk with that little revolver we found in the old fireplace hiding place. And I was chasing after Pa with a block of ice. Now why should I be after Pa with ice?" Ma shook her head, as if trying hard to rid herself of the awful picture she had in her mind. "It was all so sad-feeling. And there was so much yelling going on."

Mallie said, "Well, it's over now and everything is going to be all right."

Ma said, "The nurse said she could come only one more night."

"One more night? Who will be here to help you after that?"

"No one. Unless Greta can come. If Rolf will let her."

Rolf shook his outthrust head. "No, Walter needs her now. But we've been scouring the town for some kind of girl to help you out, Ma."

Mallie said, "Why can't the nurse keep coming?"

Rolf said, "Doc took her temporarily away from Old Pete Berger in the first place. He's worse off than Ma is. He had a stroke."

Ma kept staring straight ahead, eyes focused on an invisible image sightly above all their heads. "Did you notice him coughing a lot?"

Geoffrey blinked, cast a sidelong glance at Mallie. "A little, Ma. With his asthma, you know."

Mallie was careful not to look at any one but Ma. If Ma caught her children exchanging knowing looks about her not remembering what she'd already said, she'd catch on something was wrong with her mind. How pathetic. Mallie had to fight off tears. Her eyes traced out the outline of Ma's stubby body under the quilts. Mallie asked, "What kind of tests did the doctor give you, Ma?"

"Tests? Tests?" For a moment Ma's eyes fixed on Mallie's mouth. "He just put a cast on my leg, is all."

Geoffrey glanced down at Mallie. "You mean a test like, say, an X ray?"

Mallie nodded. "Besides your leg, did they check any other part of you?"

"Just my leg."

Mallie looked up at her brothers. For the first time it really struck her that they were all beginning to show age, wrinkles working back from the corners of their eyes and from their lips. And there were the slightly stooped shoulders. The day would soon come when all the Freylings would be dead. One was probably already dead. Mallie had privately come to believe that Pa had come to a bad end. Foul play of some kind in that wild Sioux City. If Dirk and Tressa had gone off together, they too were as good as dead. A profound sadness swept through Mallie. For herself, what was there to live for? It was obvious that she wasn't going to get a husband in time to have children.

Ma stared at something high in the corner of the bedroom. "Did you notice him coughing a lot?"

No one said a word.

"When Tressa was here last she coughed a lot."

Tane frowned, blond brows almost touching above his nose. "You already said that Ma, for godsakes."

Ma spoke sharply, "I did not."

Mallie said to Thea, "Why don't you and I go make us some coffee?"

"Sure," Ma said, "do that. I think there's still plenty in the cupboard. And I think I still got some chocolate cake in the breadbox."

539

"Good idea," Geoffrey said quickly. "I can use a cup to keep me awake driving home."

In the kitchen, Thea set out cups and saucers, and Mallie put on the coffeepot. The two daughters cried a little together.

Finally Thea said, "I think maybe I better quit my job at the Palace Theater and come home and help Ma. She's failing and she needs someone around to make sure she doesn't really hurt herself."

"I hear your boss likes your work."

"Yes, he does. But Ma needs me more."

Mallie said, "Well, this confusion of hers, that's only going to be temporary. She'll straighten out. After all, she probably got an awful bump on her head."

"Let alone an awful shock to her heart. The way she keeps talking about those two and their asthma."

Mallie considered. She let her eyes fix on the delft creamer and sugar. "I just wish I knew what is in Ma's mind behind those questions. She's thinking something private about those two."

Thea shuddered. "I don't know if I want to get into that."

"Me neither. But we have to consider what Ma's really thinking. And if it is what I hope it isn't, we're gonna have to talk her out of it. Or else slowly smooth it over."

Thea found the chocolate cake and began cutting it into slices. "It makes one wonder, doesn't it, what was going on in Pa's mind when he disappeared. We he fretting over those two too? Or was he thinking about some other trouble in our family?"

Mallie cried. She'd loved her father. "I've often wondered about that myself."

Thea put aside the cake knife. "Well, it's agreed then that I quit my job and come live with Ma?"

The coffee began to perk on the gas burner.

Mallie turned the burner down. "No. Not you. I'm gonna live with Ma. She may need a nurse for a couple of months, not just a maid, and what better than that I should be that nurse? My life has turned pretty sour too. Empty. I just work and save money and not much else. Have no social life in Sioux Falls at all any more. And living here with Ma, I'd have some again. Watch Rolf's Walter grow up. See Tane and his kids a lot. Which I don't do now. Be at the center of things in the family again. Be here should we ever get word from Dirk or Tressa. And intercept that word if it was something Ma shouldn't know about. Because obviously it wasn't the fall so much that's made Ma rattled, it's what she thinks Dirk and Tressa have done."

"Are you sure you want to quit your job at the hospital? Many a woman couldn't have got that far no matter how hard she tried. In this man's world."

"I'm sure. And then too, suppose we finally get word of what happened to Pa, shouldn't I be here to have a look at that first?"

"You're right. But I'm willing to quit my job at the Palace for Ma's sake."

Mallie smiled warm and sweet. "Oh, Thea, you've had such a rough time with life, you deserve a break. You're doing so well with Hilary Jessup. One of these days he'll have a good look at you and then he'll pop the question."

"Oh. Him. I don't think the thought's ever crossed his mind."

Mallie laughed. "What is it they say? 'There may be snow on the roof, but there's still fire in the furnace.'"

"Nah."

"Anyway, Sis, I'm kind of sick of my job. At first it's a wonderful feeling to help people get back on their feet. Through special exercises. Smiling and encouraging them. But after a while there are no more surprises. Same thing over and over. Same stale jokes by one's colleagues. Same kind of doctors, young punks, who try to get a free feel once in a while. Sometimes even the old bucks try to sneak a peek into your blouse. No, I'm sick of it and I want to quit. And if I need some spending money, I can now and then take on a local case. I've got a license to do so."

"You really want to do this, Mallie?"

"Yes. I'll resign my job tomorrow morning. I'll tell them there's a family emergency. I can be here with Ma tomorrow night."

"Well, all right then."

The Freylings were all well into their coffee and cake when Mallie made her announcement. "And," she added, "I can move into the guest room Ma has here with that separate bath. Ma and I are both living alone at the moment and that isn't right. Or good. Living together we won't have to feel so lonesome anymore."

Ma's face brightened wonderfully. "Really, Mallie?"

"Yes, Sweetie, now the two of us can at least live for each other."

53. Rolf

1946

In ten years the boy, Walter, grew up to be a healthy fellow. He resembled Fannie, his mother, more than he did his father Wallie Moon. He had almost pure white hair with brown brows and brown eyes. And mostly he was a good boy.

Walter went to the public school and was loved by his teachers. He was at the top of his class. He helped his father Rolf with the upkeep of their yard, mowing the grass and clipping the bushes and weeding their small kitchen garden. He kept a neat room upstairs. Sometimes he even made his own bed. Both Rolf and Greta couldn't believe their luck in having such a well-behaved boy. Rolf had been afraid he'd have to lay down some rules and then get after the boy to obey them. But Walter just had to hear something once and after that no bother.

Once when Rolf asked him how come he didn't backtalk like his chums sometimes did with their parents, Walter said, "I'm not wasting my time arguing to get my way when I know I'm wrong in the first place."

Rolf liked to brag about the boy, sometimes so lustily that both Tane and Geoffrey in mock disgust would hold their noses to suggest Rolf was piling it on pretty high again. They liked the boy but didn't like Rolf's bull about him.

Tane finally had to remind Rolf that he'd once sneered at the boy's real mother for having fornicated with a man who was old enough to be her grandfather. Where were all those hard words now?

Rolf growled, "I guess I can change my mind."

Greta clicked her teeth and smiled over it all.

One day Walter came home late from school. He came into the house just as Greta was setting the boiled potatoes and the broiled steaks on the table.

Rolf put aside the Sioux City *Journal* he was reading. "Well, Mother, I see our boy finally got the teacher mad and she made him stay after school."

Walter was so sweaty his hair had taken on the gray cast of soaked white chicken feathers. Sweat hung in drops from the point of his smooth pink chin. "Sorry I'm late. But coach said we had to play out the tie."

"Coach? Tie?"

Greta slowly began to wring her hands.

Walter said, "Yes, our baseball coach."

"You mean to say you're playing baseball?"

"Yes, Dad. Isn't that all right?"

"No, it ain't all right. None of us Freylings ever played sports. Ball-and-bat. Foot-te-ball. Those are games for children who have nothing else to do."

Greta sat down on her end of the table. "Isn't Walter still a child?"

Rolf said, "Child or not, I don't want him to get to like it. Because if he does, he'll become one of those bums who play for a living. And be of no good for business."

Walter stood slender near his chair. "But Dad, baseball is fun. And it's good for me. I get exercise out in the sun. Builds up my body. I want to be strong like you some day."

"Boy—"

Greta broke in. "Rolf, let the boy play. Thea's husband was a great player."

"Yeh, and look what it got him."

"He didn't die from baseball. It was from being gassed in the war."

"Well, I don't care. It's still a child's game—"

Again Greta dared to break in. "I don't think you understand what an honor it is that the coach has him playing. It's the high school team he's playing for and not just the grade school team."

Rolf stared at his boy. Spittle gathered in the crease in the middle of his thick lower lip, then formed a drop and fell on his shirt front. "You're good enough at ten to play with eighteen-year-olds?"

"Yes, Dad. They got me playing shortstop."

"Well, I swear."

Greta clicked her false teeth. "He's good, Rolf. In another year or two he'll be the best one on the high school team. His coach says."

Rolf glared at Greta. "You've been talking to the coach without telling me?"

"Well, I didn't go to the high school to talk to him. I met him at his wife's tea party. For the Bonnie Boosters."

"Oh." Rolf sucked in a second drop forming on his lower lip. "What kind of teams do you play, boy?"

542

Walter shuffled his feet. He didn't like to boast. "Oh, Rock Falls, Wodan, Sioux Center. And if we win enough games, we may even go to the state tournament."

"You mean, of the state of Iowa?"

"That's right, Dad."

"Man alive, that's hard to believe." Rolf toyed with his fork. He screwed up his eyes into little pig gimlets. "All right, go play ball-and-bat. But you got to promise me one thing. When you start high school, I want you to take all the courses you can in business. Because someday I'll need you to help me run my empire. And I got a big one, boy."

"Sure, Dad."

"Just a minute," Greta said. "Maybe he won't like business courses. Then what?"

"A son always follows his father." Rolf managed to smile at Walter. "Now, go wash off all that sweat. Meat's getting cold."

Rolf went to see Walter's home games. Rolf didn't understand the game, didn't care to learn, but he did clap his hands when everybody else cheered his boy's exploits.

A year later, going over Walter's report card, Rolf spotted a new course the boy was taking. Art.

"Hey, what's this art stuff you're taking?"

Walter brushed back his sun-blanced hair. "It's a course the teacher gave me to keep me busy. I get my lessons so easy I sometimes have nothing to do."

Rolf fixed a look at Greta. "You know about this?"

Greta gave Rolf a toothy smile. "Yes. I met her in Tillman's Mercantile the other day and she asked me if it was all right to show him how to sculpt. She saw him whittling with his jackknife on the schoolyard one day, making a stick doll. And since sculpting is her hobby, she thought it might be nice to show him the tricks of the trade."

"My kid taking up sculpting? My God in heaven, what's the world coming to?" Rolf shook his head. "Whittling is okay. 'Cause it helps you think. But sculpting?"

Greta allowed herself a cunning monkey smile. "Would we know what Jesus looked like if somebody back then hadn't made a sculpture of him? Or a painting?"

Rolf swore silently to himself. Damn. Her and her college education. When already a woman had enough woman arguments a man had trouble handling in the first place.

"Not, husband?"

"Well, yeh, I guess so."

"I see no harm in it, Rolf. I know you want to be proud of the boy. And so do I. For his own self's sake." She smiled to herself. "Wouldn't it be wonderful if our boy turned out to be our American Michelangelo?"

Rolf had heard their preacher mention Michelangelo's statuary. What? He was sitting on a boy who was going to be great like that?

"Ha, Rolf?"

Silence.

"Pa?"

"Oh, all right. But I tell you one thing, boy. When you get started cutting stone, I want you first to make a fancy gravestone for me and your ma. And of course your real ma, Fanny. With flowers cut on 'em."

543

Greta's eyes opened, resembling big white onions. "For heaven's sake, Rolf. I didn't know you ever paid attention to gravestones."

"Well, yah, sometimes I go to our cemetery and just look around a little."

"Really, Rolf?"

The boy Walter stared at his father. "Why would you do that, Pa?"

"Well, not that it means anything. But I sometimes wish that if my own pa was really dead—and I myself believe he is dead, not just missing—how nice it would be if we'd put up a gravestone for him, like about so high and so wide, with his name cut nice into it, Tunis Freyling, with flowers notched around it, along the edges, like so, how nice that would be."

Greta's mouth fell open, her uppers loosening a little.

Walter said, "Sure, Pa. I'd like that too. And someday I'll do it. But first I got to get good at it."

Rolf came down on the table with both his elbows, heavy. "You bet, boy. That's the way to think. Work at it first until you're good. And then do it. You're a boy after my own heart."

"Then I can keep on playing baseball? And learn how to cut stone? If I get to be good at business accounting?"

"All you want. I don't want you to grow up a sourpuss. Or get to be a scoffer like my brother Dirk."

54. Ana

1947

Ana lived with an Oglala Dakota family some ten miles northwest of Pine Ridge, a father and a mother, both thirty years old, and both high school teachers. They had two children, a girl of eleven and a boy of ten, both hers by a previous marriage. The father and mother still had Indian names, Mark Stone and Bright Puccoon, with their last name Let Enemy Run. Their children's first names were American, Lisa and Tommy.

When Mark Stone learned that Ana was more on their side than she was for the Bureau of Indian Affairs, he offered her a room in his bungalow. He told her he wasn't sure he liked her brand of religion, since he still believed in his own Indian religion with Wakantanka his god who was all spirit that underlay all things. What caught his eye was Ana's belief that the Oglala piercing at their sundance was almost the same thing as Christ being crucified so that mankind might be purified. Also that she said it in public at Christian worship. Further, when he learned from one of his Indian police friends that the BIA agent at Pine Ridge was heard to mutter in his beer that Ana should be shot on sight, he made it a point to be friends with her. He'd offer her protection.

Mark Stone's house was a redwood cottage. When he and his family sometimes sat on the porch facing west in the evening, the sun shining on them, their faces and the backs of their hands were the same color as the redwood. Both Mark Stone and Bright Puccoon often spoke of the redwood as Indianwood, with a little smile, and a slight nod in the direction of where Wakantanka lived, which was everywhere.

Their cottage had been set on a very high hill, with the land around sloping down and away in all directions. The sharpest descent was toward Wounded Knee. Mark Stone owned the house but not the land. The land belonged to the tribe of Oglalas. The BIA, however, paid no attention to the idea that the Oglalas owned the land. They graded roads across it, drove their jeeps everywhere, even on occasion ran telephone lines with tall poles across the Indian terrain without permits. Once when there had been an intertribal fight between two political factions, the BIA called the FBI to arrest the leaders. When the leaders made up their differences and turned on the FBI, the FBI brought their guns, including small cannon and machine guns. They built a concrete bunker with firing slits some forty feet from Mark Stone's wooden porch. For a week Mark Stone had the rare privilege of watching FBI sharpshooters firing down at his Oglala relatives living in Wounded Knee. When Ana came to live with Mark Stone, he showed her where the empty shells still lay outside the concrete casements. Mark Stone had ordered his wife and children not to pick up the empty shells and casings. He wanted them to lie just where they'd been ejected, untouched, so that people in after generations might see what the white man had done on red reservation land. Or at least so long as the shells resisted rust.

The story outraged Ana.

. . . . Ana never forgot the first time she came to visit the Let Enemy Runs. Mark Stone excused himself from teaching that afternoon to bring her to his cottage, only to find that his wife, Bright Puccoon, wasn't home. Bright Puccoon hadn't felt well that morning so he'd gone on to the high school without her. He called for her all around the house, worried that she'd been attacked by the raping white FBI. Finally he guessed that she'd walked down to Wounded Knee to get some groceries for company dinner. He shook his head. "Like always, she'll buy too much. And then will try to carry it all home. Uphill. I better go get her with the car." He told Ana to make herself to home, and if she wanted to take a nap to go ahead and lie down on his and his wife's bed. "You can at least nap until our kids come home from school."

Ana did stretch out on their bed. She was tired, not so much from work at the mission as she was from tension. She'd just dropped off to sleep when she heard the door on the porch side of the house open. She glanced at her watch. Two-thirty. Who in the world? It couldn't be one of the BIA men, or the FBI, sneaking into the house to snoop through the Let Enemy Run possessions, could it? Her heart began to beat loudly.

Then she heard whispering. It had to be Mark Stone's children, Lisa and Tommy, home early from school. Ana cracked open her off eye, looking past her nose. Sure enough. Two bronzy red faces with cherry bright eyes were staring at her from around the edge of the door.

Lisa said, "Remember what Dad said. No noise. The white lady is our friend and we must let her feel t' home."

Tommy said, "I know that. You don't have to tell me that."

"Shh, not so loud."

"Shh, yourself."

Ana couldn't help but smile. It was exactly like the whispering of her brothers and sisters long ago. With some reluctance, and though she still felt sleepy, she sat up. "Hello."

The bronze faces instantly lighted up in smiles.

"You're awake," Lisa said.

Ana rubbed her eyes. "I guess I am." She smiled. What lovely creatures of God. "School let out early?"

Lisa said, "Yes. Dad just now met us and told us to be real still. But now we don't have to."

"No, I guess not."

"Dad says you got such white hair," Lisa said.

Ana smiled some more.

Tommy said, "He said your skin was covered with real slick mouse fuzz."

Ana laughed aloud. "Yes, you people are the lucky ones. God decided to give you color but us some fuzz."

Tommy said, "I'm coloring in school. Teacher gave us new colors this morning."

"Did you bring your coloring home with you?"

Tommy shook his head.

Lisa said, "Teacher took Tommy's coloring and pasted it up on the wall, it was so good."

Ana said, "How wonderful. Maybe Tommy is going to be a great artist someday."

Tommy said, "Can you read us some stories?"

Ana got to her feet. "Sure. What story do you want me to read?"

"Little Red Ridinghood." Tommy ran to get the book. The book turned out to be spotted with drops of some kind of pop. Tommy said, "Dad always sits in his easy chair and lets us sit on the arms while he reads."

Soon all three were in the leather easy chair facing the bay window overlooking Wounded Knee.

Lisa let her cheek touch Ana's right shoulder and Tommy nuzzled against Ana's left arm. Ana had to blink away tears. If she had decided to have children this was the way she would have wanted them to take to her. Having the children would have been well worth the disgust of having a man touch her.

When Mark Stone and Bright Puccoon came home an hour later, carrying groceries, they found Ana deep in the reading of *The Story of Red Cloud*.

Tommy looked up from where he'd nuzzled his head against Ana's cheek. His snuggling had loosened her tight bun in back so that her white-gold hair had splayed out over his straight black hair. "She can read real good too, Dad. Boy!"

There was a frown around Mark Stone's glittering black eyes, but a smile at the corners of his thick lips. "I thought I told you—"

"But the white lady was already awake, Dad," Lisa said.

546 Bright Puccoon set her bag of groceries on the table in the kitchen. She was slender, had pale brown skin, had a patient expression around her black eyes. "I hope the children weren't a bother."

Ana smiled. "Not at all. They were sweethearts."

Mark Stone placed his bag on the kitchen table too.

Bright Puccoon said, "My husband says he'd like to have you board and room here."

"Why, yes."

"We don't have a garage for your Chevie. But as you know, the air out here is quite dry. And we rarely have snowstorms."

Ana nodded. She liked Bright Puccoon's gracious air. Bright Puccoon with her black hair reminded Ana of Geoffrey's Summit Avenue wife, Adela. There was no mistaking natural class no matter what the color.

"Let me show you your room then."

"Can we come with, Mother?" Lisa wanted to know.

"If you want."

Ana loved the easy way Bright Puccoon handled the child's question. So many mothers, including her own, would have snapped her off with a sharp no.

The room was under the north porch, and like the porch, its window overlooked the Wounded Knee valley. One could see for miles over the longsloping lands. On the very farthest tawny hill a man on a pony was pricking across its crest. The two looked exactly like stick figures.

"Will this cot be all right?"

"That's all I've been sleeping on at the old Pine Ridge Hotel." Ana surveyed the room. It was painted a stark white, both ceiling and walls. The floor was red linoleum, with white and black Indian throw rugs on it. There was a walnut commode in the corner under the stairwell, a single chair beside the bed, and a simple homemade desk in the far corner. "This will be fine."

"My husband is worried about you."

"He needn't be. I know I'm doing the right thing and I know the Lord will protect me."

"Let us hope so."

Back upstairs, Ana offered to help Bright Puccoon make supper.

"Oh, that isn't necessary. It won't take but a minute." Bright Puccoon smiled white teeth at her husband. "Mark, pork chops and mashed potatoes all right?"

Mark Stone had settled in his easy chair and was deep in the daily paper. The late afternoon sun fell over his shoulder onto the paper, backlighting his bronze face in such a manner that his cheeks looked like two ripe tomatoes.

Bright Puccoon smiled. "Never mind. It's the cook's choice tonight."

Mark Stone said, "I was just reading about the BIA sending a special investigator out here."

Bright Puccoon said, "Wonder what that means."

Mark Stone grunted. "I know what it means. Ha. They're out to catch our boys piercing behind the Porcupine Hills."

Ana sat up. "I'd like to see that piercing."

"But you already saw one," Mark Stone said. "I took you there."

Ana said, "Oh, but we were sitting on that hill across the creek. I couldn't see much from there. I want to sit close up."

Mark Stone frowned. "My blood brothers are afraid of letting anyone who is not of our people sit that close."

"Are they afraid I'm a spy?"

"Do you think we'd invite you to live with us if they thought that?"

"I suppose not." Ana smiled down at Tommy. He'd followed her into the kitchen and stood against her thigh. He looked up at her with shining eyes like a loving puppy might. Lisa stood a few feet away, also with admiring eyes.

They'd just sat down to supper at a linoleum-topped table, each place filled with a pork chop and a mound of mashed potatoes, when a car horn sounded outside.

"Company," Lisa said.

"Yes," Bright Puccoon said.

Footsteps sounded on the redwood porch and then four Oglala faces showed in the door, a man, a woman, and two children.

Mark Stone rose to his feet. "Hi yelo."

"We heard you had special company," the man said. He was tall and slim, full of physical power, smiled like a champion. His wife stood beside him, nodding. The two children were of Lisa's age and they stared quietly at Ana.

Mark Stone introduced them. "Running Coyote. Trembling Lily. They're teachers with us at the Pine Ridge High School. And Michael and Lea."

Bright Puccoon smiled a greeting too, and then very quietly moved the place settings already on the table closer together and set out four more. She got out a cleaver and chopped four of the pork chops in half. Lisa and Tommy meanwhile brought in four folding chairs and set them around the table.

Ana watched with astonishment. These Indians were still true Indians— ritually sharing their prepared food, whatever it was. Ana pushed her plate toward Bright Puccoon. "Here, cut mine in half too."

"But you're our special guest."

Ana shook her head politely.

Bright Puccoon ignored her offer.

Again, as all nine of them were about to begin eating, a horn sounded, and in a moment footsteps bounded up the redwood porch steps, and in came a white man and his wife.

"More company!" the children cried happily.

Lisa said, "This is a special day, isn't it, Daddy? Is it the president's birthday?"

Mark Stone grunted. "Not him."

"Crazy Horse's, then?"

"No, worse luck."

Bright Puccoon said, "Our company has come to honor our friend Ana Freyling, Lisa. Because she is a true friend."

"Is she a white apple? White outside and red inside?"

Mark Stone laughed. "That she is." Mark Stone got up and introduced the pair standing in the doorway. "Ana, this is Dr. Henry Fothergill and his wife, Dr. Nancy Wheatly. They teach in Rapid City. But someday they hope to teach in our very own Indian college. Here in Pine Ridge. They're trying to raise money for it now."

Henry Fothergill was a young-looking man of around forty with a balding high forehead. His wide face was a naturally smiling one. It was hard to imagine him frowning. "Trying is right. You can be damned sure the BIA isn't going to give us the necessary funds."

Nancy Wheatly had a narrow tight mouth. But her blue eyes twinkled in friendship. "We are on the trail of a grant from a foundation."

548

Tommy and Lisa got two more folding chairs.

Bright Puccoon once more rose to her feet and got two plates. She pinched the nine settings closer together to make room for the two plates. She got her cleaver and looked down at the already divided portions of food on the eight plates.

Ana pushed her plate toward Bright Puccoon. "Here, please take my portion and divide it for our two white friends. You don't know this, but I had a big lunch this noon."

"No, no."

"Really. I've made it a practice to eat only two meals a day. With my small bones I can ill afford to get fat."

"No."

"Please, now. I'll just have your Indian tea."

Lisa felt sorry for Ana. "Mama, maybe our lady friend Ana can have two raisin cookies with her tea. 'Stead of just one."

"Sure, honey. That's what we'll do then."

Soon all were eating the scanted food. All seemed happy. Indian sharing warmed hearts and opened lips.

The Fothergills exuded cheer. The Indians liked them, and were willing to be cheered by them, but had they been left to themselves they would have eaten with Indian decorum. When they really enjoyed a meal by themselves, they tended not to say much but would smack their lips after each hearty swallow.

Mark Stone said, "What's this new man like the BIA is sending out here?"

"Ted Jenner? A son of a bitch. Troubleshooter for the BIA. They always send him out to take care of sticky situations."

"And get rid of troublemakers."

"Right." Henry Fothergill shot a blue look at Ana. "I'm glad to learn you're going to stay here with Mark Stone. I'd be careful for the next couple of weeks. Maybe the next two months. Until they send Jenner on to the next hot spot."

Ana stiffened slightly. What? Her tough loving brothers never let the neighbors tell them what to do. Also she trusted in the Lord. Ana's chin set out. "I intend to follow my heart in all my work. Besides saving souls for Christ, I mean also to speak up for the Indians' right to worship as they please and when they please, with no interference from any other people, from any other religion."

Silence.

The children finished eating their thinned portions first and then ran outside to play.

Mark Stone called after them, "Don't play with those FBI shells now. Don't even touch them. I want them to stay exactly where they fell."

"We won't, Daddy."

Presently Henry Fothergill said, "Now that the children are out of earshot, I should maybe mention the what-else about Ted Jenner. A friend of ours living with the Navajos tells us that he raped a young girl there. Which of course he denies."

Ana said, "Didn't the Navajos bring him to court?"

"The girl involved is dead. She died in an automobile accident. And the only witness to the rape also died in an auto accident."

Mark Stone snorted. "What a coincidence!"

Henry Fothergill said, "Yes, even more of a coincidence is the fact that both were killed by the same state-owned pickup."

549

Everybody sucked in a breath.

Mark Stone sneered. "White-man justice and fair play."

Ana shivered. She hated hearing that her white people could be such devils, hated hearing the sound of hate on the Indian tongue. She bled about it for Christ's sake.

Henry Fothergill went on. "But he's effective. Wherever he shows up, trouble vanishes. All colored people fear him." He turned to Ana again. "As I say, you're wise to stay here. Because he took a room at the Pine Ridge Hotel."

Bright Puccoon looked out the window at the distant hills. "I wonder what his assignment is out here."

Mark Stone snapped, "I already told you. To catch our boys piercing. It's against their white law."

Bright Puccoon didn't snap back. "I mean, what the head of the BIA in Washington told him to look for."

Mark Stone said, "You'd think the good old USA would have been so busy in the last war trying to clobber Hitler and Hirohito that they'd have had no time to bother with us poor Indians."

Running Coyote smiled in irony. "At the same time they could take our best men and put them in their intelligence units."

Ana was surprised. "'Intelligence'?"

"Yes. The enemy knew how to crack codes too. So our Great White Father used our Indian boys to communicate in the Dakota language. Which the enemy couldn't crack."

Henry Fothergill had a question for Ana. "How come a lovely woman like you never married?"

Dr. Nancy Wheatly frowned.

Ana suffered the sting in his question for Christ's sake. She decided to repeat what an old maid in Bonnie had once said. "'You want to know why I didn't get married? Well, I have considerable money of my own. A parrot that both swears and prays. A monkey that bows to me. A stove that smokes. So you see, I'm not badly in need of a husband.'"

"All right!" Dr. Nancy Wheatly cried.

Ana went on to say, laughing, "And I guess I just never met the right man."

"Too bad. With your love for the unfortunate you'd have made a good mother."

Ana had to bite back another rejoinder. Men. "I saw how my mother got cheated out of being someone important. My father got the credit for all the good things that happened in our family." Ana decided not to mention that Pa had disappeared for his reasons, which might have been unhappy ones. Ana had a sudden vivid picture of all those shellacked fetuses up in the Bartleses' spare bedroom.

"Do you feel a chill?" Bright Puccoon asked.

"No, no."

Running Coyote had an enigmatic smile for Ana. "Perhaps Miss Freyling is one of those manly-hearted women. Our people honor them and consider the band that has one to be blessed by the gods." He smiled around shyly at his wife, Trembling Lily. "There are times when I wish my good wife was one. Then I wouldn't have to worry about white rapists attacking her while I'm at work." Running Coyote mentioned that working as a highline man for the telephone company he was gone for weeks at a time.

550

Trembling Lily sighed. "When he's gone so long it gets to be real lonesome in my little cabin on the next hill there. But I don't think any whites will bother to come out that far looking for me."

Mark Stone pursed up his lips until they touched the tip of his red nose. "That makes you all the more a sitting duck. Nobody to hear you screaming."

A flash of fire showed in Trembling Lily's black eyes. "My husband bought a high-powered rifle and has been teaching me how to shoot it."

"And she's good too," Running Coyote said. "She hit a hopping jackrabbit yesterday at a hundred yards."

Trembling Lily blushed a deep brown. "I was lucky."

"But a white man running would be easier to hit."

Ana didn't like all the shooting talk. Somehow she had to get them to talk about love things.

But the talk just wouldn't go that route. The two Indian men began to tell stories that put the white man in a bad light. Henry Fothergill joined in. It was apparent he didn't care much for the color of his own skin, nor of his white relatives.

"When the white man butchers a cow, he keeps all the meat for himself, even if it means it'll spoil before he can eat it all."

"The white man gets out his plow and tears up our mother, right across her belly. When if he'd just look around he'd see that the best place to plant corn is along the rivers, in the bottoms. If he'd just look around he'd see how even a buffalo trail will slowly unravel a hill."

"And he always has so many children. Ten. Fifteen. Even twenty. Maybe we ought to try their missionary position. Then surely we would multiply too and still lick them."

Ana didn't know what they meant by the missionary position, but she flinched anyway.

Henry Fothergill said, "Mark Stone, someday I want to talk to you about that. Just what do you Indians really do. I can never get one of you to tell me."

All the Oglalas laughed, men and women both. "You'll never find out from us. That's the one secret we mean to keep. That way our women will always be happier than the white women."

Dr. Nancy Wheatly turned to her husband. "Is it really necessary for you to know that?"

"I think so," Henry Fothergill said. "I'm just kind of curious, is all. It might explain a lot. It might even explain why the Indian resists learning how to make a living the white-man way."

"I don't think so," Dr. Nancy Wheatly said.

Mark Stone had a story to tell about how comically ridiculous the white man could be. "There was this fellow who'd worked all his life for the State Department in Washington, D.C. He'd never been west of the soft woman mountains in West Virginia. Always took his vacations on the Atlantic Ocean beaches. When his wife died, and he was single again, he decided to see the West. He bought a new car, a Pierce Arrow. You know, the car that has a kneeling Indian with a bow and arrow on the radiator cap."

Henry Fothergill said, "I remember that car. My father always wanted to own one. But he never had the money. It was the American Rolls-Royce of the day."

"Anyway," Mark Stone went on, "he takes it easy driving west. Three hundred miles a day. He has a whole month to explore the West, so there's no rush. Everything goes fine until he's past Chicago. Then he notices something. How far he can see. No grime. No smoke. It's all so unreal."

Running Coyote knew the story and laughed a short laugh; then fell silent.

"He crosses the Mississippi into Iowa. Then he notices something else. How hard it was to breathe. He thought that kind of funny since with clear air it should have been easier to breathe. He decided he maybe had a cold coming on."

Ana wondered where the story was heading. She sat very erect. She could feel a minced smile forming on her lips.

"When he crossed the Big Sioux River into South Dakota, the air got even clearer, at the same time that his breathing got worse. He coughed. He sucked air. When he stopped to eat, he found himself puffing between bites. He began to wonder if he shouldn't stop in some town somewhere and see a doctor about his bad cold."

Everybody's mouth fell open a little as they waited for the punch line.

"When he crossed the Missouri and started to drive through our reservation, his cold finally got so bad he had to pull over to the side of the road. He let his head rest on the steering wheel, puffing, puffing. He was sure he was going to die. If he could only somehow just get into the mountains. The Black Hills. Mountain air was supposed to be really good for lung problems. He lifted his head off the steering wheel and looked in the mirror over the windshield. Ye! Ye! His face was almost purple. He felt so sick to his gut he decided he needed to lie down somewhere. Forgetting to shut off the engine, he opened the door on his side and slid down onto the gravel road. He lay there a minute, puffing. And then, ye! he passed out."

"Yes?"

"Pretty soon a couple of Indian boys came along, walking down the road. They stopped to admire the kneeling Indian on the radiator cap of the Pierce Arrow. Then they noticed that the white driver had passed out and was lying on the road. They stared down at him a while. Finally one of the Indian boys said, 'We better drag him around into the ditch. Otherwise somebody is going to run over him lying here in the middle of the road.' 'Yeh,' the other Indian boy said. So they each grabbed an arm of the poor fellow and started to drag him around the rear end of the Pierce Arrow. Then, just as they dragged his purple nose past the tailpipe of the running engine, where a little blue smoke was puffing out, the white man happened to sigh, and so took in a big deep breath of the blue exhaust . . . and ye! came to." Mark Stone began to laugh; and then really laughed. And laughed and laughed. He almost slid down out of his chair, he thought the story so good.

Around eleven the company decided to leave. The children were called in from the late dusk-lighted yard outside, good-byes were said, and then silence fell on the high sloping hill.

Ana lay on her cot downstairs, hearing the red family above her murmuring together as they got ready for bed . . . .

The next day was Saturday and Ana decided she needed some personal things from the main mercantile store in Pine Ridge. She got into her Chevie around ten. She drove slowly down the long curving drive and then turned onto Highway 18.

Presently she noticed that the mailman had just gone by. He'd left packages too big for the mailbox on the ground below it.

She'd driven several miles when she had to stop to let a drove of sheep cross the road ahead of her. Dust stived up in low ochre fogs from the cloven hooves. She could barely see the drover, an Indian boy. When the dust cleared she saw that she'd stopped beside another mailbox. The mailman this time had hung a package by its string on the lid of the mailbox. She spotted a message stamped in red across the address on the package. Curious, Ana slid across the seat and opened the window on the passenger side for a closer look. It took her a moment to make out the small red letters: RETURNED UNOPENED.

As she drove on, Henry Fothergill's rude question came back to her. "How come a lovely woman like you never married?" Well, it did bother her that she'd never had children. Ma deserved to have more grandchildren. After all there was good blood in the Freyling family. She wondered what she would have done had she met the right man. She might have been able to forget those shellacked babies up in the spare bedroom in the Bartles house.

A funny thought came to her. "Ha. Now I know what I want put on my gravestone. 'Returned unopened.'"

She smiled grimly to herself.

In Pine Ridge, as she moved from shop to shop, she met several Indians who remembered her from her talk in church. They smiled at her, warm and wondering, and she smiled back. She hadn't saved many souls so far, and perhaps her church back in Bonnie might be unhappy about that for all the money they'd put up for her support, but she'd at least got some of the possible converts to smile.

The last thing she bought was a supply of facial tissues.

She was about to step into her Chevie when she spotted Father Benjamin Cobb and his wife, Sarah, talking with a sleekly dressed man a half block down the street. Ana had come to love Father Cobb and his wife because of the warm welcome they'd given her in their Episcopal church. They'd let her hold meetings in its ornate basement room. Father Cobb was a short man, barely taller than Ana, and despite his gentle round owl face, was all man. He could be quietly tough when he had to be. His wife, Sarah, plump and lively, also had steel in her. Somehow, though the rate of Indian conversion was low, the Cobbs bore up under it all with a loving air of Christian patience.

Ana thought of going over to say hello when she noted that Father Cobb and the stranger weren't getting along too well. The stranger was gesturing sharp and hard, as though he were demanding something of the Cobbs. But Father Benjamin Cobb, slowly stiffening, was declining. Sarah's full face had flushed over in anger.

"Wonder what that's all about," Ana murmured.

Then Ana caught on. Twice the stranger glanced in her direction, quick and menacing. They were talking about her. Could the man dressed in sleek gray be Ted Jenner, the BIA troubleshooter?

Suddenly the stranger stuck a finger into the front of Father Cobb's black smock. It was as if he were saying, "If you don't do it, too bad for you, Father." Father Cobb backed a step and his face turned red. Sarah made a motion as though to slap the stranger; then held back.

The gray-clad stranger wheeled and walked off in the other direction.

553

At that moment Father Cobb saw Ana. He held up his small hand to let her know he wanted to see her, then he took Sarah's elbow, and together the two hurried toward Ana. Sarah looked back several times to see if the stranger were watching them. But he had disappeared up a side alley.

"Ana!" Father Cobb said, breathing hard. "Good thing we saw you. I'm afraid we got bad news."

Ana had a smile for him. "Hello, Father. That was Ted Jenner, wasn't it?"

"It was. How did you know?"

"They were talking about him at Mark Stone's last night."

"Well, he's bad news all right. What do you suppose he asked me to do?" Father Cobb rose on his toes several times. "He asked us not to let you use our facility for your missionary work. And of course I refused. The very idea!"

"What did he really say?"

"That the Bureau of Indian Affairs was specifically asking my church not to give harbor to incendiaries, that our nation is now at work trying to recover from the last war and it's important that all its citizens pull together, and that the nation can't afford to have part of its peoples practicing a religion that is alien to it. Piercing foments civil disobedience. Piercing is a heathen practice. Piercing is against the Constitution. He said further that if we didn't forbid you use of our facility, he would have to use force of some kind."

"Force? When Christ was our gentle savior?"

"Yes, I know, Ana."

"What are you going to do?"

"Exactly as I told him. Let you hold whatever meetings you want in our church."

"Thank you, Father Cobb. But maybe I can do my missionary work back in the hills behind Porcupine."

Sarah said, "Oh, Benjamin, we can't let her do that. Some outlaw there is bound to do her hurt."

Ana said, "The Lord's will."

Father Cobb said, "Ana, you know of course that I don't hold with piercing. And while I sort of see your point that there is a similarity to Christ's suffering, the practice still really is heathen and not Christian."

Ana bristled. "Father, don't be too surprised if, as you stand before the throne of God on resurrection day, you'll see standing beside you my friends Andrew High Pine and Ben American Horse and Mark Stone Let Enemy Run. And don't be further surprised if some of our Christian friends are sent to hell while some of my Indian friends are sent to heaven. If God is as smart as we think he is, if he's got real brains, he's going to be awfully bored throughout eternity if all he has to talk to are Episcopalians."

Father Cobb's liquid brown eyes sparkled. "Aha. Ana, if I didn't know you to be a true Christian, I'd say you're almost heathen in your devotion to fair play."

"In my family we all believed in fair play. That's why we all grew up so self-assured. Even when we were wrong and hell-bent."

"Just the same, Ana, I want you to be careful. Ted Jenner is out to get you. To use his words."

"The Lord wills."

On the way home, Ana kept watching her rearview mirror to see if she were being followed. But look as she might, there were no cars on the road behind her. As she rode along she let her eyes enjoy the view on either side of the highway. There'd been a rain in early May, and the long undulant hills showed a soft faint green through the tan cover of last year's buffalo grass. She loved the mix of soft green and old tan. She saw where the fence was down in places, and she shook her head at Indian neglect. Her brother Rolf the family fence man would surely cluck his tongue at the fallen fence posts and the sagging barbwire.

Black-and-white magpies with their long tails sailed up and landed on the top of the standing fence posts, scolded Ana's Chevie raucously, and then sailed off and landed on clumps of bunch grass.

Then a car appeared behind her, coming fast. Could that be Ted Jenner? Crooking her head in thought, she decided to slow down and watch to see if the car took the Wounded Knee turn. She shifted down to intermediate. As she slowed for Mark Stone's lane and took a leisurely left, she made out that the car did take the right turn off Highway 18 and head into Wounded Knee. That had to be Jenner. No doubt he was going to ask questions about her down there.

Ana's thin lips whitened. She wasn't going to let him scare her. She was a Freyling from Siouxland. She had a brother named Tane who could handle Ted Jenner. Make him beg for mercy. She remembered how Tane had annihilated those high school bums in Bonnie who tried to torment the young Freylings as they rode home from school in their cab. And how Pa had come along and kept Tane from possibly killing those bums.

Two days later Ana was home alone. The Let Enemy Runs had gone visiting some friends on the other side of Manderson near the White River. From the way Mark Stone and Bright Puccoon hadn't been able to look her in the eye, Ana suspected they were going to a piercing.

Around eleven o'clock Ana walked down to the mailbox. The Rapid City paper and a letter from Mallie had come. From Mallie's account Ana gathered that it'd been a good move for Mallie to go live with Ma. Ma had recovered from her broken leg as well as from her confused state. She was going to church again and had even talked Mallie into taking her.

Good.

Ana read on. There still was no word on what had happened to Dirk and Tressa. More about them had better be left unsaid. As for Tane, he and his wife and boys and the hired man were doing a good job running the old homestead. Geoffrey and wife and children were doing well. Thea was happy in her new job at the Palace Theater in Whitebone. And Rolf was getting to be a pain in the neck the way he bragged about "his boy Walter." If the rest of them weren't careful, Walter was going to be the president of the United States of America some day.

Ana went out on the red porch to read the daily paper. She glanced at the headlines. The price of gas was rising now that gas rationing had been abolished. Soldiers were returning home to celebrating families. Business was still booming.

She folded the paper and placed it on the redwood table beside her. The shadow in which she sat began to narrow and soon the sun beat on her left knee and ankle. She noticed that the sun happened to catch several of the scattered empty shells outside the FBI bunker just right so that their copper shone like gold.

555

She crossed her slim legs, refolding her blue dress over her knees. What an injustice. And how like Mark Stone that he wanted the shells to remain undisturbed as a bitter memorial.

She was surprised to hear a meadowlark sing behind her. Meadowlarks hardly ever sang in the hot sun. They usually sang early in the morning. She turned. After running her eyes back and forth a few times, she spotted the meadowlark sitting on a rock. Its yellow breast was all of a part of the sunlight. It sang several more times: "What, you? What are you doing there?" Then it flew off.

The meadowlark's lovely singing evoked song in her. She hummed a few bars of "Jesus Loves Me, This I Know." Too bad Tressa wasn't around. Tressa could've sung soprano to her alto. Ana could just see the two of them standing together in church, an arm around each other's hips, Tressa with her thick full lips and she with her thin lips. Ana had often observed that full-lipped women sang soprano and thin-lipped women sang alto.

"There you are," a snappish male voice said behind her.

Ana whirled, already knowing who it was. She stood up, thinking to flee into the house and locking the door; then, deciding that was cowardly, sat down again. "What do you want, Mr. Jenner?"

Ted Jenner ascended the steps onto the redwood porch. "You."

"Well, here I am."

Ted Jenner stopped in front of her. His whitish gray eyes reminded Ana of smoldering coals about to burst into flame. There was an air about him that he was accustomed to having his way, that he would tolerate no resistance. The gray in his eyes was heightened by his immaculately pressed gray suit. He had on a blue shirt and a white tie. He was hatless, and the white of his tie intensified the hue of his sun-blanched forelock. His freckled hands hung still, ferrets ready to pound.

Ana stared back at him. She was not going to quail under his sulfureous glare. She could feel herself fill with fight. If Ted Jenner thought he could run her off the reservation he had another think coming.

Jenner said, "What you've been doing is illegal, you know."

"Under the Constitution?"

"Oh, the hell with that scrap of paper! The worst thing to ever happen to this country was when our forefathers let themselves be talked into signing that document."

"It has since became the hope of all free peoples everywhere. Including our poor Indians."

Ted Jenner's fingers remained still. "You damned religious crackpots, if you had your way, you'd show no more mercy to dissidents than our government is showing now. Same difference. Except that at the moment you're the one who's breaking the law."

Ana decided to stand up. "You can leave now."

He took a step toward her. "I'm giving you until tomorrow at sunset to get the hell off this reservation. If you're not off by then, I'm coming by and picking you up and bodily removing you."

She took a step toward him. "You wouldn't dare touch me."

"You have my warning."

"Just try touching me once. Now, if you want to."

"Lady, you're asking for it."

"Do you have a warrant for my arrest?"

"I don't need a warrant out here."

"The Constitution says you do."

"Have you read the Constitution?"

"That and the Bible, many times."

"You fanatic."

"You bigot."

They glared at each other, to the point of trembling. His eyes seared down at her and her eyes burned up at him.

Ana felt wonderful. Here at last was something she could get into with her whole heart and soul. She saw herself as the reincarnation of Joan of Arc. "Touch me."

At last a hand of his came up and he gave her a shove on the shoulder. "I'll teach you to tell me off, you snip of a witch." He gave her another shove, hard, so that she stumbled and landed in her redwood chair again.

The nerve of the guy. She popped upright and stuck her pointy nose in his face. "You pig! You cob roller!" She hit him so hard that the red imprint of her hand rose almost immediately to the surface of his bone-hard face. The blow ruffled his slicked-back ropelike hair.

Sneering, he tried to push her down again.

She fought off his push. Then she shouldered him in the belly, making him back a step. He hadn't expected such power from a little woman. She spat at him. "You stinker, you're going to pay for this! I'm going to report to the Indian police that you struck me in an Indian house where I was a guest."

The word "stinker" seemed to hit him like the smack of a fist. His whole face blackened over.

When she found that one epithet that hit home she quickly threw it at him again. "Yes, and you're a dirty hairy stinker!" The word "stinker" seemed to refer to something he wanted to forget.

He made a grab for her throat with both hands.

She ducked back; came up with her knee into his groin, hard.

He groaned; bent over for a second; then with great effort rightened himself and made another grab for her.

She dodged; then swung her elbow for his Adam's apple. She connected; but not quite right. All she did was slow him down.

He lowered his head, spread out his arms, came after her like a wrestler. He came with such a rush he caught her around the middle, and down both went with a crunch on the redwood floor of the porch.

She fought him, hissing, spitting in his face.

He found her wrists and slowly bent them down to the floor. He pressed his belly down on hers. Somehow he straddled his legs over hers in such a way that he not only spread them apart he also managed to hold them tight down on the boards. "There, you little spitcat, now I've got you where I want you."

She gathered up phlegm in her throat and spat in his face again. "Now that you think you got me, what are you going to do with me, tie me up and carry me off to jail?" She squirmed to free herself. "Well, you have another think coming, you dirty hairy stinker."

He had trouble holding her down. So he surged on her to subdue her. "You goddamned Indian lover! Before I get through with you, you'll have—"

She gathered up all her strength in her belly muscles, then her buttocks, and of a sudden pushed up, snapped up, and almost threw him off.

"Why you goddamned whorecat you!" With a mighty effort he kept her from breaking free.

She closed her eyes so tight she could feel her face wrinkling up over her cheeks.

As they wrestled his gun fell out of its shoulder holster.

"You're armed!" she cried. "Why, you came here to shoot me."

"I wear that gun for protection. From red devils out to get me."

"They don't wear guns!"

In all their wrestling, his wrath slowly changed to lust. He hardened upon her. He had her legs opened exactly right and locked into place. To free one hand to make himself ready, he took her left wrist in his mouth and clamped his teeth down on it.

"No! No!" she cried. "No."

Then that most horrible of things began to happen to her. She had a picture of herself as the hen and of him as the rooster. He had her pinned down. His beak was biting into her. It hurt. She wanted to struggle but in struggling it hurt all the worse. Then he bit her fiercely in the wrist and she fainted.

When she came to a little, vaguely she saw through half-slitted eyes the flash of sun on the revolver. She made a grab for it. And then there was a bang . . . and she spiraled off and was gone. Dead.

557

55. Thea

1948-1949

When word finally came from the Pine Ridge Reservation that sister Ana had mysteriously disappeared, Thea fell into a blue funk. She went about dispirited. She did manage to get up enough face to do her job at the Palace Theater. She liked meeting the public most times, taking tickets out front in her little booth, bagging popcorn inside, polishing the brass finishing in the lobby. She forced herself to smile because she didn't want to lose her job. But privately she grieved.

Hillary Jessup, proprietor of the Palace Theater, noticed her changed mood, and his air around her turned gentle. Thea hadn't expected that. He was a disciplinarian and had little time for sentiment. It was in the way he ran the theater. People knew that at the Palace one could enjoy a movie with no disturbance from the local rascals.

Between shows there wasn't much to do out front in her ticket booth, and Thea, to pass the time, took up knitting. She decided to make gloves for her nephew Tyson, Tane's boy, who'd taken to hunting in the wasteland along the Big Rock River.

One evening Hillary wandered out and opened the narrow door of the booth behind her. "You all right?"

"Sure, Hillary."

His glance fell on her knitting needles. "You have strange friends."

"Why?"

He smiled grudgingly. "Count the fingers on that glove once."

Thea counted. "Why, there's six."

He went on smiling. "Well," he said, "maybe you were thinking of cornhusking mittens. You know, the ones with double thumbs."

Thea blushed. "I guess I got too much on my mind."

"Still no word on what happened to your sister?"

"Not a word. Ana's just disappeared. Not even the FBI could find a trace of her."

Hillary slouched, lanky frame filling the doorway. "The FBI and the BIA work together on reservation problems. And if the BIA was behind getting rid of her, you may never see her again."

"Oh, dear. What in the world is happening to us Freylings?"

"That's the way it sometimes works in families."

Thea knew what he was thinking. When he was a boy his parents had drowned in a cloudburst near Yellow Smoke and his brother Lemuel had died in a grain elevator explosion. Those happenings had contributed to his sometimes saturnine outlook on life. He had once hoped to make up for those early calamities by living the good rich life with his wife, Mildred, having a half dozen children, all debts paid, money invested in land. But that was not to be. Mildred was killed in an automobile accident.

Thea had also heard that his life with Mildred hadn't been all that happy. Mildred turned out to be a clotheshorse. Some people said Mildred had a different dress for every day of the month. There were also rumors she had several times driven in a car alone to the town of Grub in South Dakota, and that could only mean she'd gone there to get an abortion. In fact the car accident that killed her came on her last trip to Grub. When Hillary heard that particular rumor he had driven to Grub himself to ask the coroner about it. The coroner denied it. It was all a sad business.

"Thea, why don't you take off a couple of days?" Hillary said. "A week even. Go take a trip to Pine Ridge to see what you can find out about Ana. Who knew her and so on. I know I'd hate to have that hanging in my heart without knowing what had happened to her."

"Thanks. But I'm better off keeping busy here with you. Besides, I like working for you."

Hillary's long face opened. A look came into his dark blue eyes as if he hadn't expected her to say that; also, that he wasn't sure he liked it. It was all right for him to relax from a dour outlook on life, but for anyone else to do it and to direct affection his way was to be regarded with suspicion. He had long ago sworn he was never going to get hitched again, or let any woman get close to him. The only problem with that attitude was, for whom and for what was he working so hard? When he died who would inherit it all?

"Really, I do," Thea said.

"Well, we'll see. Meanwhile, I better get back and ride herd on those rascals up in the balcony. That bunch of wild calves from Pipestone still ain't learned we got a few fences here in Whitebone."

"I noticed they were a little rowdy when they bought tickets."

"Yeh." Grumbling, Hillary closed the door behind her.

Thea looked at the six-fingered glove she'd started. She considered unraveling it; finally decided that would only make the gray yarn too unruly to use again. She'd finish it and make a joke about it. Maybe she could tell nephew Tyson that if the yarn on the trigger finger wore out he could switch to the spare. Or something like that.

Just before the first show let out, a crowd began to form a line outside the ticket booth. Thea put aside her knitting and began selling tickets again. She was proud of her patience in the booth. There were always those wise ones who tried to fob off their latest crack on her.

"That booth you're in would make a perfect hut for ice fishing in the winter."

Thea responded, saying, "If you can chop a hole in the cement here below me, maybe."

"Did you ever think of selling it to the telephone company?"

"No," Thea said, "but I have been thinking of buying it from Mr. Jessup for my coffin."

"How do you like working for that slave driver?"

"I'm a happy slave. Here's your change."

Sometimes Geoffrey and wife Adela came by. Of course they had to talk a minute. If not about Ana then about how Ma was coming along. This always caused murmuring in the waiting line behind Geoffrey and Adela. Or

Geoffrey's two boys, Tyrone and Vincent, asked Aunt Thea if they could stand inside the booth with her and watch the people buy tickets. Thea always smiled at them but always refused them. "You two boys behave upstairs in the balcony now."

What really had happened to sister Ana? Geoffrey had driven out to the Pine Ridge Reservation to investigate. But he'd found nothing. Had come home in a rage about the buck passing he'd run into. Geoffrey accused the Indians of hiding what they knew, even Mark Stone Let Enemy Run and his wife. Both whites and reds had a way of looking up and to the right or to the left and of walking away when the subject of Ana Freyling was brought up. The U.S. district attorney ordered Geoffrey out of his office when Geoffrey mentioned his sister's name.

If Ana had been assaulted and killed, then buried in a secret place, it meant that four of the ten Freylings had vanished. Pa. Then Dirk and Tressa. Now Ana. Though Dirk and Tressa were probably still alive somewhere. But because they never heard from them the two might as well be dead.

Since Hillary had also suffered family losses, Thea felt close to him. And she felt sorry for him that he lived such a lonesome life up in the apartment above the theater. She'd never seen the apartment, but she'd heard from Mildred's friends that it was opulent, rich with the best furnishings money could buy: marble sinks, wall-to-wall carpeting, maroon lamp shades, gaily colored hassocks, the latest in kitchen equipment. Wondering what he probably missed most, all the more so because Mildred hadn't even been able to serve well-steeped tea, Thea decided to bake him a cake, a chocolate three-decker with white coconut frosting.

560

Carrying the cake in a white tin container, Thea left for work a half hour early. She didn't want anybody to see her give it to him. She pushed through the side door and entered the lobby. Hillary still hadn't turned on the lights and for a moment Thea found herself in what seemed total darkness.

"What've you got there?"

His voice startled her. He'd just emerged from the theater proper. She said, "Oh, nothing much. It's for you."

"Me? Is that a package they forgot to give me at the post office?"

"No. I found it in my kitchen." Her eyes adjusted to the semidarkness and she began to see him clearly. "Here."

He took it. "What is it?"

"Open it."

He set the white tin container on the counter of the popcorn booth. He lifted the lid. "A cake!"

"Yes. You like chocolate cake, don't you?"

Slowly he looked at her with grave suspicion. "You tryin' to butter me up?"

"That isn't a pound of butter."

"Turning smart on me, are you?"

"Want me to bring it upstairs to your rooms?"

He hesitated. He stared down at the cake. For a fleeting second the tip of his dark tongue showed. "Naw. I'll bring it up myself." He replaced the white lid.

For two days he didn't have much to say. She went out of her way to be specially good at her work. He grunted at her industry. Every now and then he cast her a glittering look. After what had happened to him with Mildred, he didn't like it at all that one of his help had decided to be nice to him.

The third day, after the second movie had started and it was obvious there'd be no more customers, he came out to her little cubicle. He opened the narrow door behind her. "You can go home now if you wanna."

"Thanks."

"If any stragglers come along, I can handle them inside."

Thea turned over the proceeds for the night, a tan canvas bag full of loose change and dollar bills.

Hillary took the money and held it behind him. He never crabbed about the take, whatever it was. He usually counted his money upstairs, but so far as she could see he certainly wasn't a miser.

"Say, uh . . ." A tiny smile worked at the corners of his thin lips. And with an effort, as if he were pulling out a tooth he wanted to keep, he said, "I guess I better thank you for the cake."

"You're welcome."

"Tasted good."

"I thought maybe you might like a cake."

"Well, thanks." He turned and disappeared inside.

Thea got the impression that while he liked the chocolate cake, he didn't want to encourage her to make another.

She waited a couple of weeks, then made him some chocolate cookies. She put the cookies in a small flat paper box and, again going to work early, brought them to him.

He looked up from where he was polishing the curved brass handles to the main doors inside the theater. He'd opened the exit doors on both sides of the theater and the summer breeze coming in almost erased the odor of last night's popcorn and the stale musk of the old plush seats. "Another cake?"

"Look." Why couldn't the man relax and not be so gruff with her? She wasn't his enemy.

He humphed a gutteral cough, then unloosened the string and lifted the paper lid. "Cookies." Before he could stop himself, he added, "And my favorite kind too."

Her heart gave a pound. He did like it that she was being thoughtful.

He picked up one of the cookies and took a bite. He chewed. "Good, too."

When the weather became cold, Thea noticed that his wrists turned red. He was one of those long-armed men who could never get shirts and jackets to fit. With a knowing smile, remembering his remarks about the mittens she'd knitted for her nephew Tyson, she knitted him a pair of gray wristlets. She found out that his birthday was October 10, so on that day she gave him a third package.

He grunted when he saw the package. He shot her an angry blue glance. "Hmp. Trying to win me over through my stomach, are yuh?"

"Look."

Rocking nervously back and forth, a grimace around his nose pulling up his face, he finally did open the package. "For godsakes, woman, what's this?"

She pointed at his weather-reddened wrists. "What they look like. Wristlets for cold mornings."

Roushing to himself, he said, "Nobody's ever worried about my wrists before, for godsakes."

"Maybe it's about time then."

"Hmp!" He thrust them into his back pocket and threw the package into a nearby wastebasket.

"If they don't fit, let me know."

"Rrach. Sure." He turned his back on her and lunged into the auditorium to check the lights.

Two weeks later, Hillary showed a rerun of *Snow White and the Seven Dwarfs.* Thea had missed it the first time around. She asked Hillary if it was all right if she closed her little booth early once the second show began so she could see it.

"Of course," he snapped. "I can handle the latecomers."

About halfway through the show two young fellows behind her began to laugh. Thea didn't right away catch on what the laughter was about. Then she heard a private noise, followed by some more laughter. The two youths had become bored with the cartoon and were have a flatulating contest.

Thea was disgusted. She got up and went out front.

Hillary looked up. "You don't like the movie?"

"Sure. But I don't like the sideshow."

"What sideshow?"

Thea had trouble using the word. But she was angry, really shocked, and it popped out of her before she could use a more decorous word. "A couple of your customers were farting behind me."

He almost leaped up off the floor. His face turned black. "What!"

"Yes!"

"Who was it? Boys or girls?"

At that Thea almost choked. Girls? Girls never . . . Thea sneezed. Then she burst out laughing.

562

"Those sonsabitches!" Hillary snarled. "Follow me." He slid stealthily into the rear of the theater, Thea right behind him.

Once again there was a faint ripping sound, at the very moment that Snow White was singing a dainty feminine song. The two boys laughed raucously.

Hillary's head shot forward like a turtle snapping at a fly. "Cut out the goddam farting, you bums!"

The whole theater froze. There were gasps. Thea even thought for a second the Snow White up on the screen hesitated in her singing.

Then Hillary's two long arms reached out and he collared the two young fellows, dragged them up the aisle and out into the lobby. Thea followed them, wondering, what next? When Hillary got them to the front door, he gave each a tremendous kick in the buttocks, propelling them out onto the front sidewalk. "I don't ever want to see you rowdies in here again!" He flaffed his hands as though getting rid of disgusting dust and came back inside. Then a great good smile opened his saturnine face. He had really loved what he'd just done. It was no wonder the kids in the area behaved in the Palace Theater.

Thea went back to her seat to enjoy the rest of the movie.

When Thea went to bed that night she had several questions to ask of herself. Was she falling in love with that old fellow Hillary? If she was, what did she expect to get out of it? She was too old to have children. Unless she could pull off a biblical Sarah. Would mere companionship be enough? Would he be grouchy in bed with her like he was in the theater with her? Just what was she up to, for goodness sakes?

She wondered what Ma would say if she told her that she was marrying her boss. Or Mallie. Or the rest of the family. Geoffrey and Adela knew Hillary and liked him. Geoffrey even had him as a client and would probably approve of him.

Of course it would all be idle thinking unless Hillary popped the question.

She decided to go slowly. She'd think about it some more. Do what Mary did in the Bible. "Mary kept all these things and pondered them in her heart."

Thea began to look a little more often in the mirror. She was sixty, and though her face was somewhat lined, she still looked a young forty. At the same time Hillary, in his middle sixties, also had a healthy look about him, making him seem he was about fifty.

Around the twentieth of December Thea decided to buy Hillary a Christmas present. She knew that was a touchy thing to do. Hillary'd right away think it meant something special. He'd probably go into one of his tizzies, thinking she was making a play for him again, which she was, making him think he had to give her a present.

For two days he acted fidgety around her. He would hover around her as though he wanted to say something; then would dart off on some chore. He threw her odd looks. When she'd examine his grimaces one way, she thought he looked angry. When she'd examine them another way, she thought he looked excited and happy.

Then the third day, just as she finished taking in the last money for the night, he gave her a slender package. He'd gotten someone in the jewelry store next door to wrap it up for him in Christmas paper.

What! For godsakes. He had beat her into buying her a present. He had begun to think of her as more than just help. She was a friend then. And maybe more.

He said, "Now don't think I'm trying to butter you up." He laughed to one side like brother Tane sometimes did when he was nervous.

She could feel herself start to blush. Luckily no one was around. She looked down at the slender gift.

"Well, ain't you gonna open it?"

"You don't want me to wait until Christmas Day?"

"Oh, that's right. Sure. Wait until Christmas Day."

"After I open it I'll call you."

"Do that."

A day later Thea bought him his present. She'd noted that he'd come downstairs in the afternoon before the real work began in a pair of old bedroom slippers. The slippers were down at the heel, the toes were almost worn through, and the leather sides were all scuffed up. Any shoe polish they might have once had was worn off. She managed to have a peek into a pair of his workshoes in the janitor's cubbyhole to discover he wore size 12 A. It pleased her to learn he had such a long slim foot. The slippers she bought were expensive and well made, brown, with a box toe and very stiff sides. No cardboard in them anywhere. She recalled her husband Oliver Tice's pigeon-toed walk and his big feet. She cried. She wrapped Hillary's slippers in some specially colored Christmas wrapping.

The day before Christmas, early in the morning, Hillary called Thea at her apartment. "Say, can you play an organ?"

"I play by ear from my own amusement."

"You know that special program I planned for our town kids? The Bethlehem scene and all that, and the musicale afterwards? Betty Brower was gonna play the organ for that but she got sick."

"Didn't your wife, Mildred, play the organ in the old days? I heard her solos were popular."

"Yeh. They were. But that don't do me any good now."

Thea had a thought. "Hillary, it's too bad you didn't keep up putting on those musical solos. And musical plays. With that wonderful organ you got, and that orchestra pit, and that stage with different drops, those dressing rooms in back, it's perfect for that. There ain't many theaters around equipped for such programs."

"Them programs don't pay these days. Now it's just movies and bank nights. And maybe now and then a musicale for kids at Christmas."

Thea smiled at the black mouthpiece of her phone. "Have you opened your present yet?"

"No. You?"

So abrupt always. "No, Hillary."

He didn't hang up right away. "You're right I got a good theater here. In the old days, when traveling road shows came through, we used the organ and the pit and the drops all the time. Them was great times."

"Do you want us to open our presents together?"

Pause. "Where would we do this then?"

Thea still hadn't seen the apartment above the theater. "My place would be all right."

564

"Naw. If people saw me go up to your place, they'd be gossiping about us to a fare-thee-well."

"I suppose they would."

He growled in the phone. "I tell you what. Why don't you come by early before the kid's program. Go right upstairs and we'll do it then."

"All right."

"You'll play the organ?"

"You better get some other lady. My playing by ear isn't going to work."

It was snowing lightly when Thea walked downtown. With colored Christmas tinsel in the show windows and Christmas wreaths in all the doorways, it felt like the good old times back home, warm and comforting and sacred.

Opening the front door, she turned left and slowly went upstairs. The walls of the stairs were made of imitation black-and-white marble. She knocked on the big oak door.

He'd been waiting for her. The door opened a crack; he saw who it was; then flung open the door, letting it bang against the wall. "You made it."

She smiled. "Yes, Hillary."

"Come in, come in."

She was so struck by the beauty of the place she fell silent. The whole roomy apartment, which had once been a dance floor, was lively with maroon lamp shades, blond-wood chairs and tables and settees, celery green carpeting, salmon upholstery. The walls were papered in slow gold.

"Here," he said, "sit here on the settee. And I'll pull up a chair." He got his present from her and placed it on a hassock between them.

Thea couldn't help smiling at the lovely rooms. The low sun in the southwest had just started to edge into the west windows.

"Well, shall we open them? I gotta be downstairs pretty soon."

"Sure."

She opened his present to her first. When she slowly drew back the cover from the long slim black case, she saw an elegant Elgin lady's wristwatch. "Hillary."

He said, "I'm not hinting you're never on time, you know. I mean the thing as a reward for always being on time." He coughed several times. He found it hard to say the next words. "You're the best I ever had when it comes to that."

"You shouldn't've. So expensive."

"Oh, now, it's nothing. Though don't get any ideas."

"Thank you. Aren't you going to open yours?"

He ripped the wrapping off with a sweep of his long fingers. "My God, woman, slippers?"

"You can use them, can't you?"

"Well, sure. But . . ."

"See if they fit."

He took off a shoe and tried on one of the slippers. "Perfect."

"I'm glad."

He humphed to himself. He wanted to say more, but then remembered his theater downstairs. "Hey, I better get cracking. Customers will walk in without paying."

"Hillary, wasn't this special Christmas program going to be free today?"

"Oh, that's right. I'm so used to workdays."

Thea sighed. She wished they might have had a little more time together to wonder over their presents. But it was apparent that Hillary had become quite nervous and felt he had to break it off.

Business was brisk all through the holidays. Both Hillary and Thea were so busy they had little time to talk.

About the middle of January, when work eased off, they had time to visit a little. Hillary talked with her, even joked with her, but there still was some reserve about everything he said and did around her. When it looked like they might talk about what they meant to each other, he'd quick run off on some errand in the theater, or say he had to bank the money they'd taken in the night before.

On the first day of February a wild driving blizzard enveloped Siouxland. Hardest hit was Whitebone. There was little warning. Thea had gone early to the theater to help clean up the mess of the night before and to get out the rolls of tickets. Twice early in the afternoon Hillary sallied outside to look up at the sky and wave a hand at it as if to challenge the gods of storm to do their worst. At five they couldn't see across the street. At six, when both went to supper in the Corner Cafe, they had trouble seeing the sidewalk underfoot.

At seven o'clock it was obvious the town was locked down in a fierce snowstorm. Thea and Hillary stood looking out of the tall glass front doors watching the streaks of driven snow fly by.

Hillary said, "Jack ain't showed up yet. It's got to be pretty bad out there if he can't make it." Jack was his projectionist.

"Maybe we should put up the Closed sign."

"No. No. If just one patron shows up, I always put on the show. Come hell or

565

high water, the show must go on."

Some ten minutes later a young bachelor who lived in the apartment over the jewelry store came stumbling down through the blasting snow.

"See?" Hillary said. "Tell you what, you take his ticket and I'll go upstairs and run the projector."

The bachelor was the only one to show up. After a while Thea went in and took a back seat and watched the show too.

There was nobody for the second show.

At ten Hillary turned off the rows of lights outside on the marquee, doused the house lights, and locked the front doors.

Thea got her fur coat and slipped into it.

"Where do you think you're going?"

Thea sat down on a chair and started to pull on her black rubber boots. "Home. Where else?"

"In this storm? When not even the sparrow dares to show his beak?"

"Well, if not home, then maybe just across the corner to the Manitou Hotel."

"That'll cost you five bucks. If you make it."

"Then I don't know."

Hillary began to pace back and forth in the lobby. He licked his upper lip. "Tell you what. I got a guest room upstairs. Well, actually, it was Mildred's room."

Thea set down the black boot she had in her hand. "Mildred's room?"

"Well, you know . . ." Hillary's lank face turned red. "Mildred and I had our differences at the end, and she took to living in her own room."

"Couples sometimes do that."

He grumped to himself. "It was a roughty at the end there with her. And it helped that we could lick our sores alone in our own rooms."

"Sorry to hear that, Hillary."

"Rrach. So it goes. But come on, I'll take you upstairs and show you the room." He threw a wild gray look outside at the flying snow. "Will the people you're staying with notice it if you don't come home?"

"No. I have a separate entrance to my apartment."

"Good. Thank God that with this storm nobody will be watching to see if you stayed overnight here."

Upstairs they could hear the storm slapping on the flat tar roof. One of the windows in the west wall moaned. Hillary led her across the large living room and opened a door to the east.

Thea took one look and couldn't help but exclaim. "More of that wonderful blond furniture! Mildred had good taste."

"She did. Same way with clothes. Dresses, shoes, chapeaus. She knew how to wear it all too."

Thea said nothing.

Hillary cast her a sidelong look. "You wouldn't want to sleep in one of her nightgowns . . . Nah."

"I can sleep in my slip."

"Good." Hillary's hands kept nubbing in and out of each other. "How about a cup of hot chocolate before we hit the hay?"

"That'd be wonderful."

"By the way, you got your own bathroom here. Through that door there."

"Oh. I thought maybe that was an extra clothes closet."

"That's what it once was. But when she wouldn't use the regular bathroom, I had to build her one. Cost like the devil too. Had to run special plumbing up to it from the basement."

Again Thea said nothing. She was quite aware they were moving into a delicate time. She wished it was already morning and the storm over.

He led her out into the living room. "Have a seat and I'll be with you in a minute." He was so nervous he almost stumbled backward over a hassock.

"No rush."

Outside the storm deepened. Some of the gusts were so powerful the windows bent in as if they might give way. The brick walls were some eighteen inches thick, yet the wind was so strong they seemed to be moving.

Soon Hillary appeared from the kitchen with a tray and two mugs filled to the brim with steaming dark chocolate. There was also a plate of chocolate cookies.

Finally Hillary asked, "Are you always this good-natured?"

"I don't understand you."

"I mean, you look like a really good woman. But when you was married, was you good then too? You didn't crab and stick it into him?"

Thea choked on a bite of cookie. What? After what she'd gone through with dying husband Oliver Tice? And him at the end there as light as a pheasant? Slowly she set down her mug on the blond oak coffee table. She managed to swallow the morsel of cookie. She blinked. Blinked. And then burst into tears. In a moment—she couldn't help it—she began to cry uncontrollably.

"Now. Now. I didn't mean to hurt you feelings."

Head down, Thea lifted a hand toward him to say it was all right. He wouldn't know. But she continued to cry from the bottom of her belly.

"Really now, woman."

"Oh, Hillary, you'll never know what I went through with that poor man."

"Here, have some more hot chocolate."

When Thea got herself righted, she told him a little about Oliver. Not everything. But enough to let Hillary know her lot with a mate hadn't been easy either.

Hillary looked down at the floor. "Maybe we both deserve a break the next time around."

"Yes, we do."

"Have you ever thought to try it again?"

"Not really."

"Not? I have." Hillary looked at her directly for a second, then looked down at the floor again. "It ain't any fun waking up in a big apartment alone."

"I thought you said you two slept in different beds?"

"We did. But it was still good to know there was somebody around somewhere."

"I see what you mean."

"Well, time to go to bed. 'Night."

"Good night."

"I'll turn out the lights in here."

Thea nodded. She headed for Mildred's bedroom.

Hillary gathered up the cups and things and brought them to the sink. He flished them out and set them up on the drying rack.

Lying in bed, lights out, hearing the storm sucking at the roof above, Thea smiled to herself. Hillary had almost popped the question. And that thought made her think. Yes, she did like him a lot. And yes, she'd say yes if he asked her to marry him. She too hated waking up alone in the morning in her apartment. And smiling, still crying a little, she fell asleep. The hollooing sound overhead helped.

When she awoke in the morning, she thought she was still dreaming. Someone was preparing bacon and eggs for breakfast. Along with some strong coffee. She had to be in heaven. It'd been years since she'd awakened to the smells of cooking in the house; not since she'd lived with Pa and Ma on the old homestead. The wind was still strong outside, working on the windowpanes, soughing over the roof. That's right. Hillary had let her sleep in Mildred's room.

At that moment Hillary pushed in through the door carrying a tray loaded with steaming dishes. "Time for breakfast, lady."

Thea drew herself up on her pillows. She was quite aware that she had only a slip on, that her shoulders and arms were bare. She was too sleepy to smile about it. But there was no harm in it. "And in bed yet."

"Yup." He looked out the window. "Storm's letting up. Though maybe not fast enough for business tonight." He coughed to clear his throat. "I went down and had a look outside. Snow six feet deep outside our front door."

Thea brushed her gray-blond hair back from her forehead. "I wonder . . . could you dampen a cloth for me? I just don't feel right in the morning unless I can freshen up my cheeks."

"Sure thing." He went into her bathroom, ran some water, and in a moment was back with a dripping blue washcloth. He also brought her an amber comb.

Freshened up, Thea began to appreciate what it meant to have a man serve her in bed. Then, remembering what her brothers meant by the word "service," she blushed.

Hillary saw the color rising in her cheeks. "My," he blurted, "what a pretty woman you are. And what fun it is to have a woman in the house again."

"You were a little happy with her then?"

"Yeh. In the beginning." His nose snigged up, twice.

Thea sipped the coffee. Piping hot. And a good thick stand-up brew. Her brothers would have approved. The kind to put hair on one's chest.

Hillary said, "I almost forgot, I made up a tray for me too. Can I get it and eat with you here? I'll pull up a chair."

"Oh, yes, Hillary. That'd be wonderful."

They ate with relish, smackingly, like two old friends who'd got used to each other's eating sounds and didn't mind them.

Hillary noted the little mound of snow caught on the ledge outside the window. "It's gonna take a while to dig out of this one."

"Maybe then I can enjoy living in this lap of luxury a few days more."

"Why not? Nobody knows you're here."

Finished with breakfast, Thea handed Hillary the tray. His long strong fingers, each one with a wire-thin blue vein along the top, took it easily. He picked up his own tray and started out the door.

Thea looked up at him with yearning in her eyes. "Come back right away, will you?"

"Huh? Oh. Sure."

While he was gone, Thea quickly slipped into the bathroom. And was back in bed before he finished setting up the dishes on the drying rack.

Hillary loomed through the doorway again. "You wanted something else then?"

"Yes. Come here. Kiss me."

He stood shaking in the doorway. His frame seemed to thicken. And then, with a groan that came out of aching bone, he stepped over and leaned down and swooped her up into his arms.

He was like a bull with her. Luckily she'd been ready for him or it would have hurt.

When he came to, he said, "Now I've gone and done it."

Thea loved him up. "Done what, darling?"

"Never mind. Time to scoop snow."

Thea stayed in Mildred's room for three days. It took that long before business on Main Street returned to normal and before they could open the theater to the public again.

On the fourth day, halfway through the second show, Hillary opened the door to her ticket booth and swore. "Gotdammit, it's all over town you stayed overnight in my apartment. We can't have that."

"That can't be. Who would have known?"

"I don't know. But there it is. Even Darcy Oldre, the banker's wife, knew about it." Hillary stared haggard at her. "Woman, we got to get married right away or my business is ruined."

"All right. But is it just going to be for business reasons?"

"Naw. Naw. Because we like each other."

Thea thought it over. Hillary probably hadn't used, or thought of, the word "love" in a long while. "Where?"

"I got a friend in Blue Wing. He knows a judge there who can marry us. That way it don't get listed in the courthouse here and so won't get into our local rag. That way people can think what they want to, maybe even that we was married for some time already."

Thea nodded. Good thinking. She wasn't any more interested in being the subject of gossip than Hillary was.

The fifth day, early in the morning, Hillary got his old Ford started and they headed for Blue Wing. It was all done in a rush. By one o'clock they were back in Whitebone.

Thea wanted a wedding ring and hoped that Hillary would think of taking her around to the jeweler, but instead he was in a frenzy to get the house ready for the two shows that night. As usual Thea helped him. She didn't feel very married.

When Hillary poked his head in her stove-heated ticket booth out front around ten to tell her she was through for the night because there'd probably be no more customers, she thanked him and went upstairs. She still hadn't moved her clothes over and had no nightgown. After some thought she slipped out of the theater and walked to her apartment. A month before she'd bought herself some clothes and among them was a new pink silk nightgown. She was determined to have a new nightgown for her wedding night. She was back upstairs in Hillary's apartment before he closed down the house.

She sat in the same chair she'd sat in the first time she visited Hillary. She wondered if she should be in bed in his bedroom when he came upstairs. Or what.

Thea watched the clock show midnight. He didn't come up.

She watched it show twelve-thirty. He didn't come up.

What was going on? She dared not go down to see if he'd run into some kind of trouble or other. If he had, he'd growl at her and growling was no way to start off a marriage on the wedding night. She made herself a cup of hot chocolate and went back to waiting in her chair.

Finally at one o'clock she heard the door to the apartment creak open and then slowly close. She got up, turned, and stood waiting for him. He shot her a livid glance; then headed for his easy chair near the west window. Staying with him those five days she'd learned that the big black chair by the west window was his favorite spot. The window had a fine view of the west half of White-bone. It was also a window that allowed him to watch the weather come in.

He sat down with a groan.

With a little smile Thea went into his bedroom, found the slippers she'd given him, and then went over to where he sat. She kneeled beside him, lifted his right foot from the hassock, removed the shoe and put on a slipper, then lifted his foot back onto the hassock. She did the same with the other foot. All the while she made it a point not to look at him.

She heard a funny sound, a soft snortch in his big nose. She looked up and was astonished to see he was crying. His face was wonderfully contorted, tears trickling down past his nose. There was even a drop of moisture at the end of his nose.

570

"Why, Hillary."

"Thea."

Was he crying because Mildred used to do what she'd just done, remove his shoes and replace them with slippers? "What's the matter, Hillary?"

The words came in abrupt spurts. "Woman . . . that's . . . the fust time . . . anyone . . . ever done that for me."

"Oh, now, Hillary, really—"

"Fust time!" he broke in. "Nobody, but nobody, ever . . ."

"Oh, Hillary." She couldn't say she was sorry to hear that. It would only make him feel worse. Still on her knees, she moved closer to him and put her arms around him and kissed him. The salt in his tears was sweet on her tongue.

Then Hillary really broke down.

56. Tane

1950

Tane was asleep, and what had begun as a lovely dream, of him and Arva taking a walk in the pasture alongside the river, of meadowlarks calling cheerful cries, became a dream that slowly twisted over, like a great willow tortured by a dust devil. What had been joy slowly became pain. It was as though someone had deliberately stuck the end of a hot wire into his belly, so that the electricity in the wire extended out through every nerve of his, searing out to his fingertips and his toetips. He was on fire. He was hooked up to some great huge dynamo, direct, so that his body began to hum too.

Then he awoke.

He couldn't believe the pain he felt in his belly. Not even that time when the grade school boys had started to crucify him, driving a nail through his hand, could compare to it. The pain was both centered and spread all over him. He lay there wondering if someone had stabbed him with a pitchfork. The inside of his stomach also felt hot, as though flickerings of lightning were bounding around in it.

It got worse.

"Wife?"

Arva had apparently been awake. "Yes, Tane."

"Oh, Arva, I've got such an awful pain."

"Where?"

"Mostly in my belly. Ohh. I've never felt one like this one. It woke me up. I even dreamed about it."

"I know. You've been tossing and turning for an hour. So I couldn't sleep."

"I'm sorry. But the pain is awful."

"Where is the pain?"

"Mostly in the center of my belly."

"Not low down on the right side?"

Tane ran a hand over his naked belly. "No. It's right in the middle. God, it's awful."

"Maybe I better make some warm milk for you."

"God, no. No food."

The pain intensified. His belly muscles began to jump. Then the impulse to retch took over. "Where's that bathroom!" Two years earlier Tane and Tyson had built Arva an indoor toilet in what had been a clothes closet at the end of the bedroom.

"Where it always is, silly."

Tane erupted from the bed, and sliding on his knees, managed in the dark to

571

get his mouth over the seat. Gushes of half-digested food plopped into the water. It stunk of gall. "Acch."

"Feel better?"

"No. It still hurts."

"Vomiting should have helped."

"That jerking made it worse."

Arva got up and entered the bathroom behind him and reached up to pull on the light cord. The sudden light was blinding. She reached down and flushed the toilet. "What a mess."

"You can say that again. Smells worse even than that half-digested roughage you find in a butchered steer."

"Please! Why must you men always say things worse than they really are."

"Who'p!" Tane quickly got up and whipped his buttocks around and sat on the stool. "Now my other train is coming through."

"Good grief, Tane."

"Yeh, and the pain is even worse."

"Sounds like you got a broken 'pendix."

"Naw. Wrong place for that."

"I think we better call the doctor."

"Naw. You pay him money for medicine you already know ain't gonna help much." Tane groaned miserably. "Who'p. Now the first train wants to come through again." He got off the seat and whirled around and vomited into the stool.

"I'm going back to bed then if you won't call the doctor."

Tane nodded. In the sharp light he saw that the oatmeal he'd eaten in the morning looked like a mess of maggots. Come to think of it, an oat when it first came out of its husk did look like a maggot.

"Feeling better?"

"Worse." Tane groaned some more. "Pain like this surely takes the starch out of your piston."

Arva said nothing.

For an hour Tane had to keep reversing his position at the stool. "I wish my guts could make up their mind."

When Tane finally quit exploding at either end, he crept on hands and knees toward his side of the bed and somehow managed to climb in again. He lay on his back, holding his belly in his hands, hoping that with every cracking heartbeat the pain would get better. But it didn't. The center of the pain, where it was the worst, gradually worked throughout his whole belly. He surely was sick now.

He could feel Arva beside him hoping the pain would subside. She was breathing with him breath for breath.

He said, "Try to sleep. At least you should get some. Or maybe I should go out to the living room and sleep on the couch there."

"Maybe I better take the couch. Until you get over this."

Tane tried to sit up; couldn't quite make it. "I'm too weak."

"You didn't turn the light out."

"I know. I just didn't have it in me to reach up that high."

"I'll get the light and go out into the living room. It's probably cooler out there anyway. This July weather is getting me down."

"Well, me, I feel cold. Cover me, will you?"

"Poor man. But I think I'm going to call the doctor."

"No. I forbid you to call him. Just a lot of money thrown away. I can take the pain until it goes away."

"Suit yourself." Arva turned out the light in the bathroom and vanished into the living room.

Tane suffered it some more. He didn't dare move for fear of making it worse, and yet he had to move to relieve the pain a little.

At last dawn broke and the bedroom lighted up.

Arva came in to take off her nightgown and put on her day clothes. When she finished dressing she gave Tane a closer look. "My Lord, husband, you look like the wrath of God. So white and wrinkled."

"Like the wrath of the Devil, you mean."

"I'm going to call the doctor."

"No! I'll outlast the pain." He had to puff between words. "It'll go away."

"I'm going to call Tyson then."

"And get the army mad at him?" Tyson was in the Counter Intelligence Corps training program. Only the brightest recruits for the Korean War were sent to the CIC base at Fort Holabird near Baltimore, Maryland. "Let's not bother the boy. He needs to put his whole mind on his studies."

"I'm calling him and asking him to get a pass to come home."

"I'm not gonna die."

"Maybe Tyson can stick some sense into you." Arva left the bedroom. In a moment Tane heard her ringing the operator and placing a call to Baltimore.

Tane let go with a painful sigh. Well, at that it would be good to have Tyson home for a few days.

573

Arva finally got hold of Tyson. "Hello, son . . . It's your dad . . . He's sick in bed with a terrible pain . . . He looks a fright, Tyson . . . Do you think you could get a pass to come home quick? . . . Do try it though, will you? You know how stubborn your father can sometimes be and I think this is real serious . . . All right. Call us and I'll pick you up at the airport in Sioux Falls."

Tyson called back within the hour to say he was catching an army transport plane that was heading west and would drop him off in Sioux Falls, that he would be there in about six hours. By the time Arva left, Tane had fainted several times.

When Tane came to the last time, daughter Clairabel was sitting at his bedside. She had a job as a stenographer in the Rock Falls Community Hospital. She had grown into a real beauty: light gold hair with a touch of red in it, eyes still the color of African violets, delicate almost translucent skin, a pug nose that gave her a becoming impish look. Tane loved her almost as much as he loved Tyson. Tane was aware that Clairabel thought him a god.

"What time is?"

Clairabel looked at the clock on the bureau. "Almost two o'clock."

Tane turned a little, hoping to ease the pain.

"Can I get you anything, Daddy?"

"Oh, Clairabel, I think this is the end, it's so awful." Another dry retching grabbed his belly and shook him from head to foot. "All I'm puking now is stinky air."

Clairabel replaced the wet facecloth with a cooler one.

"Can't you make that warm? Hot?"

"Sure, Daddy." She felt his forehead and then his cheeks. "It's funny you're so chilled, Daddy, when it's so hot outdoors."

He fainted away.

When he came to, he saw Tyson standing beside his bed. Tyson was dapper in his army uniform. He'd grown into a handsome man, tall, muscular, long-armed. There was still that cowlick at the back of his head, with a corresponding curl of hair over his forehead. His hair was almost the color of Clairabel's, light blond with a touch of auburn in it. The skin over his cheekbones had toughened from all the work he'd done outdoors on the farm, though he still couldn't work up a good tan, only a warm gold.

Tyson said, "What the heck's going on with you, Dad?"

"I don't know, son. Whatever it is, it came on awful sudden. Yesterday I felt wonderful; today I'm ready to call it quits."

"Dad, Freylings never quit."

"Not, huh." Tane thought of his father, Tunis, who'd disappeared so mysteriously. On occasion Tane still had his own private thoughts about that. Because of some of the remarks Pa had let fall at the end there, Tane sometimes wondered if Pa hadn't taken his own life.

"Ma says you won't let her call the doctor."

Tane could feel himself fainting away again. "I . . . I . . ." With a last great effort he fought off encroaching darkness. He opened his eyes as wide as he could to stay conscious. Vaguely he saw that Arva and Clairabel were standing at his left, crying. He moved his head to the right and tried to make out Tyson. "Son, you make a better door than a window."

Tyson moved over a step. "Dad, this ain't a joke, you looking like that. I don't give a damn what you say, but I'm calling the doctor."

Then Tane fainted away once more.

When he came to, he found himself in a white room in a white bed with a nurse and a doctor in white gowns standing beside him. "Where am I?"

"In the Rock Falls Community Hospital."

Tane noticed the various wires attached to his chest and arms. "What's all this?"

The doctor smiled down at him. Tane vaguely remembered that their new doctor bore the name of Christopher King. "We're trying to figure out what's wrong with you."

"Broken 'pendix?"

Dr. King was a powerfully built man almost as tall as Tyson. "Your white cell count isn't really high enough for that. And it isn't a heart attack. Your pulse is strong and powerful. Your blood pressure is normal. I don't know what to make of it."

Tyson moved up beside the doctor. "Doc, I want you to go into my father and see what's wrong. Open him up."

Dr. King backed a step. "Pretty radical, that."

"My dad is an old-time cowpuncher and he'd understand."

Arva, showing up beside Tyson, wrung her hands. "Haven't you any idea what it could be?"

Dr. King threw a swift look at the nurse. "You sure he never was in the hospital before?"

"Never."

Arva said, "Tane never complains about anything. If he cuts his hand, he runs cold water over it, puts on a bandage, and goes back to work. So that you know that when he finally comes in hurt, he's hurt."

Tane could feel something slipping inside. Something bad was happening in his belly. The pain gradually let up. It scared him. Whatever part of him that had been hurting could no longer feel pain.

"Go ahead, Doc," Tyson urged. There was the sound of command in his voice. "Dad knows all about cutting. You should see him nut pigs. A quick slice and a rip, and out they are."

Arva shook her head. "Boy, why must you and your father always talk cruel like that?"

Clairabel smiled. The rough talk was old stuff to her.

Tane went along with his son's remark. "Yeh. You better cut me. I hope you brought a can of distillate along, son."

For a second a smile touched Tyson's thin lips. "I didn't mean it that way, Dad. This is serious."

"I know." Tane looked up at Dr. King. "Something just now let go in me there."

Dr. King stiffened. "All right, we're going in. Nurse, prep him. Get him onto the operating table. Now! The rest of you clear out."

Clairabel was saying something. It wasn't whispering, yet her voice sounded weak. Slowly the light in his head widened; when he opened his eyes the light truly was light and it flashed all around. He saw Clairabel's strong blue eyes not a foot away.

"Daddy?"

"Umm."

"So you're still with us. Good."

"Nnn."

She smiled into his eyes. "Well, Daddy, now I know you both inside and out."

He stared at her. "How come?"

"Dr. King let me watch the operation."

His Clairabel had been tough enough to see her father cut into?

Clairabel saw the doubt in his eyes. She laughed. "You don't know this, Daddy, but Dr. King has known for some time I want to be a nurse."

"He does?"

She smiled impishly down at him. "Oh, Daddy, you know how you always complained because I brought crippled pullets into the house. And cute little piggies, and puppies; and nursed them behind the stove. Where you said they gave off a stink. I've always wanted to help hurt creatures."

"You and Ham in the Bible. The father of Canaan. Who saw the nakedness of his father, Noah."

"Now you're making it sound like a sin."

Tane managed a laugh. "Well, at least you're even with me. I used to diaper you."

Dr. King appeared. "How's your tough old dad doing?"

"He's just now come around," Clairabel said. "And already trying to make jokes."

"Good."

Tane could feel the stitches pulling in his belly. "Well, what did you find?"

Dr. King crooked his head to one side. "Your boy was right to insist we open you up. Another night and you'd have had gangrene."

"Not really."

"First thing we saw when we entered looked like a black snake a yard long. You had a blockage of the small intestine. Due to an adhesion. And even after we cut the adhesion, it stayed black. Then we made out that that part of your small intestine had infarcted. Died. So we did a resection. Then we sewed you up. And here you are, going to be just fine."

"You mean, after you cut the dead part out, you tied up the ends of what was left?"

Dr. King laughed. His swarthy cheeks pinkened. "That's right. You can look forward to another twenty years."

But Tane didn't bounce back right away. His stitches came out in time, and the wound healed both inside and out, but his old-time pep was slow to return. He found himself taking naps, often three times a day. At night he sometimes slept ten hours straight through. When the new hired hand got behind in the work on the fields, Arva finally wrote a hardship letter to the draft board. Within two weeks Tyson was discharged from the Counter Intelligence Corps on the grounds that he was needed more on the farm to help raise produce for the Korean War than he was on the battlefield to fight the enemy.

There was talk of Tane and Arva retiring to a cottage in Bonnie. Tyson vetoed it. He wasn't going to live alone with a hired man in the big house on the big farm. He still hadn't found a girl he liked well enough to marry. And with Clairabel going off to nursing school, Tane and Arva agreed to wait.

There was no question though as to who was the head stud on the place. Tyson managed all the field work and the yard work, and assigned some jobs to the green hired hand and other jobs to Tane. Tane never demurred. Quietly, going about it slowly, taking his time, Tane fit into the scheme of things as laid out by his son.

"I ain't quite got the gaff for it any more," Tane sometimes murmured to himself.

Even Arva the mother took orders from Tyson. She sometimes wanted to protest, but didn't finally because it was all working out so well for Tane's well-being.

Tane didn't say anything either when Tyson started taking a correspondence course from the agriculture college in Ames, Iowa. Tyson said that if he was going to be a farmer, he was going to be the best one around. Tyson became a hot advocate for soil conservation like his uncle Rolf. The only way he was going to save what little good soil there was left on the hills east of Highway 75 was by contouring.

When the subject came up as to why he didn't date girls more often, Tyson had a ready answer. "Why, Ma, you know we Freylings are late bloomers."

Tane overheard that. He smiled. "Maybe we're late bloomers all right when it comes to tying the knot. But I sure as hell hope we can't be accused of that when it comes to knitting."

57. Tyson

1952

The earth turned down, and soon the sun shone on the glancing river, birds awakened in the trees, roosters crowed under the windows, and people arose early in the morning.

During the second year that Tyson took correspondence courses from the agriculture college, he noticed a new professor was reading and grading his papers. From the handwriting he knew it had to be a woman. The handwriting also suggested she might be young. Her initials were M.M.

Nothing might have come of it if M.M. hadn't finally written him a note. Among other things, she wrote: "Of all the lessons I get back, yours are by far the best. Who are you? From the profile you sent us at the beginning of your work I really can't make out much. Would you consider coming down to Ames for your finals?"

Tyson gave it some thought. It was early December. The corn was in the cribs. There really wasn't any reason why he couldn't go.

One late afternoon, while having a cup of tea, Tyson talked it over with Tane. "I've got half a notion to drive down to Ames, Dad, to take those finals. Instead of taking them in the presence of a local notary public."

Tane had a slow smile for him. "Why not? We can easy take care of winter things here on the yard while you're gone."

Arva poured them each another cup. "I agree. You've had your nose to the grindstone for quite a while now, son. It'd do you good to get away."

Tyson spilled two spoons of sugar in his green tea. "And, I'm kinda curious about this woman teacher I got."

"What if she turns out to be an old maid?"

"She can't be. She writes young. And like you once said, Dad, 'I'm a bachelor, yeh, but I don't intend to keep following the trade forever.'"

"Well, good luck. 'Just push it in and hope for the best.'"

Arva sat down with a thump. The cover on the blue teapot clattered. "Are you recommending fornication before marriage, Tane?"

Tane rocked from side to side in his armchair. "And if she bleeds all night, you'll have to keep bringing her basin after basin of warm water from the reservoir in the kitchen stove."

Tyson's eyes opened in surprise. "So that's what happened on your wedding night, eh?"

Arva jumped up. "I've heard enough. That our kids should know such things about us, huh." She left for the kitchen.

The next day, Tyson packed a suitcase and left for Ames in his silver Mercury. He took Highway 75 south to Chokecherry Corner, then Highway 18 to

Garner, then Highway 69 to Ames. It was dark when he arrived. He took a room at the Hawkeye Hotel, had himself a T-bone dinner, and went to bed.

After a good night's rest and a hearty pancake breakfast, he headed for the college. Questioning around, he finally located the office of the mysterious M.M. It was on the second floor of the Hoover Building. From the lettering on the opaque glass in the door he made out that M.M. stood for Michelle Mallam.

"What a fancy name for a farm professor," he murmured to himself as he knocked on the door.

"Come in."

He stepped inside. He saw the silhouette of a slim woman sitting at a desk. The woman was reading papers. She looked up. Because of the bright light coming off the snow outside through the window, Tyson had trouble making out her face. She had her dark wavy auburn hair done up in a knot in back, with some single hairs trailing down to the white collar of her blue jacket. He said, "I'm Tyson Freyling."

The woman stood up. She was young, thank God. "Well, what a surprise."

"I probably should've written I was coming down to take those finals. But I figured that by the time you got the letter I could be here in person."

"Good thinking." She stepped around her desk and held out her hand. She was wearing a light blue trouser suit. It was hard to make out if she had good legs or not, but she looked handsome in the suit. She would have made a good model.

Sitting near her, Tyson could at last make out her face. She was pretty. She had vivid blue eyes almost exactly like his sister Clairabel's.

578

She said, "Were the roads all right?"

"No big drifts yet."

"Good."

Tyson could see she was one of those who already had at birth lips shaped into a smile. He couldn't imagine her scowling. "I wouldn't have come down, but the folks kicked me out of the house."

"Ha. That I believe."

"Thanks. But the real reason I drove down was to see what my teacher looked like."

Her natural smile deepened, forming dimples in her cheeks. "And if you didn't like her looks?"

"Just take the finals and drive home. And chalk it up to experience." He smiled down at his hands. "Like Dad says, 'If she can't be as she should be, then she'll have to be as she is.'"

"Your father sounds like a funny man."

Tyson was about to start bragging about his father, and his sister and mother, but then remembered it might not be seemly. "Well, when do I start the finals?"

"Right now, if you wish."

"In this room?"

"Yes. At that desk over there." She pointed to a small dark oak desk in a corner. "Where I can keep an eye on you."

"I didn't ride a pony down here, so you don't have to worry."

"You Freylings sound like you might be fun people." She pulled open a drawer and drew out a sheaf of papers. "Here you are."

Tyson snapped on a desk lamp and got to work on his finals.

It didn't take him long to fill out the true-and-false tests.

"Take your time now," Michelle Mallam counseled.

"I am. They're all easy."

Her smile deepened even more.

He finished the required essay by eleven o'clock and handed over all the papers. "Still time to drive home yet today."

"You don't want to know your marks before you go?"

"I'm a little worried about being stuck here in a blizzard."

"Oh." She hesitated. "Well, I could hurry through them by lunch."

"You told me to take my time. Maybe you should too." He looked down at her. She was a pretty thing all right. And already he was beginning to feel drawn toward her. She was the first one to give him bubbles under his belt.

She asked, "How about lunch? My treat."

He smiled at her. "I suppose if I pay for the lunch it might look like I'm buying A's."

"Yes, it just might."

"Maybe I shouldn't look a gift horse in the mouth."

She turned serious. "Can you tell how old a horse is by looking at his teeth?"

"Yep."

"With tractors coming in everywhere most modern farm kids can't."

"Dad kept two teams. Plus a pony to get up the cows for milking." Tyson gave her a questioning smile. "Can you tell by looking at a horse's teeth?"

"Yes. My father taught me too."

"You a farm girl then?"

"My father was an agronomist here on the campus. And we lived on an eighty-acre farm on the edge of town."

579

It was perfect that she was an educated woman at the same time that she had a farm background.

She took him to the Commons, where she led him through a buffet line. He helped himself to pastelike potato soup, smoked red sausage, baked brown beans, blue jello, and a tall glass of orange juice. Michelle skipped the potato soup.

They ate at a table beside a tall window overlooking the campus. They didn't have much to say. But both were quietly making interior soundings.

When they finished and were sipping a second helping of orange juice, Michelle said, "There's nothing I like more than to see a man eat a hearty meal."

"Said like a true woman."

"Hey. I like that."

"You never married, did you?"

"Never found the right one."

"Still live with your parents?"

Her face darkened. "My father and mother died in an auto accident two years ago. On Highway 30 coming out of Omaha. Stupid drunk driver tried to pass a truck in their lane. Dad took to the ditch and hit a telephone pole. The drunk driver got away."

"How'd they know it was a drunk driver?"

"The trucker pulled up and afterwards told how the drunk was weaving back and forth across the road."

"Didn't the trucker get his license number?"

"Trucker was too busy pulling over so he could help my folks."

Tyson knicked his head to one side in sympathy. "You still living on the eighty then?"

"No, I rented it out. I just couldn't hack it alone out there and teach at the same time. I rented an apartment just off the campus."

As they walked back to her office, huge snowflakes the size of cabbage butterflies began to flutter down. They had to hold their heads sideways into the falling snow to keep it out of their eyes.

Tyson said, "This is going to make it tough for me to drive home this afternoon."

Michelle said, "I don't think I'd try it if I were you."

He glanced down at her stroking legs. "For once I can see the justice of you woman wearing trousers. In cold weather it must be a lot warmer than wearing a dress."

"Much warmer. I take it you don't really approve of pants for women."

"Where I live you don't see it very often. My dad is totally against it."

"So was my dad. Until that time I almost lost my life in a dress."

"Oh? How come that?"

"Back in '47, I was wearing the first fashionable long skirt that had come in again. I started to get off the bus in Des Moines when my trailing skirt got caught between the closing doors. The bus started up fast. It went almost a block before the passenger's inside got the driver to stop. If I hadn't been a guard in basketball I might never have made it. I'd learned to run hard in basketball."

580

Back in her office, Tyson looked for a telephone. "I better get a room in the Hawkeye again."

It turned out the Hawkeye had filled up that morning.

Michelle bowed her head. She had the curious habit of looking meek for a moment just before she did something daring. "If you want to, you can stay overnight in my place. I've got an extra bedroom." She also had a way of holding her hand, cupped, over her mouth, as though she wasn't quite sure she should have said what she did. "Really. You can."

He smiled at her. "May I ask a question?"

"Fire away."

"Were your parents strict?"

"Nnn, if you mean, did they lick me now and then, no. But they had rules. And you knew they meant 'em when they smiled as they reminded you about them."

Tyson nodded. "Same way with my parents." He looked through the telephone book for another hotel. "I suppose it was your father who got you into agronomy."

"Not the way you think. When I was a little kid and growing up, I thought my father was a lot like the fathers of the other kids. He had a job and he paid the bills. I had in mind to become a nurse."

"Ah, like my sister, Clairabel."

"But then one day he called me outdoors to see something. Dad kept bees. Six hives usually. Finger to his mouth for me to be real quiet, he took me out behind the toolshed where he kept the hives. And I saw something I had trouble believing. There, standing on its two hind feet, was a wise old two-stripe skunk.

It would scratch the side of the beehive, and then, as the bees emerged one by one, it would eat them."

"For godsakes. That skunk could think."

Michelle laughed. "Yes, I guess you'd have to say that. And for the first time I had a glimpse of Dad's world. It was wonderful. It told me I had a deep caring father. It wasn't long before I switched majors."

"How come some fellow in agronomy didn't spot you?"

"I don't know. Though I have noticed that most fellows in my field are quite old-fashioned. They want a helpmate, someone who can cook, and wash their clothes, and have their babies. And I guess the word got around that I'm awfully independent, and that I don't want to be just a housewife, but want work of some kind out in the world. I want all of me to be used."

Tyson finally found another hotel number. Once more he found the hotel full because of the snowstorm. "I guess I'll have to take you up on that offer of a room."

"Good." Again she held a cupped hand to her mouth, and laughed into it. "If you can stand my cooking."

While Michelle marked his finals, Tyson took a walk out in the driving snow. He stopped for a Coke in the hallway of the Commons. He looked in on an exhibit on how best to set up a dairy farm. He visited an art exhibit in a liberal arts building.

When he returned she handed him his finals. He glanced through them and saw that she'd given him two A's and a B. The B made him wince.

Michelle spotted the wince. "I had to give you that B because your exam paper showed you didn't do all the suggested outside reading."

"What do you expect in my hometown, a big-city library?"

581

"I know. But it's still a B."

Grudgingly he admired her for being firm.

She went on. "In medicine, you know, if a patient dies, a country doctor can't give as his excuse that the information wasn't available to him. He has to know if it is there to be known."

He shrugged down at her in a friendly way. "It's okay. I don't hold grudges. And you're right."

Her cooking turned out to be adequate. No fancy dishes. Just plain potatoes and meat and bread and salad and a piece of pie.

She served the potatoes baked and urged him to eat the whole potato, skin and all.

He wrinkled his lip under his nose. "But at home we give the peelings to the hogs."

"Lucky hogs. Because they got the best part of the potato."

"That's true now?"

"The inside of the potato is mostly starch. Remember when you plant potatoes you plant the eye that's in the skin? That's where the real food value sits."

He'd pretty well cleaned the meat off the bone of his pork chop. "What about this? Is there more food value in the bone than in the flesh?"

"Don't be silly. Though there is a lot of it in the marrow if you can get at it."

"So that's why Mom likes to gnaw at bones. Dad sometimes complains with a laugh that she sounds more like a dog eating at the other end of the table than a human being."

When they finished eating he helped her with the dishes.

As they worked, she in the sink and he with the dish towel, she cast him approving glances at the efficient way he polished the plates. She said, "Someday I've got to see your part of the country."

"You're welcome any time. Now that most of Grampa's family have flown the nest, we have plenty of room."

"Sounds like a mansion."

"Just a country home." He finished the last plate and hung up the towel. "Can I ask you a question?"

"Sure."

"Then you've never had a man?"

"If you mean to sleep with, no." She dried her hands and with a little laugh covered her mouth. She spoke through her fingers. "If you mean casual dates to movies and such, yes."

"What a waste."

"And you?"

"If you mean casual dates, no."

Her blue eyes opened very wide. "You joker you. I'll bet you slay women left and right."

"Don't you wish."

She started to blush. "You mean, you've never had a woman?"

"Nope. Thought of it though."

A lovely wondering look softened her eyes.

He blushed. "Well, you know, I watch horses and cows and chickens doing it all the time. And dogs. So I do get ideas."

582

"All natural. And not this hyped-up stuff we get over the radio." She led the way to the living room again. "Have a seat and I'll go check the guest room to make sure the bed is ready."

While she was gone, he noticed several magazines on the glass coffee table: *Wallace's Farmer*, *Harper's*, *Scientific American*, *Saturday Review*, *Time*. He got the *Farmer* and *Time* himself, but the others he hardly knew. On the lamp stand beside the couch were a couple of books. He picked them up and paged through them: *War and Peace*, the *Iliad*, *Giants in the Earth*. He'd read *Giants*, and had heard about the other two. He spotted several bookmarks in all three, as though Miss Mallam were using them in her classes.

Outside the brick apartment house the sound of the blizzard deepened. There were strong sucking pulls at all the windows. The roar of the straight driving wind on the roof sounded like a freight train rushing by overhead.

When she returned, he pointed at the books. "Except for *Giants* that's pretty heavy stuff."

"Not really. The *Iliad* is full of wonderful little vignettes about farming in Old Greece. And in *War and Peace* there are some really fine scenes of the Russian country."

"I'll have to read them sometime." He was impressed by the kind of rich life she was living. It was almost enough to make up for the lack of a man.

"Are you very tired? Your bed is ready," she said.

"You bet. The way that wind is kicking up, it makes a man sleepy."

"Come, I'll show you." She handed him a fresh towel and washcloth and a bar of soap. She showed him where he could get an extra blanket if it got too cold during the night. "You'll be all right now?"

"Yes."

"Good night."

" 'Night."

He saw that the bed in the spare room was going to be barely long enough for his six-foot-two frame. He undressed down to his undershirt and shorts and slid in between the white sheets. "Brr! cotton is always so cold at first."

Once he'd warmed up the sheets, he dropped off to sleep immediately.

A couple of hours later he was awakened by a loud slapping noise on the roof above. Lord, how that wind was blowing outside. Next he heard a tearing sound. It was like some berserk god of the skies was ripping up a tough piece of thick canvas, and was doing it with a vengeance. He lay there thinking about the noise, what caused it, and finally decided that the wind had somehow got under the tar surface of the flat roof and was forcing along big blips of air underneath it. Having solved the origin of the racket he went back to sleep.

Around four in the morning he was suddenly awakened by the sound of someone calling him.

"Tyson!" Fear was in the voice. *"Tyson!"*

He snapped on the bedlamp and sat up. It was Michelle in the doorway, holding her breasts in her folded arms, her face in a tight wrinkled grimace. He blinked, rubbing his eyes, looked again. "What's up?"

"Someone's trying to get into my window."

"Not really?" He couldn't help but look at her legs showing beneath her short pink nightgown. She'd played basketball all right. She had great legs. Better than his sister, Clairabel's. As good as Aunt Mallie's. It wouldn't be easy to lick her wrestling. "I don't believe it. You're up on the fourth floor here. And in this wild weather?"

"He's black too. Much as I hate seeming to be a racist."

"I'll go have a look."

"Do that."

A little embarrassed that he was wearing only his underwear, he pushed into her room. She had the light on. He stared at the window. Someone or something was out there, all right, in the flying snow. And, yes, it was black. It was some three feet out from the window so that the light from the room didn't quite catch it. How in God's name could a creature of any kind be hanging out there that far from the building and yet be looking in?

"Have you got a flashlight, Michelle?" he said over his shoulder.

"Yes. Just a sec." She ran out to the kitchen; in a moment returned with a small nickel flashlight.

"Thanks." He snapped it on and approached the window. He shone it into the flying nightdark. "Oh," he said, relieved, "I know what it is. Earlier in the night I figured out what that ripping sound was above my room. On the roof. I was right. Look. The wind has somehow got under the tar roof and has ripped it off in sheets. One of those sheets has flopped over the edge and is hanging in front of your window."

"Are you sure?"

"Come have a look."

Still hugging her breasts, she approached warily, her dark blue eyes fixed on the slapping dangling slab of black tar.

"You see?"

"Oh," she whispered. "Well, thank God it was only that. I sure was scared."

583

It went through his mind that Michelle was having old-maid problems: an intruder at her window, a rapist under her bed, a mouse showing its fangs at her pussycat. He saw how she was shaking, and much as he might console his sister, he put his arm around her and gave her a warm hug. "Everything's going to be all right. In the morning the manager will send somebody up on the roof to tack it down again." He snapped off the flashlight.

She hugged him back. It was more of a clutching at him than a hugging. After a moment she said, "Why, the flashlight is warm. It doesn't have a short in it, does it?"

He smiled above her head. He could smell sleep in her tousled hair. "That's not a flashlight between us. See?" He held up her flashlight for her to see. "And I don't think mine's shorted, either."

"Ochh!" She backed her belly away from him. "You men!" Her wild fear abruptly swung over into wild laughter. "What fun it would be to know you better. So strong. So solid you are. And with it you're a wonderfully funny man."

"In other words you're willing to give me an A for deportment." He wanted to laugh as he spoke, but his tongue had turned thick. A cough rose in his throat, and when he did cough, hunching, he inadvertently pressed himself more firmly against her.

Waves of excitement quivered in her. Her breasts pushed against him at the same time that her belly leaned away from him. "Oh, Tyson."

"Yes, Michelle." He too was torn inside. He'd never gone that far with a woman. He wanted her desperately; he was afraid. He was very aware that she was naked from her thighs on down. In hugging her he ran his hand down her back, and over the roundth of her buttocks, and then down over the back of her thighs. She had wonderful satin skin. He remembered Dad's remark: "Just push it in and hope for the best."

With a wrenching motion and a little cry, she pushed herself back from him and turned away. Her hand came up to her mouth, and she smiled into her fingers, and said, "It's so dangerous. So dangerous."

To hide himself, he turned sideways and headed for the door. "Well, back to sweet dreams." With a part-sad smile, he returned to his own room.

Once again he slid easily off into sleep, helped by the thickness he felt in his groin, by the noise of the bruising wind.

Toward morning, still dark out, the roar of the storm still mighty, he was surprised to feel someone climbing into bed with him.

"Oh, Tyson, I'm still so scared. I think there's two black things out there now."

"Just tar babies," he murmured.

"I'm scared." She shivered as she snuggled tight against him. "You feel so strong."

"Think we need to use your flashlight?"

"You."

58. *Tane*

1953–1954

Arva took the bit in her teeth and ran with it. When Tyson announced that he and Michelle Mallam were planning to get married, Arva decided that she and Tane should move to town. Michelle had driven up from Ames a half dozen times to visit Tyson, and each time both Tane and Arva had liked her more and more. Tane wasn't sure he liked all that education tucked in Michelle's head, but she'd shown him that she knew farming every bit as well as he did. Michelle was easy to be around.

Arva brought it up again after supper. A light November snow was falling outdoors. Their new hired hand, Mandus Solon, had left for a movie in Rock Falls. Tane and Tyson were still sipping their tea when Arva said, "Husband, tomorrow let's go look up those six acres for sale on the north edge of town."

Tane set his cup in his saucer. "What for?"

"I'm not going to live any longer in a house where there's two head studs. Life's not worth it having a tight belly all day long wondering when you two are going to have your next fight."

Tane leaned back in his creaking swivel chair. "We don't fight."

"Oh? What do you call those hard words you two had at breakfast this morning?"

Tane grimaced, drawing up the cords under his chin. Arva was right. There had been a devil of a wrangle that morning.

. . . . Tane said, "Son, I'm not going to put a mortgage on this place so my son can buy himself a big all-purpose tractor. And a combine. And God knows what else. My dad bought this place with hard cash and the Freylings have never owed a cent on it, never had big debts. And by the balls of Satan himself, we're not gonna let those banks get a holt on us where the hair is short."

Tyson took a sip of tea. "Well, Dad, then whoever farms this is slowly going to lose out."

Tane hated what he was going to say next. He truly did like Michelle; already considered her his daughter. "All those highfalutin ideas from that farm campus . . . I'll bet Michelle's the one who's been secretly sticking them into you."

Tyson set his cup down slowly and turned on his father. "I never heard that."

Arva said, "Now, Pa."

Tane reached down and petted the head of Shep, their golden-haired dog. Shep always whined until given permission to nap under Tane's chair. "The whole world's going to the dogs. Everybody thinks they gotta be in debt to belong."

"I only want to get ahead, Dad."

"That a little farmer might need to go into debt to catch up, that I always understood. But, son, we're big enough not to have to go into debt. We got six hundred and forty acres, not just a quarter section."

"Dad, the time is coming when even a whole section won't be enough land to support a family. Those big farm operators who farm a couple thousand acres will always beat us."

Tane lashed out an arm at an invisible enemy. "Then you want us to go into debt so that they can all the easier wipe us out?"

"Dad, I want that machinery so I can get ahead and buy up some of the farms around us. Now that Clate Bartles is dead, I think I can pick up that quarter from his sister Hettie for a song."

"But them's all sand hills they got."

"Dad, that's why we can get them cheap. And with soil contouring, Michelle and I think we can salvage that farm."

Tane shot a work-crooked finger at Tyson. "See, bless her soul, Michelle is too behind all this modern crap of yours."

"Dad, we can't make it with that little Fordson tractor of yours and those five horses you've kept." Tyson stood up. "And I don't want to hear anything more against Michelle. She's already agreed to step down from being a professor to being just a farmer's wife."

Arva whirled around from where she was working at the sink. "'Just'?"

"Well, Ma, she is giving up an awful lot. A really good salary. With extra benefits. But she loves our homestead. And she's already been talking about what a wonderful time our children, your grandchildren, will have growing up here."

Tane muttered, "For them tain't gonna be like when you grew up on it, let me tell you. You're getting rid of the horses, you're getting rid of the cattle, you're getting rid of the chickens, getting rid of everything that's alive, and instead are just going to raise crops with stinking bigwheel tractors. In diversified farming you at least had a chance that one thing would work for you in a bad year."

Tyson turned to his mother. "Maybe we ought to worry more about having two head mares in the house than two head studs. Men can somehow get along on the yard, but in the house . . . oh, no."

Arva poured herself a cup of tea and sat down at her end of the table. "Well, the truth is I've thought about that. All the more reason why Pa and me should move to town."

Tane hit the table with his fist. "No!" In the old days before his operation he would have made the dishes jump, maybe even made the sugar fly out of the sugar bowl.

Arva slowly settled down her chin. "Husband, let the new generation have their head. Tyson is smart. So is Michelle. And they'll know best for their time what they should do to make a go of it on the farm. If Tyson has to borrow money from the bank, he won't want you leaning over his shoulder with you breathing down his shirt every time he wants to turn over a dollar. Husband, we're going."

"No."

"You've worked hard enough in your life. Time for you to take it easy."

Tane snarled, "And have me be like all those other farmers who retire and then within the year drop dead on Main Street? My body ain't used to coasting. With nothing to do I'll have a heart attack sure as shootin'" . . . .

Tane and Tyson had two days left of picking corn in the bottoms along the river. It was cold out. The sky was heavy and more light snow was falling. Three inches of snow already on the ground made the going slippery. Tyson was up on the two-row corn picker and Tane was up on the Fordson pulling a box wagon along to catch the ears of corn.

They had to stop to replace a link in a chain above the gathering rollers. After a minute or so, the cold wrenches made their hands numb despite wearing wool-lined mittens. They couldn't help but be clumsy.

Finally a nut fell into the fallen stalks below. Tane tried to pick it up with his mittened fingers but couldn't quite nab it. Finally he took off his mitten and picked it up. "Goddam this cold weather. Why couldn't it have held off a couple more days, until we'd finished? But I guess that's the way the cookie crumbles."

Shep had his long black nose nearby, as if to check out Tane's work.

Tane gave the dog a light kick. "Get out of the way, hound."

Shep didn't like the rough treatment. He barked.

Tane growled, "Dog, go home and watch the yard."

Tyson said, "You don't have to take it out on him. If we'd have had that new big tractor with the four-row attachment, we'd have long ago been done."

"Yeh, and that big tractor with all its weight would have packed down the ground and killed all the angleworms. You can't have good land unless the worms help you work it up."

"That's why they're coming out with those big wide rubber wheels to offset all that weight."

An hour later the Fordson tractor mysteriously quit popping and they were stopped again.

Tane got down off the tractor seat and looked into the engine. "Now what the devil is wrong with you? Dirt in your carburetor?" Moving around, Tane almost stumbled over a fallen cornstalk. "Goddamit!"

Shep, still underfoot, jumped up at Tane and barked.

Tane snarled, "Why you sonofabitch you! I'll teach you to bark at me." Tane's hand shot out like a striking snake, grabbed Shep by the nape of his neck, and threw him into the still-running picker. There was an anguished yowl; then an explosion of blood; and then silence.

Too late Tyson shut off the engine in the picker. He whirled around in his high seat, shocked. "Dad!"

Tane stared at all the blood, at the mangled form of Shep, at the saw-edged white bone ends sticking out of the opened flesh.

"Dad."

"Yeh. I guess I lost my temper."

Two weeks later Tane was milking the last four cows they owned. Tane was aware that both wife Arva and son Tyson were talking about him behind his back.

"Well, they better be worried," Tane muttered as he ping-panged streams of milk into an empty pail. He was milking Betsy. "I don't like the way things are going at all. Huh. Lucky Pa. He disappeared when he reached seventy. That leaves me three more years to go."

Betsy was a black-and-white Frisian-Holstein who had the nervous habit of switching her tail for what seemed no reason at all.

"Still! you old witch you. I'm not a bull about to put the shot to you when you're not ready."

Betsy continued to switch her mean tail.

Tane checked over her four tits. No sores that he could see. "Stand! you silly old she-devil you."

Betsy stood still for a dozen or so squirts; Tane relaxed and buried his head in her flank again, and began wondering what retired life in Bonnie would be like. He'd miss being the boss of a farmyard. Running a section of land was like being the president of a country, while living in town would be like boy's play again. Though it would be nice to live near Ma and Mallie, stop by for coffee now and then, maybe help them turn over the garden in the spring. And live near brother Rolf and kid him about being a millionaire, and razz him about the future of his adopted artist son.

Betsy usually pranced around once or twice before switching her tail, and that gave Tane time to turn his head and shoulder away from the flailing whip. But the next time she didn't. She let fly with a long sweeping swish just as the cow next down the line lifted her tail and lowered her rump to piss into the gutter. Betsy's tail flished through the falling yellow stream twice, once going out and once coming back; and continuing on, came around and caught Tane squarely around his right cheek and over his nose and mouth. The long hairs at the end of her tail were loaded with moisture. The tip of her tail hit like the plaited lash at the end of a bullwhip. Really mean.

God, it stung. And stunk.

Tane let out a roar; jumped up; threw his one-legged stool to one side and set his pail down; and in a flash of rage got out his jackknife and grabbed Betsy's tail and with a slashing motion cut the tail back to a stump. He wiped the blade of the knife on his pantleg and then closed the knife and dropped it in his pocket.

Betsy's rear went up and she kicked out. And then she stood still. Blood began to run out of the end of the stump.

"Serves you right!" Tane picked up his stool and pail again, and once more went back to milking.

Betsy didn't swing her stump again. Good thing too, or she'd have showered him with blood.

Later, when Tyson came by to help Tane carry the milk to the milk shed he spotted the bleeding stump. "What happened?"

Tane said through set teeth, "She switched her tail once too often."

Tyson slowly stiffened erect. He stared, and stared, at Tane. He wanted to say something but bit it back.

Clairabel came home. When she learned what her father had done to Shep and Betsy, she immediately took sides with Tyson and Ma.

Tane had an awful time saying no to his darling daughter and at last agreed to take a look at that six-acre place on the north edge of Bonnie.

The cottage on the six acres turned out to be well built. The Keiths, who'd owned it, were neat Scots. They'd had no children to ruin the woodwork. The house and the one-car garage had recently been painted a cream white with green trim and the little barn had been painted a bright red with white trim. There were four ash trees on the place, and they formed a row on the south side, providing shade over the little porch and the wide lawn. The garden south of the trees had been faithfully manured every fall and looked rich enough to grow Tane and Arva all the fresh vegetables they'd need.

Tane liked the five-acre pasture. Walking over it he found the fences tight and the sod in good shape.

Arva was standing beside the red barn when Tane returned from his inspection. "Maybe we can rent that pasture out to someone who wants to keep a cow."

"What! Never. I'm taking my favorite team to town with me."

"You mean the bays, Old Fred and Old Frank?"

"You bet."

"But what will you do with them? Nobody uses horses anymore. Especially not in town."

Tane stared at her. "I'll need them to haul manure."

"What manure?"

"I'll be putting them up in the barn in the winter and that'll make for manure."

Arva started to laugh. "You mean you're gonna keep horses in town so they can make manure and then you have to have them around to haul it away? You muddlehead you."

Tane waved her off. "I'm looking in the barn next. See if it's winter-tight."

Arva said, "I thought maybe you could use the barn to make birdhouses. It's the thing these days to put up birdhouses in the backyard for martins and bluebirds."

"Me build birdhouses? Never."

"Well, you're so handy with the saw I thought maybe it'd make a good hobby for you. Give you something to do."

"Yeh, and get me out of the house, like you women always do." Tane shook his head at woman law. "I suppose you're gonna have a house where everything's new and perfect, never used, so a man dassent dare to sit down even for a cup of tea. Let alone crawl into a perfect bed. No, lady, this barn was meant for animals, and I think Fred and Frank will know how to appreciate it. And, lady, I'm sittin' in the house when I feel like it, in my favorite corner, in my favorite chair, and goddammit you're not gonna be able to budge me out of it until I drop dead on Main Street."

Arva fell silent.

Tyson and Michelle were married in January at the Episcopal church in Whitebone. They took the plane in Sioux Falls to Miami and had themselves a week's honeymoon in warm air on a beach. When they returned, Tane and Arva moved to town, along with the horses Old Fred and Old Frank.

In the middle of May Tane bought himself a flat spade and began cutting up some sod behind the barn. He piled the squares of grass on a wheelbarrow and went across to the lumberyard on the west end of town and sold them as sodding.

By the time Arva came out of the house to see what in the world Tane was up to, he'd cut the sod from a square some twenty by twenty feet. She had relaxed around him a little after a couple of months in town, but still wasn't altogether

589

free of worry about his sanity. She stared at the bare ground. "What are you doing here?"

Tane twitched up his nose. "You'll see." As usual when nervous, he waggled his butt back and forth a couple of times.

"When will that be?"

"In time." Tane set his spade to one side and then with a garden rake began to rough up the bare black soil, making the surface crumbly and soft.

Arva smiled. "Aha, now I see. This is where you're gonna plant potatoes. Instead of south of the house by the garden."

"Nope. Guess again."

Arva picked up a handful of the black earth. "Rich enough for potatoes."

"Well, if we was to plant potatoes here, I'd have to put up a fence around it to keep the horses from stomping 'em into the ground."

"Well, what for then?"

"You'll see after I feed the horses tonight."

Just before supper, Tane went out and called in his bays Old Fred and Old Frank to feed them some shelled corn he'd brought along from the farm. The two horses trusted and loved him, and they came trotting up to enter the barn one behind the other. Tane haltered them, watched them mouth the golden kernels, and then headed for the house.

When he and Arva finished supper he smiled and got to his feet. "Now, wife, if you'll just watch me through your window over the sink there, the one you're always watching me from when I'm puttering around on the yard, you'll see a thing of real beauty."

"Humph. You're starting to talk like Rolf's boy, Walter."

"Just watch."

Tane went out to the barn. He talked softly. "Ready for a little dust roll, huh, boys, huh?" He called out their names, and then circumspectly slid between them and loosened the head straps to their halters. Both Old Fred and Old Frank had near-white muzzles. They whinnied and ran outside. They had one look around, then headed straight for the square of soft dirt. Once again they whinnied in delight, and kneeling front feet first, then rear legs, they lay down and began trying to roll over on their backs. Neither one made it on the first try, nor the second, but on the third they managed to roll up on their arched spines. They hung there a moment, perfectly balanced, legs slack, like puppies begging to be tickled in their pale bellies, and at last with a hollow intestinal whump fell to the other side. They rolled back and forth several times, and then with a satisfied loose-lipped grimace slowly got up front feet first. They rippled their hides in shuddering folds, ridding themselves of most of the dust and dirt.

When Tane went back into the house, Arva said, "What was so wonderful about that? I've seen that many times before."

"A dust roll is always wonderful to watch. It's when a horse is happy, and so trusting he don't worry about showing his belly."

"So?"

"Your belly is the first thing you protect when it looks like somebody is going to jump you." Tane balled a fist and pretended he was about to hit her in her midsection. Arva flinched; hunched over and covered her belly with her arms. "See? Well, those horses of mine know I'd never hurt them. Boy, sometimes when they're dust-rolling like that I wanna go over there and tickle 'em in the belly. Friendly-like, you know."

It could be seen that Arva wanted to make a biting remark of some kind but held it back.

Tyson and Michelle decided to take a jaunt down to Ames on the Fourth of July holiday. Michelle still hadn't sold her furniture, stored in a warehouse, and still had some of her books to get. There were also some friends to visit. Tyson asked Tane if he'd watch the yard of the old homestead while they were gone. The hired hand, Mandus Solon, had also asked for that weekend off.

Tane, thinking it might be fun to play boss again on the old place, agreed to come. There weren't many chores to do, what with no milk cows, workhorses, or fattener hogs on the yard anymore. The only livestock left were a hundred yearling shorthorn grassers running in the pasture. And Michelle was raising a couple hundred white Wyandotte chickens.

Tane got up at 4:30, ate a hearty breakfast of bacon and eggs and American fries and a couple of slices of sprouted-wheat bread. It was going to be wonderful driving out to the old Freyling empire that early in the morning.

Arva poured him a second cup of coffee. "Good thing there's a phone out there. If you get mixed up in something you can always quick call me."

Tane wrinkled shut his eyes. There it was again. Behind Arva's remark was the thought that he might do something crazy wild again. He decided to ignore it. He looked out at old Fred and old Frank already out in the early dawn grazing in their little pasture. "What's the temperature stick say outside your window there?"

"Eighty-one degrees."

"Wow. It's gonna be a cooker today."

"Then you be careful. No chasing after the grassers. Just go out on the old porch with a pitcher of lemonade and just sit there. Like a fat slug in the garden."

Tane rubbed his thumb across the calluses of his fingers.

Arva winced. "Must you make that noise?"

"What noise?"

"That squinchy noise. It gets on my nerves. Sometimes you do it in your sleep at night and I'm ready to jump out of my skin."

Tane decided to make a joke of it. "Hey, that I'd like to see, you with both your clothes and your skin off."

"You sex-crazed men."

Tane sipped his coffee. "Wife, how long has it been now?"

"Get out of here. The kids are probably waiting for you to show up so they can take off."

When Tane showed up on Tyson's yard, he found a note tacked on the door:

Dad,
We left early. Raid the fridge to your stomach's content.

Michelle

Before it got too hot Tane decided to take a walk over the old yard. He went about it slowly, smiling to himself in memory.

After a while, though, as he walked through the wide alley of the barn, he shook his head. How he missed the sounds of livestock: the lowing cattle, the whickering horses, the onking hogs, the cats meowing for milk.

"The farm has become a factory," he muttered.

He went out to the pump in the night yard. He remembered the hours he'd spent working the pump handle up and down to water the cows and horses. He used to play games with the pumping, to break the tedium. "After a hundred strokes, the water should be six inches deep. After two hundred strokes twelve inches deep." The only trouble was the livestock would hear him pumping and they'd crowd around the metal tank and drink the water as fast as he pumped it in. Then he'd groan. Because the rule was, according to Pa, the pumper was not to leave the tank until it was running-over full.

"What a great thing it was when Pa bought that little Fairbanks-Morse two-horse engine. It'd pump water for us when there was no wind." There often were days when it was calm out.

He went to the toolshed and got the potato fork and strolled into the corn-field north of the barn. The green corn was more than knee high. In the old days it was the hope of every farmer to have corn "knee high by the Fourth of July." But with the modern hybrid corn the stalks were often hip high by the Fourth of July. About ten rows in, Tane dug around a little with the potato fork. Turn up black earth as he might, he found no angleworms, those silent and patient underground husbandmen of the soils.

"See?" Tane said aloud as though Tyson might be standing near. "That's what all them chemicals are doing to the earth. That and all them terrible heavy tractors. And you gotta have worms for aeration and enrichment."

He stood a moment, hand to his brow, looking around at his old stomping grounds.

"Though I will say his theory of not plowing in the fall, and of tilling the soil instead in the spring, is a good up-to-date idea. Wind can't get at the top humus as easy. Nor is there much runoff during a heavy rain."

At noon he raided Michelle's icebox for coldcuts of ham and potato salad and what he liked to call roughage or hay, a bowl of lettuce.

Stomach full, he retired to a recliner wicker chair on the east porch. To keep the light out of his eyes, he pulled a pillow over his face and lay back to catch a nap. Housesitting for the kids was turning out to be snap.

He heard chickens cackle, and wasn't sure he was hearing it for real or in a dream. He longed to make the nap last as long as possible, it was so sweet to have on a hot day. But then he noticed the noise the chickens were making wasn't their usual racket. Something was bothering them. A weasel or a fox.

He lay considering the racket a few moments, hanging between sleep and wakefulness, thinking that maybe Michelle's theory of keeping the chickens locked up with special fly-proof fencing was a good thing. It made them lay more eggs and the eggs were easier to find.

He sat up. What? A fox inside that fenced-in area? When Tyson had dug the bottom edge of the chicken wire a good two feet down in the ground? Impos-sible. He blinked. Blinked again. Finally managed a good clear look.

He couldn't believe what he was seeing. A new blue Ford pickup was stand-ing backed up to the gate of the little chicken yard and two men were unloading some crates. And one of them was Mandus Solon, the hired hand. Why, that dirty sneaking sonofabitching thief. Robbing his own boss. Thinking that with the boss and wife gone for the Fourth, he and his buddy could rob the place to their heart's content. Mandus must not have heard Tyson make arrangements for someone to housesit the place.

Tane hadn't liked Mandus the first time he saw him. But since hired men were hard to find, what with factories paying such high wages in the big cities, Tane'd had to take him. And Tyson, when he took over, kept Mandus on. Mandus came from near Sioux City and knew the country well. He was a slight fellow, as quick as a mink, and had muscles as tough as braided buckskin. He had narrow-set brown eyes, and when he tried to talk with one, eyeball to eyeball, his eyelids would close in a series of flutters.

Tane was a little surprised that Mandus hadn't seen him napping on the porch. Perhaps having that pillow over his eyes had helped hide him.

Tane lay a moment wondering what to do. His first impulse was to cry out and scare them off. But then he remembered what Tyson and Arva had been thinking that he flew off the handle too quick, that he didn't think things out. What Tane really wanted to do was to catch them red-handed with some chickens in a crate and loaded onto the Ford pickup.

Tane watched Mandus and his crony as they went into the chicken house and carried out pairs of white chickens caught by the feet, heads down. They'd filled one crate and had another half full when it came to Tane what to do. Tyson had earlier that year bought a 12-gauge shotgun to knock off the rabbits that were getting into Michelle's garden. It hung on a nail in the kitchen over the door. A box of shells stood beside the alarm clock on a shelf nearby.

Tane waited until both men had disappeared into the chicken house for another couple of handfuls of white chickens, then stealthily slipped out of the recliner chair and headed for the kitchen. He reached for the gun, a Browning automatic, filled it with five shells.

"Now, you sonsabitches."

He decided to go at them from the back door. He stood behind the screen door and waited until they'd filled the two crates and had carried the two crates onto the pickup. He had to catch them with the evidence on the pickup, like he'd planned. His thought was to march them into the house near the telephone, make them lie on the floor belly down, and then call the sheriff.

"Hyar!" he roared as he stepped outside.

Mandus flashed around like a cornered fox. He took one look at Tane, then jumped for the driver's seat of the blue pickup. The other fellow broke out of his stance then too and piled in on the passenger side. The new Ford pickup started on the first push of the starter button and with a roar it started off with spinning wheels kicking dust and gravel backward. For a second the pickup looked like a horse taking off in a sulky race. Up the lane it shot toward the highway.

"Why! those sneaky devils," Tane cried. Then he ran for his own car, an ivory gray Ford two years old, which he'd parked in the corn crib alley out of sight. "We'll soon see who can go the fastest." He placed the loaded Browning on the seat beside him. Luckily his car started at the first push of the starter button too. And in a moment two swirls of dust chased up the level highway toward Bonnie, the rear swirl slowly gaining on the first swirl.

On the outskirts of Bonnie, Mandus hung a sharp left, heading up Highway 167 for Highway 75. He almost tipped over. The two crates in the back of the pickup moved to the right but didn't quite slide out.

Tane took the corner on two wheels too. He soon discovered when righted and going downhill that his Ford had the edge. Going uphill the Ford pickup had the edge. About a half mile from the corner of 75, taking the passing lane, he pulled up even with the pickup and yelled for Mandus to stop. Mandus ducked his head away, daring Tane to do something. Tane picked up the Browning with his right hand and placed it on the windowsill on the passenger side. He drove one-handed with his left hand.

Then, out of the corner of his eye, Tane saw that a car was taking the turn off 75 and heading toward him in the passing lane. In a moment he could make out the face of the driver in the oncoming car. It was an old man, and his eyes were opening wider and wider. The astonished look of the old codger was so funny Tane almost laughed. Then quickly Tane slowed down and fell behind the pickup again.

Soon the two racing automobiles were headed south down 75 and up the first long slope. Tane rammed the footfeed to the floor. But lean forward as he might over the steering wheel, he couldn't gain an inch on the flying blue pickup.

Two miles farther along the road the two cars topped a hill. Below lay a long wide valley. One look and Tane saw no cars coming. He swung out and swiftly caught up with the pickup. When he drew even with Mandus again, he lifted up the automatic with his right hand and roared, "Pull up or I'll shoot your brains out!"

Again Mandus ducked away, driving with his head held sideways.

Tane fired a warning shot over the top of the pickup. Blam!

Mandus continued to keep his head ducked away.

Once more out of the corner of his eye, Tane saw that an oncoming car had topped the farther hill and was headed for him in the passing lane. Tane had to slow down and pull in behind the pickup.

The two cars roared past Chokecherry Corner. Several tourists, standing beside their cars under the canopy of a filling station, stared with open mouths at the flying vehicles.

A quarter of a mile more and Tane once again saw a clear road ahead and drew up even with Mandus. Tane kept a wary eye on the narrow ever-varying space between the two vehicles to keep from colliding.

"Pull up, damn you," Tane shouted, "or I'll kill you!"

Mandus skulked away and down, and kept on driving.

Tane aimed for the top of the pickup. Blam! Dozens of pellet holes suddenly showed in the blue top.

Mandus dropped his head even lower. The other man, apparently the owner of the new blue pickup, gestured violently for Mandus to stop. Mandus finally did let up.

The two cars pulled to a stop abreast of each other.

Tane quickly snapped on his headlights to let oncoming as well as following cars know something was up. Then, still holding his Browning in his left hand, he slid along the seat, got out on the passenger side, and stuck his gun into the cab of the pickup. Quickly he snaked in his right hand and plucked the pickup's keys from the ignition. "All right, one at a time, slide out the other door and lay out flat in the ditch there. Face down. Get! Or goddam you . . ."

The two men got out and lay down in the ditch.

A farmer's wife standing on the yard of a farm across the road saw it all. She ran into the house and called the sheriff.

That night, after Arva heard all the details, she decided it might be a good idea to be nice to Tane. She woke him up around midnight and enticed him to make love. It didn't take Tane long to know a good thing. Tane roared his delight.

59. *Thea*

1957

Thea first noticed it when Hillary came down with colds in the summertime. The flu bug he'd had the past winter had weakened him. Somehow she had to make sure he got plenty of rest through the last of the warm months to build up his strength for the tough winter ahead.

She also made Hillary go to the doctor. But their doctor, David Cottam, son of the famous pioneer doctor at Rock Falls, couldn't find anything wrong. He prescribed some vitamin pills and suggested a vacation. "Get lots of rest," Dr. Cottam said.

"As if I didn't already know that," Hillary growled. Hillary had never thought much of either doctors or lawyers. Hillary thought doctors were mere advance men for the undertakers and lawyers were bird dogs for the bankers.

Thea and Hillary were having a chocolate milk nightcap. Both were in their nightclothes and sitting together on the sofa. Hillary had closed up the theater downstairs and had placed the night's take in the black office safe.

Thea wanted to pep him up with cheerful remarks. At the same time she thought: "Dear God, must I once again suckle a husband who's slowly withering away? I don't want another shriveled-up pheasant on my hands like Oliver Tice."

Hillary coughed. He took a sip from his cup of hot chocolate. But the sip made him cough worse. He coughed until his face and neck turned a sickly purple. When he finally got his throat clear, he muttered, "Much as I hate hospitals, I better go to the Mayo Clinic at that."

"You'll be all right, husband. We'll fill you with vitamins and I'll run the theater for you a couple of weeks. You just lie around here and rest."

"I dunno. I think I'm slipping. Old age is catching up with me."

"Dear God, man, you haven't aged a hair."

"I dunno."

"More hot chocolate?"

Hillary thought to himself a moment. "You know, there's one thing I can still try." He got up and went to the cupboard in the kitchen.

"What's that?"

"My Pa's sure-fire cure for colds. A hot sling." He opened various doors. "What did you do with that flask of pure alcohol I had?"

"It's on the bottom shelf next to the vinegar jug."

"Aha. Good." He got himself another mug and poured in a generous shot of the pure alcohol, then added several spoons of sugar and a long splash of hot water. "Now to drink it as hot as I can stand."

Thea smiled. "That sling of your father's is a pretty radical treatment."

"Yeh." Hillary sipped at the hot drink cautiously. "Maybe I also ought to add Pa's kerosene treatment."

"For goodness sakes, what's that?"

"Soak a piece of flannel in kerosene and wrap it around my neck."

"That's even more drastic."

"Or, better yet, take an old stinking stocking and soak it."

"Now you're teasing me."

Hillary's face broke into a wide thin smile. With a wink, he finished off the powerful hot sling.

But Hillary continued to fail.

A month later, Thea agreed they should go visit the Mayo Clinic. She hired a young couple just out of college to run the theater for them.

Thea drove their old white Cadillac east on Highway 16. Hillary groused all the way to Rochester.

Hillary also complained throughout the exhaustive checkup. He grumbled in his room.

The tests and X rays were negative.

Neither Thea nor Hillary were satisfied. There had to be something wrong. Hillary had lost forty pounds in the past two months.

Finally a young blond doctor named Donald Mulder suggested that he take one more look, using a gastroscope to examine Hillary's stomach at close range. Hillary hated having the long cold tubular instrument stuck down his throat. It was torture.

596 Dr. Mulder looked long and patiently; at last he removed the hollow gastroscope.

"Well?"

"I think I've spotted it. And it explains why the X rays didn't pick it up. And it isn't good news, I'm sorry to say. The lining of your stomach seems to be dotted over with tiny cancers. At least that's what I think they are."

Both Thea and Hillary looked bleakly at the young doctor.

"What I'd like to do is some exploratory surgery. Take a close-up look around in there to make sure."

Hillary thought a while. Thea placed a hand on his wrist and he placed his other hand on hers. Finally Hillary said, "Well, if it must be, it must be. Let's do it. Because I know something's wrong with me losing all that weight. With no pep at all. Right now I couldn't lick a hummingbird."

Three hours later they knew the worst. Besides the lining of his stomach, almost all the organs in Hillary's abdominal cavity were peppered with little cancers.

On the way home, Hillary murmured to himself, "By golly, after that young Dr. Mulder saw what he saw, all he did was sew me back up and send me home. To die."

Thea cried. She had trouble seeing the road as she drove the old white Cadillac. "Oh, Hillary, darling, there wasn't anything else he could do."

"Yeh, I know. Too late for that cobalt treatment. Too late for them new chemicals they got."

She placed a hand on his bone-sharp knee.

Hillary looked down at her hand, and then gently lifted it away. "You know, wife, you had better get used to not having me around much longer. So don't call me darling and don't touch me. You're throwing your good love away after bad luck."

"Husband, this is not like in the banking business, where you don't throw good money after bad money."

Hillary went fast. Within a week after his return from the Mayo Clinic he had trouble negotiating the stairs. He'd take three steps and then would have to stop and puff a while.

In desperation Thea drove to Sioux Falls and bought an electric stair lift.

Hillary liked riding up and down in the stair lift. For several days he played with it like a boy might. A little pink showed up high in his cheeks and his weak blue eyes shone.

Soon, though, the corners of his lips turned down. "You won't need this contraption after I'm gone."

"That's no way to talk." Thea had read in *Time* there had been several instances where sheer will power had aroused the body's resistance and the body had thrown off the cancer. "Hillary, you've got to believe that you're going to be all right."

"Well, wife, it's kinda nice to dream that. But it's no use. It's close by now."

Later, when Thea was alone, she broke down and cried. It was terribly hard for her to watch the crumbling away into dust of what had once been a powerful man. This wonderful man, who'd once run his corner of the block as though it were a sovereign nation, was beginning to look more and more like a mummified baby.

Thea took him out riding in the country. Hillary loved the green rolling hills of Siouxland, the long slopes of black loam on the higher elevations, the pink and purple rock outcroppings on top of the Blue Mounds, the lazy windings of the Big Rock River.

"Say," Hillary rasped. "Can you take me east of town? There's a ravine in Norton's pasture where some bobolinks live."

"Sure, husband."

They parked below the ravine. Thea shut off the engine. After the wildlife got used to the white car standing silent along the narrow grassy road, exuberant happy bird cries burst forth again. Soon several male birds, black feathers below and white above, rose out of the bluestem grass and began singing on the wing. Their song was a melodious bubbling, as though someone were blowing through an oboe.

Thea loved the reedy sounds. "What are those?"

"Bobolinks, like I mentioned." He leaned past her to look up at the sky. "They always look like they put on their tuxedo backwards."

"Look," Thea said. "There's one of them hanging in one spot in the sky like it's been pinned there. While it's singing its heart out."

"That's the papa bird. When we kids saw one of them hanging and singing in one spot like that, then we knew where to find the mama bird on her nest. She's directly below him. To within the inch almost."

"Isn't that sweet."

Hillary sat watching the bobolinks for an hour; then, almost fainting away, he asked to be driven home.

As she pulled into their garage behind the Palace Theater, Hillary murmured, "You know, wife, it's asking too much to have you diaper a vegetable. It's best to be able to clean up after one's self all the way to the end."

"What are you talking about?" Thea was afraid he was thinking suicide.

"Just that I hope I go so fast I still got a clear head at the end there."

Around four one morning Thea was awakened by a rustling sound in bed beside her. She listened a moment, and then made out that Hillary had reached down to the floor for the nickel urinal and was trickling in it. Good, she thought.

An hour later, turning over, wondering if Hillary was all right, Thea reached over a hand, and discovered his nose was cold. She next felt his brow. Then his throat. He was cold all over.

She snapped on the bed lamp above them. "Hillary?"

But he was gone. He'd died in his sleep. His face, in death, was slowly composing itself into a peaceful, even benign, expression.

Later, when brother Geoffrey hurried over, Thea was too sad to cry.

Geoffrey had aged into a handsome man. His rusty blond hair had turned silver gold. His blue eyes still were grave and steady. It was only in the corners of his mouth that he'd begun to show fifty-plus years. Tiny wrinkles flowed into his cheeks and sometimes when he shaved he didn't quite get all the hairs in the cracks.

Geoffrey was wise enough not to say anything for a while. Sitting across from Thea, with some flowers between them on the coffee table, he sighed several times.

598

Thea looked down at where her hand caressed her knee.

"Well, Sis," Geoffrey said finally, "I'm really sorry."

"Don't be. After all, I was lucky to have eight years with Hillary. After what I went through with Oliver, I'd never expected to be happy with a man again."

Geoffrey's blue eyes squinted up into squares.

"But I had those eight happy years with Hillary. Very happy years. And what a man he was. And lover? He'd always first be like a lamb and then after a while he'd turn into a lion."

Geoffrey shifted uncomfortably in his chair. He wasn't sure he liked hearing about the intimate side of his sister's marriage. "Well, Sis, that's life. I hear so many sad stories in my office. Like sadness might be the usual thing." He shook his head gravely. "So many strange and terrible turns. Like I heard last week about Old Hettie Bartles. It appears she set fire to her own house and let herself be cremated in it. When they poked through the ashes, wondering where she might be, they found her bones. The local dentist identified the dental work he'd done for her. But what was the strangest, and really the saddest thing they found, was the charred remains of a half dozen babies. All stillborn, they think."

Thea played with the ends of her blue belt. She hardly heard her brother. "I've had a look around at life and it has struck me there aren't many happy marriages. Take, now, Pa and Ma. And take Tressa and that stern Wallie Starnes. And then the many other couples I've seen in the theater here. Maybe only one marriage in ten is happy. Well, as I say, at least I had those eight great years with a king, and I am thankful to God I at least had that."

60. Geoffrey

1962

Late that summer it was decided the whole family, Geoffrey, Adela, and the boys, Tyrone and Vincent, should take a vacation together. The boys were home for the summer. Tyrone had only a year to go for his doctorate in electronics and Vincent had two more years to go for his degree in law, both at the University of Minnesota.

When the boys were younger the whole family had often taken summer vacations together, but once the boys had enrolled in college, there'd been no more great times together.

Over the years Geoffrey had mellowed. He no longer was always willing to take on hard-luck cases. Sometimes he took the side of bankers and moneyed people. Yet in his profession he was regarded as a man of integrity. He was known as "a good lawyer," and in his case it went both ways. He could be as canny and slippery as the next lawyer, and he could also argue that the law was meant to provide justice, even truth, in some instances. Somehow. Geoffrey wasn't always sure that adversary law was good law, and he was heard to remark, even to a judge right in the middle of a trial, that neither he nor his honorable opponent should be out to win points to prevail, but that both of them, and the judge, should be out first of all to find all the truth, even it if meant a counselor should give his adversary information that would damage his side of a case, and vice versa.

Adela had aged into a beautiful woman. Her black hair had turned white-silver, but her skin was still smooth, her black eyes still sparkled merriment, and she walked with the easy tripping swing of an English lady. She still helped her husband in his legal office several days a week. She served on the county library board and on the Whitebone school board. Sundays she played the organ at the Episcopalian church. Best of all, she was a reader. She took the best magazines and from them gleaned the latest news of the literary world. She had her own money to buy books and bookcases, and the house on Estey was overrun with classics as well as best-sellers. Her influence on the town library was considerable. She helped the librarian clean out the junk books and had them replaced with good editions of Emily Dickenson, Walt Whitman, Herman Melville, Washington Irving, and Nathaniel Hawthorne, as well as the better moderns. At the same time she suggested that the library purchase certain selected best-sellers, even if a trifle junky, on the grounds that surely the ignorant should have something to read too, because it just might happen that among such people there might be a good lost mind, who, if he or she read long enough, would gradually educate themselves into having good taste. "But keep replacing those silly books as fast as you can. Don't let them push out the good stuff on your shelves."

Tyrone had grown up slender and tall, walked with his mother's grace, and had her way of going at things. He read. But his reading tended to be in the sciences. He even dipped into the philosophy of science. Once he'd caught a glimpse of what Bohr and Einstein and Schrödinger and Dirac were uncovering in quantum mechanics, he began to bombard his brother, and his father and mother, with all sorts of tricky theoretical propositions. It led to some furious arguments at the dinner table. Tyrone had girlfriends but he wasn't serious about any one of them.

Vincent too was tall and slender and blond. He smiled a lot. But as the youngest in the family he sometimes had to resort to strategem, even trickery, to get in his say. They were all stronger than he was, and more experienced. From his lawyer father he learned to set traps of considerable complication. There was a game called Monopoly the family sometimes played together, and it was there that he was unbeatable. Vincent too had girlfriends but he was quite casual about dating them.

Tyrone and Vincent differed on almost every subject. But they were also laughers together, and they missed each other terribly when one or the other wasn't around.

Geoffrey and Adela wisely let them go. When the two boys had been very little they'd been instructed not to bite each other, or hit each other, or steal from each other, and if it did happen they broke those rules they were encouraged to forgive and make up.

Geoffrey several times remarked to Adela in the privacy of their bedroom that as the boys got older they'd gradually get over their incessant penchant for tugging at each other. "Their good sense will win out."

"I agree they'll get over it," Adela said from her side of the bed, "but it will be class that will win out."

"Maybe good sense is class."

Adela laughed softly. "Of course class is good sense, my husband."

The vacation was to last three weeks. With no deadlines. If they only drove fifty miles one day because of interesting things to see, so be it. Their intent was to follow all four noses. If necessary, each in turn.

It took them six days to drive across South Dakota. It took them another three days to drive across Montana.

They stayed in a motel in Missoula near the University of Montana. In the morning after breakfast the two boys took a stroll across the grounds of the university. The boys reported that the western campus was interesting but nothing like Minnesota's, even if there were lovely mountains to all sides.

Toward noon they headed for Glacier National Park. Tyrone was at the wheel, Vincent beside him, with Geoffrey and Adela in back. Geoffrey still liked to sit at ease with his shoes off. As they rolled north, Tyrone filled them in with what they were seeing on the lower hills: bunch grass, which grew in yellow withered tufts, leaving the ground bare around it; furlike buffalo grass; tall elegant bluestem; occasional patches of feathery sagebrush. In the bottoms along the streams grew tall stiff cottonwoods and bending willows. Higher up on the first slopes of the mountains, among barren rocks, loomed dark yellow pine and red fir and scruffy tamarack. The variety of greens was a pleasing visual symphony: the silverish green of headed grain, the dark green of corn, the shadowed green of the conifers, the silver-gray of the sage.

They didn't see much wildlife, but Tyrone, who'd read all the brochures, talked about them anyway: the predators, grizzly bears, black bears, wolves, mountain lions, and lynx; and the wild game, mountain sheep, antelope, and deer.

Vincent, a little tired of listening to Tyrone, turned on the radio. There weren't many stations they could get in the mountains, but to all their surprise the one thing they could get was rock music. Little Richard and Elvis had hit the country a few years before and already the Far West had picked up the fad.

Geoffrey winced in back. He hated the new music. He glanced at Adela beside him. "Can you bear that, dear?"

"Not really," she said. "But it seems that at the moment we're at the mercy of the young. One of them is in the driver's seat and the other one is boss of the radio."

"Yes. And too bad."

Tyrone looked up in the rearview mirror. "You want to drive, Dad?"

"No, no. You're doing fine. It's just that your music gets us down. If one can call it music. I'll be glad when this 'age of awful music' passes on."

"Oh, Dad, come off it. It's the thing these days. Listen to the beat. Once you catch the beat of it, it's like you got your finger on the pulse of the universe."

"It all sounds alike to me," Geoffrey said. "Bang bang bang bang. With a lot of shouting going on, even some shrieking. And guys strumming guitars while they're making clever jumps around on the stage."

Vincent joined in. "But listen to it closely, Dad. Besides the beat try to catch the melody too."

601

"No," Geoffrey said. "Tain't worth it."

"Dad, you've been spoiled by opera singers."

Adela smiled her quiet lofty smile. "Husband dear, your ears haven't been trained for it."

Geoffrey continued to screw up his face in wrinkles. "Watching them on television is enough to make one vomit. Especially when what you call a female vocalist carries that nickel penis around and holds it close to her mouth and sings intimately into it."

The boys in front were shocked. "Dad! What do you mean . . . nickel penis?"

"That nickel microphone. Sometime just watch that. The way she fondles it as she sings to it, and looks at it, and plays with it."

Adela drew an inch away from Geoffrey. "Evil is in the mind of the beholder."

Geoffrey snorted. "Not if the holder is depraved enough to look like she might have once practiced fellatio."

Tyrone gave Vincent a certain smile. "I think we just now heard a hint as to what kind of sex our parents practice."

Vincent turned in his seat and looked back at his father. "Where in the world do you get such ideas?"

"Son, that's one of the drawbacks of practicing law. You run into some pretty hairy things. Or like you kids now say, heavy things."

Tyrone slapped the steering wheel in pretended shock. "To think that our father has finally learned the secrets of life."

Geoffrey went on. "And if you look closely enough you'll notice something odd about those jumping jacks while they're strumming their guitars. It's like they consider their guitars enormous penises. With their left hand they're tickling the glans of their great horse cocks and with their right hand they're stroking their testicles." Then in a falsetto voice Geoffrey imitated a television troubadour: "'I'm gonna get my sweet guitar, and play with it all night long.'"

"Oh, my God," Tyrone moaned. "This dialogue has deteriorated into pure smut."

Vincent shook his head. "That our father should have such thoughts."

Geoffrey wasn't done. "And the way modern people kiss, both on television and what a person can't help but see at drive-in movie theaters. Godd! They kiss like guppies lipping each other."

Adela gave Geoffrey a wrinkled look of distaste. "I'll never be able to watch television again."

"Good," Geoffrey said. "Good."

They climbed a hogback. Tyrone spotted a lookout point facing the Mission Range and pulled into it. It was as good a way as any to change the subject. All four got out of the old black Packard, with Geoffrey quick slipping into his oxfords. They brushed out the seats of their clothes and stretched their limbs. They strolled over to a stone wall and looked out. Far to the east of them Cardinal Peak and Scapegoat Mountain poked up out of the Lolo National Forest.

For a little while nothing was said. They stood and looked, and strolled around and looked. The odors wafting up from the valley below were heady: sacramental sage, the drying just-mown hay, the mushy fermenting sloughs.

Vincent said, "Tyrone, do you mean to tell me that that peak over there, Cardinal Peak, is there only because we're looking at it, and that if we turn our backs on it, it might not be there?"

Tyrone's eyes lighted up with mischief. "That's right."

"And if I turn my back on it and not you, it still might not be there for me?"

"That's right."

"And that white half-moon up there, which we can just barely see in the sky, it won't be there if I turn my back on it?"

"Possibly."

"But for you, standing beside me this instant and facing it, it will be there for you?"

"Right."

"I think," Vincent said slowly with a sly smile, "I think you're arguing that reality likes to play tricks on me but not on you. You're sort of reality's pet."

Tyrone pushed his upper lip up against the two openings of his nose. "It'd be the same if we changed roles, man."

"No, it wouldn't. Because you see, me being in your place, the manipulator, I'd start out thinking that the Cardinal Peak and the moon, and the earth I stood on, would be there even if I'd never been born."

"But you wouldn't know that until you looked."

Vincent said, "Oh, yes I would. Because when I do look I find them there. And no matter how often I looked I'd always find them there."

"But there might be one time not."

"Can you be as sure of that as I can of my side of the argument?"

"No, I guess I can't because I can't be you."

"And there is a possibility I might be right?"

"Yes."

"Well, if so, you can't rule out, absolutely, my kind of finding?"

Tyrone ran his tongue along his upper lip. "Your having taken all those courses in legal argument isn't going to change the nature of reality."

Vincent drew up his blue summer pants with his hands in his pockets. He smiled some more and slowly turned his back on his brother. "Do you mean to tell me, now that I'm not looking at you, you're not there?"

"For you, no, I'm not here."

"Even though I can hear your voice?"

"So long as you don't see my lips and tongue move you can't prove I'm speaking. It might be a virtual voice you're hearing in your imagination."

"In other words, even though you call it a virtual voice, it's not there?"

"Well . . ."

"And even though I can smell you?"

"Same thing," Tyrone said.

"Even though I can sense you?"

"Ditto."

"If I were to look at you, then turn my back on you, one thousand times, couldn't I be sure you're there the thousandth-and-first time I turn my back on you?"

"Not if you did it a million and one times."

Vincent turned around and looked at his brother again. "This state is full of sites where they find dinosaur bones. You mean to tell me that when I finally go to some museum and look at those bones, they weren't there until I looked at them?"

"That's right."

"Do you think that if you were to testify to that before a jury that they'd believe you?"

"No. But jury decisions don't change the nature of the universe."

"You know, Tyrone, you're as bad as the fanatic Christian who argues that the world is only six thousand and sixty-two years old. And when you can show that Christian by carbon dating that those bones are more than two hundred million years old, he says God created them that old when he created the heavens and the earth. Your argument is just as silly. There is no way you can mesh with such people in a discussion. If you don't finally in the end there rely on good sense, you're in for a lot of trouble. Even to the point of wiping yourself out as you defend what you think is 'truth.'"

Adela spotted something in the valley below to the southwest. She went back to the car and got a pair of binoculars. She looked a moment. "Why, I do believe there's a wedding about to take place in that quaint old church down there."

Geoffrey said, "Let me have a look." He too examined the tan church below. "You're right. The groom and the best man are already standing on the church steps. And the bride is just arriving with the bridesmaids."

Tyrone went to the car too and got a map of Montana. "Aha. The Saint Ignatius Church. Built in 1854. Spanish design."

Adela asked for the binoculars again. She looked some more. "Wouldn't it be fun to go see that wedding? A real country wedding?"

The menfolk said nothing.

"Let's go see it. Indulge your mom for once."

Geoffrey smiled. The trip in the first place had been pretty much Adela's idea. She wanted one more taste of how it had been when they were first married with two little grave-eyed boys in the car. Geoffrey was proud of his family, and happy that years ago he had dared to ask Adela Sharples from Mount Curve to marry him. The two boys had picked up from Adela the low-key airs of the aristocrat. The two boys could wear almost anything, baggy tweeds, jackets with patched elbows, old trench raincoats, and still look well-dressed. They were at home any place they happened to land. Geoffrey finally said, "Yeh, let's go see that wedding. There we'd get a good chance to see a cross section of the people around here. The farmer, the lumberjack, the miner, the banker, the clergy, the merchant. Most everybody probably goes to a wedding out here."

Tyrone shrugged agreeably. "Maybe even spot us two pretty fillies, eh, Dad?"

"Maybe. Look where I spotted your mother. Of all places, in a law office."

Adela stood a moment listening. "I've been noticing something else that's rather wonderful. The different kind of background noises in this Montana silence. We live a good quiet life in Whitebone as compared to life on Mount Curve. But if you'll listen carefully at home, especially after you go to bed, you'll hear the fridge running, or the water heater downstairs humming, or the air conditioner cracking, while standing on this point there's a low incessant whirring of insects, like someone is lightly running a bow back and forth over some slack strings. And then overhead all the calls of birds." Then Adela got into the car.

They pulled up in the parking lot just as the last of the celebrants at the wedding had been ushered into the tan brick church under its spearing tower. The four of them quietly entered the vestibule. An usher, dressed like a male mannekin in a store window, smiled at them with borrowed joy. "Bride or groom?"

"Neither," Geoffrey said. "We just happened by and thought it make be nice to take in a wedding."

"This way please."

They were led toward the bride's side of the church. As they walked past the font, Adela slowed and dipped her fingers in the water and lightly touched her forehead and stomach and her two breasts.

After they were seated in back, Geoffrey whispered, "I didn't know you were Catholic. Here I've been living with you all this time and never a hint of it."

"I'm not. I'm an Episcopalian, remember? But my mother's mother was Catholic. I used to go to church with her. And I guess I was doing it before I knew it. Old habit."

The wedding service began. Geoffrey looked over the crowd. There were about forty souls sitting on the bride's side and some thirty on the groom's side. Some were at ease in their best clothes and smiled indulgently when the tremulous little flower girl almost dropped the floral cluster. But most sat stiff, men as well as women. There were several single women on both sides. A couple of them were crying. Geoffrey guessed they were either divorced or thinking of it.

A huge fat woman came in late. She shuffled heavily past where the Freylings sat. She moved one leg and one arm at a time, and then had to stop and puff. There was no shape to her breasts, just great slags of loose flesh hanging down; nor to her buttocks, just two bushel baskets of lard swinging obscenely. Her face was flushed a deep purple, with the purple waxing as she took a step and waning when she rested a moment. Her florid ears, large as lily pads, waggled under a knot of black hair. Finally she sat down, the bench making an explosive cracking sound, so loud the priest paused and looked over his spectacles at the huge creature. A murmur of unrest moved through the benches ahead of the fat woman.

Tyrone whispered to Vincent, just loud enough for Geoffrey and Adela to hear, "How would you like to have sex with her?"

Vincent whispered back, low behind a hand, "It'd be like having intercourse with a hill."

"Shh," Adela whispered, also under a hand. "That's scandalous."

Geoffrey have Adela a nudge with his elbow and leaned over to whisper into her ear, "That's really kind of funny, though."

"I don't care. You men are so like an ever-ready flashlight it's disgusting."

Geoffrey indulged himself in looking at all the different colors in the church: the light blue of the walls and the gold of the soaring arches and lofty nave, the scarlet and gold of the pulpit up on one side, the artery reds and vein blues and bile greens of the luminous parallelograms in the windows, the brisk maroon carpeting in the middle aisle. The lilac blue colors everywhere was like a sky blooming over them. The unctuous old priest wore an immaculate cream white stole. A ruby on his right ring finger flashed ecclesiastical warnings every time he gestured. Below him, with a humble air, in white silk and white serge, stood the fresh-cheeked bride and the strong-browed groom.

The ceremony seemed to last a long time.

Soon Geoffrey found himself looking at his fingernails to see if he'd trimmed them that morning. Next he noticed that where he'd placed his hands his thighs seemed to have thinned over the years. Or was it that his knees, due to mild rheumatism, had thickened? There was a time when Geoffrey had been proud of the way his legs shaped up in well-tailored trousers.

605

The priest with a fatherly part-leering smile at last pronounced the bride and groom married. The two turned to kiss each other; then, to the rising surge of the pipe organ, they began their triumphant wedding march back to the front door.

Geoffrey liked the pretty bride: dark curly hair, high blue eyes, good chin and nose, full bosom, tall. Her husband, though, had the look of a hired hand who'd just scrubbed himself clean with a harsh soap, and then had inched himself into a rented suit with a shoehorn. Geoffrey thought: "He'd better not swell with pride. Or whatever."

The two male ushers gestured for the audience to get up and leave, a row at a time on each side of the aisle. Everyone had a smile of sorts, wide for those who loved weddings and who were probably happy in their marriage, a bit pinched for those who'd come out of duty.

Geoffrey studied the various faces as though they were a panel of citizens from which he might have to choose a jury. He didn't see one he'd object to.

Then an older couple, whose set of shoulders seemed vaguely familiar when seen from the back, got up. With them were two young ladies in their early twenties. The moment the older couple turned into the aisle, Geoffrey recognized them. He'd so little expected to see them in Montana, or anywhere ever, that it took several seconds for it to soak in.

Adela recognized them too. Instantly she woke up to what she was seeing. She drew in a deep gasp, then yet another, before she turned to Geoffrey in elegant amazement. "Why! It's your brother Dirk. And . . ."

Geoffrey's tongue stirred. "Yeh." His glance switched to the two young ladies following Dirk and Tressa. Could those two be their children? Eyes narrowed, flicking back and forth from Dirk to Tressa, and then to the two young ladies, Geoffrey saw they had to be. The girls both had the happy blend of Dirk's whimsical grimace and Tressa's compassionate smile. Both girls had Dirk's complexion and Tressa's rusty gold hair. They had Dirk's slender build and Tressa's full bosom. For once the offspring of a brother and a sister had made for good breeding.

Both Tyrone and Vincent had got to their feet to leave, but when they saw how their father and mother were staring at four people coming down the aisle toward them, they hesitated.

The four people were smiling together, happy and laughing, as they drifted toward the exit. Dirk had said some teasing thing to the two young ladies, and they'd laughed and given him a push in protest. Tressa smiled indulgently at it all.

Then Dirk, blue eyes always alert, spotted Geoffrey; and then Adela. He stiffened; and stopped. He grabbed Tressa by the arm, and in so doing stopped the two young ladies too. Dirk's eyes next flicked a searching look at Tyrone and Vincent.

Geoffrey broke out of his freeze, and slowly got to his feet. Adela rose to her feet too.

Dirk's gray head rolled a little, as though he were trying to shrug off an animal of some sort that had latched itself onto his back. Then Dirk collected his mastership, and got his sails squared around to the wind, and the old witty fellow in him spoke up. "Well, well, look what the rabbits chased into the church. My own legal beagle brother."

606

Geoffrey couldn't help but laugh. "Yes, sometimes rabbits will turn on you."

"These your sons all growed up?"

"Yes."

"Married?"

"No." Geoffrey glanced at the left ring fingers of the girls. "Just like your two girls."

"Oh." Dirk took a deep breath. He looked at Tressa as though already apologizing for giving away a secret they meant to keep. "Yes. Our pride and joy. The twins, Tansy and Lara."

Before anyone could say anything, Adela remarked, "What interesting names." Adela had instantly caught on who the two girls were named after.

Tansy and Lara looked wonderingly at Geoffrey and Adela: then switched their attention to Tyrone and Vincent. They smiled at the young men, and Tyrone and Vincent smiled back.

Geoffrey caught the look of intense interest between the four young folk. He cleared his throat. "Ahh, Dirk, don't you think you ought to—"

"Yes," Dirk broke in. "I guess I better. Wife, shall we tell the four youngsters here who they are to each other?"

Tressa slowly nodded. "Why not? You can't stop them from getting acquainted now, and sooner or later they'll find out."

Dirk stretched his lips thin with a wincing look. "Tansy, Lara, like I've already hinted, this man and I are brothers. So that makes these two young whippersnappers your cousins." Dirk looked at Geoffrey. "What's their names again?"

"Tyrone and Vincent."

The four young people looked at each other astonished.

Dirk waggled his head to one side, so sharply his gray hair fell out of its parting. "Yes, this is your uncle Geoffrey, my youngest brother, and this is aunt Adela, his wife." Dirk tried out a laugh. "To mix you up even more, since your mother and I are cousins, which you already know, your mother is also the cousin of Geoffrey here." A nervous cough kept him from saying more.

Geoffrey thought: "So that's how Dirk and Tressa passed off to their children what they did. Not brother and sister running off together, but cousins."

The four young people continued to stare at each other, smiles working at the corners of their lips.

Dirk said, "Geoff, how did you happen to luck onto this church?"

Geoffrey explained how they came to be there.

Dirk cocked his eyes sideways at Geoffrey. "As an officer of the court, you weren't chasing after some rascal or other?"

"On my vacation with my family? Never."

Adela sidled over to Tressa, and after a moment graciously slid an arm around Tressa's waist and gave her a light hug. Tears abruptly rimmed Tressa's blue eyes.

Geoffrey's heart gave a jump. He called on his courtroom manner to remain cool and collected. "Dirk, what do you do for a living up here so high on the map?"

"What else but run a little weekly newspaper. Saint Ignatius *News*. I've managed to build it up to over two thousand subscribers in the valley here. The paper pays for itself pretty much. But we make our real living doing printing jobs."

"Well, good, good."

Dirk was about to put an arm around Tressa too, then thought the better of it, and made the motion of his arm seem part of brushing back his forelock. "We can easy put you four up, you know, if you've got the time. Then we can catch up on all the news."

There was a silence.

Geoffrey looked at his two young nieces. They were lovely. They were obviously identical twins all right, and one would not have been able to tell them apart if Tansy hadn't had slightly protruding upper teeth, and over the years had learned to shape her upper lip over them in such a way that it wasn't too apparent. Already Geoffrey's heart went out to them. Gramma Clara Freyling would be proud of them. Gramma so far then had six handsome bright grandchildren. And of course Grampa Tunis Freyling had them too.

Adela gave Tressa another soft hug. "Truth to tell, we're on a sort of schedule, and we've got to get back in time for Geoffrey here to fight an important case . . . so I think we perhaps should ask for a raincheck."

Tyrone and Vincent looked at their mother with barely masked astonishment. Ma was lying.

Geoffrey caught Adela's drift. She was thinking that perhaps their boys shouldn't find out that Dirk and Tressa were not cousins but brother and sister—it would color their feelings about the family forever. And even worse, the girls, Tansy and Lara, should absolutely not find out. It might wreck them. "Ya. I'm sorry, Dirk, but even stopping at this church was going to cut into the time we had left. So, maybe some other time, huh?"

Tressa caught on to what Adela had in mind, and in obvious relief nodded that perhaps, yes, some other time.

The old priest came along then, and with a courteous smile asked Dirk, "Well, did you get their names for your paper?"

"Yes," Dirk quickly said.

"Spelled right?"

"What? You ask that of an old newsman?"

"Just joking, Dirk, just joking."

The priest's interruption broke up the meeting between Geoffrey and his brother and sister, and with firm handshakes and soft good-byes, each family went its way.

Afterward in their car, as they continued on their way to Glacier National Park, Tyrone and Vincent were angry that Dad and Mother hadn't accepted Dirk's offer to stay with them.

Tyrone wheeled the old black Packard along in a fussy manner. "What's the harm in us getting acquainted with our cousins? They look like such great chicks."

"Yeh." Vincent turned in his seat to face his father and mother. "You two acted like we was thinking of dating them."

Tyrone went on. "Suppose we did get to like them a lot, and later on wanted to marry them, what's the harm in cousins marrying? Their father and mother did."

Geoffrey drew himself up very erect. "No."

Adela said, more softly, "I'm afraid it's a no, boys."

Geoffrey thought: "Ma must never find out. So it's a no."

Vincent said, "You two are hiding something, aren't you? Lying?"

"Maybe we are," Geoffrey said. "But in any case, you must never mention who we ran into in front of Gramma."

Vincent said, "Dad, I never ever heard you mention that you had a cousin named Tressa. Like our missing Aunt Tressa."

It wasn't until they were about to enter the Glacier National Park that Vincent went back to his earlier tussle with Tyrone. "In other words, brother, if you can't prove to me you exist when my back is turned on you, then I can safely ignore your quantum mechanics theory."

"Hey. That's solipsism. We physicists have little or no time for philosophic theories."

"And I suppose if we turn our backs on Uncle Dirk and Aunt Tressa, they don't exist either?"

"Well, our parents seem to believe that."

"Nor those two double cousins of ours?"

Tyrone stared at his younger brother. Then caught on to what he meant.

Geoffrey also caught on. Vincent had figured out that Uncle Dirk and Aunt Tressa weren't cousins after all, but were brother and sister. "Double cousins." The boys now knew that there weren't two Tressas, only one.

61. Clara

March 3, 1966

Most of them were there on her one hundredth birthday: Tane and Arva with their children, Tyson and Clairabel; Thea, who had taken up residence with Ma; Rolf and wife Greta with their adopted son, Walter; Mallie, who was the first to go back and live with Ma; and Geoffrey and Adela and their two sons, Tyrone and Vincent.

Over the years Clara had almost managed to blot out the memory of her husband, Tunis, as well as the memory of Dirk and Tressa. Ana, it appeared, had become a martyr in the Lord's cause and for her Clara often grieved in her bed at night.

There was also a baby in the house, Truman, a beautiful baby, a great-grandchild born to Tyson and his wife, Michelle. Clara wished it might have been born a girl. But perhaps a boy was all right. By the third generation the blood of that wild man Tunis surely had been thinned out.

Clara sat in her favorite place, in an upholstered armchair that Tane had improved specially for her. Compared to her children and her children's children Clara was a shorty. She once complained to Tane that she always felt like she was sitting or standing in a hole when talking to members of her family. Couldn't her favorite chair, a red plush thing with curled wing sides, be somehow raised several inches? Even six inches? Tane took a look at the legs and agreed. He removed the four legs, and then in his toolshop shaped a new set of four some five inches longer. When he finished, Clara tried it out. She had to raise herself on her toes to slide herself onto the chair. Tane started to laugh. "First chair I ever did see wearing lifters," he said. Clara decided she liked the new height. When she sat erect her eyes were above those of her family. It made her feel more in control.

Clara was as surprised as any one that she'd reached a hundred. She'd known all along that she had a tough heart. Her heart had to have been tough for her to have survived all the rough times she'd lived through. But reach a hundred? So far as she knew none of her relatives in Weldon, or back in Old England, had reached that venerable age.

Now and then, when she looked in a mirror, she always smiled at how well-preserved her face was. She hardly looked seventy. People who dropped in on her often remarked about how in the pink she looked. "You sure don't look your years, Mrs. Freyling." When newsmen from the local weeklies in the county called on her to write her up, they asked her what her secret was for longevity. She tried not to smile. There was no secret. Unless the Lord knew what it was. Her milk white hair had thinned, but not so that one could see the scalp, as was so often true of old people.

Clara was also proud of the way she could still agitate around, as she called it, despite the stiffness of her right thigh. The broken thighbone had healed just fine, but it left the hip joint sore, as though she might have a touch of rheumatism in it. She still walked downtown to get the mail, get the groceries, and to attend the meetings of the Bonnie Boosters.

Clara sat at the head of the living room, next to the upright piano, and looked over her remarkable brood. What a handsome bunch they were. In her eyes they resembled more her Shortridge side of the family than Tunis's side. Too bad they couldn't've borne the Shortridge name. Her father would have been so proud of them. Even little baby Truman already had the look that he would someday be a stalwart handsome man with rusty hair. It was also obvious that the little one had her grave gray eyes.

Tane and Rolf were laughing together in the corner by the television set about the old days when the Bonnie Omaha train crossed their homestead. They lamented that the railroad company had decided to discontinue the run between Bonnie and Whitebone, had torn up the tracks and returned the right-of-way to the farms on either side of it.

Tane laughed some more. "Yeah, I guess I was going on seven when the funniest thing happened. Not counting that time when it jumped the track and started tearing up the earth like an old boar gone crazy. Pa was telling about it."

Tyrone broke in. "Uncle Tane, you mean our grampa?"

"That's who. A few miles south of Hackberry Run, a young lady rode a small gray horse up alongside the engine and trotted even with it for a mile or so. Easy. This was too much for old Suddaby, the engineer. No horse was going to run with his steamer, timetable or no timetable. So he let her went. Pulled back on the steam handle."

610

Tyrone got set for a laugh. So did his brother, Vincent, and his cousin Tyson.

"Well," Tane said wiggling in his armchair, "the faster the iron horse went the faster the little white nag stretched herself. Even-steven all the way. For two miles or so. Huffing-puffing; clippety-clop. The time card was smashed to smithereens. But still the young lady held her own on the nag. And by golly if she didn't gallop across the tracks at Hackberry Run ahead of the train. An easy winner."

Rolf had a question. "How come I never heard Pa tell that?"

Tane shrugged. "He probably just forgot with you. There was so many funny stories to tell about our old Toonerville Trolley."

Mallie and Thea went out to the kitchen, where they had various pots and kettles steaming for dinner.

Rolf looked fondly at his adopted son, Walter. "To, son, talk a little with your cousins. You with your arithmetic should get along good with Tyrone and his science."

Clairabel had a request to make. "Before Aunt Thea and Aunt Mallie bring out the food, I'd like to take some pictures. Gramma, how about a four-generation picture of you, of my father, Tane, of my brother, Tyson, and the baby, Truman?"

Clara held her head to one side. "Must you? I'm not all that crazy to have my picture taken."

"Oh, come on, Gramma," Tyson said, "tain't often a person can take a four-generation picture. C'mon. Dad, you take this chair next to Gramma here. And I'll kneel in front of you holding Truman."

It was done. Clairabel took several black-and-whites for framing, and then with another camera took a couple of colored slides for a projector.

Clara felt her old heart beating faster than usual, large and full. She had an idea. "How about a picture with the baby on my lap? The cute little thing." Clara reached for Truman, and Tyson, with an indulgent laugh, settled the baby in her lap. Clara felt the baby's bottom. "So far so good." She gave it a cozy tender hug. "What a little darling." As she nuzzled the baby Clairabel quickly snapped the picture.

Soon Thea and Mallie had the food all set out on card tables in the living room. In an orderly warm family fashion, everyone lined up buffet-style. So much food had been set out the legs of the card tables looked rickety: baked potatoes, red running prime beef, creamed carrots and peas, cracked wheat bread and butter and chokecherry jelly, a salad of lettuce and watercress, red slices of pickled apple, and pecan pie topped off with a large dollop of vanilla ice cream. It was a feast fit for a queen.

Clara's three grandsons fought over the honor of bringing her a tray of food. "Now, Gramma, this is your day. You stay sitting right there. Don't you move. Not even Queen Victoria had as much right for the honor."

"But I don't want my grandsons fighting over it. Why don't you draw straws?"

"Good idea. Clairabel, will you get a couple of Gramma's lucifers in the kitchen and break them off at different lengths?"

Clairabel got three red-tipped matches, broke off the red ends at different lengths, and then with a smile held them out to the three grandsons in turn. The lot fell to Vincent. With a whoop, he got Gramma her tray of food.

There were spurts of talk about many things.

Clara was halfway through the food when she noticed a lapse of time. Aha. Another little pinprick stroke. She knew about them but had never mentioned them to either Thea or Mallie. The first time she had one she became aware of it when it seemed all sound had ceased around her, even in her head. She didn't know for how long it'd been silent inside. She'd quickly looked at Thea and Mallie to see if they'd noticed. They hadn't. Same thing now. For a few moments the sound of joyous laughter and talk had vanished. It was as if she had been sitting in a movie house with the sound turned off but with the people up there on the screen still talking and laughing and kissing.

611

Presently she continued eating and smiling at her wondrous family.

The little stroke stirred up the memory of a strange dream she'd had two nights before. It was about her husband, Tunis. She often dreamt about him, vaguely, and always with him as the bad guy. But this time in the dream to her surprise he came on as a tender hero, and she was once again in love with him, like in the old days when she'd first met him. They'd made love, and were lying together in the dark catching their breaths, when he suddenly said, "Clara, honey, I'm sorry if I misread you. Sometimes when you cuddle up close to me, you just want to be close to me, just be touching your skin against my skin. No more. But the old bull in me misinterprets what you want, thinks what you want is for me to jump you and shoot my seed into you. Thinks that what you need is some sex. Honey, I'm sorry. Teach me how to read a woman so that I may know what she really wants." Then Tunis had taken her hand and stroked it gently over the back, and then he'd raised her hand and kissed it on the back. "Honey?"

But the dream didn't end there. There was a little bit of an explosion in her head. It instantly changed the scene, and she next saw her husband Tunis taking a walk over a very long bridge. Below rushed a foaming angry yellow river. Suddenly four men confronted him. They came from the rowdy dives in South Sioux City, across the river. All four had knives. Tunis whipped out his pistol, the one she'd found in the bricks beside the old fireplace. It had only three bullets. He fired, fired, fired; and three of the four men dropped. But the fourth man kept on coming. The fourth man had an awful ruffian face with a black handlebar moustache and tuberthick lips. Tunis tried to hit the ruffian. Tunis missed, and slipped and fell. The ruffian jumped on Tunis and stabbed him. Then as Tunis's life ebbed away, the ruffian gave him a tremendous kick— the ruffian appeared to be twice as tall and muscular as Tunis—so that Tunis rolled underneath the bridge railing and fell into the rushing roaring river below. "Now I know where Pa went!" she'd cried; and woke up.

For a whole day she considered telling Geoffrey about the dream. Would it be worthwhile to have a search party go look for Tunis's skeleton on both sides of the Missouri River below the Sioux City bridge?

But as the dream faded in memory so too did her idea to get up a search party.

Secretly, though, she thought she knew where Tunis's body was. He had not run away from her or from the family after all, but had been the victim of foul play in Sioux City.

The girls Thea and Mallie might not have noticed the pinprick strokes. But they noticed something else. Clara had lately become terribly stubborn about silly little things, like trying to get out of taking the weekly bath, or of refusing to brush her teeth, or of declining to wear her glasses. She hated those glasses. Her reading suffered, but not her viewing of television.

She'd come to love the classical programs coming over the public television stations, especially the series dealing with English life in Great Britain. Sometimes the English characters on television were so real she forgot where she was, forgot her age, forgot her family. There were times when it seemed to her that if she had one more erg of willpower she could transport herself back to those old times. Sitting erect in her armchair, in the very center of it, she sometimes imagined that the red wings of the chair were real feather wings, her very own angel wings, and that she could fly anywhere she wanted to.

She found herself listening to the joshing talk between Tyson and Tyrone and Vincent. They were having so much fun about some modern thing. She wondered how much they really knew about the history of the Freyling homestead. Had anyone ever told them about the Indians who once visited the place? About that dying white woman who was buried Indian fashion up on that fat limb of their great old veteran cottonwood in the pasture by the river?

Clara cleared her throat. "Boys?"

"Yes, Gramma."

"Did anyone ever tell you that there's a body buried under that great cottonwood in our pasture?"

"There is?"

Clara told a little about how Her New Man appeared one day with a remnant band of Yankton Indians, that there was actually a white woman with them who was dying, and how her bones had first been put up on a limb of the cottonwood and later reburied under the limb.

"Really." Vincent turned to his father Geoffrey. "How come you never told us about that?"

Clara went on, happy to be the raconteur yet once more. "Yes, and did your father ever tell you that there's a big red stone on top of the east hill that has an image of some kind on it? A petroglyph?"

"No!"

"Well, there is." Clara told how after Her New Man had placed the body of his mother up on the limb, he had climbed the high hill and had prayed to the petroglyph.

Tyson said, matter-of-factly, "I knew about it. Dad once told me."

Tyrone said, "Well, we didn't. Because our Dad never mentioned it."

Clara was into her pecan pie and ice cream when she noticed there'd been another lapse of time in her head, a little pinprick irruption. Because two of her grandsons were having a lively discussion about what they thought was truly real.

Tyrone was saying, "How could you have seen it? You had your back turned on it."

Vincent said, "I have eyes in the side of my head."

"You mean in the back of your head."

"No. I mean peripheral vision."

Tyrone said, "Well, anyway, there are as many universes as there are people. If there are three billion people on earth then there are three billion universes."

Walter broke in. "Suppose there were no human minds around to understand what you are saying, then there'd be only one universe around."

Tyrone finished the last bite of his pie and set his plate on the blue-carpeted floor at his feet. "No, then there'd be no universes around."

613

Vincent said, "All right. But how about this then. The human mind that understands what you are saying couldn't just have popped out of nowhere. It had to pop out of some kind of mass in space. And if that is so, then couldn't some kind of mass in space have been there before your brain came along?"

Tyrone shook his head loftily. "The truth is that scientists now think there are virtual protons and virtual electrons. Not here one moment, then here the next moment, then gone a moment later. Same thing with a universe."

The talk bewildered Clara. Except for one thing. With her little strokes coming and going there were times when she was not there one moment and then a moment later she was there again. Clara smiled to herself. What bright grandchildren she had.

All of a sudden Tyrone said something that burned in the end of her nose. Tyrone said, "Well, the best chick I ever saw was a double cousin of ours."

Tyson said, "You mean my sister, Clairabel?"

"No, no, not her. Though she's a love too. No, I mean Uncle Dirk's twin daughters, Tansy and Lara. Now there, there really were two beauties."

Tyson, and Clairabel, who'd drawn near when she heard her name mentioned, stared at Tyrone. "Where did you meet them?"

"In Montana. Uncle Dirk and his wife, Tressa, introduced them to us in a Spanish church there." Abruptly Tyrone realized he spilled some beans he'd promised not to spill. Tyrone looked at his father across the room.

Geoffrey heard him. Geoffrey's face turned dark. Then Geoffrey shot a look at his mother, Clara.

Clara's heart banged and tumbled about in her chest. What? Geoffrey and Adela and their boys had seen Dirk? In Montana? With his wife, Tressa? And Dirk and Tressa had twin girls? Why, then they had finally run off together and had gotten married. Brother and sister. And they'd had children. So . . . wrongful mingling of the flesh had shown up in her family after all.

Clara rose a little in her red wing chair. She could feel her eyes widen, widen so much they stung in the corners.

There was a sudden collapsing of a wall in her head and then the rapid sound of a surge of water rushing around her eyes. And then she felt herself tipping forward and falling out of her chair, her tray with its unfinished piece of pecan pie and ice cream sliding to the floor ahead of her. Dirk and Tressa . . .

62. Geoffrey

July 1966

Geoffrey found that he'd been named executor of his mother's estate. After he'd made sure all of her debts had been paid, he then divided up the estate as she'd directed.

On the way home from Bonnie, going north up the old King's Trail, Geoffrey abruptly pulled up near the end of the lane of the Freyling homestead. Out of the corner of his eye he'd noticed a flash of sunlight on the big red boulder high up on the hill to the right. It was the boulder Ma had talked about just before she'd died of a stroke. The half-breed named Her New Man had once prayed to a scratching on it right after his mother, Judith, had died under the big cottonwood tree in the pasture.

Geoffrey got out of his car, brushed down his gray-green jacket in back, and went through a gate into the east field. He started up the hill along a fence line. He remembered the great rock all right. After he left home to go to college and law school, he'd often thought of going up there and sitting on the boulder and having a look around at the Freyling place, but somehow he'd never got around to it. And the few times he had gone up there as a boy he hadn't paid much attention to the petroglyph on the great stone.

Halfway up the hill he had to stop to catch his breath. His heart had also begun to beat wild and fast. So. He was getting old. As a boy he could run up and down hills as though they were flat land.

Breath back, heart beating steady again, he continued climbing. He went slower, stopping now and then to have a look around. As he rose he could see more and more of the slowly curving valley running from northeast to southwest with its leisurely wriggling river. Elms and maples fringed the river as far as he could see in both directions. At the north edge of the homestead was a thickening of trees. The wasteland. Pa had once seen a cougar in its dense growth. And Rolf had once uncorked a gas gusher there while digging a corner post.

At last Geoffrey reached the great red boulder. It shone in the late afternoon sun as though a lapidary had worked on it with a polishing rag. From an anthropologist at the Pipestone National Monument, north of Whitebone, Geoffrey had learned to see the difference between a rock polished by glacial action and one polished by buffalo rubbing their oily hides on it to get rid of winter hair. Geoffrey leaned down for a closer look. Why! it was a buffalo rubbing rock. All these years the family hadn't known they had a rub stone on their place. And it was the sun reflecting off that buffalo polished part that had caught his eye when he came up the King's Trail.

Gleaming as though it had been shellacked, then polished, it was a beautiful stone. The wavy grain of pink and purple resembled flesh just skinned out, then frozen.

Geoffrey rubbed his hand over it. So smooth. So slick. It invited one to rest on it, even press one's cheek against it.

Then, rubbing it, he saw the petroglyph. He knelt to study the glyph better. A very long time ago someone had pecked out with a hard sharp-edged stone a horizontal line with a circle set on it. For heaven's sake. The petroglyph was similar to something in the Pipestone National Monument that one ranger had declared was the Egyptian hieroglyph for the rising sun. Leaning down, Geoffrey made out something else. A line had been pecked out on the right going up a ninety-degree angle and another line on the left also going up at a ninety-degree angle. Hey. That could represent the summer and winter solstices. He looked to the northeast, then to the southeast, to see if he could spot two other boulders. But so far as he could see there were none. Had there been two such marker boulders they would have been in Rodman's alfalfa field. Well, had they been there Rodman by now would probably have removed them.

Geoffrey backed off a couple of steps. At this very spot, underfoot, Her New Man had knelt and prayed to the sacred stone.

That prayer was lost forever.

Geoffrey thought of sitting down on the cool stone; then, with a sigh and a sweep of his fingers through his gray hair, rejected it. One didn't sit on the Episcopalian church's baptismal font or on a table prepared for the Lord's Supper.

He turned to look down at the farmyard below where nephew Tyson and his wife, Michelle, lived. Tyson was letting the land on the high east hill go wild. Tyson knew it was virgin land, that the only tampering that had been done on it was to mow it for hay during a rainy year.

Red-purple coneflowers, softened with a chocolate dusting, nodded all around Geoffrey. Blue vervain flowed with the gently persistent south wind. There were several compass plants, a rare prairie flower, showing where true north and true south lay. In some places bluestem grass stood hip high.

Geoffrey turned back to the big fleshy stone with its aboriginal petroglyph. He tried to conceive what it might have meant to those Old Ones. Had some shaman pecked it out and then in late June and late December performed some kind of religious rite at the site? If so, the shaman's people below at the foot of the hill would have waited for his message, like the people of Israel had waited for Moses to come down from Mt. Sinai with a message.

As Geoffrey stood silently amid the flowers and wild grasses, with his mother just dead, he wondered if he too shouldn't kneel and pray like Her New Man had.

Geoffrey didn't want to kneel in his neatly pressed gray-green gabardine suit. He stood. And repeated parts of the funeral service that the minister from the Episcopal church in Whitebone had recited at Mother's funeral:

"For a thousand years in thy sight are but as yesterday, when it is past, and as a watch in the night. As soon as thou scatterest them they are even as a sleep; and fade away suddenly like the grass.

"The days of our age are threescore and ten; and though men be so strong that they come to fourscore years, yea, even fivescore years, yet is their strength then but labour and sorrow; so soon it passeth away, and we are gone.

"For in the time of trouble he shall hide me in a secret place and set me upon a rock of stone.

"Grant unto us thy servants that we may at length fall asleep peacefully in thee."

Geoffrey again brushed gray hair out of his eyes as he stared down at the petroglyph.

He whispered aloud, "That circle set on a straight line had to mean something about the sun and its light." Geoffrey studied to himself. "Perhaps young Her New Man prayed only a very simple prayer. Something like: 'Light is life and life is light. Hi yelo, my mother's light is gone. The wind and the birds take up her flesh and pass it on.'"

Geoffrey thought he heard someone call. Turning, looking down the hill, he spotted Michelle below, standing on the old family stoop holding up baby Truman. With her free hand she was waving at him.

Smiling, Geoffrey waved back.

Then Michelle picked up the hand of her little one and helped it wave up to him. Geoffrey could see her lips move. He guessed she was saying: "There's Uncle Geoffrey. Wave to him. Say hi to him."

Geoffrey's smile deepened. He waved vigorously, with exaggerated up and down gestures, to make sure little Truman Freyling would see him.

As an officer of the court of justice, not law, Geoffrey felt like a shaman for a moment.

617